CliffsNotes®

AP® Chemistry

CliffsNotes®

AP® Chemistry

by
Angela Woodward Spangenberg, M.S.

Houghton Mifflin Harcourt
Boston • New York

About the Author

Angela Woodward Spangenberg has a Master of Science in Chemistry from the University of North Carolina. Having taught advanced chemistry in high school and currently working as a research chemist at the University of Texas, she tutors AP Chemistry students in the Austin, Texas, area.

Acknowledgments

I am grateful to the following contributors for their time and expertise: Charles Griste, Ben Shoulders, Alan Campion, Ian Riddington, John Ketcham, and the members of the AP Chemistry Teacher Community. I owe a debt of gratitude to my technical editor, Fatima Fakhreddine, not only for her excellent suggestions, but also for being a mentor. I thank Christina Stambaugh for her patience and help. Among other things, she is responsible for the absence of hundreds of errors. I thank Lynn Northrup, Kelly Rosier, and Donna Wright for their hard work and attention to detail. I am grateful to Joy Gilmore for giving me this opportunity. This work would not have been completed without the support and assistance of my mom and dad. Finally, I lovingly thank Kyle for holding our life together while I wrote. This book is dedicated to Eddie and Billy...may you each grow up to find your own fulfilling purpose.

Editorial

Executive Editor: Greg Tubach

Senior Editor: Christina Stambaugh

Production Editor: Erika West

Copy Editor: Lynn Northrup

Technical Editors: Fatima Fakhreddine, Ph.D., and Kelly Rosier

Proofreader: Donna Wright

CliffsNotes® AP® Chemistry

Table of Contents

Chapter 4: Kinetics (Big Idea 4)   184

Chapter 5: Thermodynamics (Big Idea 5) 227

Introduction

Your decision to take AP Chemistry says a lot about you. You seek out coursework that represents the highest educational challenge available to you, and you are willing to put forth an effort to excel. You are cognizant of the financial advantage of receiving college credit before you begin your university experience, and you are preparing yourself to enter your higher education years with the study skills required for success in courses that come easily to very few. These traits will serve you well. Your teachers, parents, and college admissions committees will be impressed.

Of the resources available to you, no textbook, study guide, website, or YouTube tutorial is as important as your classroom teacher. This person has undergone years of training both in chemistry and in teaching, not to mention a grueling course audit, in order to call his or her course "AP Chemistry." Your teacher is your greatest ally: He or she has a vested interest in your success because his or her professional accomplishment is intertwined with student achievement. When you feel that there are shortcomings in your understanding, never hesitate to approach your teacher for clarification. You will both be glad that you did.

The intent of this study guide is to provide you with plenty of opportunities for self-assessment so that you can pinpoint your weaknesses and overcome them. The complete solution to each practice question has a reference to one or more of the Essential Knowledge (EK) items from the *AP Chemistry Course and Exam Description* that was published in 2013 for the revised exam. This document is available on the College Board's AP Chemistry webpage, https://apstudent.collegeboard.org/apcourse/ap-chemistry/course-details. You are encouraged to look it over and familiarize yourself with its organization. You can refer to the Essential Knowledge (EK) categories, which are specific components of the AP Chemistry learning objectives, to target your problem areas and polish your skills. Practice, practice, and practice some more.

Each question in this revised edition of *CliffsNotes AP Chemistry* was designed specifically to assess some content component of the current course. There is ample coverage of newly introduced topics such as spectroscopy, chromatography, and Coulomb's law. On the other hand, colligative properties, organic reaction prediction, and quantum numbers, to name a few, are important and interesting topics, but since they are excluded from the curriculum, they are excluded from this guide. An exception has been made for the Nernst equation, which proved to be advantageous to students on both the May 2014 and 2015 administrations of the AP Chemistry exam. Despite its formal exclusion from the curriculum framework, the Nernst equation is covered here at the end of Big Idea 6 (Chapter 6, "Chemical Equilibrium").

Whether you are using this book as a supplement throughout your school year or you are picking it up a few weeks or days before the exam, it is my hope that this revised edition of *CliffsNotes AP Chemistry* will provide a valuable supplement to your teacher's instruction. Pick up your favorite pencil (remember, it's loaded with graphite, a soft network covalent compound with sheetlike layers) and start practicing!

Topics Covered in a Typical AP Chemistry Course

In most cases, the AP Chemistry course you are taking will not follow the sequence set forth in the *AP Chemistry Course and Exam Description*. The six Big Ideas in the course description, which were introduced in 2013, represent an inventory of concepts that students need to master in order to be successful on the exam, not a timetable for study of these concepts. There is no need to work through the Big Ideas in the sequence that they are presented, although it is certainly possible to do so. The table below shows a typical AP Chemistry Course sequence and the likely timing of the coverage of Essential Knowledge. You can use these items to determine which Big Idea and Essential Knowledge your course topic fits into, and when working the practice problems in this book, you can quickly refer to your class notes for review.

Topic	Essential Knowledge
Atoms, Molecules, and Ions	1.A.1, 1.A.2, 1.A.3
Chemical Equations and Stoichiometry	1.E.1, 1.E.2 3.A.1, 3.A.2 3.B.1 3.C.1
Gases	2.A.2
Liquids and Solids	2.A.1, 2.A.3
Intermolecular Forces	2.B.1, 2.B.2, 2.B.3 5.D.1, 5.D.2, 5.D.3
Thermochemistry (Enthalpy and Calorimetry)	3.C.2 5.A.1, 5.A.2 5.B.1, 5.B.2, 5.B.3, 5.B.4 5.C.1, 5.C.2 5.D.1
Atomic Structure and Periodicity	1.B.1, 1.B.2 1.C.1, 1.C.2 1.D.1, 1.D.2, 1.D.3
Bonding and Molecular Structure	2.C.1, 2.C.2, 2.C.3, 2.C.4 2.D.1, 2.D.2, 2.D.3, 2.D.4
Kinetics	4.A.1, 4.A.2, 4.A.3 4.B.1, 4.B.2, 4.B.3 4.C.1, 4.C.2, 4.C.3 4.D.1, 4.D.2
Acids and Bases	3.B.2 6.C.1
Thermodynamics	5.E.1, 5.E.2, 5.E.3, 5.E.4, 5.E.5 6.D.1
General Equilibrium	6.A.1, 6.A.2, 6.A.3, 6.A.4 6.B.1, 6.B.2 6.D.1
Acid/Base Equilibrium	6.C.1, 6.C.2
Solubility Equilibrium	6.C.3
Electrochemistry	3.B.3 3.C.3 6.D.1

Other topics that are excluded from the exam may be included in your course. These include nuclear chemistry, organic reactions, transition metal and coordination chemistry, and colligative properties. These are topics that will be very important in university-level chemistry. Thank your teacher for taking the time to cover them!

Format of the AP Chemistry Exam

The AP Chemistry exam is divided into two sections. Calculators are not permitted on Section I, but you may use your calculator on Section II. Throughout the exam, you will have access to the *AP Chemistry Equations and Constants* sheet (pages 365–366). You should refer to this list of important equations and constants frequently as you study for the exam.

	Section Weight	Type of Question	Number of Questions	Recommended Time per Question	Total Time Allowed
Section I	50%	Multiple choice	60	1.5 minutes	90 minutes
Section II	50%	Long free response	3	22 minutes	105 minutes
		Short free response	4	9 minutes	

Exams are graded on a scale of 1 to 5, with 5 being the highest score. Most colleges require a minimum score of 3 or 4 to offer a student credit for chemistry or allow the student to skip one or two semesters of introductory chemistry. Check with the chemistry departments at the universities that you will apply to in order to determine whether they award credit for the exam.

The distributions of student scores on recent administrations of the exam are shown below.

	Exam Grade	Approximate Percentage of Exam Points Earned	Approximate Percentage of Students Earning the Grade
Extremely Well Qualified	5	72–100	8–10
Well Qualified	4	58–71	15–16
Qualified	3	42–57	25–28
Possibly Qualified	2	27–41	25–26
No Recommendation	1	0–26	21–22

Strategies for Multiple-Choice Questions

- **Carefully read the background information when answering question set items.** There are two types of questions in the multiple-choice section: stand-alone questions and question sets. Stand-alone questions are single questions with four choices lettered A–D. Question sets begin with a prompt indicating which question numbers belong to the set. A prompt might read, "Use the following information to answer questions 2–4." Make sure that you refer to the background information while answering all of the questions in the set.

- **Do not leave any answers blank.** There is no penalty for guessing, so eliminate any choices that are obviously wrong and choose one of the remaining choices. If you cannot eliminate any choices, just make a guess. You have one chance in four of guessing correctly.

- **Do not spend too much time on one question.** Even if you are sure you can figure out the answer to a long question, put a mark by the question in your booklet, strike through any incorrect choices, and come back after you have worked quickly through the rest of the exam. You may be able to answer several easy questions and earn multiple points in the time it takes to answer one difficult question for a single point.

- **Don't overthink easy questions.** The questions range in difficulty from very easy to difficult. If a question seems too easy, do not assume that it is a trick. Don't second-guess yourself.

- **Review True and False items carefully.** Some questions may ask "which of the following is true" or "which of the following is false." Write a T or an F beside each answer choice to avoid confusion.

- **Check your bubbling carefully and obsessively.** Every time you turn the page, check to make sure that the question number at the top corresponds to the correct bubble that you are filling in on your answer sheet. Rather than bubbling circles completely as you work through a page, place a light hash mark across the correct answer. At the end of the page, check your question numbers and then darken the bubbles completely. This way, if you do make a bubbling error, you can erase it quickly and completely before correcting your work.

Multiple-Choice Math Strategies

Calculators are not allowed on the multiple-choice section of the exam, but calculations are still required. This can be one of the most intimidating aspects of the AP Chemistry exam, but it does not have to be. Practice working problems without a calculator. Start early in the school year to gain comfort doing this. The math is simple. You just need to know the tricks.

Estimating

Suppose a question asks for the pressure exerted by a 10-gram sample of F_2 in a 4-L container at 385 K. You know that this is an ideal gas law problem and that $PV = nRT$. The number of moles, n, is equal to the number of grams divided by the molar mass, 38.00 g·mol^{-1}. The value of the gas constant, R, is found on the *AP Chemistry Equations and Constants* sheet (pages 365–366). Begin by solving the equation for P and plugging in the appropriate values for V, n, R, and T.

$$P = \frac{nRT}{V} = \frac{\left(\dfrac{10}{38}\right)(0.08206)(385)}{4}$$

Notice that in the numerator, 385 divided by 38 is approximately 10.

$$\frac{\left(\dfrac{10}{38}\right)(0.08206)\left(385^{10}\right)}{4} \approx \frac{(10)(0.08206)(10)}{4}$$

Next, recognize that 0.08 divided by 4 is 0.02.

$$(10)(0.02)(10) = 2$$

If you had used your calculator, you would have determined the answer to be 2.078. The estimated numerical value will only be close to one of the answer choices.

Working with Exponents

Be comfortable with the rules for working with exponents.

- When two numbers are multiplied, their exponents are added.

$$(6 \times 10^{-11})(3 \times 10^8) = (6)(3) \times 10^{(-11 + 8)} = 18 \times 10^{-3} = 1.8 \times 10^{-2}$$

- When two numbers are divided, the exponent of the number in the denominator is subtracted from the exponent of the number in the numerator.

$$\frac{3 \times 10^8}{6 \times 10^{-11}} = 0.5 \times 10^{(8-(-11))} = 0.5 \times 10^{19} = 5 \times 10^{18}$$

- To take a square root of an exponent, divide the exponent by 2.

$$\sqrt{1 \times 10^{-18}} = 1 \times 10^{-9}$$

- In order to raise an exponent to the power of another exponent, multiply the two exponents.

$$(1 \times 10^{-6})^3 = 1 \times 10^{(-6 \times 3)} = 1 \times 10^{-18}$$

Working with Logarithms

Logarithms are another operation that appears on the exam, usually in the context of pH or pK. The log of a number is the power to which 10 must be raised in order to give that number.

$$\log (1000) = \log (10^3) = 3$$

$$\log (0.001) = \log (10^{-3}) = -3$$

Sometimes it is necessary to estimate the log of a number that is not a multiple of 10.

$$\log (2.3 \times 10^{-4})$$

The value 2.3×10^{-4} is greater than 1×10^{-4} and smaller than 1×10^{-3}, so the value of the log is larger than log (1×10^{-4}) and smaller than log (1×10^{-3}). The value can be estimated to lie between -3 and -4. The actual value is -3.63.

Strategies for Free-Response Questions

The free-response section is 105 minutes long, and calculators *are* allowed.

Significant Figures

Free-response calculations should be reported with the correct numbers of significant figures. When counting significant figures, zeros to the left of the first nonzero value are not significant. (The underlined digits are significant.)

$$0.0001\underline{1055} \qquad \text{Four significant figures}$$

Zeros at the end of a number and to the left of a decimal point are not significant unless there is a decimal point.

$$\underline{1,055},000 \qquad \text{Four significant figures}$$

$$\underline{1,055,000}. \qquad \text{Seven significant figures (more precise)}$$

Rounding

When two measured values are multiplied or divided, the result should be rounded to reflect the number of significant figures as the least precise measurement.

$$\frac{10,553(0.023)}{31.8526} = 7.6$$

When two measurements are added or subtracted, the result should be rounded to reflect the left-most decimal place that contains an uncertain digit.

$$84 + 38,\underline{6}00 + 9.005 = 38,700$$

This may be easier to visualize using a stacked equation in which all values are aligned at the decimal point.

$$
\begin{array}{r}
84 \\
38{,}600 \\
9.005 \\
\hline
38{,}693.005 \quad \text{(unrounded answer)} \\
38{,}700 \qquad \text{(correct number of significant figures)}
\end{array}
$$

When performing a series of calculations, it is always best to carry out all the arithmetical operations before rounding to avoid propagation of error.

Example:

> Divide 25.398 by 142.04. Divide 1.38 by 58.44. Add the two results and divide the answer by 0.10000. Report the final answer with the correct number of significant figures.

The first division operation results in five significant figures.

$$\frac{25.398}{142.04} = 0.17881 \quad \text{(unrounded value to be carried to the next step: 0.1788087863)}$$

The second division operation results in three significant figures because it is limited by the value 1.38.

$$\frac{1.38}{58.44} = 0.0236 \quad \text{(unrounded value to be carried to the next step: 0.023613963)}$$

The two results are added, and the result has four significant figures because it is limited by the value 0.0236.

$$
\begin{array}{l}
0.1788087868 \\
0.023613963 \\
\hline
0.2024227498 \quad \text{(unrounded answer)} \\
0.2024 \qquad \text{(correct number of significant figures)}
\end{array}
$$

When the result is divided by 0.10000, the final answer can be reported to four significant figures, because it is limited by the value 0.2024.

$$\frac{0.2024227498}{0.10000} = 2.024$$

There are four significant figures in the final answer. Note that no rounding occurred until the last step of the calculation.

Additional Free-Response Strategies

Free-response questions are not traditional essay questions. You should answer each question with a sentence or two, a calculation, or a quick sketch.

- **Read each question carefully.** Circle key information and jot key words in the margins. Do not assume that you know what the question is asking without *thinking* carefully.
- **Number your responses.** Clearly label your responses with the correct question number and question part.

- **Write clearly and neatly.** You are not penalized for poor grammar, spelling, or handwriting, but if it interferes with the readers' ability to interpret your response, you may lose valuable points.

- **Follow the directions precisely.** When a question asks for an answer and an explanation, you must explain your answer in order to earn credit. This also applies to questions that ask you to justify your responses by referring to data, calculations, and drawings. Refer to the data explicitly. If a question asks for a justification and you do not refer to the data, you *may* fail to earn points, even if your answer is technically correct.

- **Include a sketch when helpful or when requested.** Some questions may be best answered with a sketch. If you feel that your answer would be clarified for the reader with an illustration, provide one. Make sure to neatly label the parts of your sketch and explain how the drawing answers the question. If, on the other hand, a sketch is *requested*, you must provide one or you will not earn credit.

- **Show your work.** Be sure to use the factor-label method of dimensional analysis to check your work and show the reader that you know the material. For example, a question might ask you to calculate the number of moles of hydrochloric acid required to react with 30.0 grams of calcium carbonate. Show your work, as demonstrated below.

$$2\,HCl + CaCO_3 \rightarrow CaCl_2 + H_2O + CO_2$$

$$30.0 \ \cancel{g\,CaCO_3} \times \frac{1 \ \cancel{mol\,CaCO_3}}{100.09 \ \cancel{g\,CaCO_3}} \times \frac{2 \ mol\ HCl}{1 \ \cancel{mol\,CaCO_3}} = 0.599 \ mol\ HCl$$

- **Do not answer more than what is asked.** You will not get extra credit, and you will waste valuable time.

- **Read and attempt to answer every part of each question.** Even if you do not know how to answer an early part, you can still earn credit for knowing how to answer the parts that come later. If you need to make up numbers for the early parts of the question in order to proceed to the parts that you do know how to work, state what you have done and carry the number through the rest of the calculations. Glean every available point.

Finally, believe in what you have learned. Sleep well the night before the exam, eat well the morning of the exam, and breathe deeply. Read carefully, think carefully, write clearly, and use this opportunity to show how much you have practiced!

Chapter 1

Structure of Matter (Big Idea 1)

Big Idea 1: Atomic structure is the basis for understanding the properties of the elements

The central concept in chemistry is that matter is composed of atoms. Atoms do not undergo a change in identity during chemical reactions. The characteristics of elements are a consequence of the structure of the atoms that make up the elements. This chapter will review the fundamentals of atomic theory as they are covered in the AP Chemistry curriculum. Some of the material in this chapter is a review of Pre-AP Chemistry concepts that are assumed to be prior knowledge on the AP Chemistry exam.

Atoms: The Fundamental Building Blocks of Matter

Matter, anything that has mass and volume, is composed of atoms. An **atom** is the smallest unit of matter that retains its elemental identity through all physical and chemical processes. Atoms are the basic units of **elements,** pure substances such as carbon or gold that cannot be decomposed into simpler substances by ordinary chemical or physical changes.

Atoms are composed of three types of fundamental **subatomic particles:** protons, neutrons, and electrons. The **nucleus** is the central region of an atom. It is comprised of positively charged **protons** and neutral **neutrons.** A proton and a neutron each have a mass of approximately one **atomic mass unit** (amu), 1.66×10^{-27} kg. The amu is defined as one-twelfth the mass of a neutral atom of carbon-12, which has six protons and six neutrons.

Electrons are negatively charged subatomic particles located in the space outside of the nucleus. The mass of an electron is negligible compared with the mass of a proton or a neutron.

The **atomic number,** Z, of an element is the number of protons in the nucleus of an atom of that element. Elements are tabulated systematically on the periodic table according to increasing atomic number, and the identity of an element is determined by its atomic number.

The **mass number,** A, of an atom is equal to the total number of protons and neutrons in that atom. The number of neutrons, n^0, is equal to the difference between the mass number and the atomic number. The mass number and the atomic number are always whole numbers.

For a neutral atom, the number of protons, p^+, is equal to the number of electrons, e^-.

Atomic Symbol

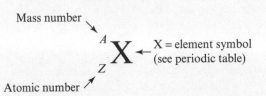

Mass number

Atomic number

$$^{A}_{Z}X$$

X = element symbol
(see periodic table)

An element's symbol on the periodic table is accompanied by the atomic number and the atomic weight of the element. The **atomic mass,** or **atomic weight,** is the weighted average of the masses of the naturally occurring isotopes of the element. **Isotopes** are atoms of the same element that have different numbers of neutrons. The atomic mass is numerically equal to the **molar mass,** which is the mass in grams of one mole of the atoms of an element.

The Element Sodium as it Appears on the Periodic Table

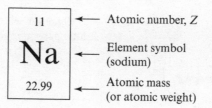

11 ← Atomic number, Z

Na ← Element symbol (sodium)

22.99 ← Atomic mass (or atomic weight)

PRACTICE:

How many protons, neutrons, and electrons are in a neutral atom of $^{26}_{12}\text{Mg}$?

There are 12 protons, 14 neutrons, and 12 electrons in a neutral atom of $^{26}_{12}\text{Mg}$. The atomic number, Z, at the lower left, is equal to the number of protons, 12. The number at the upper left is the mass number, A, which equals the number of protons plus the number of neutrons. There are 14 neutrons.

$$A = 12 + n^0 = 26$$
$$n^0 = 14$$

In a neutral atom, the number of protons equals the number of electrons, so the number of electrons in a neutral atom of magnesium is 12.

A **pure substance** is matter that cannot be broken down into simpler substances by any *physical* means. Elements and compounds are pure substances.

A **compound** is a pure substance composed of two or more different elements in a fixed ratio. It can be broken down into elements by *chemical* means. Some examples of compounds are H_2O, CH_4, and $Cr_2(SO_4)_3$.

A **molecule** is the simplest group of bonded atoms making up a pure substance that can exist independently and retain all the characteristics of the pure substance. Examples of molecules include simple ones like H_2, S_8, H_2O, and CH_4 and very complicated ones like chlorophyll ($C_{55}H_{72}N_4O_5Mg$) or proteins and nucleic acids. Notice that the **subscripts** give the number of atoms of each element in a molecule. There are eight atoms of sulfur in a molecule of S_8, and there are two atoms of hydrogen and one oxygen atom in a molecule of H_2O.

Some compounds exist as **hydrates.** They contain fixed numbers of associated water molecules. The general formula for a hydrate is

$$\text{Compound} \cdot n\,H_2O$$

For example, there are seven molecules of water associated with each formula unit of magnesium sulfate heptahydrate, $MgSO_4 \cdot 7\,H_2O$. A substance that has no associated water is said to be **anhydrous.**

Mixtures are obtained by mixing two or more pure substances. Mixtures may be either homogeneous or heterogeneous. **Homogeneous mixtures,** such as salt water or air, have the same properties throughout. **Heterogeneous mixtures,** such as oatmeal cookies or marble, do not look uniform and have different regions with different properties.

A mixture is usually separable into its component atoms or compounds by physical means. Common physical methods for separating mixtures are filtration, evaporation, distillation, and chromatography.

Filtration is a technique for separating heterogeneous mixtures such as sand and water. A liquid component is passed through a filter and a solid is retained in the filter. In the filtration apparatus below, a sidearm flask is connected to a vacuum source. The mixture is poured into the Büchner funnel that has been fitted with filter paper. The liquid, or **filtrate,** is pulled through the funnel into the flask, while the solid remains on the paper in the funnel.

Filtration Apparatus

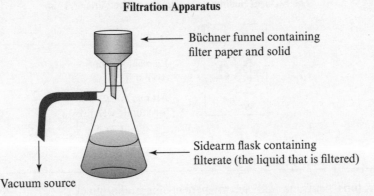

Büchner funnel containing filter paper and solid

Sidearm flask containing filterate (the liquid that is filtered)

Vacuum source

Evaporation is a separation technique in which a liquid is boiled away or allowed to evaporate away from a solid. Salt may be separated from a homogeneous saltwater solution by boiling away the water. Both homogeneous and heterogeneous mixtures may be separated in this way.

Distillation and chromatography are methods for separating mixtures that will be discussed in the context of intermolecular forces in Big Idea 2 (Chapter 2, "Bonding and Intermolecular Forces"). To summarize, matter is divided into two categories, pure substances and mixtures. Pure substances are further classified as elements and compounds while mixtures can be homogeneous and heterogeneous.

Classification of Matter

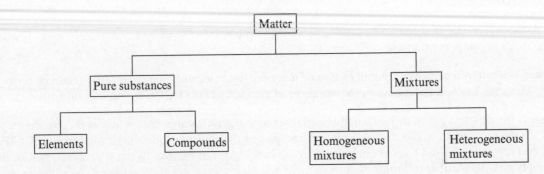

Law of Conservation of Mass

Matter cannot be created or destroyed in ordinary physical processes. This **law of conservation of mass** is the reason chemical equations must be balanced, a skill that is discussed further in Big Idea 3 (Chapter 3, "Chemical Reactions"). The law of conservation of mass does not apply to nuclear transformations.

Consider the reaction between sodium, a soft metal, and chlorine, a diatomic gas, to form sodium chloride. This may be represented as a chemical equation. Notice that the same number of sodium atoms and chlorine atoms appear in both reactants and products.

$$2\ Na(s) + Cl_2(g) \rightarrow 2\ NaCl(s)$$

The **reactants** are the reacting species to the left of the arrow, Na and Cl_2, and the **products** are the species formed, NaCl(s). The **coefficients** are the numbers in front of each species that indicate the relative number of units of that species that react. The arrow shows that a chemical reaction occurs. The **state symbols** following each species indicate the state of that species in the reaction. Solids, liquids, gases, and aqueous solutions (solutions in water) are given the symbols (s), (l), (g), and (aq), respectively.

The law of conservation of mass can be seen in natural phenomena such as the hydrologic cycle. Earth has a relatively constant mass of water over time. One water molecule may travel from the ocean to the atmosphere via evaporation. It will eventually fall as rain. It may even be consumed by an organism before being excreted and re-entering the cycle.

Law of Definite Proportions

The **law of definite proportions** states that a particular compound always contains the same mass percentages of elements. Every gram of water, H_2O, is always composed of 0.89 gram of oxygen and 0.11 gram of hydrogen. In other words, it is 89% oxygen and 11% hydrogen by mass. The fixed percent of each element by mass for a compound is called the **percent composition.**

$$\text{Mass percent} = \frac{\text{mass of one element}}{\text{total mass of compound}} \times 100\%$$

PRACTICE:

> A 52.1-gram sample of a compound is composed of 20.8 grams of carbon, 3.5 grams of hydrogen, and 27.8 grams of oxygen. What is the percent composition of the sample?

The percent composition of each element is its percentage of the total mass.

$$\text{Percent carbon} = \frac{20.8 \text{ grams C}}{52.1 \text{ grams total}} \times 100\% = 39.9\% \text{ C}$$

$$\text{Percent hydrogen} = \frac{3.5 \text{ grams H}}{52.1 \text{ grams total}} \times 100\% = 6.7\% \text{ H}$$

$$\text{Percent oxygen} = \frac{27.8 \text{ grams O}}{52.1 \text{ grams total}} \times 100\% = 53.4\% \text{ O}$$

Experimentally determined percent composition can also be an indicator of the purity of a sample. If the sample of the compound in the practice problem above, $C_2H_4O_2$, was determined experimentally to have different mass percentages than the one shown, this would be good evidence for the presence of impurities in the sample.

Law of Multiple Proportions

John Dalton was a teacher, chemist, and physicist who made observations about the ratios of the masses of elements that combine to form compounds. His contributions to chemistry include the **law of multiple proportions,** which states that when two elements form more than one compound, such as H_2O and H_2O_2, the ratio of the masses of the second element that combine with a fixed amount of the first element is always a small, whole-number ratio.

In the example of H_2O and H_2O_2, 1 gram of hydrogen combines with 8 grams of oxygen to form H_2O, and 1 gram of hydrogen combines with 16 grams of oxygen to form H_2O_2. The two masses of oxygen that combine with 1 gram of hydrogen can be simplified to a small, whole-number ratio.

$$\frac{\text{Mass of oxygen in } H_2O_2}{\text{Mass of oxygen in } H_2O} = \frac{16 \text{ g}}{8 \text{ g}} = \frac{2}{1}$$

PRACTICE:

> One gram of carbon is found to combine with 0.336 gram of hydrogen in Compound A and with 0.252 gram of hydrogen in Compound B. Show that these compounds obey the law of multiple proportions.

To demonstrate that two compounds adhere to the law of multiple proportions, show that the masses of hydrogen that combine with 1 gram of carbon can be simplified to a whole-number ratio. It is necessary to recognize that $0.3\bar{3}$ is $\frac{1}{3}$. The ratio must be multiplied by $\frac{3}{3}$ in order to obtain the small whole-number ratio.

$$\frac{\text{Mass of hydrogen in Compound A}}{\text{Mass of hydrogen in Compound B}} = \frac{0.336 \text{ g H}}{0.252 \text{ g H}} = \frac{1.3\bar{3}}{1} \times \frac{3}{3} = \frac{4}{3}$$

Dalton's Atomic Theory

Dalton's work supported the concept that compounds were composed of atoms, and his discoveries prompted him to present a comprehensive atomic theory in the early nineteenth century. The postulates of atomic theory have been refined since Dalton's original proposal, but the fundamental accuracy of most of his ideas has been verified experimentally.

Dalton's Atomic Theory

- All matter is composed of atoms.
- Atoms cannot be created or destroyed.*
- The atoms of a given element are identical in mass, but different from other elements.**
- Atoms combine in simple, whole-number ratios to form compounds.
- Atoms are reorganized, not fundamentally changed, in chemical reactions.

*It was later discovered that mass and energy could be interconverted in nuclear transformations.

**Dalton proposed that atoms of the same kind of element were identical. It was shown later, with mass spectrometry and the discovery of isotopes, that this was incorrect.

Counting Particles: The Mole

Atoms, molecules, and other submicroscopic particles are incomprehensibly small. They are so tiny that a special method is necessary to count them. Consider a tablespoon (roughly 15 mL) of water. At ambient temperature and pressure, that tablespoon contains on the order of 5×10^{23} molecules of H_2O. This enormous number cannot possibly be counted directly. The **mole,** which is the number of carbon atoms found in exactly 12 grams of carbon-12, is used to circumvent this problem. A mole, abbreviated "mol," contains a number of particles equal to Avogadro's constant, N_A. It works just like "a dozen."

$$N_A = 6.022 \times 10^{23} \text{ particles} = 1 \text{ mole of particles}$$

Consider the following examples:

$$1 \text{ mol of Na} = 6.022 \times 10^{23} \text{ atoms of Na}$$
$$1 \text{ mol of } H_2O = 6.022 \times 10^{23} \text{ molecules of } H_2O$$

These can be written as ratios for use in **dimensional analysis,** a technique by which units for a value are converted. The value to be converted is multiplied by unit factors. A **unit factor** is a ratio in which the numerator and denominator are equal. An expression can be multiplied by a unit factor without changing its value.

From the equalities above, we can write the following unit factors:

$$\frac{6.022 \times 10^{23} \text{ atoms of Na}}{1 \text{ mol Na}} \text{ or } \frac{1 \text{ mol Na}}{6.022 \times 10^{23} \text{ atoms of Na}} \text{ or } \frac{1 \text{ mol } H_2O}{6.022 \times 10^{23} \text{ molecules of } H_2O}$$

$$\text{or } \frac{6.022 \times 10^{23} \text{ molecules of } H_2O}{1 \text{ mol } H_2O}$$

In order to determine the number of sodium atoms in 0.150 mole of sodium, we multiply the number of moles of sodium by the unit factor that relates number of atoms to moles.

$$\frac{6.022 \times 10^{23} \text{ atoms of Na}}{1 \text{ mol Na}} = 1$$

$$0.150 \text{ mol Na} \times \frac{6.022 \times 10^{23} \text{ atoms of Na}}{1 \text{ mol Na}} = 9.03 \times 10^{22} \text{ atoms of Na}$$

PRACTICE:

> How many CO_2 molecules make up 1.5 moles of CO_2?

One mole of CO_2 = 6.022×10^{23} molecules of CO_2. In order to find the number of CO_2 molecules in 1.5 moles of CO_2, the number of moles is multiplied by the unit factor relating moles of CO_2 to molecules of CO_2.

$$\frac{6.022 \times 10^{23} \text{ molecules } CO_2}{1 \text{ mol } CO_2} = 1$$

$$1.5 \text{ mol } CO_2 \times \frac{6.022 \times 10^{23} \text{ molecules } CO_2}{1 \text{ mol } CO_2} = 9.0 \times 10^{23} \text{ molecules } CO_2$$

Atomic Weight and Molar Mass

Macroscopic quantities such as mass and volume can be measured using such instruments as a balance and a graduated cylinder. Mass and volume can be related to the number of particles of a substance via the mole.

Just as a dozen bowling balls weigh more than a dozen tennis balls, a mole of iron atoms weighs more than a mole of lithium atoms. The **atomic weight** is the average weight of a particular kind of atom in amu. It is a weighted average of the exact masses of the naturally occurring isotopes. The mass of one mole of atoms of an element in grams is called the **molar mass**. It has the same numerical value as its atomic weight and is expressed in $g \cdot mol^{-1}$. It is used to convert mass, a quantity that can be measured in a laboratory, to moles.

PRACTICE:

> Find the mass in grams of 1.0×10^{13} atoms of sodium.

The number of grams of sodium can be determined using the relationship between moles and number of atoms and using the atomic mass of sodium found on the periodic table.

$$1 \text{ mol of Na} = 6.022 \times 10^{23} \text{ atoms of Na}$$
$$1 \text{ mol of Na} = 22.99 \text{ g Na}$$

We can multiply the number of sodium atoms by the appropriate unit factor ratios.

$$1.0 \times 10^{13} \text{ atoms Na} \times \frac{1 \text{ mol Na}}{6.022 \times 10^{23} \text{ atoms Na}} \times \frac{22.99 \text{ g Na}}{1 \text{ mol Na}} = 3.8 \times 10^{-10} \text{ g Na}$$

PRACTICE:

> What is the mass in grams of 0.15 mole of helium atoms?

The mass is determined by multiplying the number of moles of helium by the molar mass.

$$0.15 \text{ mol He} \times \frac{4.00 \text{ g He}}{1 \text{ mol He}} = 0.60 \text{ g He}$$

The mass of a mole of molecules is given by the sum of the atomic weights of the constituent elements. In a molecule of glucose, $C_6H_{12}O_6$, there are 6 carbon atoms, 6 oxygen atoms, and 12 hydrogen atoms. That means that in 1 mole of glucose, there are 6 moles of carbon atoms, 6 moles of oxygen atoms, and 12 moles of hydrogen atoms. To determine the **molar mass, M,** or **molecular weight** for a compound or **formula weight** for an ionic formula, the number of moles of each element is multiplied by the atomic weight of that element.

Suppose a student needs to determine the molar mass of glucose, $C_6H_{12}O_6$. There are 6 moles of carbon, 12 moles of hydrogen, and 6 moles of oxygen in each mole of $C_6H_{12}O_6$.

$$M_{C_6H_{12}O_6} = \left(\frac{6 \text{ mol C}}{1 \text{ mol } C_6H_{12}O_6} \right)\left(\frac{12.01 \text{ g}}{1 \text{ mol C}} \right) + \left(\frac{12 \text{ mol H}}{1 \text{ mol } C_6H_{12}O_6} \right)\left(\frac{1.01 \text{ g}}{1 \text{ mol H}} \right) +$$

$$\left(\frac{6 \text{ mol O}}{1 \text{ mol } C_6H_{12}O_6} \right)\left(\frac{16.00 \text{ g}}{1 \text{ mol O}} \right)$$

$$M_{C_6H_{12}O_6} = 180.18 \frac{\text{g}}{\text{mol}}$$

PRACTICE:

Find the molar masses of the following compounds.

(a) H_2O

(b) $(NH_4)_3PO_4$

(c) $CaSO_4 \cdot 2 H_2O$

(a) There are 2 moles of hydrogen atoms and 1 mole of oxygen atoms per mole of water.

$$M_{H_2O} = \left(\frac{2 \text{ mol H}}{1 \text{ mol } H_2O} \right)\left(\frac{1.01 \text{ g H}}{1 \text{ mol H}} \right) + \left(\frac{1 \text{ mol O}}{1 \text{ mol } H_2O} \right)\left(\frac{16.00 \text{ g O}}{1 \text{ mol O}} \right)$$

$$M_{H_2O} = 18.02 \frac{\text{g}}{\text{mol}}$$

(b) The parentheses indicate that there are three ammonium ions, NH_4^+, for every phosphate ion, PO_4^{3-}. This means that there are 3 moles of nitrogen atoms, 12 moles of hydrogen atoms, 1 mole of phosphorus atoms, and 4 moles of oxygen atoms per mole of the formula.

$$M_{(NH_4)_3PO_4} = \left(\frac{3 \text{ mol N}}{1 \text{ mol } (NH_4)_3PO_4} \right)\left(\frac{14.01 \text{ g N}}{1 \text{ mol N}} \right) + \left(\frac{12 \text{ mol H}}{1 \text{ mol } (NH_4)_3PO_4} \right)\left(\frac{1.01 \text{ g H}}{1 \text{ mol H}} \right) +$$

$$\left(\frac{1 \text{ mol P}}{1 \text{ mol } (NH_4)_3PO_4} \right)\left(\frac{30.97 \text{ g P}}{1 \text{ mol P}} \right) + \left(\frac{4 \text{ mol O}}{1 \text{ mol } (NH_4)_3PO_4} \right)\left(\frac{16.00 \text{ g O}}{1 \text{ mol O}} \right)$$

$$M_{(NH_4)_3PO_4} = 149.12 \frac{\text{g}}{\text{mol}}$$

(c) This compound is a **dihydrate**. The prefix *di-* indicates that there are 2 water molecules associated with each calcium sulfate formula unit.

$$M_{CaSO_4 \cdot 2H_2O} = \left(\frac{1 \text{ mol Ca}}{1 \text{ mol } CaSO_4 \cdot 2H_2O}\right)\left(\frac{40.08 \text{ g Ca}}{1 \text{ mol Ca}}\right) + \left(\frac{1 \text{ mol S}}{1 \text{ mol } CaSO_4 \cdot 2H_2O}\right)\left(\frac{32.06 \text{ g S}}{1 \text{ mol S}}\right) +$$

$$\left(\frac{6 \text{ mol O}}{1 \text{ mol } CaSO_4 \cdot 2H_2O}\right)\left(\frac{16.00 \text{ g O}}{1 \text{ mol O}}\right) + \left(\frac{4 \text{ mol H}}{1 \text{ mol } CaSO_4 \cdot 2H_2O}\right)\left(\frac{1.01 \text{ g H}}{1 \text{ mol H}}\right)$$

$$M_{CaSO_4 \cdot 2H_2O} = 172.18 \frac{g}{mol}$$

Density

Volume is another quantity that can be measured in a laboratory. The volume of a substance is related to the number of grams of that substance by its **density,** the mass of the substance per unit volume.

$$\text{Density} = \frac{\text{mass}}{\text{volume}}$$

The density of PCl_3 is 1.57 g·mL^{-1} near 25 °C. There are 1.57 grams of PCl_3 in every milliliter of PCl_3. The density can be written as two different ratios that can be used in dimensional analysis.

$$\frac{1.57 \text{ g } PCl_3}{1 \text{ mL } PCl_3} = 1 \quad \text{or} \quad \frac{1 \text{ mL } PCl_3}{1.57 \text{ g } PCl_3} = 1$$

If a pipette is used to deliver 5.0 mL of PCl_3 to a reaction vessel, the number of grams that has been added is the product of the volume and the density. The mass can then be converted to moles using the molar mass.

$$5.0 \text{ mL } PCl_3 \times \frac{1.57 \text{ g } PCl_3}{1 \text{ mL } PCl_3} \times \frac{1 \text{ mol } PCl_3}{137.32 \text{ g } PCl_3} = 0.59 \text{ mol } PCl_3$$

PRACTICE:

> A chemist needs to use 0.030 mole of Br_2 in a reaction. How many milliliters are required? The density of Br_2 is 3.01 g·mL^{-1}.

The number of moles is first converted to grams. The density is then used to determine the volume.

$$0.030 \text{ mol } Br_2 \times \frac{159.80 \text{ g } Br_2}{1 \text{ mol } Br_2} \times \frac{1 \text{ mL } Br_2}{3.01 \text{ g } Br_2} = 1.6 \text{ mL } Br_2$$

The densities of fluids dictate which immiscible (unable to mix) fluids will float on top of others. Vegetable oil is less dense than water, so it forms a layer above water in a container. It does not mix with water for reasons that will be reviewed in Big Idea 2 (Chapter 2, "Bonding and Intermolecular Forces").

Empirical and Molecular Formulas

The **molecular formula** of a compound is the actual number of atoms of each element in a molecule or formula unit of that compound. The **empirical formula** of a compound is the lowest whole-number ratio of atoms in that compound. Sucrose, or table sugar, has a molecular formula of $C_6H_{12}O_6$. When each subscript is divided by six, the molecular formula simplifies to the empirical formula, CH_2O.

PRACTICE:

> The molecular formula of crotonic acid is $C_4H_6O_2$. What is the empirical formula?

Division of each of the subscripts in the formula by two gives the simplest possible whole-number ratio of the atoms in the formula, C_2H_3O.

Empirical and Molecular Formula Determination

Empirical formulas can be determined from the mass percent, or percent composition of a compound. Suppose a compound is found to be 54.5% carbon, 9.2% hydrogen, and 36.3% oxygen by mass. The molar mass of the compound is found to be 264.24 g·mol⁻¹. We can use this information to first determine empirical formula.

A methodical approach to this type of problem is to first determine the number of moles of each element in 100.0 grams of the compound. Any mass may be chosen, but 100.0 grams is a simple mass to work with because in 100.0 grams of the compound there are 54.5 grams of carbon, 9.2 grams of hydrogen, and 36.3 grams of oxygen. These masses are multiplied by atomic mass unit factors obtained from the periodic table.

$$54.5 \text{ g C}\left(\frac{1 \text{ mol C}}{12.01 \text{ g C}}\right) = 4.54 \text{ mol C}$$

$$9.2 \text{ g H}\left(\frac{1 \text{ mol H}}{1.01 \text{ g H}}\right) = 9.1 \text{ mol H}$$

$$36.3 \text{ g O}\left(\frac{1 \text{ mol O}}{16.00 \text{ g O}}\right) = 2.27 \text{ mol O}$$

Next, find the simplest whole-number ratio by first dividing each number of moles by the smallest number. In this case, divide by 2.27 moles.

$$\frac{4.54 \text{ mol C}}{2.27 \text{ mol}} \approx 2$$

$$\frac{9.1 \text{ mol H}}{2.27 \text{ mol}} \approx 4$$

$$\frac{2.27 \text{ mol O}}{2.27 \text{ mol}} = 1$$

These integer values give an empirical formula of C_2H_4O.

Now that the empirical formula has been determined, we can find the molecular formula using the molar mass of the compound and the empirical formula molar mass. The molar mass of the compound was given above: 264.24 g·mol⁻¹. We must determine the molar mass of the empirical formula.

$$M_{C_2H_4O} = \left(\frac{2 \text{ mol C}}{1 \text{ mol } C_2H_4O}\right)\left(\frac{12.01 \text{ g C}}{1 \text{ mol C}}\right) + \left(\frac{4 \text{ mol H}}{1 \text{ mol } C_2H_4O}\right)\left(\frac{1.01 \text{ g H}}{1 \text{ mol H}}\right) + \left(\frac{1 \text{ mol O}}{1 \text{ mol } C_2H_4O}\right)\left(\frac{16.00 \text{ g O}}{1 \text{ mol O}}\right)$$

$$M_{C_2H_4O} = 44.06 \frac{\text{g}}{\text{mol}}$$

Next, the molar mass of the compound is divided by the empirical formula molar mass.

$$\frac{264.24 \ g \cdot \cancel{mol^{-1}}}{44.06 \ g \cdot \cancel{mol^{-1}}} \approx 6$$

The subscripts in the empirical formula are multiplied by the result to give the molecular formula, $C_{12}H_{24}O_6$.

The AP Chemistry curriculum makes specific mention of the use of percent composition information to draw conclusions about the percent purity of a sample. It is very important to understand that any two compounds with the same empirical formula must have identical percent composition.

PRACTICE:

A research group discovers and purifies a small molecule from a marine plant species in the Caribbean Sea. It has an empirical formula of $C_{10}H_{11}O_2$. They name it *Caribbeanium*. Another research group attempts to reproduce these results. They isolate a 0.892-mg sample that has the elemental composition shown in the table below. What conclusions can be drawn from these results regarding the identity and purity of the sample isolated by the second group?

Element	Mass (mg)
C	0.573
H	0.064
O	0.255
Total	**0.892**

If the sample isolated by the second group is a pure sample of *Caribbeanium*, the percent composition should match that of *Caribbeanium*.

The percent composition of *Caribbeanium* is determined first. When using an empirical formula to determine percent composition, one method is to assume the number of grams of compound present is the same as the empirical molar mass.

$$M_{C_{10}H_{11}O_2} = \left(\frac{10 \ \cancel{mol \ C}}{1 \ mol \ C_{10}H_{11}O_2}\right)\left(\frac{12.01 \ g \ C}{1 \ \cancel{mol \ C}}\right) + \left(\frac{11 \ \cancel{mol \ H}}{1 \ mol \ C_{10}H_{11}O_2}\right)\left(\frac{1.01 \ g \ H}{1 \ \cancel{mol \ H}}\right)$$

$$+ \left(\frac{2 \ \cancel{mol \ O}}{1 \ mol \ C_{10}H_{11}O_2}\right)\left(\frac{16.00 \ g \ O}{1 \ \cancel{mol \ O}}\right) = 163.21 \frac{g}{mol}$$

The mass of each element present in 163.21 grams (1 mole) of *Caribbeanium* is

$$\left(\frac{10 \ \cancel{mol \ C}}{1 \ mol \ C_{10}H_{11}O_2}\right)\left(\frac{12.01 \ g \ C}{1 \ \cancel{mol \ C}}\right) = 120.10 \ g \ C$$

$$\left(\frac{11 \ \cancel{mol \ H}}{1 \ mol \ C_{10}H_{11}O_2}\right)\left(\frac{1.01 \ g \ H}{1 \ \cancel{mol \ H}}\right) = 11.11 \ g \ H$$

$$\left(\frac{2 \ \cancel{mol \ O}}{1 \ mol \ C_{10}H_{11}O_2}\right)\left(\frac{16.00 \ g \ O}{1 \ \cancel{mol \ O}}\right) = 32.00 \ g \ O$$

The percent composition of *Caribbeanium* is

$$\text{Percent C} = \frac{120.10 \text{ g C}}{163.21 \text{ g C}_{10}\text{H}_{11}\text{O}_2} \times 100\% = 73.6\% \text{ C}$$

$$\text{Percent H} = \frac{11.11 \text{ g H}}{163.21 \text{ g C}_{10}\text{H}_{11}\text{O}_2} \times 100\% = 6.8\% \text{ H}$$

$$\text{Percent O} = \frac{32.00 \text{ g O}}{163.21 \text{ g C}_{10}\text{H}_{11}\text{O}_2} \times 100\% = 19.6\% \text{ O}$$

The percent composition of the unknown sample is determined and compared.

$$\text{Percent C} = \frac{0.573 \text{ mg C}}{0.892 \text{ mg unknown}} \times 100\% = 64.2\% \text{ C}$$

$$\text{Percent H} = \frac{0.064 \text{ mg H}}{0.892 \text{ mg unknown}} \times 100\% = 7.2\% \text{ H}$$

$$\text{Percent O} = \frac{0.255 \text{ mg O}}{0.892 \text{ mg unknown}} \times 100\% = 28.6\% \text{ O}$$

The percent composition of the sample isolated by the second group does not match that of *Caribbeanium*. Two conclusions may be drawn about the identity and purity of the unknown sample:

1. The unknown sample *may* contain *Caribbeanium,* but if it does, it must also contain impurities that cause the percent composition to differ.

2. The unknown sample *may not* contain *Caribbeanium*. No conclusion may be drawn about the purity of the sample if this is the case.

Combustion Analysis

In a combustion reaction, a compound reacts rapidly with oxygen while generating heat and light.

Combustion analysis is a method for determining the percent composition and empirical formula of a compound. When the data from a combustion analysis are used in conjunction with molar mass information, the molecular formula of a compound can be determined. Mass spectrometry, a technique for determining the molar mass of a compound, will be discussed later in this chapter (page 48).

In a combustion reaction of a **hydrocarbon,** a compound that contains carbon and hydrogen atoms bound together, carbon dioxide, CO_2, and water vapor, H_2O, are generated according to the equation below.

$$C_x H_y + z \, O_2 \rightarrow x \, CO_2 + \frac{y}{2} \, H_2O$$

Although balancing chemical reactions is a topic that will be addressed in Big Idea 3 (Chapter 3, "Chemical Reactions"), there are two very important features of this reaction to note in the context of combustion analysis. First, the number of moles of carbon dioxide produced, x, is equal to the number of moles of carbon that were initially present in the sample. Second, the number of moles of H_2O produced is equal to half the number of moles of hydrogen atoms, y, that were present in the original sample. (We will see in Chapter 3 that the coefficients must be multiplied by a factor to convert any fractional coefficients to the smallest possible whole numbers.) When oxygen atoms are present in the unknown compound, the difference between the mass of the original sample and the mass that can be attributed to carbon and hydrogen is equal to the mass of the oxygen in the sample. All the atoms in the reactants are also present in the products, and *the law of conservation of mass is obeyed*.

PRACTICE:

An unknown compound contains only carbon, hydrogen, and oxygen. Combustion of a 30.0-gram sample of the compound in excess oxygen yields 80.1 grams of CO_2 and 12.6 grams of H_2O. What is the empirical formula of the compound?

The number of moles of carbon in the original sample can be determined from the grams of CO_2 obtained. The number of moles of hydrogen can be determined from the mass of water.

$$\text{moles of carbon} = 80.1 \ \text{g} \ CO_2 \times \frac{1 \ \text{mol} \ CO_2}{44.01 \ \text{g} \ CO_2} \times \frac{1 \ \text{mol C}}{1 \ \text{mol} \ CO_2} = 1.82 \ \text{mol C}$$

$$\text{moles of hydrogen} = 12.6 \ \text{g} \ H_2O \times \frac{1 \ \text{mol} \ H_2O}{18.02 \ \text{g} \ H_2O} \times \frac{2 \ \text{mol H}}{1 \ \text{mol} \ H_2O} = 1.40 \ \text{mol H}$$

The masses of carbon and hydrogen can be used to find the mass of oxygen in the sample since the total mass is known.

$$\text{mass of carbon} = 1.82 \ \text{mol C} \times \frac{12.01 \ \text{g C}}{1 \ \text{mol C}} = 21.9 \ \text{g C}$$

$$\text{mass of hydrogen} = 1.40 \ \text{mol H} \times \frac{1.01 \ \text{g H}}{1 \ \text{mol H}} = 1.41 \ \text{g H}$$

$$\text{Total mass of sample} = \text{mass of carbon} + \text{mass of hydrogen} + \text{mass of oxygen}$$
$$30.0 \ \text{g} = 21.9 \ \text{g} + 1.41 \ \text{g} + \text{mass of oxygen}$$
$$\text{Mass of oxygen} = 6.7 \ \text{g}$$

The mass of oxygen is used to find the number of moles of oxygen in the sample.

$$\text{moles of oxygen} = 6.7 \ \text{g} \ O \times \frac{1 \ \text{mol O}}{16.00 \ \text{g} \ O} = 0.42 \ \text{mol O}$$

The final step in determining the empirical formula is division of the number of moles of each element by the smallest number of moles.

$$\text{Carbon:} \quad \frac{1.82}{0.42} = 4.33$$

$$\text{Hydrogen:} \quad \frac{1.40}{0.42} = 3.33$$

$$\text{Oxygen:} \quad \frac{0.42}{0.42} = 1$$

The number 0.33 should be recognized as $\frac{1}{3}$, so the simplest ratio can be determined by multiplying each number by 3.

$$\text{Carbon:} \quad 4.33 \times 3 = 13$$
$$\text{Hydrogen:} \quad 3.33 \times 3 = 10$$
$$\text{Oxygen:} \quad 1 \times 3 = 3$$

The empirical formula, therefore, is $C_{13}H_{10}O_3$.

The Evolution of Scientific Models

Scientific models are based on experimental evidence and are refined over time as new data becomes available. Chemists' understanding of the structure of the atom has changed dramatically since Dalton published his atomic theory in 1808. At that time, Dalton imagined the atom to be an indivisible particle, not unlike a small marble. Subsequent discoveries and observations led to the adaptation of scientists' model of the internal structure of the atom. The history of the atomic model is used here to illustrate how a scientific model evolves to reflect new experimental results.

The Discovery of the Electron

In the 1890s, J. J. Thomson, a physicist working with **cathode ray tubes,** noticed that when a voltage was applied to a low-pressure sample of gas, a beam of light was generated. When a magnet or charged plates were placed near the tube, the beam could be moved around inside the glass. By studying how cathode rays were deflected in a magnetic field, Thomson deduced that the beam was comprised of electrons, negatively charged subatomic particles that were components of atoms.

Cathode Ray Tube

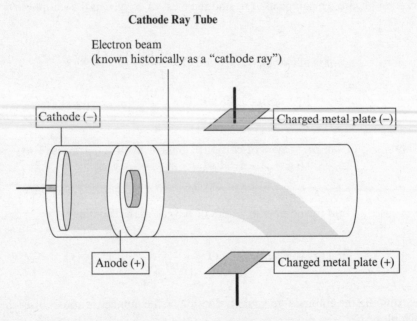

Thomson's cathode ray experiments enabled him to determine the mass-to-charge ratio for an electron. His work led to a revision of the marblelike model of the atom. In this **"plum pudding model,"** the electrons were envisioned as being suspended in a sphere of positively charged mass like blueberries suspended in a muffin.

The "Plum Pudding Model" of the Atom

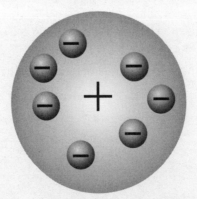

The Thomson model of the atom was refined again in 1909 with the determination of the mass of the electron by Robert Millikan. In his famous oil drop experiment, he calculated the mass of a single electron by measuring the voltage required to suspend a charged oil droplet between two charged plates.

The Nuclear Atom

A milestone in scientists' understanding of the internal structure of the atom was reached in 1911 with Ernest Rutherford's work with alpha particles. When Rutherford directed a beam of **alpha particles** (particles composed of two protons and two neutrons) from a radioactive source at a thin sheet of gold foil, the vast majority of the alpha particles passed through the atoms. Surprisingly, a small fraction of the alpha particles were deflected. Rutherford reasoned that there must be a very small, dense, positively charged **nucleus** at the center of the electron cloud of the atom.

The Rutherford Gold Foil Experiment

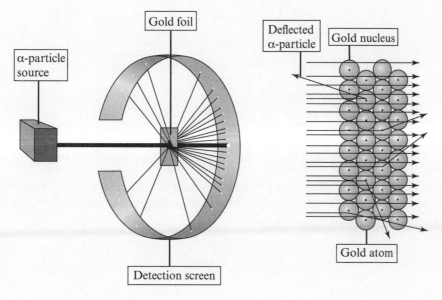

The accounts of the discoveries of electrons and the nucleus serve to illustrate an important point. A scientific model such as that of the atom is a representation that best reflects all the known experimental information. A model is not necessarily static; it is continually evolving to incorporate additional data as it becomes available. This point is emphasized in the AP Chemistry curriculum.

The Quantum Nature of the Atom

The model of the atom following Rutherford's discovery was one in which the electrons orbited the nucleus in elliptical paths like planets orbiting a star. The structure of the atom is currently understood to be a more complicated picture of electrons behaving as waves. At the AP Chemistry level, **electronic orbitals** can be visualized as three-dimensional regions surrounding the nucleus where the probability of finding an electron is high. They are not elliptical. Instead, orbitals are understood to be shaped like diffuse spheres, petals, and donuts. This section will briefly review the evolution of the atomic model from the Rutherford solar system description to the current quantum mechanical understanding.

Electromagnetic Radiation

Electromagnetic radiation played a crucial role in shaping current ideas of atomic structure. **Electromagnetic radiation** is radiant energy that is composed of oscillating electric and magnetic fields. Visible light, radio waves, x-rays, gamma rays, and ultraviolet and infrared radiation are all electromagnetic radiation. It is both wavelike and particlelike in nature. A **photon** is a unit of electromagnetic radiation that has a **quantum,** or fixed amount, of energy.

Electromagnetic radiation can be described in terms of its frequency, wavelength, speed, amplitude, and energy. The **wavelength,** λ, is the distance between two consecutive crests or troughs. The **amplitude** is the distance from crest to trough.

Wavelength and Amplitude

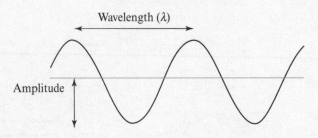

Electromagnetic radiation can have a continuous spectrum of wavelengths, but the common units for wavelengths of visible light are the nanometer ($1 \text{ nm} = 10^{-9} \text{ m}$) and the Ångstrom ($1 \text{ Å} = 10^{-10} \text{ m}$).

The **frequency** of a wave, ν, is the number of waves that pass a fixed point in space per second. The units of frequency are hertz (abbreviated Hz). Hertz are cycles per second, also represented as s^{-1}.

All electromagnetic radiation travels at the **speed of light,** c, and this speed is related to the wavelength and frequency. This equation, in addition to the value for the speed of light, is included on the *AP Chemistry Equations and Constants* sheet (pages 365–366).

$$c = \lambda\nu$$
$$c = 2.998 \times 10^8 \text{ m} \cdot \text{s}^{-1}$$

It follows that wavelength and frequency are inversely proportional. The higher the frequency, the shorter the wavelength.

PRACTICE:

> Find the frequency of an infrared photon that has a wavelength of 750 nm.

The equation for the speed of light ($c = \lambda\nu$) can be rearranged to solve for frequency.

$$\nu = \frac{c}{\lambda} = \frac{2.998 \times 10^8 \text{ m} \cdot \text{s}^{-1}}{750 \text{ nm}} \times \frac{10^9 \text{ nm}}{1 \text{ m}} = 4.0 \times 10^{14} \text{ s}^{-1}$$

The **energy,** E, of a photon is related to its frequency by the Planck relation and Planck's constant, $h = 6.626 \times 10^{-34} \text{ J} \cdot \text{s}^{-1}$. Both the energy equation and the value of Planck's constant are provided on the exam.

$$E = h\nu$$

Substitution for ν gives the relationship between the energy, the wavelength, and the speed of light.

$$E = \frac{hc}{\lambda}$$

The energy of a photon is directly proportional to the frequency and inversely proportional to the wavelength.

PRACTICE:

> What is the energy of a photon that has a wavelength of 620 nm?

The energy can be found using the Planck relationship.

$$E = \frac{hc}{\lambda} = \frac{(6.626 \times 10^{-34}\,\text{J} \cdot \cancel{\text{s}})(2.998 \times 10^{8}\,\cancel{\text{m} \cdot \text{s}^{-1}})}{620\,\cancel{\text{nm}}} \times \frac{10^{9}\,\cancel{\text{nm}}}{1\,\cancel{\text{m}}} = 3.2 \times 10^{-19}\,\text{J}$$

The electromagnetic spectrum should be remembered in terms of the energy ranking of the classifications of electromagnetic radiation. Memorization of specific wavelengths or frequencies is not necessary, but students should know the order of decreasing energy (increasing wavelength) of electromagnetic radiation.

Gamma rays   <   X-rays   <   Ultraviolet   <   Visible   <   Infrared   <   Microwaves   <   Radio

(highest energy, lowest λ)   (lowest energy, highest λ)

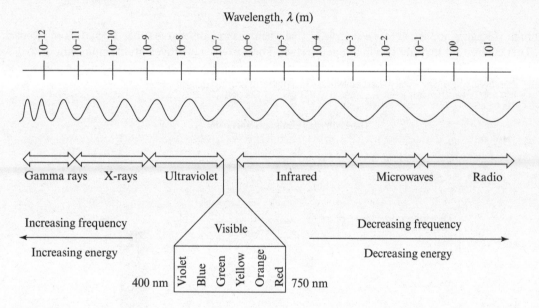

The Electromagnetic Spectrum

In the sections and chapters that follow, the chemistry applications of several of these classes of electromagnetic radiation will be reviewed.

Emission and Absorption Spectra: The Bohr Model of the Atom

The study of the emission of ultraviolet and visible light by excited hydrogen atoms was the foundation for the quantum mechanical model of the atom. When white light, which is comprised of the continuous spectrum of visible wavelengths, is passed through a prism, it is separated into a rainbow of wavelengths.

Separation of White Light into the Visible Spectrum

When a high voltage is applied across a sample of hydrogen gas in a discharge tube, the hydrogen atoms are excited. This means that they are in a high-energy state. These excited hydrogen atoms emit light as they relax to lower-energy states. When the light emitted by hydrogen is passed through a prism, only discrete wavelengths are observed. These wavelengths comprise the emission spectrum of hydrogen.

The Hydrogen Emission Spectrum

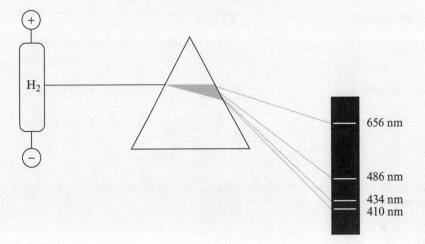

Furthermore, when white light is passed through a sample of hydrogen gas, some of the wavelengths are absorbed. The missing wavelengths in the light that emerges from the sample coincide exactly with the wavelengths that are produced in the emission spectrum. The spectrum in which the absorbed frequencies are absent is called the **absorption spectrum** of hydrogen.

The Hydrogen Absorption Spectrum

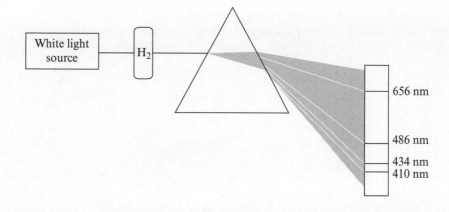

The **Bohr model** of the atom, presented in 1913 by Danish physicist Niels Bohr, is a quantum model that provides an explanation for the absorption and emission spectra of hydrogen. According to the Bohr model, an electron orbits the nucleus in a fixed, circular path. Orbits are only located at discrete distances from the nucleus, and each orbit has an associated energy. In other words, the energy is **quantized.** The electrons orbiting the nucleus either occupy the lowest-energy **ground state,** $n = 1$, which is the configuration closest to the nucleus, or they occupy an excited, higher-energy state, $n = 2, 3, 4,...\infty$. The positive integer, n, is called the **principal quantum number,** and it describes the main energy level than an electron occupies.

When the electron in the ground state of a hydrogen atom is excited by an applied voltage, it is promoted to a higher-energy level. The electron relaxes back to the ground state, and the transition gives off a photon that is equal in energy to the energy difference between the excited state and a lower-energy state. Since only certain energies are allowed, this accounts for the characteristic wavelengths that are observed in the emission spectrum of hydrogen.

The Bohr Model of a Hydrogen Atom: Atomic Emission

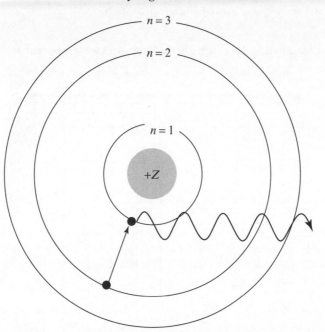

The absorption spectrum is generated when the hydrogen electron absorbs a photon with an energy exactly equal to the difference in energy between two levels. The light that passes through the sample is missing the wavelengths that correspond to photons that are absorbed.

The Bohr Model of a Hydrogen Atom: Atomic Absorption

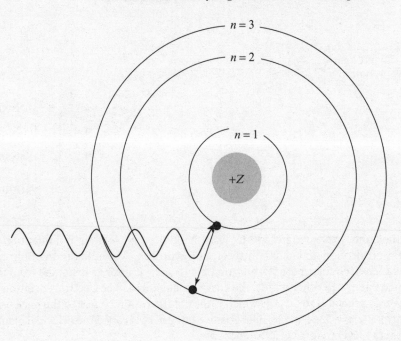

Higher-energy levels in a hydrogen atom become increasingly close in energy. In other words, the energy difference between the $n = 2$ level and the $n = 3$ level is less than the energy difference between the $n = 1$ and $n = 2$ energy levels.

Transitions from higher-energy levels to the $n = 1$ energy level emit wavelengths in the ultraviolet region of the electromagnetic spectrum. This set of spectral lines is referred to as the **Lyman series.** Transitions from higher-energy levels to the $n = 2$ level emit lower-energy wavelengths. These are referred to as the **Balmer series,** and four of these lines are in the visible region of the spectrum.

Characteristic Wavelengths in the Hydrogen Emission Spectrum

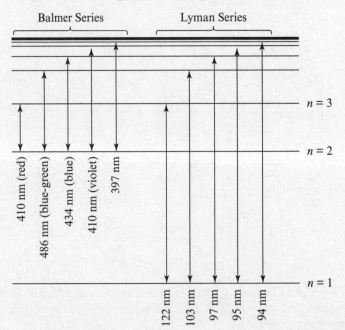

The Bohr model works well for the electronic energy transitions in hydrogen, but it does not work when applied to atoms with more than one electron. The problem is that *electrons do not orbit the nucleus in fixed circular or elliptical orbits*. The circular orbit picture is based on classical mechanics, which describe the motion of large objects such as projectiles, roller coasters, and planets. An acceleration in classical mechanics is a change in the speed or direction of an object in motion. An orbiting electron would be in a continuous state of acceleration due to its circular path, and so it would be expected to constantly emit electromagnetic radiation. In this way, it would lose energy and spiral into the nucleus. Because this does not happen, it is clear that the Bohr model is not fully correct, although it is still a useful way to keep track of the quantization of electronic energy in single-electron atoms.

The Quantum Mechanical Atom

A complete revolution in atomic theory occurred in the 1920s with the development of **quantum mechanics,** the study of the energy and motion of subatomic particles. Quantum mechanical descriptions are applied to very small particles that can only exist in certain energy states and can change their energy by absorbing or emitting electromagnetic radiation. The energies and positions of electrons in atoms are described by wave functions. **Wave functions** are solutions to the **Schrödinger equation,** a mathematical model of electronic motion that was based on the treatment of electrons as waves. Wave functions describe **atomic orbitals.** Each atomic orbital is composed of a maximum of two electrons.

For each wave function, there is a certain probability of finding an electron at a certain distance from the nucleus. The squares of the wave functions are related to the probability of finding an electron in each point in space surrounding the nucleus.

The lowest-energy atomic orbitals in each main energy level, or **shell,** beginning with $n = 1$, are the s orbitals. *S* **orbitals** are spherically symmetrical orbitals surrounding the nucleus. It should be noticed that the radius at which the electron has the highest probability of existing increases with the energy of the electron. As the principal energy level of the electron increases, so does the number of **nodes,** or regions at which the electron has zero probability of existing.

Electron Density Distributions for *s* Orbitals

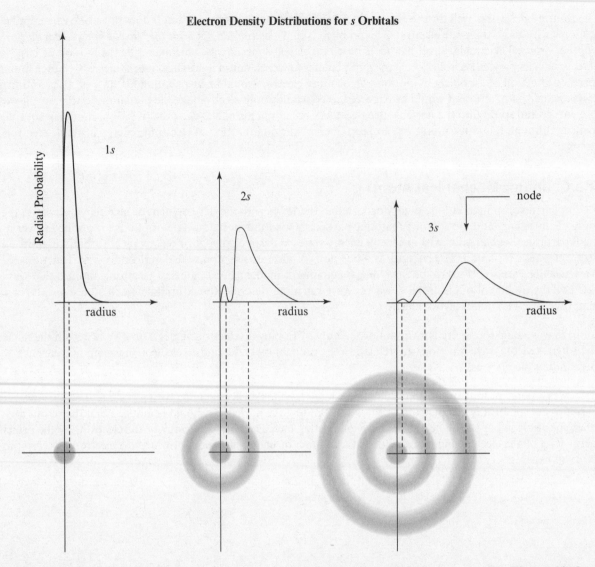

The second principal energy level, $n = 2$, contains an *s* orbital and three *p* orbitals, p_x, p_y, and p_z. The **p orbitals** are oriented along *x*, *y*, and *z* axes with respect to one another and are shaped like two equal-sized balloons tied together at their ends. Since each orbital is composed of a maximum of two electrons, the entire $n = 2$ shell can contain a maximum of eight electrons (two electrons in the *s* orbital and a total of six in the *p* orbitals).

Each shell beginning with $n = 3$ has a set of five *d* orbitals. The **d orbitals** are either shaped like four equal-sized balloons tied together at their ends (a three-dimensional four-leaf clover) or, as in the case of the d_{z^2} orbital, like two equal-sized balloons surrounded by a donut-shaped region.

The Shapes of Atomic Orbitals

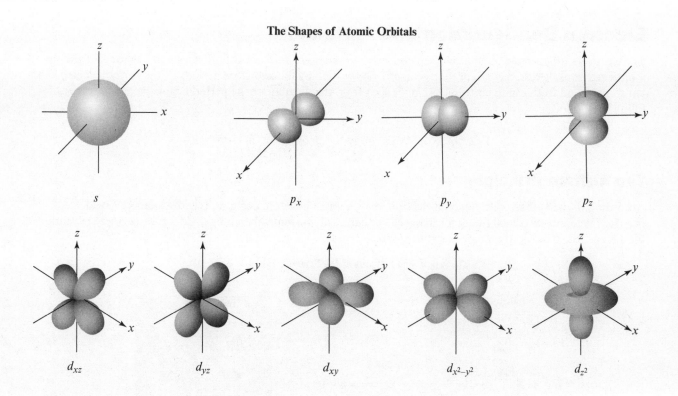

s p_x p_y p_z

d_{xz} d_{yz} d_{xy} $d_{x^2-y^2}$ d_{z^2}

The f orbitals have complicated shapes and names. Students will *not* need to know the shapes or names of the f orbitals for the AP Chemistry exam. They will only need to know that there are seven f orbitals in each shell, starting with $n = 4$.

Each type of orbital designation, s, p, d, or f, present within a shell represents a **subshell** or **sublevel.** Then number of subshells within a particular shell is equal to the shell number, n. The number of orbitals in the shell is equal to n^2, and the total possible number of electrons in a shell is equal to $2n^2$.

This pattern is summarized below.

Shell, n	Orbitals Present	Number of Subshells (n)	Number of Orbitals in the Shell (n^2)	Total Possible Number of Electrons in the Shell ($2n^2$)
1	$1s$	1 (s)	1	2
2	$2s$ $2p_x$, $2p_y$, $2p_z$	2 (s and p)	4	8
3	$3s$ $3p_x$, $3p_y$, $3p_z$ $3d_{xy}$, $3d_{yz}$, $3d_{xz}$, $3d_{x^2-y^2}$, $3d_{z^2}$	3 (s, p, and d)	9	18
4	$4s$ $4p_x$, $4p_y$, $4p_z$ $4d_{xy}$, $4d_{yz}$, $4d_{xz}$, $4d_{x^2-y^2}$, $4d_{z^2}$ $4f$ ora (There are seven $4f$ orbitals, for a maximum total of 14 electrons in the $4f$ subshell.)	4 (s, p, d, and f)	16	32

Electron Configuration and Periodicity

The **electron configuration** of an atom provides a shorthand description of the energies and positions of the atom's electrons. Electron configurations can *often* be written by following the periods of the periodic table from left to right and from top to bottom. As can be seen from the diagram of the periodic table below, the order of filling is as follows:

$$1s^2 2s^2 2p^6 3s^2 3p^6 4s^2 3d^{10} 4p^6 5s^2 4d^{10} 5p^6 6s^2 4f^{14} 5d^{10} 6p^6 7s^2 5f^{14} 6d^{10}$$

The Aufbau Principle

According to the **aufbau principle,** each electron in a ground state atom occupies the lowest-energy available orbital. The order of orbital filling for many atoms can easily be remembered by dividing the periodic table into the s block, the p block, the d block, and the f block.

The s, p, d, and f Blocks of the Periodic Table

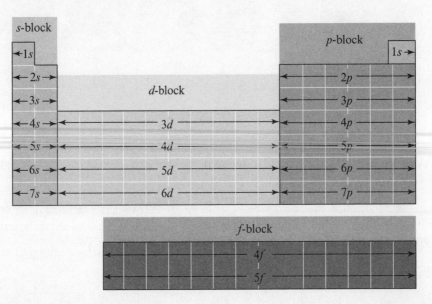

A hydrogen atom's single electron is in the lowest-energy ($n = 1$) s orbital in the ground state. The electron configuration for the ground state of hydrogen is $1s^1$, where the superscript denotes the number of electrons occupying the orbital. A helium atom has two electrons in the $n = 1$ shell. The electron configuration of helium is $1s^2$. A neutral atom of lithium has three electrons. In the ground state, two of the electrons are in the $n = 1$ shell and one is in the $n = 2$ shell. The electron configuration of lithium is $1s^2 2s^1$.

Suppose we would like to write the electron configuration for the ground state of arsenic. Arsenic is located in the third row of the p block of the periodic table, as shown below. Counting hydrogen and helium gives $1s^2$. Next are lithium and beryllium: $2s^2$. Continued counting in order of atomic number from boron through zinc results in $2p^6 3s^2 3p^6 4s^2 3d^{10}$. Arsenic is the third element in the $4p$ sublevel, so the last three electrons are designated $4p^3$. The full electron configuration for arsenic is $1s^2 2s^2 2p^6 3s^2 3p^6 4s^2 3d^{10} 4p^3$. (In order to emphasize the increase in orbital energy as a function of the main energy level, some teachers prefer the following grouping: $1s^2 2s^2 2p^6 3s^2 3p^6 3d^{10} 4s^2 4p^3$. Both configurations will earn credit on the AP Chemistry exam.)

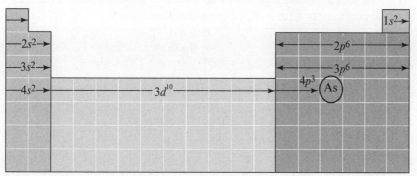

The Electron Configuration of Arsenic Based on Periodic Table Position

There are exceptions to this filling order. Students are not required to write electron configurations on the AP Chemistry exam for elements that do not follow this pattern, but they should recognize when an electron configuration does not follow the conventional order and understand why these deviations occur. To illustrate, the electron configuration of copper is expected to be $1s^2 2s^2 2p^6 3s^2 3p^6 \mathbf{4s^2 3d^9}$. Instead, the actual configuration of copper is $1s^2 2s^2 2p^6 3s^2 3p^6 \mathbf{4s^1 3d^{10}}$. An element's order of orbital filling is the electronic arrangement that minimizes electron-electron repulsions and achieves the lowest-energy configuration overall.

Noble gas notation is a shorthand method of writing electron configurations. For noble gas notation, the symbol of the previous noble gas is written in brackets, and then the electron configuration is continued. The noble gas configuration for the arsenic example is $[Ar]4s^2 3d^{10} 4p^3$.

PRACTICE:

> Write the full electron configuration and the noble gas notation configuration of the ground state of cobalt, Co.

Cobalt is found in the fourth period of the table. The full notation is $1s^2 2s^2 2p^6 3s^2 3p^6 4s^2 3d^7$. Counting back to the previous noble gas, argon, gives the noble gas configuration $[Ar]4s^2 3d^7$.

Hund's Rule and the Pauli Exclusion Principle

Electron configurations can be represented using **orbital notation** in which the electrons are depicted by arrows. Two electrons in an orbital must spin in opposite directions. Arrows pointing up and down denote spin-up and spin-down electrons, respectively. The orbital notation for oxygen is shown below.

Oxygen Orbital Notation

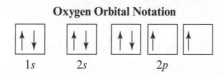

This example illustrates both Hund's rule and the Pauli Exclusion Principle. **Hund's rule** states that in the ground state, electrons occupy each orbital in a subshell singly before pairing up. In addition, the first electrons in the separate orbitals of a subshell have parallel spins. In other words, each orbital of a subshell is occupied by a spin-up electron before any orbital in the subshell gets a spin-down electron.

According to the **Pauli Exclusion Principle,** a single orbital cannot hold two spin-up or two spin-down electrons. A pair of electrons may only exist together in an orbital if they have opposite spins.

PRACTICE:

> Write the electron configuration for sulfur using orbital notation.

The electron configuration for sulfur is $1s^2 2s^2 2p^6 3s^2 3p^4$.

Sulfur Orbital Notation

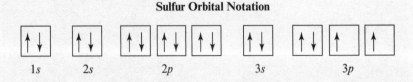

Exceptions to the aufbau principle and Hund's rule occur when an electron is in an **excited state,** or higher-energy state. Below, carbon is shown in two excited states. The first is a violation of the aufbau principle and the second is a violation of Hund's rule.

Excited States of Carbon

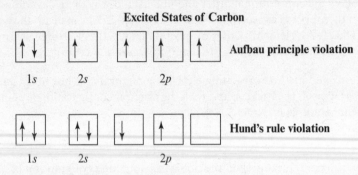

Violations of the Pauli Exclusion Principle are forbidden.

PRACTICE:

> Which of the following is a ground state, which is an excited state, and which is forbidden?
>
> **(a)** $1s^2 2s^2 2p^5$
>
> **(b)** $1s^2 2s^2 2p^2 3s^3$
>
> **(c)** $1s^2 2s^1 2p^6$

(a) The configuration $1s^2 2s^2 2p^5$ is in the ground state. The aufbau principle and the Pauli Exclusion Principle are presumably obeyed.

(b) The configuration $1s^2 2s^2 2p^2 3s^3$ is forbidden. The $3s$ orbital holds more than two electrons, so the Pauli Exclusion Principle is violated.

(c) The configuration $1s^2 2s^1 2p^6$ is an excited state since one of the electrons in the $2s$ sublevel has been promoted to the $2p$ sublevel. The Pauli Exclusion Principle is presumably obeyed.

Magnetism

A spinning charged particle such as an electron has an associated magnetic moment. The behavior of elements in a magnetic field can be predicted based on electron configuration. There are three types of magnetism to be aware of: ferromagnetism, paramagnetism, and diamagnetism.

Ferromagnetism is permanent magnetism exhibited by some solid metals. Iron, nickel, and cobalt are ferromagnetic elements. The presence of an external magnetic field magnetizes a ferromagnetic sample by aligning the spins of the electrons. The spins remain aligned and the sample remains magnetized when the external magnetic field is removed.

Paramagnetic substances are those that contain unpaired electrons in one or more orbitals. When a paramagnetic element is placed in an external magnetic field, the spins of its electrons align with the field. When the magnetic field is removed, the electron spins become random and the element's magnetism is lost.

Diamagnetic elements are those that are repelled by a magnetic field. These elements do not have unpaired electrons.

PRACTICE:

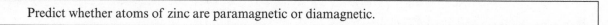

Predict whether atoms of zinc are paramagnetic or diamagnetic.

The first step in making this prediction is to write the electron configuration of zinc: $[Ar]4s^2 3d^{10}$. Orbital notation for zinc is written as follows.

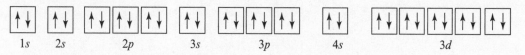

Since there are no unpaired electrons in zinc, it is a diamagnetic element.

PRACTICE:

Predict whether manganese atoms are paramagnetic or diamagnetic.

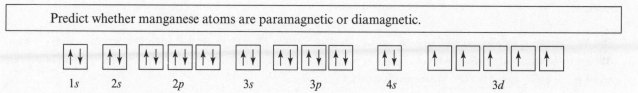

There are five unpaired electrons in the $3d$ orbital of manganese, so it is a paramagnetic element.

The Periodic Table

The periodic table was first arranged by Dmitri Mendeleev in 1869. He systematically organized the elements according to atomic weight and realized that there was a regular, periodic repetition of the chemical and physical properties of the elements. Mendeleev even left spaces in the periodic table for elements that had yet to be discovered. This regular repetition of properties is called the **periodic law.** In the twentieth century, Henry Moseley reorganized the periodic table by atomic number. It is now understood that the regular repetition of properties, or **periodicity,** of the elements is a consequence of the electron configurations of the elements.

The general layout of the periodic table, including the locations of the metals, nonmetals, and metalloids, should be very familiar to AP Chemistry students.

Horizontal rows on the periodic table are referred to as **periods.**

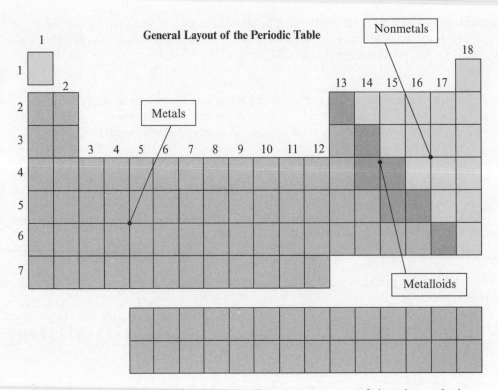

General Layout of the Periodic Table

The properties of any element on the periodic table are a direct consequence of that element's electron configuration. Electron configurations of the elements in **groups** (vertical columns) of the periodic table are similar, so the elements in a group may display similar chemical properties. Groups on the periodic table are also referred to as **families.**

Tip: The group numbers *do not* appear on the periodic table that is provided with the AP Chemistry exam. Students should be familiar with the main group layout of the periodic table. (The Roman numerals do not need to be memorized for the transition metals.)

The Locations of Main Groups, Transition Metals, and Inner Transition Metals

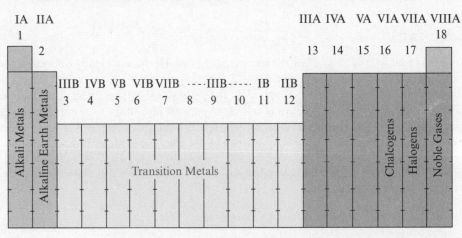

The **main groups** are groups 1, 2, and 13 through 18. The older designations for these groups are IA, IIA, and IIIA through VIIIA. Elements within the same main group have the same number of valence electrons. The **valence electrons** are the electrons in the outermost shell of an atom. These valence electrons are responsible for the reactivity of the elements. For example, a neutral atom of phosphorus has an electron configuration of $1s^2 2s^2 2p^6 3s^2 3p^3$. Phosphorus has five electrons in the highest energy level ($n = 3$).

PRACTICE:

How many valence electrons are in a neutral atom of silicon?

The electron configuration of silicon is $1s^2 2s^2 2p^6 3s^2 3p^2$. The total number of electrons in the $n = 3$ shell is four.

The groups and their properties are summarized below.

Group	Valence Electron Configuration	Elements	Characteristics
1 (IA) Alkali metals	ns^1 for $n \geq 2$	Li, Na, K, Rb, Cs, Fr	Highly reactive elements that tend to lose a single electron to form M^+ ions with noble gas electron configurations. This tendency increases down the group.
2 (IIA) Alkaline earth metals	ns^2 for $n \geq 2$	Be, Mg, Ca, Sr, Ba, Ra	Less reactive than the alkali metals. Tend to lose two electrons to form M^{2+} ions with noble gas electron configurations. This tendency increases down the group.
16 (VIA) Chalcogens	$ns^2 np^4$ for $n \geq 2$	O, S, Se, Te, Po	Tend to gain two electrons to form X^{2-} ions with noble gas. This tendency decreases down the group. Form a large variety of molecular compounds with nonmetals.
17 (VIIA) Halogens	$ns^2 np^5$ for $n \geq 2$	F, Cl, Br, I, At	Tend to gain one electron to form X^- ions. This tendency decreases down the group. Form diatomic molecules, X_2, but are not found in elemental form in nature due to their high reactivity.
18 (VIIIA) Noble gases	$ns^2 np^6$ for $n \geq 2$ ($1s^2$ for helium)	He, Ne, Ar, Kr, Xe, Rn	Do not usually form compounds except under special conditions. They exist in their monatomic form in nature.

Certain elements always occur as diatomic molecules, X_2. These are H_2, N_2, O_2, F_2, Cl_2, Br_2, and I_2; the locations of these elements on the periodic table can be used to memorize them.

The most stable electron configuration for many main group atoms is a **noble gas configuration,** either $1s^2$ or $ns^2 np^6$. When the main group elements form ions, as shown in the table below, they lose or gain electrons as necessary to achieve this electron configuration.

Electron Configurations of Common Main Group Ions

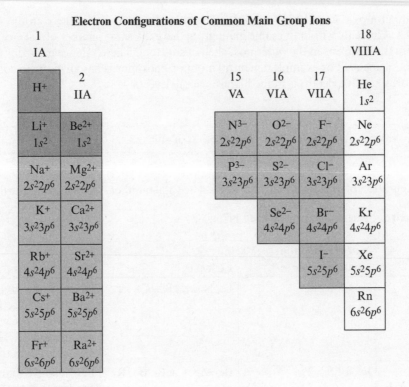

The **transition metals** make up the *d* block of the periodic table. Transition metals generally lose electrons to form cations, but ionization patterns for the transition metals are not as regular and predictable as they are for the main group elements. From left to right across a period, electrons are being added to an inner shell rather than to an outer shell, so the transition metals do not demonstrate the striking group characteristics that the main group elements display. In addition, many transition metals can have more than one oxidation state. For instance, when copper ionizes, it can form either Cu^+ or Cu^{2+}.

Cobalt, for example, can form either Co^{2+} cations or Co^{3+} cations. The *s* electrons, which are highest in energy, are lost.

Electron configuration of Co^0: $[Ar]4s^2 3d^7$

Electron configuration of Co^{2+}: $[Ar]3d^7$

Electron configuration of Co^{3+}: $[Ar]3d^6$

PRACTICE:

> Anions with a −2 charge are most likely to be formed from which main group elements on the periodic table?

When elements with the electron configuration ns^2np^4 gain two electrons, they achieve a noble gas configuration (ns^2np^6), so the main group elements are most likely to be the chalcogens (group VIA).

Periodic Trends

Trends in atomic properties are rationalized using coulombic arguments. Shielding and effective nuclear charge are key ideas that students should be comfortable using in their discussions of the periodic trends. A trend itself should never be offered as an explanation for observed properties.

According to **Coulomb's law,** the energy required to remove an electron from an atom is proportional to the product of the charge of the electron and the effective nuclear charge, and inversely proportional to the distance from the nucleus to the electron.

$$E \propto \frac{q_1 q_2}{r}$$

In this equation, q_1 and q_2 are the charge of the electron and the effective nuclear charge, and r is the distance between the charges. The higher the effective nuclear charge, the more energy is required to remove the oppositely charged electron. Electrons that are more distant from the nucleus require less energy to remove.

Shielding from nuclear attraction accounts for the ease with which a valence electron is removed from a neutral atom when compared with that of an inner shell electrons, or **core electrons.** Since like charges repel, electrons experience repulsion from one another. The larger the number of core electrons between a valence electron and the nucleus, the easier the valence electron is to remove because it is shielded from the positive charge of the nucleus by the core electrons.

PRACTICE:

> Which electron in phosphorus is easier to remove from the atom, a $2p$ electron or a $3p$ electron?

Two effects make the $3p$ electron easier to remove than the $2p$ electron. The $3p$ electron is more distant from the nucleus than the $2p$ electron, so the $3p$ electron experiences less coulombic attraction to the nucleus and requires less energy to remove. The second effect is that of shielding. The $2p$ electron is shielded from the nucleus by the $n = 1$ shell, but the $3p$ electron is shielded by both the $n = 1$ and the $n = 2$ shells. For this reason, also, the $3p$ electron experiences less coulombic attraction to the nucleus and is easier to remove.

Effective nuclear charge, Z_{eff}, is the apparent nuclear charge experienced by an electron after inner shell electron repulsions have been accounted for. It is the difference between the atomic number, Z, and the number of inner shell electrons or core electrons.

$$Z_{eff} = Z - (\text{number of core electrons})$$

PRACTICE:

> What is the effective nuclear charge experienced by a valence electron in a phosphorus atom?

The atomic number of phosphorus, Z, is 15. The core electrons are in the $n = 1$ and $n = 2$ shells. This is a total of 10 core electrons. The effective nuclear charge experienced by the $n = 3$ electrons is

$$Z_{eff} = 15 - 10 = 5$$

As we have seen, shells are further divided into subshells. For atoms with multiple electrons, the subshells within a shell have slightly different energies. This can be understood in terms of the **penetration effect.** A comparison of the radial distributions of orbitals within the second shell shows that the $2s$ electrons penetrate the cloud of $1s$ core electrons more than the $2p$ electrons. Due to their greater penetration and greater degree of exposure to the positive charge of the nucleus, the $2s$ electrons experience more attraction to the nucleus and are slightly lower in energy than the $2p$ electrons.

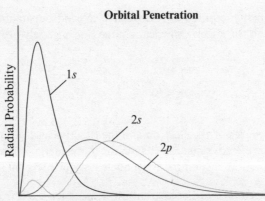

Orbital Penetration

This pattern holds true for the *d* and *f* subshells, too. The *p* subshell electrons experience a greater coulombic attraction to the nucleus and are lower in energy than the *d* subshell electrons in the same shell due to a higher degree of penetration. Likewise, the *d* subshell electrons are lower in energy than the *f* subshell electrons in the same shell.

Ionization Energy

The energy required to remove the highest-energy outermost electron from an atom in the gas phase to form a +1 cation, as represented in the equation below, is called the **first ionization energy,** IE_1.

$$X(g) \rightarrow X^+(g) + e^- \qquad IE_1$$

Across a period on the periodic table, first ionization energy tends to increase. Increased effective nuclear charge going from left to right causes a greater coulombic attraction between the electrons and the nucleus.

Down a group, ionization energy tends to decrease. The highest-energy electrons occupy increasingly higher shells. With a greater number of shells shielding the valence electrons from the nucleus, more electron-electron repulsion and less nuclear attraction is experienced by the outermost electrons. Additionally, the distance of the outermost electrons from the nucleus increases down a group, so the energy required to remove these electrons decreases.

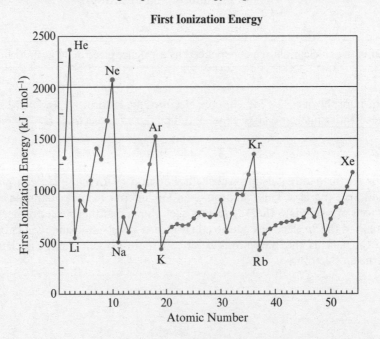

First Ionization Energy

PRACTICE:

> Would the expected first ionization energy be higher for sodium or potassium?

Sodium would be expected to have a higher ionization energy because its outermost electrons are less shielded from the positively charged nucleus than those of potassium, making them harder to remove. In addition, sodium's outermost electrons are in the $n = 2$ shell (compared to the $n = 3$ shell for potassium), so they are closer to the nucleus and subject to higher coulombic attraction. The effective nuclear charge is the same for sodium and potassium, so Z_{eff} is inconsequential in this situation.

The energies required to remove subsequent electrons to form +2 and +3 cations are called **second** and **third ionization energies.** After the atom loses one electron, subsequent ionizations become increasingly difficult because of decreased electronic repulsion and increased attraction of the remaining electrons to the positively charged nucleus. Ionization energies increase substantially as more and more electrons are removed.

The equations for second and third ionization energies, IE_2 and IE_2, are given by

$$X^+(g) \rightarrow X^{2+}(g) + e^- \qquad IE_2$$
$$X^{2+}(g) \rightarrow X^{3+}(g) + e^- \qquad IE_3$$

Notice the increases in subsequent ionization energies in the ionization data for the first five elements, shown in the table below. Also, if we compare the effect of shells on ionization energy, we see that removal of an electron from a core configuration requires substantially more energy than electrons that occupied a higher-energy shell.

Consider helium, for instance. The second ionization energy is a little over two times the first. It requires more energy to remove a second electron from a positively charged He^+ ion.

For lithium and other elements with electrons in higher shells, the additional effect can be seen. The second ionization energy for lithium is *fourteen times* the first. Not only does it require more energy to remove a second electron from an already positively charged lithium ion, the energy increase is substantial because the second electron is being removed from a noble gas core electron configuration.

Ionization Energies (kJ·mol⁻¹)					
	IE_1	IE_2	IE_3	IE_4	IE_5
H	1312				
He	2372	5250			
Li	520	7297	11,810		
Be	899	1757	14,845	21,000	
B	800	2426	3659	25,020	32,820

PRACTICE:

> Consider the first four ionization energies below for an unknown element. To what group of the periodic table does the element likely belong?

Ionization Energies (kJ·mol⁻¹)			
IE_1	IE_2	IE_3	IE_4
737	1450	7731	10,545

The second ionization energy is about two times the first ionization energy for this element. The third ionization energy is more than five times the second ionization energy. The fourth ionization energy is less than twice the third ionization energy. The relatively large increase between IE_3 and IE_2 indicates that after the second ionization, a noble gas core electron configuration has been achieved. This indicates that the element is probably a member of group IIA. (Indeed, the data is for magnesium.)

Electron Affinity

Electron affinity is the energy released upon the addition of an electron to an atom in the gas phase according to the following equation.

$$X(g) + e^- \rightarrow X^-(g)$$

The more negative the electron affinity, the more energy is released when the electron combines with the atom. In other words, the more negative the electron affinity, the more easily the electron is added to the atom. The trend is not as pronounced as that for ionization energy, but the explanation may be provided using similar arguments.

Across a period on the periodic table, electron affinity generally tends to become more negative. Increased effective nuclear charge from left to right across the period increases the coulombic attraction between the electrons and the nucleus, so electrons are added more easily.

Down a group, electron affinity becomes less negative. (The addition of an electron becomes less favorable.) Down a group, electrons are being added to increasingly higher shells. With a greater number of shells between the outermost electrons and the nucleus, shielding is increased. More electron-electron repulsion and less nuclear attraction is experienced by the outermost electrons. The distance of the outermost electrons from the nucleus is again increasing, causing a decrease in coulombic attraction.

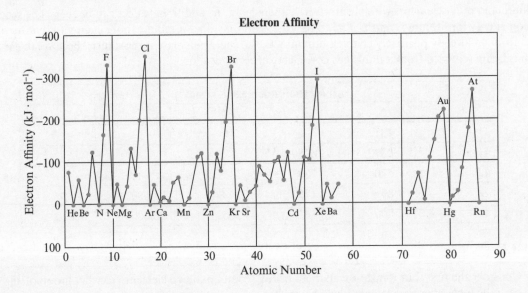

PRACTICE:

Is more energy released with the addition of an electron to a fluorine atom or to an oxygen atom?

Adding an electron to a fluorine atom releases more energy than adding an electron to an oxygen atom. Fluorine has a more negative electron affinity because it has a higher effective nuclear charge than oxygen. An electron is being added to the same shell, $n = 2$, for both fluorine and oxygen, so shielding is irrelevant.

Atomic Radii

The **atomic radius,** or covalent radius, is defined as one-half the distance between the nuclei of two atoms of the same element bound by a single covalent bond or a metallic bond.

Atomic radius

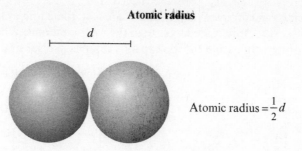

$$\text{Atomic radius} = \frac{1}{2}d$$

Across a period on the periodic table, atomic radii tend to decrease due to increasing effective nuclear charge. The electrons experience greater coulombic attraction to the nucleus, so they are held more closely.

Down a group, atomic radii increase due to increased shielding. The larger the number of shells between the outermost electrons and the nucleus, the greater the electronic repulsions and the greater the distance between the valence electrons and the nucleus. The electrons are held less tightly due to decreased coulombic attraction.

Atomic Radii

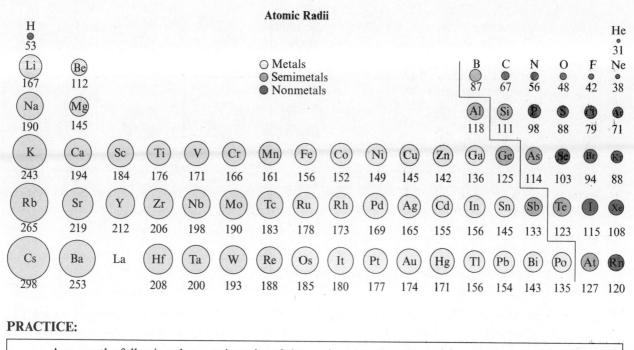

PRACTICE:

> Arrange the following elements in order of decreasing atomic radius: calcium, barium, and beryllium.

$$\text{radius}_{Ba} > \text{radius}_{Ca} > \text{radius}_{Be}$$

The radius of beryllium (Be) is the smallest, calcium (Ca) has an intermediate radius, and the radius of barium (Ba) is the largest. Since barium is closest to the bottom of the periodic table, there are more shells shielding its outer electrons from the nucleus. The electronic repulsions and the distance of the outermost electrons from the nucleus is the greatest, so the coulombic attraction is the smallest. The electrons of beryllium are the least shielded, so they are held most tightly by the nucleus.

Ionic Radii

Within a period or a group, ionic radii follow the same general trend as atomic radii. They decrease from left to right, and they increase from top to bottom. The shielding and coulombic arguments are similar.

Cations are smaller than their parent atoms. When electrons are lost, there is less electronic repulsion and the atom contracts from its neutral size. Anions are larger than their parent atoms. When electrons are gained, there are more repulsive electronic interactions and the ion expands from its neutral size.

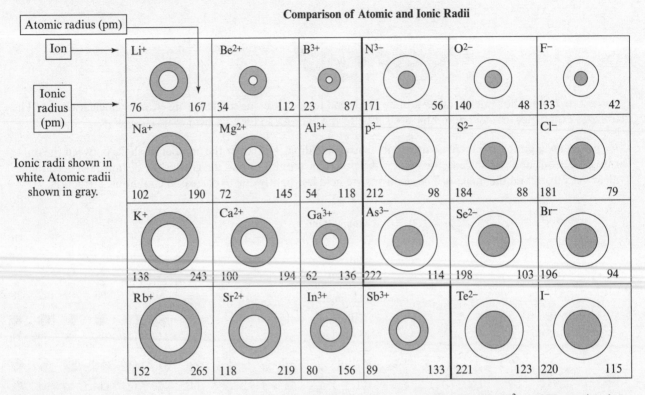

Comparison of Atomic and Ionic Radii

Isoelectronic species are atoms or ions that have equal numbers of electrons. For example, O^{2-} and Ne are isoelectronic. When the radii of isoelectronic species are compared, as the nuclear charge increases, the size decreases.

PRACTICE:

Rank the following ions from largest to smallest: K^+, Cl^-, Ca^{2+}, S^{2-}.

The correct ranking of the ions from largest to smallest is S^{2-}, Cl^-, K^+, Ca^{2+}. All the ions are isoelectronic and have a $[Ne]3s^2 3p^6$ electron configuration, while the nuclear charge increases with atomic number from sulfur to calcium.

Electronegativity

Electronegativity is a measure of how strongly an atom draws electrons toward itself in a covalent bond. The higher the electronegativity of an element, the more it attracts shared electrons.

The **Pauling electronegativity scale** is one that is very commonly used. Pauling electronegativities range from less than 1 for the group IA metals, which are not very electronegative, to 4.0 for fluorine, the most electronegative element. Electronegativities of noble gases are not discussed since the group VIIIA elements rarely participate in covalent bonding. The consequences of electronegativity differences between bonded atoms will be discussed further in Big Idea 2 (Chapter 2, "Bonding and Intermolecular Forces").

Pauling Electronegativities

1 **H** 2.2																	
3 **Li** 1.0	4 **Be** 1.5											5 **B** 2.0	6 **C** 2.5	7 **N** 3.0	8 **O** 3.4	9 **F** 4.0
11 **Na** 0.9	12 **Mg** 1.2											13 **Al** 1.5	14 **Si** 1.9	15 **P** 2.2	16 **S** 2.6	17 **Cl** 3.1
19 **K** 0.9	20 **Ca** 1.0	21 **Sc** 1.3	22 **Ti** 1.5	23 **V** 1.6	24 **Cr** 1.6	25 **Mn** 1.6	26 **Fe** 1.8	27 **Co** 1.9	28 **Ni** 1.9	29 **Cu** 1.9	30 **Zn** 1.7	31 **Ga** 1.8	32 **Ge** 2.0	33 **As** 2.2	34 **Se** 2.6	35 **Br** 2.9
37 **Rb** 0.8	38 **Sr** 1.0	39 **Y** 1.2	40 **Zr** 1.3	41 **Nb** 1.6	42 **Mo** 2.1	43 **Tc** 1.9	44 **Ru** 2.2	45 **Rh** 2.3	46 **Pd** 2.2	47 **Ag** 1.9	48 **Cd** 1.7	49 **In** 1.8	50 **Sn** 1.8	51 **Sb** 2.0	52 **Te** 2.1	53 **I** 2.6
55 **Cs** 0.8	56 **Ba** 0.9	57 **La** 1.1	72 **Hf** 1.3	73 **Ta** 1.5	74 **W** 2.3	75 **Re** 1.9	76 **Os** 2.2	77 **Ir** 2.2	78 **Pt** 2.3	79 **Au** 2.5	80 **Hg** 2.0	81 **Tl** 1.6	82 **Pb** 1.9	83 **Bi** 2.0	84 **Po** 2.0	85 **At** 2.2
87 **Fr** 0.7	88 **Ra** 0.9																

Across a period on the periodic table, electronegativity increases. Increasing effective nuclear charge going from left to right increases attractions between the electrons and the nucleus.

Down a group, electronegativity decreases. Electrons are more shielded from the nucleus, so they experience a weaker nuclear attraction. The distance of the outermost electrons from the nucleus increases down a group, causing the coulombic attraction of the outermost electrons to the nucleus to decrease.

PRACTICE:

> Which is more electronegative, sulfur or phosphorus?

Sulfur is more electronegative than phosphorus. The effective nuclear charge of sulfur is greater than that of phosphorus, which causes sulfur to attract electrons more strongly. Both sulfur and phosphorus are in the same period, so shielding arguments do not apply.

Periodic Trend Anomalies

Some elements do not follow the periodic trends for ionization energy or electron affinity. The explanations for anomalous variations in these periodic properties are sometimes best explained using orbital notation. For example, the first ionization energies in the second period generally increase from left to right, but two elements in the second period, beryllium and nitrogen, do not follow the trend.

Beryllium has a higher ionization energy than boron. The decrease in ionization energy between beryllium and boron is due to the ease of removal of an electron from a 2*p* orbital in boron compared with a 2*s* orbital in beryllium. The 2*s* orbital is slightly lower in energy than a 2*p* orbital. Electrons in an *s* orbital penetrate closer to the nucleus than in a *p* orbital. This leads to a higher coulombic attraction between the 2*s* electrons and the nucleus.

Nitrogen has a higher ionization energy than oxygen. When two electrons occupy the same orbital, there is a certain amount of electron-electron repulsion between them. When an electron is removed from a $2p$ orbital of an oxygen atom, the repulsion it experiences from the other electron in the $2p$ orbital is relieved. Nitrogen's $2p$ orbitals, however, are all singly occupied and the electrons do not experience the additional relief of repulsive interactions when an electron is removed.

Ionization of Nitrogen and Oxygen

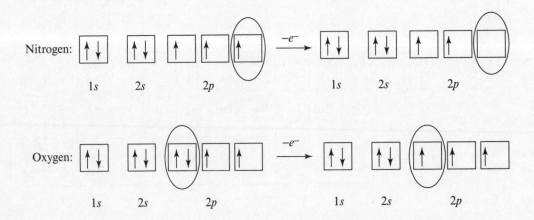

PRACTICE:

The electron affinity of nitrogen is less negative than that of carbon. Provide an explanation for this exception to the periodic trend.

It is more difficult to add an electron to nitrogen than it is to add one to carbon; this exception to the trend has a similar explanation to the one for the anomalous ionization energies of nitrogen and oxygen.

When two electrons occupy the same orbital, there is some repulsion between them. When an electron is added to carbon, the result is three singly occupied $2p$ orbitals. When an electron is added to nitrogen, however, that electron is forced to pair with an existing electron in one of the already singly occupied $3p$ orbitals. The increased electronic repulsion results in a less negative electron affinity for nitrogen compared to carbon.

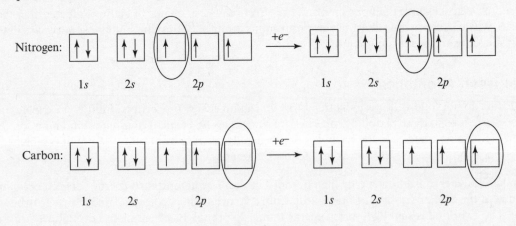

Photoelectron Spectroscopy

Experimental evidence for the shell and subshell energies and populations of electrons in atoms comes from a technique called **photoelectron spectroscopy,** or PES.

Photoelectron spectroscopy has its basis in the photoelectric effect. The **photoelectric effect** is the ability of photons of a certain minimum energy to cause electrons to be ejected from a metal. Photons with insufficient energy are incapable of ejecting electrons.

The Photoelectric Effect

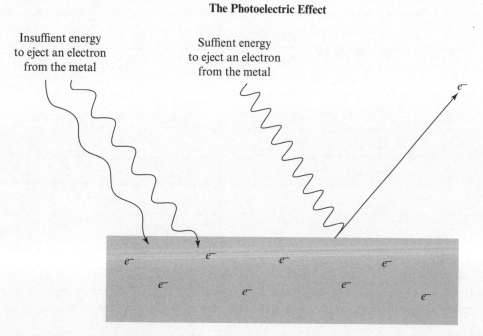

In a photoelectron spectroscopy experiment, atoms are bombarded with beams of x-ray photons with a known energy. The energy of the photons is sufficiently high that when a photon collides with any electron in a neutral atom, it causes the electron to be ejected.

The **kinetic energy,** KE, of the ejected electrons (their energy of motion) is measured in a detector. The difference between the energy of the photon used, hv, and the kinetic energy of the electron is equal to the ionization energy, IE, the amount of energy that was required to eject the electron.

$$IE = hv - KE$$

A useful feature of PES is the fact that any electron can be ejected by this technique. The photons are not limited to ejecting the lowest-energy outer electrons. The ionization energies, also called the **binding energies,** of electrons from all of the subshells of an atom are detected. The relative number of electrons with a given energy is recorded.

Only a single electron is ejected from a neutral atom. When an atom has been ionized in a PES experiment, no subsequent electrons are removed from that atom.

The PES spectra of hydrogen, helium, lithium, and magnesium are shown below.

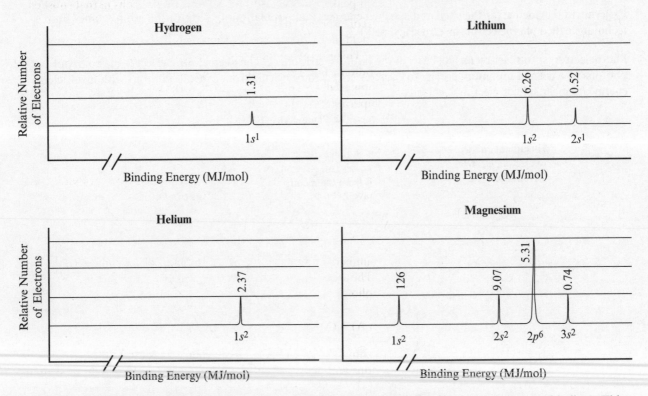

PES Spectra of Hydrogen, Lithium, Helium, and Magnesium

The PES signal for the $1s$ electron of hydrogen is half as intense as the signal for the $1s$ electrons of helium. This is because there are twice as many $1s$ electrons in a helium atom as there are in a hydrogen atom.

The binding energy of the $1s$ electrons in the helium atom is also greater than that of hydrogen. Helium has a higher nuclear charge than hydrogen, so its electrons are more strongly attracted to the nucleus.

When answering questions about spectra, students should draw on their knowledge of periodic trends and electron configurations. PES spectra should be viewed by students as experimental evidence for shells, subshells, and electron configurations of atoms.

PRACTICE:

(a) The PES data below are for which element?

(b) The $2s$ electrons for sodium have a binding energy of 6.84 MJ/mol. Explain why that value is different from the energy of the $2s$ electrons of this element.

Binding Energy (MJ/mol)	Relative Number of Electrons
0.42	1
2.38	6
3.93	2
29.1	6
37.1	2
347	2

(a) The data are for potassium. The electron configuration of potassium is $1s^2 2s^2 2p^6 3s^2 3p^6 4s^1$. One peak is expected for each subshell, and the height of each peak corresponds to the number of electrons in that subshell.

(b) The energy of the $2s$ electrons for potassium corresponds to the second peak in the spectrum, 37.1 MJ/mol. The larger value means that the $2s$ electrons are held more tightly to potassium than they are to sodium, which has a $2s$ electron binding energy of 6.84 MJ/mol. This is because the nuclear charge experienced by the $2s$ electrons is greater for potassium than it is for sodium. This results in an increased coulombic attraction between the $2s$ electrons of potassium and the nucleus compared with that of sodium. Notice that although we are comparing atoms in the same group, we are comparing similar orbitals, so in this case, shielding arguments are irrelevant.

Atomic Nuclei

As mentioned previously, the nucleus of an atom is the small, positively charged region at the center that is comprised of protons and neutrons. Atomic nuclei have been studied using a technique called mass spectrometry.

Isotopes

Atoms of the same element that have different numbers of neutrons are called **isotopes**. The **atomic weight** is the weighted average of the masses of the isotopes. The atomic weight of a hypothetical element with naturally occurring isotopes A, B, and C is calculated as follows:

$$\text{Atomic weight} = (\text{Mass A} \times \text{Fraction A}) + (\text{Mass B} \times \text{Fraction B}) + (\text{Mass C} \times \text{Fraction C})$$

Naturally occurring carbon atoms exist as approximately 99% carbon-12 (which has 6 protons and 6 neutrons in its nucleus) and 1% carbon-13 (which has 6 protons and 7 neutrons in its nucleus). The atomic weight of carbon can be calculated from this data.

$$\text{Atomic weight} = [(12 \text{ amu}) \times 0.99] + [(13 \text{ amu}) \times 0.01] = 12.01 \text{ amu}$$

Notice that this agrees with the atomic weight of carbon on the periodic table.

PRACTICE:

> Naturally occurring chlorine consists of two isotopes, ^{35}Cl and ^{37}Cl. Use the periodic table (page 364) to determine the fractions of atoms in a chlorine sample that are ^{35}Cl and ^{37}Cl.

The sum of all the fractions must add up to one. Since there are two isotopes, the fraction of one of the isotopes, say ^{35}Cl, can be assigned x, and the fraction of the other isotope, ^{37}Cl, can be $1 - x$. The atomic weight of chlorine according to the periodic table is 35.45 amu. The fractions can then be determined.

$$\text{Atomic weight} = 35.45 \text{ amu}$$
$$35.45 \text{ amu} = [(35 \text{ amu})(x)] + [(37 \text{ amu})(1 - x)]$$
$$35.45 = 35x + 37 - 37x$$
$$2x = 1.55$$
$$x = 0.78$$

Therefore, the fraction of naturally occurring chlorine that is ^{35}Cl is 0.78, or 78%. The fraction of chlorine that is ^{37}Cl is $1 - x = 1 - 0.78 = 0.22$, or 22%.

Mass Spectrometry

Mass spectrometry is an experimental technique that allows chemists to determine atomic masses, molecular masses, and isotope patterns in atoms and molecules.

In a mass spectrometer, vaporized molecules are first ionized by one of a variety of means, usually to form positive ions. They are then accelerated through a magnetic field. This causes them to separate based on their mass-to-charge ratio, m/z. More massive species experience less deflection than less massive species. The ions are detected, and their degree of deflection is reported in a **mass spectrum.**

Mass Spectrometer

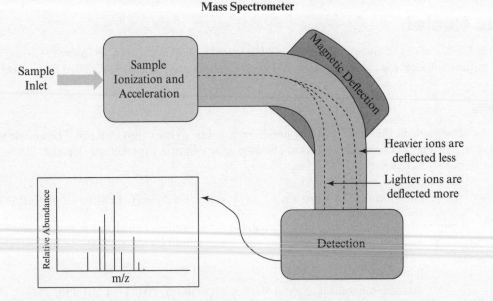

AP Chemistry students should be aware that mass spectrometry provides proof that all atoms of an element are not necessarily identical, contrary to what John Dalton believed. Instead, many elements are composed of isotopes. Students should expect to answer questions regarding the isotopic compositions of different elements based on mass spectra.

The simulated mass spectrum of copper is shown below. There are two naturally occurring, stable isotopes of copper; these account for the two peaks in the spectrum. The relative heights of the peaks reflect the relative number of atoms of each isotope. This data can be used to calculate the average atomic weight.

The Mass Spectrum of Copper

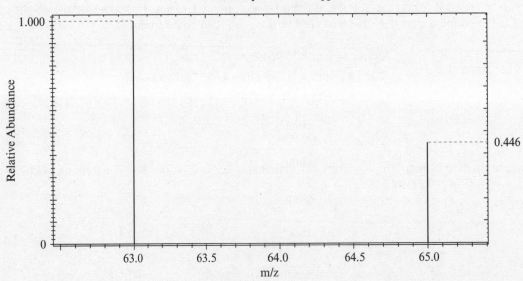

The fractions of each isotope are given by the relative abundances of each, divided by the sum of the heights of the peaks.

$$\text{fraction}_{^{63}Cu} = \frac{1.000}{1.000 + 0.446} = 0.6916$$

$$\text{fraction}_{^{65}Cu} = \frac{0.446}{1.000 + 0.446} = 0.3084$$

These fractions correspond to the natural abundance percentages of the isotopes of copper, 69.16% and 30.84%.

The average atomic mass of an element can be found by determining the weighted average of the mass-to-charge ratios expressed in units of amu. Each fraction is multiplied by the corresponding mass-to-charge ratio. The sum of the results gives the average atomic weight of the element.

Average atomic mass of copper = $(0.6916 \times 63.0 \text{ amu}) + (0.3084 \times 65.0 \text{ amu}) = 63.6 \text{ amu}$

PRACTICE:

Based on the following mass spectrum, determine the percent abundance of each isotope and the atomic weight of zinc.

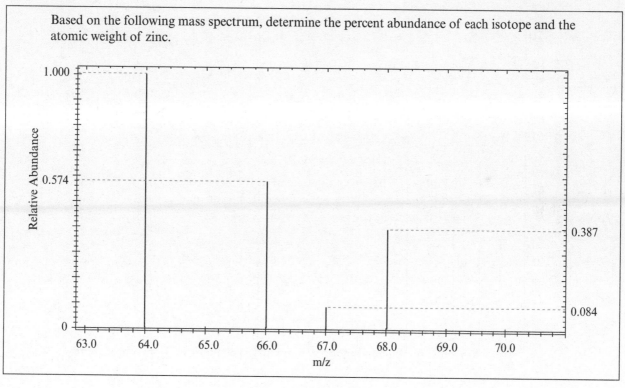

The isotope fractions are determined from the ratios of the heights of the peaks to the sum of the heights.

$$\text{fraction}_{^{64}Zn} = \frac{1.000}{2.045} = 0.489$$

$$\text{fraction}_{^{66}Zn} = \frac{0.574}{2.045} = 0.281$$

$$\text{fraction}_{^{67}Zn} = \frac{0.084}{2.045} = 0.041$$

$$\text{fraction}_{^{68}Zn} = \frac{0.387}{2.045} = 0.189$$

These fractions can be converted to percent abundances when multiplied by 100. The percentages of the isotopes of zinc are 48.9% ^{64}Zn, 28.1% ^{66}Zn, 4.1% ^{67}Zn, and 18.9% ^{68}Zn.

The atomic weight is the weighted average of the masses of the isotopes.

$$Atomic\ weight = \left(\frac{1.00}{2.045} \times 64.0\ amu\right) + \left(\frac{0.574}{2.045} \times 66.0\ amu\right) + \left(\frac{0.084}{2.045} \times 67.0\ amu\right) + \left(\frac{0.387}{2.045} \times 68.0\ amu\right)$$

$$= 31.296 + 18.525 + 2.752 + 12.868\ \text{(Additional significant figures shown for illustration.)}$$

$$= 65.4\ amu$$

Mass spectrometry is also one of the most important analytical techniques available to chemists for determining the masses of molecules. The mass spectrum of caffeine, $C_8H_{10}N_4O_2$ (molecular mass = 194 amu), is shown below. The peak corresponding to the **molecular ion** (a molecule that has lost an electron), is the tall peak with the mass-to-charge ratio of 194. The other small peaks at 195 and 196 amu are due to forms of caffeine in which one or more naturally occurring ^{13}C atoms have replaced ^{12}C isotopes in the molecule. The other peaks at 109, 82, 67, and 55 are due to fragments of the molecule that resulted when covalent bonds were broken during ionization.

The Mass Spectrum of a Compound

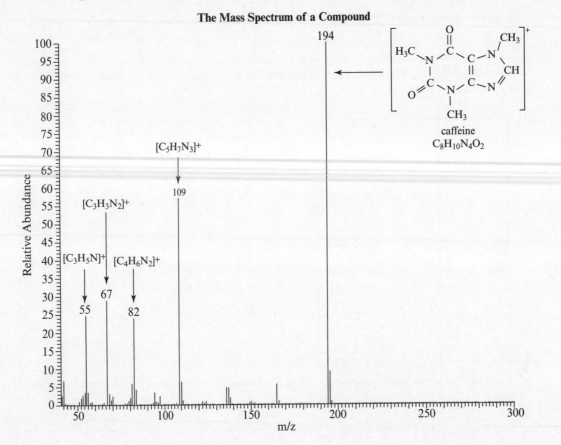

PRACTICE:

> The mass spectrum of a compound shows a molecular ion peak at m/z = 144. Combustion analysis provides an empirical formula of $C_3H_4O_2$. What is the molecular formula of the compound?

The mass spectrum information gives the molecular mass of the compound, 144 amu. Division by the empirical formula weight will provide the factor by which the subscripts should be multiplied.

$$(3 \times 12.01\ amu) + (4 \times 1.01\ amu) + (2 \times 16.00\ amu) = 72.07\ amu$$

$$\frac{144\ amu}{72.07\ amu} \approx 2$$

Multiplication of each subscript by 2 results in a molecular formula of $C_6H_8O_4$.

Review Questions

Multiple Choice

1. Which of the following neutral elements has 26 protons and 32 neutrons?

   A.   Germanium, Ge
   B.   Cerium, Ce
   C.   Nickel, Ni
   D.   Iron, Fe

2. Two samples of potassium chloride are analyzed for chlorine content and found to contain different mass percentages of chlorine. Which of these is the best explanation?

   A.   The two samples came from different sources.
   B.   One of the samples has a different percentage of potassium isotopes.
   C.   One of the samples contains impurities.
   D.   One of the samples has a different empirical formula.

The following representations are atomic models that have been accepted at different times in the past 200 years. Use these figures to answer questions 3–4.

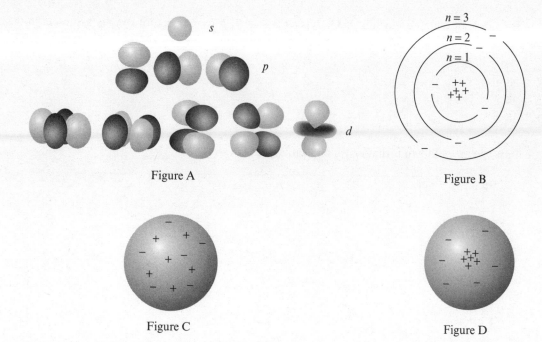

Figure A

Figure B

Figure C

Figure D

3. When Ernest Rutherford observed the dramatic deflection of alpha particles by atoms of gold foil, he proposed that the most accurate picture of the atom was not depicted by _____, as previously thought, but by a model more closely resembling _____.

   A.   Figure D, Figure B
   B.   Figure B, Figure A
   C.   Figure C, Figure A
   D.   Figure C, Figure D

4. The currently accepted depiction of the atom is one that incorporates the experimental observations of Thomson, Rutherford, Bohr, and Schrödinger. It most closely resembles

    A. Figure A

    B. Figure B

    C. Figure C

    D. Figure D

5. Which of the following electron configurations represents an electronic excited state due to a violation of Hund's rule?

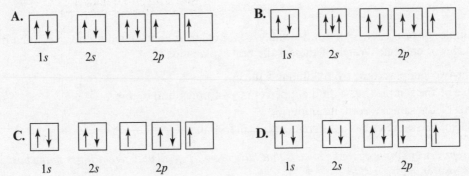

6. A pure sample of aluminum oxide, Al_2O_3, has a mass of 51 g. What mass of oxygen is present in the sample?

    A. 8 g

    B. 20 g

    C. 24 g

    D. 48 g

7. The mass spectrum shown is that of which element?

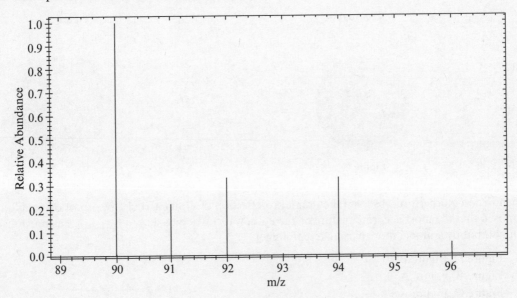

    A. Y

    B. Zr

    C. Nb

    D. Mo

8. A neutral element is magnetized in a magnetic field, but when the field is removed, the element is no longer magnetic. The most probable ground state electron configuration for this element is

    A. $[Xe]4f^{14}5d^36s^2$

    B. $[Ar]4s^2$

    C. $[Ar]4s^23d^{10}$

    D. $[Kr]5s^24d^{10}5p^6$

9. The first six ionization energies are shown for an element. What is the identity of the element?

Ionization	Ionization Energy (kJ·mol^{-1})
First	600
Second	1800
Third	2700
Fourth	11,600
Fifth	14,800
Sixth	18,400

    A.   Al

    B.   Na

    C.   Mg

    D.   C

10. Which of the following figures best represents the three-dimensional shape of an orbital in the highest-energy sublevel of a neutral atom of oxygen in the ground state?

Figure 1

Figure 2

Figure 3

Figure 4

    A.   Figure 1

    B.   Figure 2

    C.   Figure 3

    D.   Figure 4

11. The photoelectron spectrum of an element contains the following peaks:

MJ/mol	Relative Intensity
433	2
48.5	2
39.2	6
5.44	2
3.24	6
0.77	1
0.63	2

This element is best described as a(an)

A. transition metal.

B. element that exists in elemental form as a molecule.

C. alkali metal.

D. non-metal.

12. The ground state electron configuration of a neutral copper atom is $[Ar]4s^13d^{10}$. Which of the following is a ground state configuration for an ion commonly formed by copper?

A. $[Ar]4s^23d^9$

B. $[Ar]4s^23d^8$

C. $[Ar]4s^13d^9$

D. $[Ar]3d^{10}$

13. Waves A and B represent the wavelengths of photons that may be emitted when an electron in an atom relaxes from an excited state to the ground state. Which of the following best describe the waves?

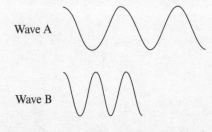

Wave A

Wave B

A. Photon A was generated by a transition from a higher energy level in the element than photon B.

B. Photon B was generated by a transition from a higher energy level in the element than photon A.

C. Photon A has greater amplitude and a longer wavelength than photon B.

D. Photon B has a greater amplitude and a higher frequency than photon A.

14. The orbital configuration below depicts

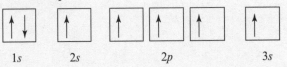

$1s$ $2s$ $2p$ $3s$

A. oxygen in the ground state.

B. sodium in the ground state.

C. nitrogen in an excited state.

D. fluorine in an excited state.

15. Nitrogen forms many compounds of the form NR_3, where R is hydrogen or a hydrocarbon group like CH_3. Which of the following elements is likely to form similar compounds?

    A. Si

    B. S

    C. Al

    D. As

16. The photoelectron spectrum of a certain pure element, X, is shown below:

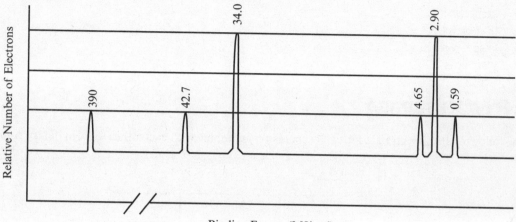

Binding Energy (MJ/mol)

When two elements combine to form an ionic compound, the sum of their charges is zero. For example, Mg^{2+} and Cl^- form the neutral compound $MgCl_2$. Element X will most likely form which of the following compounds?

    A. MgX, KX_2

    B. MgX_2, KX

    C. XO, XCl_2

    D. X_2O, XCl

17. Which of the following arrangements shows the listed atoms in order of increasing first ionization energy?

    A. Na < Ne < Ar

    B. Ne < Ar < Na

    C. Ar < Ne < Na

    D. Na < Ar < Ne

18. Which phrase best completes the following statement?

The energy required to eject a $2s$ electron from a neutral atom of nitrogen in a PES experiment is _____ the fourth ionization energy, IE_4, of nitrogen.

    A. greater than

    B. less than

    C. equal to

    D. four times

19. Which of the following electron configurations represents the element with the greatest electronegativity?

    A. $1s^2 2s^2 2p^5$

    B. $1s^2 2s^2 2p^6 3s^2 3p^3$

    C. $1s^2 2s^2 2p^6 3s^2 3p^4$

    D. $1s^2 2s^2 2p^4$

20. For an element exposed to x-ray irradiation, an electron ejected from which sublevel of an atom will have the greatest kinetic energy?

    A. $4s$ sublevel

    B. $4p$ sublevel

    C. $4d$ sublevel

    D. $4f$ sublevel

Long Free Response

1. The following PES spectra are for two elements that combine with each other to form binary compounds.

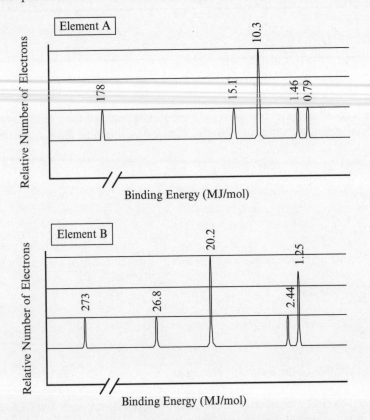

    a.   Write the electron configurations of elements A and B. Identify the two elements.

    b.   Why do the $2s$ electrons have different energies for the two elements?

    c.   A compound contains 1.00 gram of element A and 5.05 grams of element B. A second compound contains 1.00 gram of element A and 3.79 grams of element B. How many moles of element A are present in 1.00 gram?

   d.   Determine the number of moles of element B that react with 1.00 gram of element A in each of the two compounds.

   e.   **i.**   Write the empirical formulas for the two compounds.

        ii.   Use ratios to show that the two compounds demonstrate the law of multiple proportions.

   f.   The mass spectrum of element A contains a peak at 28.00 amu with an intensity of 1.000, a second peak at 29.00 amu with an intensity of 0.05074, and a third peak at 30.00 amu. What is the relative intensity of the third peak?

   g.   The mass spectrum of element B contains five peaks. Four of the peaks correspond to 35, 37, 70, and 72 amu. The fifth peak reflects a species with what mass? Justify your answer.

2.   The formula of a certain hydrate, $NaC_xH_yO_z \cdot nH_2O$, contains one sodium atom per formula unit. A 25.00-gram sample of the hydrate is heated in a 3.00-gram crucible. After 10 minutes of heating, the crucible is cooled and weighed. The following data are collected.

	Mass of Sample + Crucible (grams)
After 1st heating	21.12
After 2nd heating	20.43
After 3rd heating	20.40
After 4th heating	20.40

The sample is then treated with dilute hydrochloric acid to replace each sodium atom with a hydrogen atom. The sample is purified to remove the resulting NaCl. The pure $C_xH_{(y+1)}O_z$ is dried and found to have a mass of 12.72 grams.

Complete combustion of this final sample in excess oxygen yields 18.63 grams of CO_2 and 7.63 grams of H_2O. The compound has a molar mass of 60.06 g·mol^{-1}.

   a.   Why is the heating of the original sample repeated four times?

   b.   What is the final mass of the sodium salt?

   c.   What is the empirical formula of the pure $C_xH_{(y+1)}O_z$?

   d.   What is the molecular formula of the pure $C_xH_{(y+1)}O_z$?

   e.   What is the formula of the original sodium salt? (Your answer should include the correct values for x, y, z, and n.)

Short Free Response

3.   Pictured below are an atom of calcium, an atom of sulfur, and a formula unit of calcium sulfide, CaS.

  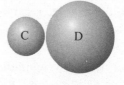

   a.   Clearly label A, B, C, and D as the correct atom or ion.

   b.   Discuss your assignment in terms of the atomic and ionic radii of the species.

   c.   How many grams of sulfur are expected to be present in 180.3 grams of calcium sulfide?

Answers and Explanations

Multiple Choice

1. **D.** (EK 1.B.1) Iron has an atomic number of 26, which corresponds to 26 protons. An element is defined by its atomic number.

2. **C.** (EK 1.A.2) Potassium ionizes by losing a single electron to achieve a stable, noble gas electron configuration. Chlorine gains a single electron. Binary compounds of potassium and chlorine with empirical formulas other than KCl are not formed. Naturally occurring potassium should have a relatively fixed isotopic abundance, regardless of the source of the KCl. The two samples may have come from different sources, but this in itself is not the reason the compositions are different. Two samples of pure KCl from two different sources are expected to have identical composition. The most likely reason for the difference is the presence of impurities in one of the samples.

3. **D.** (EK 1.D.1) Rutherford's discovery of the nucleus at the center of the atom replaced the "plum pudding" model of the atom, shown in Figure C, with a nuclear model, shown in Figure D. The quantized nature of the energy of the electrons, which led to the models in Figures A and B, had yet to be elucidated.

4. **A.** (EK 1.C.2, 1.D.1) The current depiction of the atom is one in which electrons are described as waves. Orbital pictures depict the three-dimensional regions surrounding the nucleus where electrons have a high probability of being located. The shapes of the atomic orbitals resulting from quantum mechanical calculations are shown in Figure A.

5. **D.** (EK 1.C.1) Hund's rule states that each orbital in a sublevel must be filled singly before electrons are paired and that all electrons in singly occupied orbitals within a sublevel must have parallel spins. The configuration in choice D shows two electrons with antiparallel spins in singly occupied p orbitals. Choices A and C depict ground states, and choice B is forbidden.

6. **C.** (EK 1.A.1, 1.A.2, 1.A.3) The formula for aluminum oxide is Al_2O_3. The molar mass is about $102 \text{ g} \cdot \text{mol}^{-1}$. The number of grams of oxygen present in 51 grams of sample can be determined by dimensional analysis.

$$51 \text{ g } Al_2O_3 \times \frac{1 \text{ mol } Al_2O_3}{102 \text{ g } Al_2O_3} \times \frac{3 \text{ mol O}}{1 \text{ mol } Al_2O_3} \times \frac{16.00 \text{ g O}}{1 \text{ mol O}} = 24 \text{ g O}$$

7. **B.** (EK 1.D.2) The weighted average of the masses can be estimated to obtain the atomic weight of the element. It is greater than 90 amu, so yttrium (88.91 amu) cannot be the correct answer. The average mass is significantly less than about 93 amu, so the answer is not niobium or molybdenum (92.91 and 95.94 amu, respectively). The correct answer must be zirconium (91.22 amu).

8. **A.** (EK 1.B.2, 1.C.2) An element that is magnetized in a magnetic field but loses magnetization when the magnetic field is removed is paramagnetic. It must contain unpaired electrons. The electron configuration given in choice A is that of tantalum, Ta. The $5d$ orbitals of tantalum contain only three electrons, so these electrons must be unpaired.

9. **A.** (EK 1.B.1, 1.B.2) The ionization energies for the first three electrons much smaller than the fourth ionization energy. Removing a fourth electron disrupts the noble gas configuration of the ion, so the element must be in group IIIA of the periodic table. The element is Al.

10. **C.** (EK 1.B.2, 1.C.2) The highest-energy sublevel of a noble gas atom is a p sublevel. A p orbital is shaped like two inflated balloons joined at their tied ends (Figure 3).

11. **A.** (EK 1.B.1, 1.B.2) There are seven distinct energy sublevels in the atom. The element is in the d block of the periodic table and has the electron configuration $1s^2 2s^2 2p^6 3s^2 3p^6 4s^2 3d^1$. Notice that the $4s$ electrons are lower in energy than the $3d$ electron. The principal quantum number determines the relative energy of the sublevel. This element, scandium, is a transition metal.

12. **D.** (EK 1.B.1) The ground state electron configuration of Cu^+, one of the cations formed by copper, is that in which the $4s$ electron has been lost, $[Ar]3d^{10}$.

13. B. (EK 1.D.3) Wave B has a shorter wavelength than wave A, so wave B is higher in energy. It is emitted during a larger transition from a higher-energy orbital to the ground state than wave A. (Both waves have the same amplitude.)

14. C. (EK 1.B.2, 1.C.1) The electron configuration shows seven electrons. The element is a neutral nitrogen atom. Instead of a $1s^2 2s^2 2p^3$ electron configuration, one of the electrons has been promoted to the $3s$ orbital. This indicates an excited state.

15. D. (EK 1.C.1) Arsenic, As, is in the same group on the periodic table as nitrogen. It displays similar chemical behavior due to its similar np^3 electron configuration.

16. C. (EK 1.C.1, 1.B.1) Electrons with higher binding energy are located in energy levels closer to the nucleus. The electrons with a binding energy of 290 MJ/mol correspond to the $1s$ electrons. The relative height of that peak corresponds to two electrons. The resulting electron configuration, $1s^2 2s^2 2p^6 3s^2 3p^6 4s^2$, indicates that the element is calcium. When calcium ionizes, it loses its two valence electrons to form a cation. Calcium cation, Ca^{2+}, forms calcium oxide with O^{2-}, CaO, and it forms calcium chloride with Cl^-, $CaCl_2$.

17. D. (EK 1.B.1, 1.B.2, 1.C.1) Neon's (Ne) outermost electron is in a lower shell than the outermost electrons of argon (Ar) and sodium (Na). Neon will be less shielded and experience a relatively high coulombic attraction to the nucleus. It has the highest first ionization energy. Sodium has the smallest effective nuclear charge and has the lowest ionization energy of the three elements.

18. B. (EK 1.B.1, 1.B.2, 1.C.1) Less energy is required to remove a $2s$ electron from a neutral atom than to remove a $2s^1$ electron from a N^{3+} ion. The coulombic attraction of the remaining electrons with the +3 charge of the ion makes removal of a fourth electron more difficult than removal of a single $2s$ electron from a neutral atom of nitrogen.

19. A. (EK 1.B.1, 1.B.2, 1.C.1) The electron configuration in choice A corresponds to a fluorine atom. Fluorine is the most electronegative element because it has a very high effective nuclear charge, a high coulombic attraction between its outermost electrons and the nucleus, and low shielding by inner shell electrons relative to atoms of the other elements.

20. D. (EK 1.B.1, 1.B.2) Of the electrons in the $n = 4$ shell, a $4f$ electron is highest in energy and most loosely held by the nucleus. A relatively small fraction of the energy of the x-ray photon is expended in ionizing the $4f$ electron. More energy is converted to the kinetic energy of the ejected electron.

Long Free Response

1. a. (EK 1.B.1, 1.B.2, 1.C.1) Element A has the electron configuration $1s^2 2s^2 2p^6 3s^2 3p^2$. Element A is silicon. Element B has the electron configuration $1s^2 2s^2 2p^6 3s^2 3p^5$. Element B is chlorine.

b. (EK 1.B.1, 1.B.2, 1.C.1) The $2s$ electron for silicon has a lower ionization energy than that of chlorine because chlorine has a higher effective nuclear charge. The larger effective nuclear charge results in a greater coulombic attraction between the outermost electrons and the nucleus.

c. (EK 1.A.3) The molar mass is used in the determination of the number of moles of silicon in 1.00 gram.

$$1.00 \ \cancel{g \ Si} \times \frac{1 \ mol \ Si}{28.09 \ \cancel{g \ Si}} = 0.0356 \ mol \ Si$$

d. (EK 1.A.1) The number of moles of chlorine that combine with 1.00 gram of silicon in each compound is determined as follows:

$$5.05 \ \cancel{g \ Cl} \times \frac{1 \ mol \ Cl}{35.45 \ \cancel{g \ Cl}} = 0.142 \ mol \ Cl$$

$$3.79 \ \cancel{g \ Cl} \times \frac{1 \ mol \ Cl}{28.09 \ \cancel{g \ Cl}} = 0.107 \ mol \ Cl$$

e. i. (EK 1.A.2) The smallest whole-number ratio for the first compound is determined by dividing each number of moles by the smallest number of moles, 0.0356 mol Si.

Silicon: $\dfrac{0.0356}{0.0356} = 1$

Chlorine: $\dfrac{0.142}{0.0356} = 4$

The empirical formula for the first compound is $SiCl_4$.

The smallest whole-number ratio for the second compound is determined the same way.

Silicon: $\dfrac{0.0356}{0.0356} = 1$

Chlorine: $\dfrac{0.107}{0.0356} = 3$

The empirical formula for the second compound is $SiCl_3$.

e. ii. (EK 1.A.1) The law of multiple proportions states that when two elements form two different binary compounds, the ratio of the masses of the second element that combine with a fixed amount of the first element is always a small whole-number ratio. The ratio of the masses of the chlorine that combine with 1.00 gram of silicon must be determined and converted to a whole-number ratio.

$$\frac{5.05 \text{ g}}{3.79 \text{ g}} = \frac{1.33}{1} \times \frac{3}{3} = \frac{4}{3}$$

Chlorine combines with silicon in a 4:3 mass ratio for the two compounds.

f. (EK 1.D.2) Let x be the unknown intensity. The atomic weight of silicon, 28.09 amu, can be found on the periodic table. This atomic weight is the weighted average of the masses in the spectrum. The sum of the intensities for this calculation is $1.000 + 0.05074 + x$.

$$28.09 = \left(28.00 \times \frac{1.000}{1.000 + 0.05074 + x}\right) + \left(29.00 \times \frac{0.05074}{1.000 + 0.05074 + x}\right) + \left(30.00 \times \frac{x}{1.000 + 0.05074 + x}\right)$$

$$28.09 = \frac{28.00 + 1.4714 + 30.00x}{1.05074 + x}$$

$$x = 0.02154$$

g. (EK 1.B.1, 1.D.2) Chlorine has an atomic weight of 35.45 amu, which is a weighted average of the two naturally occurring isotopes, ^{35}Cl and ^{37}Cl. Elemental chlorine exists as a diatomic molecule, Cl_2, and the three Cl_2 peaks correspond to $^{35}Cl-^{35}Cl$, which has a peak in the mass spectrum at 70 amu; $^{35}Cl-^{37}Cl$ at 72 amu; and $^{37}Cl-^{37}Cl$. The third molecule has a mass of 74 amu.

2. a. (EK 1.E.1) The sample is heated, cooled, and weighed multiple times in order to ensure that the sample is completely anhydrous. When all the water has been lost, the mass of the sample remains constant.

b. (EK 1.E.1) The final mass of the sodium salt is the mass of the anhydrous sample minus the mass of the crucible.

Mass of anhydrous sample = (Mass of anhydrous sample + crucible) – mass of the crucible

Mass of anhydrous sample = 20.40 g – 3.00 g = 17.40 g

c. (EK 1.A.2) The empirical formula for the compound is determined from the simplest whole-number ratio of the numbers of moles of carbon, hydrogen, and oxygen.

$$\text{moles of carbon} = 18.63 \ \text{g } CO_2 \times \frac{1 \ \text{mol } CO_2}{44.01 \ \text{g } CO_2} \times \frac{1 \ \text{mol C}}{1 \ \text{mol } CO_2} = 0.423 \ \text{mol C}$$

$$\text{moles of hydrogen} = 7.63 \ \text{g } H_2O \times \frac{1 \ \text{mol } H_2O}{18.02 \ \text{g } H_2O} \times \frac{2 \ \text{mol H}}{1 \ \text{mol } H_2O} = 0.847 \ \text{mol H}$$

The masses of carbon and hydrogen are used to find the mass of oxygen in the sample.

$$\text{mass of carbon} = 0.423 \ \text{mol C} \times \frac{12.01 \ \text{g C}}{1 \ \text{mol C}} = 5.08 \ \text{g C}$$

$$\text{mass of hydrogen} = 0.847 \ \text{mol H} \times \frac{1.01 \ \text{g H}}{1 \ \text{mol H}} = 0.855 \ \text{g H}$$

Total mass of sample = mass of carbon + mass of hydrogen + mass of oxygen

12.72 g = 5.08 g + 0.855 g + mass of oxygen

Mass of oxygen = 6.79 g

The mass of oxygen is used to find the number of moles of oxygen in the sample.

$$6.79 \ \text{g } O_2 \times \frac{1 \ \text{mol } O_2}{32.00 \ \text{g } O_2} \times \frac{2 \ \text{mol O}}{1 \ \text{mol } O_2} = 0.424 \ \text{mol O}$$

The final step in determining the empirical formula is dividing the number of moles of each element by the smallest number of moles, 0.423 in this case, and finding the simplest whole-number ratio of moles.

$$\text{Carbon:} \quad \frac{0.423}{0.423} = 1$$

$$\text{Hydrogen:} \quad \frac{0.847}{0.423} = 2$$

$$\text{Oxygen:} \quad \frac{0.424}{0.423} = 1$$

The empirical formula, therefore, is CH_2O.

d. (EK 1.A.2) The empirical formula weight is

$$(12.01 \ \text{g·mol}^{-1} \times 1) + (1.01 \ \text{g·mol}^{-1} \times 2) + (16.00 \ \text{g·mol}^{-1} \times 1) = 30.03 \ \text{g·mol}^{-1}$$

The molecular formula is determined by dividing the molar mass by the empirical formula weight and multiplying the subscripts in the empirical formula by the resulting integer.

$$\frac{60.06 \ \text{g·mol}^{-1}}{30.03 \ \text{g·mol}^{-1}} = 2$$

The molecular formula is $C_2H_4O_2$.

e. (EK 1.A.3, 1.E.1, 1.E.2) In order to find the number of molecules of water associated with each formula unit of the sodium salt, the mass of the sodium salt must be determined. One hydrogen atom per formula unit replaced one sodium atom, so the formula of the original sodium salt must have been $NaC_2H_3O_2$. The molar mass of this compound is 82.04 g·mol^{-1}. The number of moles of $NaC_2H_3O_2$ in the original sample can be determined from the mass of anhydrous sodium salt.

$$17.40 \ \text{g NaC}_2\text{H}_3\text{O}_2 \times \frac{1 \ \text{mol NaC}_2\text{H}_3\text{O}_2}{82.04 \ \text{g NaC}_2\text{H}_3\text{O}_2} = 0.212 \ \text{mol NaC}_2\text{H}_3\text{O}_2$$

The number of grams of water (which can be converted to moles) is the difference between the original mass of the sample and the mass of the $NaC_2H_3O_2$. The ratio of moles of water to moles of $NaC_2H_3O_2$ gives the number of water molecules in the hydrate.

Mass of original sample = mass of sodium salt + mass of water

25.00 g = 17.40 g + mass of water

Mass of water = 7.60 g

$$7.60 \ \text{g H}_2\text{O} \times \frac{1 \ \text{mol H}_2\text{O}}{18.02 \ \text{g H}_2\text{O}} = 0.422 \ \text{mol H}_2\text{O}$$

$$\frac{0.422 \ \text{mol H}_2\text{O}}{0.212 \ \text{mol NaC}_2\text{H}_3\text{O}_2} = 2 \ \text{moles of H}_2\text{O per mole of NaC}_2\text{H}_3\text{O}_2$$

There are two molecules of water associated with each formula unit of the sodium salt. The correct formula is $NaC_2H_3O_2 \cdot 2H_2O$.

Short Free Response

1. a. (EK 1.C.1, 1.E.1) Species A represents a neutral calcium atom, species B represents a neutral sulfur atom, species C represents a Ca^{2+} cation, and species D represents an S^{2-} anion.

   b. (EK 1.C.1, 1.E.1) The neutral calcium atom is larger than the neutral sulfur atom because its outermost electrons are in a higher principle quantum level and experience more shielding from the nucleus. In addition, the effective nuclear charge is less for calcium than it is for sulfur. For these reasons, the outermost electrons are held more closely to the nucleus in sulfur than they are in calcium. The two ions, Ca^{2+} and S^{2-}, are isoelectronic. Ionic radii of isoelectronic species decrease with increasing atomic number and nuclear charge, so Ca^{2+} is smaller than S^{2-}.

   c. (EK 1.A.1, 1.A.2) The number of moles of sulfur present in 180.3 grams of CaS is determined using the molecular formula and the molar mass.

   $$M_{\text{CaS}} = (1 \times 40.08 \ \text{g·mol}^{-1}) + (1 \times 32.06 \ \text{g·mol}^{-1}) = 72.14 \ \text{g·mol}^{-1}$$

   $$180.3 \ \text{g CaS} \times \frac{1 \ \text{mol CaS}}{72.14 \ \text{g CaS}} \times \frac{1 \ \text{mol S}}{1 \ \text{mol CaS}} \times \frac{32.06 \ \text{g S}}{1 \ \text{mol S}} = 80.13 \ \text{g S}$$

Chapter 2

Bonding and Intermolecular Forces (Big Idea 2)

Big Idea 2: Bonding and intermolecular interactions determine physical and chemical properties

Atoms and ions interact with one another to form substances with properties that can be attributed to these interactions. Big Idea 2 focuses on bonding, intermolecular interactions, and solution behavior. The impact of these characteristics on the physical and chemical properties of solids, liquids, and gases, are discussed. The chapter will begin with a review of chemical nomenclature.

Nomenclature

Naming compounds is not a skill that will be tested directly on the AP Chemistry exam, but it is a prerequisite for success. Organic nomenclature and prediction of organic reactions are no longer a requirement. The organic compounds themselves, however, remain an important part of the curriculum. Organic functional groups determine intermolecular forces and are important in biological chemistry, materials chemistry, and many other areas. This section is a review of nomenclature and interpretation of chemical structures.

Inorganic Nomenclature

Compounds are composed of more than one type of element and can be broadly classified as ionic or covalent. The ionic or covalent nature of a compound, in turn, determines how the compound is named.

Ionic Nomenclature

Ionic compounds are those that are formed between positively charged ions, or **cations,** and negatively charged ions, or **anions.** Many times, ionic compounds are formed between metal cations and nonmetal anions. They may also be formed from polyatomic ions, which are ions that are composed of more than one atom. The names of ionic compounds begin with the name of the cation and end with the name of the anion. The ending of the name of a monatomic anion is changed to -*ide*.

For example, the ionic compound formed from potassium and sulfur is potassium sulfide. Since potassium is in group IA, it forms K^+. Sulfur is in group VIA, so it forms S^{2-}. The sum of the charges for an ionic compound must equal zero, so there must be two potassium cations and one sulfur anion. The formula is K_2S.

PRACTICE:

> Name and write the formulas for the ionic compounds formed between the following:
>
> **(a)** lithium and nitrogen
> **(b)** strontium and bromine

(a) Lithium nitride is the name of the ionic compound formed between lithium and nitrogen. Lithium is in group IA, so it forms Li^+, and nitrogen is in group VA, so it forms N^{3-}. The formula for lithium nitride that leads to an overall charge of zero is Li_3N.

(b) Strontium bromide is the name of the ionic compound formed between strontium and bromine. Strontium is in group IIA, so it forms Sr^{2+}, and bromine is in group VIIA, so it forms Br^-. The formula for strontium bromide that gives an overall charge of zero is $SrBr_2$.

In order to understand the nomenclature of ionic compounds, students must memorize some important polyatomic ions and their charges.

Polyatomic Ion Name	Formula
Acetate	$C_2H_3O_2^-$
Ammonium	NH_4^+
Carbonate	CO_3^{2-}
Hydrogen carbonate (also known as bicarbonate)	HCO_3^-
Perchlorate	ClO_4^-
Chlorate	ClO_3^-
Chlorite	ClO_2^-
Hypochlorite	ClO^-
Chromate	CrO_4^{2-}
Dichromate	$Cr_2O_7^{2-}$
Dihydrogen phosphate	$H_2PO_4^-$
Hydrogen phosphate	HPO_4^{2-}
Phosphate	PO_4^{3-}
Hydrogen sulfate	HSO_4^-
Sulfate	SO_4^{2-}
Sulfite	SO_3^{2-}
Hydroxide	OH^-
Nitrate	NO_3^-
Nitrite	NO_2^-
Oxalate	$C_2O_4^{2-}$
Permanganate	MnO_4^-
Peroxide	O_2^{2-}

In addition to the polyatomic ions, students should know that many metals that can have multiple oxidation states. Many transition metals and some others exhibit this behavior. For instance, iron cations can exist as Fe^{2+} or as Fe^{3+}. To name a compound containing an iron ion, a roman numeral is used to show the charge of the ion. For example, the name of $Fe(OH)_2$ is iron(II) hydroxide and the name of $Fe(OH)_3$ is iron(III) hydroxide.

Metal	Common Ion(s)
Antimony	Sb^{3+}, Sb^{5+}
Bismuth	Bi^{3+}, Bi^{5+}
Cadmium	Cd^{2+}
Cobalt	Co^{2+}, Co^{3+}
Copper	Cu^+, Cu^{2+}
Iron	Fe^{2+}, Fe^{3+}
Lead	Pb^{2+}, Pb^{4+}
Mercury*	Hg_2^{2+}, Hg^{2+}
Nickel	Ni^{2+}
Silver	Ag^+
Tin	Sn^{2+}, Sn^{4+}
Zinc	Zn^{2+}

*Note that mercury(I) is Hg_2^{2+} and mercury(II) is Hg^{2+}.

PRACTICE:

Write formulas for the following ionic compounds:

(a) aluminum sulfate
(b) sodium peroxide
(c) iron(II) nitrate
(d) mercury(I) acetate

The formulas are as follows:

(a) $Al_2(SO_4)_3$

(b) Na_2O_2

(c) $Fe(NO_3)_2$

(d) $Hg_2(C_2H_3O_2)_2$

Ionic hydrates are named as usual for ionic compounds, and the number of water molecules is specified with a Greek prefix. For instance, there are five water molecules in copper(II) sulfate pentahydrate, $CuSO_4 \cdot 5\,H_2O$.

Number	Greek Prefix
1	*mono-*
2	*di-*
3	*tri-*
4	*tetra-*
5	*penta-*
6	*hexa-*
7	*hepta-*
8	*octa-*
9	*nona-*
10	*deca-*

PRACTICE:

Write the formula for cobalt(II) chloride hexahydrate.

The *hexa-* prefix indicates six water molecules are associated with the cobalt(II) chloride. The formula is $CoCl_2 \cdot 6\,H_2O$.

Binary Covalent Nomenclature

Binary covalent compounds are neutral compounds composed of two nonmetals. The same Greek prefixes used in hydrate nomenclature denote the number of atoms of each element in a binary covalent molecule. Usually, the less electronegative element is named first, followed by the more electronegative element. The end of the name of the second element is changed to *-ide*.

When there is only one atom of the first element, however, the prefix *mono-* is not used. For example, CO_2 is called "carbon dioxide," not "monocarbon dioxide."

When a prefix ending in an "a" or an "o" precedes the name of an element that begins with a vowel, the "a" or "o" is dropped. For example, CO is called "carbon monoxide," not "carbon monooxide."

PRACTICE:

Name the following compounds:

(a) N_2O_5
(b) P_4O_{10}
(c) $SiCl_4$
(d) CS_2

The names of the compounds are

(a) dinitrogen pentoxide

(b) tetraphosphorus decoxide

(c) silicon tetrachloride

(d) carbon disulfide

Organic Nomenclature

Organic compounds are broadly defined as compounds containing carbon and usually hydrogen. The term *organic* encompasses a vast number of molecules that may or may not be associated with life processes. The definition is generally understood to exclude alloys like steel, which is composed of carbon atoms interspersed among iron atoms, and simple carbon-oxygen molecules like carbon dioxide and carbonate ions.

Hydrocarbons are a class of organic compounds that consist of only hydrogen and carbon. **Alkanes** are hydrocarbons that consist of singly bonded carbon atoms. These are also called **saturated hydrocarbons.** The molecular formula for a saturated hydrocarbon is C_nH_{2n+2}. The names of alkanes begin with the appropriate Greek prefix and end in *-ane*. Propane is the name of the saturated hydrocarbon that contains three carbons and the maximum possible number of hydrogen atoms. The formula for propane is C_3H_8. Butane is the name of the hydrocarbon C_4H_{10}. It is not necessary to name organic compounds on the AP Chemistry exam; however, familiarity with organic compounds is advantageous.

The Simplest Unbranched Saturated Hydrocarbons

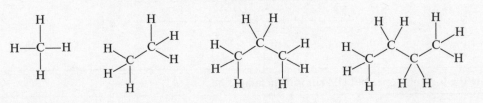

Methane CH_4 Ethane C_2H_6 Propane C_3H_8 Butane C_4H_{10}

Name of Alkane	Molecular Formula		Name of Alkane	Molecular Formula
Methane	CH_4		Hexane	C_6H_{14}
Ethane	C_2H_6		Heptane	C_7H_{16}
Propane	C_3H_8		Octane	C_8H_{18}
Butane	C_4H_{10}		Nonane	C_9H_{20}
Pentane	C_5H_{12}		Decane	$C_{10}H_{22}$

Organic compounds may also contain **functional groups,** which are groups of atoms in a molecule that give the molecule characteristic physical and chemical properties. There is no need to memorize the systematic nomenclature for these compounds, but recognition of the various functional groups conveys an advantage in terms of compound property prediction. Many of the characteristics mentioned here will be reviewed in greater detail later in this chapter, so it is a good idea to refer to this table later.

Functional Group	Structure	Characteristics	Example
Alcohol	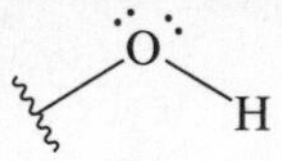	Alcohols are relatively polar since they are capable of donating and accepting hydrogen bonds.	Methanol 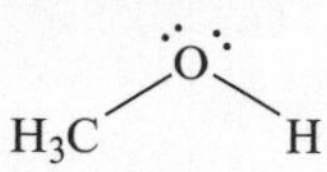
Amine	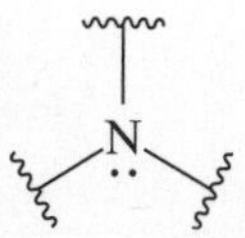	Amines are important in acid-base chemistry because they behave as weak bases.	Ethylamine 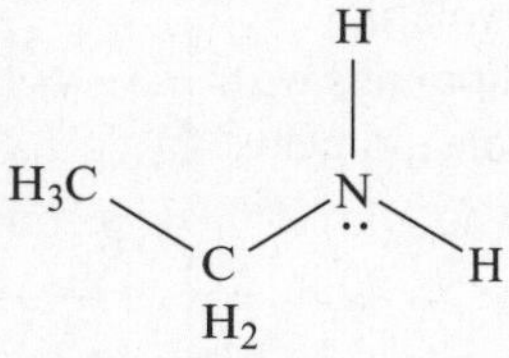
Alkyl halide	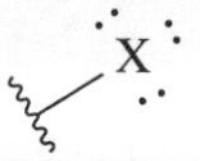 Where X = F, Cl, Br, or I	Alkyl halides are important reactants in organic chemistry.	2-Chlorobutane 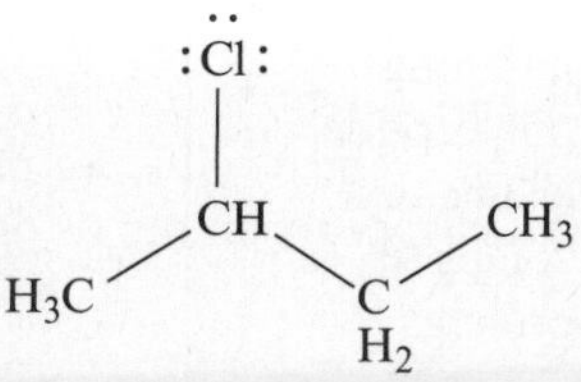
Ether	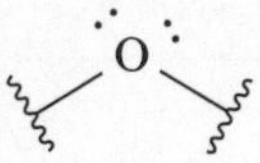	Small molecular weight ethers are volatile compounds with dipole moments.	Diethyl ether 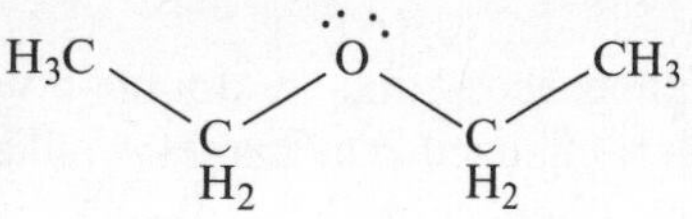
Aldehyde	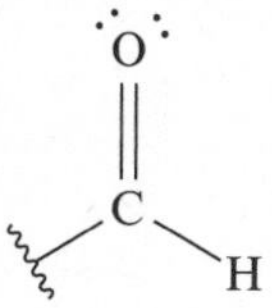	Small molecular weight aldehydes are volatile compounds with dipole moments.	Pentanal 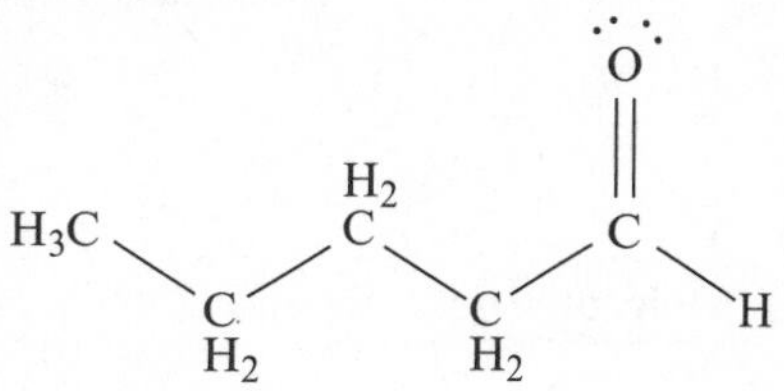
Ketone	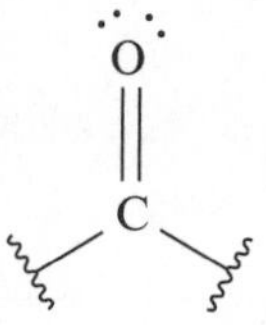	Small molecular weight ketones are volatile compounds with dipole moments.	3-Hexanone 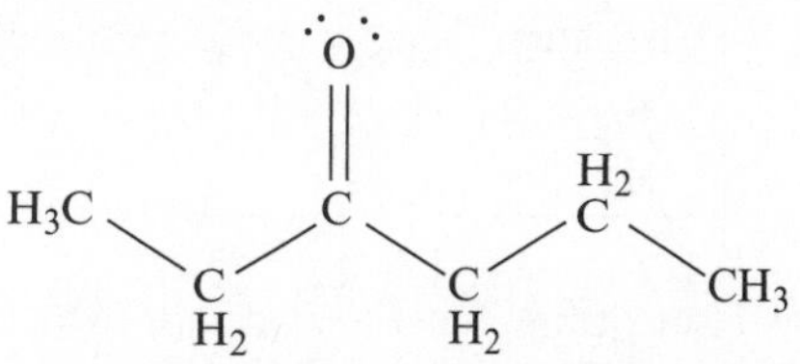

continued

67

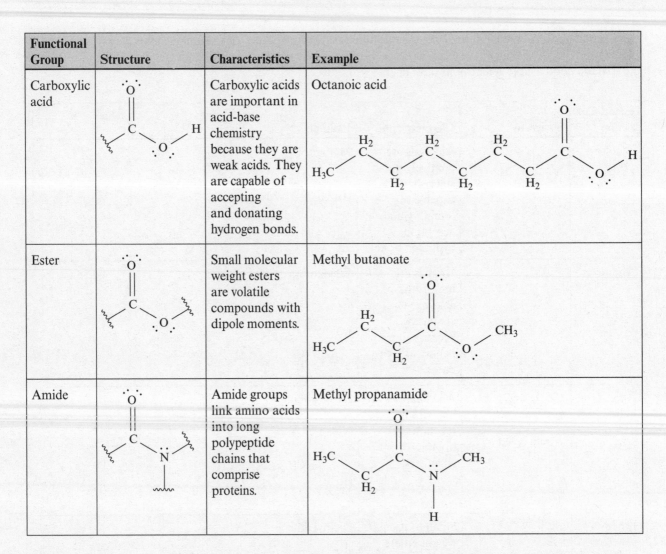

Functional Group	Structure	Characteristics	Example
Carboxylic acid		Carboxylic acids are important in acid-base chemistry because they are weak acids. They are capable of accepting and donating hydrogen bonds.	Octanoic acid
Ester		Small molecular weight esters are volatile compounds with dipole moments.	Methyl butanoate
Amide		Amide groups link amino acids into long polypeptide chains that comprise proteins.	Methyl propanamide

Hydrocarbons may also contain carbons that are double-bonded or triple-bonded to one another. In these cases, the ending of the parent chain is changed. The names of alkenes, which are molecules that contain double bonds, end in -*ene*. The names of triple bond–containing alkynes are changed to -*yne*.

Double and Triple Bonds

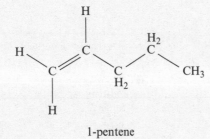

1-pentene

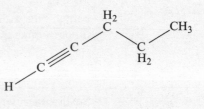

1-pentyne

PRACTICE:

Refer to the earlier table (pages 67–68), if necessary, to match the structures below with one of the following names: 1-butene, triethylamine, 1-heptyne, propanoic acid, 2-hexanol.

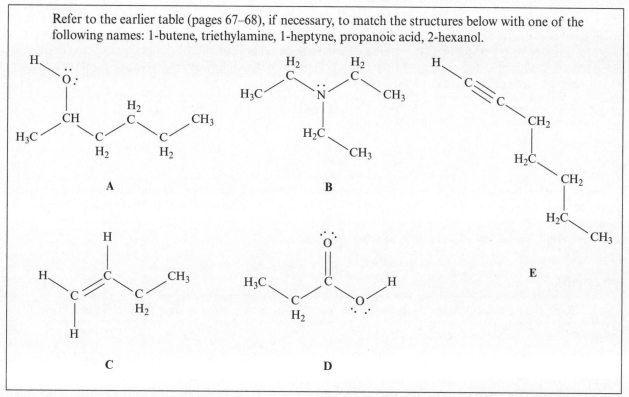

Structure A is 2-hexanol, a 6-carbon alcohol. Structure B is triethylamine, an amine with three 2-carbon chains. Structure C is 1-butene, a 4-carbon alkene. Structure D is propanoic acid, a 3-carbon carboxylic acid. Structure E is 1-heptyne, a 7-carbon alkyne.

Chemical Bonds

Chemical bonds are forces that hold atoms together in compounds. A bond results from the sharing or transfer of electrons between two atoms. The distinction between covalent and ionic bonding is not concrete. Rather, bonds can be classified on a continuum between covalent and ionic based on the characteristics and electronegativity differences between the two atoms involved in the bonding.

Covalent Bonding

Covalent bonding occurs when two nonmetallic atoms share at least one pair of electrons. In general, for a bond to be classified as covalent, the distribution of electron density between the two atoms participating in the bond is not unequal to the extent that the atoms would be considered ionized. Usually the two atoms have an electronegativity difference of about 1.7 or less. The Pauling electronegativity of a hydrogen atom is about 2.2, and the electronegativity of chlorine is about 3.1. The difference in electronegativity, ΔEN, between chlorine and hydrogen is 0.9. Hydrogen and chlorine form a covalent bond in a molecule of hydrochloric acid, HCl. For a review of electronegativity, refer to page 42 in Big Idea 1 (Chapter 1, "Structure of Matter").

$$\Delta EN = 3.1 - 2.2 = 0.9$$

Polar and Nonpolar Covalent Bonds

Polar covalent bonds are covalent bonds in which the electron pair(s) are shared unequally by the two atoms due to differences in electronegativity greater than about 0.4 and less than 1.7. The hydrogen-chlorine bond discussed previously is a polar covalent bond. The greater effective nuclear charge of chlorine draws the electron density of the bond toward the chlorine nucleus. The polarity of the bond is shown by an arrow pointing from the less electronegative atom to the more electronegative atom.

Nonpolar covalent bonds are bonds in which electron pair(s) are shared equally by the two atoms due to very small or no differences in electronegativity between the bonded atoms. The covalent bonds in H_2, O_2, and Cl_2 are nonpolar because there is no difference in electronegativity between two atoms of the same element. The carbon-hydrogen bond is generally considered to be nonpolar covalent.

PRACTICE:

Rank the following single covalent bonds in order of increasing polarity: H-F, H-P, H-O, and H-S.

Phosphorus is the least electronegative of the four heavy atoms, F, P, O, and S. It experiences more shielding of the nucleus by core electrons than fluorine and oxygen, and it has the lowest effective nuclear charge, so the H-P bond can be assumed to be the least polar. By contrast, the fluorine atom is the most electronegative because it has the highest effective nuclear charge. Its valence electrons are less shielded than those of sulfur and phosphorus. The H-F bond is the most polar. Oxygen is more electronegative than sulfur because its valence electrons experience less shielding, so the correct order of increasing bond polarity is H-P < H-S < H-O < H-F.

Bond Length

The **bond length,** or the average distance between the nuclei of two bonded atoms, is the distance at which the potential energy of the two atoms is at a minimum. The lower the potential energy, the more stable the arrangement and the stronger the bond. When the atoms are very far apart, there is no interaction between them and the potential energy is zero. At closer distances, the nucleus of each atom begins to attract the electron cloud of the other atom. As the atoms approach one another, their potential energy decreases. At the equilibrium distance, the attractive and repulsive forces are balanced and the energy is at a minimum. For two hydrogen atoms, this distance is 0.074 nm. At distances closer than the bond length, on the other hand, the repulsive forces between electron clouds and nuclei increase the potential energy.

Bond Length: Potential Energy Versus Internuclear Distance

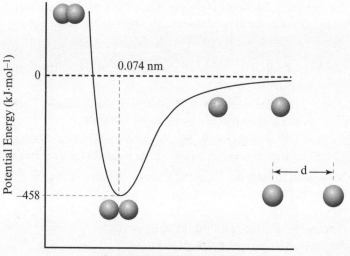

The energy required to separate the two atoms completely is 458 kJ·mol^{-1}.

Lewis Dot Structures

The number of valence electrons is an important factor in the bonding behavior of the elements because they are the electrons that are available to be transferred or shared between atoms. **Lewis dot structures** for elements consist of the symbol of the element surrounded by dots representing the valence electrons. The number of valence electrons for the main group elements is equal to the main group number. The only exception is helium, which has two valence electrons. Notice that the positions of the first four electrons are spaced as far apart as possible before the electrons are paired.

Lewis Dot Diagrams of the Main Group Elements

I	II				III	IV	V	VI	VII	0
H·										He:
Li·	·Be·				·B·	·C·	·N·	:O·	:F·	:Ne:
Na·	·Mg·				·Al·	·Si·	·P·	:S·	:Cl·	:Ar:
K·	·Ca·				·Ga·	·Ge·	·As·	:Se·	:Br·	:Kr:
Rb·	·Sr·				·In·	·Sn·	·Sb·	:Te·	:I·	:Xe:
Cs·	·Ba·				·Tl·	·Pb·	·Bi·	:Po·	:At·	:Rn:

The Lewis dot structures for the *d* and *f* block elements are not discussed in the AP Chemistry curriculum.

The Lewis structures of molecules and polyatomic ions consist of the symbols for the atoms surrounded by dots and lines. The lines represent the bonds, and the dots represent the unshared electrons.

A large number of molecules follow the **octet rule.** This is the tendency for main group elements to achieve noble gas electron configurations. Hydrogen follows the **duet rule.** It can have a maximum of two electrons.

Drawing Lewis Structures of Molecules and Polyatomic Ions

The majority of chemical structures follow the octet rule. When the octet rule is obeyed, each atom except for hydrogen has eight valence electrons in the most stable configuration. There are six steps in writing a correct Lewis structure:

1. Arrange the atom labels in a reasonable, symmetrical skeleton, with the least electronegative elements in the central positions. Hydrogen is never central.

2. Calculate the total number of valence electrons, N, needed in the molecule. Each atom except for hydrogen needs eight valence electrons. Hydrogen needs two valence electrons.

3. Calculate the number of available electrons, A, by adding the number of valence electrons for each atom. Add an electron for each negative charge, and subtract an electron for each positive charge.

4. Calculate the number of shared electrons, S, using $S = N - A$. The number of bonds, indicated by lines, is half the number of shared electrons. In other words, there are two shared electrons per bond. Add the bonds to the structure.

5. Place the rest of the available electrons around the atoms in order to achieve an octet for each atom except hydrogen. These electrons are called **lone pairs.**

6. Assign formal charges to each atom in the molecule. The sum of the formal charges in a neutral molecule is zero. The sum of the formal charges in an ion equals the overall charge of the ion. The formal charge of each element is determined by subtracting the number of bonds and unshared electrons from the main group number for the element.

   Formal charge = number of valence electrons – number of bonds – number of unshared electrons

The six-step method can be used to draw the Lewis structure of a carbonate ion:

1. Carbonate ion, CO_3^{2-}, has one carbon and three oxygens. Carbon is the least electronegative, so it is drawn as the center of a symmetrical skeleton.

$$
\begin{array}{ccc}
O & & O \\
 & C & \\
 & O &
\end{array}
$$

2. There are four atoms in the ion, and each atom needs eight electrons, so

$$N = 4 \times 8 = 32$$

3. The number of available electrons is the sum of the valence electrons contributed by each atom plus the two extra electrons indicated by the –2 charge. Carbon is in group IVA, so it contributes four valence electrons. Oxygen is in group VIA, so each of the three oxygens contributes six electrons.

$$A = (1 \text{ carbon} \times 4) + (3 \text{ oxygens} \times 6) + 2 = 24$$

4. The number of shared electrons is

$$S = N - A = 32 - 24 = 8$$

The number of bonds is four, since each bond is composed of two electrons. For a carbonate ion, this corresponds to two single bonds and one double bond. It does not matter which bond is drawn as a double bond.

5. The difference between the number of available electrons, 24, and the number of shared electrons, 8, is the number of electrons that occur as lone pairs. There are 16 nonbonded electrons, or 8 lone pairs.

It is equally correct to draw the bonds as pairs of dots rather than lines. Both methods will earn credit on the AP Chemistry exam.

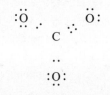

6. Each singly-bonded oxygen atom has a formal charge of –1. The sum of the formal charges in a carbonate ion is –2.

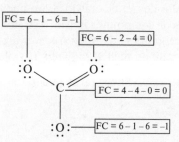

PRACTICE:

Draw Lewis structures for the following species. Be sure to include formal charges.

(a) ONF
(b) NOF
(c) HCN
(d) HNC

Notice that in ONF and HNC, nitrogen is the central atom. In NOF, oxygen is central, and in HCN, carbon is central.

The position of the central atom has an effect on the formal charges of the atoms, as can be seen when formal charges are assigned.

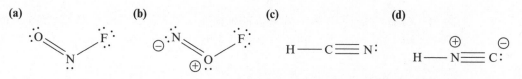

Resonance Structures

Some molecules, such as the carbonate ion shown in the last example, can be drawn as several different valid structures. The bond lengths for a carbonate ion are intermediate between the expected single- and double-bond lengths. In addition, the four pairs of shared electrons are distributed equally throughout the molecule. This is called **delocalization,** and the structure is said to exhibit **resonance.** In order to fully describe the bonding in such **hybrid structures,** all **resonance structures** must be drawn with the resonance relationship indicated by double-headed arrows. It is important to recognize that the double bonds are not exchanging positions. In the carbonate ion, all three bonds are of equal length. The bonds are shorter than carbon-oxygen single bonds, but they are longer than carbon-oxygen double bonds.

Resonance Structures of Carbonate

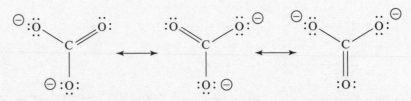

In some cases, not all resonance structures are equal, and some resonance forms contribute more to the overall hybrid structure than others. Thionyl chloride can be drawn as two unequal resonance forms. *Note:* When students are asked to draw Lewis structures of compounds in which strict adherence to the octet rule by all atoms is possible, the structure on the right is acceptable. Only when students are asked to compare the relative contributions of resonance structures is the structure on the left required. It violates the octet rule.

Resonance Structures of Thionyl Chloride

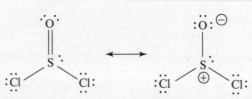

The structure that makes the larger contribution is the one in which:

- each second period element has a complete octet
- the formal charge on each atom is as close to zero as possible (referred to as "least separation of charge")
- negative charges occur on more electronegative elements

In the case of thionyl chloride, the structure on the left makes the greater contribution to the hybrid structure because it has the least separation of charge.

PRACTICE:

For each of the pairs of resonance structures below, select the structure in each box that makes the greater contribution to the hybrid.

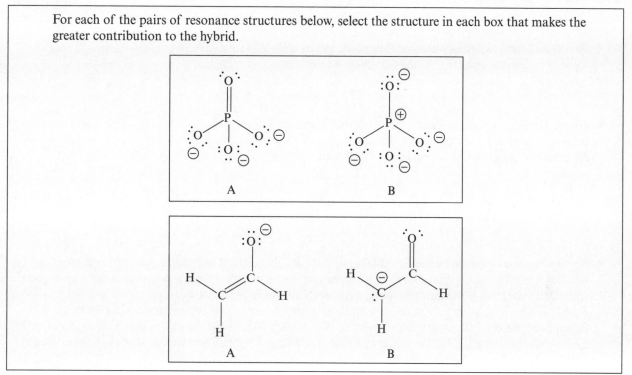

In the first pair, structure A makes the greater contribution to the PO_4^{-3} resonance hybrid. There is less separation of charge in this structure than there is in structure B, and two of the atoms, P and O, have formal charges of zero.

In the second pair, structure A makes the greater contribution to the $H_3C_2O^-$ resonance hybrid. The negative formal charge occurs on oxygen, the more electronegative element.

Many common organic compounds contain a six-membered ring. Benzene, C_6H_6, can be represented as two resonance structures that make equal contributions to the hybrid. In bottom representations, it is understood that each vertex of the hexagon is a carbon atom bound to one hydrogen and two carbons.

Resonance Structures of Benzene

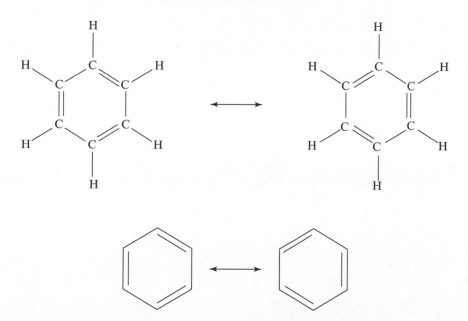

The structure of benzene is an intermediate between the two resonance forms shown above.

75

Limitations of the Octet Rule

In some cases, atoms form compounds without achieving octets.

- Beryllium forms two bonds with no lone pairs. Beryllium needs four electrons rather than eight, so the number of needed electrons, N, for beryllium is four.

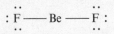

- Group IIIA elements, including boron and aluminum, tend to form three covalent bonds. These elements need six electrons rather than eight, so the number of needed electrons, N, is six. The compounds formed have no lone pairs on the central group IIIA atom.

- Some p block elements in period 3 and higher form compounds that have more electrons available than the number needed to satisfy the octet rule. If the number of shared electrons, S, is less than the number needed to bond all the atoms, S is changed to the number of electrons needed to bond all the atoms. After all other octets have been satisfied, any remaining available electrons are placed around the central atom. In the example below, XeF_2, there are three atoms, so $N = 3 \times 8 = 24$. The number of available electrons, A, is 7 for each fluorine atom and 8 for the xenon atom ($A = (7 \times 2) + 8 = 22$). The number of shared electrons, S, is determined by subtracting A from N.

$$S = A - N = 24 - 22 = 2$$

Because four electrons are needed to participate in bonding between xenon and the fluorine atoms, this compound violates the octet rule.

PRACTICE:

> Which of the following molecules do not obey the octet rule: $AlCl_3$, PCl_3, PCl_5, SF_2, SO_4^{2-}?

The compounds that do not obey the octet rule are $AlCl_3$, PCl_5, and SO_4^{2-}.

Aluminum is in group IIIA. It only needs six valence electrons.

Phosphorus pentachloride needs to share ten electrons in order to bond all the chlorine atoms to the central phosphorus. The calculated number of shared electrons (8) is less than the minimum number needed to bond all the chlorine atoms to the phosphorus atom. In this case, five bonds are drawn, representing the minimum number of shared electrons. The available electrons (A) are then added to provide each chlorine atom with an octet.

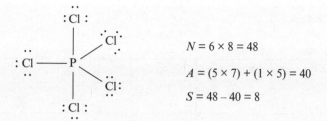

$$N = 6 \times 8 = 48$$
$$A = (5 \times 7) + (1 \times 5) = 40$$
$$S = 48 - 40 = 8$$

Some species, such as the sulfate ion, can be drawn with strict adherence to the octet rule by all atoms (and this is permissible on the AP Chemistry exam if a question merely asks for a Lewis structure), but the resulting structure has a great deal of separation of charge. All four oxygen atoms in this structure have negative charges, and the sulfur atom has a +2 charge. The more important contributors to the hybrid structure are those that have negative charges on only two of the oxygen atoms.

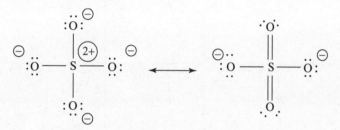

The other compounds, PCl_3 and SF_2, obey the octet rule.

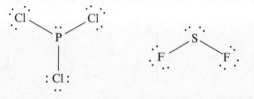

Lewis structures are limited in that they only work well for molecules that have an even number of valence electrons. Other models of bonding, such as molecular orbital theory, are needed to describe the bonding in molecules with odd numbers of valence electrons, but the details of molecular orbital theory are now excluded from the AP Chemistry curriculum.

The VSEPR Model

Once the Lewis structure of a molecule has been established, the molecular shape and polarity of a molecule can be determined using the **valence shell electron pair repulsion (VSEPR) model.** This is a powerful system for prediction of molecular geometry, and it requires memorization. Bonds and electron pairs are treated as regions of electron density around the nucleus of an atom. These regions of electron density are oriented as far apart as possible in order to minimize repulsions. In addition, lone pairs of electrons on a central atom will take up more space than bonding pairs of electrons.

Steps in Predicting the Molecular Geometry of a Molecule

1. Draw the Lewis structure.
2. Count the regions of high electron density. Each atom, X, bound to the central atom, A, is counted as one region of electron density, regardless of whether the bond to that atom is single, double, or triple. Each lone pair, E, counts as one region.
3. Determine the **electronic geometry** based on the total number of regions of electron density, X + E.
4. Determine the **molecular geometry** by considering only the bonding pairs of electrons, X.

The following electronic geometries and molecular geometries must be memorized. (Hybridization about the central atom will be discussed below in the section entitled "Orbital Hybridization.")

Electronic Geometry	Hybridization About the Central Atom	Formula	Molecular Geometry	Structure	Examples
Linear	*sp*	AX_2	Linear		$BeCl_2$, CO_2, HCN
Trigonal planar	sp^2	AX_3	Trigonal planar		BF_3, SO_3, CO_3^{2-}
		AX_2E	Bent		SO_2, O_3, NO_2^-
Tetrahedral	sp^3	AX_4	Tetrahedral		CH_4, NH_4^+, SO_4^{2-}
		AX_3E	Trigonal pyramidal		NH_3, PCl_3, SO_3^{2-}
		AX_2E_2	Bent		H_2O, OF_2, NH_2^-
Trigonal bipyramidal	sp^3d (not tested on the AP Chemistry exam)	AX_5	Trigonal bipyramidal		PCl_5, PF_5
		AX_4E	Seesaw-shaped (diphenoidal)		SF_4, XeF_4, IF_4^+
		AX_3E_2	T-shaped		BrF_3, ICl_3

continued

Electronic Geometry	Hybridization About the Central Atom	Formula	Molecular Geometry	Structure	Examples
		AX_2E_3	Linear		I_3^-, XeF_2
Octahedral	sp^3d^2 (not tested on the AP Chemistry exam)	AX_6	Octahedral		SF_6, PCl_6^-
		AX_5E	Square pyramidal		IF_5, $XeOF_4$
		AX_4E_2	Square planar		XeF_4, ICl_4^-

The molecular geometry of more complicated organic structures can be elucidated by considering each central atom in turn. For example, the molecular geometry of acetic acid, CH_3CO_2H, can be determined by considering the two carbon atoms individually. The geometry with respect to the $–CH_3$ carbon is tetrahedral (AX_4), while the geometry of the $–CO_2H$ carbon is trigonal planar (AX_3).

A Three-Dimensional Model of an Acetic Acid Molecule

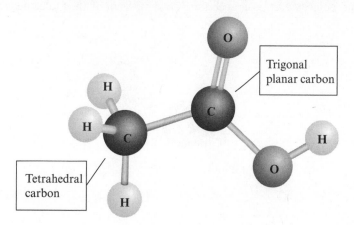

PRACTICE:

Predict the electronic and molecular geometries around each of the central atoms in NO_2^-, N_2O, XeO_3, and XeO_4^{2-}. Notice that each species can be correctly drawn as more than one resonance structure.

Draw each Lewis structure and count the numbers of atoms and lone pairs surrounding the central atoms.

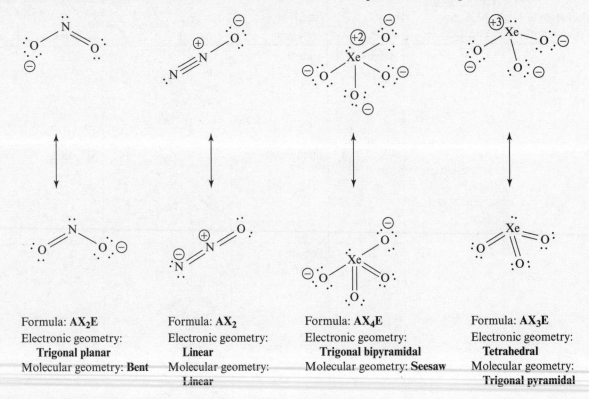

Formula: AX_2E	Formula: AX_2	Formula: AX_4E	Formula: AX_3E
Electronic geometry:	Electronic geometry:	Electronic geometry:	Electronic geometry:
Trigonal planar	**Linear**	**Trigonal bipyramidal**	**Tetrahedral**
Molecular geometry: **Bent**	Molecular geometry: **Linear**	Molecular geometry: **Seesaw**	Molecular geometry: **Trigonal pyramidal**

Dipole Moment

Once the molecular geometry of a molecule or polyatomic ion has been established, the polarity of the molecule can be predicted. The **dipole moment** is a measure of the inequality of charge distribution in a molecule. The polarity of the molecule is indicated by a vector that points in the direction of the more negative region of the molecule.

The overall dipole moment of a molecule is the vector sum of the individual bond dipoles. In symmetric molecules, such as CO_2, the bond polarity vectors cancel, the dipole moment of the molecule is zero, and the molecule is nonpolar.

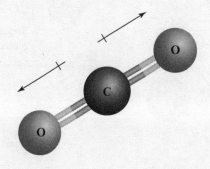

When the arrangement of bonds and lone pairs around the central atom is asymmetric, as is the case for ammonia, the overall dipole moment is nonzero and the molecule is polar.

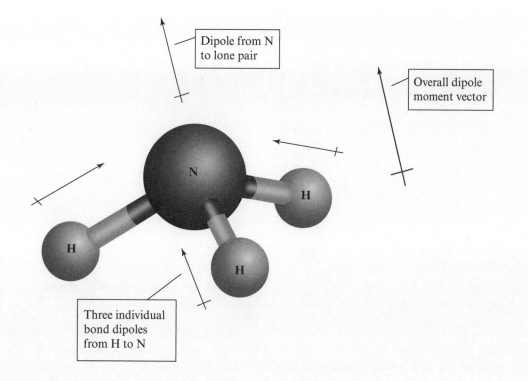

PRACTICE:

The structures below represent *ortho*-dichlorobenzene and *para*-dichlorobenzene. Which of these molecules below is polar? The Pauling electronegativity of chlorine and carbon are 3.1 and 2.5, respectively.

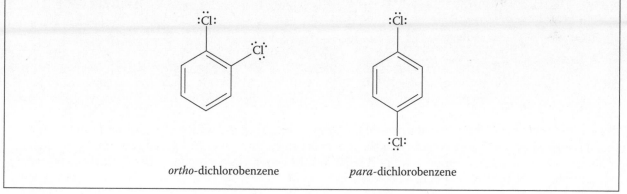

ortho-dichlorobenzene   *para*-dichlorobenzene

The C-C and C-H bonds are nonpolar, so the only bonds that need to be considered are the C-Cl bonds. Chlorine is substantially more electronegative than carbon. The bond dipole vectors point from the carbon atoms toward the chlorine atoms. The vectors cancel in *para*-dichlorobenzene, so it is nonpolar. Since the vectors do not cancel in *ortho*-dichlorobenzene, it is a polar molecule.

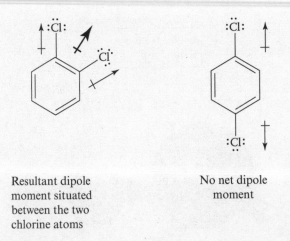

Resultant dipole
moment situated
between the two
chlorine atoms

No net dipole
moment

Orbital Hybridization

When bonding occurs, atomic orbitals are thought to combine to form molecular **hybrid orbitals.** The number of hybrid orbitals equals the number of atomic orbitals that were combined.

A simple method for determining the hybridization about a central atom is to count the number of regions of electron density. Central atoms such as the beryllium atom in BeF_2 have two regions of electron density, bond angles of 180°, and are *sp* hybridized. Central atoms surrounded by three regions of electron density, such as the carbon atom in carbonate, are sp^2 hybridized and have bond angles close to 120°. Central atoms with tetrahedral electronic geometry and bond angles close to 109.5°, such as the nitrogen in ammonia, are sp^3 hybridized.

Orbital Hybridization

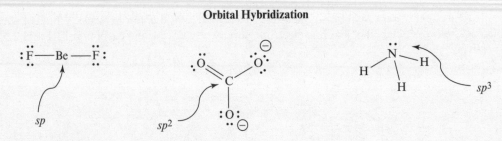

Sigma and Pi Bonds

Sigma (σ) bonds are cylindrically symmetric bonds formed from head-on overlap of two atomic orbitals. A $\sigma_{s\text{-}s}$ bond is formed between two *s* orbitals, as is the case in H_2. In HF, a $\sigma_{s\text{-}p}$ bond is formed between the *s* orbital of hydrogen and a *p* orbital of fluorine. A $\sigma_{p\text{-}p}$ orbital is formed between two *p* orbitals, as in F_2. It is acceptable to simply refer to any of these simply as a "σ bond."

Sigma Bonding

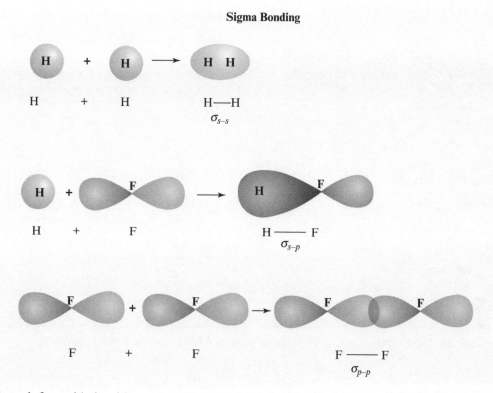

$$\sigma_{s-s}$$

$$\sigma_{s-p}$$

$$\sigma_{p-p}$$

Pi (π) bonds result from side-by-side overlap of *p* orbitals. Each π bond contains a pair of electrons and is perpendicular to a line drawn between the nuclei of the two bonded atoms (the internuclear axis). Pi bonds can only form between atoms that are already participating in σ bonding. They are weaker than σ bonds because there is not as much overlap between the π-bonded *p* orbitals.

A π bond occupies a region both above and below the internuclear axis. This representation should not be confused with two separate π bonds.

Pi Bonding

$$\pi_{p-p}$$

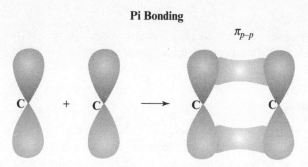

In atoms that participate in double and triple bonding, the first bond formed between the atoms is a σ bond, and the second and third bonds are π bonds. In addition, atoms joined by only σ bonds can rotate around those bonds, but atoms joined by π bonds cannot rotate without breaking the bonds. For this reason, a molecule like 1-chloropropane, which is connected by only σ bonds, can be drawn several different ways without changing the structure. A molecule like 1-chloropropene, however, which has a σ and a π bond between carbons 1 and 2, exists in two discrete forms called **geometric isomers.**

Geometric Isomerism

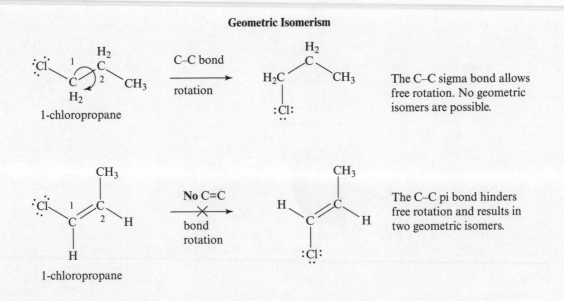

1-chloropropane

The C–C sigma bond allows free rotation. No geometric isomers are possible.

1-chloropropane

The C–C pi bond hinders free rotation and results in two geometric isomers.

PRACTICE:

Identify the σ and π bonds in the following structure. Which bonds allow free rotation?

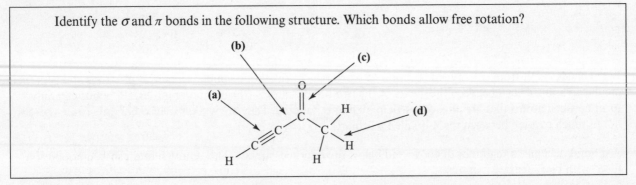

Bond **(a)** is a triple bond composed of one σ and two π bonds. Bonds **(b)** and **(d)** are single bonds, each composed of one σ bond. Bond **(c)** is a double bond composed of one σ and one π bond. Only **(b)** and **(d)**, the single bonds, allow free rotation.

Multiple Bond Strengths

In general, when comparing single, double, and triple bonds between a given pair of atoms, the larger the number of electrons shared between the atoms, the shorter and stronger the bond. In general, single bonds are the longest and weakest since they consist of only one σ bond, and triple bonds are the strongest and shortest since they are composed of one σ and two π bonds. **Bond enthalpy** is a measure of the strength of a bond. It is the energy required to break a bond. The higher the bond enthalpy, the stronger the bond. Shown below are the bond enthalpies and average bond lengths of carbon-carbon single, double, and triple bonds for comparison.

Bond	Bond Enthalpy (kJ·mol⁻¹)	Approximate Bond Length (pm)
C——C	348	154
C══C	614	147
C≡≡≡C	839	137

Infrared Spectroscopy

Covalent bonds in molecules vibrate. Two covalently bonded atoms can be visualized as suspended marbles connected by a spring. The spring stretches and recoils with a certain frequency. For a covalent bond, this frequency lies in the infrared region of the electromagnetic spectrum. In general, bonds between large atoms vibrate with lower frequencies than bonds between small atoms.

Marbles Connected by a Spring

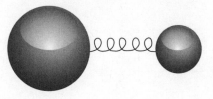

When photons matching the vibrational frequencies of bonds are absorbed, the absorbed energy causes molecules to transition from vibrational ground states to vibrational excited states. The vibrational states are quantized, which means that the vibrations of bonds can have only certain allowed frequencies. This is the basis for **infrared spectroscopy,** a technique that provides chemists with one method for determining the types of functional groups present in a molecule.

As discussed previously, a **functional group** is a group of atoms that determines the chemical properties of a compound. Some examples of the types of bonds that are easily identified by infrared spectroscopy are C-H, C-C, C=C, C-N, C-O, C=O, and O-H bonds. The different types of bonds have different characteristic vibrational frequencies in the infrared region.

An **infrared spectrometer** is a device that measures the frequencies of infrared radiation that are absorbed by a sample. An **infrared spectrum,** which is characteristic of the molecules in the sample, is produced.

The infrared region encompasses photon frequencies of $4.3 \times 10^{14} - 3.0 \times 10^{11}$ s^{-1}. These frequencies are very large, so they are generally expressed as **wavenumbers,** cm^{-1}. The wavenumber is just the frequency divided by the speed of light in cm·s^{-1}. Students will *not* be expected to calculate wavenumber, but they should know that wavenumber is proportional to frequency.

The percent transmittance, which shows the portion of infrared radiation that is not absorbed by a sample, is plotted on the vertical axis of an infrared spectrum.

The infrared spectrum below is the spectrum of methanol, CH_3OH. From a table of characteristic IR frequencies, some of the peaks can be identified. Students are only required to know that different kinds of bonds absorb different characteristic IR frequencies and that these absorptions can help in the identification of the functional groups present in a compound.

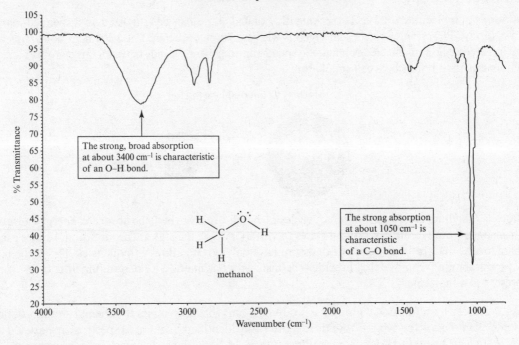

The Infrared Spectrum of Methanol

Ionic Bonding

Ionic bonds are electrostatic attractions between positive and negative ions. The electronegativity difference between atoms participating in an ionic bond is usually greater than 1.7. Ionic bonds are formed when electrons are transferred between two or more atoms. The resulting charged species are attracted to one another by **coulombic** attractions.

The energy released when a cation and an anion in the gas phase come together to form an ionic solid is called the **lattice energy.** It is the measure of the strength of an ionic bond. It can be represented using the form of Coulomb's law that was introduced in Big Idea 1 (Chapter 1, "Structure of Matter"):

$$E \propto \frac{q_1 q_2}{r}$$

The lattice energy, E, is proportional to the product of the ionic charges, q_1 and q_2, and is inversely proportional to the distance, r, between the centers of the ions. When the ions have charges that are opposite in sign, the lattice energy is negative, indicating an attractive force and a release of energy when the ionic solid forms. The more negative the lattice energy, the stronger the ionic bond.

PRACTICE:

Predict the order of increasing lattice energy magnitude for $CaCl_2$, Fe_2O_3, KCl, and FeO.

There are two factors to consider when answering this question. The first is the charge of each ion, and the second is the radius. Since the radii of the cations (ranging from 116 pm for Na^+ and 80 pm for Fe^{3+}) and the radii of the anions (126 pm for O^{2-} and 167 pm for Cl^-) have similar orders of magnitude, the product of the charges, $q_1 q_2$, will be the more important determinant in this example.

Compound	Cation	Anion	q_1q_2	Lattice Energy (kJ·mol^{-1})
$CaCl_2$	Ca^{2+}	Cl^-	$(2 \times -1) = -2$	-2268
Fe_2O_3	Fe^{3+}	O^{2-}	$(3 \times -2) = -6$	$-14{,}309$
KCl	K^+	Cl^-	$(1 \times -1) = -1$	-701
FeO	Fe^{2+}	O^{2-}	$(2 \times -2) = -4$	-3795

Since the value of q_1q_2 becomes more negative progressing from KCl to Fe_2O_3, the order of increasing lattice energy magnitude is KCl < $CaCl_2$ < FeO < Fe_2O_3. Actual reported values for the lattice energies are shown for comparison.

Ionic solids form in such a way as to maximize attractive forces between oppositely charged ions and minimize repulsive forces. This leads to orderly crystal structures in which each cation is surrounded by anions and each anion is surrounded by cations. The regular positions occupied by the ions are referred to as **lattice points.**

The Structure of an Ionic Crystal

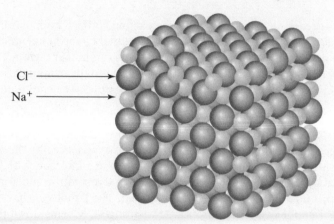

Cl$^-$

Na$^+$

Metallic Bonding

Metallic bonding is characterized by a regular three-dimensional array of metal cations surrounded by freely moving valence electrons. The outermost electrons are delocalized, which accounts for many of the observable physical properties of solid metals, such as conductivity and malleability. The properties will be discussed in greater detail in the section "Metallic Solids" later in this chapter (page 104).

The Electron Sea Model of Metallic Bonding

Intermolecular Forces

Intermolecular forces, also known as **IMFs,** are weak attractions between covalent molecules or discrete atoms. *They are not to be confused with bonds.* Bonds are intramolecular forces within molecules. When bonds are broken or formed, the identity of the species is changed. When intermolecular forces between molecules are broken or formed, the molecules themselves remain unchanged.

When molecular solids such as ice melt, for instance, some of the intermolecular forces (called hydrogen bonds) between the H_2O molecules are broken, but the covalent bonds between hydrogen and oxygen are not. Additional intermolecular forces are overcome in order to separate the H_2O molecules completely into the gas phase when water evaporates or boils, but again, no covalent bonds are broken. The amount of energy required to break a covalent O-H bond is much greater than the amount of energy required to overcome the intermolecular forces between molecules.

Physical properties such as the miscibility of compounds are a direct consequence of the types of intermolecular forces present between molecules of the substances. In general, because stronger intermolecular forces require more energy to overcome than weaker intermolecular forces, they lead to higher boiling points, higher melting points, higher viscosities, higher surface tensions, and lower vapor pressures.

London Dispersion Forces

London dispersion forces are the weakest of the intermolecular forces. They are present between any molecules that are in proximity of one another.

London dispersion forces are the only intermolecular forces acting between nonpolar molecules and single atoms such as noble gases. They are a result of **instantaneous dipoles** caused by the momentary and reversible accumulation of electron density in one region of a molecule at the expense of another region. This fleeting dipole moment causes the electron density in surrounding molecules to be attracted to the temporary partial positive region. This results in additional instantaneous dipoles in the neighboring molecules. The end result is a net attraction between the molecules.

Polarizability refers to how easily electrons can be displaced within a molecule. The more polarizable the electron density is in a molecule, the stronger the London dispersion forces experienced by the molecule. A molecule with greater surface area and with many electrons is more polarizable than a molecule with less surface area and fewer electrons. This is illustrated by the phases of the halogens at room temperature and atmospheric pressure. F_2 and Cl_2 are gases at room temperature, Br_2 is a liquid, and I_2 is a solid. The I_2 molecule has the most electrons and is the most polarizable, so its London dispersion forces are the strongest. Moving down the group, each halogen has more electrons and is more polarizable. The London dispersion forces become increasingly strong, and the halogens have more of a tendency to stick together.

Shown below are two organic molecules called pentane and neopentane. Although both molecules are composed of five carbons and twelve hydrogens, pentane has a higher boiling point than neopentane because of its larger surface area and greater polarizability.

Comparison of the London Dispersion Forces in Pentane and Neopentane

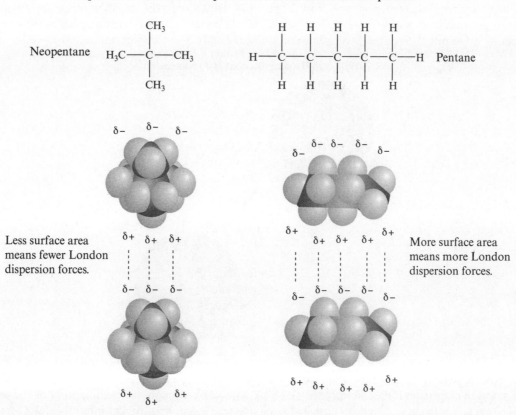

Less surface area means fewer London dispersion forces.

More surface area means more London dispersion forces.

Dipole-Dipole Attractions

Dipole-dipole attractions are intermolecular forces between polar molecules. The partial positive portion of one molecule is attracted to the partial negative end of a neighboring molecule. The more polar the molecules, the stronger the dipole-dipole attraction.

Dipole-Dipole Attractions Between HCl Molecules

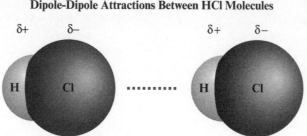

Dipole-Induced Dipole Attractions

Dipole-induced dipole attractions are interactions between polar and nonpolar molecules. Proximity to a polar molecule causes an instantaneous dipole in the polarizable electrons of a nonpolar molecule, resulting in an attraction. Nonpolar oxygen molecules are capable of dissolving in polar water molecules because of dipole-induced dipole interactions.

Hydrogen Bonds

Hydrogen bonding, a subset of dipole-dipole attractions, occurs in molecules that have hydrogen bound to N, O, or F. These elements are so electronegative and remove so much of the electron density from the hydrogen atom that the hydrogen begins to behave like a bare proton. It experiences a strong attraction to the electron pairs of the N, O, or F atoms of adjacent molecules, and the resulting attraction is the strongest of the intermolecular forces. Hydrogen bonds are still very weak, however, when compared to ionic or covalent bonds. It cannot be stressed enough: Despite their name, hydrogen bonds are *not* bonds. They are intermolecular forces.

Hydrogen Bonding Between H_2O Molecules

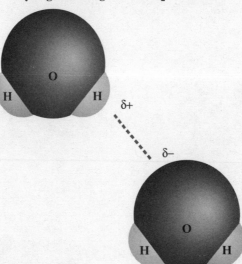

The implications of hydrogen bonding are seen as boiling point anomalies for the second-period hydrides HF, H_2O, and H_3N. In general, boiling points for the hydrides increase down a group on the periodic table due to increased London dispersion forces. For groups VA, VIA, and VIIA, though, the boiling point of the period 2 hydride is much larger than expected. Because hydrogen bonding is a much stronger intermolecular force than dipole-dipole interactions or London dispersion forces, the energy required to convert NH_3, HF, or H_2O from the liquid to the gas phase is higher than would be predicted based on the trend.

Boiling Point Trends for the Groups 14–17 Hydrides

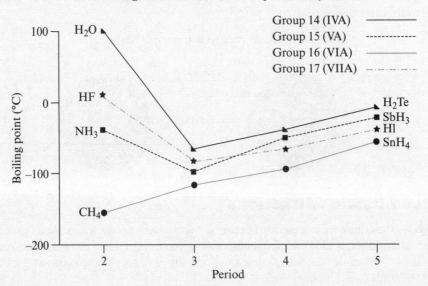

Hydrogen bonding is very important in biology, and there is emphasis on this fact in the AP Chemistry curriculum. Noteworthy examples include hydrogen bonding between the base pairs of the DNA molecule, as shown below. Adenine and thymine form two hydrogen bonds, and cytosine and guanine form three hydrogen bonds.

The Role of Hydrogen Bonding in the Structure of DNA

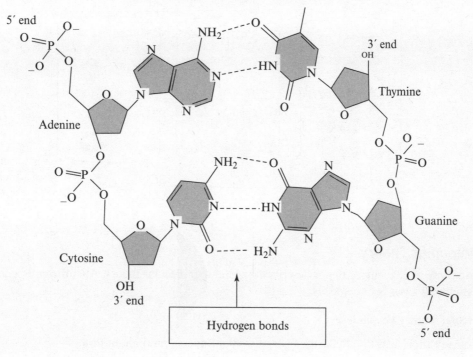

PRACTICE:

Rank the listed substances in order of increasing melting point. Justify your ranking.

XeF_2, CO_2, CS_2

The correct order of increasing melting point is $CO_2 < CS_2 < XeF_2$. Carbon disulfide, carbon dioxide, and xenon difluoride are all nonpolar, linear molecules. None has a dipole moment because the symmetrical arrangement of the regions of electron density around the central atoms cancels any net dipole. Xenon difluoride, however, has the most electrons and is the most polarizable, so its London dispersion forces are stronger than those in CS_2 and CO_2. It has the highest melting point. Carbon disulfide has more electrons and is more polarizable than carbon dioxide, so the melting point of carbon dioxide is the lowest.

$$\ddot{O} = C = \ddot{O} \qquad \ddot{S} = C = \ddot{S} \qquad :\!\ddot{F} - \ddot{X}e - \ddot{F}\!:$$

Physical States of Matter

Solids and liquids are **condensed states** of matter. The densities of solids and liquids are much higher than those of gases, and they are relatively noncompressible (this means that increasing pressure does not substantially decrease their volume). Solids are rigid and hold their shape, whereas liquids conform to the shape of the bottom of their container and assume a flat surface due to gravity.

Gases, by contrast, are diffuse and compressible. Compared with solids and liquids, there is much more space between the molecules of a gas. The particles will spread out and evenly fill a container. The properties of gases are much different from those of solids or liquids.

Particulate Comparison of the Solid, Liquid, and Gas States

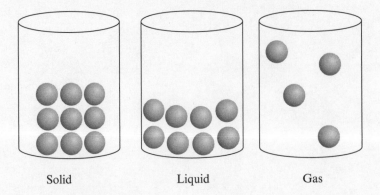

Solid   Liquid   Gas

Gases

Kinetic Molecular Theory

Ideal gases are those with behavior that is described by kinetic-molecular theory. At sufficiently high temperatures and low pressures, all gases behave ideally.

Kinetic Molecular Theory Postulates:

- The atoms or molecules that make up a gas are in continuous, random motion.
- All collisions between gas particles or between gases and the walls of their container are perfectly elastic (no energy is lost due to the collisions).
- The pressure exerted by a gas is due to collisions of the particles with the walls of the container.
- The volume of individual gas particles is negligible compared to the empty space between the particles.
- The temperature of a gas is a measure of the average kinetic energy of the particles.

Samples of gases can be described by four variables: pressure, temperature, volume, and number of moles.

Pressure, which is due to the collisions of gas molecules with the walls of their container, is a measure of force exerted by a gas per unit area. At sea level, the height of mercury in a mercury barometer that is supported by the atmosphere, or the **barometric pressure,** is 760 mm Hg. This is equal to 760 torr, 1 atmosphere (atm), or 101 kiloPascals (kPa). The necessary conversion factors will be provided in the *AP Chemistry Equations and Constants* sheet (pages 365–366) on the exam or within the questions themselves.

Mercury Barometer

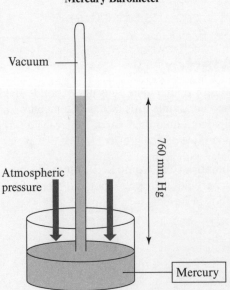

Vacuum

Atmospheric pressure

760 mm Hg

Mercury

Kinetic energy is energy of motion. **Temperature** is a measure of the **average kinetic energy** of the particles in a sample. In all gas law calculations, the temperature in **Kelvin** must be used. The temperature in Kelvin is given by

$$K = °C + 273$$

The kinetic energy, *KE,* for a single particle is given by

$$KE = \frac{1}{2}mv^2$$

Where *m* is the mass of the particle and *v* is the speed or velocity of the particle. Not all of the particles in a sample are moving at the same speed. The distribution of the speeds of the particles in a sample can be described by a **Maxwell-Boltzmann curve.**

The Maxwell-Boltzmann Distributions of Two Samples of Gas at Different Temperatures

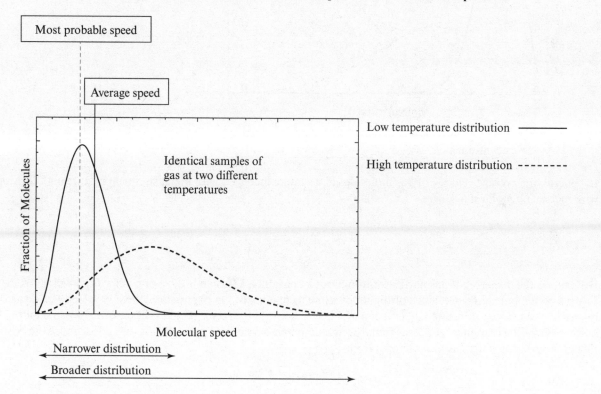

The two curves shown here represent two otherwise identical gas samples at two different temperatures. The areas under the two curves are equal, but the average speed of the particles in the high-temperature sample is greater than that of the particles in the low-temperature sample. It should also be noted that as the temperature increases, the range of velocities broadens. In addition, the average velocity is slightly higher than the most probable velocity since the curve is not symmetrical and is skewed toward higher speeds.

The Maxwell-Boltzmann distribution may also be used to describe the speeds of different types of molecules at one temperature. In this case, molecules with higher molar mass tend to move at speeds closer to their average velocity, while molecules with lower molar mass tend to have a broader range of velocities.

The Maxwell-Boltzmann Distributions of Two Samples of Gas with Different Molar Masses

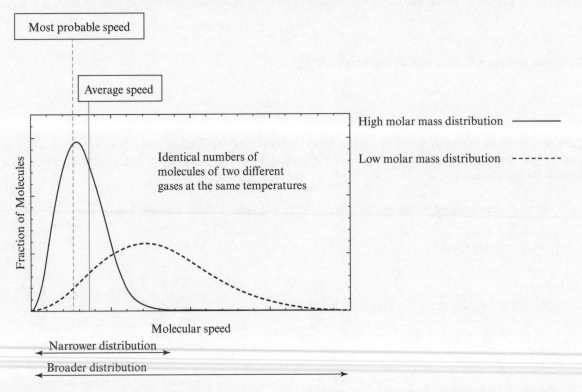

In general, the average velocity of gas molecules in a sample increases with increasing temperature and decreases with increasing molar mass, *M*.

$$\text{Average velocity} \propto \sqrt{\frac{T}{M}}$$

Diffusion is the dispersal of gas particles throughout a container. **Effusion** is the escape of gas particles through tiny pores in a barrier from regions of higher pressure to regions of lower pressure. Average velocity of a gas is related to the rates of diffusion and effusion of the gas, because the faster the particles are moving, the more quickly they fill a container or pass through an opening in a barrier. All gases diffuse and effuse more quickly at higher temperatures than at lower temperatures.

Diffusion and Effusion

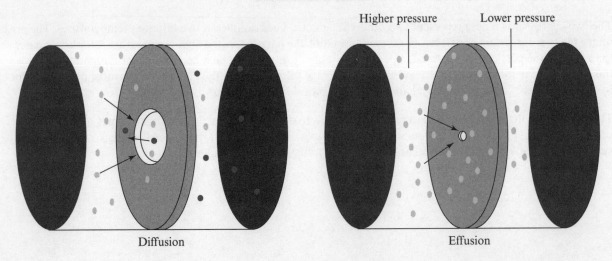

Small molecular weight gases effuse and diffuse faster than higher molecular weight gases. The relationship between rates of motion of two gases is given by **Graham's law.** In this equation, rate$_A$ and rate$_B$ **refer** to the rates of diffusion or effusion of gases A and B, respectively, and *M* refers to the molar mass. This equation is *not* available on the *AP Chemistry Equations and Constants* sheet (pages 365–366).

$$\frac{\text{rate}_A}{\text{rate}_B} = \sqrt{\frac{M_B}{M_A}}$$

PRACTICE:

> A mixture of helium and nitrogen is contained in a balloon. A microscopic hole is punctured in the balloon. What is the ratio of the rates of effusion of helium to nitrogen?

The molar mass of helium, a noble gas, is 4.00 g·mol^{-1}. The molar mass of nitrogen, N$_2$, is 28.02 g·mol^{-1}. The ratio of the rates can be determined using Graham's law.

$$\frac{\text{rate}_{He}}{\text{rate}_{N_2}} = \sqrt{\frac{28.02 \ \text{g·mol}^{-1}}{4.00 \ \text{g·mol}^{-1}}} = 2.65$$

Helium diffuses through the opening 2.65 times as fast as nitrogen.

Boyle's Law

The product of the volume and the pressure of a gas is constant. At constant temperature the volume, *V*, of a gas sample is inversely proportional to its pressure, *P*. This relationship is named **Boyle's law** after its discoverer, Robert Boyle.

$$P \propto \frac{1}{V}$$

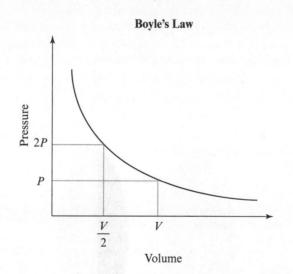

Boyle's Law

Charles' Law

Charles' law states that the volume of a sample gas is directly proportional to the absolute Kelvin temperature of the gas at constant pressure.

$$V \propto T$$

The graph of volume versus temperature can be extrapolated to a temperature at which volume is theoretically zero. This temperature, 0 Kelvin or **absolute zero,** is –273 °C. Temperatures of 0 K have not been attained in a laboratory.

Charles' Law

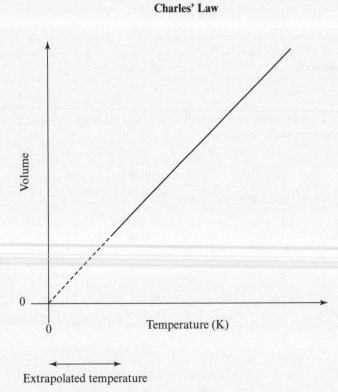

Extrapolated temperature

Avogadro's Law

Equal volumes of gases at the same temperature and pressure contain identical numbers of moles of gas molecules. This relationship is known as **Avogadro's law:** The number of moles of gas, n, is directly proportional to the volume.

$$n \propto V$$

Ideal Gas Law

The experimental observations of Boyle, Charles, and Avogadro are summarized in the **ideal gas law,** the equation from which any ideal gas conditions can be determined.

$$PV = nRT$$

The **universal gas constant,** R, is 0.08206 L·atm·mol^{-1}·K^{-1}. The ideal gas law and the value of R are given on the *AP Chemistry Equations and Constants* sheet (pages 365–366).

For example, the pressure exerted by 0.50 mole of an ideal gas occupying 3.0 L at 200 K can be found by rearranging the ideal gas equation.

$$P = \frac{nRT}{V}$$

$$P = \frac{0.50 \ \cancel{mol} \times 0.08206 \ \cancel{L} \cdot atm \cdot \cancel{mol^{-1}} \cdot \cancel{K^{-1}} \times 200 \ \cancel{K}}{3.0 \ \cancel{L}} = 2.7 \ atm$$

PRACTICE:

> Find the number of liters occupied by 0.22 mole of an ideal gas at a temperature of 42 °C and 3800 torr.

The pressure must first be converted to atmospheres.

$$3800 \text{ torr} \times \frac{1 \text{ atm}}{760 \text{ torr}} = 5.0 \text{ atm}$$

The temperature must be expressed in Kelvin.

$$42 \text{ °C} + 273 = 315 \text{ K}$$

The ideal gas equation is rearranged to solve for volume.

$$V = \frac{nRT}{P} = \frac{(0.22 \text{ mol})(0.08206 \text{ L} \cdot \text{atm} \cdot \text{mol}^{-1} \cdot \text{K}^{-1})(315 \text{ K})}{5.0 \text{ atm}} = 1.1 \text{ L}$$

Since R is constant, rearranging the ideal gas equation gives a form that allows for useful calculations.

$$R = \frac{PV}{nT}$$

The initial conditions of a gas, P_i, V_i, n_i, and T_i, are related to the final conditions, P_f, V_f, n_f, T_f, by

$$\frac{P_i V_i}{n_i T_i} = \frac{P_f V_f}{n_f T_f}$$

Any of the four variables that remain constant can be cancelled out of the equation. For instance, a problem may provide an initial volume and pressure. The question may then ask for a final pressure at a new volume, assuming the number of moles and temperature are held constant. The number of moles and the temperature cancel out of the equation since $n_i = n_f$ and $T_i = T_f$.

$$\frac{P_i V_i}{n_i T_i} = \frac{P_f V_f}{n_f T_f}$$

$$P_i V_i = P_f V_f$$

$$P_f = \frac{P_i V_i}{V_f}$$

In this way, any of the ideal gas laws can be quickly derived from the ideal gas equation given on the *AP Chemistry Equations and Constants* sheet (pages 365–366).

PRACTICE:

> A rigid 5.0-L container holds 2.0 moles of gas at 800.0 torr. What is the new pressure if an additional 1.5 moles of gas are added at constant temperature?

Since both the volume and the temperature are held constant, the needed equation relates pressure to number of moles. The final number of moles, n_f, is equal to the initial number of moles, n_i, plus 1.5 moles, which is the number that has been added.

$$\frac{P_i \cancel{V_i}}{n_i \cancel{T_i}} = \frac{P_f \cancel{V_f}}{n_f \cancel{T_f}}$$

$$P_i n_f = P_f n_i$$

$$P_f = \frac{P_i n_f}{n_i}$$

$$P_f = \frac{800.0 \text{ torr} \times (2.0 \cancel{\text{ mol}} + 1.5 \cancel{\text{ mol}})}{2.0 \cancel{\text{ mol}}} = 1400 \text{ torr}$$

Standard Temperature and Pressure

By convention, **standard temperature and pressure,** STP, for the purposes of gas law calculations, are 0 °C (273 K) and 1 atm.

PRACTICE:

Find the volume occupied by 1.0 mole of an ideal gas at STP.

Standard temperature is 273 K, and standard pressure is 1 atm.

Rearranging the ideal gas equation gives the expression for volume.

$$V = \frac{nRT}{P} = \frac{1.0 \cancel{\text{ mol}} \times 0.08206 \text{ L} \cdot \text{atm} \cdot \cancel{\text{mol}^{-1}} \cdot \cancel{\text{K}^{-1}} \times 273 \cancel{\text{ K}}}{1.0 \cancel{\text{ atm}}} = 22.4 \text{ L}$$

This is a very useful relationship, because at STP, the volume of one mole of *any* ideal gas is 22.4 L.

Gas Density

The density, D, of a gas is equal to the mass of gas that will occupy a given volume at a certain temperature and pressure.

$$D = \frac{m}{V}$$

A relationship can be derived between the temperature, pressure, density, and molar mass using the ideal gas law. Since molar mass, M, is equal to grams per mole, the relationship between the number of moles, n, and the mass, m, is given by the following relationship.

$$n = \frac{m}{M}$$

This relationship can be substituted into the ideal gas law.

$$PV = \left(\frac{m}{M}\right) RT$$

Rearrangement gives an equation for the molar mass, and D can be substituted for $\frac{m}{V}$.

$$M = \frac{mRT}{VP}$$

$$M = \frac{DRT}{P}$$

A common laboratory investigation in AP Chemistry involves determination of the molar mass of a volatile liquid by elucidation of its density at a known temperature and pressure. A container with a known volume is weighed together with a small piece of aluminum foil punctured with a pinhole. A small amount of the liquid is placed in the bottom of the container and the container is covered with the foil. The flask is gently heated to a recorded temperature until the entire sample of liquid is vaporized. It is assumed that the pressure reached by the vapor is equal to the barometric pressure in the room and that the entire volume of the container is filled with vapor. The flask is allowed to cool to room temperature so that the vapor that filled the flask condenses. The mass of the flask and foil is subtracted from the mass of the flask, foil, and liquid to give the mass of the vapor.

PRACTICE:

> A student obtains a 10-mL sample of an unknown liquid. She weighs an Erlenmeyer flask and a square of aluminum foil on a balance and obtains a combined mass of 55.21 grams. The student places the liquid into the flask, covers the flask with aluminum foil, and then places the flask into a water bath at 90. °C. Once the liquid has completely vaporized, the student removes the flask and allows it to reach room temperature. Droplets of the volatile liquid form on the walls of the flask. The flask, foil, and liquid are weighed and found to have a mass of 55.31 grams. The student rinses out the flask and fills it to the brim with water. She carefully pours the water into a graduated cylinder and finds that the water has a volume of 57.4 mL. The atmospheric pressure in the room is 1.00 atm. What is the molar mass of the liquid?

The mass of the vapor is the difference between the empty flask with foil and the flask with foil and the condensate.

$$m = 55.31 \text{ g} - 55.21 \text{ g} = 0.10 \text{ g}$$

The temperature is expressed in Kelvin.

$$T = 90. \text{ °C} + 273 = 363 \text{ K}$$

The density of the vapor is the mass per unit volume. The mass of the re-condensed liquid is the same as the mass of the vapor that occupied the flask at the high temperature.

$$D = \frac{0.10 \text{ g}}{57.4 \text{ mL}} = 0.0017 \text{ g} \cdot \text{mL}^{-1}$$

$$(0.00174216)$$

Finally, the molar mass is determined using the equation derived from the ideal gas law.

$$M = \frac{DRT}{P} = \frac{(0.00174126 \text{ g} \cdot \text{mL}^{-1})(0.08206 \text{ L} \cdot \text{atm} \cdot \text{mol}^{-1} \cdot \text{K}^{-1})(363 \text{ K})}{1.00 \text{ atm}} \times \frac{1000 \text{ mL}}{1 \text{ L}} = 52 \text{ g} \cdot \text{mol}^{-1}$$

Dalton's Law of Partial Pressures

Dalton's law states that the total pressure of gas in a mixture of gases is equal to the sum of the pressures that the individual gases would exert by themselves. For gases A, B, and C in a mixture, the total pressure, P_{total}, is equal to the sum of the partial pressures.

$$P_{total} = P_A + P_B + P_C$$

The **partial pressure** of a gas is equal to the total pressure multiplied by the **mole fraction, X,** of that gas in the mixture. The following equation is included on the *AP Chemistry Equations and Constants* sheet (pages 365–366).

$$P_A = P_{total} \times X_A, \text{ where } X_A = \frac{\text{moles A}}{\text{total moles}}$$

$$X_A = \frac{n_A}{n_A + n_B + n_C}$$

PRACTICE:

> A 50-mL tube inverted over a dish of water contains CO_2 and water vapor at STP. The partial pressure of H_2O is 24 torr. What is the mole fraction of CO_2 in the tube?

The partial pressure of CO_2 is given by the difference between the total pressure (atmospheric pressure) and the partial pressure of water.

$$P_{CO_2} = P_{total} - P_{H_2O}$$

$$P_{CO_2} = 760 \text{ torr} - 24 \text{ torr} = 736 \text{ torr}$$

Since the partial pressure of CO_2 is the mole fraction of CO_2 times the total pressure, the mole fraction can be calculated.

$$X_{CO_2} = \frac{P_{CO_2}}{P_{total}} = \frac{736 \text{ torr}}{760 \text{ torr}} = 0.968$$

Questions like the one in the previous example apply to laboratory situations in which the gaseous product(s) of a reaction (usually a decomposition) are collected in a tube over water. The gas that displaces water in the inverted tube contains water vapor with a partial pressure equal to the vapor pressure of water at that temperature. The rest of the gases collected in the inverted tube are products of the reaction.

Collection of the Gaseous Products of a Decomposition Reaction

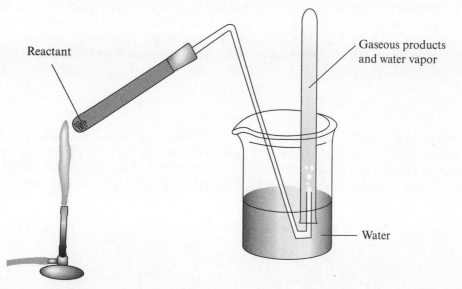

Real Gases

The particles of an ideal gas have no volume and have no interaction with the particles around them other than perfectly elastic collisions. They experience no intermolecular forces. *In reality, no gases are ideal.* **Real gas** particles experience intermolecular attractions (and repulsions at sufficiently close distances). They also occupy space. Some gases behave more ideally than others, however. Helium, for instance, occupies less volume and is less polarizable than CH_4, so its behavior is better described by the ideal gas law.

Gas particles are attracted to other gas particles because of intermolecular forces. The stronger the intermolecular forces between the molecules of the gas, the more the behavior of the gas deviates from that predicted by the ideal gas law. In addition, the larger the molecule, the less accurately the behavior of the gas is predicted by the ideal gas law.

As the average kinetic energy (or temperature) of a sample of gas particles increases, the particles move faster. The faster the gas molecules move, the more energetic their collisions are. Faster-moving gas particles are better able to overcome intermolecular attractions, and so at higher temperatures gas behavior is better predicted by the ideal gas law. At very low temperatures, some of the collisions between the gas molecules are not energetic enough to overcome the strength of the intermolecular forces. Collisions are more inelastic (the molecules stick together). At temperatures close to those at which a gas is expected to condense to the liquid state, a gas deviates from ideal behavior. At higher pressures, molecules are closer together, and intermolecular attractions have an increased influence on the behavior of the gas than at lower pressures. At very high pressures, gases deviate from ideal behavior.

It is important to remember that gases deviate from ideal behavior as their temperature is decreased and their pressure is increased. In other words, the ideal gas law becomes less useful for predicting gas behavior as the gas approaches the liquid state.

PRACTICE:

> Rank the following gases from least to greatest deviation from ideal behavior at STP and explain your ranking: Cl_2, CH_4, H_3COCH_3, C_4H_{10}. (It may help to sketch Lewis structures.)

The correct ranking from least to greatest deviation from ideal behavior is $CH_4 < Cl_2 < C_4H_{10} < H_3COCH_3$. London dispersion forces are the primary intermolecular forces experienced by Cl_2, CH_4, and C_4H_{10}, but

H_3COCH_3 is a bent molecule with two lone pairs on the central oxygen. It is expected to have a dipole moment and experience dipole-dipole interactions, so it is the gas that deviates most from ideal behavior. Butane, C_4H_{10}, has more surface area and electrons than Cl_2 and CH_4, so its polarizability is greatest. Its London dispersion forces are stronger than those of Cl_2 and CH_4, so it deviates more from ideal behavior. Methane, CH_4, has the fewest electrons and is least polarizable of all the gases, so its London dispersion forces are weakest and it deviates least from ideal behavior.

Solids

Solid substances can be classified as either **amorphous** or **crystalline.** Amorphous solids are solids like glass that are relatively disordered on the particulate level. **Crystalline solids** are regular three-dimensional arrangements of atoms, ions, or molecules. Sodium chloride, for instance, is a crystalline solid. Each particle is said to occupy a **lattice point** in the three-dimensional array. For sodium chloride, each lattice point is occupied by a sodium or a chloride ion.

Crystalline and Amorphous Solids

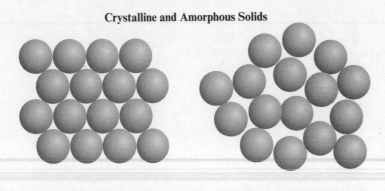

Crystalline   Amorphous

Solids can be further subcategorized as four general types: ionic, network covalent, metallic, and molecular. Each type of solid has properties that can be explained based on the type of bonding and intermolecular forces that dominate.

Ionic Solids

Ionic solids are three-dimensional arrays of alternating cations and anions held together by coulombic attractions. These electrostatic attractions, discussed earlier in the section on ionic bonding (page 86), are relatively strong and give ionic solids high melting points and boiling points.

Ionic solids are hard and brittle. When an ionic solid is struck hard enough for the ions to slip past one another, repulsive attractions between like charges cause the crystal to break.

Breaking an Ionic Crystal

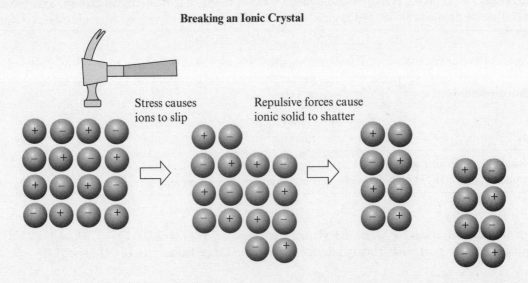

Stress causes ions to slip

Repulsive forces cause ionic solid to shatter

Electrical conductivity is a measure of how well a material transmits an electric current. Ions or electrons must be able to move in order for a substance to conduct electricity. The ions in ionic solids are fixed in place, so ionic solids are nonconductive. By contrast, molten, or melted, ionic solids as well as dissociated ions in aqueous solutions are mobile and conductive.

Network Covalent Solids

Network covalent solids are arrays of atoms held together by covalent bonds. An example is quartz, a crystalline form of SiO_2.

Network covalent solids have extremely high melting points since disruption of the atoms requires breaking covalent bonds. They also tend to be extremely hard and insoluble in water.

Diamond and graphite are both allotropes of carbon. **Allotropes** are different bonding forms of the same element in the same phase. Diamond is composed of sp^3 hybridized, σ-bonded carbon. It is not electrically conductive since the electrons are localized between covalently bound atoms. Graphite is a different allotrope of carbon, consisting of fused six-carbon rings with delocalized single and double bonds. It is a conductive network solid because it is composed of layers of two-dimensional sheets of rings in which the π-bonded electrons are free to move. The attractive forces between the graphite sheets are relatively weak London dispersion forces.

The Structures of Diamond and Graphite

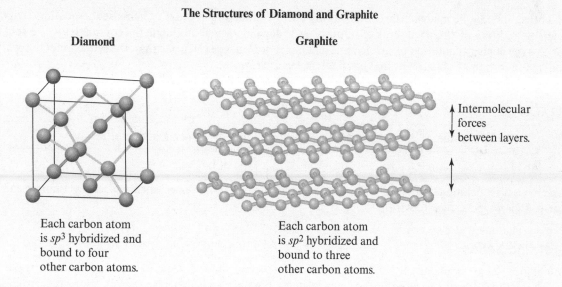

Diamond

Graphite

Each carbon atom is sp^3 hybridized and bound to four other carbon atoms.

Each carbon atom is sp^2 hybridized and bound to three other carbon atoms.

Intermolecular forces between layers.

Elemental silicon is another important network covalent solid. Silicon is a **semiconductor,** which means that its electrical conductivity is greater than that of an electrical insulator like diamond, but less than that of a conductor like pure copper.

As its temperature is raised, silicon's electrical conductivity increases. To understand why this is the case, it is useful to envision bands of adjacent molecular orbitals. The **valence band** of orbitals contains the valence electrons, and the conduction band is a higher-energy band in which conductive electrons can move through the solid. The **band gap** is a range of energies in which no orbitals occur.

In covalent networks, the band gap is too large for any of the electrons in the valence band to be promoted to the conduction band. In metals, the band gap is generally very small, and electrons easily escape the valence band to enter the conduction band. In semiconductors such as silicon, however, the band gap is such that when the material is warmed, electrons gain the energy to move from the valence band to the conduction band.

A Comparison of the Band Gaps in Metals, Semiconductors, and Insulators

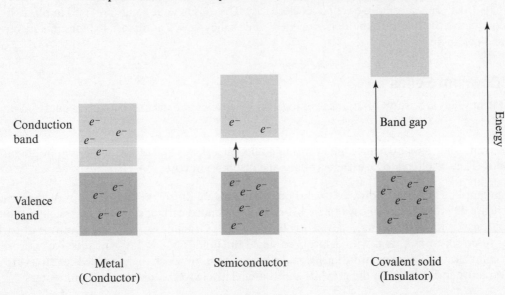

Modifications can be made to the composition of semiconductors in order to increase their conductivity. **Doping** refers to addition of small amounts of impurities, or **dopants,** which modulate the conductivity of a semiconductor. *N*-type doping is addition of an element that has more valence electrons than the semiconductor, while *p*-type doping is addition of an element that has fewer valence electrons.

PRACTICE:

> A small amount of gallium is added to arsenic. What type of semiconductor results?

Arsenic is a semiconducting metalloid. Gallium is the dopant. It has fewer valence electrons than arsenic, so this results in a *p*-type semiconductor.

Metallic Solids

Metallic solids are made up of the *s* block, *d* block, and some *p* block elements such as aluminum and lead. They are characterized by the **electron sea model** of metallic bonding, in which a crystal of cations is surrounded by loosely held, delocalized (or mobile) electrons. This electron mobility explains the electrical conductivity of metals.

The electron sea model explains the high malleability and ductility of metals. **Malleability** is the ability to be pounded into sheets, and **ductility** is the ability to be drawn into wires. When the material is pounded or stretched, the loose electron cloud allows the metallic nuclei to easily slide past one another.

The melting points of metals vary widely, ranging from very low to quite high. Mercury, for example, melts at –39 °C, while tungsten melts at 3422 °C.

Alloys are mixtures of metal atoms and other metallic or nonmetallic elements. They are prepared by mixing molten elements that produce a homogeneous solid solution when cooled. In general, the disruption of the regular crystal lattice of pure metal atoms by atoms of another element makes it more difficult for the layers of nuclei to slip past one another. In other words, most alloys are harder, less malleable, and less ductile than pure metals.

The two major classes of alloys are substitutional and interstitial. **Substitutional alloys** result when a metal is mixed with an element of similar atomic radius. Usually the atomic radii of the atoms in the mixture are within 15% of one another.

Brass, a mixture of copper and zinc, is an example of a substitutional alloy. Copper and zinc atoms are both transition metals, and they have similar radii. The densities of substitutional alloys are intermediate between those of their constituent elements. Different compositions of brass have densities between 8.4 and 8.7 $g \cdot mL^{-1}$. Brass is less dense than pure copper ($d = 8.96 \ g \cdot mL^{-1}$) and more dense than pure zinc ($d = 7.13 \ g \cdot mL^{-1}$).

Interstitial alloys result when much smaller atoms, usually nonmetals such as carbon, boron, and nitrogen, are mixed with a metal with a larger atomic radius. **Steel,** a mixture of iron and carbon, is an interstitial alloy.

Substitutional and Interstitial Alloys

Substitutional Alloy

Some atoms in the crystal are substituted with atoms os similar size.

Interstitial Alloy

Much smaller atoms occupy the interstices (spaces).

PRACTICE:

Sterling silver is composed of about 93% silver and 7% copper. Is this a substitutional or interstitial alloy?

Since silver and copper atoms are both metals with fairly similar atomic radii, sterling silver is a substitutional alloy.

Molecular Solids

Molecular solids are composed of discrete covalent molecules. The individual molecules are held together by intermolecular forces, so molecular solids are softer and lower-melting than the other three types of solids. They may be amorphous, like wax, or crystalline, like ice or solid sucrose (table sugar). Other examples include solid CO_2 (dry ice), I_2 (iodine crystals), and $C_9H_8O_4$ (aspirin).

Although most solids tend to be denser than their corresponding liquid phase, solid water (ice) is a rare and notable exception. Each oxygen is covalently bound to two hydrogens and experiences hydrogen bonding with two additional water molecules. Due to the empty spaces in the crystal structure of ice, solid water is less dense than its liquid phase.

The Crystal Structure of Ice

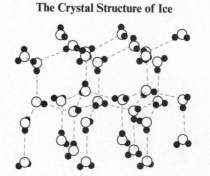

Polymers are sequences of small molecules (monomers) covalently bound in long chains. Polymers are a class of very large molecules that do not fit neatly into the network covalent category since discrete polymer molecules usually do not span the entire solid. They are held together by weak intermolecular forces, and many have relatively low melting points. Polymers are better described as molecular solids.

Polysaccharides are biopolymers, polymers that come from biological sources. They are composed of long chains of simple sugar monomers such as glucose. The glucose biopolymer shown here, amylose, is a component of starch. Amylose is a solid powder isolated from vegetable matter. It is soluble in water and can be used to detect triiodide ions in lab solutions.

Amylose, a Polymer of Glucose

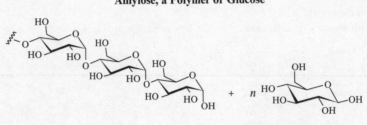

Glucose monomers

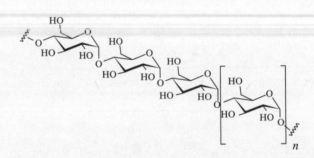

Amylose, a polysaccharide

Other polymers are can be synthetic, or produced in a lab. Common useful examples are polypropylene, made from monomers of propene, and acrylic, made from monomers of methyl methacrylate. These are thermoplastic materials, which are tough and rigid solids at low temperatures due to a large number of intermolecular forces. These materials become flexible and pliable at high temperatures due to disruption of their intermolecular forces.

Synthetic Polymers

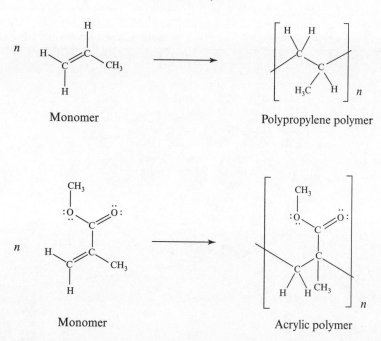

Monomer

Polypropylene polymer

Monomer

Acrylic polymer

Polymers can be synthesized with a variety of properties to serve many different purposes. Students should be familiar with the conventional polymer structure notation (*n* repeating units, with repeating units enclosed in brackets or parentheses). The specific names of these molecules and mechanisms for their formation are beyond the scope of the AP Chemistry curriculum.

Liquids

In the **liquid** state, molecules have interactions with their nearest neighbors, but these interactions are dynamic. The shape of a liquid substance is not fixed. The volume of a liquid is relatively constant; it is only minimally compressible. Particles tend to arrange themselves in such a way as to minimize the surface area of the liquid. Liquids form flat surfaces in open containers and spherical droplets when suspended.

Surface Tension

Surface tension refers to tendency of a liquid to resist an increase in surface area. A molecule within the liquid interacts with surrounding molecules on all sides. These intermolecular forces are called **cohesive forces,** attractions between like molecules. Molecules on the surface, by contrast, only experience cohesive forces with the molecules below them in the liquid. This unbalanced attraction of the surface molecules causes them to be constantly drawn down into the liquid, resulting in flattening of a liquid surface and formation of spherical droplets. The stronger the intermolecular forces between the liquid molecules, the greater the surface tension.

Surface Tension

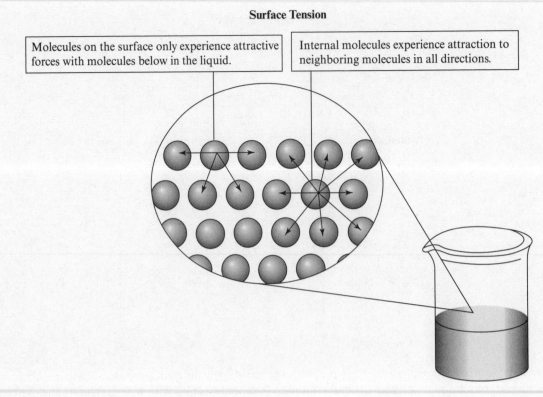

Molecules on the surface only experience attractive forces with molecules below in the liquid.

Internal molecules experience attraction to neighboring molecules in all directions.

Surfactants are molecules that accumulate at the surface of a liquid and disrupt the surface tension. Soaps, detergents, and anti-fogging agents all behave as surfactants.

Viscosity

Viscosity is the resistance of a liquid to flow. The stronger the intermolecular forces between the liquid molecules, the more viscous they are. Honey, which is a mixture of very polar sugar molecules and water, is more viscous than pure water. In addition, long molecules are more likely to become entangled with one another, resulting in high viscosity.

Viscosity of liquids is reduced at higher temperatures. When the temperature is raised, the average kinetic energy of the molecules is increased. This leads to greater motion and a greater ability to overcome intermolecular forces.

Capillary Action

Capillary action refers to the behavior of liquids in narrow tubes.

When a narrow glass tube is placed in water, capillary action causes the water to rise in the tube. This is due to **adhesive forces,** which are intermolecular forces between the molecules of the water and the surface of the glass. Since adhesive forces between water and glass are stronger than cohesive forces between the molecules, the meniscus is concave.

Mercury, by contrast, has a convex meniscus since the cohesive forces between the mercury atoms are stronger than the adhesive forces between the mercury and the glass.

Capillary Action

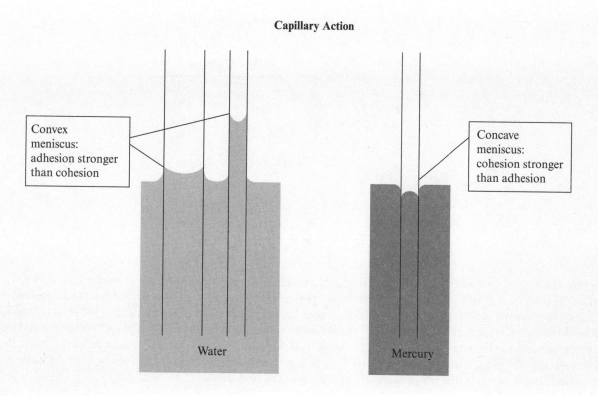

Phase Changes

Phase changes, including freezing, melting, boiling, condensation, sublimation, and deposition, involve the transfer of energy to or from a substance. The thermodynamic term, **enthalpy,** H, is used to describe the energy of a system at constant pressure. At constant pressure, **enthalpy change,** ΔH, is equal to heat transferred to or from a system. The final enthalpy of the system is H_f and the initial enthalpy of the system is H_i.

$$\Delta H = H_f - H_i$$

During melting, vaporization, boiling, and sublimation, intermolecular forces are broken. In order to overcome these attractions, energy must be gained by the substance. The final enthalpy of the substance is greater than the initial enthalpy, so the change in enthalpy, ΔH, is greater than zero. These processes are said to be **endothermic.**

The reverse is true for freezing, condensation, and deposition. When molecules come together due to intermolecular attractions, energy is released. The change in enthalpy is less than zero, and the process is **exothermic.**

A **heating curve** is a useful way to represent the temperature change associated with the transfer of energy that occurs during phase transitions. The heating curve below shows the variation in temperature as heat energy is added to water.

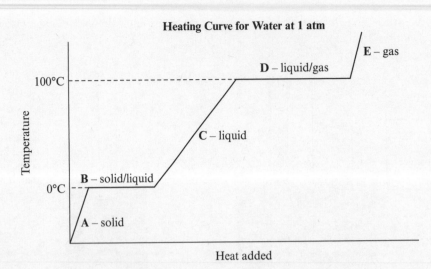

As heat is added to solid ice, the closely packed ice molecules begin to vibrate faster and the temperature rises (A). When the solid reaches 0 °C, the melting point, the temperature stops rising, even though heat is still being added (B). All the added energy at this temperature is used to disrupt the intermolecular forces and convert the solid to liquid. Once the solid has been completely melted, the temperature rises again as more heat is added (C). A second and longer plateau occurs at the liquid-gas transition temperature (D). Boiling requires more heat than melting because the intermolecular forces need to be completely overcome to separate the molecules in space. Finally, once the water is converted completely to steam, the temperature of the gas begins to rise again (E).

The heating curve will be revisited in Big Idea 5 (Chapter 5, "Thermodynamics").

Vapor Pressure

Vaporization, or **evaporation,** is a phase change from liquid to gas that occurs at the surface of a liquid. In a closed container, liquid begins to evaporate: Molecules at the surface are released into the gas phase. The rate of evaporation is greater than the rate of condensation until the temperature-dependent equilibrium vapor pressure is reached. Also referred to as simply the **vapor pressure,** this is the pressure of a gas in equilibrium above its liquid phase at a given temperature. At the equilibrium vapor pressure, the rate of evaporation and the rate of condensation are equal. The concept of equilibrium is the theme of Big Idea 6 (Chapter 6, "Chemical Equilibrium").

Vapor Pressure

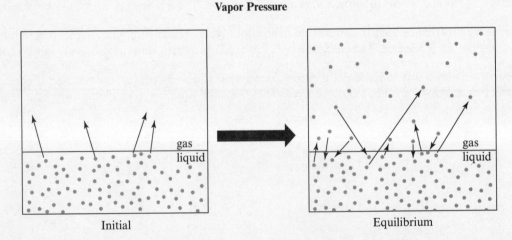

Vapor pressure depends on the strength of the intermolecular forces between the liquid molecules. The stronger the intermolecular forces, the more difficult it is for a liquid molecule to escape the attraction of its neighbors and transition to the vapor phase. For this reason, water, a hydrogen-bonding molecule, will have a lower vapor pressure at room temperature than ethanol, CH_3CH_2OH, a molecule of intermediate polarity, or diethyl ether, $CH_3CH_2OCH_2CH_3$, a polar molecule that is incapable of hydrogen bonding. Diethyl ether, which experiences the weakest intermolecular forces of the three substances, has the highest vapor pressure.

The Vapor Pressures of Three Substances as Functions of Temperature

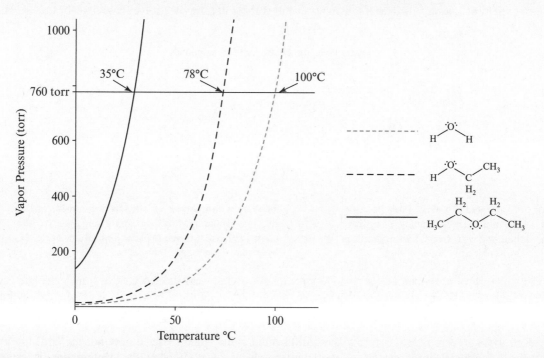

As temperature increases, the vapor pressure of a liquid increases. This is because at higher temperatures, a higher fraction of the molecules have sufficient energy to overcome the intermolecular forces at the surface of the liquid to enter the vapor phase. The **boiling point** is the temperature at which the vapor pressure of the liquid equals the external pressure, which is usually the atmospheric pressure. Notice from the curves above that diethyl ether, the least polar of the three molecules shown, has the highest vapor pressure at all temperatures. Its boiling point at 760 torr or 1 atm is the lowest at 35 °C. The boiling point of water at 760 torr is 100 °C.

Solutions

A **solution** is a homogeneous mixture of a major component and one or more minor components. The major component is called the **solvent** and the minor components are called **solutes.**

Solutions may be solids, liquids, or gases. An alloy such as bronze, which is composed of 88% copper and 12% tin, is an example of a solid solution. Vinegar is an example of a liquid solution. Vinegar is a solution of 5% acetic acid dissolved in water. The atmosphere at sea level is a gaseous solution of 78% nitrogen, 21% oxygen, and smaller amounts of carbon dioxide, neon, and other gases. Bodies of freshwater are solutions of dissolved oxygen and other gases.

Many AP Chemistry questions will deal with **aqueous solutions,** those in which solutes are dissolved in water.

Solubility and Intermolecular Forces

When an element or compound is capable of being dissolved in a particular solvent, it is said to be **soluble** in that solvent. Solubility depends on the strength of attractive interactions between solute and solvent particles. The degree of solubility varies with temperature from solute to solute in a particular solvent.

In general, molecules with similar intermolecular forces are **miscible** (capable of being mixed). This is the principle behind the phrase "like dissolves like." Ionic and polar solutes tend to be soluble in polar solvents. Oxalic acid, shown below, is soluble in water because it is capable of forming hydrogen bonds with water.

Nonpolar solutes tend to be soluble in nonpolar solvents. Fats, oils, and other nonpolar compounds, such as the major component of beeswax, are insoluble in water but soluble in nonpolar solvents such as hexane, C_6H_{12}, and benzene, C_6H_6.

Hydrophilic and Hydrophobic Compounds

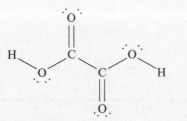

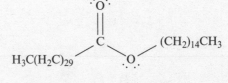

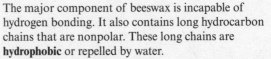

Oxalic acid is water-soluble because the molecules are capable of hydrogen bonding with water. This molecule is **hydrophilic** or "water-loving."

The major component of beeswax is incapable of hydrogen bonding. It also contains long hydrocarbon chains that are nonpolar. These long chains are **hydrophobic** or repelled by water.

Solutes in aqueous solutions can be classified as strong electrolytes, weak electrolytes, or nonelectrolytes. An **electrolyte** is a solute that when dissolved in water makes a conductive solution. Electricity is conducted by the motion of charged particles. If the solute does not break into ions, it is a nonelectrolyte.

Strong electrolytes are strong acids, strong bases, and soluble salts. When these compounds are added to water, they dissociate completely into ions. An additional intermolecular force, the **ion-dipole interaction,** is responsible for the solvation of the ions by water molecules. As the name suggests, ion-dipole interactions are coulombic attractions between cations and the electron-rich regions of polar molecules, and between anions and the electron-poor regions of polar molecules.

Sodium chloride is a soluble ionic compound. When a crystal of NaCl is added to water, the Na^+ and Cl^- ions dissociate. They are completely solvated by water. The ability to produce a simplified particulate sketch similar to the one shown below is a valuable skill for AP Chemistry students.

The Solvation of Sodium Chloride by Water

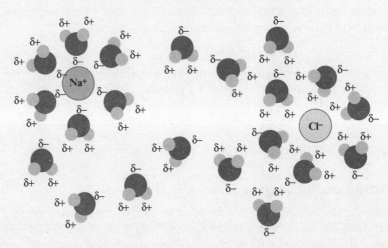

Molecular compounds that do not dissociate into ions in aqueous solutions are nonelectrolytes. Covalent molecules like sucrose, which break up into discrete neutral molecules in water but do not dissociate into ions, are **nonelectrolytes.**

Weak electrolytes are compounds that undergo incomplete dissociation into ions in aqueous solution. In other words, a fraction of the molecules ionize, but the rest do not. Weak electrolytes include weak acids and bases and slightly soluble salts.

Strong electrolytes are highly conductive in aqueous solution. They allow a current to flow through the solution. A complete circuit with a power source that passes through a strong electrolyte solution allows a light bulb to shine brightly. Weak electrolytes allow only some of the current to flow, so the light bulb shines dimly. Nonelectrolytes allow so little current to flow that no light can be detected from the bulb.

Electrolytes and Nonelectrolytes

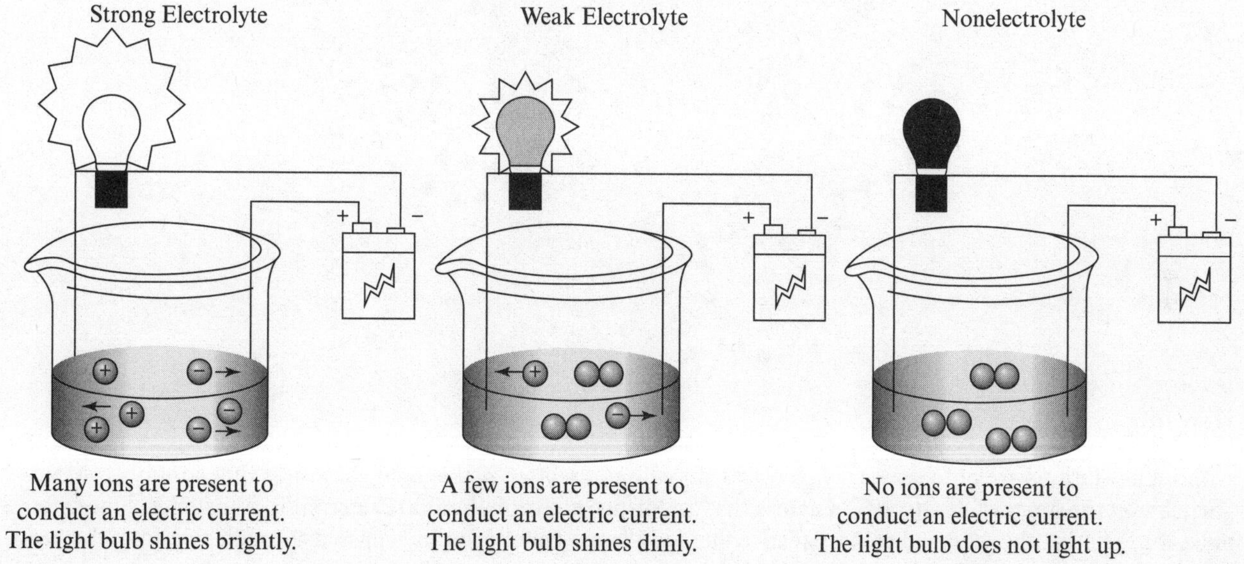

Strong Electrolyte	Weak Electrolyte	Nonelectrolyte
Many ions are present to conduct an electric current. The light bulb shines brightly.	A few ions are present to conduct an electric current. The light bulb shines dimly.	No ions are present to conduct an electric current. The light bulb does not light up.

PRACTICE:

A student would like to classify two unknown solids, A and B, as ionic or covalent. The student adds distilled water to a sample of each solid and discovers that A is soluble in water, but B is not. The student uses a conductivity meter to determine that the aqueous solution of A is conductive. Finally, the student finds that a sample of A is insoluble in hexane, C_6H_{14}, but that a sample of B is soluble. What types of bonding are most likely present in compounds A and B?

Since compound A forms a conductive solution when it dissolves in water and since it is insoluble in the nonpolar hydrocarbon solvent, it may either be a water-soluble ionic compound or an acid or base. Compound B's insolubility in water alone does not eliminate the possibility that it could be an ionic solid, since not all ionic compounds are water-soluble. Compound B is soluble in hexane, which is a nonpolar solvent. Since a nonpolar solvent is incapable of dissolving ionic compounds, compound B must be covalent rather than ionic.

Biochemical Implications of Solubility

The water solubility of many biologically important molecules can have profound effects on biological structures and processes. For instance, proteins, which are polymers of amino acids, may have some portions that are hydrophobic and other portions that are hydrophilic. Since cytosol, the fluid portion of a cell, is an aqueous solution, proteins will arrange so that the hydrophilic portions are in contact with the solution and the hydrophobic portions associate with one another.

Protein Folding in Aqueous Solution

Black = hydrophobic amino acids
White = hydrophilic amino acids

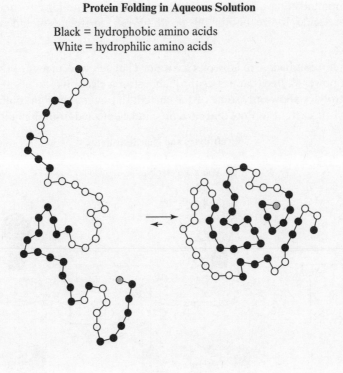

Colloids

Although solutions are not necessarily colorless, they do not scatter visible light. Mixtures that contain suspended particles on the order of 10^{-9} to 10^{-6} m across that are dispersed throughout are referred to as **colloids.** Smoky air, milk, fog, gelatin, and whipped cream are all colloids. When a beam of light is passed through a colloid, the beam is scattered in a way that is visually detectable.

The Scattering of a Beam of Light by a Colloid

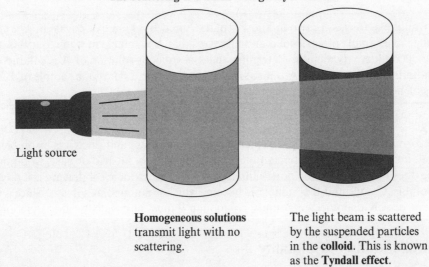

Light source

Homogeneous solutions transmit light with no scattering.

The light beam is scattered by the suspended particles in the **colloid**. This is known as the **Tyndall effect**.

Thermodynamics of Solution Formation

Formation of a solution may be exothermic or endothermic. The temperature of a solution increases during an exothermic dissolution ($\Delta H_{soln} < 0$), and the temperature of a solution decreases during an endothermic dissolution ($\Delta H_{soln} > 0$).

When a solution is formed, three processes contribute to the overall change in enthalpy:

1. Intermolecular forces or ionic bonds between solute particles are disrupted.
2. Intermolecular forces between solvent particles are disrupted.
3. Interactions between solute and solvent particles are formed.

Disruption of interactions (either ionic bonds or intermolecular forces) requires an input of energy. Formation of interactions releases energy. The overall enthalpy change, $\Delta H_{solution}$, for the dissolution process is the sum of the enthalpy changes for the three processes.

$$\Delta H_{solution} = \Delta H_1 + \Delta H_2 + \Delta H_3$$

The Enthalpy of Solution Formation

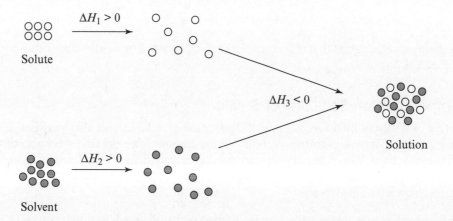

Usually, dilute solutions of ionic compounds are considered. For a dilute solution, the enthalpy change associated with interruption of solvent-solvent interactions, ΔH_2, can be ignored.

The enthalpy change associated with disrupting intermolecular forces between solute particles, in the case of an ionic solute, is the lattice energy, ΔH_L. Recall that this is the energy required to separate the ionic compound into separate gas-phase ions.

$$\Delta H_1 = \Delta H_L$$

The enthalpy change associated with formation of interactions between solute and solvent particles is the enthalpy of hydration, $\Delta H_{hydration}$.

$$\Delta H_3 = \Delta H_{hydration}$$

Substituting these values into the equation for the enthalpy of solution gives the following equation.

$$\Delta H_{solution} = \Delta H_L + \Delta H_{hydration}$$

The thermodynamic favorability of these processes will be discussed in Big Idea 5 (Chapter 5, "Thermodynamics").

PRACTICE:

The lattice energy of $CaCl_2$ is 2270 kJ·mol^{-1}. Given the following data for the enthalpies of hydration of gaseous ions, will the temperature of an aqueous solution increase or decrease as $CaCl_2$ is dissolved?

Ion	$\Delta H_{hydration}$ (kJ·mol^{-1})
Ca^{2+}	−1653
Cl^-	−338

The lattice energy, 2270 kJ·mol^{-1}, is the enthalpy change for the dissociation of one mole of $CaCl_2$ into its constituent ions.

$$CaCl_2(s) \rightarrow Ca^{2+}(g) + 2\ Cl^-(g)$$

The overall enthalpy of hydration for a mole of $CaCl_2$ is the sum of the $\Delta H_{hydration}$ values for each mole of ions. One mole of Ca^{2+} and two moles of Cl^- are hydrated for each mole of $CaCl_2$ dissolved.

$$\Delta H_{hydration} = -1653\ \text{kJ·mol}^{-1} + 2(-338\ \text{kJ·mol}^{-1}) = -2329\ \text{kJ·mol}^{-1}$$

The overall enthalpy change for the dissolution is

$$\Delta H_{solution} = \Delta H_L + \Delta H_{hydration}$$

$$\Delta H_{solution} = 2270\ \text{kJ·mol}^{-1} - 2329\ \text{kJ·mol}^{-1} = -59\ \text{kJ·mol}^{-1}$$

The negative enthalpy change means that this is an exothermic process. The temperature of an aqueous solution will increase as $CaCl_2$ is dissolved.

Effect of Temperature on Solubility of Solids

As the temperature of a solvent increases, the rate of dissolution of solid solutes also increases. For many solids, an increase in temperature also increases the solubility, or the amount of solute that is capable of being dissolved in a certain volume of solvent. This is because the increased average kinetic energy leads to an increased number and strength of collisions between solvent and solute particles. These collisions disrupt intermolecular and electrostatic attractions between solute particles.

This is a simplification, however. Some solids become less soluble as the temperature increases. This complication is due to the enthalpy change of the dissolution. Exothermic dissolution is favored at lower temperatures and endothermic dissolution is favored at higher temperatures. This concept will be reviewed further in the context of Big Idea 6 (Chapter 6, "Chemical Equilibrium") and Le Chatelier's principle.

Effects of Temperature and Pressure on Solubility of Gases

The number of moles of a gas that will dissolve in a liter of liquid solution is directly proportional to the partial pressure of the gas in the space above the solution. This is known as **Henry's law.** As gas pressure increases, more gas particles collide with the surface of the solvent and are incorporated into the solution.

The Solubility of Gases in Water as a Function of Pressure

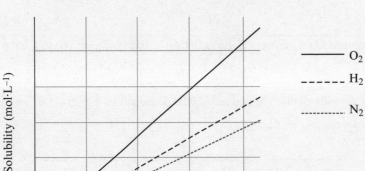

Temperature also has an effect on gas solubility. An increase in temperature leads to a decrease in the solubility of gases. As the kinetic energy of a solution increases, more collisions between solvent and solute particles cause the gaseous solute to be ejected into the space above the surface of the solvent. Dissolution of gases is exothermic. As we will review in Big Idea 6 (Chapter 6, "Chemical Equilibrium"), it is, therefore, favored at low temperatures and decreases as the temperature increases.

Solution Concentration

There are several ways of expressing the concentration of a solution, but in AP Chemistry, the only ones that are needed are mole fraction, X, and molarity, M. Mole fraction was reviewed earlier in the chapter in the context of Dalton's law of partial pressures (page 100). **Molarity** is the number of moles of solute dissolved in enough solvent to make exactly one liter of solution.

Any time a species is shown in brackets, molarity is implied. A 2.0 M solution of OH^- is indicated by $[OH^-] = 2.0\ M$.

Volumetric flasks, flasks that are calibrated to hold a precise volume at a particular temperature, are used to prepare solutions of known molarity. In order to make a known concentration of a solution, the solid solute is weighed on a balance and placed into a volumetric flask. Solvent is added to the mark on the neck of the flask.

Volumetric Flask

Precise volumes of liquid solutes or concentrated solutions are delivered using **pipettes.**

Pipettes

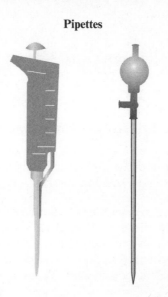

PRACTICE:

> A student weighs 101.7 g of magnesium chloride hexahydrate in a weigh boat on a balance and then pours the salt into a 100.0-mL volumetric flask. The student adds about 50 mL of distilled water, swirls the mixture until the solid dissolves completely, and then fills the flask with water to the 100-mL mark. What is the molarity of the resulting solution?

The molar mass of $MgCl_2 \cdot 6H_2O$ is 203.32 g·mol^{-1}. The number of moles is found by multiplying the mass of the salt by the molar mass.

$$101.7 \text{ g } MgCl_2 \cdot 6H_2O \times \frac{1 \text{ mol } MgCl_2 \cdot 6H_2O}{203.33 \text{ g } MgCl_2 \cdot 6H_2O} \times \frac{1 \text{ mol } MgCl_2}{1 \text{ mol } MgCl_2 \cdot 6H_2O} = 0.5002 \text{ mol } MgCl_2$$

The molarity is the number of moles divided by the volume.

$$\frac{0.5002 \text{ mol } MgCl_2}{100.0 \text{ mL}} \times \frac{1000 \text{ mL}}{1 \text{ L}} = 5.002 \text{ } M$$

Sometimes a solution is made by dilution of a more concentrated solution. Dilution is a decrease in concentration of a solute by addition of solvent. The dilution equation, which can be used to calculate the final concentration of a solution after dilution, is a consequence of the fact that the number of moles of solute does not change.

$$M_1 \times V_1 = M_2 \times V_2$$

PRACTICE:

> A 5.00–mL volumetric pipette is used to deliver 12.0 M HCl to a 25.0–mL volumetric flask. Distilled water is added to the 25.0-mL mark. What is the resulting concentration of the dilute solution?

The initial molarity and volume of HCl, M_1 and V_1, are 12.0 M and 5.00 mL, respectively. The final volume of dilute HCl solution is 25.0 mL. The final molarity can be determined by rearranging the dilution equation.

$$M_2 = \frac{M_1 \times V_1}{V_2}$$

$$M_2 = \frac{(12.0 \text{ } M) \times (5.00 \text{ mL})}{25.0 \text{ mL}} = 2.40 \text{ } M$$

Measuring Concentration Using Spectrophotometry

Some solutions have color because they absorb certain wavelengths of visible light. (The color of a solution is complementary to the wavelength that is absorbed.) Information about the concentration of a colored solute can be elucidated from the amount of visible light a solution absorbs.

A **spectrophotometer** is an instrument used to determine the absorbance of a solution. It contains a source of light that can be separated into discrete wavelengths. A wavelength is selected that corresponds to an electronic energy level transition in a molecule under investigation. (The solution to be measured is placed in a **cuvette,** a small vial of known width. The cuvette with the sample is inserted into the spectrometer and the amount of light that is transmitted through the sample is detected and used to determine the amount of light that is absorbed.

Components of a Spectrophotometer

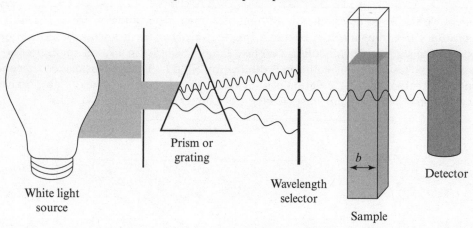

When the absorbed wavelength is passed through a solution, the amount of light that is absorbed by the sample is directly proportional to the concentration of the sample. This relationship, which is known as **Beer's law,** is provided on the *AP Chemistry Equations and Constants* sheet (pages 365–366) of the exam.

$$A = abc$$

In this equation, A is the **absorbance,** a is the **molar absorptivity,** b is the **path length** or the width of the cuvette, and c is the concentration.

PRACTICE:

> The molar absorptivity, a, of $[Fe(C_{12}H_8N_2)_3]^{2+}$ at its maximum absorption wavelength is 1.11×10^4 L·mol^{-1}·cm^{-1}. What is the molarity of a sample that has an absorbance, A, of 5.55×10^2 in a 1.0 cm cuvette?

The concentration can be determined by rearranging the Beer's law equation.

$$c = \frac{A}{ab}$$

$$c = \frac{5.55 \times 10^2}{(1.11 \times 10^4 \text{L} \cdot \text{mol}^{-1} \cdot \cancel{\text{cm}^{-1}}) \times (1.0 \ \cancel{\text{cm}})} = 0.050 \ M$$

To determine the concentration of an unknown sample, a calibration curve using absorptions of a series of solutions of known concentration is needed. The absorptions are plotted versus their concentration. The slope of the resulting line gives the molar absorptivity for the solute. Once the absorptivity is known, the concentration of the unknown can be determined.

PRACTICE:

A student would like to determine the amount of copper in a sample of brass. The student creates a calibration curve, shown below, by measuring the absorbances of known concentrations of $Cu(NO_3)_2$. The student then dissolves a 0.212-g sample of brass in a small amount of concentrated nitric acid. The resulting Cu^{2+} solution is diluted to 25.0 mL. The student makes a second dilution in which 2.00 mL of the Cu^{2+} solution is diluted to 500. mL. She measures an absorbance of 4.375 using a 1.0-cm cuvette. What is the percentage of copper in the original sample?

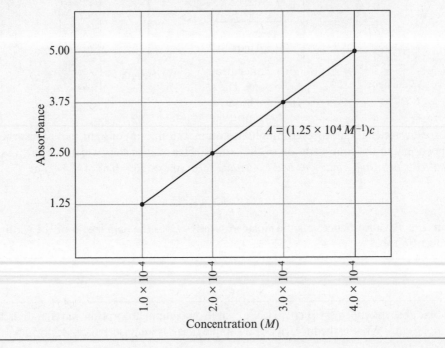

In order to find the concentration of the 500.-mL Cu^{2+} solution, the student must determine the slope of the concentration versus absorbance graph. The slope, which is equal to the product ab, may be determined by choosing any two points on the graph and finding the difference.

$$ab = \frac{\Delta A}{\Delta c} = \frac{5.00 - 1.25}{4.0 \times 10^{-4}\,M - 1.0 \times 10^{-4}\,M} = 1.25 \times 10^4\,M^{-1}$$

Since ab has been determined, the concentration of Cu^{2+} in the final solution may be found using the measured absorbance.

$$c = \frac{A}{ab} = \frac{4.375}{1.25 \times 10^4\,M^{-1}} = 3.50 \times 10^{-4}\,M$$

The measured concentration, M_2, was the result of diluting 2.00 mL (V_1) of the original 25.0-mL solution to a volume of 500. mL (V_2). The concentration of the 25.0-mL solution can be found using the dilution equation.

$$M_1 = \frac{M_2 \times V_2}{V_1} = \frac{3.50 \times 10^{-4}\,M \times 500.\,\cancel{mL}}{2.00\,\cancel{mL}} = 0.0875\,M$$

The concentration of the 25.0-mL solution is next used to determine the number of moles of copper present in the original sample.

$$0.0250\,\cancel{L} \times \frac{0.0875\,mol}{1\,\cancel{L}} = 0.00219\,mol\ Cu$$

The number of moles of copper is converted to grams, and this mass is used in the determination of the mass percent of the original sample.

$$0.00219 \ \text{mol Cu} \times \frac{63.55 \ \text{g Cu}}{1 \ \text{mol Cu}} = 0.139 \ \text{g Cu}$$

$$\text{Percent copper} = \frac{0.139 \ \text{g Cu}}{0.212 \ \text{g sample}} \times 100\% = 65.6\% \ \text{Cu}$$

Measuring Concentration Using Titration

Titration is a technique by which an unknown concentration of an **analyte** is determined by reaction with an accurately known amount of a standard, or **titrant.** The setup usually involves a known volume of the analyte in an Erlenmeyer flask. The titrant is added using a buret, a specialized piece of glassware that allows measured volumes of titrant to be added. The titrant is added until the endpoint of the titration is reached. The **endpoint** is some indication, usually a color change or sharp pH change, that the reaction is complete.

Titration

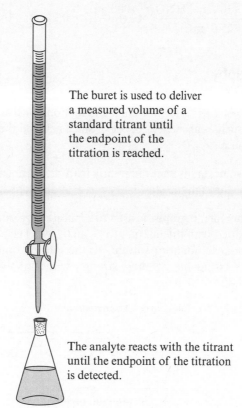

The buret is used to deliver a measured volume of a standard titrant until the endpoint of the titration is reached.

The analyte reacts with the titrant until the endpoint of the titration is detected.

In many cases, an indicator is added to the analyte. An **indicator** is a substance that changes color at or near the equivalence point of the reaction. The **equivalence point** is the point in which stoichiometric amounts of titrant and analyte have reacted. A balanced chemical equation is necessary to determine the stoichiometric ratio of titrant to analyte. This concept will be reviewed in Big Idea 3 (Chapter 3, "Chemical Reactions").

Phenolphthalein is a common indicator that is used to detect the endpoints of titrations of strong acids with strong bases. It changes from colorless in acidic solutions to pink in basic solutions.

PRACTICE:

A 25.0-mL sample of HNO_3 is titrated with a standardized solution of 0.460 M NaOH. The endpoint of the titration is indicated by a phenolphthalein color change when 13.1 mL of NaOH solution have been added. What is the molarity of the HNO_3 solution? The balanced equation for the reaction of NaOH with HNO_3 is shown.

$$HNO_3(aq) + NaOH(aq) \rightarrow NaNO_3(aq) + H_2O(l)$$

The balanced chemical equation shows that for each mole of HNO_3, one mole of NaOH reacts.

$$13.1 \ \text{mL NaOH} \times \frac{1 \ \text{L NaOH}}{1000 \ \text{mL NaOH}} \times \frac{0.460 \ \text{mol NaOH}}{1 \ \text{L NaOH}} \times \frac{1 \ \text{mol HNO}_3}{1 \ \text{mol NaOH}} = 6.03 \times 10^{-3} \ \text{mol HNO}_3$$

The concentration of HNO_3 is determined using the number of moles and the original volume.

$$\frac{6.03 \times 10^{-3} \ \text{mol HNO}_3}{25.0 \ \text{mL}} \times \frac{1000 \ \text{mL}}{1 \ \text{L}} = 0.241 \ M \ HNO_3$$

Separation by Chromatography

Chromatography refers to a class of laboratory techniques in which the components of a solution are separated based on differences in the strengths of their intermolecular interactions with a stationary phase and a mobile phase. A **stationary phase** is a solid such as absorbent paper or silica gel, and the **mobile phase** is a liquid or gas that is passed over the stationary phase.

Because different components of a solution interact differently with the stationary and mobile phases, the components travel with the mobile phase through the stationary phase at different speeds and can be separated.

Thin-layer chromatography or **paper chromatography** is used to separate very small amounts of a mixture. The bottom of a thin strip of paper is dotted with the mixture to be analyzed. The paper is the polar **stationary phase.** It is sealed in a jar and dipped in a small amount of solvent. As the solvent, or **mobile phase,** begins to creep up the paper, some components of the mixture interact more strongly with the solvent than with the paper. These components move up the paper with the solvent.

Thin-Layer Chromatography

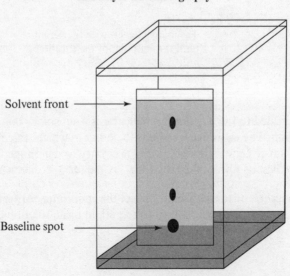

Solvent front

Baseline spot

Different components of a mixture will have different **retention factors** (R_f) in a particular solvent system. The R_f for a compound is calculated by dividing the distance travelled by that compound by the distance travelled by the solvent front.

The Calculation of R_f in Thin-Layer Chromatography

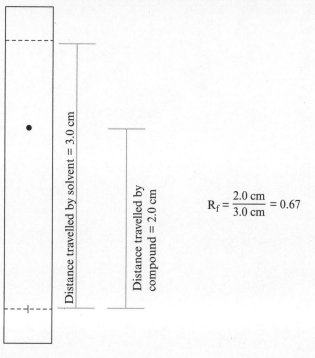

$$R_f = \frac{2.0 \text{ cm}}{3.0 \text{ cm}} = 0.67$$

PRACTICE:

> A mixture contains a polar component and a nonpolar component. Paper chromatography is performed on the mixture in which a relatively nonpolar solvent is used. The R_f for component A is 0.80, and the R_f for component B is 0.20. Identify components A and B as polar or nonpolar.

Since the R_f of component A indicates that it travelled further up the paper, it interacts more strongly with the nonpolar solvent than with the paper. Therefore, component A is the nonpolar component, and compound B is the polar component.

Separation by Evaporation and Distillation

A nonvolatile solute can be recovered from a solution by a simple **evaporation**, in which the volatile solvent is allowed to evaporate or is gently boiled away. Sodium chloride can be recovered from a saltwater solution in this way.

If the solvent needs to be recovered, however, or if a solution of two volatile components needs to be separated, distillation is a better choice. **Distillation** is a separation method that is based on differences in vapor pressures and boiling points among the components of the solution.

The mixture is placed in a round-bottom flask equipped with a condenser and a receiving vessel. The mixture in the round-bottom flask is heated to the boiling point of the more volatile component. This volatile component remains in the vapor phase until it is cooled in the condenser. The vapor then forms liquid droplets on the inner surface of the cooled condenser. The liquid, or **distillate**, drips into the receiving vessel, where it is collected.

Distillation

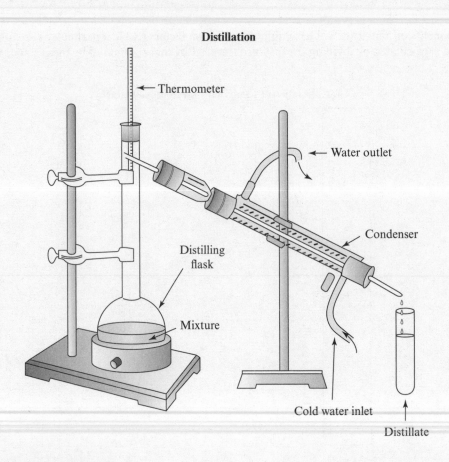

Review Questions

Multiple Choice

1. Which of the following polyatomic species has the same molecular geometry as a sulfate anion?

    A. Carbonate

    B. Ammonium

    C. Sulfur trioxide

    D. Xenon tetrafluoride

2. Which of the following is the most important contributing structure to the thiocyanate resonance hybrid? The Pauling electronegativities of carbon, nitrogen, and sulfur are about 2.5, 3.0, and 2.6, respectively.

    A. $\overset{..}{\underset{..}{S}} = C = \overset{\ominus}{\underset{..}{N}} ..$

    B. $: \overset{\oplus}{S} \equiv C - \overset{..}{\underset{..}{N}} \overset{2\ominus}{} :$

    C. $: \overset{\ominus}{\underset{..}{S}} - C \equiv N :$

    D. $\overset{..}{\underset{..}{S}} = \overset{\oplus}{C} - \overset{..}{\underset{..}{N}} \overset{2\ominus}{} :$

3. Identify the species that contains two π bonds.

    A. H_2ClO

    B. I_3^-

    C. CN^-

    D. NO_3^{2-}

4. A sample of gas at constant volume is heated from 230 K to 690 K. Which of the following best describes the effect on the gas?

    A.   The final pressure is triple the initial pressure, and the average kinetic energy of the molecules is tripled.

    B.   The final pressure is triple the initial pressure, and the average kinetic energy of the molecules is constant.

    C.   The final pressure is the cube root of the initial pressure, and the average kinetic energy of the molecules is tripled.

    D.   The final pressure is the cube root of the initial pressure, and the average kinetic energy of the molecules is constant.

5. The Maxwell distribution for two gases at the same temperature is shown below. Which of the following is true?

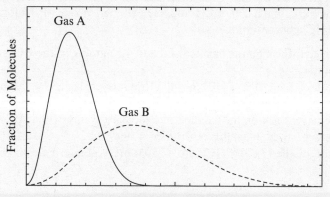

    A.   Gas A has a higher average kinetic energy than gas B.

    B.   Gas B has a higher average kinetic energy than gas A.

    C.   Gas A has a higher molar mass than gas B.

    D.   Gas B has a higher molar mass than gas A.

6. Which of the following correctly ranks four gases in order of increasingly ideal behavior at constant temperature and pressure?

    A. $Ne < N_2 < CO < NH_3$

    B. $Ne < CO < N_2 < NH_3$

    C. $NH_3 < N_2 < CO < Ne$

    D. $NH_3 < CO < N_2 < Ne$

7. The following figure represents a submicroscopic view of a mixture of gases. If the total pressure is 1 atm, what is the partial pressure of the gas represented by the white circles?

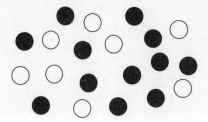

  A.   2.5 atm
  B.   0.40 atm
  C.   1.5 atm
  D.   0.67 atm

8. An analytical chemist needs to make a 0.5000 M HCl solution. The chemist has a 12.00 M solution available in addition to distilled water, a balance, an Erlenmeyer flask, a variety of graduated pipettes, a 250.0-mL volumetric flask, and a 250.-mL graduated cylinder. Which of the following procedures would result in the correct HCl concentration?

  A.   Place the volumetric flask on the balance and add 4.56 grams of the HCl solution. Dilute to the mark with distilled water.
  B.   Pipette 10.42 mL of the 12.00 M HCl into the Erlenmeyer flask. Use the graduated cylinder to add 239.6 mL of distilled water.
  C.   Place the Erlenmeyer flask on the balance and add 4.56 grams of the HCl solution. Use the graduated cylinder to add 245.4 mL of distilled water.
  D.   Pipette 10.42 mL of the 12.00 M HCl into a 250.0-mL volumetric flask. Dilute to the mark with distilled water.

9. A food scientist would like to test the claim by a candy manufacturer that only one dye is used in the production of a certain variety of green candy. Which separation technique would be the most appropriate method for determining whether more than one pigment is present in a one piece green candy?

  A.   gravimetric analysis
  B.   Paper chromatography
  C.   Evaporation
  D.   Distillation

10. The ionic radii for four different hypothetical ions are tabulated below. Based on this information, which choice correctly predicts the order of increasing melting point for the ionic compounds?

Ion	M^+	N^+	X^-	Y^-
Radius (pm)	50	70	120	170

  A.   NX < NY < MX < MY
  B.   MY < MX < NY < NX
  C.   NY < MY < NX < MX
  D.   MX < NX < MY < NY

11. Which of the following processes is endothermic? (The system under investigation is shown in italics.)

  A.   *Iodine gas* undergoes deposition on the outside surface of an ice-filled test tube.
  B.   When *sodium hydroxide* is dissolved in water, the temperature of the water rises.
  C.   Solid CO_2, also known as dry ice, sublimes at room temperature.
  D.   *Melted butter* solidifies in a refrigerator.

12. Match the curves relating vapor pressure to temperature for the following compounds.

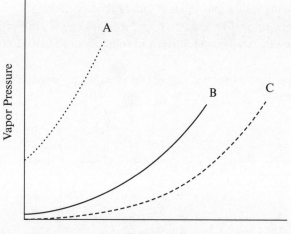

A. A = SiH$_4$, B = H$_2$S, C = NH$_3$
B. A = NH$_3$, B = H$_2$S, C = SiH$_4$
C. A = SiH$_4$, B = NH$_3$, C = H$_2$S
D. A = H$_2$S, B = NH$_3$, C = SiH$_4$

Use the following particulate diagrams to answer questions 13–14.

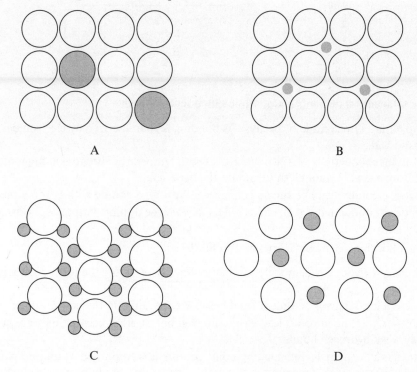

13. A jeweler uses an alloy of silver and zinc to solder a silver bracelet closed. The alloy is low-melting, and its density lies between that of silver and zinc. The solid form of this alloy is best represented by which solid?

A. A
B. B
C. C
D. D

14. Which statement is most likely to describe the solids represented by the particulate diagrams?

  A. Solids A and D are malleable, and solids B and C are brittle.
  B. Solids A and B are malleable, and solids C and D are low-melting.
  C. Solids A and D are electrically conductive, and solids B and C are electrical insulators.
  D. Solids A and B are electrically conductive, and solids C and D are electrical insulators.

15. Which of the following polymer structures would be expected to have the highest density?

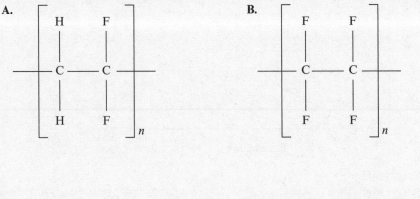

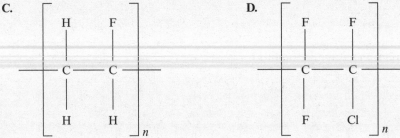

16. Which of the following statements about semiconductors is correct?

  A. Pure copper is a semiconductor because its bonding is characterized by electron delocalization and a small band gap.
  B. The electrical conductivity of silicon increases with temperature because at higher temperatures its electrons are energetic enough to surmount the band gap.
  C. The electrical conductivity of silicon is improved by n-type doping with boron atoms.
  D. The electrical conductivity of silicon is reduced by n-type doping with phosphorus atoms.

17. Which of the following statements is true of graphite?

  A. Graphite is a network covalent material that is conductive in its solid form due to delocalized π electrons.
  B. Graphite is a hard network covalent solid because every atom in the network is sp^3 hybridized.
  C. The layers of graphite in pencil lead easily slip past one another because they are held together by relatively weak hydrogen bonds.
  D. Graphite has an extremely high melting point because it is composed of ionized particles that are arranged in a manner that maximizes coulombic attractions and minimizes coulombic repulsions.

18. Bonds in molecules are promoted to higher vibrational states due to the absorption of photons in which region of the electromagnetic spectrum?

   A. X-ray
   B. Ultraviolet
   C. Visible
   D. Infrared

19. Consider the Lewis structures of H_3CCN and H_3CNH_2. Which statement best describes the bonding in these two molecules?

   A. The C-N bond in H_3CNH_2 allows free rotation. It is shorter and stronger than the C-N bond in H_3CCN.
   B. The C-N bond in H_3CNH_2 hinders free rotation. It is longer and weaker than the C-N bond in H_3CCN.
   C. The C-N bond in H_3CNH_2 allows free rotation. It is longer and weaker than the C-N bond in H_3CCN.
   D. The C-N bond in H_3CNH_2 hinders free rotation. It is shorter and stronger than the C-N bond in H_3CCN.

20. Two 20-mL containers of a carbonated beverage are opened to the atmosphere. One container is placed in a 40 °C refrigerator and the other is placed in a warm window. After 8 hours, the refrigerated liquid still retains some carbonation. The container in the warm window has very little detectable carbonation. Which of the following is the best explanation for these observations?

   A. The solubility of dissolved gases increases with increased partial pressure of water vapor above the liquid.
   B. The solubility of dissolved gases increases with increased pressure of the gas above the liquid.
   C. The solubility of dissolved gases decreases with increasing concentration of nongaseous solutes because the solutes change the nature of the intermolecular forces between the solvent and the gas.
   D. The solubility of dissolved gases decreases with increasing temperature because the increased strength and frequency of molecular collisions force the gas molecules out of the solution.

Long Free Response

1. A sample of helium, initially at 25 °C and 760. torr, initially occupies a volume of 2.50 L.

   a. How many moles of helium are present?
   b. If the helium sample is compressed to 1.50 L and the temperature is held constant, what is the change in pressure in atm?
   c. If the volume and temperature remain constant at 1.50 L and 25 °C, what is the resulting partial pressure of xenon if 0.050 mole of xenon gas is added to the container?
   d. Is the final pressure of the real gas mixture expected to be closer to the value predicted by the ideal gas law at very high or very low temperatures? Explain your answer.
   e. A 10.0-mL portion of distilled water is introduced into the container and the container is allowed to expand until the total pressure is 0.500 atm. The vapor pressure of water is 23.8 torr at 25 °C. What is the mole fraction of the water vapor in the gas mixture?
   f. The container is punctured with a tiny pinhole. Which of the three gases (helium, xenon, or water) is expected to escape the fastest and why?

Short Free Response

2. Hydrochloric acid is a strong acid. It reacts with sodium hydroxide to form sodium chloride and water. A researcher is preparing a hydrochloric acid solution and accidentally spills too much water into the solution. The researcher would like to determine the new concentration. A standardized solution of 0.250 *M* sodium hydroxide is available.

    a.   Write the net ionic equation for the neutralization reaction between sodium hydroxide and hydrochloric acid. See Big Idea 3 (Chapter 3, "Chemical Reactions") for more about net ionic equations and neutralization reactions.

    b.   The researcher finds that 26.1 mL of the sodium hydroxide solution are required to titrate 10.0 mL of the hydrochloric acid. What is the molarity of the hydrochloric acid solution?

    c.   The final neutralized solution is found to conduct electrical current. Draw and label a particle diagram of the final solution that illustrates why this is the case, and discuss why this diagram illustrates a conductive solution.

3. The compounds shown below, methyl cinnamate and cinnamic acid, are solids at room temperature. Notice that lone pairs of electrons are not shown in the structures.

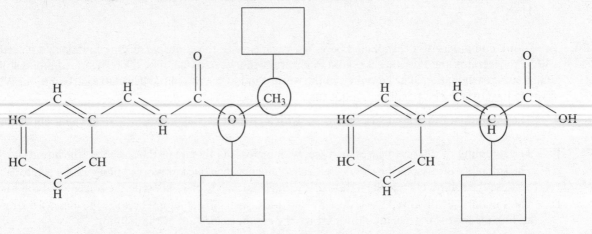

Methyl cinnamate   Cinnamic acid

    a.   In the boxes, predict the bond angles and hybridization at the circled C and O atoms.

    b.   One of the compounds is insoluble in water. The other is slightly soluble. Explain which compound is insoluble and which is soluble based on the principles of intermolecular interactions.

    c.   The more volatile compound contributes to the fragrance of strawberries. Which compound has the higher vapor pressure and why?

    d.   How might IR spectroscopy and mass spectrometry be used to differentiate between the two compounds?

4. A compound is composed of one atom of chlorine, one atom of oxygen, and one atom of hydrogen.

    a.   In the box on the left, draw a complete Lewis structure for the compound in which chlorine is central. In the box on the right, draw a complete Lewis structure for the compound in which oxygen is central.

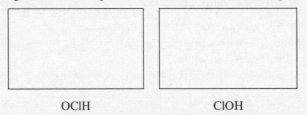

               OClH   ClOH

    b.   Which of these two compounds is the more likely structure? Use the two Lewis structures to justify your response.

    c.   What are the molecular geometry and the bond angle of the stable structure?

Answers and Explanations

Multiple Choice

1. B. (EK 2.C.4) Sulfate, SO_4^{2-}, has tetrahedral molecular geometry. Ammonium, NH_4^+, is the only other species in the list that is tetrahedral. Carbonate, CO_3^{2-}, and sulfur trioxide, SO_3, are trigonal planar; xenon tetrafluoride, XeF_4, is square planar.

2. A. (EK 2.C.4) Choices B and D can be eliminated based on the large separation of charge within their structures. They make very little contribution to the hybrid structure. Choices A and C contribute to the hybrid, but choice A is predicted to make a greater contribution since the negative charge is located on the more electronegative element.

3. C. (EK 2.C.4) The Lewis structures of the species show that only the cyanide ion (choice C) has a triple bond, which is composed of a σ bond and two π bonds.

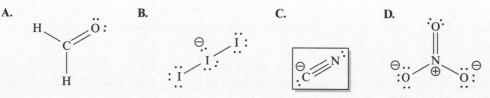

4. A. (EK 5.A.1, 2.A.2) Average kinetic energy has tripled since the temperature has tripled. The equation relating temperature to pressure is

$$\frac{P_1}{T_1} = \frac{P_2}{T_2}$$

$$P_2 = \frac{P_1 T_2}{T_1}$$

Since $T_2 = 3 \times T_1$, the final pressure becomes

$$P_2 = \frac{3\cancel{T_1}P_1}{\cancel{T_1}}$$

$$P_2 = 3P_1$$

5. C. (EK 2.A.2) Because the two gases have the same temperature, their average kinetic energies are the same. Since a larger number of molecules has a higher velocity for gas B, it has a lower molar mass than gas A.

6. D. (EK 2.A.2, 2.B.1, 2.B.2) Because NH_3 participates in hydrogen bonding, it deviates the most from ideal behavior. CO is polar, so its deviation is greater than N_2 and Ne, which are both nonpolar and experience only London dispersion forces. N_2 is a larger molecule than Ne and it has more electrons, so it is more polarizable. It also occupies a slightly greater volume, so it deviates more from ideal behavior than Ne. The correct order is, therefore, $NH_3 < CO < N_2 < Ne$.

7. B. (EK 2.A.2) According to Dalton's law of partial pressures, the partial pressure is the mole fraction of the gas multiplied by the total pressure. There are a total of 20 circles, 8 of which are white. The mole fraction is simply $\frac{8}{20}$ or $\frac{2}{5}$.

$$P_{white} = P_{total} \times X_{white}$$

$$P_{white} = \frac{2}{5} \times 1 \text{ atm} = 0.40 \text{ atm}$$

8. D. (EK 2.A.3) The correct concentration can be achieved with pipettes for measuring 10.42 mL of the 12.00 M HCl and a volumetric flask for the final dilution. The balance, graduated cylinder, and Erlenmeyer flask are inappropriate for achieving an accurate or precise dilution in this situation.

9. B. (EK 2.A.3) Separation of the dyes in green candy is most easily achieved via paper chromatography. The colored dyes in the mixture can be separated on the basis of the relative strengths of their interactions with the stationary and mobile phases.

10. C. (EK 2.C.2) Estimation of the increasing melting point should follow a decrease in the distance between the two nuclei because the coulombic attraction decreases with increased internuclear distance. The largest ions, N^+ and Y^-, should form a compound with the lowest melting point, and the smallest ions, M^+ and X^-, should form a compound with the highest melting point. The distance between the nuclei in NX is less than that in MY, so MY should have a lower melting point than NX. The correct order, therefore, is NY < MY < NX < MX.

11. C. (EK 2.A.1, 2.A.3) CO_2 gains energy in transitioning from the solid to the gas phase. This input of energy disrupts the intermolecular forces between the CO_2 molecules. The change in enthalpy is positive, and the process is endothermic.

12. A. (EK 2.B.3) SiH_4 (curve A) is nonpolar and experiences only London dispersion forces. It has the highest vapor pressure. H_2S (curve B) is polar, so its vapor pressure is between that of SiH_4 and NH_3. NH_3 (curve C) has the lowest vapor pressure since it participates in hydrogen bonding, the strongest intermolecular force.

13. A. (EK 2.D.2) Since both silver and zinc are metals and since neither is a small atom such as hydrogen, boron, carbon, or nitrogen, the alloy is substitutional rather than interstitial. Solid A best represents the solid form of this alloy.

14. D. (EK 2.C.2, 2.C.4, 2.D.2) Solids A and B represent alloys, which are primarily metallic and conductive. Solid C represents an insulating molecular solid, and solid D represents an insulating ionic solid. Ionic compounds are only conductive in the molten state or in aqueous solutions.

15. D. (EK 2.D.4) The polymer with the highest density is the one that has the heaviest elements incorporated into the structure. In this case, the polymer with F and Cl substitution, shown in choice D, is the densest.

16. B. (EK 2.D.3) As the temperature of a semiconductor increases, its conductivity increases. This is because the energy of the electrons in the valence band becomes sufficient to enter the conduction band.

17. A. (EK 2.D.3) The extended π system of graphite is responsible for its electrical conductivity. Graphite is a network covalent solid composed of sp^2 hybridized carbon atoms.

18. D. (EK 1.D.3) Infrared spectroscopy is used to determine the types of functional groups present in a molecule by measuring the absorption of electromagnetic radiation due to the vibrations of covalent bonds.

19. C. (EK 2.C.4) The C-N bond in H_3CNH_2 allows free rotation because it is a single bond. The C-N bond in H_3CCN is a triple bond. Single bonds tend to be longer and weaker than triple bonds.

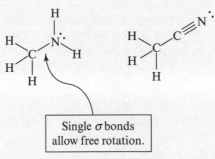

Single σ bonds allow free rotation.

20. D. (EK 2.A.1) The solubility of dissolved gases decreases with increasing temperature. As the average kinetic energy in a solution of dissolved gas increases, the gas particles escape the solution and enter the vapor phase.

Long Free Response

1. a. (EK 2.A.2) The number of moles of helium present can be determined using the ideal gas law. Recognizing that 760. torr is equal to 1.00 atm simplifies the task and eliminates the need to convert units.

$$PV = nRT$$

$$n = \frac{PV}{RT} = \frac{1.00 \text{ atm} \times 2.50 \text{ L}}{(0.08206 \text{ L} \cdot \text{atm} \cdot \text{mol}^{-1} \text{K}^{-1}) \times (25 + 273 \text{ K})} = 0.102 \text{ mol He}$$

b. (EK 2.A.2) The new pressure can be determined using Boyle's law.

$$P_1 V_1 = P_2 V_2$$

$$P_2 = \frac{P_1 V_1}{V_2} = \frac{1.00 \text{ atm} \times 2.50 \text{ L}}{1.50 \text{ L}} = 1.67 \text{ atm}$$

The change in pressure is the difference between the final pressure, P_f, and initial pressure, P_i.

$$\Delta P = P_f - P_i = 1.67 \text{ atm} - 1.00 \text{ atm} = 0.67 \text{ atm}$$

c. (EK 2.A.2) The total number of moles of gas present after the addition of xenon is

$$n_{total} = 0.102 \text{ mole He} + 0.050 \text{ mole Xe} = 0.152 \text{ mole}$$

The new pressure is

$$P = \frac{nRT}{V} = \frac{0.152 \text{ mol} \times (0.08206 \text{ L} \cdot \text{atm} \cdot \text{mol}^{-1} \cdot \text{K}^{-1}) \times (25 + 273 \text{ K})}{1.50 \text{ L}} = 2.48 \text{ atm}$$

The partial pressure of xenon, P_{Xe}, is equal to the mole fraction of xenon, X_{Xe}, multiplied by the total pressure.

$$P_{Xe} = X_{Xe} \times P_{total} = \left(\frac{n_{Xe}}{n_{total}} \right) \times P_{total}$$

$$P_{Xe} = \left(\frac{0.050 \text{ mol}}{0.152 \text{ mol}} \right) \times 2.48 \text{ atm} = 0.82 \text{ atm}$$

d. (EK 2.A.2) The final pressure of the gas mixture is expected to be closer to the value determined by the ideal gas law at very high temperatures. At high temperatures, the gas particles are moving faster and their collisions are energetic enough to overcome the intermolecular attractions that would otherwise cause their behavior to deviate from that predicted by the ideal gas law.

e. (EK 2.A.2) The vapor pressure of the water is equal to the partial pressure of water vapor in the gas mixture. The pressure must be converted to atmospheres first.

$$23.8 \text{ torr} \times \left(\frac{1 \text{ atm}}{760 \text{ torr}} \right) = 0.0313 \text{ atm}$$

Since the vapor pressure is equal to the partial pressure of water vapor, we can use it to determine the mole fraction of the water vapor.

$$P_{H_2O} = X_{H_2O} \times P_{total}$$

$$X_{H_2O} = \frac{P_{H_2O}}{P_{total}} = \frac{0.0313 \text{ atm}}{0.500 \text{ atm}} = 0.0626$$

f. (EK 2.A.2) Of the three gases in the container, helium escapes the fastest. The rate of effusion of a molecule is inversely proportional to the square root of its molar mass.

$$\text{rate} \propto \sqrt{\frac{T}{M}}$$

Since the molar mass of helium is the smallest, 4.00 g·mol^{-1} (compared to 18.01 g·mol^{-1} for H$_2$O and 131.29 g·mol^{-1} for Xe), its rate of diffusion is the highest.

Short Free Response

2. a. (EK 1.E.2) The neutralization of HCl with NaOH produces water and NaCl.

Overall equation: $HCl(aq) + NaOH(aq) \rightarrow H_2O(l) + NaCl(aq)$

Cancellation of spectator ions in the total ionic equation gives the net ionic equation. See Big Idea 3 (Chapter 3, "Chemical Reactions").

Total ionic equation: $H^+ + \cancel{Cl^-} + \cancel{Na^+} + OH^- \rightarrow H_2O + \cancel{Na^+} + \cancel{Cl^-}$

Net ionic equation: $H^+ + OH^- \rightarrow H_2O$

b. (EK 1.E.2, 2.A.3, 3.A.2) The balanced equation shows that for every mole of NaOH added, one mole of HCl reacts. At the endpoint of the titration, the number of moles of NaOH is equal to the number of moles of HCl.

$$\text{moles of HCl} = 26.1 \ \cancel{\text{mL NaOH}} \times \frac{1 \ \cancel{\text{L NaOH}}}{1000 \ \cancel{\text{mL NaOH}}} \times \frac{0.250 \ \cancel{\text{mol NaOH}}}{1 \ \cancel{\text{L NaOH}}} \times \frac{1 \ \text{mol HCl}}{1 \ \cancel{\text{mol NaOH}}}$$

$$= 0.00653 \ \text{mol HCl}$$

The concentration is determined by dividing the number of moles by the volume.

$$\frac{0.00653 \ \text{mol HCl}}{10.0 \ \cancel{\text{mL HCl}}} \times \frac{1000 \ \cancel{\text{mL HCl}}}{1 \ \text{L HCl}} = 0.653 \ M \ \text{HCl}$$

c. (EK 2.A.3) The final solution conducts an electrical current because it contains Na$^+$ cations and Cl$^-$ anions dissociated in water. An ionic solution is conductive because the charges are free to move through the solution. A student's sketch should look like the particle diagram shown below. The lone pairs on the oxygen atoms of H$_2$O are oriented toward the Na$^+$ cations, and the hydrogen atoms are oriented toward the Cl$^-$ anions.

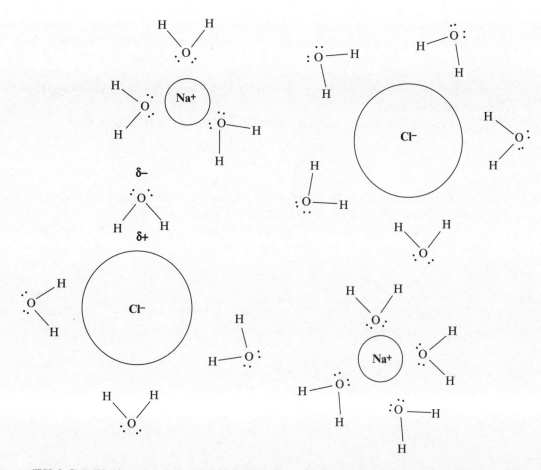

3. a. (EK 2.C.4) The bond angles and hybridizations are shown below. Remember that lone pairs must be taken into account when determining the number of regions of electron density. The circled oxygen atom has two lone pairs, so it is sp^3 hybridized.

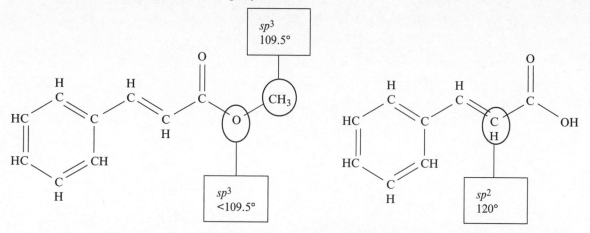

b. (EK 2.B.2, 2.B.3) Cinnamic acid is a slightly water-soluble compound. It has an O-H bond that is capable of forming hydrogen bonds with water molecules. Methyl cinnamate is a polar molecule, but it is incapable of hydrogen bonding. Methyl cinnamate is water-insoluble.

c. (EK 2.B.3) The hydrogen bonding between molecules of cinnamic acid results in a lower vapor pressure for cinnamic acid than for methyl cinnamate. Methyl cinnamate experiences dipole-dipole attractions that are weaker than hydrogen bonds, so the methyl cinnamate molecules more easily overcome the intermolecular attractions and escape into the gas phase.

d. (EK 1.D.3) Infrared spectroscopy gives informations about the types of bonds present in molecules. The IR spectrum of cinnamic acid would be expected to have an IR absorption due to the O-H peak, while the spectrum of methyl cinnamate will lack the O-H absorbance. Methyl cinnamate would have an O-CH$_3$ single bond absorbance that would not be expected in the spectrum of cinnamic acid. Mass spectrometry would indicate a larger molecular mass for methyl cinnamate (162 amu) than for cinnamic acid (148 amu).

4. a. (EK 2.C.4) The correct Lewis structures and their formal charges are shown below.

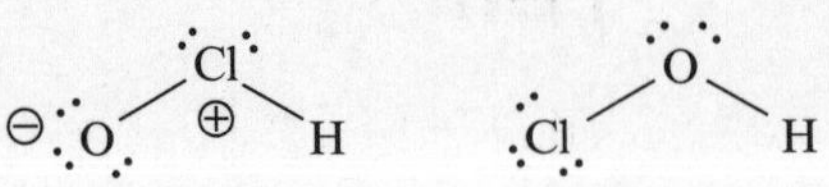

b. (EK 2.C.4) The compound on the right is the more stable structure since it has no formal charges. The structure on the left has a greater separation of charge.

c. (EK 2.C.4) The central atom has AX$_2$E$_2$ tetrahedral electronic geometry. The molecular geometry is bent with a bond angle that is compressed by the lone pairs on the central atom. The angle is less than 109.5°.

Chapter 3

Chemical Reactions (Big Idea 3)

Big Idea 3: Chemical reactions involve changes in bonding and changes in energy

During a physical change, intermolecular interactions between atoms or compounds are formed or disrupted. No change takes place to the structure or bonding arrangement of individual molecules. By contrast, during a **chemical change,** bonds are broken and formed. This leads to a fundamental change in the identity of the participating pure substances.

A combustion reaction, for example, transforms glucose and oxygen to carbon dioxide and water. When the combustion is complete, all of the carbon, oxygen, and hydrogen atoms still exist, but they exist in the form of CO_2 and H_2O. No glucose remains.

A chemical change is accompanied by a change in the energy of the reactants as they are transformed to products. When the products of a reaction are lower in energy than the reactants, energy is released and the reaction is exothermic. When the products are higher in energy, the reaction is endothermic.

Evidence for Chemical Change

It can sometimes be difficult to tell whether a chemical change has occurred, and entire chemical research projects are devoted to finding out.

There are four general clues that strongly suggest that a chemical change has occurred:

1. *Production of heat or light* usually indicates an exothermic chemical reaction. When glucose is rapidly burned in oxygen, both heat and light are given off. (This evidence is not definitive by itself, though. When a current is passed through the tungsten filament of an incandescent light bulb, both heat and light are emitted, but no chemical reaction takes place.)

2. *Formation or consumption of a gas,* usually observed as a change in pressure or volume, indicates a chemical reaction has occurred. Formation of bubbles in a liquid generally indicates a chemical change. (Physical changes such as sublimation and vaporization create gases, too, so this evidence should be used cautiously, as well.)

3. *Color changes* can also be indicators of a chemical change. The acid-base indicator phenolphthalein changes from colorless to pink when it undergoes a chemical reaction in the presence of a base. (Again, this evidence should be used with care. When yellow dye is added to blue dye, the mixture turns green, but no chemical change has occurred.)

4. *Formation of a **precipitate,*** an insoluble solid, can indicate a chemical reaction has occurred. When a solution containing Ag^+ ions is added to a solution containing Cl^- ions, solid AgCl forms and settles to the bottom of the container. (Again, however, a solid can form from a homogeneous solution due to physical changes, too. Honey, an aqueous sugar solution, crystallizes under certain conditions.)

PRACTICE:

> Which of the following is likely to be a chemical change?
>
> (a) When a voltage is applied across a glass tube filled with neon, a bright orange glow is observed.
>
> (b) When a sample of ammonium dichromate is ignited with a splint, the substance gives off heat, light, and gases as it changes from a crystalline orange solid to a green solid.
>
> (c) When a flavored drink packet is added to water, the water turns red.

Only choice b, the decomposition of ammonium dichromate, is a chemical change. Several lines of evidence suggest this is the case, including color change, production of heat and light, and formation of gases. Lighting a neon light (choice a) and dissolving a drink packet in water (choice c) are physical changes.

Balancing Chemical Equations

In order to work with chemical reactions, students must be able to write and balance chemical equations. Because atoms are conserved in ordinary (non-nuclear) chemical changes, the atoms of each element on the reactant side of the equation must equal the atoms on the product side of the equation. This is achieved with **coefficients,** numbers indicating the number of particles or moles of each species in an equation.

There are several methods for successfully balancing a chemical equation. The following tips will make the task simpler:

- Balance elements that appear in only one place on each side of the equation first.
- Balance hydrogen, oxygen, and atoms in their free elemental form last.
- Balance polyatomic ions, such as NO_3^- and SO_4^{2-}, as units.
- Make sure that the sum of the charges of the reactants is equal to the sum of the charges of the products.

Consider the unbalanced equation for the oxidation of aluminum.

$$\text{Unbalanced: } Al + O_2 \rightarrow Al_2O_3$$

We can tabulate the number of atoms of each element. When oxygen is present, it is usually easiest to balance it last. Since there are two aluminum atoms in the products, a coefficient of 2 will balance the aluminum in the reactants.

$$\text{Still unbalanced: } 2\,Al + O_2 \rightarrow Al_2O_3$$

There are 3 oxygen atoms on the right and 2 on the left. A coefficient of 1.5 will equalize the number of oxygen atoms.

$$\text{Still unbalanced: } 2\,Al + 1.5\,O_2 \rightarrow Al_2O_3$$

Finally, each coefficient is multiplied by the factor that will result in the lowest whole-number ratio, 2 in this case.

$$\text{Balanced: } 4\,Al + 3\,O_2 \rightarrow 2\,Al_2O_3$$

It is always best to double-check that there are the same number of atoms of each element on both sides of the equation.

PRACTICE:

Balance the following equation using the lowest whole-number coefficients: $C_4H_{10} + O_2 \rightarrow CO_2 + H_2O$.

Carbon should be balanced first.

$$C_4H_{10} + O_2 \rightarrow 4\,CO_2 + H_2O$$

Hydrogen can be balanced second.

$$C_4H_{10} + O_2 \rightarrow 4\,CO_2 + 5\,H_2O$$

Because oxygen exists as a free element on the left, it should be balanced last. There are 13 oxygen atoms on the right, so the O_2 on the left must be multiplied by 6.5 in order to balance.

$$C_4H_{10} + 6.5\,O_2 \rightarrow 4\,CO_2 + 5\,H_2O$$

Multiplication of each coefficient by 2 converts the coefficients to the lowest set of whole numbers.

$$2\,C_4H_{10} + 13\,O_2 \rightarrow 8\,CO_2 + 10\,H_2O$$

Double-check that there are 8 carbon atoms, 20 hydrogen atoms, and 26 oxygen atoms on each side of the equation.

More difficult equations can be balanced systematically, as well. Consider the unbalanced equation for the explosive decomposition of nitroglycerin, $C_3H_5N_3O_9$. Fill in the blanks to balance.

$$\_\_\,C_3H_5N_3O_9 \rightarrow \_\_\,N_2 + \_\_\,H_2O + \_\_\,CO_2 + \_\_\,O_2$$

We can begin by balancing carbon.

$$\underline{1}\,C_3H_5N_3O_9 \rightarrow \_\_\,N_2 + \_\_\,H_2O + \underline{3}\,CO_2 + \_\_\,O_2$$

Next, balance the nitrogen. For now, do not worry about using a fractional coefficient.

$$\underline{1}\,C_3H_5N_3O_9 \rightarrow \underline{1.5}\,N_2 + \_\_\,H_2O + \underline{3}\,CO_2 + \_\_\,O_2$$

Now, consider hydrogen.

$$\underline{1}\,C_3H_5N_3O_9 \rightarrow \underline{1.5}\,N_2 + \underline{2.5}\,H_2O + \underline{3}\,CO_2 + \_\_\,O_2$$

Deal with oxygen last since it appears in multiple species in the products. Take an inventory of the number of oxygen atoms on each side. There are 9 in the reactants. On the product side, there is oxygen in H_2O, CO_2, and O_2. Set up an equation to balance the oxygen atoms and solve for the coefficient, n.

$$9 = (2.5 \times 1) + (3 \times 2) + (n \times 2)$$
$$9 = 2.5 + 6 + 2n$$
$$0.5 = 2n$$
$$0.25 = n$$

$$\underline{1}\,C_3H_5N_3O_9 \rightarrow \underline{1.5}\,N_2 + \underline{2.5}\,H_2O + \underline{3}\,CO_2 + \underline{0.25}\,O_2$$

Notice that the coefficients can be converted to smallest whole numbers when multiplied by 4.

$$\underline{4}\,C_3H_5N_3O_9 \rightarrow \underline{6}\,N_2 + \underline{10}\,H_2O + \underline{12}\,CO_2 + O_2$$

PRACTICE:

> Balance the equation below using the smallest whole-number coefficients.
>
> $$\_\_\,C_5H_{17}N_5O_2 + \_\_\,O_2 \rightarrow \_\_\,N_2 + \_\_\,H_2O + \_\_\,CO_2$$

Again, a systematic method is to begin by balancing carbon, nitrogen, and hydrogen using fractions, if necessary.

$$1 \ C_5H_{17}N_5O_2 + \_\_ \ O_2 \rightarrow 2.5 \ N_2 + 8.5 \ H_2O + 5 \ CO_2$$

Set up an equation to determine n, the coefficient for O_2.

$$(1 \times 2) + (n \times 2) = (8.5 \times 1) + (5 \times 2)$$
$$2 + 2n = 8.5 + 10$$
$$2n = 16.5$$
$$n = 8.25$$

$$1 \ C_5H_{17}N_5O_2 + 8.25 \ O_2 \rightarrow 2.5 \ N_2 + 8.5 \ H_2O + 5 \ CO_2$$

Multiply each coefficient by 4 to obtain the smallest whole-number ratio.

$$4 \ C_5H_{17}N_5O_2 + 33 \ O_2 \rightarrow 10 \ N_2 + 34 \ H_2O + 20 \ CO_2$$

PRACTICE:

Practice balancing as many equations as you can find. Some examples include:

$$Si + S_8 \rightarrow Si_2S_4$$
$$As + NaOH \rightarrow Na_3AsO_3 + H_2$$
$$Mg_3N_2 + H_2O \rightarrow Mg(OH)_2 + NH_3$$
$$V_2O_5 + Ca \rightarrow CaO + V$$
$$H_3BO_3 \rightarrow H_4B_6O_{11} + H_2O$$
$$Ca_3(PO_4)_2 + SiO_2 \rightarrow P_4O_{10} + CaSiO_3$$
$$Fe_2(C_2O_4)_3 \rightarrow FeC_2O_4 + CO_2$$

$$4 \ Si + S_8 \rightarrow 2 \ Si_2S_4$$
$$2 \ As + 6 \ NaOH \rightarrow 2 \ Na_3AsO_3 + 3 \ H_2$$
$$Mg_3N_2 + 6 \ H_2O \rightarrow 3 \ Mg(OH)_2 + 2 \ NH_3$$
$$V_2O_5 + 5 \ Ca \rightarrow 5 \ CaO + 2 \ V$$
$$6 \ H_3BO_3 \rightarrow H_4B_6O_{11} + 7 \ H_2O$$
$$2 \ Ca_3(PO_4)_2 + 6 \ SiO_2 \rightarrow P_4O_{10} + 6 \ CaSiO_3$$
$$Fe_2(C_2O_4)_3 \rightarrow 2 \ FeC_2O_4 + 2 \ CO_2$$

A balanced chemical equation can be represented symbolically by a **particle diagram,** which is a picture that represents reacting atoms or molecules as circles or spheres. The AP Chemistry curriculum is brimming with references to particulate representations of chemical phenomena, so it is in a student's best interest to be familiar with such drawings and to know how to produce them.

$$N_2 + 3 \ H_2 \rightarrow 2 \ NH_3$$

Particulate Representation of a Reaction

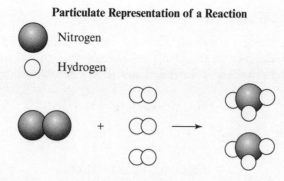

Classification of Chemical Reactions

Chemical equations can be classified as one or more of six types: synthesis, decomposition, combustion, single replacement, double replacement, and acid-base. In addition to fitting into one or more of these categories, some reactions may be redox reactions. These will be reviewed in much greater detail in the sections on oxidation-reduction reactions and electrochemistry a bit later in this chapter.

Synthesis Reactions

A **synthesis reaction** is one in which reactants combine to form a single product. The reaction between nitrogen and hydrogen on page 140 is classified as a synthesis reaction. Many synthesis reactions occur when elements are heated with oxygen, and some of these reactions are redox, as will be discussed later in this chapter.

Examples of synthesis reactions include:

$$2\,Mg + O_2 \rightarrow 2\,MgO$$
$$C + O_2 \rightarrow CO_2$$
$$2\,Li + H_2 \rightarrow 2\,LiH$$
$$Cl_2 + H_2 \rightarrow 2\,HCl$$

The reactions of metal and nonmetal oxides are important examples of synthesis reactions in AP Chemistry. Metal oxides are often called **basic anhydrides** because they react with water to form hydroxides. *Anhydride* means "without water."

$$Na_2O + H_2O \rightarrow 2\,NaOH$$
$$CaO + H_2O \rightarrow Ca(OH)_2$$

Nonmetal oxides are called **acid anhydrides** because they react with water to form acids.

$$Cl_2O_7 + H_2O \rightarrow 2\,HClO_4 \text{ (perchloric acid)}$$
$$SO_3 + H_2O \rightarrow H_2SO_4 \text{ (sulfuric acid)}$$
$$N_2O_5 + H_2O \rightarrow 2\,HNO_3 \text{ (nitric acid)}$$

Acid anhydrides react with basic anhydrides to form salts.

$$Li_2O + SO_3 \rightarrow Li_2SO_4$$
$$6\,Na_2O + P_4O_{10} \rightarrow 4\,Na_3PO_4$$

Decomposition Reactions

Decomposition reactions can be thought of as the reverse of synthesis reactions. In these reactions, one reactant forms two or more products. In many cases, this is due to heating or electrolysis, in which an electrical current is passed through a solution. The electrolysis of water is classified as a decomposition reaction:

$$2\ H_2O\ (l) \rightarrow 2\ H_2\ (g) + O_2\ (g)$$

Other examples of decompositions include:

$$Cu(OH)_2 \rightarrow CuO + H_2O$$
$$2\ Na_2O_2 \rightarrow 2\ Na_2O + O_2$$
$$2\ KClO_3 \rightarrow 2\ KCl + 3\ O_2$$
$$(NH_4)_2CO_3 \rightarrow 2\ NH_3 + CO_2 + H_2O$$

Sometimes unstable products are formed during the course of a reaction that decompose further to produce water and gases. Three unstable products to be aware of are carbonic acid, H_2CO_3, sulfurous acid, H_2SO_3, and ammonium hydroxide, NH_4OH.

$$H_2CO_3 \rightarrow H_2O + CO_2$$
$$H_2SO_3 \rightarrow H_2O + SO_2$$
$$NH_4OH \rightarrow H_2O + NH_3$$

These reactions are important to be aware of in acid-base chemistry. For instance, in the reaction between acetic acid, $H_3C_2O_2H$, and sodium bicarbonate, $NaHCO_3$ (vinegar and baking soda), the carbonic acid that is generated immediately decomposes to form carbon dioxide and water.

$$H_3C_2O_2H + NaHCO_3 \rightarrow NaH_3C_2O_2 + CO_2 + H_2O$$

Combustion Reactions

Combustion reactions are reactions in which elements or compounds react exothermically with oxygen. Usually "combustion" refers to the burning of hydrocarbon and other organic (carbon- and hydrogen-containing) molecules to yield carbon dioxide and water, but it may also refer to the burning of other combustible materials. A spark is required to initiate these processes.

$$CH_4 + 2\ O_2 \rightarrow CO_2 + 2\ H_2O$$
$$CH_4O + O_2 \rightarrow CO_2 + 2\ H_2O$$
$$SiH_4 + 2\ O_2 \rightarrow SiO_2 + 2\ H_2O$$

These reactions give off a great deal of energy, and they are used extensively for energy production. Gasoline, wood, coal, and natural gas are all examples of combustible fuels. Combustion reactions are also classified as redox reactions.

Single Replacement Reactions

Single replacement reactions are redox reactions in which one element in a compound is replaced by another, more active element. Whether a single replacement is expected to occur can be determined based on a table of measured oxidation-reduction potentials. This will be covered in more depth in the section on electrochemistry that begins on page 162.

$$A + BC \rightarrow AB + C$$

Single Replacement Reaction

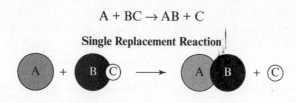

Examples of single replacement reactions include:

$$Cu + 2\,AgNO_3 \rightarrow Cu(NO_3)_2 + 2\,Ag$$
$$Mg + 2\,HCl \rightarrow MgCl_2 + H_2$$

In the first reaction, Cu is replacing Ag^+ in $AgNO_3$. In the second reaction, Mg is replacing H^+ in HCl.

Single replacement reactions readily occur between the group I metals and water. (Remember, group IA metals have an ns^1 valence electron configuration, so they readily ionize to achieve a noble gas configuration.) When a group IA metal is added to water, it reacts vigorously to form the metal hydroxide and hydrogen gas. The reaction is exothermic, and enough heat can be given off to cause the hydrogen above the surface of the water to ignite.

Moving down group IA from lithium to cesium, the elements become more reactive with water. (Francium, which is below cesium, is very unstable and very rare.) The reactivity can be explained by increasing shielding and decreasing ionization energy down the group.

$$K + H_2O \rightarrow KOH + H_2$$

Fluorine is the most active halogen and iodine is the least active halogen. Group VIIA elements closer to the top of the periodic table are more likely to gain an electron than those at the bottom. (Group VIIA elements have an ns^2np^7 valence electron configuration. They achieve a noble gas configuration by gaining one electron.) Chlorine, which is closer to the top of the periodic table and has a greater electron affinity, replaces bromide as the sodium salt in a single replacement reaction.

$$2\,NaBr + Cl_2 \rightarrow 2\,NaCl + Br_2$$

Double Replacement Reactions

Double replacement reactions are reactions in which cationic and anionic portions of two compounds are exchanged.

$$AB + CD \rightarrow AD + CB$$

Double Replacement Reaction

Double replacement reactions occur under any of the following circumstances:

- A precipitate is formed. A precipitate is an insoluble solid that forms when two solutions of ions are mixed. The reaction between $AgNO_3$ and KCl is an example. Alone, each reactant is soluble in water, but when they are mixed, the AgCl formed is insoluble. It is a solid that settles at the bottom of the container.

$$AgNO_3(aq) + KCl(aq) \rightarrow AgCl(s) + KNO_3(aq)$$

- Water, a weak acid, a weak base, or some other weakly-ionizing compound forms. The strong base, NaOH, reacts with a strong acid, $HClO_3$, to produce a salt, $NaClO_3$, and water, which is weakly ionizing. This is also classified as an acid-base reaction. An **acid-base reaction** is one in which an acid reacts with a base to form a solution of salt and water.

$$NaOH(aq) + HClO_3(aq) \rightarrow NaClO_3(aq) + H_2O(l)$$

- An intermediate forms that can decompose to a gas. Sulfurous acid, H_2SO_3, was one of the three compounds mentioned earlier that decomposes to water and gas. (The other two species were H_2CO_3 and NH_4OH.) It is a transient (or fleeting) product of the reaction of K_2SO_3 with HCl, a strong acid. As soon as the intermediate H_2SO_3 is formed, it decomposes to SO_2 and water.

$$K_2SO_3(aq) + 2\ HCl(aq) \rightarrow 2\ KCl(aq) + SO_2(g) + H_2O(l)$$

Ionic Solubility Rules

The solubility of ionic substances varies from compound to compound. Some substances such as AgCl are minimally soluble in water. Solubility will be explored further in Big Idea 6 (Chapter 6, "Chemical Equilibrium"), but for now, it is important to note that ionic compounds that are poorly soluble in water are referred to as "insoluble," despite the fact that they may dissociate to a slight extent.

Other ionic compounds **dissociate,** or break up into ions, almost completely in an aqueous solution. These are the strong electrolytes. A dissociation equation shows the ionic compound breaking up into ions when it is added to water.

$$NaCl(s) \rightarrow Na^+(aq) + Cl^-(aq)$$

The AP Chemistry curriculum requires memorization of only a few solubility rules:

- Sodium salts are soluble in water. Examples include NaF, Na_2SO_4, and NaCN.
- Potassium salts are soluble in water. Examples include KCl, K_2CO_3, and K_3PO_4.
- Ammonium salts are soluble in water. Examples include NH_4Cl and $NH_4CH_3CO_2$.
- Nitrate salts are soluble in water. Examples include $AgNO_3$, $Cu(NO_3)_2$, and $Pb(NO_3)_2$.

Acids and Bases

Six strong acids should be memorized. These are HCl, HBr, HI, $HClO_4$, H_2SO_4, and HNO_3. Other strong, oxygen-containing ternary acids (made up of three elements) can be recognized by the fact that they are composed of at least two more oxygen atoms than hydrogen atoms. Both $HClO_3$ and $HBrO_4$ are strong acids. They each have at least two more oxygen atoms than hydrogen atoms.

Strong bases dissociate completely in water. They are the group IA hydroxides, LiOH, NaOH, KOH, RbOH, and CsOH. Two hydroxides from group IIA, $Ba(OH)_2$ and $Sr(OH)_2$, also dissociate completely and are considered to be strong bases.

Strong acids and strong bases dissociate completely into ions in water. Strong acids and bases are strong electrolytes.

A weak acid is any acid that partially ionizes in an aqueous solution. Some weak acids are HF, H_2CO_3, H_3PO_4, and HNO_2, among many others. In addition, all carboxylic acids, which contain the functional group $-CO_2H$, are weak acids.

Bases that are not strong are either weakly-soluble hydroxides or weak bases. Weakly-soluble hydroxides include compounds such as $Mg(OH)_2$ or $Al(OH)_3$. Ammonia, NH_3, and the amines are common weak bases discussed in AP Chemistry. The amines have the general formula NR_3, where R is either hydrogen or a hydrocarbon group. Examples of amines are CH_3NH_2, $(CH_3)_2NH$, and $(CH_3)_3N$.

Weak acids and bases and weakly-soluble hydroxides are weak electrolytes.

Reactions of Acids and Bases

Chemists employ several definitions of acids and bases, but the most important one for AP Chemistry is the Brønsted-Lowry definition. Familiarity with the older Arrhenius acid-base theory facilitates understanding of Brønsted-Lowry acids and bases.

An **Arrhenius acid** is a species that releases a proton. The word "proton" is synonymous with "hydrogen ion," or "H^+." All of the acids discussed above (HCl, H_2SO_4, H_2CO_3, CH_3CO_2H, etc.) are Arrhenius acids. The ionization of an acid in water produces a **hydrogen ion, H^+**, and the anion of the acid.

$$HCl(aq) \rightarrow H^+(aq) + Cl^-(aq)$$

Arrhenius bases are species that release a hydroxide ion, OH^-, upon dissociation. Strong soluble bases such as $NaOH$, KOH, and $Ba(OH)_2$ are Arrhenius bases. The dissociation of basic hydroxide produces hydroxide ion, OH^-.

$$NaOH(aq) \rightarrow Na^+(aq) + OH^-(aq)$$

A **Brønsted-Lowry acid** is a proton donor, exactly like an Arrhenius acid. The anion that is produced upon the release of the proton is the **conjugate base** of the acid. It is called the conjugate base because it could accept a proton under appropriate conditions. In the ionization reaction of HCl in water below, Cl^- is the conjugate base of HCl and H_3O^+ is the conjugate acid of H_2O. A conjugate acid/base pair differs by one H^+.

Conjugate Acid/Conjugate Base Relationships

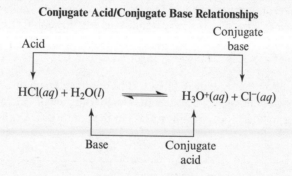

A **Brønsted-Lowry base** is a proton acceptor. A Brønsted-Lowry base such as ammonia, NH_3, reacts with water by accepting a proton. The resulting ammonium ion, NH_4^+, is called the **conjugate acid** of the base, because it could donate a proton under appropriate conditions. The conjugate base of water, OH^-, is produced in the reaction.

Conjugate Acid/Conjugate Base Relationships

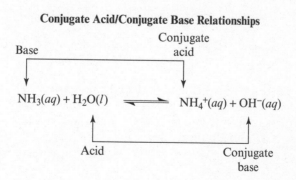

Water is behaving as a base in the reaction with HCl and as an acid in the reaction with NH_3. Water is an amphoteric species. An **amphoteric** species can act as both an acid and a base. It is also an **amphiprotic** species, one that can either donate or accept a proton. (Since all amphiprotic species are amphoteric, but not all amphoteric species are amphiprotic, it is best to use "amphoteric" in free-response answers.)

PRACTICE:

> Which of the following species are amphoteric? Write two equations for each amphoteric species. One equation should show the species reacting with water as a Brønsted-Lowry acid, and the other equation should show the species reacting with water as a Brønsted-Lowry base.
>
> $$HCO_3^-, SO_4^{2-}, HPO_4^{2-}$$

HCO_3^- and HPO_4^{2-} are both amphoteric species. SO_4^{2-} can accept a proton, but it does not have a proton to donate, so it is not amphoteric.

The reactions of HCO_3^- and HPO_4^{2-}, in which the species are behaving as acids, are

$$HCO_3^- + H_2O \rightarrow CO_3^{2-} + H_3O^+$$
$$HPO_4^{2-} + H_2O \rightarrow PO_4^{3-} + H_3O^+$$

The reactions of HCO_3^- and HPO_4^{2-}, in which the species are behaving as bases, are

$$HCO_3^- + H_2O \rightarrow H_2CO_3 + OH^-$$
$$HPO_4^{2-} + H_2O \rightarrow H_2PO_4^- + OH^-$$

The stronger an acid, the weaker its conjugate base. The stronger a base, the weaker its conjugate acid. HCl is a very strong acid, and its conjugate base, Cl^-, is a very weak base. Acetic acid, CH_3CO_2H, is a weaker acid than HCl. Its conjugate base, $CH_3CO_2^-$, is a stronger base than Cl^-. Notice that this refers to relative strength. Acetate anion, $CH_3CO_2^-$, is not a strong base. It is merely a stronger base than Cl^-.

Ammonia, NH_3, is a stronger base than acetate, $CH_3CO_2^-$. The conjugate acid of ammonia, NH_4^+, is a weaker acid than acetic acid, CH_3CO_2H, the conjugate acid of acetate. Further review of acid and base strength will be covered in Big Idea 6 (Chapter 6, "Chemical Equilibrium") in the context of K_a and K_b.

PRACTICE:

> Determine the weaker acid in each of the following pairs:
>
> (a) H_2O or NH_4^+
> (b) $(CH_3)_2NH$ or $(CH_3)_2NH_2^+$

To determine the weaker acid, look for the stronger conjugate base in each pair.

(a) In this pair, the conjugate bases are OH^- and NH_3. The hydroxide ion is a much stronger base than ammonia, a weak base. Water, the conjugate acid of hydroxide, is a weaker acid than NH_4^+, the conjugate acid of ammonia.

(b) In this pair, the conjugate bases are $(CH_3)_2N^-$ and $(CH_3)_2NH$, respectively. The stronger conjugate base is $(CH_3)_2N^-$. When a weakly basic amine such as $(CH_3)_2NH$ loses a proton, the resulting anionic species is strongly basic. The conjugate base of the second species is $(CH_3)_2NH$. It is a weak base, so its conjugate acid is the stronger acid. The first species, $(CH_3)_2NH$, is the weaker acid.

PRACTICE:

> Determine the weaker base in each of the following pairs:
>
> **(a)** H_2O or HSO_3^-
> **(b)** Cl^- or CN^-

To determine the weaker base, look for the stronger conjugate acid in each pair.

(a) In this pair, the conjugate acids are H_3O^+ and H_2SO_3. Hydronium, H_3O^+, is a strong acid, and H_2SO_3 is a weak acid. Therefore, water is a weaker base than HSO_3^-.

(b) In this pair, the conjugate acids are HCl and HCN. HCl is a strong acid and HCN is a weak acid. Therefore, chloride, Cl^-, is a weaker base than CN^-.

Net Ionic Equations

Net ionic equations are a very useful way of representing double replacement, single replacement, and acid-base reactions in aqueous solutions. They show only the species involved in the reaction. **Spectator ions,** which are ions that do not participate in the reaction, are not shown.

Consider the double replacement reaction between aqueous potassium iodide and aqueous lead nitrate. An insoluble solid precipitate, lead iodide, is formed.

The overall equation is first written and balanced. State symbols are included here to emphasize the nature of the precipitation reaction, but they are not required for credit on the AP Chemistry exam.

$$Pb(NO_3)_2(aq) + 2\ KI(aq) \rightarrow PbI_2(s) + 2\ KNO_3(aq)$$

Next, any strong electrolytes, which include soluble salts, strong acids, and strong bases, are written as dissociated ions in the total ionic equation. Remember that all nitrates and potassium salts are soluble.

$$Pb^{2+}(aq) + 2\ NO_3^-(aq) + 2\ K^+(aq) + 2\ I^-(aq) \rightarrow PbI_2(s) + 2\ K^+(aq) + 2\ NO_3^-(aq)$$

Finally, the spectator ions, which appear in both the reactants and the products, are cancelled for the net ionic equation.

$$Pb^{2+}(aq) + 2\ \cancel{NO_3^-(aq)} + 2\ \cancel{K^+(aq)} + 2\ I^-(aq) \rightarrow PbI_2(s) + 2\ \cancel{K^+(aq)} + 2\ \cancel{NO_3^-(aq)}$$
$$Pb^{2+}(aq) + 2\ I^-(aq) \rightarrow PbI_2(s)$$

PRACTICE:

> Write balanced net ionic equations and classify the following reactions.
>
> **(a)** Solid aluminum reacts with aqueous hydrochloric acid to form aqueous aluminum chloride and hydrogen gas.
>
> **(b)** When aqueous sodium hydroxide is added to an aqueous solution of magnesium sulfate, magnesium hydroxide precipitate is formed.

(a) The reaction between aluminum and hydrochloric acid is a single replacement reaction.

Overall equation:

$$2\ Al(s) + 6\ HCl(aq) \rightarrow 2\ AlCl_3(aq) + 3\ H_2(g)$$

Total ionic equation:

$$2\ Al(s) + 6\ H^+(aq) + 6\ \cancel{Cl^-(aq)} \rightarrow 2\ Al^{3+}(aq) + 6\ \cancel{Cl^-(aq)} + 3\ H_2(g)$$

Net ionic equation:

$$2\ Al(s) + 6\ H^+(aq) \rightarrow 2\ Al^{3+}(aq) + 3\ H_2(g)$$

Alternative net ionic equation without state symbols:

$$2\ Al + 6\ H^+ \rightarrow 2\ Al^{3+} + 3\ H_2$$

(b) The reaction between sodium hydroxide and magnesium sulfate is a double replacement reaction.

Overall equation:

$$MgSO_4(aq) + 2\ NaOH(aq) \rightarrow Mg(OH)_2(s) + Na_2SO_4(aq)$$

Total ionic equation:

$$Mg^{2+}(aq) + \cancel{SO_4^{2-}(aq)} + 2\ \cancel{Na^+(aq)} + 2\ OH^-(aq) \rightarrow Mg(OH)_2(s) + 2\ \cancel{Na^+(aq)} + \cancel{SO_4^{2-}(aq)}$$

Net ionic equation:

$$Mg^{2+}(aq) + 2\ OH^-(aq) \rightarrow Mg(OH)_2(s)$$

Alternative net ionic equation without state symbols:

$$Mg^{2+} + 2\ OH^- \rightarrow Mg(OH)_2$$

Oxidation-Reduction (Redox) Reactions

Oxidation-reduction reactions, also known as **redox reactions,** involve the transfer of electron(s) from a species that is oxidized to a species that is reduced. An easy mnemonic is "oil rig." **O**xidation **i**s **l**oss of electrons. **R**eduction **i**s **g**ain of electrons. It is important to remember that since electrons are negatively charged, the species that is reduced becomes more negative and the species that is oxidized becomes more positive.

Although the terms "oxidizing agent" and "reducing agent" will no longer be tested on the AP Chemistry exam, these phrases are important for anyone working with laboratory chemicals. An oxidizing agent is a chemical that is easily reduced, and a reducing agent is easily oxidized. This terminology is included on the material safety data sheet (MSDS) for many compounds such as peroxides, permanganates, and nitrates.

Assigning Oxidation Numbers

A prerequisite skill for identifying which species in a reaction is oxidized and which is reduced is the ability to assign oxidation numbers to each element in a compound.

The following rules are used for assigning oxidation numbers:

- A free element such as Fe, H_2, or S_8 has an oxidation number of zero.
- The oxidation number of a monatomic ion is equal to the charge on that ion. The oxidation number of Na^+ is +1 and the oxidation number of S^{2-} is –2.

- In compounds, hydrogen generally has an oxidation number of +1 when it is combined with non-metals and –1 when it is combined with metals. The oxidation number of hydrogen in HCl is +1 and the oxidation number of hydrogen in KH is –1.
- Oxygen generally has an oxidation number of –2 except in peroxides, in which it has an oxidation number of –1. Oxygen has an oxidation number of –2 in H_2O, but it has an oxidation number of –1 in H_2O_2.
- The sum of the oxidation numbers of the element in a polyatomic ion is equal to the charge of that ion. The sum of the oxidation numbers of the atoms in MnO_4^- is –1.
- The sum of the oxidation numbers of the elements in a neutral compound such as CO_2 or Fe_2O_3 is zero.

The species that is reduced in a redox reaction can be identified by its decrease in oxidation number. The species that is oxidized has an increase in oxidation number.

PRACTICE:

Assign oxidation numbers to each element in the following:

(a) Na_2SO_4

(b) $Cr_2O_7^{2-}$

(c) $KMnO_4$

(a) For Na_2SO_4, each sodium atom has an oxidation number of +1 and each oxygen atom has an oxidation number of –2. That leaves the oxidation number of sulfur, which can be assigned the variable x. Since the sum of the oxidation numbers is zero, an equation can be written.

$$2(+1) + x + 4(-2) = 0$$
$$2 + x - 8 = 0$$
$$x = 6$$

The oxidation number of sulfur in Na_2SO_4 is +6.

(b) For $Cr_2O_7^{2-}$, oxygen again has an oxidation number of –2. Let x be the oxidation number of chromium. The overall charge on the ion is –2, so the sum of the oxidation numbers is –2.

$$2x + 7(-2) = -2$$
$$2x - 14 = -2$$
$$2x = 12$$
$$x = 6$$

The oxidation number of chromium in $Cr_2O_7^{2-}$ is +6.

(c) For $KMnO_4$, the oxidation number of potassium is +1 and the oxidation number of oxygen is –2. Let x be the oxidation number of manganese. Again, the overall charge of the compound is zero.

$$1(+1) + x + 4(-2) = 0$$
$$1 + x - 8 = 0$$
$$x = 7$$

The oxidation number of manganese in $KMnO_4$ is +7.

PRACTICE:

Determine which element is oxidized and which element is reduced in the following reaction:

$$2 \, Zn + 2 \, HCl \rightarrow 2 \, ZnCl + H_2$$

This equation is easiest to deal with in net ionic equation form, since spectator ions are not oxidized or reduced.

Total ionic equation:

$$2\,Zn + 2\,H^+ + 2\,Cl^- \rightarrow 2\,Zn^{2+} + 2\,Cl^- + H_2$$

Net ionic equation:

$$2\,Zn + 2\,H^+ \rightarrow 2\,Zn^{2+} + H_2$$

In the reactants, zinc has an oxidation number of zero, and in the products it has an oxidation number of +2. The oxidation number has increased. Zinc has lost electrons and has been oxidized.

In the reactants, hydrogen has an oxidation number of +1, and in the products it has an oxidation number of zero. The oxidation number has decreased. Hydrogen has gained electrons and has been reduced.

Balancing Redox Equations

Balancing redox equations is most easily accomplished using a systematic technique called the **half reaction method.** Once a reaction has been identified as redox, the overall reaction is divided into two: an oxidation half-reaction and a reduction half reaction.

Often a redox reaction occurs in acidic or basic solution. All balancing is first performed as if the solution were acidic. Then, if the solution is basic, the acidic form of the balanced equation is modified to suit the basic conditions.

Steps for balancing redox reactions:

1. Write the net ionic form of the unbalanced equation.
2. Using oxidation numbers, divide the equation into oxidation and reduction half reactions
3. Balance all atoms other than hydrogen and oxygen.
4. Balance oxygen by adding one H_2O for every missing oxygen.
5. Balance hydrogen by adding one H^+ for every missing hydrogen.
6. Balance charge by adding the appropriate number of electrons to the side that has a more positive overall charge.
7. Multiply the half reactions by a factor that will equalize the number of electrons.
8. Add the half reactions back together. The electrons on both sides must cancel.
9. If the reaction is in basic solution, add enough OH^- to both sides of the equation to neutralize all the H^+. Simplify the number of water molecules.
10. Check to make sure that the number of each type of atom is equal in the products and the reactants. The overall charge must be the same on both sides of the equation.

Consider the reaction in basic solution between sulfite and chromate. A chromium(III) hydroxide precipitate and a sulfate solution are formed.

1. First, write the unbalanced equation. State symbols are not required for credit and are excluded here for clarity.

$$SO_3^{2-} + CrO_4^{2-} \rightarrow SO_4^{2-} + Cr(OH)_3$$

2. Divide the reaction into oxidation and reduction half reactions. The oxidation number of sulfur increases from +4 to +6, and the oxidation number of chromium decreases from +6 to +3. Sulfur is oxidized and chromium is reduced.

$$\text{oxidation: } SO_3^{2-} \rightarrow SO_4^{2-} \qquad \text{reduction: } CrO_4^{2-} \rightarrow Cr(OH)_3$$

3. Balance all atoms other than hydrogen and oxygen. In this case, sulfur and chromium are balanced, so no coefficients are needed.

$$SO_3^{2-} \rightarrow SO_4^{2-} \qquad CrO_4^{2-} \rightarrow Cr(OH)_3$$

4. Balance oxygen by adding H_2O.

$$SO_3^{2-} + \mathbf{H_2O} \rightarrow SO_4^{2-} \qquad CrO_4^{2-} \rightarrow Cr(OH)_3 + \mathbf{H_2O}$$

5. Balance hydrogen by adding H^+.

$$SO_3^{2-} + H_2O \rightarrow SO_4^{2-} + \mathbf{2\,H^+} \qquad CrO_4^{2-} + \mathbf{5\,H^+} \rightarrow Cr(OH)_3 + H_2O$$

6. Balance charge by adding electrons.

$$SO_3^{2-} + H_2O \rightarrow SO_4^{2-} + 2\,H^+ + \mathbf{2\,e^-} \qquad CrO_4^{2-} + 5\,H^+ + \mathbf{3\,e^-} \rightarrow Cr(OH)_3 + H_2O$$

7. Multiply the half reactions by a factor that will equalize the number of electrons.

$$\mathbf{3}[SO_3^{2-} + H_2O \rightarrow SO_4^{2-} + 2\,H^+ + 2\,e^-] \qquad \mathbf{2}[CrO_4^{2-} + 5\,H^+ + 3\,e^- \rightarrow Cr(OH)_3 + H_2O]$$

$$3\,SO_3^{2-} + 3\,H_2O \rightarrow 3\,SO_4^{2-} + 6\,H^+ + 6\,e^- \qquad 2\,CrO_4^{2-} + 10\,H^+ + 6\,e^- \rightarrow 2\,Cr(OH)_3 + 2\,H_2O$$

8. Add the half reactions back together. The electrons on both sides must cancel. The resulting equation is balanced in acidic solution.

$$3\,SO_3^{2-} + \cancel{3}^{1}\,H_2O + 2\,CrO_4^{2-} + \cancel{10}^{4}\,H^+ + \cancel{6\,e^-} \rightarrow 3\,SO_4^{2-} + \cancel{6\,H^+} + \cancel{6\,e^-} + 2\,Cr(OH)_3 + \cancel{2\,H_2O}$$

$$3\,SO_3^{2-} + H_2O + 2\,CrO_4^{2-} + 4\,H^+ \rightarrow 3\,SO_4^{2-} + 2\,Cr(OH)_3$$

9. If the reaction is in basic solution, add enough OH^- to both sides of the equation to neutralize all of the H^+. Simplify the number of water molecules.

$$3\,SO_3^{2-} + H_2O + 2\,CrO_4^{2-} + 4\,H^+ + \mathbf{4\,OH^-} \rightarrow 3\,SO_4^{2-} + 2\,Cr(OH)_3 + \mathbf{4\,OH^-}$$

$$3\,SO_3^{2-} + H_2O + 2\,CrO_4^{2-} + 4\,H_2O \rightarrow 3\,SO_4^{2-} + 2\,Cr(OH)_3 + 4\,OH^-$$

$$3\,SO_3^{2-} + 2\,CrO_4^{2-} + 5\,H_2O \rightarrow 3\,SO_4^{2-} + 2\,Cr(OH)_3 + 4\,OH^-$$

10. *Always* double-check to ensure that the number of each type of atom is equal in the products and the reactants. The overall charge must be the same on both sides of the equation.

Reaction Stoichiometry

Reaction stoichiometry refers to the relationship between the quantities of reactants and products in chemical reactions.

Dimensional analysis, as we have seen, is the use of unit factors to convert a quantity with certain units to an equal quantity with different units. It is used extensively in stoichiometric calculations. An additional source of conversion factors is used in reaction stoichiometry: the balanced chemical equation. Consider the coefficients in the balanced equation for the decomposition of potassium chlorate upon heating.

$$2 \ KClO_3(s) \rightarrow 2 \ KCl(s) + 3 \ O_2(g)$$

The coefficients have multiple meanings. They are a molecular ratio. Two molecules of $KClO_3$ decompose to produce two molecules of KCl and three molecules of O_2. They are also a mole ratio. Two moles of $KClO_3$ decompose to produce two moles of KCl and three moles of O_2. The following is an incomplete list of the equalities that can be obtained from this balanced equation:

2 molecules $KClO_3$ reacted = 2 molecules KCl formed

2 molecules KCl formed = 3 molecules O_2 formed

2 moles $KClO_3$ reacted = 3 moles of O_2 formed

The number of moles of O_2 formed when 8.75 moles of $KClO_3$ decompose according to the equation above can be determined using the relationship between the number of moles of $KClO_3$ and the number of moles of O_2 in the balanced equation.

$$8.75 \ \cancel{mol \ KClO_3} \times \frac{3 \ mol \ O_2}{2 \ \cancel{mol \ KClO_3}} = 13.1 \ mol \ O_2$$

In real situations, moles cannot be measured directly. Mass and volume are quantities that can be measured. They must be converted to moles using molar masses, concentrations, densities, or gas law relationships. The stoichiometry roadmap below summarizes the relationships between moles, masses, volumes, and particles of generic substances A and B that participate in a chemical reaction.

Stoichiometry Roadmap

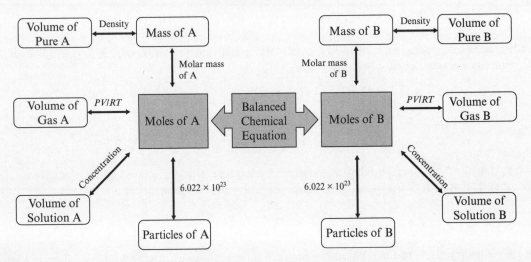

PRACTICE:

How many liters of O_2 are produced at 27 °C and 0.975 atm when 12.0 grams of $KClO_3$ decompose, according to the equation below?

$$2 \ KClO_3(s) \rightarrow 2 \ KCl(s) + 3 \ O_2(g)$$

Begin by converting the mass of $KClO_3$ to moles using the molar mass. The number of moles of $KClO_3$ is related to the number of moles of O_2 by the stoichiometric coefficients in the balanced equation.

$$12.3 \ \text{g} \ \cancel{KClO_3} \times \frac{1 \ \text{mol} \ \cancel{KClO_3}}{122.55 \ \text{g} \ \cancel{KClO_3}} \times \frac{3 \ \text{mol} \ O_2}{2 \ \text{mol} \ \cancel{KClO_3}} = 0.151 \ \text{mol} \ O_2$$

The number of moles of O_2 can then be converted to liters using the rearranged ideal gas law.

$$V = \frac{nRT}{P} = \frac{(0.151 \ \cancel{mol})(0.08206 \ \text{L} \cdot \text{atm} \cdot \cancel{mol^{-1}} \cdot \cancel{K^{-1}})(27+273 \ \cancel{K})}{0.975 \ \cancel{atm}} = 3.80 \ \text{L}$$

PRACTICE:

> What mass of CO_2 results from the combustion of 5.0 mL of pure benzene, C_6H_6, with excess oxygen (enough oxygen for complete combustion)? The density of benzene is 0.877 g·mL^{-1}.

It is first necessary to balance the combustion equation.

$$2 \ C_6H_6 + 15 \ O_2 \rightarrow 12 \ CO_2 + 6 \ H_2O$$

The volume of benzene must be converted to moles, and then the moles of benzene can be used to find the number of moles of CO_2. The moles of CO_2 are multiplied by the molar mass of CO_2 to give the mass produced in the reaction.

$$5.0 \ \cancel{mL \ C_6H_6} \times \frac{0.877 \ \text{g} \ \cancel{C_6H_6}}{1 \ \cancel{mL \ C_6H_6}} \times \frac{1 \ \text{mol} \ \cancel{C_6H_6}}{78.12 \ \text{g} \ \cancel{C_6H_6}} \times \frac{12 \ \text{mol} \ \cancel{CO_2}}{2 \ \text{mol} \ \cancel{C_6H_6}} \times \frac{44.01 \ \text{g} \ CO_2}{1 \ \text{mol} \ \cancel{CO_2}} = 15 \ \text{g} \ CO_2$$

Redox Titrations

As reviewed in Big Idea 2 (Chapter 2, "Bonding and Intermolecular Forces"), titration is a technique for the determination of an unknown concentration of an analyte by reaction with an accurately known amount of a standard, or titrant. A **redox titration** is a titration that relies on a redox reaction between the analyte and the standard.

Hydrogen peroxide, H_2O_2, is an active ingredient in consumer bottles of antiseptic solution. It decomposes over time due to exposure to light, heat, and trace amounts of transition metals.

Redox titration of H_2O_2 with permanganate, MnO_4^-, is a method for determining the concentration of hydrogen peroxide in a solution. The oxygen atoms in hydrogen peroxide are oxidized from a −1 oxidation state to an oxidation state of zero. The manganese atoms in the permanganate ions are reduced from a purple +7 oxidation state to a colorless +2 oxidation state. The permanganate serves as both a titrant and as an indicator.

$$H_2O_2 \rightarrow O_2 + 2 \ H^+ + 2 \ e^- \qquad \text{(oxidation)}$$
$$MnO_4^- + 8 \ H^+ + 5 \ e^- \rightarrow Mn^{2+} + 4 \ H_2O \qquad \text{(reduction)}$$

In order to balance the overall equation, the hydrogen peroxide oxidation must be multiplied by a factor of 5 and the permanganate reduction must be multiplied by a factor of 2 before the reactions can be added.

$$5(H_2O_2 \rightarrow O_2 + 2 \ H^+ + 2 \ e^-) \qquad 2(MnO_4^- + 8 \ H^+ + 5 \ e^- \rightarrow Mn^{2+} + 4 \ H_2O)$$

$$5 \ H_2O_2 \rightarrow 5 \ O_2 + 10 \ H^+ + 10 \ e^- \qquad 2 \ MnO_4^- + 16 \ H^+ + 10 \ e^- \rightarrow 2 \ Mn^{2+} + 8 \ H_2O$$

Add the half reactions back together. The electrons on both sides must cancel.

$$5\,H_2O_2 + 2\,MnO_4^- + \cancel{16}^{\,6}\,H^+ + \cancel{10\,e^-} \rightarrow 5\,O_2 + \cancel{10\,H^+} + \cancel{10\,e^-} + 2\,Mn^{2+} + 8\,H_2O$$

$$5\,H_2O_2 + 2\,MnO_4^- + 6\,H^+ \rightarrow 5\,O_2 + 2\,Mn^{2+} + 8\,H_2O$$

The balanced equation shows that for every five moles of hydrogen peroxide present, two moles of permanganate react.

In the titration, an exact volume of hydrogen peroxide solution is diluted with a small volume of water. The volume of water added does not affect the result. The hydrogen peroxide solution is acidified with a small amount of sulfuric acid. A precisely known concentration of potassium permanganate solution is then added drop-wise to the hydrogen peroxide via a buret. The endpoint of the titration is reached when the hydrogen peroxide solution turns light pink and remains pink. At this point, no peroxide is left to react with additional Mn^{+7}, so the pink color lingers.

PRACTICE:

> Titration of a dilute, acidified, 2.00-mL-aliquot of a commercial hydrogen peroxide solution requires 13.4 mL of 0.050 M $KMnO_4$. Assume the commercial solution has a density of 1.00 g·mL^{-1}.
>
> **(a)** What is the molarity of the H_2O_2 solution?
>
> **(b)** What is the mass percent of the H_2O_2 solution?

The volume of titrant required is used to determine the number of moles of H_2O_2 in the aliquot.

$$13.4\ \cancel{mL\ KMnO_4} \times \frac{1\ \cancel{L\ KMnO_4}}{1000\ \cancel{mL\ KMnO_4}} \times \frac{0.050\ \cancel{mol\ KMnO_4}}{1\ \cancel{L\ KMnO_4}} \times \frac{5\ mol\ H_2O_2}{2\ \cancel{mol\ KMnO_4}} = 0.0017\ mol\ H_2O_2$$

$$(0.001675)$$

(a) The molarity is determined by dividing the moles of H_2O_2 by the volume of the commercial sample used. (If we had been asked to report the number of moles of peroxide, we would report only two significant figures. The value is used before rounding in the following calculation, however.)

$$\text{Molarity of } H_2O_2 = \frac{0.001675\ mol\ H_2O_2}{2.00\ \cancel{mL\ H_2O_2}} \times \frac{1000\ \cancel{mL\ H_2O_2}}{1\ L\ H_2O_2} = 0.84\ M\ H_2O_2$$

(b) The mass percent is the percentage of the total mass of the solution that is H_2O_2.

$$\text{mass of } H_2O_2 = 0.001675\ mol\ H_2O_2 \times \frac{34.02\ g\ H_2O_2}{1\ mol\ H_2O_2} = 0.057\ g\ H_2O_2$$

$$(0.05698)$$

Since the density of the solution is assumed to be 1.00 g·mL^{-1}, the mass of the solution is 2.00 grams. Again, the answer is limited to two significant figures by the molarity of $KMnO_4$, but in order to avoid propagation of error, the entire calculated mass of H_2O_2 is used in the calculation of mass percent.

$$\text{percent by mass } H_2O_2 = \frac{\text{mass } H_2O_2}{\text{mass solution}} \times 100\% = \frac{0.05698\ g\ H_2O_2}{2.00\ g\ solution} \times 100\% = 2.8\%$$

Gas Stoichiometry

A convenient shortcut is to remember that the volume of a gas at a particular temperature and pressure is proportional to the number of moles. With this in mind, gas-phase reaction stoichiometry can be simplified by using volumes in place of moles whenever the gases under investigation are at the same temperature and pressure.

When hydrogen and oxygen gases are ignited, they form water.

$$2 H_2(g) + O_2(g) \rightarrow 2 H_2O(g)$$

How many liters of oxygen at STP must be available to completely react with 3.0 liters of hydrogen at STP?

The balanced equation shows that 2.0 liters of hydrogen react with exactly 1.0 liter of oxygen at a given temperature and pressure.

$$3.0 \ \cancel{L H_2} \times \frac{1 \ L \ O_2}{2 \ \cancel{L H_2}} = 1.5 \ L \ O_2$$

PRACTICE:

> Acetylene gas, C_2H_2, undergoes combustion in oxygen to form carbon dioxide and water. How many liters of oxygen must be present at STP to react completely with 4.0 liters of acetylene?

The first step in solving this problem is to write and balance the equation for the combustion of acetylene.

$$2 C_2H_2(g) + 5 O_2(g) \rightarrow 4 CO_2(g) + 2 H_2O(g)$$

Next, the coefficients in the balanced equation are used as a volume ratio to determine the stoichiometric amount of oxygen needed.

$$4.0 \ \cancel{L \ C_2H_2} \times \frac{5 \ L \ O_2}{2 \ \cancel{L \ C_2H_2}} = 10. \ L \ O_2$$

Heat of Reaction

Reaction stoichiometry is used in calculations of thermal energy gained or lost by a reacting system. When a reaction has a known enthalpy change per mole of product formed, the associated change in enthalpy for a specified amount of reactant consumed or product formed can be determined. Consider ΔH for the exothermic reaction of gaseous hydrogen and oxygen again.

$$H_2(g) + \frac{1}{2} O_2(g) \rightarrow H_2O(g)$$

$$\Delta H = -242 \ kJ \cdot mol^{-1}$$

Here, the stoichiometric coefficients refer to the number of moles of reactants consumed and products formed to produce the reported enthalpy change. The "mol^{-1}" refers to a "mole of this reaction as it is written." An enthalpy change of –242 kJ is a consequence of the reaction of one mole of $H_2(g)$. One-half of a mole of $O_2(g)$ is consumed for every 242 kJ released. Because everything is read in terms of moles, the use of fractional coefficients is allowed when balancing the chemical equation. Notice that the negative change in enthalpy indicates a release of heat to the surroundings. This is detected as an increase in the temperature of the surroundings.

The enthalpy change, ΔH, can be used as a ratio in dimensional analysis.

$$\Delta H = \frac{\text{heat transferred (kJ)}}{\text{moles of reaction (mol)}}$$

If a 10.0-L balloon holds pure hydrogen at STP, how much energy will be released if the hydrogen reacts with excess oxygen?

The first step is to calculate the number of moles of H_2 present using the standard molar volume. Next, the number of moles of hydrogen is multiplied by the change in enthalpy. One mole of H_2 reacts per mole of reaction and 242 kJ are released per one mole reaction.

$$10.0 \ \text{L } H_2 \times \frac{1 \ \text{mol } H_2}{22.4 \ \text{L } H_2} \times \frac{1 \ \text{mol rxn}}{1 \ \text{mol } H_2} \times \frac{242 \ \text{kJ}}{1 \ \text{mol rxn}} = 108 \ \text{kJ}$$

PRACTICE:

> A 46-gram sample of solid sodium reacts with excess oxygen to form sodium oxide. How much energy is released or absorbed in this process?
>
> $$4 \ Na(s) + O_2(g) \rightarrow 2 \ Na_2O(s)$$
> $$\Delta H = -832 \ \text{kJ·mol}^{-1}$$

The negative value of ΔH indicates that energy is released in this reaction. Four moles of sodium are consumed and 832 kJ of heat are released per mole of reaction. The number of grams of sodium are first converted to moles; then the number of moles of sodium is converted to moles of reaction. Finally, the number of moles of reaction are multiplied by the value of ΔH:

$$46.0 \ \text{g } Na \times \frac{1 \ \text{mol } Na}{22.99 \ \text{g } Na} \times \frac{1 \ \text{mol rxn}}{4 \ \text{mol } Na} \times \frac{-832 \ \text{kJ}}{1 \ \text{mol rxn}} = -416 \ \text{kJ}$$

Some chemical reactions are endothermic. When thionyl chloride, $SOCl_2$, is added to cobalt chloride hexahydrate, the resulting chemical reaction causes the temperature of the solution to decrease. The thermometer, which is part of the surroundings, loses heat to the system.

$$CoCl_2 \cdot 6H_2O + 6 \ SOCl_2 + \text{energy} \rightarrow CoCl_2 + 12 \ HCl + 6 \ SO_2$$

Endothermic and exothermic reactions are often depicted in **potential energy diagrams.** Energy is plotted on the vertical axis, and reaction coordinate is shown on the horizontal axis. **Reaction coordinate** can be interpreted as progress of a reaction or as time, usually with reactants on the left and products on the right. For endothermic reactions, the energy of the products is higher than the energy of the reactants. Energy is absorbed during the progress of the reaction. The opposite is true for an exothermic reaction. Energy of the reactants is greater than the energy of the products. Energy is lost during the course of the reaction.

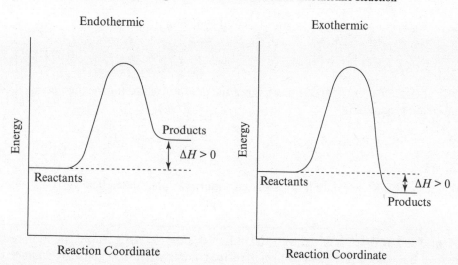

Potential Energy Diagrams for Endothermic and Exothermic Reaction

Limiting Reagent

The **limiting reagent** (or limiting reactant) is the substance that runs out first in a chemical reaction. It determines the maximum amount of product that can be produced, or **theoretical yield,** of a reaction.

To find the limiting reagent in a chemical reaction, the theoretical yield of one of the products is calculated using the amounts of each reactant given. Any reactant that is "in excess" is not the limiting reagent. *Whenever a question provides the amounts of two or more starting materials, the procedure for determining limiting reagent and theoretical yield must be followed.*

Steps for determining limiting reagent and theoretical yield:

1. Write the balanced chemical equation.
2. Choose one of the products. Use reaction stoichiometry to convert the amount of one of the reactants to moles of the chosen product.
3. Repeat step 2 with each reactant in turn. Always convert to moles of the same product.
4. The smallest number of moles of the chosen product is the theoretical yield of that product.
5. The reactant that gave the theoretical yield is the limiting reagent.

Suppose a question asks for identification of the limiting reagent and the theoretical yield in grams of P_4O_{10} in the reaction between 12.3 grams of $KClO_3$ and 12.3 grams of P_4. We can use this example to illustrate the steps for determining limiting reagent and theoretical yield.

1. The first step is to write the balanced equation.

$$3\,P_4 + 10\,KClO_3 \rightarrow 3\,P_4O_{10} + 10\,KCl$$

2. The second step is to convert each reactant to moles of product. Although either product will work in this step, the theoretical yield of P_4O_{10} is required. It is best to choose this product in order to minimize the effort. Notice that although the numbers of moles of P_4O_{10} can only be reported with three significant figures, it is better to use the unrounded value in subsequent calculations.

$$12.3 \text{ g } KClO_3 \times \frac{1 \text{ mol } KClO_3}{122.55 \text{ g } KClO_3} \times \frac{3 \text{ mol } P_4O_{10}}{10 \text{ mol } KClO_3} = 0.0301 \text{ mol } P_4O_{10}$$

(0.030110)

3. The amount of P_4 is also converted to number of moles of product.

$$12.3 \ \cancel{g \, P_4} \times \frac{1 \ \cancel{mol \, P_4}}{123.88 \ \cancel{g \, P_4}} \times \frac{3 \ mol \, P_4O_{10}}{3 \ \cancel{mol \, P_4}} = 0.0993 \ mol \ P_4O_{10}$$

(0.0992896)

4. The theoretical yield of P_4O_{10} is 0.0301 mole. Since the question asked for the theoretical yield in grams, a simple conversion is required.

$$0.030110 \ \cancel{mol \, P_4O_{10}} \times \frac{283.88 \ g \ P_4O_{10}}{1 \ \cancel{mol \, P_4O_{10}}} = 8.55 \ g \ P_4O_{10}$$

5. The limiting reagent is $KClO_3$ since it is associated with the smaller theoretical yield.

PRACTICE:

> 100. mL of 0.600 M $BaCl_2$ is mixed with 100. mL of 0.250 M K_3AsO_4. A precipitation reaction occurs, and the solid $Ba_3(AsO_4)_2$ that forms is filtered, dried completely, and weighed. What mass of precipitate is formed? The molar mass of $Ba_3(AsO_4)_2$ is 689.82 $g \cdot mol^{-1}$.

The first step is to write the balanced equation.

$$3 \ BaCl_2 + 2 \ K_3AsO_4 \rightarrow Ba_3(AsO_4)_2 + 6 \ KCl$$

Next, each reagent is converted to moles of $Ba_3(AsO_4)_2$.

$$100. \ \cancel{mL \, BaCl_2} \times \frac{1 \ \cancel{L \, BaCl_2}}{1000 \ \cancel{mL \, BaCl_2}} \times \frac{0.600 \ \cancel{mol \, BaCl_2}}{1 \ \cancel{L \, BaCl_2}} \times \frac{1 \ mol \ Ba_3(AsO_4)_2}{3 \ \cancel{mol \, BaCl_2}} = 0.0200 \ mol \ Ba_3(AsO_4)_2$$

$$100. \ \cancel{mL \, K_3AsO_4} \times \frac{1 \ \cancel{L \, K_3AsO_4}}{1000 \ \cancel{mL \, K_3AsO_4}} \times \frac{0.250 \ \cancel{mol \, K_3AsO_4}}{1 \ \cancel{L \, K_3AsO_4}} \times \frac{1 \ mol \ Ba_3(AsO_4)_2}{2 \ \cancel{mol \, K_3AsO_4}} = 0.0125 \ mol \ Ba_3(AsO_4)_2$$

Since the smaller number of moles of $Ba_3(AsO_4)_2$ is produced by complete reaction of the K_3AsO_4, the theoretical yield of $Ba_3(AsO_4)_2$ is 0.0125 mole. The limiting reagent is K_3AsO_4.

To determine the mass of precipitate formed, the number of moles is converted to grams using the molar mass.

$$0.0125 \ \cancel{mol \, Ba_3(AsO_4)_2} \times \frac{689.83 \ g \ Ba_3(AsO_4)_2}{1 \ \cancel{mol \, Ba_3(AsO_4)_2}} = 8.62 \ g \ Ba_3(AsO_4)_2$$

Often students are asked to determine the amount of the excess reactant that is left over. In this case, the theoretical yield of product is used to determine the number of moles of excess reagent that is consumed in the reaction. The number of moles that reacted is subtracted from the number of moles of excess reagent that were present at the start of the reaction. The difference is the amount that is left over.

PRACTICE:

> In the preceding question, which reactant is in excess and what is the molarity of this reactant when the reaction is complete?

Since K_3AsO_4 is the limiting reagent, $BaCl_2$ is in excess. In order to find the molarity of this reactant at the end of the reaction, we need to know how many moles are left over and the volume of the combined solution.

The amount of $BaCl_2$ left over is equal to the difference between the initial amount and the amount that was consumed.

$$\text{Initial moles of } BaCl_2 = 100. \text{ mL } BaCl_2 \times \frac{1 \text{ L } BaCl_2}{1000 \text{ mL } BaCl_2} \times \frac{0.600 \text{ mol } BaCl_2}{1 \text{ L } BaCl_2} = 0.0600 \text{ mol } BaCl_2$$

The amount of $BaCl_2$ that was consumed can be determined from the number of moles of product that were produced.

$$\text{Moles of } BaCl_2 \text{ reacted} = 0.0125 \text{ mol } Ba_3(AsO_4)_2 \times \frac{3 \text{ mol } BaCl_2}{1 \text{ mol } Ba_3(AsO_4)_2} = 0.0375 \text{ mol } BaCl_2$$

$$\text{Moles of } BaCl_2 \text{ left over} = 0.0600 \text{ mol} - 0.0375 \text{ mol} = 0.0225 \text{ mol } BaCl_2$$

The final concentration of $BaCl_2$ is the number of moles divided by the total volume, 200. mL of combined solution.

$$\frac{0.0225 \text{ mol } BaCl_2}{200. \text{ mL}} \times \frac{1000 \text{ mL}}{1 \text{ L}} = 0.113 \text{ } M \text{ } BaCl_2$$

Percent Yield

Percent yield is a measure of the efficiency of a reaction. It indicates how much of the desired product of a reaction was obtained compared to how much was expected. Often, less product is obtained than anticipated. This can be due to incomplete reaction, competing side reactions, impure starting materials, or difficult purification of products. A yield greater than 100% is not possible.

$$\text{Percent yield} = \frac{\text{Actual yield of product}}{\text{Theoretical yield of product}} \times 100\%$$

As long as the units of actual yield and theoretical yield are the same, either grams or moles may be used.

When 56.1 grams of 1-butene, C_4H_8, are allowed to react with 240. grams of bromine, Br_2, the reaction yields 200. grams of product, $C_4H_8Br_2$. In order to determine the percent yield, we must first find the theoretical yield. Since the amounts of both starting materials are given, we must treat this as a limiting reagent problem.

$$C_4H_8 + Br_2 \rightarrow C_4H_8Br_2$$

$$56.1 \text{ g } C_4H_8 \times \frac{1 \text{ mol } C_4H_8}{56.12 \text{ g } C_4H_8} \times \frac{1 \text{ mol } C_4H_8Br_2}{1 \text{ mol } C_4H_8} = 1.00 \text{ mol } C_4H_8Br_2$$

$$240.0 \text{ g } Br_2 \times \frac{1 \text{ mol } Br_2}{159.8 \text{ g } Br_2} \times \frac{1 \text{ mol } C_4H_8Br_2}{1 \text{ mol } Br_2} = 1.50 \text{ mol } C_4H_8Br_2$$

Since fewer moles of product are expected to form based on the initial amount of 1-butene, the theoretical yield of $C_4H_8Br_2$ is 1.00 mole. The actual yield, 200.0 grams of $C_4H_8Br_2$, must be divided by the theoretical yield of $C_4H_8Br_2$ in grams.

$$\text{Theoretical yield} = 1.00 \text{ mol } C_4H_8Br_2 \times \frac{215.92 \text{ g } C_4H_8Br_2}{1 \text{ mol } C_4H_8Br_2} = 216 \text{ g } C_4H_8Br_2$$

$$\text{Percent yield} = \frac{200. \text{ g } C_4H_8Br_2}{216 \text{ g } C_4H_8Br_2} \times 100\% = 92.6\%$$

PRACTICE:

> The reaction below can be used to produce hydrazine, N_2H_4. A group of chemists would like to prepare 10.0 kg of hydrazine. If the expected yield of hydrazine is 70.0%, how many moles of chloramine, NH_2Cl, must the chemists use?
>
> $$NH_2Cl + NH_3 + NaOH \rightarrow N_2H_4 + H_2O + NaOH$$

The solution to this problem begins with the desired mass of hydrazine. The actual yield of N_2H_4 must be 10.0 kg. The percent yield equation can be rearranged to calculate the theoretical yield that must be planned.

$$\text{Theoretical yield} = \frac{\text{Actual yield}}{\text{Percent yield}} \times 100\% = \frac{(10.0 \text{ kg } N_2H_4)}{70.0\%} \times 100\% = 14.3 \text{ kg } N_2H_4$$

The theoretical yield is used to calculate the number of moles of chloramine that must be used.

$$14.2857 \text{ kg } N_2H_4 \times \frac{1000 \text{ g } N_2H_4}{1 \text{ kg } N_2H_4} \times \frac{1 \text{ mol } N_2H_4}{32.06 \text{ g } N_2H_4} \times \frac{1 \text{ mol } NH_2Cl}{1 \text{ mol } N_2H_4} \times \frac{51.48 \text{ g } NH_2Cl}{1 \text{ mol } NH_2Cl}$$

$$\times \frac{1 \text{ kg } NH_2Cl}{1000 \text{ g } NH_2Cl} = 22.9 \text{ kg } NH_2Cl$$

Atom Economy

Green chemistry refers to the movement toward sustainability in chemical processes and products. Green chemistry focuses on safety and renewability in addition to minimization of waste, byproducts, and energy usage.

Atom economy is a measure of how efficient a process is from a waste minimization standpoint. It is different from percent yield because it takes the total mass of the atoms used, not just the theoretical yield, into account. In a reaction with 100% atom economy, every atom of the reactants theoretically ends up incorporated into the products.

$$\text{Percent atom economy} = \frac{\text{Mass of wanted products}}{\text{Total mass of products}} \times 100\%$$

For simplicity, masses in the above equation are usually calculated based on the number of moles in the balanced chemical equation. For example, in the bromination of 1-butene, discussed above, the only product formed is the desired product, $C_4H_8Br_2$. The total mass of product is equal to the total mass of wanted product, so the percent atom economy is 100%.

Consider the reaction between 2-bromo-2-methylpropane, C_4H_9Br, and sodium ethoxide, C_2H_5ONa. The desired product is isobutene, C_4H_8. The undesired byproducts are ethanol, C_2H_5OH, and sodium bromide, NaBr.

In order to perform an atom economy calculation, assume that the number of moles of desired product is equal to the stoichiometric coefficient. This simplifies the calculation, because the molar mass of that product in grams is formed. The total mass of all products is the sum of the molar masses of products multiplied by their stoichiometric coefficients.

$$C_4H_9Br + C_2H_5ONa \rightarrow C_4H_8 + C_2H_5OH + NaBr$$

Product	Desired?	Molar Mass $(g \cdot mol^{-1})$	Stoichiometric Coefficient	Theoretical Mass of Product Formed (g)
C_4H_8	Yes	56.11	1	56.11
C_2H_5OH	No	46.07	1	46.07
NaBr	No	102.89	1	102.89
Total				205.07

The percent atom economy is

$$\text{Percent atom economy} = \frac{56.11}{205.07} \times 100\% = 27.36\%$$

From an atom economy standpoint, this is a relatively inefficient reaction that generates a lot of waste.

PRACTICE:

Phosphorus tribromide, PBr_3, is used to convert butanol, C_4H_9OH, to bromobutane, C_4H_9Br. The byproduct of this reaction is phosphorous acid, H_3PO_3. A chemistry student sets up a reaction in which 200. grams of C_4H_9OH are treated with 271 grams of PBr_3. The student isolates 300. grams of C_4H_9Br. What are the percent yield and percent atom economy for this reaction?

$$3\ C_4H_9OH + PBr_3 \rightarrow 3\ C_4H_9Br + H_3PO_3$$

The theoretical yield must be calculated by determining the limiting reagent.

$$200.\ \text{g } C_4H_9OH \times \frac{1\ \text{mol } C_4H_9OH}{74.14\ \text{g } C_4H_9OH} \times \frac{3\ \text{mol } C_4H_9Br}{3\ \text{mol } C_4H_9OH} = 2.70\ \text{mol } C_4H_9Br$$

$$271\ \text{g } PBr_3 \times \frac{1\ \text{mol } PBr_3}{270.67\ \text{g } PBr_3} \times \frac{3\ \text{mol } C_4H_9Br}{1\ \text{mol } PBr_3} = 3.00\ \text{mol } C_4H_9Br$$

The limiting reagent is C_4H_9OH, and the theoretical yield of C_4H_9Br is 2.70 moles. The theoretical yield is converted to grams and used to determine the percent yield.

$$2.70\ \text{mol } C_4H_9Br \times \frac{137.03\ \text{g } C_4H_9Br}{1\ \text{mol } C_4H_9Br} = 370.\ \text{g } C_4H_9Br$$

$$\text{Percent yield} = \frac{300.\ \text{g } C_4H_9Br}{370.\ \text{g } C_4H_9Br} \times 100\% = 81.1\%$$

Percent atom economy is determined using the masses of both products.

Product	Desired?	Molar Mass $(g \cdot mol^{-1})$	Stoichiometric Coefficient	Theoretical Mass of Product Formed (g)
C_4H_9Br	Yes	137.03	3	411.09
H_3PO_3	No	82.00	1	82.00
Total				493.09

$$\text{Percent atom economy} = \frac{411.09}{493.09} \times 100\% = 83.4\%$$

Electrochemistry

Electrochemistry is the study of the electron movement and energetics of redox processes.

There are two kinds of redox processes: those that are thermodynamically favorable and those that are thermodynamically unfavorable. For now, it is sufficient to know that a thermodynamically favorable process will happen without any continuous input of energy. A thermodynamically unfavorable process will not happen without an external source of energy. The idea of thermodynamic favorability will be further developed in Big Idea 5 (Chapter 5, "Thermodynamics").

Standard Cell Potential

An **electrochemical cell** is an apparatus in which the oxidation and reduction half reactions of a redox process are separated in space. An electrochemical cell in which the redox process is thermodynamically favorable is a **galvanic cell,** also called a voltaic cell. A cell in which the redox process must be supplied with energy from an external power source, such as a battery, is an **electrolytic cell.**

In electrochemical cells, there are two electrodes where the half reactions take place. The **cathode** is the electrode where reduction occurs, and the **anode** is the electrode where oxidation occurs. A useful mnemonic for this relationship is "red cat": <u>Red</u>uction always occurs at the <u>cat</u>hode.

The **standard cell potential,** $E°_{cell}$, for a redox process provides a quantitative measure of the favorability of that process. The more positive the standard cell potential, the more favorable the process. An unfavorable process has a negative cell potential.

$$E°_{cell} = E°_{reduction} - E°_{oxidation}$$

or

$$E°_{cell} = E°_{cathode} - E°_{anode}$$

The naught or ° symbol indicates that the cell potentials are measured for all reactants and products in their standard states (1 atm for gases, 1.0 M for solutions and at 298 K). Non-standard cells will be reviewed in more detail in the context of chemical equilibrium in Big Idea 6, (Chapter 6, "Chemical Equilibrium"). The $E°_{cathode}$ and the $E°_{anode}$ represent the standard reduction potentials for both electrodes.

Some standard reduction potentials are tabulated below. The unit is **volts,** V, the unit of electrical potential equal to joules of work per coulomb of charge transferred.

Half Reaction	Standard Reduction Potential, $E°$ (V)
$Al^{3+} + 3\,e^- \rightarrow Al$	–1.66
$Ca^{2+} + 2\,e^- \rightarrow Ca$	–2.76

These values can be used to determine the cell potential for the electrochemical cell in which Al^{3+} is reduced to Al and Ca is oxidized to Ca^{2+}. (The oxidation reaction of calcium is just the reverse of the reduction, $Ca \rightarrow Ca^{2+} + 2\,e^-$.)

$$2\,Al^{3+} + 3\,Ca \rightarrow 2\,Al + 3\,Ca^{2+}$$

$$E°_{cell} = E°_{reduction} - E°_{oxidation} = -1.66\text{ V} - (-2.76) = +\,1.10\text{ V}$$

The positive cell potential indicates a thermodynamically favored process. This procedure will always work for finding the correct reduction potential, and many teachers and textbooks use it. There are other procedures for finding cell potentials that involve changing the sign of one of the cell half reaction reduction potentials. *If you have been presented with one of these other methods by your instructor and are comfortable with it, use it exclusively to avoid confusion.*

Standard reduction potentials for half reactions, such as those given for Ca^{2+} and Al^{3+} above, are measured against a **standard hydrogen electrode,** which is an inert platinum electrode immersed in a 1 M solution of H_3O^+ under a 1 atm partial pressure of hydrogen gas. The reaction that is defined by chemists to have a cell potential of zero is the reduction of H^+.

$$2\,H^+ + 2\,e^- \rightarrow H_2 \qquad E^\circ_{cell} = 0.00\ V$$

PRACTICE:

> Based on their standard reduction potentials, which of the following species have a greater tendency to be reduced than H^+?

Half Reaction	Standard Reduction Potential, E° (V)
$O_2 + 4\,H^+ + 4\,e^- \rightarrow 2\,H_2O$	1.23
$Ag^+ + e^- \rightarrow Ag$	0.80
$Co^{2+} + 2\,e^- \rightarrow Co$	−0.28

As indicated by their positive standard reduction potentials, both O_2 and Ag^+ have a greater tendency to be reduced than H^+. Cobalt ion, Co^{2+}, has a negative reduction potential, so it has a lesser tendency to undergo reduction than H^+.

Galvanic/Voltaic Cells

A **galvanic cell** is one in which a redox process occurs spontaneously. A galvanic cell, also called a **voltaic cell,** has a positive cell potential, E°_{cell}. Galvanic cells produce electrical energy by causing electrical current to move through the wire connecting the anode and the cathode. Batteries are galvanic cells. As we will see in Big Idea 5 (Chapter 5, "Thermodynamics"), the change in Gibbs free energy, ΔG°_{rxn}, is less than zero for a redox process with a positive cell potential.

Shown below is a picture of a galvanic cell. In this cell, a strip of copper immersed in a solution of 1 M copper(II) sulfate is connected by a wire to a strip of zinc in a solution of 1 M zinc sulfate.

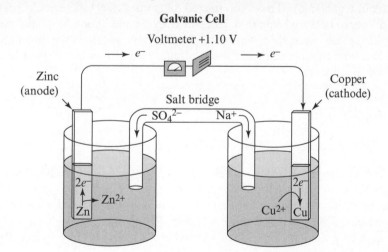

The standard reduction potentials for the Cu^{2+} and Zn^{2+} ions are given below. Because the cell is galvanic, E°_{cell} is positive. In order for this to be true, copper, which has the higher standard reduction potential, must be reduced at the cathode, and zinc, which has the lower reduction potential, must be oxidized at the anode.

Half Reaction	Standard Reduction Potential, $E°$ (V)
$Cu^{2+} + 2\,e^- \rightarrow Cu$	0.34
$Zn^{2+} + 2\,e^- \rightarrow Zn$	–0.76

$$E°_{cell} = E°_{cathode} - E°_{anode} = 0.34\text{ V} - (-0.76\text{ V}) = 1.10\text{ V}$$

Overall equation: $Cu^{2+} + Zn \rightarrow Cu + Zn^{2+}$

Electrons flow from the zinc electrode, where oxidation is occurring, to the copper electrode, where reduction is occurring. *Electrons always flow from the anode to the cathode, regardless of whether the cell is galvanic or not.*

As electrons are gained by the Cu^{2+} in solution at the cathode, the Cu^{2+} ions leave the solution and become solid copper, which deposits on the Cu electrode. This adds copper mass to the cathode. As electrons leave the zinc electrode, solid zinc atoms leave the electrode as they become Zn^{2+} ions in solution. The zinc anode loses mass.

When both the reactant and the product of a half reaction remain in solution, or when a reactant or product is a gas, an inert (unreactive) electrode such as platinum or graphite is used. Inert electrodes do not participate in the redox reaction; they just provide the surface where half reactions occur.

In order to maintain charge balance, a **salt bridge** connects the two half-cells. The salt bridge consists of a soluble salt embedded in a gel. The ions of the salt can move into the solutions, but the solutions themselves are prevented from mixing. Because Cu^{2+} ions are leaving the solution at the anode, the positive charges are replaced by cations (Na^+) from the salt bridge. Because Zn^{2+} ions are entering the solution at the anode, the positive charges are balanced by anions (SO_4^{2-}) from the salt bridge.

A picture like the galvanic cell image above is *not* referred to as a "cell diagram." A **cell diagram** is a shorthand method for describing an electrochemical cell in which the anode is written first, the cathode is written last, cathode and anode are separated by a double vertical line, ‖, and phase boundaries are denoted by single vertical lines, |. The diagram for the galvanic cell pictured above is shown below.

$$Zn(s) \mid Zn^{2+}(1\ M) \parallel Cu^{2+}(1\ M) \mid Cu(s)$$

PRACTICE:

> Sketch a picture of a galvanic cell based on the cell diagram: $Pt(s) \mid Cr^{2+}(aq), Cr^{3+}(aq) \parallel H^+(aq) \mid H_2(g) \mid Pt(s)$. Write the overall balanced equation, label the cathode and anode, and label each half-cell with the reaction taking place. Show the direction of electron flow and show the direction of cation and anion flow to and from the solution and the salt bridge. Finally, is either of the electrodes gaining or losing mass? Why or why not?

The overall balanced equation is

$$2\ Cr^{2+} + 2\ H^+ \rightarrow 2\ Cr^{3+} + H_2$$

The electron flow is from the anode, where Cr^{2+} is being oxidized to Cr^{3+}, to the cathode, where H^+ is being reduced to H_2, which bubbles out of the solution. Anions flow from the salt bridge to the anode to offset the positive charges that result from the oxidation of Cr^{2+}. Cations flow from the salt bridge to the cathode to offset the loss of H^+ from the solution. (*Electrons should never be shown flowing to or from the salt bridge.*) Neither of the platinum electrodes is gaining mass. The Cr^{2+}, when oxidized to Cr^{3+}, remains in solution. The H^+, when reduced, forms a gas that bubbles out of the solution.

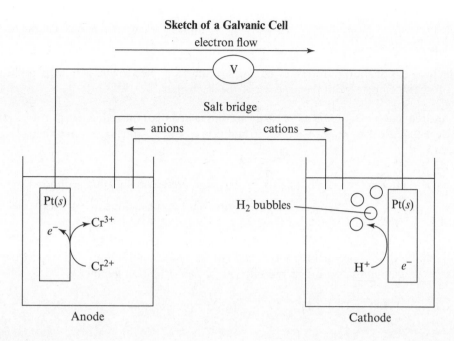

Sketch of a Galvanic Cell

Electrolytic Cells

Electrolytic cells are electrochemical cells that involve a thermodynamically disfavored redox process. Electrolytic cells require an external source of energy, such as a battery, in order to force the electrolysis reaction to proceed. An electrolytic cell has a negative cell potential. The change in Gibbs free energy, ΔG°_{rxn}, is greater than zero for a redox process with a negative cell potential (again, this concept will be reviewed in Big Idea 5, Chapter 5, "Thermodynamics").

The electrolysis of molten sodium chloride, which occurs industrially in a Downs cell, is shown in the picture below. The cell potential is negative, and the species with the more negative standard reduction potential, Na^+, is being reduced to molten sodium at the cathode. Chloride ions, Cl^-, are being oxidized to chlorine gas at the anode. Electrons still flow from the anode to the cathode, but they do not move spontaneously. The battery or electrical energy source forces the electrons to move. The two half reactions do not require separation in an electrolytic cell, so there is no need for a salt bridge.

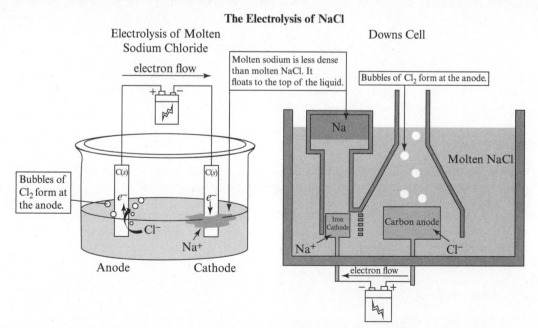

The Electrolysis of NaCl

Prediction of the products of electrolysis of molten salts is simple. The cation is reduced at the cathode and the anion is oxidized at the anode.

Prediction of the products of the electrolysis of aqueous solutions of electrolytes is more complicated, because the electrolysis of water competes with the reaction of the electrolyte.

At the cathode, the reduction of water is more easily accomplished than the reduction of the cations of active metals. The **active metals** are the group IA metals, in addition to Ca, Sr, and Ba. Formation of H_2 and OH^- is the reaction that occurs.

$$2\,H_2O + 2\,e^- \rightarrow H_2 + 2\,OH^- \qquad \text{(occurs preferentially at the cathode)}$$
$$Na^+ + e^- \rightarrow Na \qquad \text{(does not occur in aqueous solution)}$$

At the anode, the oxidation of water to form O_2 is more easily accomplished than the oxidation of polyatomic ions such as SO_4^{2-} and NO_3^-. Notice that the sulfur and nitrogen atoms in these anions are already highly oxidized. Sulfur has an oxidation number of +6 and nitrogen has an oxidation number of +5.

$$2\,H_2O \rightarrow O_2 + 4\,H^+ + 4\,e^- \qquad \text{(occurs preferentially at the anode)}$$

PRACTICE:

> An electrolytic cell is assembled in which an aqueous solution of silver nitrate is electrolyzed. Write and label the half reaction at the anode and at the cathode. Write the overall balanced equation. Is either of the electrodes gaining or losing mass? Why or why not?

The reduction of Ag^+ ions occurs at the cathode. Since silver is not a group IA or group IIA metal, the reduction of water is not a competing process.

$$\text{Cathode: } Ag^+ + e^- \rightarrow Ag$$

The oxidation water occurs at the anode. Nitrate, a polyatomic anion, is more difficult to oxidize than water.

$$\text{Anode: } 2\,H_2O \rightarrow O_2 + 4\,H^+ + 4\,e^-$$

The equation for reduction of silver must be multiplied by 4 in order to balance the number of electrons in the reactants and the products. After the addition of the two half reaction equations, the overall equation can be written.

$$\text{Overall: } 4\,Ag^+ + 2\,H_2O \rightarrow 4\,Ag + O_2 + 4\,H^+$$

The cathode, where Ag^+ is undergoing reduction to solid silver, is gaining mass; as the Ag^+ ions gain electrons, the neutral atoms plate onto the surface of the electrode. The oxidation of water at the anode produces oxygen gas, which bubbles out of the solution, and H^+ ions, which remain in the solution.

Faraday's Law

Faraday's law of electrolysis states that the number of moles of a product that can be formed in an electrolytic reaction has a stoichiometric relationship with the number of electrons supplied.

The number of electrons supplied in an electrolysis reaction can be determined by the amount of current supplied over a known amount of time. **Current**, I, is a measure of the amount of charge, q, transferred per unit time, t. It is measured in amperes (A). One **ampere** is equal to one coulomb (C) of charge per second.

$$I = \frac{q}{t}$$

$$1 \text{ ampere} = \frac{1 \text{ coulomb}}{1 \text{ second}}$$

The **Faraday constant,** *F,* is the amount of charge supplied by one mole of electrons. The equation for current and the value of Faraday's constant are both included on the *AP Chemistry Equations and Constants* sheet (pages 365–366).

$$F = \frac{96,485 \text{ coulombs}}{1 \text{ mol } e^-}$$

The answer to any quantitative question regarding the amount of products formed, reactants consumed, current, time, or charge can be determined using the equation for current, the balanced redox equation, and dimensional analysis.

Suppose the electrolysis of an aqueous solution of silver nitrate results in the deposit of a mass of 10.8 grams of silver at the cathode. How much current is required in order for this process to be complete in exactly 5.00 hours?

The balanced equation for the reduction of silver cations is

$$Ag^+ + e^- \rightarrow Ag$$

One mole of electrons is required to reduce one mole of silver cations. The charge, *q*, in coulombs is calculated first.

$$10.8 \text{ g Ag} \times \frac{1 \text{ mol Ag}}{107.87 \text{ g Ag}} \times \frac{1 \text{ mol } e^-}{1 \text{ mol Ag}} \times \frac{96,485 \text{ C}}{1 \text{ mol } e^-} = 9660 \text{ C}$$

Since the current is expressed as coulombs per second, the time must be converted to seconds.

$$5.00 \text{ h} \times \frac{3600 \text{ s}}{1 \text{ h}} = 1.80 \times 10^4 \text{ s}$$

The current is determined using the appropriate equation.

$$I = \frac{q}{t} = \frac{9660 \text{ C}}{1.80 \times 10^4 \text{ s}} = 0.537 \text{ A}$$

PRACTICE:

An electrolytic cell is constructed in which electrodes are placed into an aqueous solution of $CuSO_4$. A current of 3.00 A is applied. How long must the electrolysis proceed in order to plate 5.00 grams of copper at the cathode?

The balanced half reaction is needed to give the number of moles of electrons required for the reduction of one mole of copper atoms.

$$Cu^{2+} + 2 e^- \rightarrow Cu$$

In order to solve for time, begin with the number of grams of copper needed. Convert the grams of copper to moles, convert moles of copper to moles of electrons, and then use Faraday's constant to find the charge transfer required, *q*.

$$5.00 \text{ g Cu} \times \frac{1 \text{ mol Cu}}{63.55 \text{ g Cu}} \times \frac{2 \text{ mol } e^-}{1 \text{ mol Cu}} \times \frac{96,485 \text{ C}}{1 \text{ mol } e^-} = 1.52 \times 10^4 \text{ C}$$

$$(1.518253 \times 10^4)$$

The equation for current is rearranged to solve for time.

$$t = \frac{q}{I} = \frac{1.518253 \times 10^4 \ \cancel{C}}{3.00 \ \cancel{C} \cdot s^{-1}} = 5.06 \times 10^3 \ s$$

Redox Reactions in Energy Production

The flow of electrons between chemical species in redox reactions provides a means for doing useful technological and biochemical work. The combustion of hydrocarbons provides energy for manufacturing, heating, cooling, lighting, and transportation. Batteries provide a portable source of power for such devices as lights, computers, and phones. Biological systems harness the energy released in redox reactions to power the processes essential to life.

Fossil fuels such as petroleum, natural gas, and coal result from the decomposition of biological matter buried underground. They are the main source of energy in contemporary society. Energy is released when the electrons of C–C and C–H bonds are transferred to oxygen. The combustion of isooctane, for instance, takes place with a decrease in the oxidation number of oxygen and an increase in the oxidation number of carbon.

$$2 \ C_8H_{18} + 25 \ O_2 \rightarrow 16 \ CO_2 + 18 \ H_2O + energy$$

The carbon in this process goes from an oxidation state of $+\frac{9}{4}$ in C_8H_{18} to +4 in CO_2. Oxygen goes from an oxidation state of zero in O_2 to –2 in H_2O and in CO_2. In Big Idea 5 (Chapter 5, "Thermodynamics"), we will review how to calculate the amount of energy released in this reaction based on the numbers and types of bonds formed and broken.

Batteries are an additional source of energy that originates from redox reactions. A **battery** is a galvanic cell or series of galvanic cells that allows the movement of electrons from a species undergoing oxidation to a species undergoing reduction. The energy that is released is used to power an external process. One of the most familiar batteries are alkaline dry cell batteries. A zinc casing serves as the anode, and a graphite inner rod (or powdered graphite) serves as the cathode. Between the anode and the cathode is a paste of MnO_2 and KOH. The following reactions take place at the anode, where zinc is oxidized from Zn^0 to Zn^{2+}, and at the cathode, where manganese is reduced from Mn^{+4} to Mn^{+3}.

$$Zn + 2 \ OH^- \rightarrow Zn(OH)_2 + 2 \ e^- \qquad \text{(anode)}$$
$$2 \ MnO_2 + H_2O + 2 \ e^- \rightarrow Mn_2O_3 + 2 \ OH^- \qquad \text{(cathode)}$$

In biological systems, **catabolism** refers to the utilization of nutrient molecules to provide energy for cellular processes. (Catabolism is part of a more general process, **metabolism,** which is the sum of all fuel production and breakdown processes in a cell.) Living cells use fuel molecules such as glucose, C_6H_{12}, as a source of electrons. The electrons are removed by enzymes, or biological catalysts, which transfer the electrons to other chemical species such as O_2. This process is coupled to the synthesis of ATP, the cell's energy "currency," in mitochondria.

$$C_6H_{12}O_6 + 6 \ O_2 \ \rightleftharpoons \ 6 \ CO_2 + 6 \ H_2O + energy$$

Descriptive Chemistry

There are several chemical observations that have historically appeared on AP Chemistry exams. These include colors of various solutions, tests for gases and halogens, and colors of common pH indicators. Students have probably made many of these observations firsthand in their AP Chemistry lab work.

Tests for Common Gases

- Hydrogen gas, H_2, when produced in a test tube, makes a pop or "bark" when ignited with a burning splint.
- Carbon dioxide, CO_2, when produced in a test tube, extinguishes a burning splint.
- Oxygen gas, O_2, when produced in a test tube, reignites a glowing splint.

Tests for Acids and Bases

- **Litmus paper** turns red in contact with acids and blue in contact with bases.
- **Universal indicator paper** has a color range across the visible spectrum. Acids turn universal indicator red. The indicator changes from red to orange to green as solutions increase in pH from acidic to neutral (see Big Idea 6—Chapter 6, "Chemical Equilibrium"). More basic solutions turn universal indicator darker green to blue to purple.
- **Phenolphthalein** is colorless in acidic solutions and pink in basic solutions.

Colors of Various Oxidation States of Transition Metals

Although exam questions often refer to the colors of transition metals, students should not be concerned with memorizing the colors.

- Cr^{2+} ions tend to be blue, Cr^{3+} ions tend to be green, CrO_4^{2-} ions are yellow, and $Cr_2O_7^{2-}$ ions are orange.
- Mn^{2+} is pink, Mn^{6+} is green, and Mn^{7+} is purple.
- Fe^{3+} is light orange. When a pale yellow solution of thiocyanate, SCN^-, ions is added, the resulting $Fe(SCN)^{2+}$ complex is dark red.
- Cu^{2+} solutions are blue and Ni^{2+} solutions are green.
- When a few drops of aqueous ammonia are added to a solution of Cu^{2+}, a light blue precipitate forms. Upon continued addition of ammonia, the precipitate re-dissolves and the solution turns dark blue.

Flame Test Colors

A flame test is a qualitative test for the presence of a metal ion based on the metal's characteristic emission spectrum (see Big Idea 1—Chapter 1, "Structure of Matter"). A small sample of the compound to be tested is placed on a nichrome (nickel-chromium alloy) wire. The sample is then placed in a colorless flame and the color of the flame produced by the metal is observed. It is unlikely that students will need to draw on memory to answer questions about the color of a flame produced by a particular metal.

- Yellow flames are produced by Na^+.
- Red flames are produced by Li^+, Ca^{2+}, and Sr^{2+}.
- Violet flames are produced by K^+, Rb^+, and Cs^+.
- Green flames are produced by Cu^{2+} compounds other than halides (chlorides, bromides, and iodide). Green flames may also be indicative of Ba^{2+}.
- Blue flames are produced by copper(II) halides.
- White flames are produced by Mg^{2+}.

Halogens and Halides

- Fluorine gas, F_2, a highly reactive substance, is pale yellow-green. Chlorine gas is pale green. Bromine, a liquid at STP, is red-brown. Iodine, I_2, is a lustrous gray solid. When iodine sublimes, it forms a purple vapor.
- A test for halide ions, X^-, involves the addition of drops of aqueous $AgNO_3$ to the solution under investigation. A white or yellow precipitate is a positive test for halides.

$$Ag^+(aq) + X^-(aq) \rightarrow AgX(s)$$

Review Questions

Multiple Choice

1. Three 0.5-mL samples of different unknown clear, colorless solutions are contained in vials labeled A, B, and C. Twenty drops of an aqueous solution of ammonium chloride are added to each vial. Based on the following data, which statement is most likely to be true?

Vial	A	B	C
Observation	A gas is evolved, which turns damp litmus paper blue.	No detectable change occurs.	A white precipitate forms.

   A. A chemical change occurs in vial A, while the processes in vials B and C are physical.
   B. Chemical changes probably only occur in vials A and C.
   C. Chemical changes occur in all three vials.
   D. A chemical change only occurs in vial C.

Use the following particulate diagram to answer questions 2 and 3. The reaction takes place in aqueous solution, but water is not shown. The black circles represent copper, the gray circles represent nickel, and the white circles represent sulfate anions.

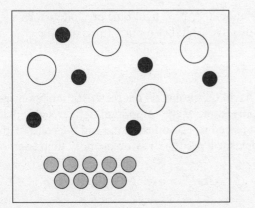 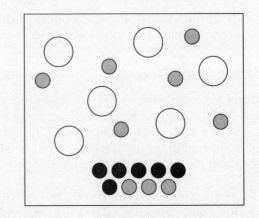

2. Which type of chemical reaction is most likely represented by the particulate diagram above?

   A. Synthesis
   B. Decomposition
   C. Redox
   D. Precipitation

3. Which of the following statements is true?

    A. Copper ions are the limiting reagent.
    B. Nickel ions are the limiting reagent.
    C. Solid copper is the limiting reagent.
    D. Solid nickel is the limiting reagent.

Refer to the unbalanced redox reaction between tin and periodate ions in acidic solution to answer questions 4 and 5.

$$Sn^{2+} + IO_4^- + H^+ \rightarrow Sn^{4+} + I^- + H_2O$$

4. Which statement regarding this reaction is true?

    A. Tin is being reduced.
    B. Iodine is being reduced.
    C. Oxygen is being reduced.
    D. Hydrogen is being reduced.

5. How many Sn^{2+} ions are required when the equation is balanced with the smallest possible whole-number coefficients?

    A. 1
    B. 2
    C. 4
    D. 8

6. For which of the following reactions is a net ionic equation least appropriate?

    A. A double replacement reaction between $MgSO_4$ and $NaOH$, in which a precipitate of $Mg(OH)_2$ forms
    B. A redox reaction between $NaClO$ and KI in an HCl solution to form I_2, KCl, $NaCl$, and water
    C. An acid-base reaction between H_3PO_4 and $NaOH$ to form Na_3PO_4 and H_2O
    D. A combustion reaction between C_2H_3F and oxygen, in which CO_2, H_2O, and HF are formed

Use the following equation for the oxidation of iron to answer questions 7 and 8. The enthalpy change for the formation of one mole of Fe_2O_3 by this synthesis reaction is –826 kJ·mol⁻¹.

$$\_\_ Fe + \_\_ O_2 \rightarrow \_\_ Fe_2O_3$$

7. What quantity of heat is transferred in this reaction when a 27.9-gram sample of iron reacts with 11.2 L of O_2 at STP?

    A. –103 kJ
    B. –207 kJ
    C. –275 kJ
    D. –413 kJ

8. Which of the following sketches best represents the potential energy profile for the reaction of iron with oxygen to form Fe_2O_3?

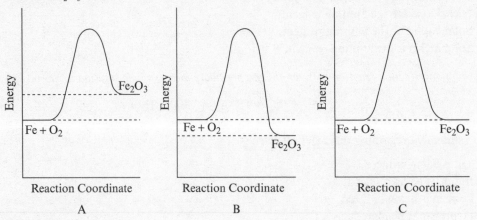

A   B   C

A.   Energy profile A
B.   Energy profile B
C.   Energy profile C
D.   The energy profile cannot be predicted based on the information given.

9. A student prepares 1.0 M aqueous solutions of each of the following salts: HCO_2Na, NH_4Cl, $NaNH_2$, and CaI_2. Which choice shows the correct ranking of the solutions from most acidic to most basic?

	Most Acidic			Most Basic
A.	HCO_2Na	NH_4Cl	$NaNH_2$	CaI_2
B.	HCO_2Na	NH_4Cl	CaI_2	$NaNH_2$
C.	NH_4Cl	CaI_2	HCO_2Na	$NaNH_2$
D.	NH_4Cl	HCO_2Na	$NaNH_2$	CaI_2

Use the following information to answer questions 10 and 11.

Phosphorus trichloride, PCl_3, a reagent used in organic chemistry, is synthesized by the reaction of white phosphorus, P_4, with chlorine gas, Cl_2. The data below shows the mass of PCl_3 formed when varying amounts of P_4 are used. The mass of chlorine is the same in each trial.

$$\_P_4 + \_Cl_2 \rightarrow \_PCl_3$$

Mass of PCl_3 Formed versus Mass of P_4 Reacted

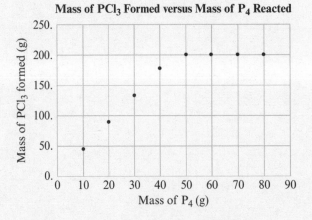

10. Which statement about the limiting reagent in these trials is correct?

- **A.** In the first four trials, phosphorus is the limiting reagent and chlorine is in excess.
- **B.** In the first four trials, chlorine is the limiting reagent and phosphorus is in excess.
- **C.** In the last four trials, stoichiometric ratios of phosphorus and chlorine are available to react.
- **D.** No reliable conclusion regarding the limiting reagent can be drawn from this data set.

11. What mass of chlorine is used in the trials?

- **A.** 39 grams
- **B.** 77 grams
- **C.** 103 grams
- **D.** 155 grams

12. The decomposition of $C_3H_5N_3O_9$ results in the formation of nitrogen, carbon dioxide, oxygen, and water.

$$4\,C_3H_5N_3O_9 \rightarrow 6\,N_2 + 10\,H_2O + 12\,CO_2 + O_2$$

If the volume of oxygen produced by the decomposition of 454.2 grams of $C_3H_5N_3O_9$ is 8.4 L at STP, what is the percent yield for this reaction? The molar mass of $C_3H_5N_3O_9$ is 227.1 g·mol^{-1}.

- **A.** 38%
- **B.** 67%
- **C.** 75%
- **D.** 100%

13. Atom economy is a measure of how much of the reactants in a reaction end up in the products. Assuming there is only one desired product in each case, for which type of reaction is the theoretical atom economy equal to 100%?

- **A.** Synthesis
- **B.** Decomposition
- **C.** Brønsted acid-base
- **D.** Double replacement

14. Consider the following redox potentials. Which of the reactions below is most thermodynamically favorable as written?

Half Reaction	E^o (V)
$2\,H_2O + 2\,e^- \rightarrow H_2 + 2\,OH^-$	−0.83
$Br_2 + 2\,e^- \rightarrow 2\,Br^-$	1.07
$Au^{3+} + 3\,e^- \rightarrow Au$	1.50

- **A.** $2\,Au^{3+} + 6\,Br^- \rightarrow 2\,Au + 3\,Br_2$
- **B.** $2\,Au + 6\,H_2O \rightarrow 3\,H_2 + 6\,OH^- + 2\,Au^{3+}$
- **C.** $3\,Br_2 + 2\,Au \rightarrow 6\,Br^- + 2\,Au^{3+}$
- **D.** $H_2 + 2\,OH^- + Br_2 \rightarrow 2\,Br^- + 2\,H_2O$

15. A student places a few drops of solutions of copper(II) sulfate, magnesium sulfate, and lead(II) nitrate into several small test tubes. The student places a sample of solid copper into a tube containing Mg^{2+} and another into a tube containing Pb^{2+}. The student places samples of solid lead into tubes containing Cu^{2+} and Mg^{2+}. Finally, the student places samples of solid magnesium into tubes containing Cu^{2+} and Pb^{2+}. The results of the experiment are tabulated below.

	$Cu^{2+}(aq)$	$Mg^{2+}(aq)$	$Pb^{2+}(aq)$
$Cu(s)$		No reaction	No reaction
$Mg(s)$	Reaction occurs		Reaction occurs
$Pb(s)$	Reaction occurs	No reaction	

Based on this data, which of the following rankings of the half reactions is the correct order of standard reduction potentials, from most negative to most positive?

	Lowest (Most Negative) Reduction Potential		Highest (Most Positive) Reduction Potential
A.	$Cu^{2+} + 2\,e^- \rightarrow Cu$	$Pb^{2+} + 2\,e^- \rightarrow Pb$	$Mg^{2+} + 2\,e^- \rightarrow Mg$
B.	$Mg^{2+} + 2\,e^- \rightarrow Mg$	$Pb^{2+} + 2\,e^- \rightarrow Pb$	$Cu^{2+} + 2\,e^- \rightarrow Cu$
C.	$Pb^{2+} + 2\,e^- \rightarrow Pb$	$Cu^{2+} + 2\,e^- \rightarrow Cu$	$Mg^{2+} + 2\,e^- \rightarrow Mg$
D.	$Mg^{2+} + 2\,e^- \rightarrow Mg$	$Cu^{2+} + 2\,e^- \rightarrow Cu$	$Pb^{2+} + 2\,e^- \rightarrow Pb$

16. A 2.0-A current is passed through a solution of $M(NO_3)_2$ for exactly 2 hours and 42 minutes. If 6.4 grams of metal are plated onto the cathode, what is the identity of the metal cation, M^{2+}?

A. Fe^{2+}
B. Cu^{2+}
C. Zn^{2+}
D. Sn^{2+}

17. An aqueous solution of K_2SO_4 is electrolyzed in a slightly acidic solution. Which statement correctly describes the reaction that occurs?

A. Water is reduced at the cathode and water is oxidized at the anode.
B. K^+ is reduced at the cathode and water is oxidized at the anode.
C. Water is reduced at the cathode and sulfate is oxidized at the anode.
D. K^+ is reduced at the cathode and sulfate is oxidized at the anode.

18. Which of the following choices shows a conjugate acid/conjugate base pair?

A. HCO_3/CO_2
B. H_3O^+/OH^-
C. $H_2AsO_4^-/HAsO_4^{2-}$
D. H_3AsO_4/AsO_4^{2-}

19. The reaction between 3.0 liters of $SO_2(g)$ and 1.0 liter of O_2 gas in a piston produces the maximum amount of $SO_3(g)$. At constant temperature and pressure, which statement describes the change in the volume of the piston?

A. The volume of the piston increased by 2.0 liters.
B. The volume of the piston increased by 1.0 liter.
C. The volume of the piston decreased by 2.0 liters.
D. The volume of the piston decreased by 1.0 liter.

20. A student is trying to identify the metal cation present in a clear, colorless aqueous solution. When sodium hydroxide is added to a small aliquot of the unknown, no precipitate forms. Which course of action would give the student the most information about the identity of the cation?

    A. Evaporate the water from the sample and subject it to a flame test.

    B. Add a few drops of ammonia to a small aliquot of the sample.

    C. Add a few drops of silver nitrate to a small aliquot of the sample.

    D. Add a crystal of I_2 to a small aliquot of the sample.

Long Free Response

1. A study is conducted in which varying volumes of 0.500 M sodium hypochlorite, NaOCl, solution are added to varying volumes of a sodium thiosulfate solution. The sodium thiosulfate is 0.500 M $Na_2S_2O_3$ in 0.200 M NaOH. The products of the reaction are sodium sulfate, sodium chloride, and water.

    a.   **i.** Write and balance the net ionic equation for the reaction between OCl^-, $S_2O_3^{2-}$ and OH^- to form SO_4^{2-}, Cl^- and H_2O.

          ii. What advantage does the net ionic equation have over the total equation?

    b. The initial temperature of the solutions is 25.0 °C. When various volumes of the solutions are mixed, the resulting temperature change is recorded. Is this reaction endothermic or exothermic? Explain your answer based on the tabulated data below.

Trial	Volume of 0.500 M NaOCl (mL)	Volume of 0.500 M $Na_2S_2O_3$ (mL)	Final Temperature (°C)
1	0	50.0	25.0
2	5.0	45.0	28.9
3	10.0	40.0	33.1
4	15.0	35.0	36.3
5	20.0	30.0	39.7
6	25.0	25.0	43.8
7	30.0	20.0	47.6
8	35.0	15.0	52.6
9	40.0	10.0	56.9
10	45.0	5.0	37.0
11	50.0	0	25.0

    c. A plot of the temperature changes for the trials is constructed. Explain the shape of the plot in terms of limiting reagent before and after trial 9.

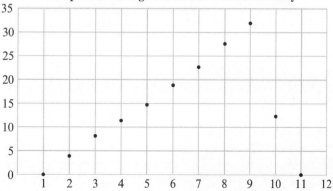

Temperature Change versus Reaction Stoichiometry

    d. What conclusion about reagent ratio and theoretical yield can be drawn from the maximum temperature change in trial 9?

    e. The final volume of the mixture is kept constant throughout the trials. Why is it important to maintain a constant volume throughout the experiment?

Short Free Response

2. Aspirin is a common pain-relieving medication. A student synthesizes a sample of aspirin, acetylsalicylic acid (ASA) by reacting salicylic acid (SA) with acetic anhydride (AA).

Aspirin Synthesis

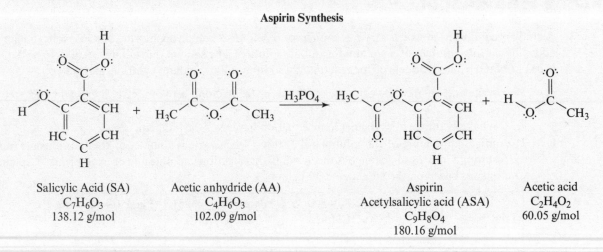

Salicylic Acid (SA)	Acetic anhydride (AA)	Aspirin	Acetic acid
$C_7H_6O_3$	$C_4H_6O_3$	Acetylsalicylic acid (ASA)	$C_2H_4O_2$
138.12 g/mol	102.09 g/mol	$C_9H_8O_4$	60.05 g/mol
		180.16 g/mol	

The student begins by heating 2.00 grams of salicylic acid with 5.00 mL acetic anhydride ($d = 1.08$ g·mL^{-1}). The reagents are mixed with a catalytic amount of H_3PO_4. This means that the H_3PO_4 facilitates the reaction but it is not consumed. This will be discussed in Big Idea 4 (Chapter 4, "Kinetics"). When the reaction is complete, the student dilutes the mixture with water and cools it to 0 °C in an ice bath.

The student filters the crystals that form and washes them with additional cold water. This removes any leftover acetic anhydride, H_3PO_4, and acetic acid from the synthesis. The solid is dried. It is composed of a mixture of ASA and unreacted SA.

The unreacted SA can be quantified by spectrophotometry. When a solution of $FeCl_3$ is added to the mixture of ASA and SA, the Fe^{3+} complexes with the unreacted SA to produce a violet solution. The Fe^{3+} does not react with ASA.

The concentration of SA can be determined using a Beer's law analysis. The standard absorbance curve of known concentrations of pure SA with $FeCl_3$ is shown below. The student finds that when excess $FeCl_3$ solution is added to a 0.220-gram sample of the ASA/SA mixture to give a final volume of 200. mL, the absorbance is 0.497.

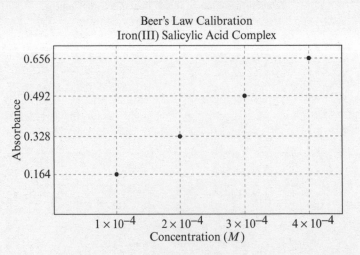

Beer's Law Calibration
Iron(III) Salicylic Acid Complex

a. Aspirin is soluble in water at high temperature but forms insoluble crystals at 0 °C. Explain this observation in terms of the kinetic energy of solvent and solute particles. What does this suggest about the enthalpy of dissolution of aspirin in water? (*Hint:* This requires knowledge of Big Idea 6—Chapter 6, "Chemical Equilibrium.")

b. What is the theoretical yield of ASA from the student's synthesis in moles?

c. What is the concentration of SA in the 200.-mL solution?

d. What is the percent SA by mass in the ASA/SA mixture?

3. A voltaic cell is constructed according to the cell diagram: $Ni \mid Ni^{2+}$ (1.00 M) $\parallel Ag^+$ (1.00 M) $\mid Ag$.

Half Reaction	Standard Reduction Potential, E^o (V)
$Ag^+ + e^- \rightarrow Ag$	0.80
$Ni^{2+} + 2\,e^- \rightarrow Ni$	−0.25

a.   i. Write the balanced net ionic equation for the reaction.

     ii. Determine the cell potential, E^o_{cell}.

b. Which electrode is losing mass? Explain what is happening to this mass.

c. When the concentration of Ag^+ has reached 0.822 M, what is the concentration of Ni^{2+}?

Answers and Explanations

Multiple Choice

1. **B.** (EK 3.C.1) Chemical changes probably only occur in vials A and C. The gas formation in vial A and the precipitate formation in vial C are indicative of chemical changes. The absence of any change in vial B is evidence that no chemical change is occurring, but further testing would be required to prove this definitively. The best answer is choice B.

2. **C.** (EK 3.A.1, 3.B.1, 3.B.3) Copper starts out in the solution. The copper ions are found in a 1:1 ratio with sulfate ions, which have a −2 charge, so the copper ions must be Cu^{2+}. The nickel is shown as a solid crystal at the bottom of the container. On the product side, some of the nickel has been replaced by copper, which has been reduced. The nickel that has been replaced has entered the solution as Ni^{2+}. The net ionic equation for the reaction shown is

$$Cu^{2+} + Ni \rightarrow Cu + Ni^{2+}$$

3. **A.** (EK 3.A.2) Copper ions gain electrons from nickel and replace them as the metallic solid. In this drawing, Cu^{2+} ions react with Ni^0. The Cu^{2+} is completely consumed to form products, but some Ni^0 remains. The copper ions, therefore, are the limiting reagent.

4. **B.** (EK 3.B.3) Iodine is going from a +7 oxidation state in the periodate ion to a −1 oxidation state as iodide. This decrease in oxidation number is due to a gain of electrons.

5. **C.** (EK 3.B.3) The coefficient for tin is 4. The balanced redox equation as determined by the half reaction method is shown.

$$4\,Sn^{2+} + IO_4^- + 8\,H^+ \rightarrow 4\,Sn^{4+} + I^- + 4\,H_2O$$

6. **D.** (EK 3.A.1) The presence of spectator ions, which do not participate in the chemistry of a reaction, necessitate the use of net ionic equations. The only reaction in which there are no spectator ions is the last equation, the combustion of C_2H_3F. Na^+ and SO_4^{2-} are spectators in the double replacement reaction, K^+ and Na^+ are spectators in the redox reaction, and Na^+ is a spectator in the acid-base reaction.

7. B. (EK 3.A.2, 3.C.2) The equation for the reaction must be balanced first.

$$4\ Fe + 3\ O_2 \rightarrow 2\ Fe_2O_3$$

The problem gives the amount of heat released by one mole of Fe_2O_3, as indicated by the negative value of the enthalpy change. The next step in the solution is determining the number of moles of Fe_2O_3 that are generated based on the amounts of starting materials, 27.9 grams of iron and 11.2 L of O_2 at STP.

$$27.9\ \text{g Fe} \times \frac{1\ \text{mol Fe}}{55.85\ \text{g Fe}} \times \frac{2\ \text{mol Fe}_2O_3}{4\ \text{mol Fe}} = 0.250\ \text{mol Fe}_2O_3$$

$$11.2\ \text{L O}_2 \times \frac{1\ \text{mol O}_2}{22.4\ \text{L O}_2} \times \frac{2\ \text{mol Fe}_2O_3}{3\ \text{mol O}_2} = 0.333\ \text{mol Fe}_2O_3$$

Iron is the limiting reagent. The amount of heat released is calculated from the theoretical yield of Fe_2O_3.

$$0.250\ \text{mol Fe}_2O_3 \times \frac{-826\ kJ}{1\ \text{mol Fe}_2O_3} = -207\ kJ\ \text{released}$$

8. B. (EK 3.C.2) Energy profile B represents an exothermic reaction. The negative enthalpy change indicates a product energy that is lower than the energy of the reactants, so heat has been released over the course of the reaction.

9. C. (EK 3.B.2) NH_4^+ ions are slightly acidic, aqueous CaI_2 is neutral, HCO_2^- is weakly basic, and NH_2^- is strongly basic. It is best to approach this problem by first recognizing that Na^+, Cl^-, Ca^{2+}, and I^- do not affect the pH of the solution since they are the conjugates of strong acids (**HCl** and **HI**) and bases (**NaOH** and **Ca(OH)$_2$**). NH_4^+, is the conjugate acid of ammonia, a weak base (NH_3). It forms a weakly acidic solution. CaI_2, is composed of Ca^{2+}, the cation of a strong base, $Ca(OH)_2$, and I^-, the conjugate base of a strong acid, HI, so it is a neutral salt. HCO_2^-, is the conjugate base of a weak acid, HCO_2H. It forms a weakly basic solution. NH_2^-, is the conjugate base of ammonia, which is already weakly basic and is an amphoteric species. The deprotonated form of ammonia is strongly basic, and this solute is the most basic of the four species.

10. A. (EK 3.A.2) The amount of PCl_3 formed levels off when the stoichiometric ratio of P_4 to Cl_2 is reached. Before this point, the limiting reagent is P_4, because as more P_4 is added, more product is formed. After this point, the amount of product formed does not increase with increasing quantities of P_4. In these cases, chlorine is the limiting reagent.

11. D. (EK 3.A.2) The first step in any stoichiometry problem is to balance the chemical equation.

$$P_4 + 6\ Cl_2 \rightarrow 4\ PCl_3$$

The maximum amount of chlorine available is used in the final four trials to form the maximum amount of product, 200. grams. The number of grams of chlorine can be calculated from the number of grams of product that are formed.

$$200.\ \text{g PCl}_3 \times \frac{1\ \text{mol PCl}_3}{137.32\ \text{g PCl}_3} \times \frac{6\ \text{mol Cl}_2}{4\ \text{mol PCl}_3} \times \frac{70.90\ \text{g Cl}_2}{1\ \text{mol Cl}_2} = 155\ g$$

Without a calculator, we can make an estimation. The molar mass of chlorine is approximately $\frac{140}{2}$.

$$200 \times \frac{1}{140} \times \frac{3}{2} \times \frac{140}{2} = \frac{300}{2} = 150$$

The closest choice is 155 grams.

12. **C.** (EK 3.A.2) Theoretical yield and actual yield are needed in order to determine percent yield. The theoretical yield of oxygen is determined using the mass of the reagent.

$$454.2 \text{ g C}_3\text{H}_5\text{N}_3\text{O}_9 \times \frac{1 \text{ mol C}_3\text{H}_5\text{N}_3\text{O}_9}{227.1 \text{ g C}_3\text{H}_5\text{N}_3\text{O}_9} \times \frac{1 \text{ mol O}_2}{4 \text{ mol C}_3\text{H}_5\text{N}_3\text{O}_9} \times \frac{22.4 \text{ L O}_2}{1 \text{ mol O}_2} = 11.2 \text{ L O}_2$$

The actual yield of O_2 is 8.4 L.

$$\frac{8.4 \text{ L O}_2}{11.2 \text{ L O}_2} \times 100\% = 75\%$$

13. **A.** (EK 3.A.2, 3.B.1) In a synthesis reaction, every atom in the starting material is theoretically incorporated into the products. This should be a 100% atom economical process. For each of the other types of reactions, multiple products are formed. If only one of the products is desired in these other processes, the atom economy is less than 100%.

14. **D.** (EK 3.C.3) The reaction with the most positive cell potential, $E°_{cell}$, is the most spontaneous as written. Inspect the direction of each half reaction to determine which potential applies to the cathode and which applies to the anode.

	Reduced Species (Cathode)	Oxidized Species (Anode)	$E°_{cathode} - E°_{anode} = E°_{cell}$ (V)
A.	Au^{3+}	Br^-	$1.50 - 1.07 = 0.43$
B.	H_2O	Au	$-0.83 - 1.50 = -2.33$
C.	Br_2	Au	$1.07 - 1.50 = -0.43$
D.	Br_2	H_2	$1.07 - (-0.83) = 1.90$

The reaction with the highest cell potential is the redox reaction between Br_2 and H_2 in basic solution (choice D).

15. **B.** (EK 3.C.3) The solids in this question have oxidation states of zero, and the ions have oxidation states of +2. If a reaction occurs, the solid metal is oxidized and the ion is reduced in a single replacement reaction. Cu^{2+} has the highest reduction potential because it is reduced by both Mg and Pb. Mg^{2+} has the lowest reduction potential; it is reduced by neither Cu nor Pb.

16. **B.** (EK 3.C.3) The number of electrons transferred is determined using the equation for current. The equation relating current, charge, and time $\left(I = \dfrac{q}{t} \right)$ is found on the *AP Chemistry Equations and Constants* sheet (pages 365–366). The number of electrons transferred is used to calculate the number of moles of metal, M. The molar mass, *M*, of the metal can be obtained by dividing the mass by the number of moles of metal. The molar mass, 64 g/mol, most closely matches that of copper, so the metal cation is Cu^{2+}.

$$q = t \times I = (162 \text{ min}) \frac{60 \text{ s}}{1 \text{ min}} \times \frac{2.0 \text{ C}}{1 \text{ s}} \times \frac{1 \text{ mol } e^-}{96,485 \text{ C}} \times \frac{1 \text{ mol M}}{2 \text{ mol } e^-} = 0.101 \text{ mol M}$$

$$M = \frac{6.4}{0.101 \text{ mol}} = 64 \text{ g} \cdot \text{mol}^{-1}$$

Without a calculator, the calculation can be simplified. Using scientific notation is one way to deal with large numbers.

$$\frac{160 \times 60 \times 2}{96,000 \times 2} = \frac{9.6 \times 10^3}{9.6 \times 10^4} \approx 0.1$$

17. A. (EK 3.C.3) The electrolysis of a solution of K_2SO_4 will result in water being both oxidized and reduced. K^+ is an active group IA metal ion that accepts an electron with more difficulty than H_2O. SO_4^{2-} is a highly oxidized sulfur-species. The oxidation number of sulfur is +6. Water is oxidized more easily than SO_4^{2-}.

18. C. (EK 3.B.2) A conjugate acid/conjugate base pair is a pair of species in which one proton (H^+) can be transferred from the acid to the base. They differ by one H^+. For the $H_2AsO_4^-/HAsO_4^{2-}$ pair, a single H^+ is transferred from $H_2AsO_4^-$ to produce $HAsO_4^{2-}$.

19. D. (EK 3.A.1, 3.A.2) The chemical equation must first be written and balanced.

$$2\,SO_2 + O_2 \rightarrow 2\,SO_3$$

Next, determine the limiting reagent.

$$3.0\ \text{L}\,\cancel{SO_2} \times \frac{2\ \text{L}\ SO_3}{2\ \text{L}\,\cancel{SO_2}} = 3.0\ \text{L}\ SO_3$$

$$1.0\ \text{L}\,\cancel{O_2} \times \frac{2\ \text{L}\ SO_3}{1\ \text{L}\,\cancel{O_2}} = 2.0\ \text{L}\ SO_3$$

The maximum amount of SO_3 that can be produced is 2.0 L. O_2 is the limiting reagent, so the entire volume of O_2 reacts. The amount of SO_2 that reacts must be calculated.

$$2.0\ \text{L}\,\cancel{SO_3} \times \frac{2\ \text{L}\ SO_2}{2\ \text{L}\,\cancel{SO_3}} = 2.0\ \text{L}\ SO_2$$

One methodical approach to determining how many liters are present at the end of the process is to set up a table to take an inventory of the species present before and after the reaction. Equilibrium (or "R.I.C.E.") tables will be considered in Big Idea 6 (Chapter 6, "Chemical Equilibrium").

Species	SO_2	O_2	SO_3
Before Reaction	3.0 L	1.0 L	0 L
Change	–2.0 L	–1.0 L	+2.0 L
After Reaction	1.0 L	0 L	2.0 L

Before the reaction, there are 4.0 L of gas ($SO_2 + O_2$) in the piston; after the reaction, there are 3.0 L of gas ($SO_2 + SO_3$). There is a decrease of 1.0 L.

20. A. (EK 3.C.1) The addition of sodium hydroxide would cause any cation other than that of a strong soluble base to precipitate, but the group IA metals and the heavier group IIA metals would remain in solution. Adding ammonia, nitrate, or I_2 to any of these cations would have no effect. A flame test, however, would result in different flame colors for different cations. Yellow flames are produced by Na^+; red flames are produced by Li^+, Ca^{2+}, and Sr^{2+}; and violet flames are produced by K^+, Rb^+, and Cs^+. Of the methods listed, the flame test would provide the most information about the identity of the cation.

Long Free Response

1. a. i. (EK 3.B.3) The change in oxidation states of the atoms in the species shows that this is a redox reaction in basic solution.

First, write the unbalanced net ionic equation. Notice that the oxidation number of sulfur goes from +2 to +3, and the oxidation number of chlorine goes from +1 to –1. Sulfur is oxidized and chromium is reduced. Recognizing that Na^+ is always a spectator ion in aqueous solution will expedite the task.

$$OCl^- + S_2O_3^{2-} + OH^- \rightarrow SO_4^{2-} + Cl^- + H_2O$$

Divide the reaction into oxidation and reduction half reactions. Balance all atoms other than hydrogen and oxygen.

$$\text{oxidation: } S_2O_3^{2-} \rightarrow 2\,SO_4^{2-} \qquad \text{reduction: } OCl^- \rightarrow Cl^-$$

Balance oxygen by adding H_2O.

$$S_2O_3^{2-} + 5\,H_2O \rightarrow 2\,SO_4^{2-} \qquad OCl^- \rightarrow Cl^- + H_2O$$

Balance hydrogen by adding H^+.

$$S_2O_3^{2-} + 5\,H_2O \rightarrow 2\,SO_4^{2-} + 10\,H^+ \qquad OCl^- + 2\,H^+ \rightarrow Cl^- + H_2O$$

Balance charge by adding electrons.

$$S_2O_3^{2-} + 5\,H_2O \rightarrow 2\,SO_4^{2-} + 10\,H^+ + 8\,e^- \qquad OCl^- + 2\,H^+ + 2\,e^- \rightarrow Cl^- + H_2O$$

Multiply the half reactions by a factor that will equalize the number of electrons.

$$1(S_2O_3^{2-} + 5\,H_2O \rightarrow 2\,SO_4^{2-} + 10\,H^+ + 8\,e^-) \qquad 4(OCl^- + 2\,H^+ + 2\,e^- \rightarrow Cl^- + H_2O)$$

$$S_2O_3^{2-} + 5\,H_2Ov\,2\,SO_4^{2-} + 10\,H^+ + 8\,e^- \qquad 4\,OCl^- + 8\,H^+ + 8\,e^- \rightarrow 4\,Cl^- + 4\,H_2O$$

Add the half reactions back together. The electrons on both sides must cancel.

$$S_2O_3^{2-} + 5\,H_2O + 4\,OCl^- + \cancel{8\,H^+} + \cancel{8\,e^-} \rightarrow 2\,SO_4^{2-} + {}^2\cancel{10}\,H^+ + \cancel{8\,e^-} + 4\,Cl^- + 4\,H_2O$$

$$S_2O_3^{2-} + 5\,H_2O + 4\,OCl^- \rightarrow 2\,SO_4^{2-} + 2\,H^+ + 4\,Cl^- + 4\,H_2O$$

The reaction is in basic solution. Add enough OH^- to both sides of the equation to neutralize all the H^+. Simplify the number of water molecules.

$$S_2O_3^{2-} + 5\,H_2O + 4\,OCl^- + 2\,OH^- \rightarrow 2\,SO_4^{2-} + 2\,H^+ + 4\,Cl^- + 4\,H_2O + 2\,OH^-$$

$$S_2O_3^{2-} + 5\,\cancel{H_2O} + 4\,OCl^- + 2\,OH^- \rightarrow 2\,SO_4^{2-} + 4\,Cl^- + {}^1\cancel{6}\,H_2O$$

$$\mathbf{S_2O_3^{2-} + 4\,OCl^- + 2\,OH^- \rightarrow 2\,SO_4^{2-} + 4\,Cl^- + H_2O}$$

ii. (EK 3.A.1) The net ionic equation has the advantage of omitting spectator ions that do not undergo any reaction.

b. (EK 3.C.2) An increase in temperature reflects a transfer of heat from the reacting system to the thermometer, which is part of the surroundings. In all cases when reactants are mixed, heat is given off, so this reaction is exothermic and energy is released as a product of the process.

c. (EK 3.A.2) Before trial 9, the heat released increases as the ratio of $S_2O_3^{2-}$ to OCl^- increases. In these trials, OCl^- is the limiting reagent since adding more OCl^- from one trial to the next increases the amount of heat released. After trial 9, $S_2O_3^{2-}$ is the limiting reagent. At this point, there is not enough $S_2O_3^{2-}$ to react with the larger quantity of OCl^-.

d. (EK 3.A.2) The maximum temperature change in trial 9 indicates that a perfect stoichiometric ratio of OCl^- and $S_2O_3^{2-}$ has been added. The concentrations of both reactants are the same, so the 4:1 volume ratio of trial 9 corresponds to a 4:1 mole ratio of OCl^- to $S_2O_3^{2-}$. This means that the maximum theoretical yield is expected.

e. (EK 3.C.2, 5.B.2) It is important to maintain a constant final volume in this experiment so that no correction must be made for heat transferred to varying amounts of the solvent. If more solvent was available in a trial the same amount of heat would be released in the reaction, but more heat would be transferred to the solvent. This would result in a smaller heat transfer to the thermometer to register as a temperature change relative to a trial with a smaller volume of solvent.

Short Free Response

2. a. (EK 2.A.3, 5.A.1, 6.B.1) Aspirin is more soluble at high temperatures because the average kinetic energy of aspirin and water particles is greater, causing an increase in the number of collisions that are energetic enough to disrupt solute-solute intermolecular forces. This suggests that the dissolution is an endothermic process. An endothermic dissolution process is shifted toward products when additional heat is supplied to the system. This is an application of Le Chatelier's principle, which says that when a stress is applied to a system at equilibrium, the equilibrium shifts in such a way as to relieve that stress.

b. (EK 3.A.2) The theoretical yield is determined by finding the number of moles of aspirin expected if each reactant was converted completely to product.

$$2.00 \text{ g SA} \times \frac{1 \text{ mol SA}}{138.12 \text{ g SA}} \times \frac{1 \text{ mol ASA}}{1 \text{ mol SA}} = 0.0145 \text{ mol ASA}$$

$$5.00 \text{ mL AA} \times \frac{1.08 \text{ g AA}}{1 \text{ mL AA}} \times \frac{1 \text{ mol AA}}{102.09 \text{ g AA}} \times \frac{1 \text{ mol ASA}}{1 \text{ mol AA}} = 0.0529 \text{ mol ASA}$$

Less aspirin (ASA) is expected from the complete reaction of SA than from that of AA, so SA is the limiting reagent. The theoretical yield of ASA is 0.0145 mole.

c. (EK 1.D.3) The slope of the straight line from the standard curve is equal to ab.

$$ab = \frac{\Delta A}{\Delta c} = \frac{0.656 - 0.164}{4 \times 10^{-4} M - 1 \times 10^{-4} M} = 1640 \ M^{-1}$$

The concentration is found by rearranging the Beer's law equation and using the measured absorbance, A, and the slope, ab, of the standard curve to solve for c.

$$c = \frac{A}{ab} = \frac{0.497}{1640 \ M^{-1}} = 3.03 \times 10^{-4} \ M$$

d. (EK 1.E.2, 2.A.3) The mass of SA is needed to determine the percent by mass in the mixture. This can be determined from the volume and the concentration.

$$200. \text{ mL solution} \times \frac{1 \text{ L solution}}{1000 \text{ mL solution}} \times \frac{3.03 \times 10^{-4} \text{ mol SA}}{1 \text{ L solution}} \times \frac{138.12 \text{ g SA}}{1 \text{ mol SA}} = 0.00837 \text{ g SA}$$

$$\frac{0.00837 \text{ g SA}}{0.220 \text{ g mixture}} \times 100\% = 3.81\% \text{ SA by mass}$$

3. a. i. (EK 3.B.3, 3.C.3) The balanced net ionic equation is

$$\text{Ni} + 2\,\text{Ag}^+ \rightarrow \text{Ni}^{2+} + 2\,\text{Ag}$$

ii. (EK 3.C.3) One reliable method for finding the cell potential is as follows.

$$E^\circ_{\text{cell}} = E^\circ_{\text{cathode}} - E^\circ_{\text{anode}} = 0.80 \text{ V} - (-0.25 \text{ V}) = 1.05 \text{ V}$$

b. (EK 3.C.3) Mass is being lost from the anode, the electrode where oxidation of nickel solid to Ni^{2+} is occurring. As the electrons leave the nickel and it is converted to cations, it becomes soluble in the aqueous solution. The Ni^{2+} ions leave the solid anode and enter the solution.

c. (EK 3.A.2) Both Ag^+ and Ni^{2+} begin as 1.00 M solutions. As Ag^+ is reduced, its concentration decreases, and as nickel is oxidized, the Ni^{2+} concentration increases. When the concentration of Ag^+ has fallen to 0.822 M, the amount of Ag^+ per liter that has reacted is the difference between the initial concentration and the new concentration.

$$[\text{Ag}^+] = 1.00\ M - 0.822\ M = 0.178\ M\ \text{Ag}^+$$

The amount of Ni^{2+} formed is determined by the reaction stoichiometry.

$$\frac{0.178\ \text{mol Ag}^+\ \text{reacted}}{1\ \text{L solution}} \times \frac{1\ \text{mol Ni}^{2+}\ \text{formed}}{2\ \text{mol Ag}^+\ \text{reacted}} = \frac{0.0890\ \text{mol Ni}^{2+}\ \text{formed}}{1\ \text{L solution}}$$

The new concentration of Ni^{2+} is the sum of the concentration formed as a result of the redox reaction and the initial concentration.

$$[\text{Ni}^{2+}] = 1.00\ M + 0.0890\ M = 1.09\ M$$

Chapter 4

Kinetics (Big Idea 4)

Big Idea 4: Chemical kinetics is the study of the factors that influence the rates of chemical reactions

Chemical reactions occur at a wide variety of speeds. The explosive reaction of gunpowder in fireworks occurs almost instantly, while the decomposition of diamond to graphite occurs on a geologic timescale. **Chemical kinetics** is the study of the rates of reactions. The manner in which molecules collide, the energy with which those collisions occur, and the stepwise sequence of events that lead to a particular transformation are all within the scope of kinetics.

Rates of Reactions

A **rate** is a change in a quantity per unit time. A familiar example is the rate that is displayed on the speedometer in a car. This rate refers to change in position over time. If a car is travelling at 70 miles per hour, then in 1 hour the car's position has changed by 70 miles.

In chemistry, the **rate of a reaction** is expressed as a change in amounts of reactants or products per unit time. As an aid to visualization, imagine a catering service is preparing sandwiches at a rate of one sandwich per minute according to the following "equation."

$$2 \text{ slices of bread} + 3 \text{ slices of cheese} \rightarrow 1 \text{ sandwich}$$

The rate of sandwich production is expressed as a change in quantity per unit time.

$$\text{rate of sandwich production} = \frac{\text{sandwiches}}{\text{time}} = \frac{1 \text{ sandwich}}{\text{minute}}$$

The rate of sandwich production can be related to the rate of disappearance of bread and cheese slices. Since the amounts of bread and cheese decrease as sandwiches are produced, Δ bread and Δ cheese are less than zero. The rates of change of the ingredients are negative.

As one sandwich is produced, two slices of bread disappear. Alternatively stated, the rate of sandwich production is one-half the rate of bread disappearance.

$$\text{rate of sandwich production} = -\frac{1}{2} \frac{\text{bread}}{\text{time}}$$

As one sandwich is produced, three slices of cheese disappear. The rate of cheese disappearance is one-third the rate of sandwich production.

$$\text{rate of sandwich production} = -\frac{1}{3} \frac{\text{cheese}}{\text{time}}$$

By this analogy, for the general reaction

$$a\text{A} + b\text{B} \rightarrow c\text{C} + d\text{D}$$

the rate expression in terms of concentrations of reactants and products is:

$$\text{rate of reaction} = -\frac{1}{a} \frac{[\text{A}]}{t} = -\frac{1}{b} \frac{[\text{B}]}{t} = \frac{1}{c} \frac{[\text{C}]}{t} = \frac{1}{d} \frac{[\text{D}]}{t}$$

PRACTICE:

> The equation for a hypothetical reaction is shown below. Using the tabulated data provided, determine the coefficients b, c, and d.

$$3\,A + b\,B \rightarrow c\,C + d\,D$$

Change	Rate of Change ($M \cdot s^{-1}$)
$\dfrac{\Delta[A]}{\Delta t}$	−0.750
$\dfrac{\Delta[B]}{\Delta t}$	−1.00
$\dfrac{\Delta[C]}{\Delta t}$	0.500
$\dfrac{\Delta[D]}{\Delta t}$	0.250

Since the coefficient of A is known, the rate of change of the concentration of A can be used to determine the rate of the reaction.

$$\text{rate of reaction} = -\frac{1}{a}\left(\frac{\Delta[A]}{\Delta t}\right) = -\frac{1}{3}\left(-0.750\ M \cdot s^{-1}\right) = 0.250\ M \cdot s^{-1}$$

Once the rate of reaction is known, it can be used to determine the coefficients b, c, and d.

$$0.250\ M \cdot s^{-1} = -\frac{1}{b}\left(-1.00\ M \cdot s^{-1}\right)$$
$$b = 4$$
$$0.250\ M \cdot s^{-1} = \frac{1}{c}\left(0.500\ M \cdot s^{-1}\right)$$
$$c = 2$$
$$0.250\ M \cdot s^{-1} = \frac{1}{d}\left(0.250\ M \cdot s^{-1}\right)$$
$$d = 1$$

Consider the following hypothetical reaction between reactants A and B.

$$A + B \rightarrow C + D$$

At any time in the reaction, the **instantaneous rate** with respect to a reactant or product is given by the slope of the tangent line to the concentration versus time curve. Let's calculate the instantaneous rate of disappearance of B at 1 second and at 5 seconds of reaction time.

The Concentration of B as a Function of Time

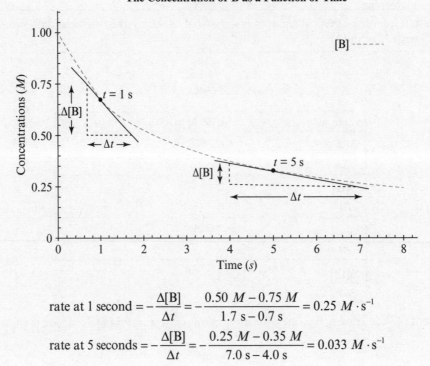

$$\text{rate at 1 second} = -\frac{\Delta[B]}{\Delta t} = -\frac{0.50\ M - 0.75\ M}{1.7\ s - 0.7\ s} = 0.25\ M \cdot s^{-1}$$

$$\text{rate at 5 seconds} = -\frac{\Delta[B]}{\Delta t} = -\frac{0.25\ M - 0.35\ M}{7.0\ s - 4.0\ s} = 0.033\ M \cdot s^{-1}$$

Notice also that the rate of disappearance of B decreases with time.

PRACTICE:

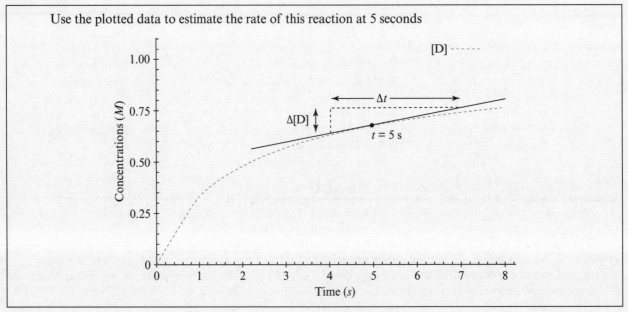

Use the plotted data to estimate the rate of this reaction at 5 seconds

The slope of the tangent line at 5 seconds is used to calculate the rate.

$$\text{rate at 5 seconds} = \frac{\Delta[D]}{\Delta t} = \frac{0.75\ M\ -\ 0.65\ M}{7.0\ \text{s} - 4.0\ \text{s}} = 0.033\ M \cdot \text{s}^{-1}$$

Now, imagine another hypothetical reaction between reactants A and B in aqueous solution.

$$A + 2\,B \rightarrow C + 2\,D$$

The concentrations of the reactants and products can be measured and plotted as a function of time.

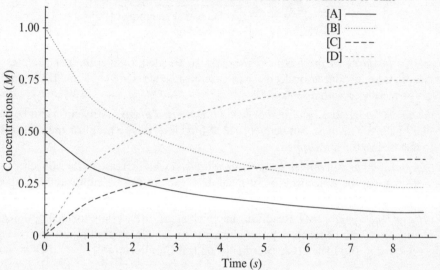

The rate of disappearance of B at any instant is twice the rate of the disappearance of A, and the rate of appearance of D is twice the rate of the appearance of C. In this case, the rates of disappearance of reactants and the rates of appearance of products are decreasing with time. In other words, as concentrations of reactants decrease, the rate of the reaction also decreases. When the concentrations of reactants and products stop changing, after 8 seconds in this case, equilibrium has been established. At **equilibrium,** the rates of the forward and reverse reactions are no longer changing, (chemical reactions proceed both in the forward and in the reverse direction; the reversibility of chemical reactions will be the focus of Big Idea 6—Chapter 6, "Chemical Equilibrium"). In the plot above, equilibrium is reached after about 8 seconds.

Measuring the Rates of Reactions

There are several methods for determining the rate of a chemical reaction experimentally, and all of them involve measuring the change in some observable quantity over time.

Some quantities that can be monitored to deduce the rate of a reaction include:

- *Volume of a gas produced.* A reaction that produces a gas as a product can be set up in an Erlenmeyer flask with a stopper and an empty syringe. The plunger of the syringe is pushed out by the pressure of the gas produced, and the volume of gas in the syringe is recorded at regular time intervals during the reaction.

Apparatus for Measurement of the Rate of Gas Production

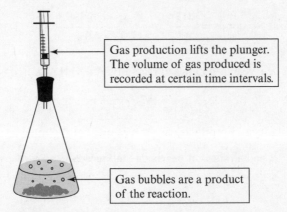

Gas production lifts the plunger. The volume of gas produced is recorded at certain time intervals.

Gas bubbles are a product of the reaction.

- *Change in pressure as gases are produced or consumed.* In a sealed, rigid container, the pressure will increase as gaseous products are produced or decrease as gaseous reactants are consumed. The total pressure in the container can be measured with a sensor.

- *Change in the mass of a reaction as a solid or liquid is converted to gas.*. A reaction can be carried out in a container on a balance. The mass can be recorded at time intervals to monitor the rate at which gaseous products are released to the atmosphere.

- *Change in concentration as determined by spectrophotometry.* An increase in the concentration of a colored product or a decrease in the concentration of a colored reactant can be monitored in a spectrophotometer. The values of the concentrations are determined using Beer's law analysis of a known calibration curve.

- *Change in pH as a reaction proceeds.* Reactions in which acids or bases are formed or consumed will undergo a change in pH as the reaction proceeds. A pH meter can be used to monitor the change. The pH scale will be reviewed in Big Idea 6 (Chapter 6, "Chemical Equilibrium").

PRACTICE:

> A group of art conservation researchers is interested in determining the rate at which a red pigment in a sample of watercolor paint fades upon exposure to ultraviolet light. The group has access to a pure sample of the pigment. Propose a general method by which the researchers might determine the rate at which the pigment fades.

Since the pigment is water-soluble, the researchers might use spectrophotometry to determine how the concentration of the red pigment in an aqueous solution decreases after periods of ultraviolet exposure. After determining the maximum visible wavelength of absorbance of the pigment, a calibration curve should be constructed using known concentrations of the pigment. The absorbance of a solution of a known concentration should be measured, and then it should be exposed to UV light for a fixed length of time. The absorbance should then be measured again. The pigment solution should be exposed to UV light and measured several more times to determine how the concentration changes with time of exposure.

Factors That Influence Rates of Reactions

Reactions can occur at an enormous variety of rates, and the rate of a single reaction can vary, depending on the conditions. Consider a novelty glow stick. It consists of a thin glass tube of one reagent inside a flexible plastic casing that contains a second reagent. When the tube is bent, the inner stick breaks and the reagents mix. The reaction mixture glows until the reaction is complete. At room temperature, the reaction is complete in several hours and the stick stops glowing, but in the freezer, the stick may continue to glow for days. The rate of the reaction is temperature-dependent.

Novelty Glow Stick

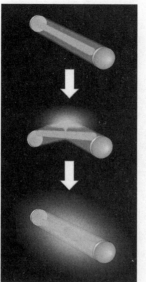

The light-emitting glow stick reaction begins when the inner glass tube is broken.

The reaction reaches completion faster at room temperature than it does at cooler temperatures.

There are several experimental factors that have important effects on the measured rates of chemical reactions.

- *The physical state of the reactants has an effect on the rate of a reaction.* Mixing aqueous solutions of $Pb(NO_3)_2$ and KI will form a precipitate, PbI_2, but if solid $Pb(NO_3)_2$ and KI are brought together, no reaction will occur because the ions are unable to collide in their solid crystalline forms. In aqueous solutions, the reactants are dissociated into free ions and are capable of colliding.

The Effect of Physical States on Reaction Rate

Ions in solution move and collide.
The reaction is faster in solution.

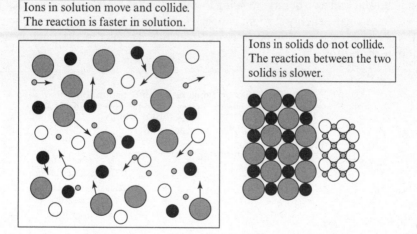

Ions in solids do not collide.
The reaction between the two solids is slower.

The reaction of butyl bromide, C_4H_9Br, with azide, N_3^-, is observed to proceed 5,000 times faster in acetonitrile, CH_3CN, a polar solvent, than in methanol, CH_3OH, a solvent capable of hydrogen bonding. The reasons for this are complicated and beyond the scope of the AP Chemistry exam, but students should be aware of the ability of a solvent to affect the rate of a reaction due to differences in intermolecular forces between different solvents, reactants, and products.

A change in the surface area of the reactants has an effect on the rate, as well. A piece of chalk that has been crushed has more surface area and reacts much more quickly with aqueous acid than a stick of chalk that is intact. This is because more of the chalk particles in the crushed chalk are at the surface and are exposed to the acid. The acid particles can only collide with the surface of the chalk.

Surface Area

Two cubes have the same volume, but the cube on the right
has a greater surface area. For the same reason, a crushed
reactant has more surface area than a single, intact solid.

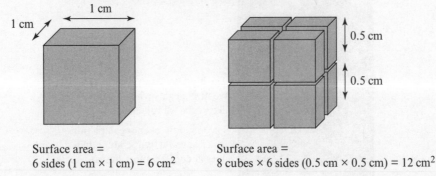

Surface area =
6 sides (1 cm × 1 cm) = 6 cm^2

Surface area =
8 cubes × 6 sides (0.5 cm × 0.5 cm) = 12 cm^2

- *The concentrations or partial pressures of the reactants have an impact on the rates of nonzero order reactions.* For reactions in which reactant particles must collide, an increase in the number of particles will increase the frequency of collisions.

- *The temperature at which a reaction is carried out affects the rate of the reaction.* At higher temperatures, reactions proceed faster than at lower temperatures. An increase in temperature is an increase in the average kinetic energy of the molecules. The higher the average kinetic energy, the higher the frequency and energy of the collisions. A larger number of molecules collide with sufficient energy for a reaction to occur. *For reactions at or near room temperature, a 10 °C increase in temperature will, in many cases, double the reaction rate.*

The **activation energy,** E_a, is the minimum energy the reactants must achieve to reach the transition state for a reaction to occur. The transition state represents a high-energy activated complex, in which reactants' bonds are being broken and new bonds are being formed. The reagents in the glow stick mentioned above have a higher average kinetic energy at room temperature than they do in the freezer, so collisions with sufficient activation energy for the reaction occur more frequently. This is why the reaction proceeds more quickly at room temperature.

The Effect of Temperature on Reaction Rate

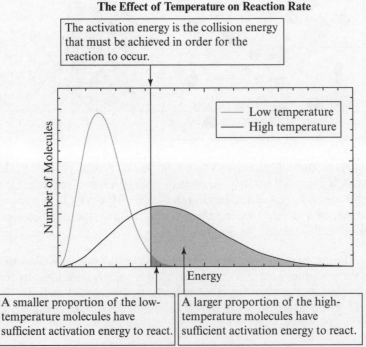

■ *The presence of a catalyst increases the rate of a reaction.* A catalyst is a substance that provides an alternate route, or mechanism, that leads to a different activated complex for a reaction. This activated complex, or transition state, is lower in energy than the activated complex of the uncatalyzed reaction. Catalysts will be discussed in more detail in the final section of this chapter.

The Effect of Catalyst on Reaction Rate

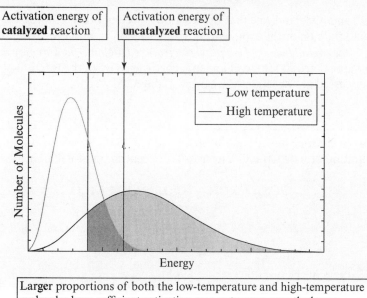

Larger proportions of both the low-temperature and high-temperature molecules have sufficient activation energy to overcome the lower barrier of the catalyzed reaction.

The Rate Law

A **rate law** (also called the **differential rate law** or **rate expression**) is a mathematical expression of the relationship between the rate of a reaction and the concentration of the reactants.

For the general reaction

$$a\,A + b\,B + c\,C \rightarrow \text{products}$$

where A, B, and C are reactants and a, b, and c are stoichiometric coefficients, the rate law has the form

$$\text{rate} = k[A]^x[B]^y[C]^z$$

The constant, k, is called the **rate constant** for a reaction. It is an experimentally determined factor that is characteristic of a particular reaction *at a certain temperature*. The exponents are the **orders** of the reaction with respect to each reactant. The **overall reaction order** is given by the sum of the exponents.

The reaction between chlorine dioxide and hydroxide ion is shown to illustrate

$$2\,ClO_2 + 2\,OH^- \rightarrow ClO_3^- + ClO_2^- + H_2O$$

The rate law for this reaction at 25 °C is

$$\text{rate} = (230\ M^{-2} \cdot s^{-1})[ClO_2]^2[OH^-]$$

Notice first that $k = 230\ M^{-2} \cdot s^{-1}$. Again, the numerical value of the rate constant has been determined experimentally for this reaction at this temperature. The units of k are chosen so that the rate has units of $M \cdot s^{-1}$. Considering only the units,

$$\text{rate} \propto k \cdot M^3$$
$$M \cdot s^{-1} = k \cdot M^3$$
$$(M \cdot s^{-1})M^{-3} = k$$
$$M^{-2} \cdot s^{-1} = k$$

The exponents for $[ClO_2]$ and $[OH^-]$ indicate that the reaction is second order with respect to ClO_2 and first order with respect to OH^-. Since the sum of the exponents is 3, the reaction is third order overall. *The orders are unrelated to the coefficients in the overall balanced equation since the reaction mechanism may not occur in a single step.* (The orders of reactions are related to the stoichiometric coefficients when the reaction occurs via a single step mechanism, as will be discussed in "Reaction Mechanisms," page 206.)

PRACTICE:

A reaction between chlorine dioxide and hydroxide ion at 25 °C, shown below, initially has a chlorine dioxide concentration of 0.020 M and a hydroxide concentration of 0.400 M.

$$2\ ClO_2 + 2\ OH^- \rightarrow ClO_3^- + ClO_2^- + H_2O$$

The rate law is

$$\text{rate} = (230\ M^{-2} \cdot s^{-1})[ClO_2]^2[OH^-]$$

What is the initial rate of the reaction?

The initial rate can be found by solving the rate law expression using the initial concentrations.

$$\text{rate} = (230\ M^{-2} \cdot s^{-1})[ClO_2]^2[OH^-]$$
$$\text{rate} = (230\ M^{-2} \cdot s^{-1})(0.020\ M)^2(0.400\ M) = 0.037\ M \cdot s^{-1}$$

The value of the rate constant provides information about the relative speed of a reaction. The larger the rate constant, the faster the reaction. A reaction with a rate constant on the order of 10^3 at 10 °C, for instance, is much faster than a reaction with a rate constant of 10^{-3} at the same temperature.

Sometimes the rate of a reaction is independent of the concentration of one (or more) of the reactants. In this case, the order of a reaction with respect to that reactant is zero.

The rate law for a hypothetical reaction is shown. Notice that the order with respect to reactant B is zero. In this reaction, the rate of the reaction is independent of the concentration of B.

$$A + B \rightarrow \text{products}$$

$$\text{rate} = k[A]^2[B]^0 = k[A]^2$$

PRACTICE:

A reaction between molecules X, Y, and Z has the following rate law.

$$\text{rate} = k[X][Y]^3$$

What will happen to the reaction rate if the concentrations of X and Z are doubled and the concentration of Y is halved?

Because the reaction is zero-order in Z, we can disregard Z. Let X_1, and Y_1 be the initial concentrations and let X_2, and Y_2 be the final concentrations of X and Y. We can establish relationships between the initial concentrations and the final concentrations based on the wording of the problem.

$$[X_2] = 2[X_1]$$

$$[Y_2] = \left[\frac{1}{2}Y_1\right]$$

We would like to know the ratio of the rate of the final reaction to the initial reaction, so we can set up an equation and substitute the values of X_1 and Y_1 for X_2 and Y_2, respectively.

$$\frac{\text{rate}_2}{\text{rate}_1} = \frac{k[X_2][Y_2]^3}{k[X_1][Y_1]^3}$$

$$\frac{\text{rate}_2}{\text{rate}_1} = \frac{k\left(2[X_1]\right)\left[\frac{1}{2}Y_1\right]^3}{k[X_1][Y_1]^3} = 2\left(\frac{1}{2}\right)^3 = \frac{1}{4}$$

When the concentrations of X and Z are doubled and the concentration of Y is halved, the rate of the reaction decreases to $\frac{1}{4}$ the initial rate.

There are several methods for using experimental data to determine the rate law for a process. These are the method of initial rates and the integrated rate equations. A third technique will also be introduced, in which a proposed reaction mechanism is used to write the rate law (see "Reaction Mechanisms," page 206).

Method of Initial Rates

The **method of initial rates** involves the use of initial concentrations and initial rates of a reaction to deduce its rate law and the value of its rate constant. As will be further discussed in Big Idea 6 (Chapter 6, "Chemical Equilibrium"), chemical reactions proceed both in the forward and in the reverse direction. Before any products have appeared, though, the reverse reaction can be neglected. When the initial rates of reactions are measured, the complication of the reverse reaction can be avoided.

The initial rates of reaction and initial concentrations of reactants A, B, and C are measured experimentally and tabulated.

$$A + 3B + 2C \rightarrow \text{products}$$

Trial Number	Initial Concentration of A (M)	Initial Concentration of B (M)	Initial Concentration of C (M)	Initial Rate of Reaction ($M \cdot s^{-1}$)
1	0.010	0.012	0.010	1.2×10^{-5}
2	0.010	0.024	0.010	2.4×10^{-5}
3	0.020	0.012	0.010	4.8×10^{-5}
4	0.010	0.012	0.020	1.2×10^{-5}

The reaction orders are determined first. Let the orders with respect to A, B, and C be x, y, and z, respectively.

Begin by choosing two sets of data in which the concentration of only one of the reactants changes. Only the concentration of B changes between trials 1 and 2, so these trials can be chosen to determine y, the order with respect to B. A ratio is set up between the rate laws, and since the concentration of B is greater in trial 2 than it is in trial 1, it may be easier to put trial 2 in the numerator and trial 1 in the denominator.

$$\frac{\text{rate}_2}{\text{rate}_1} = \frac{k[A]_2^x[B]_2^y[C]_2^z}{k[A]_1^x[B]_1^y[C]_1^z}$$

$$\frac{2.4\times10^{-5}}{1.2\times10^{-5}} = \frac{\cancel{k}\ \cancel{(0.010)^x}\ (0.024)^y\ \cancel{(0.010)^z}}{\cancel{k}\ \cancel{(0.010)^x}\ (0.012)^y\ \cancel{(0.010)^z}}$$

$$2 = 2^y$$

$$y = 1$$

The reaction is first order with respect to B.

Between trials 1 and 3, only the concentration of A changes, so these trials can be used to determine x, the order with respect to A.

$$\frac{\text{rate}_3}{\text{rate}_1} = \frac{k[A]_3^x[B]_3^y[C]_3^z}{k[A]_1^x[B]_1^y[C]_1^z}$$

$$\frac{4.8\times10^{-5}}{1.2\times10^{-5}} = \frac{\cancel{k}\ (0.020)^x\ \cancel{(0.012)^y}\ \cancel{(0.010)^z}}{\cancel{k}\ (0.010)^x\ \cancel{(0.012)^y}\ \cancel{(0.010)^z}}$$

$$4 = 2^x$$

$$x = 2$$

The reaction is second order with respect to A.

Finally, trials 1 and 4 can be used to determine the order with respect to C.

$$\frac{\text{rate}_4}{\text{rate}_1} = \frac{k[A]_4^x[B]_4^y[C]_4^z}{k[A]_1^x[B]_1^y[C]_1^z}$$

$$\frac{1.2\times10^{-5}}{1.2\times10^{-5}} = \frac{\cancel{k}\ \cancel{(0.010)^x}\ \cancel{(0.012)^y}\ (0.020)^z}{\cancel{k}\ \cancel{(0.010)^x}\ \cancel{(0.012)^y}\ (0.010)^z}$$

$$1 = 2^z$$

$$z = 0$$

The order with respect to C is zero, so the rate is independent of the concentration of C. The rate law, therefore, has the general form

$$\text{rate} = k[A]^2[B]$$

Any of the four trials can be chosen to find the rate constant. The data from the selected trial is used to solve the rate expression for k. The data from trial 1 is selected as an example.

$$1.2\times10^{-5}\,M\cdot\text{s}^{-1} = k(0.010M)^2(0.012M)$$

$$k = \frac{1.2\times10^{-5}\,\cancel{M}\cdot\text{s}^{-1}}{(0.010M)^2(0.012\,\cancel{M})} = 10.\ M^{-2}\cdot\text{s}^{-1}$$

In cases where there is not more than one trial in which the concentrations of one of the reagents is the same, solve for the order of that reagent last.

PRACTICE:

The initial rates and concentrations for the reaction between C_5H_5N and CH_3I at 25 °C are shown below.

(a) What are the rate law and the value of the rate constant for this reaction?

(b) What is the rate of the reaction in trial 3 when the concentration of C_5H_5N has decreased to 7.60×10^{-4} M?

$$C_5H_5N + CH_3I \rightarrow [C_5H_5NCH_3]^+ + I^-$$

Trial Number	Initial Concentration of C_5H_5N (M)	Initial Concentration of CH_3I (M)	Initial Rate of Reaction ($M{\cdot}s^{-1}$)
1	3.70×10^{-4}	3.70×10^{-4}	1.03×10^{-5}
2	1.11×10^{-3}	1.11×10^{-3}	9.24×10^{-5}
3	1.11×10^{-3}	2.22×10^{-3}	1.85×10^{-4}

(a) The general form of the rate expression for this reaction is

$$\text{rate} = k[C_5H_5N]^x[CH_3I]^y$$

Since the concentration of C_5H_5N is the same in trials 2 and 3, these two trials can be used to determine the order with respect to CH_3I.

$$\frac{\text{rate}_3}{\text{rate}_2} = \frac{k[C_5H_5N]_3^x[CH_3I]_3^y}{k[C_5H_5N]_2^x[CH_3I]_2^y}$$

$$\frac{1.85 \times 10^{-4}\ \cancel{M{\cdot}s^{-1}}}{9.24 \times 10^{-5}\ \cancel{M{\cdot}s^{-1}}} = \frac{\cancel{k}\ \cancel{(1.11 \times 10^{-3}\ M)^x}\ (2.22 \times 10^{-3}\ \cancel{M})^y}{\cancel{k}\ \cancel{(1.11 \times 10^{-3}\ M)^x}\ (1.11 \times 10^{-3}\ \cancel{M})^y}$$

$$2 = 2^y$$

$$y = 1$$

At this point, either of the other two combinations of trials (1 and 2 or 1 and 3) can be selected. Either choice will provide the correct order of the reaction with respect to C_5H_5N.

$$\frac{\text{rate}_3}{\text{rate}_1} = \frac{k[C_5H_5N]_3^x[CH_3I]_3^y}{k[C_5H_5N]_1^x[CH_3I]_1^y}$$

$$\frac{1.85 \times 10^{-4}\ \cancel{M{\cdot}s^{-1}}}{1.03 \times 10^{-5}\ \cancel{M{\cdot}s^{-1}}} = \frac{\cancel{k}(1.11 \times 10^{-3}\ \cancel{M})^x(2.22 \times 10^{-3}\ \cancel{M})^1}{\cancel{k}(3.70 \times 10^{-4}\ \cancel{M})^x(3.70 \times 10^{-4}\ \cancel{M})^1}$$

$$3 = 3^x$$

$$x = 1$$

The rate expression is

$$\text{rate} = k[C_5H_5N][CH_3I]$$

The value of k can be determined using the data from any of the three trials. Trial 1 is used as an example here.

$$1.03 \times 10^{-5}\ M{\cdot}s^{-1} = k\left(3.70 \times 10^{-4}\ M\right)\left(3.70 \times 10^{-4}\ M\right)$$

$$k = \frac{1.03 \times 10^{-5}\ \cancel{M}{\cdot}s^{-1}}{\left(3.70 \times 10^{-4}\ \cancel{M}\right)\left(3.70 \times 10^{-4}\ M\right)} = 75.2\ M^{-1}{\cdot}s^{-1}$$

(b) From the one-to-one stoichiometry of the reaction, it is apparent that the rates of consumption of C_5H_5N and CH_3I are equal.

$$-\frac{\Delta[C_5H_5N]}{\Delta t} = -\frac{\Delta[CH_3I]}{\Delta t}$$

The change in concentration of C_5H_5N is determined.

$$\Delta[C_5H_5N] = 7.60 \times 10^{-4}\ M - 1.11 \times 10^{-3}\ M = -3.50 \times 10^{-4}\ M$$

This change is equal to that of $\Delta[CH_3I]$.

$$\Delta[CH_3I] = [CH_3I]_{final} - [CH_3I]_{initial}$$

$$\Delta[CH_3I] = -3.50 \times 10^{-4}\ M = [CH_3I]_{final} - 2.22 \times 10^{-3}\ M$$

$$[CH_3I]_{final} = -3.50 \times 10^{-4}\ M - (-2.22 \times 10^{-3}\ M) = 1.87 \times 10^{-3}\ M$$

Now the two final concentrations can be used in the rate law to determine the new rate.

$$\text{rate} = k[C_5H_5N][CH_3I] = \left(75.2\ M^{-1} \cdot s^{-1}\right)\left(7.60 \times 10^{-4}\ M\right)\left(1.87 \times 10^{-3}\ M\right) = 1.07 \times 10^{-4}\ M \cdot s^{-1}$$

Integrated Rate Laws

The integrated rate equation is used to determine how much of a certain reactant remains after a specific time t has elapsed.

The integrated rate equations for first and second order reactions are shown on the *AP Chemistry Equations and Constants* sheet (pages 365–366), but they are not labeled as such. It is the student's responsibility to know which equation corresponds to which reaction order. It is also in the student's best interest to know the similar integrated rate law for zero order kinetics.

Integrated rate laws may also be used to determine reaction **half-life, $t_{1/2}$,** the time it takes for a quantity of a reactant to decrease by half. The half-life equation shown on the *AP Chemistry Equations and Constants* sheet is for a first order reaction.

Zero Order Reactions

For the zero order reaction

$$A \rightarrow products$$

the rate is

$$\text{rate} = k[A]^0 = k$$

The units of the rate constant must be $M \cdot s^{-1}$, just like the rate itself.

This rate is independent of the concentration of A. A plot of the concentration, [A], versus time, t, gives a straight line.

A Plot of [A] versus t for a Zero Order Decay

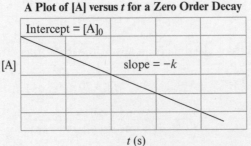

The absolute value of the slope of the plot gives the rate constant, k, and the intercept gives the initial concentration, $[A]_0$, of the reactant before any reaction time has elapsed.

The integrated rate law of a zero order process, which relates the concentration of A at time t, $[A]_t$, to the initial concentration, $[A]_0$, is not given on the *AP Chemistry Equations and Constants* sheet, but it is very likely to be important in AP Chemistry nonetheless.

$$[A]_t - [A]_0 = -kt$$

The half-life of a zero order reaction can be determined by recognizing that when half of reactant A is consumed,

$$[A]_t = \frac{[A]_0}{2}$$

This value can be substituted into the integrated rate law to find the half-life.

$$\frac{[A]_0}{2} - [A]_0 = -kt_{1/2}$$

$$\frac{[A]_0}{2} - \frac{2}{2}[A]_0 = -kt_{1/2}$$

$$-\frac{[A]_0}{2} = -kt_{1/2}$$

$$t_{1/2} = \frac{[A]_0}{2k}$$

First Order Reactions and Nuclear Decay

For the first order reaction

$$A \rightarrow products$$

the rate is

$$rate = k[A]$$

A plot of [A] versus time, t, gives a curve and not a straight line. This shows that, unlike the rate of a zero order reaction, the rate of a first order reaction decreases as the reaction progresses. The rate of a first order reaction is concentration-dependent. The unit of the rate constant is s^{-1}.

A Plot of [A] versus *t* for a First Order Decay

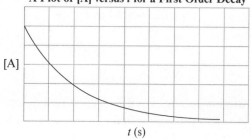

[A]

t (s)

The plot of the natural logarithm of [A] versus time gives a straight line.

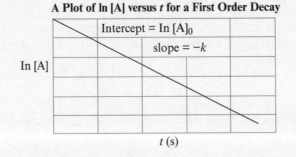

A Plot of ln [A] versus *t* for a First Order Decay

The absolute value of the slope of the plot gives the rate constant, k, and the intercept gives the natural log of the initial reactant concentration, $\ln [A]_0$, before any reaction time has elapsed.

The integrated rate law of a first order process is given on the *AP Chemistry Equations and Constants* sheet. Again, it is not labeled as such, so students must be able to recognize it.

$$\ln [A]_t - \ln [A]_0 = -kt$$

The half-life of a first order reaction is again determined when the concentration of the reactant is half of the initial concentration. Although the derivation of this equation is not necessary since it is also given on the *AP Chemistry Equations and Constants* sheet (pages 365–366), it is derived as shown below.

$$\ln \frac{[A]_0}{2} - \ln[A]_0 = -kt_{1/2}$$

$$\ln \left(\frac{\frac{[A]_0}{2}}{[A]_0} \right) = -kt_{1/2}$$

$$\ln \left(\frac{1}{2} \right) = -kt_{1/2}$$

$$\ln 2 = kt_{1/2}$$

$$\frac{0.693}{k} = t_{1/2}$$

Second Order Reactions

For the second order reaction

$$A \rightarrow products$$

the rate is

$$rate = k[A]^2$$

Again, the rate of a second order reaction decreases as the reaction progresses; it is concentration-dependent. The units of the rate constant are $M^{-1} \cdot s^{-1}$.

The plot of $\frac{1}{[A]}$ versus time for a second order process gives a straight line.

A Plot of ln [A] $^{-1}$ versus t for a Second Order Decay

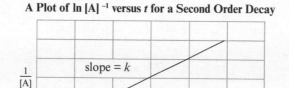

The absolute value of the slope of the plot gives the rate constant, k, and the intercept gives the reciprocal of the initial reactant concentration, $\frac{1}{[A]_0}$, before any reaction time has elapsed.

The integrated rate law of a second order process is given on the *AP Chemistry Equations and Constants* sheet (pages 365–366), but it is not labeled as such, so students will need to recognize it.

$$\frac{1}{[A]_t} - \frac{1}{[A]_0} = kt$$

The half-life of a second order reaction is again determined when the concentration of the reactant is half of the initial concentration.

$$\frac{1}{\left(\dfrac{[A]_0}{2}\right)} - \frac{1}{[A]_0} = kt_{1/2}$$

$$\frac{2}{[A]_0} - \frac{1}{[A]_0} = kt_{1/2}$$

$$\frac{1}{k[A]_0} = t_{1/2}$$

Summary of Integrated Rate Laws

The following table summarizes the integrated rate law for zero, first, and second order reaction rates.

Reaction Order	Differential Rate Law	Integrated Rate Law	Linear Plot	Half-Life*	Units of Rate Constant
Zero	rate = k	$[A]_t - [A]_0 = -kt$	$[A]$ versus t	$t_{1/2} = \dfrac{[A]_0}{2k}$	$M \cdot s^{-1}$
First	rate = $k[A]$	$\ln [A]_t - \ln [A]_0 = -kt$	$\ln [A]$ versus t	$t_{1/2} = \dfrac{0.693}{k}$	s^{-1}
Second	rate = $k[A]^2$	$\dfrac{1}{[A]_t} - \dfrac{1}{[A]_0} = kt$	$\dfrac{1}{[A]_t}$ versus t	$t_{1/2} = \dfrac{1}{k[A]_0}$	$M^{-1} \cdot s^{-1}$

*Tip: Don't be concerned with memorization of the half-life equations. It is only important to notice that zero and second order half-lives are concentration-*dependent* and that the half-life of a first order reaction is concentration-*independent*. In the unlikely event that an exam question asks for a half-life calculation for a zero order or second order reaction, simply use the method of setting the concentration of A at the half-life to half the initial concentration and solve for $t_{1/2}$, as demonstrated in the text above.

PRACTICE:

The decomposition of a reactant, X, occurs by the following reaction.

$$X \rightarrow products$$

The reaction was monitored over the course of 10.0 hours at constant temperature and the data obtained is shown in the table below. The information is plotted in the graphs that follow.

(a) What is the order of the reaction with respect to X? Justify your response.

(b) Write the rate law for the reaction and calculate the specific rate constant with appropriate units.

(c) Calculate the concentration of X after 14.0 hours have elapsed.

Time (hours)	[X]	ln [X]	$[X]^{-1}$
0.0	0.368	−1.00	2.72
1.0	0.247	−1.40	4.06
2.0	0.165	−1.80	6.05
3.0	0.111	−2.20	9.03
5.0	0.0498	−3.00	20.1
7.0	0.0224	−3.80	44.7
10.0	0.00674	−5.00	148

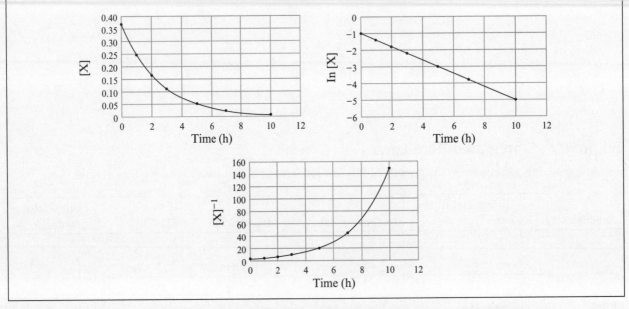

(a) The reaction is first order with respect to X. The plot of ln [X] versus time produces a straight line.

(b) The general form of the rate law for a reaction that is first order in X is

$$rate = k[X]$$

The specific rate constant is given by the absolute value of the slope of the plot of ln [X] versus time. Any two points can be chosen to determine the slope of the graph.

$$k = \left| \frac{-5.00 - (-1.00)}{10.0 - 0.0} \right| = 0.400 \text{ h}^{-1}$$

Since rate is reported in units of concentration per unit time, the rate constant must have units of h^{-1}.

(c) The concentration of X after 14.0 hours have elapsed can be calculated using the equation for a first order reaction.

$$\ln [X]_{14\,h} - \ln [X]_0 = -kt$$
$$\ln [X]_{14\,h} - \ln (0.368 \ M) = -(0.400 \text{ h}^{-1})(14.0 \text{ h})$$
$$\ln [X]_{14\,h} = -5.60 - 1.00$$
$$[X]_{14\,h} = e^{-6.60} = 0.0014 \ M$$

Reactions Between Multiple Reactants

The integrated rate laws discussed so far have been for reactions involving single reactants. Many times, more than one reactant is required, and this complicates the measurement of the rate law. One way to handle the problem is by using conditions in which one reagent is so much less concentrated than the others that it experiences a substantially greater change in concentration as the reaction proceeds. The concentration of the other reactant changes so little that it is approximately constant.

For visualization purposes, imagine a "reaction" occurs between a grain of rice and a small glass bead. Now, imagine that there is a 2-liter container filled with rice grains (an estimated 126,000 grains) and 126 glass beads. The number of rice grains is 1000 times greater than the number of beads.

Rice grain + Glass bead → Imaginary product

R + G → P

When 63 of the glass beads have reacted, the "concentration" of beads has decreased by half. A decrease of 63 rice grains, however, still leaves approximately 126,000 grains of rice (rounded to three significant figures). The rate law for this reaction is

rate = $k[R]^x[G]^y$

Since the concentration of R appears to be constant, the product, k', of $[R]^x$ and k appears constant as well.

$k' = k[R]^x$

The rate law can be rewritten

rate = $k'[G]^y$

Now, the concentration of G can be measured experimentally as a function of time and the order with respect to G can be determined using the integrated rate law method. The slope of the plot of [G], ln [G], or $\frac{1}{[G]}$ versus time gives k' rather than k.

PRACTICE:

Bromophenol blue is an acid-base indicator that is blue in basic solution. Upon prolonged exposure to alkaline conditions, the blue molecule fades to a colorless form. Two solutions of 1.00×10^{-3} M bromophenol blue (BB) in 1.00 and 0.500 M hydroxide (OH$^-$), respectively, are monitored spectrophotometrically. The concentrations at various times are tabulated below. Note that although students are required to understand these concepts in order to do well on the AP Chemistry exam, generation of these plots is more likely to be an AP Chemistry laboratory or classroom requirement.

Determine the rate law for the fading of bromophenol blue in hydroxide by

(a) finding the order with respect to BB.

(b) finding the apparent rate constant, k', for the fading in 1.00 M OH$^-$.

(c) finding the apparent rate constant for the fading in 0.500 M OH$^-$.

(d) using the apparent rate constants to determine the order with respect to OH$^-$.

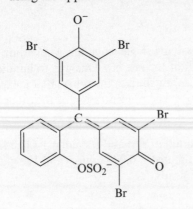 + OH$^-$ $\longrightarrow$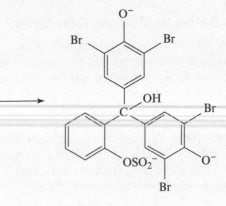

Blue   Colorless

1.00 M OH$^-$ Solution	
Time (min)	[BB] (M)
0	1.00×10^{-3}
1	9.33×10^{-4}
3	8.12×10^{-4}
5	7.07×10^{-4}
10	5.00×10^{-4}
20	2.50×10^{-4}

0.500 M OH$^-$ Solution	
Time (min)	[BB] (M)
0	1.00×10^{-3}
1	9.66×10^{-4}
3	9.01×10^{-4}
5	8.41×10^{-4}
10	7.07×10^{-4}
20	4.99×10^{-4}

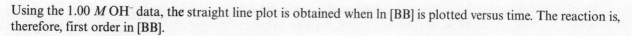

(a) The order of the reaction with respect to BB can be determined using either set of data. Three plots are generated from the chosen data set. The concentration, [BB], versus time, ln [BB] versus time, and $[BB]^{-1}$ versus time are plotted. The order is determined by the plot that gives a straight line.

Using the 1.00 M OH⁻ data, the straight line plot is obtained when ln [BB] is plotted versus time. The reaction is, therefore, first order in [BB].

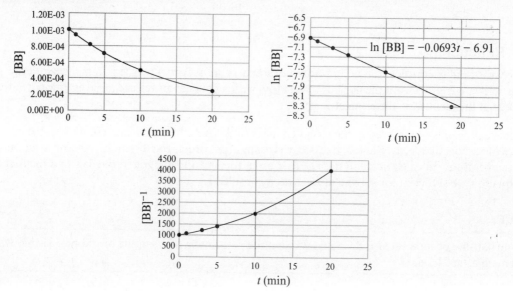

(b) The apparent rate constant for the fading of BB in 1.00 M OH⁻ is the absolute value of the slope of the plot of ln [BB] versus time.

$$\text{rate} = k'[BB]$$

where the slope of the line is given in the equation of the line on the plot.

$$k' = k[OH^-]^x = |\text{slope}| = 0.0693 \text{ min}^{-1}$$

(c) The apparent rate constant for the fading of BB in 0.500 M OH⁻ is the absolute value of the slope of the plot of ln [BB] versus time.

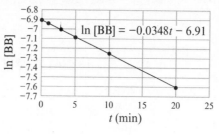

$$\text{rate} = k'[BB]$$

where

$$k' = k[OH^-]^x = |\text{slope}| = 0.0348 \text{ min}^{-1}$$

(d) There are two equations for k' at two different concentrations of OH⁻.
For [OH⁻] = 1.00 M,

$$k[OH^-]^x = 0.0693 \text{ min}^{-1} = k[1.00]^x$$

For [OH⁻] = 0.500 M,

$$k[OH^-]^x = 0.0348 \text{ min}^{-1} = k[0.500]^x$$

The ratio of the rate constants can be used to determine the order, x, with respect to OH^-.

$$\frac{0.0693 \text{ min}^{-1}}{0.0348 \text{ min}^{-1}} = \frac{\cancel{k}[1.00]^x}{\cancel{k}[0.500]^x}$$

$$1.99 = 2^x$$

$$x = 1$$

Nuclear Reactions

Nuclear decay, or **radioactive decay,** is an important example of a first order process. In a nuclear decay, sub-atomic particles are emitted from the nucleus of an atom with a concurrent release of large amounts of energy and a change in the identity of the element.

The only nuclear chemistry included in the recent changes to the AP Chemistry curriculum is in the context of the kinetics of radioactive decay. Radioactive decay is always first order. Furthermore, nuclear reactions are unaffected by temperature, pressure, or catalysts. The first order form of the integrated rate law and the first order half-life equation are sufficient for solving nuclear decay problems.

PRACTICE:

> The half-life of iodine-131 is 8.02 days. Predict the percentage of a sample of iodine-131 that will remain after 21.2 days.

The rate constant for this first order process can be calculated from the half-life.

$$t_{\frac{1}{2}} = \frac{0.693}{k}$$

$$k = \frac{0.693}{8.02 \text{ days}} = 0.0864 \text{ day}^{-1}$$

Let A_0 represent the initial amount of iodine-131. Before any time has elapsed, the sample is assumed to be 100% iodine-131, so $A_0 = 1$. Let A represent the fraction that remains after 21.2 days. The first order integrated rate law equation can be solved for A.

$$\ln A - \ln A_0 = -kt$$

$$\ln A - \ln 1 = -\left(0.0864 \text{ day}^{-1}\right)\left(21.2 \text{ day}\right)$$

$$\ln A = -1.83$$

$$A = e^{-1.83} = 0.160$$

The fraction that remains after 21.2 days is 0.160 or 16.0%.

Collision Theory

In order for two molecules to react with one another to form a product, the molecules must collide. Collisions between particles, however, do not guarantee that a reaction will occur. In order for a collision to successfully result in a reaction, two minimum conditions must be met:

1. The collision between the particles must have energy greater than or equal to the activation energy in order for the reaction to occur. The activation energy, E_a, is a potential energy barrier that the reactants must overcome to achieve the necessary transition state, the high-energy arrangement of atoms in which bond breaking and/ or bond formation occurs. The lower the activation energy of a reaction, the faster the rate of the reaction.

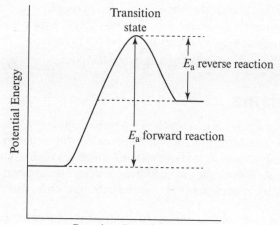

Just as it takes more energy to jump over a high hurdle than a short one, it takes more energy for reactants to overcome a higher activation barrier. The higher the kinetic energy of the reacting particles, the higher the likelihood that a collision between the two particles will lead to a reaction.

2. The reactants must collide with an effective orientation.

Consider the reaction between HI molecules and Cl atoms in the gas phase.

$$HI + Cl \rightarrow HCl + I$$

The reaction can only occur if the chlorine collides with the hydrogen. If the iodine is oriented toward the colliding chlorine atom, the collision will be ineffective and no reaction will occur.

Effective Orientation of Reactants During Collisions

Correct orientation during collision results in reaction.

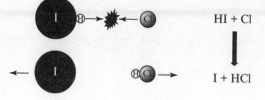

Incorrect orientation during collision results in no reaction.

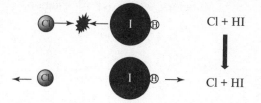

PRACTICE:

Explain in terms of collision theory how an increase in temperature leads to an increase in the rate of a reaction.

The higher the temperature of a reaction mixture, the higher the average kinetic energy of the particles. The higher the kinetic energy, the greater the frequency of collisions that have the correct molecular orientation and that are sufficiently energetic to overcome the activation barrier for the reaction. At higher temperature, the reaction rate will increase.

Reaction Mechanisms

Most chemical reactions occur by a process that involves more than one step. This is why the rate law cannot be deduced from the stoichiometric coefficients of a balanced equation. A **reaction mechanism** is a step-by-step sequence of bond breaking, bond formation, and other transformations that result in an overall reaction. A reaction mechanism is made up of steps showing colliding or decomposing particles. These steps are called **elementary reactions.** The stoichiometric coefficients for an elementary reaction determine the rate law of that step.

An elementary step in which one reactant decomposes to products is a **unimolecular** step. An elementary step in which two reactants collide and react is a **bimolecular** step. **Termolecular** steps, those in which three reactants simultaneously collide and react, are extremely unlikely.

Molecularity	Elementary Step	Possible Rate Law(s) for the Elementary Step
Unimolecular	A → products	Rate = $k[A]$
Bimolecular	A + A → products A + B → products	Rate = $k[A]^2$ Rate = $k[A][B]$
Termolecular	A + A + A → products A + A + B → products A + B + C → products	Rate = $k[A]^3$ Rate = $k[A]^2[B]$ Rate = $k[A][B][C]$

Imagine a hypothetical reaction between reactants A and B to form a product, E.

$$2A + B \rightarrow 2E$$

The reaction between A and B below might occur in the following series of elementary steps.

$$A + A \rightarrow C$$
$$B + C \rightarrow D$$
$$D \rightarrow E + E$$

These elementary steps can be "added" together to give the overall equation.

$$A + A \rightarrow \cancel{C}$$
$$B + \cancel{C} \rightarrow \cancel{D}$$
$$\cancel{D} \rightarrow E + E$$

Species C and D, which are produced in an earlier elementary step and then consumed later in the mechanism, are called **reaction intermediates.**

The rate of an overall reaction is determined by the rate of the slowest step in the process. The slowest step, for this reason, is called the **rate-determining step.** Visualize an assembly line in which three workers are assembling bicycles. Worker 1 attaches the fork and handlebars to the frame of the bicycle, worker 2 assembles the wheels and gears, and worker 3 attaches the seat. Suppose that the task of worker 2 is the most difficult and takes the longest amount of time. The bicycles can be produced only as fast as worker 2 can perform the task. The assembly of the wheels and gears is the rate-determining step.

The rate-determining step has the highest activation energy of any step in a reaction mechanism. The reaction profile for a hypothetical multistep process is shown below. This process is a three-step reaction with three transition states (activated complexes) and two intermediates.

Reaction Profile for a Three-Step Reaction

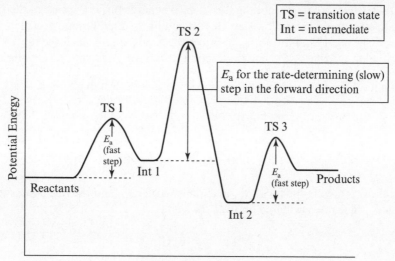

For a hypothetical reaction mechanism, the rate law is determined by the slow step.

$$A + A \rightarrow C \text{ (slow)}$$

$$B + C \rightarrow D \text{ (fast)}$$

$$D \rightarrow E + E \text{ (fast)}$$

The rate law for the overall transformation is based on the stoichiometry of the slow step.

$$\text{rate} = k[A]^2$$

The mechanisms for overall reactions can be very difficult to elucidate experimentally. A rate law is determined for an overall process using either the method of initial rates or measurement of change in amounts of reactants and products with time. A proposed mechanism must be consistent with the observed rate law.

PRACTICE:

$$2\,NO + Br_2 \rightarrow 2\,NOBr$$

The rate law for the reaction shown above between NO and Br_2 is determined experimentally to be

$$\text{rate} = k[NO][Br_2]$$

Which mechanism, A or B, is consistent with this rate law?

Mechanism A:	$NO + NO \rightarrow N_2O_2$	(slow)
	$N_2O_2 + Br_2 \rightarrow NOBr + NOBr$	(fast)
Mechanism B:	$NO + Br_2 \rightarrow NOBr_2$	(slow)
	$NO + NOBr_2 \rightarrow NOBr + NOBr$	(fast)

Mechanism B is consistent with the observed rate law. The rate law based on the slow step of mechanism B is the one that is observed. The rate law based on the slow step of mechanism A, on the other hand, is

$$\text{rate} = k[\text{NO}]^2$$

In some cases, the rate-determining step is not the first step. Whenever this is the case at the AP Chemistry level, the elementary reactions that precede the slow step are fast equilibria. **Equilibrium,** as will be reviewed in Big Idea 6 (Chapter 6, "Chemical Equilibrium"), describes the condition in which the rate of a reaction in the forward direction is equal to the rate of the reverse reaction. It is designated with an **equilibrium arrow,** $\rightleftharpoons$.

Consider the following mechanism in which the first step is a fast equilibrium reaction.

$$A + A \underset{k_{-1}}{\overset{k_1}{\rightleftharpoons}} B \qquad \text{(fast)}$$

$$B + C \overset{k_2}{\longrightarrow} D \qquad \text{(slow)}$$

The rate constant for the first step in the forward direction is written k_1, and the rate constant for the first step in the reverse direction is k_{-1}. The rate law based on the slow step is

$$\text{rate} = k_2[\text{B}][\text{C}]$$

but there is a problem. Intermediates do not generally appear in the rate law at the AP Chemistry level. This issue is easily solved by recognizing that the forward rate of the first reaction is equal to the reverse rate.

$$\text{rate}_1 = \text{rate}_{-1}$$

$$k_1[\text{A}]^2 = k_{-1}[\text{B}]$$

Now, [B] can be calculated and substituted into the solution into the rate law that was written based on the slow step.

$$[\text{B}] = \frac{k_1[\text{A}]^2}{k_{-1}}$$

$$\text{rate} = k_2\left(\frac{k_1[\text{A}]^2}{k_{-1}}\right)[\text{C}]$$

The product of the constants $k_2 \cdot k_1 \cdot \dfrac{1}{k_{-1}}$ is the apparent rate constant, k, observed in rate experiments. The overall rate law is

$$\text{rate} = k[\text{A}]^2[\text{C}]$$

PRACTICE:

Chlorine reacts with chloroform to generate carbon tetrachloride and hydrogen chloride.

$$\text{Cl}_2 + \text{CHCl}_3 \rightarrow \text{CCl}_4 + \text{HCl}$$

The proposed mechanism follows. Based on this mechanism, determine the rate law for the reaction.

$$\text{Cl}_2 \underset{k_{-1}}{\overset{k_1}{\rightleftharpoons}} 2\,\text{Cl} \qquad \text{(fast, equilibrium)}$$

$$\text{Cl} + \text{CHCl}_3 \overset{k_2}{\longrightarrow} \text{HCl} + \text{CCl}_3 \qquad \text{(slow)}$$

$$\text{CCl}_3 + \text{Cl} \overset{k_3}{\longrightarrow} \text{CCl}_4 \qquad \text{(fast)}$$

The overall rate of the reaction is based on the slow step.

$$rate = k_2[Cl][CHCl_3]$$

For the first step in the mechanism, the rates of the forward and reverse steps are equal since the reaction is at equilibrium.

$$rate_1 = rate_{-1}$$

$$k_1[Cl_2] = k_{-1}[Cl]^2$$

Since the chlorine atom is an intermediate, it should not be included in the rate law.

$$[Cl] = \left(\frac{k_1[Cl_2]}{k_{-1}} \right)^{\frac{1}{2}}$$

$$rate = k_2 \left(\frac{k_1[Cl_2]}{k_{-1}} \right)^{\frac{1}{2}} [CHCl_3]$$

$$rate = k_2 \left(\frac{k_1}{k_{-1}} \right)^{\frac{1}{2}} [Cl_2]^{\frac{1}{2}} [CHCl_3]$$

$$rate = k'[Cl_2]^{\frac{1}{2}} [CHCl_3]$$

The Transition State

The **transition state,** or **activated complex,** is the highest-energy configuration that a group of atoms must achieve in order to break or form bonds. Along the reaction coordinate, it is the state that is achieved by colliding molecules with sufficient activation energy and correct orientation. At this point, bonds are at the process of breaking or forming, so they are longer and weaker than regular covalent bonds.

$$CH_3Br + OH^- \rightarrow CH_3OH + Br^-$$

In the exothermic reaction with methyl bromide, CH_3Br, hydroxide, OH^-, collides with the carbon atom on the side opposite the bromine. When the collision occurs with sufficient energy to overcome the activation barrier, the C-Br bond breaks as the C-O bond forms. The dotted bonds in the activated complex indicate partially formed or partially broken bonds.

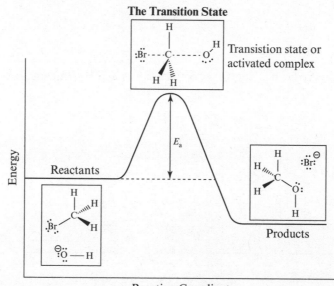

Temperature and Reaction Rate

As temperature increases, reaction rate increases because more reactant molecules collide more frequently with a favorable orientation for reaction and with sufficient energy to overcome the activation barrier. In other words, the rate constant, k, is temperature-dependent. The **Arrhenius equation** is an expression that relates the rate constant for a reaction to the temperature. Calculations involving the Arrhenius equation have been excluded from the AP Chemistry curriculum, but an understanding of the implications and graphical results is explicitly required.

The Arrhenius equation relates k to the **pre-exponential factor,** A, which gives the frequency with which collisions occur with the proper orientation for a reaction. As temperature increases, the fraction of molecules with the minimum critical activation energy increases exponentially as a function of $e^{-\frac{E_a}{RT}}$, where E_a is the activation energy, R is the gas constant, $8.314 \text{ J} \cdot \text{mol}^{-1} \cdot \text{K}^{-1}$, and T is the temperature in kelvin.

The Arrhenius equation has the form

$$k = Ae^{-\frac{E_a}{RT}}$$

Taking the natural log of both sides gives

$$\ln k = -\left(\frac{E_a}{R}\right)\left(\frac{1}{T}\right) + \ln A$$

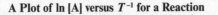

When the rate constants for a reaction are measured at different temperatures, a plot of $\ln k$ versus $\frac{1}{T}$ results in a straight line with a slope of $-\frac{E_a}{R}$.

A Plot of ln [A] versus T^{-1} for a Reaction

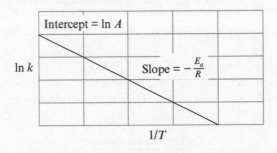

PRACTICE:

The plot below shows Arrhenius plots for two reactions, A and B. Which reaction has a higher activation energy?

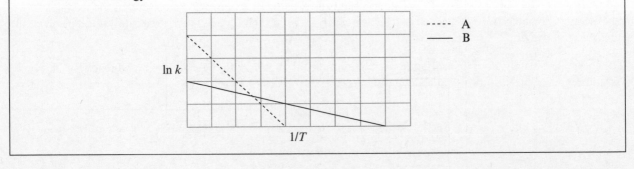

Reaction A has a higher activation energy. The steeper slope of plot A shows that the magnitude of $\left| -\dfrac{E_a}{R} \right|$ is larger than it is for B.

Catalysts

A catalyst is a substance that increases the rate of a reaction by providing an alternative transition state with a lower activation energy than that of the uncatalyzed reaction. The effect of a catalyst on reaction rate in the forward direction is shown below. The rates of the forward and reverse reactions are both increased.

The General Effect of a Catalyst on Activation Energy

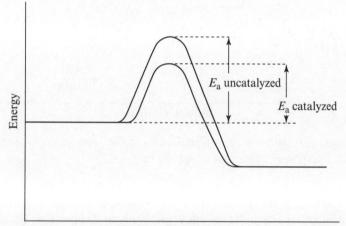

In a reaction mechanism, a catalyst is a substance that is used in an early step and regenerated in a later step. Since a catalyst is regenerated in the mechanism, it can react again and again. For this reason, only a small (sub-stoichiometric, or less than stoichiometric) amount is usually necessary to increase the rate of a reaction. A catalyst will not change the thermodynamics of a reaction or the position of equilibrium (how far a reaction will proceed before the forward and reverse rates equalize).

For an overall reaction, a catalyst is shown above the reaction arrow.

$$A + B \xrightarrow{\text{catalyst}} AB$$

The mechanism for this reaction, in which C is the catalyst, might be

$$A + C \to AC$$
$$AC + B \to AB + C$$

In this example, the catalyst, C, is the substance that is used in the first step and regenerated in the second step, and the intermediate, AC, is generated and subsequently consumed. It is common for the catalyst to appear in the rate law for a reaction.

The energy of a catalyzed transformation can be compared with the energy of an uncatalyzed reaction. Notice that the ‡ symbol in the figure that follows indicates a transition state.

The Effect of a Catalyst on a Reaction Mechanism

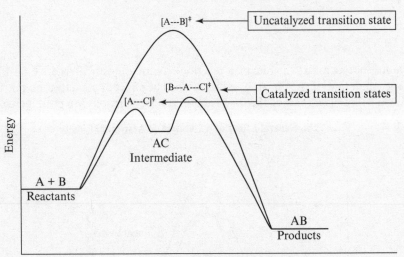

The activation energies for the formation of the intermediate and the product are lower than that of the uncatalyzed process. The decreased activation barrier increases the rate.

The two major catalyst classifications are homogeneous and heterogeneous catalysts. A **homogeneous catalyst** is in the same phase or physical state as the reactants and a **heterogeneous catalyst** is in a different phase than the reactants. Examples of homogeneous catalysts include acids, bases, and enzymes in solution. Catalytic converters in cars, in which solid catalysts speed conversion of unburned gaseous fuel, carbon monoxide, and nitrogen oxides to carbon dioxide, water, and nitrogen, are heterogeneous catalysts.

Acid-Base Catalysis

Acid-base catalysis can be homogeneous or heterogeneous catalysis. In an acid- or base-catalyzed reaction, the rate is increased by transfer of proton, H^+, to or from a reactant. An example is the acid-catalyzed hydration of an alkene.

Acid-Catalyzed Hydration of an Alkene

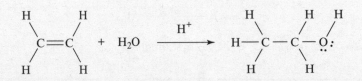

The rate of the reaction of an alkene with water is increased when the alkene is activated by a proton. This results in a positively charged intermediate that reacts quickly with water in the second step of the mechanism. Regeneration of the proton in the third step leads to the alcohol product. Notice that there is no *net* consumption or production of H^+ in the reaction. (Since H^+ is both consumed in the first step and regenerated in the last step, they cancel.)

$$C_2H_4 + H^+ \rightarrow C_2H_5^+$$

$$C_2H_5^+ + H_2O \rightarrow C_2H_7O^+$$

$$C_2H_7O^+ \rightarrow C_2H_6O + H^+$$

Enzyme Catalysis

Enzymes are catalysts that occur in biological systems. Enzyme catalysis is homogeneous catalysis, which usually occurs under mild conditions in an aqueous solution like intracellular fluid. Enzymes are usually composed mostly of proteins, which are biopolymers of amino acids. Intermolecular forces within the protein hold the large molecule in a defined three-dimensional reactive shape.

Enzymes have reactive sites that bind to specific reactants, which are called **substrates.** The reacting substrates are bound in a favorable geometric orientation and modified to make reaction faster. Once the product is formed, it is released from the enzyme into the solution.

Enzyme Catalysis

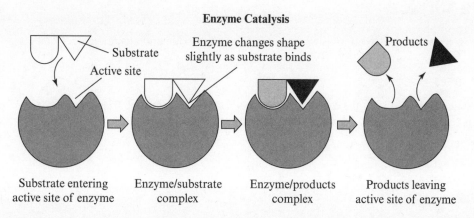

| Substrate entering active site of enzyme | Enzyme/substrate complex | Enzyme/products complex | Products leaving active site of enzyme |

It is important to note that both the forward and the reverse reaction rates are increased by an enzyme. Consider the enzyme **carbonic anhydrase.** Carbon dioxide, CO_2, is a product of cellular respiration. Addition of water (referred to as **hydration**) to CO_2 is necessary in order for CO_2 to be transported from the cells to the lungs via the circulatory system, since CO_2 is insoluble in aqueous solution and H_2CO_3, the hydrated form, is soluble. The uncatalyzed hydration is too slow to remove the CO_2 efficiently. Carbonic anhydrase increases the rate of the reaction. Once the hydrated CO_2 reaches the lungs, the reverse reaction is catalyzed, in which H_2CO_3 is converted back to CO_2. Carbonic anhydrase is responsible for increasing the rate of both the forward and the reverse reactions. The double reaction arrow indicates reversibility.

$$CO_2 + H_2O \rightleftharpoons H_2CO_3$$

Heterogeneous Catalysis

A heterogeneous catalyst is in a different phase or physical state than the reactants. There are many practical examples of heterogeneous catalysts, such as the catalytic converters in cars and the polymerization of propene (also known as propylene) to form polypropylene.

The process of heterogeneous catalysis begins with the adsorption of the reactant to the catalyst. **Adsorption** refers to the binding of reactant molecules to the surface of the catalyst. The second step in heterogeneous catalysis is activation of the adsorbed reactants. The reaction then occurs while the activated reactant is adsorbed, and the activation energy is lower than that of the uncatalyzed process. Finally, the product molecule undergoes **desorption,** or release from the surface of the catalyst.

An example of heterogeneous catalysis is used in the production of ammonia from hydrogen and nitrogen gases. This reaction is carried out at very high temperatures in the presence of a solid iron catalyst. The hydrogen and nitrogen adsorb to the iron surface and their bonds break. New bonds between hydrogen and nitrogen form on the surface and the resulting ammonia is released.

Heterogenous Catalysis

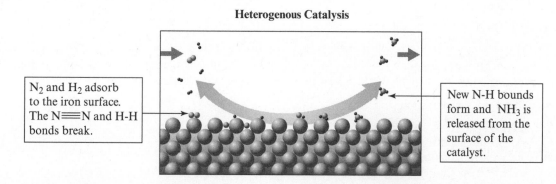

N_2 and H_2 adsorb to the iron surface. The N≡N and H-H bonds break.

New N-H bounds form and NH_3 is released from the surface of the catalyst.

Review Questions

Multiple Choice

1. Dinitrogen pentoxide decomposes to form dinitrogen tetroxide and oxygen gas.

$$2 N_2O_5 \rightarrow 2 N_2O_4 + O_2$$

In an experiment at 45 °C, the concentration of N_2O_5 decreases from 0.0200 M to 0.0071 M in 0.10 second. What is the average rate of formation of O_2 during this time period?

   A. $1.29 \times 10^{-2}\ M \cdot s^{-1}$
   B. $6.45 \times 10^{-2}\ M \cdot s^{-1}$
   C. $1.29 \times 10^{-1}\ M \cdot s^{-1}$
   D. $2.58 \times 10^{-1}\ M \cdot s^{-1}$

2. When the kinetics of the reaction $2 HI \rightarrow H_2 + I_2$ are studied using the method of initial rates, the following data is obtained. What is the rate law for the reaction?

Trial	$[HI]_0$ (M)	Initial Rate of Formation of I_2 ($M \cdot s^{-1}$)
1	0.010	4.0×10^{-6}
2	0.020	1.6×10^{-5}
3	0.030	3.6×10^{-5}

   A.   rate = k
   B.   rate = $k[HI]$
   C.   rate = $k[HI]^2$
   D.   rate = $k[HI]^{0.5}$

3. Which of the following reactions is least likely to be an elementary step in a reaction mechanism?

   A. $A \rightarrow B$
   B. $2 A \rightarrow B$
   C. $A + B \rightarrow C$
   D. $2 A + B \rightarrow C$

4. The reaction $A \rightarrow B$ is zero order. When $[A]_0 = 0.25\ M$, the initial rate of the reaction is found to be 0.40 $M \cdot s^{-1}$. What is the expected initial rate when $[A]_0 = 0.75\ M$?

   A. $0.28\ M \cdot s^{-1}$
   B. $0.40\ M \cdot s^{-1}$
   C. $1.2\ M \cdot s^{-1}$
   D. $3.6\ M \cdot s^{-1}$

5. A researcher is searching for a set of conditions that would cause an increase in the rate of a desired reaction. An increase in which of the following is NOT expected to increase the rate of a reaction?

   A.   Reactant concentration
   B.   Surface area of a reactant
   C.   Activation energy of the reaction
   D.   Temperature of the reaction

The nuclear decay of sulfur-35 was monitored and plotted below. Use this data to answer questions 6–8.

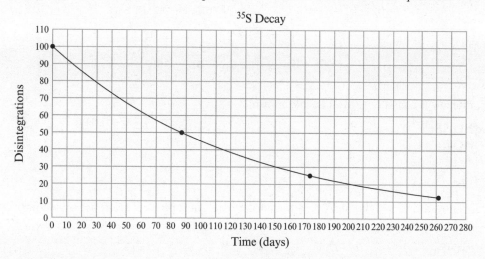

^{35}S Decay

6. What is the approximate half-life for the decay of sulfur-35?

    A.   44 days

    B.   87 days

    C.   130 days

    D.   260 days

7. What is the rate constant for the decay of sulfur-35?

    A. $0.004\ \text{day}^{-1}$

    B. $0.008\ \text{day}^{-1}$

    C. $0.04\ \text{day}^{-1}$

    D. $0.08\ \text{day}^{-1}$

8. A pure sample of sulfur-35 has a mass of 2.00 grams. How much will remain after 348 days?

    A.   0.125 gram

    B.   0.250 gram

    C.   0.500 gram

    D.   1.00 gram

9. The rate of a particular chemical reaction at 320 K is found to be four times faster than the rate of the same reaction at temperature, T. What is the likely value of T?

    A.   0 K

    B.   273 K

    C.   300 K

    D.   350 K

10. An oxidoreductase is an enzyme that catalyzes redox reactions. Which reaction below is likely to be faster in the presence of an oxidoreductase?

    A. $P_2O_7^{4-} + H_2O \rightarrow 2\ HPO_4^{2-}$

    B. $CO_2 + H_2O \rightarrow H_2CO_3$

    C. $2\ H_2O_2 \rightarrow 2\ H_2O + O_2$

    D. $C_4H_2O_4 + H_2O \rightarrow C_4H_4O_5$

11. A proposed mechanism for the reaction of nitrogen monoxide with bromine is:

$$2\,NO \underset{k_{-1}}{\overset{k_1}{\rightleftharpoons}} N_2O_2 \qquad \text{(fast)}$$

$$N_2O_2 + Br_2 \xrightarrow{k_2} 2\,NOBr \quad \text{(slow)}$$

Which rate law is consistent with this mechanism?

A. $k[NO]^2[Br_2]$
B. $k[NO][Br_2]$
C. $k[NO]^2$
D. $k[Br_2]$

12. The concentration of a reactant, A, in a zero order reaction is plotted as a function of time. Which of the following graphs results?

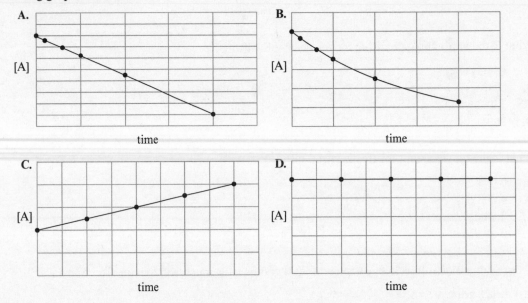

13. Which is necessarily true of the reaction represented by the energy profile below?

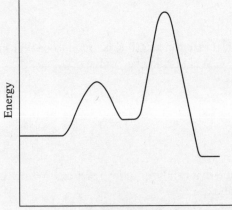

A. The reaction mechanism has a single transition state and two intermediates.
B. The reaction mechanism has two catalysts and two intermediates.
C. The reaction mechanism has two transition states and one intermediate.
D. The reaction mechanism has two catalysts and no intermediates.

14. The reaction mechanism below takes place in aqueous solution. The role of H_3O^+ in the reaction is best described as that of a(n) _____.

$$C_7H_6O + H_3O^+ \rightarrow C_7H_7O^+ + H_2O$$
$$C_7H_7O^+ + C_8H_8O \rightarrow C_{15}H_{15}O_2^+$$
$$C_{15}H_{15}O_2^+ + H_2O \rightarrow C_{15}H_{14}O_2 + H_3O^+$$

  A. heterogeneous catalyst
  B. acid catalyst
  C. intermediate
  D. reactant

Molecules of X decompose to form Y and Z in a certain chemical reaction. The rate of this reaction was studied at 200 °C, and the data that were obtained were plotted. Use this information to answer questions 15–17.

$$X \rightarrow Y + Z$$

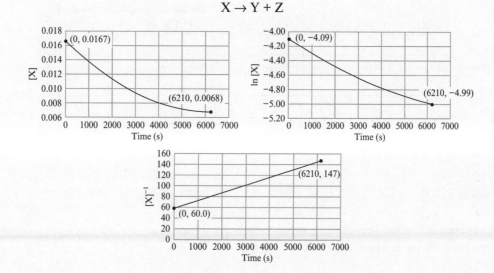

15. Doubling the concentration of X will _____ the rate of the reaction.

  A. have no effect on
  B. double
  C. triple
  D. quadruple

16. The magnitude of the rate constant for this reaction is approximately _____ at this temperature.

  A. 2.0×10^{-6}
  B. 1.6×10^{-4}
  C. 1.4×10^{-2}
  D. 6.7×10^{1}

17. The rate constant of this reaction has units of _____.

  A. $mol \cdot L^{-1} \cdot s^{-1}$
  B. $L \cdot mol^{-1} \cdot s^{-1}$
  C. s^{-1}
  D. $L^2 \cdot mol^{-2} \cdot s^{-1}$

18. The rate law for a reaction is rate = $k[A]^2$. The magnitude rate constant is 1.0×10^{-3} at 25 °C. If the initial concentration of reactant A is 4.0 M, what is the expected concentration after 250 s?

    A.   0 M

    B.   0.25 M

    C.   0.50 M

    D.   2.0 M

19. Propene, C_3H_6, undergoes an addition reaction with HCl according to the following equation.

$$C_3H_6 + HCl \rightarrow C_3H_7Cl$$

At a certain temperature, the method of initial rates was used to determine the rate expression for this reaction. The following initial rate data was collected.

Trial	$[C_3H_6]_0$ (M)	$[HCl]_0$ (M)	Initial Rate of Formation of C_3H_7Cl ($M \cdot s^{-1}$)
1	0.010	0.010	5.0×10^{-8}
2	0.010	0.020	4.0×10^{-7}
3	0.020	0.010	1.0×10^{-7}

The rate law for the addition of HCl to C_3H_6 is rate = _____.

    A. $k[C_3H_6]^3[HCl]$

    B. $k[C_3H_6][HCl]$

    C. $k[C_3H_6][HCl]^3$

    D. $k[C_3H_6][HCl]^2$

20. Select the reaction energy profile that corresponds to the slowest reaction. All reaction coordinates proceed from reactants on the left to products on the right.

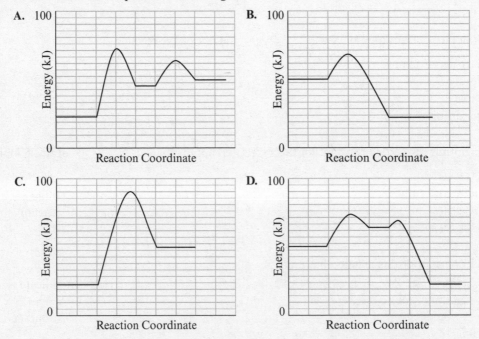

Long Free Response

1. At 2000 K, cyclopropane rearranges to form propene with a specific rate constant of $1.24 \times 10^8 \text{ s}^{-1}$.

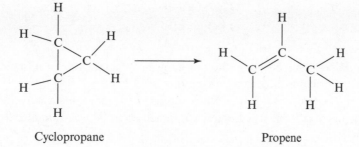

Cyclopropane   Propene

    a.   Is this reaction relatively fast or slow at 2000 K? Briefly describe your reasoning.

    b.   What is the order of the reaction with respect to cyclopropane? How do you know?

    c.   If the initial mass of cyclopropane is 2.00 grams and no propene is initially present, how long will it take for the mass of propene to reach 1.00 gram?

    d.   At 500 K, the rate of this reaction increases in the presence of boron trichloride, BCl_3, but BCl_3 is not consumed.

        i.   What is the likely role of BCl_3 in the reaction?

        ii.   On a single plot, sketch energy profiles for the reactions in the presence and the absence of BCl_3 at 500 K. Label products, reactants, axes, and activation energies. Clearly indicate which reaction is taking place in the presence of BCl_3. The reaction is exothermic.

    e.   The rate constant of the uncatalyzed reaction was measured at various temperatures and used to generate the plot shown below. What is the activation energy of the uncatalyzed formation of propene from cyclopropane? Include units in your response. (Temperatures are in Kelvin.)

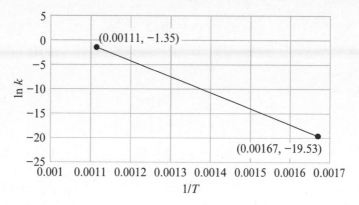

Short Free Response

2. The following reaction occurs at 1000 K. It is a second order process. When equilibrium has been established, the concentrations of products are greater than the concentration of the reactants.

$$2 \text{ A}(g) \rightleftharpoons 2 \text{ B}(g) + \text{C}(g)$$

    a.   Sketch a graph that shows how the concentrations of products and reactants change with time when pure A is placed in a piston with a fixed volume. Be sure to label both axes and indicate which concentration each curve represents.

    b.   What would be the effect of running the reaction with the same initial mass of A, but increasing the volume of the piston at constant temperature? Explain your answer.

    c.   What would be the effect of decreasing the temperature of the reaction on the rate at constant volume? Support your answer with a discussion of activation energy and a plot of number of molecules versus energy. Make sure to label the high temperature and low temperature curves.

3. An atmospheric researcher would like to investigate a reaction that is expected to occur by the following mechanism.

$$O_3 \rightleftharpoons O_2 + O \quad \text{(fast)}$$
$$O + O_3 \rightarrow 2O_2 \quad \text{(slow)}$$

    a.   Write the overall reaction based on this mechanism. When the rate of disappearance of O_3 is $2.0 \times 10^{-3} \; M \cdot s^{-1}$, what is the rate of appearance of O_2?

    b.   What is the rate law for this reaction if it proceeds by the mechanism shown?

    c.   What two factors determine whether a reaction will occur between a molecule of O_3 and an O atom by this mechanism?

    d.   Chlorine atoms in the atmosphere catalyze this reaction. What effect would the catalyst have on the rate? Explain your answer in terms of activation energy.

Answers and Explanations

Multiple Choice

1. B. (EK 4.A.1) The relationship between the rates of N_2O_5 consumption and O_2 production are given by the expression

$$\text{rate} = \frac{\Delta[O_2]}{\Delta t} = -\frac{1}{2}\left(\frac{\Delta[N_2O_5]}{\Delta t}\right) = -\frac{1}{2}\left(\frac{0.0071 \; M \; - \; 0.0200 \; M}{0.10 \; s}\right) = \frac{0.0129}{0.20} = 6.45 \times 10^{-2} \; M \cdot s^{-1}$$

2. C. (EK 4.A.2) The general form of the rate law is

$$\text{rate} = k[HI]^x$$

Any two of the trials can be chosen to determine the order with respect to HI. Using trial 2 and trial 1 as an example,

$$\frac{\text{rate}_2}{\text{rate}_1} = \frac{\cancel{k}}{\cancel{k}}\left(\frac{[HI]_{0_2}}{[HI]_{0_1}}\right)^x$$
$$\frac{1.6 \times 10^{-5}}{4.0 \times 10^{-6}} = \left(\frac{0.020}{0.010}\right)^x$$
$$4 = 2^x$$
$$x = 2$$

3. D. (EK 4.B.1) Trimolecular collisions, those in which three molecules collide simultaneously, are exceedingly rare. The simultaneous collision between two molecules of A and one molecule of B (choice D) is a trimolecular step, while the other choices depict unimolecular and bimolecular steps. The trimolecular step is least likely to occur in a reaction mechanism.

4. B. (EK 4.A.1, 4.A.2) In a zero order reaction, the rate is independent of reactant concentration. The initial rate when the concentration of reactant is $0.25 \; M$ is the same as when the initial concentration is $0.75 \; M$; therefore, choice B, $0.40 \; M \cdot s^{-1}$, is correct.

5. C. (EK 4.A.1, 4.B.2) An increase in the activation energy of a reaction would slow the reaction rather than speed it up. At a given temperature, fewer molecules would have sufficient energy to overcome a higher activation energy barrier than a lower activation barrier.

6. B. (EK 4.A.3) Half-life is the amount of time it takes for the initial number of disintegrations to decrease by half. The time it takes for the initial number of disintegrations, 100, to decrease to 50 is between 85 and 90 days according to the graph. The best choice is 87 days.

7. B. (EK 4.A.3) This reaction is first order because all nuclear decay processes occur with first order kinetics. The relationship between half-life for a first order decay and the rate constant is given on the *AP Chemistry Equations and Constants* sheet (pages 365–366).

$$t_{1/2} = \frac{0.693}{k}$$

$$k = \frac{0.693}{t_{1/2}} = \frac{0.693}{87\text{ days}} \approx \frac{0.7}{90} \approx 0.008\text{ day}^{-1}$$

8. A. (EK 4.A.3) The easiest way to approach this problem is to recognize that 348 days corresponds to four half-lives (87 days × 4 = 348 days). After the first half-life, the number of grams of sulfur-35 has decreased to 1.00 gram. After two half-lives, the amount has decreased to 0.500 gram. After three half-lives, the amount has decreased to 0.250 gram, and after four half-lives, the amount has decreased to 0.125 gram.

9. C. (EK 4.B.2, 4.B.3) For many chemical reactions near room temperature, a 10-kelvin increase in temperature results in a twofold increase in the rate of a reaction. Since the reaction rate has quadrupled, this means that a temperature of 320 K must be 20 kelvins higher than the previous temperature.

10. C. (EK 4.D.2) A catalyst such as an enzyme increases the rate of a reaction, so an oxidoreductase increases the rate of a redox reaction. The only redox reaction in the answer choices is the decomposition of H_2O_2. The oxidation number of hydrogen decreases from +1 to zero, and the oxidation number of oxygen increases from –1 to zero.

11. A. (EK 4.B.1, 4.C.2, 4.C.3, 4.C.4) The rate law based on the slow step is

$$\text{rate} = k_2[N_2O_2][Br_2]$$

Since N_2O_2 is an intermediate, however, it is not included in the rate law.

The rate of the first step in the forward direction is equal to the rate in the reverse direction.

$$k_1[NO]^2 = k_{-1}[N_2O_2]$$

Solving for the intermediate results in

$$[N_2O_2] = \frac{k_1[NO]^2}{k_{-1}}$$

Substitution into the rate law gives

$$\text{rate} = \frac{k_1[NO]^2[Br]}{k_{-1}}$$

$$\text{rate} = k[NO]^2[Br]$$

12. A. (EK 4.A.2) A plot of concentration versus time for a zero order reaction results in a straight line with a negative slope. The concentration of A decreases steadily, but the rate of the reaction does not change.

13. C. (EK 4.B.3, 4.C.3) The energy profile shows two transition states and one intermediate, as labeled in the plot below. The transition states are at the energy maxima, and the intermediate is at an energy minimum between the two transition states.

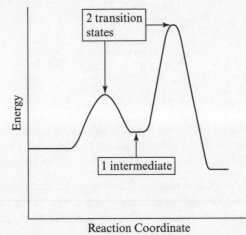

14. B. (EK 4.D.1, 4.D.2) The H_3O^+ reacts in the first step and is regenerated in a subsequent step, so it is a catalyst in this mechanism. It activates the reactant by donating a proton, so it is specifically an acid catalyst.

15. D. (EK 4.A.2) The plot of $[X]^{-1}$ versus time is linear, so the rate is second order with respect to X.

$$\text{rate} = k[X]^2$$

If the concentration of X is doubled, the rate will increase by a factor of 4.

$$\frac{\text{rate}_2}{\text{rate}_1} = \frac{\cancel{k}(2 \times \cancel{[X]})^2}{\cancel{k}\,\cancel{[X]^2}}$$

$$\frac{\text{rate}_2}{\text{rate}_1} = 2^2$$

$$\text{rate}_2 = 4 \times \text{rate}_1$$

16. C. (EK 4.A.3) The slope of the plot of $[X]^{-1}$ versus time provides the rate constant, k. The slope can be approximated

$$\frac{\Delta t}{\Delta[X]^{-1}} = \frac{147 - 60}{6210 - 0} = \frac{87}{6210} \approx \frac{9}{6} \cdot \frac{10^1}{10^3} = \frac{3}{2} \times 10^{(1-3)} = 1.5 \times 10^{-2}$$

The closest response is 1.4×10^{-2}, which is the calculator result.

17. B. (EK 4.A.3) The rate constant must have units that can be multiplied by the square of the concentration to result in units of rate, $M \cdot s^{-1}$, or $\text{mol} \cdot L^{-1} \cdot s^{-1}$.

$$\frac{\text{mol}}{L \cdot s} = k\left(\frac{\text{mol}}{L}\right)^2$$

$$\frac{\cancel{\text{mol}}}{\cancel{L} \cdot s} \times \frac{L^{\cancel{2}}}{\text{mol}^{\cancel{2}}} = k = \frac{L}{\text{mol} \cdot s}$$

18. D. (EK 4.A.2, 4.A.3) The relationship between initial concentration and concentration at time, t, for a second order reaction is given on the *AP Chemistry Equations and Constants* sheet (pages 365–366).

$$\frac{1}{[A]} - \frac{1}{[A]_0} = kt$$

$$\frac{1}{[A]} - \frac{1}{4.0\ M} = (1.0 \times 10^{-3}\ M^{-1} \cdot s^{-1})(250\ s) = 0.25\ M^{-1}$$

$$\frac{1}{[A]} - 0.25\ M^{-1} = 0.25\ M^{-1}$$

$$\frac{1}{[A]} = 0.50\ M^{-1}$$

$$[A] = 2.0\ M$$

19. C. (EK 4.A.2) The overall rate of the reaction is given by

$$\text{rate} = k[C_3H_6]^x[HCl]^y$$

Select two trials (trials 1 and 3) in which HCl does not change in order to solve for x.

$$\frac{\text{rate}_3}{\text{rate}_1} = \frac{k(0.020)^x\,(0.010)^y}{k(0.010)^x\,(0.010)^y} = \frac{1.0 \times 10^{-7}}{5.0 \times 10^{-8}}$$

$$2^x = 2$$

$$x = 1$$

The order with respect to HCl can be determined using trials 1 and 2.

$$\frac{\text{rate}_2}{\text{rate}_1} = \frac{k\,(0.010)^x\,(0.020)^y}{k\,(0.010)^x\,(0.010)^y} = \frac{4.0 \times 10^{-7}}{5.0 \times 10^{-8}}$$

$$2^y = 8$$

$$y = 3$$

The rate law for the reaction is

$$\text{rate} = k[C_3H_6][HCl]^3$$

20. C. (EK 4.B.2) The profile with the highest activation energy going from reactants on the left to products on the right is the profile shown in choice C.

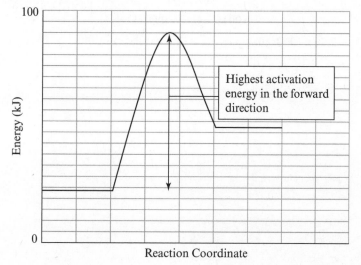

Reaction Coordinate

Long Free Response

1. a. (EK 4.A.3) The reaction is fast, as indicated by the very large rate constant on the order of 10^8.

    b. (EK 4.A.2, 4.A.3) The reaction is first order with respect to cyclopropane. The units associated with the rate constant, s^{-1}, must be multiplied by M to result in units of rate, $M \cdot s^{-1}$.

    c. (EK 4.A.2, 4.A.3) The time it takes for the concentration to decrease by half is the half-life of a reaction. Since the molar masses are identical for each gram of cyclopropane that is consumed, 1 gram of propene is produced. The time for the cyclopropane to decrease from 2 grams to 1 gram is the half-life. This reaction is first order, so the half-life is given by

$$t_{\frac{1}{2}} = \frac{0.693}{k} = \frac{0.693}{1.24 \times 10^8 \ s^{-1}} = 5.59 \times 10^{-9} \ s$$

    d. i. (EK 4.D.1) Because BCl_3 increases the rate of the reaction without being consumed, it is a catalyst. It changes the reaction mechanism to one with lower activation energy than the uncatalyzed process.

       ii. (EK 4.D.1) Your answer should resemble the sketch below. Notice that the activation energy for the reaction in the presence of BCl_3 is lower than that of the reaction in the absence of BCl_3. Since the reaction is exothermic, product potential energy is lower than reactant potential energy.

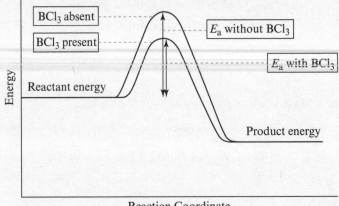

    e. (EK 4.B.3) The activation energy of a reaction can be determined from the slope of the plot of $\ln k$ versus T^{-1}.

$$\text{slope} = -\frac{E_a}{R}$$

$$E_a = -\text{slope} \times R = -\left(\frac{-19.53 - (-1.35)}{0.00167 \ K^{-1} - 0.00111 \ K^{-1}} \right) \times 8.314 \ J \cdot mol^{-1} \cdot K^{-1}$$

$$E_a = 2.70 \times 10^5 \ J \cdot mol^{-1}$$

Short Free Response

2. a. (EK 4.A.1) The sketch should clearly show that A disappears at approximately the same rate that B appears. The rate of appearance of C is half the rate of appearance of B.

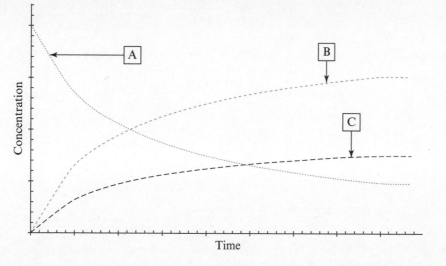

b. (EK 4.A.1) Because the volume of the vessel is increased, the concentration of A is decreased. A decreased concentration of reactant leads to a decrease in the rate of the reaction when the rate is not zero order.

c. (EK 4.B.2) At a higher temperature, a larger number of molecules will have sufficient kinetic energy to overcome the activation energy barrier and react, while at the lower temperature, a smaller number of molecules will have sufficient kinetic energy to do so. This results in an increased reaction rate at high temperature.

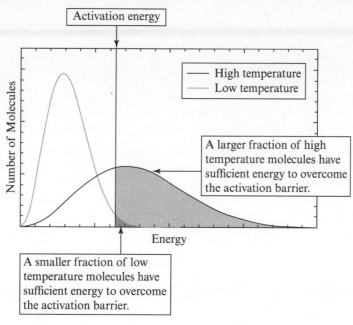

3. a. (EK 4.A.1) The overall rate of the reaction is

$$O_3 \rightleftharpoons O_2 + \cancel{O}$$
$$\cancel{O} + O_3 \rightarrow 2\,O_2$$
$$\overline{2\,O_3 \rightarrow 3\,O_2}$$

The rate of disappearance of O_3 is related to the rate of appearance of O_2 by

$$\text{rate of reaction} = -\frac{1}{2}\left(\frac{\Delta[O_3]}{\Delta t}\right) = \frac{1}{3}\left(\frac{\Delta[O_2]}{\Delta t}\right)$$

$$-\frac{1}{2}\left(-2.0\times10^{-3}\ M\cdot s^{-1}\right) = \frac{1}{3}\left(\frac{\Delta[O_2]}{\Delta t}\right)$$

$$\frac{\Delta[O_2]}{\Delta t} = 3.0\times10^{-3}\ M\cdot s^{-1}$$

b. (EK 4.C.1) The rate is determined by the slow step.

$$\text{rate} = k_2[O][O_3]$$

Since the rate law should not contain an intermediate, it is necessary to recognize that the rate of the forward reaction for the first step is equal to the rate of the reverse.

$$k_1[O_3] = k_{-1}[O_2][O]$$

$$[O] = \frac{k_1[O_3]}{k_{-1}[O_2]}$$

Substituting the expression into the rate law gives

$$\text{rate} = \frac{k_1 k_2}{k_{-1}}[O_3]^2[O_2]^{-1} = k[O_3]^2[O_2]^{-1}$$

c. (EK 4.B.2) The two factors that determine whether a collision between O_3 and O will result in a reaction are the energy of the molecules and the orientation. The energy of the collision must be sufficient to overcome the activation barrier for the reaction. The molecules must collide with an orientation that makes bond formation and bond breaking possible.

d. (EK 4.D.1) The catalyst increases the rate of the reaction by providing an alternative mechanistic route from reactants to products. This alternative route would have a decreased activation energy relative to the activation energy of the uncatalyzed process. A decrease in activation energy means that at a given temperature, a larger number of molecules has sufficient kinetic energy to overcome the activation barrier.

Chapter 5

Thermodynamics (Big Idea 5)

Big Idea 5: Thermodynamics is the study of energy changes in systems

Energy is the ability to transfer heat or do work. **Thermodynamics** is the study of the energy changes that accompany physical and chemical processes. The transfer of energy into and out of systems has implications for the spontaneity, or thermodynamic favorability, of processes.

The First Law of Thermodynamics

The amount of matter and energy in the universe is fixed. This is one statement of the **first law of thermodynamics.** In ordinary physical and chemical processes, when energy is absorbed or released by a system as heat or work, this energy must be transferred between the system and the surroundings. In other words, *energy is conserved in ordinary chemical and physical changes*. In order to better understand this, some key definitions are crucial.

Temperature

As discussed in Big Idea 2 (Chapter 2, "Bonding and Intermolecular Forces"), the kinetic energy of an object is its energy by virtue of its motion. The kelvin **temperature** of a system is a measure of the average kinetic energy of the particles that make up the system.

The Kinetic Energy of the Particles that Make Up a System

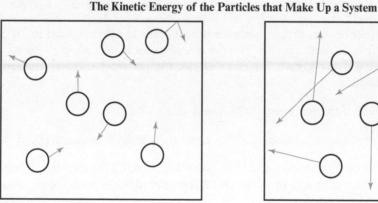

Lower temperature
Lower average kinetic energy

Higher temperature
Higher average kinetic energy

The average speeds of the particles in a sample are distributed in a manner described by the Maxwell-Boltzmann distribution. The sample with the lower average kinetic energy has a narrower distribution of molecular speeds, and the sample with the higher average kinetic energy has a broader distribution of molecular speeds.

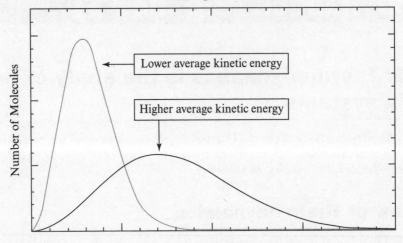

The Distribution of Molecular Speeds as a Function of Temperature

Lower average kinetic energy

Higher average kinetic energy

Number of Molecules

Molecular Speed

As the temperature of a sample approaches zero kelvin, the motion of the particles in the sample decreases. At the theoretical temperature of zero kelvin, the particles in a sample are completely motionless.

Heat

When two samples at different temperatures are in contact with one another, the particles at the interface between the two samples collide. If one of the samples has a higher average kinetic energy than the other, the collisions between the particles of the two samples result in the transfer of energy from the higher-energy sample to the lower-energy sample. **Heat** is this transfer of thermal energy from a warmer substance to a cooler substance.

The kinetic energy of the particles of the warmer substance will continue to be transferred to the particles of the cooler substance until the particles of both samples have the same average kinetic energy. This condition is referred to as **thermal equilibrium.** Two objects in contact with one another are at thermal equilibrium when they have achieved the same temperature.

The symbol for heat, the amount of thermal energy transferred, is q.

At constant pressure, a transfer of heat to or from a system is equal the **enthalpy change,** ΔH, of the process.

As discussed in Big Idea 2 (Chapter 2, "Bonding and Intermolecular Forces"), the transfer of heat to a system is an endothermic process. The potential energy of the products is greater than the potential energy of the reactants.

The release of heat by a system to the surroundings is an exothermic process. The potential energy of the products is lower than the potential energy of the reactants.

Work

Work, w, is the product of a force acting on an object or a system over a distance; the term encompasses energy transfers that are not heat transfers. In AP Chemistry, work will be limited to gas pressure-volume work. This is work that happens when a system expands or contracts against a constant external pressure. When a system expands against its surroundings, the system is doing work on the surroundings. When the system contracts, the surroundings are doing work on the system. This pressure-volume work only occurs when there is a change in the volume of the gas.

The equation for work is

$$w = -P\Delta V$$

where P is the external pressure and ΔV is the change in volume, $V_f - V_i$. This gives work in units of L·atm, which can be converted to joules:

$$1 \text{ L·atm} = 101.3 \text{ J}$$

In the event that a work calculation is required on the AP Chemistry exam, either L·atm will be appropriate units *or* this conversion factor is likely to be included in the question. Be sure to read carefully.

System and Surroundings

A **system** is a sample or a region under investigation, and the **surroundings** are everything else. There are sign conventions associated with heat transfer to a system from surroundings or to surroundings from a system.

The heat transferred to a system is equal in magnitude and opposite in sign to the heat transferred from the surroundings.

$$q_{sys} = -q_{surr}$$

Likewise, the work done on a system is equal in magnitude and opposite in sign to the work done by the surroundings.

By convention, when heat, q, is transferred from the surroundings to a system, $q > 0$. When heat is transferred from a system to the surroundings, $q < 0$. Likewise, when work is done by the surroundings on a system, $w > 0$. When work is done by the system on the surroundings, $w < 0$.

Transfer of Heat and Work Between System and Surroundings

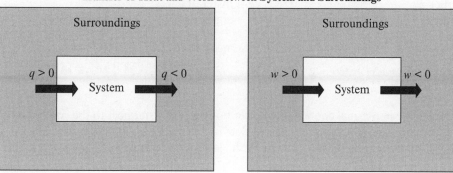

Both the system and the surroundings taken together make up the **thermodynamic universe.** The first law of thermodynamics states that energy of the universe is constant. It can be transferred between the system and the surroundings, but it cannot be created or destroyed in ordinary chemical or physical processes.

PRACTICE:

> A piston expands from a volume of 2.50 L to a volume of 3.10 L against a constant external pressure of 1.0 atm. How much work is performed? Express your answer in joules (101.3 J = 1 L·atm). Is work done by the system or on the system?

Using the equation for work,

$$w = -P\Delta V = -(1.00 \text{ atm})(3.10 \text{ L} - 2.50 \text{ L}) = -0.60 \text{ L} \cdot \text{atm}$$

$$-0.60 \text{ L·atm} \times \frac{101.3 \text{ J}}{1 \text{ L·atm}} = -61 \text{ J}$$

The negative value indicates that work is done by the system. This will always be the case when a system expands.

Heat Capacity

The **heat capacity** of a substance is the heat required to raise the temperature of a quantity of the substance by 1 K.

The amount of heat required to raise the temperature of *one gram* of the substance by one kelvin (or 1 °C) is called the **specific heat capacity**, c, and is reported in units of $J \cdot g^{-1} \cdot K^{-1}$ or $J \cdot g^{-1} \cdot °C^{-1}$. The amount of heat required to raise the temperature of *one mole* of the substance by one kelvin (or 1 °C) is called the **molar heat capacity** and is reported in units of $J \cdot mol^{-1} \cdot K^{-1}$ or $J \cdot mol^{-1} \cdot °C^{-1}$.

The higher the specific heat capacity of a substance, the greater the heat required to raise the temperature of the substance. For example, liquid water has a specific heat capacity of $4.18 \ J \cdot g^{-1} \cdot K^{-1}$. Copper has a specific heat capacity of $0.385 \ J \cdot g^{-1} \cdot K^{-1}$. It requires less heat to raise the temperature of 1 gram of copper than it does to raise the temperature of 1 gram of water.

The amount of heat absorbed or released by a chemical or physical process is given by

$$q = mc\Delta T$$

where m is the mass of the substance, c is the specific heat capacity of the substance, and T is the change in temperature, $T_{final} - T_{initial}$. This equation is given on the *AP Chemistry Equations and Constants* sheet.

PRACTICE:

> What quantity of heat is needed to raise the temperature of 10.0 g of water from 25 °C to 50 °C? The specific heat capacity of water is $4.18 \ J \cdot g^{-1} \cdot °C^{-1}$.

The equation for heat is used.

$$q = mc\Delta T = (10.0 \ \cancel{g})(4.18 \ J \cdot \cancel{g}^{-1} \cdot \cancel{°C}^{-1})(50.0 \ \cancel{°C} - 25.0 \ \cancel{°C}) = 1050 \ J$$

When two substances are in thermal contact, the hotter body will transfer heat to the cooler body until both substances have reached the same temperature. The heat lost by the higher-temperature substance, q_{lost}, is equal in magnitude and opposite in sign to the heat gained by the lower-temperature substance, q_{gained}.

$$q_{lost} = -q_{gained}$$

Suppose a student would like to measure the specific heat of aluminum. A 5.00-gram block of aluminum at 100.0 °C is placed in 20.0 grams of water at 30.0 °C. The temperature of the water increases until it reaches 33.6 °C before it begins to decrease to room temperature.

The heat transferred from the aluminum to the water is equal in magnitude to the heat gained by the water. Although both substances are at different initial temperatures, at thermal equilibrium their final temperature, T_f, is the same.

$$q_{aluminum} = -q_{water}$$

Substituting $mc\Delta T$ for water and for aluminum allows us to solve for c, the specific heat capacity of aluminum.

$$m_{Al}c_{Al}\Delta T_{Al} = -m_{H_2O}c_{H_2O}\Delta T_{H_2O}$$

$$(20.0 \ \cancel{g})(4.18 \ J \cdot \cancel{g}^{-1} \cdot \cancel{°C}^{-1})(33.6 \ \cancel{°C} - 30.0 \ \cancel{°C}) = -c_{H_2O}(5.0 \ g)(33.6 \ °C - 100.0 \ °C)$$

$$c_{H_2O} = 0.91 \ J \cdot g^{-1} \cdot °C^{-1}$$

PRACTICE:

A 100.-gram block of aluminum at 20.0 °C is placed in contact with a 10.0-gram block of iron at 60.0 °C. Assuming that no heat is lost to the surroundings, what is the final temperature of the two metals? The specific heat of aluminum is 0.897 J·g^{-1}·°C^{-1} and the specific heat of iron is 0.450 J·g^{-1}·°C^{-1}.

The heat lost by the iron is equal in magnitude and opposite in sign to the heat gained by the aluminum. The final temperature, T_f, is the same for both metals.

$$q_{lost} = -q_{gained}$$
$$m_{Fe}c_{Fe}\Delta T_{Fe} = -m_{Al}c_{Al}\Delta T_{Al}$$
$$(10.0 \text{ g})(0.450 \text{ J} \cdot \text{g}^{-1} \cdot °\text{C}^{-1})(T_f - 60.0 \text{ °C}) = -(100. \text{ g})(0.897 \text{ J} \cdot \text{g}^{-1} \cdot °\text{C}^{-1})(T_f - 20.0 \text{ °C})$$
$$T_f = 21.9 \text{ °C}$$

Calorimetry

Calorimetry is a technique for the measurement of the amount of heat transferred to or from a system. In most AP Chemistry classrooms, the type of calorimeter used is the **coffee cup calorimeter.** A reaction is carried out in a well-insulated disposable foam cup. The insulation is important so that heat transfer to or from the surroundings is minimized. Pressure (atmospheric) is constant in this kind of calorimetry experiment, so the change in enthalpy of the system is equal to the heat lost or gained in the reaction under investigation. Here, q_p represents the heat transferred to or from the system at constant pressure.

$$\Delta H = q_p$$

Coffee cup calorimetry deals with reactions in solution. The distinction between system and surroundings is sometimes a source of confusion for students. The system is specifically the reactants and products of the reaction, and the surroundings include the solvent, the thermometer, and the calorimeter. When the temperature of the solvent increases, it is because energy is being released by the reactants as they form products in an exothermic process. When the temperature of the solution decreases, the decrease is due to the uptake of energy from the surroundings by the reactants as they form products in an endothermic process.

Coffee Cup Calorimeter

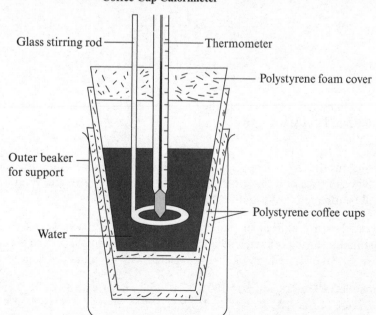

Glass stirring rod — — Thermometer

— Polystyrene foam cover

Outer beaker for support —

— Polystyrene coffee cups

Water —

Since a coffee cup calorimeter is not a perfectly insulated apparatus, some heat will be transferred to or from the surroundings. The value of ΔH calculated in a calorimetry experiment can differ from the actual value when a significant amount of heat transfer between the system and surroundings occurs.

PRACTICE:

> 100. mL of a 1.00 M HCl solution was mixed with 100. mL of 1.00 M NaOH in a coffee cup calorimeter. Before mixing, the temperatures of the HCl and NaOH solutions were both 30.0 °C. At the end of the experiment, the maximum temperature reached by the combined solutions was 40.0 °C. Assume that the densities and specific heats of the HCl and NaOH solutions were the same as that for water, 1.00 $g \cdot mL^{-1}$ and 4.18 $J \cdot g^{-1} \cdot °C^{-1}$, respectively.
>
> **(a)** What is the enthalpy of reaction for the neutralization of HCl with NaOH? Report the value in units of $J \cdot mol^{-1}$.
>
> **(b)** Is the reaction endothermic or exothermic?
>
> **(c)** If a significant amount of heat transfer with the surroundings occurs, will the enthalpy of neutralization calculated be too high or too low?

(a) The heat given off in the reaction is equal to the heat gained by the solution. Since the reaction occurs at constant pressure (atmospheric pressure), this heat is equal to the enthalpy change for the reaction. Because the density of the solution is 1.00 $g \cdot mL^{-1}$, 100. mL of solution has a mass of 100. grams.

$$q_{rxn} = -q_{soln} = -m_{soln} c_{soln} \Delta T_{soln}$$

$$q_{rxn} = -(100. \; g + 100. \; g)(4.18 \; J \cdot g^{-1} \cdot °C^{-1})(40.0 \; °C - 30.0 \; °C)$$

$$q_{rxn} = -8360 \; J$$

The amount of heat given off per mole of HCl or NaOH reacted is reported as the enthalpy change per mole reaction.

$$HCl(aq) + NaOH(aq) \rightarrow H_2O(l) + NaCl(aq)$$

The same number of moles of HCl and NaOH are present.

$$100. \; mL \; HCl \times \frac{1 \; L}{1000 \; mL} \times \frac{1.00 \; mol \; HCl}{1 \; L \; HCl} = 0.100 \; mol \; HCl$$

$$\Delta H_{rxn} = \frac{q_{rxn}}{n} = \frac{-8360 \; J}{0.100 \; mol} = -8.36 \times 10^4 \; J \cdot mol^{-1}$$

(b) The negative enthalpy change and the fact that the final temperature of the solution was higher than the initial temperature both indicate an exothermic reaction.

(c) If a significant amount of heat is lost to the surroundings, the temperature of the solution will not increase as much as expected. This means that ΔT will appear to be smaller than the true value, and the calculated magnitude of q_{rxn} will be too low. Since the reaction is exothermic and the value is negative, however, the calculated value of the enthalpy change will be too high (less negative than the true value).

Careful calibration of a coffee cup calorimeter results in measurement of a **calorimeter constant,** c_{cal}, the amount of heat that is lost or gained by the calorimeter. This can be done by using a heater to deliver a precise amount of heat or by careful measurement of the energy change associated with a standard reaction.

For example, a student adds 25.0 mL of water at 100.0 °C to 25.0 mL of water at 23.2 °C in a coffee cup calorimeter. The temperature of the water and the calorimeter rises from 23.2 °C to 58.7 °C. We can calculate the calorimeter constant in units of $J \cdot °C^{-1}$. The quantity of heat lost by the hot water as it mixes with the cold is equal to the heat that is gained by the cold water and the calorimeter.

$$q_{hot} = -(q_{cold} + q_{cal})$$
$$m_{hot}c_{H_2O}\Delta T_{hot} = -(m_{cold}c_{H_2O}\Delta T_{cold} + c_{cal}\Delta T_{cold})$$

$$(25.0 \text{ g})(4.18 \text{ J} \cdot \text{g}^{-1} \cdot °C^{-1})(58.7 °C - 100.0 °C) =$$
$$-[(25.0 \text{ g})(4.18 \text{ J} \cdot \text{g}^{-1} \cdot °C^{-1})(58.7 °C - 23.2 °C) + c_{cal}(58.7°C - 23.2 °C)]$$
$$c_{cal} = 17.1 \text{ J} \cdot °C^{-1}$$

PRACTICE:

A coffee cup calorimeter is calibrated and found to have a calorimeter constant of 27.3 $J \cdot °C^{-1}$. When 15.0 mL of 0.200 M $AgNO_3$ at 24.50 °C are added to 30.0 mL of 0.120 M NaCl, also at 24.50 °C, in this calorimeter, the temperature of the solution in the calorimeter reaches 25.43 °C. What is the heat of reaction? Report the result in units of kJ per mole of AgCl formed. Assume that the densities and specific heats of the solutions are the same as that for water, 1.00 $g \cdot mL^{-1}$ and 4.18 $J \cdot g^{-1} \cdot C^{-1}$, respectively.

The net ionic equation for the reaction that occurs is

$$Ag^+(aq) + Cl^-(aq) \rightarrow AgCl(s)$$

The amount of heat given off by the reaction is equal to the combined heat that raises the temperature of the solution and that is lost to the calorimeter.

$$q_{rxn} = -(q_{soln} + q_{cal})$$

The combined volume of the two reactant solutions is

$$15.0 \text{ mL} + 30.0 \text{ mL} = 45.0 \text{ mL}$$

Because the density is assumed to be 1.00 $g \cdot mL^{-1}$, this volume has a mass of 45.0 g.

$$q_{rxn} = -[(m_{soln}c_{soln}\Delta T) + (c_{cal}\Delta T)]$$
$$q_{rxn} = -[(45.0 \text{ g})(4.18 \text{ J} \cdot \text{g}^{-1} \cdot °C^{-1})(25.43 °C - 24.50 °C) + (27.3 \text{ J} \cdot °C^{-1})(25.43 °C - 24.50 °C)]$$
$$q_{rxn} = -2.0 \times 10^2 \text{ J}$$

In order to report the enthalpy change per mole of AgCl formed, the limiting reagent and theoretical yield must be determined. Both reactant quantities are converted to moles of AgCl formed.

$$15.0 \text{ mL AgNO}_3 \times \frac{0.200 \text{ mol AgNO}_3}{1000 \text{ mL AgNO}_3} \times \frac{1 \text{ mol AgCl}}{1 \text{ mol AgNO}_3} = 0.00300 \text{ mol AgCl}$$

$$30.0 \text{ mL NaCl} \times \frac{0.120 \text{ mol NaCl}}{1000 \text{ mL NaCl}} \times \frac{1 \text{ mol AgCl}}{1 \text{ mol NaCl}} = 0.00360 \text{ mol AgCl}$$

The theoretical yield of AgCl is 0.00300 mole, so the enthalpy of reaction can be determined.

$$\Delta H_{rxn} = \frac{-2.0 \times 10^2 \text{ J}}{0.00300 \text{ mol AgCl}} \times \frac{1 \text{ kJ}}{1000 \text{ J}} = -67 \text{ kJ} \cdot \text{mol}^{-1}$$

Enthalpy Changes in a System

AP Chemistry students must be familiar with energy changes that accompany heating and cooling, phase changes, and chemical reactions.

Heating and Cooling Curves

The enthalpy changes that accompany simple heating and cooling and phase changes for a substance with changes in temperature are portrayed graphically on heating and cooling curves. The heating curve of water was discussed previously in Big Idea 2 (Chapter 2, "Bonding and Intermolecular Forces"). A heating curve can be used to determine the energy transfer required to heat or cool a substance by a certain amount or the energy transfer required to cause a phase change.

When energy is added to or removed from a substance to raise or lower its temperature, the amount of heat transferred can be determined using

$$q = mc\Delta T$$

Notice that the specific heat capacity of a substance depends on the physical state (solid, liquid, or gas) of the substance.

When a substance freezes or melts, however, the temperature is constant and the protocol for determining the heat transfer is different. The amount of heat transferred is determined by the number of moles of the substance, n, multiplied by the **enthalpy of fusion,** ΔH_{fus}, which is the energy transferred during the conversion of one mole of a substance from a solid to a liquid at its freezing temperature.

$$q = n\Delta H_{fus}$$

Sometimes the enthalpy of fusion is given as the energy transferred during the conversion of 1 gram of a substance from a solid to a liquid at its freezing temperature. In this case, the heat transfer is determined by the product of the mass of the substance, m, and the enthalpy of fusion.

$$q = m\Delta H_{fus}$$

When a substance boils or condenses, the amount of heat transferred is determined by the number of moles multiplied by the **enthalpy of vaporization,** ΔH_{vap}. The enthalpy of vaporization is the energy required to convert one mole of a substance from liquid to gas at its boiling temperature.

$$q = n\Delta H_{vap}$$

The enthalpy of vaporization may also be expressed in grams. In this case, the heat transfer is determined by the product of the mass of the substance, m, and the enthalpy of vaporization.

$$q = m\Delta H_{vap}$$

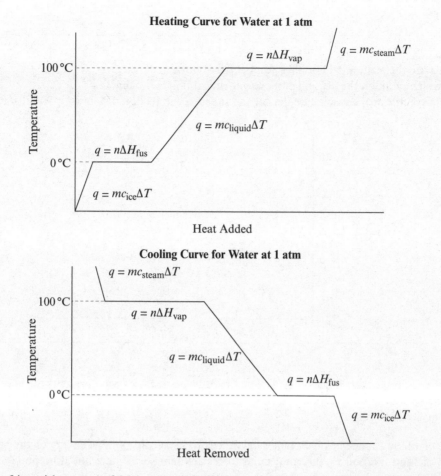

Suppose a block of ice with a mass of 25.0 grams is initially at a temperature of –15 °C. The amount of energy that is required to convert the ice to steam with a temperature of 102 °C at atmospheric pressure can be calculated. The heat of fusion of ice, the heat of vaporization of steam, and the specific heat capacities of ice, liquid water, and steam are all known. (ΔH_{fus} = 6.01 kJ·mol^{-1}, ΔH_{vap} = 40.7 kJ·mol^{-1}, c_{ice} = 2.1 J·g^{-1} · °C^{-1}, c_{liq} = 4.18 J·g^{-1} · °C^{-1}, and c_{steam} = 2.0 J·g^{-1} · °C^{-1}.)

The number of kilojoules of heat required is the sum of the amounts of heat needed to raise the temperature of the block of ice from –15 °C to 0 °C, melt the ice at 0 °C, raise the temperature of the liquid water from 0 °C to 100 °C, convert the liquid to steam at 100. °C, and then raise the temperature of the steam from 100. to 102 °C.

$$q = mc_{ice}\Delta T + n\Delta H_{fus} + mc_{liq}\Delta T + n\Delta H_{vap} + mc_{steam}\Delta T$$

$$q = [(25.0 \ g)(2.1 \ J \cdot g^{-1} \cdot °C^{-1})(0 \ °C - (-15 \ °C))] + \left[\left(25.0 \ g \times \frac{1 \ mol}{18.02 \ g}\right)(6.01 \ kJ \cdot mol^{-1})\left(\frac{1000 \ J}{1 \ kJ}\right)\right] +$$

$$[(25.0 \ g)(4.18 \ J \cdot g^{-1} \cdot °C^{-1})(100 \ °C - 0 °C)] + \left[\left(25.0 \ g \times \frac{1 \ mol}{18.02 \ g}\right)(40.7 \ kJ \cdot mol^{-1})\left(\frac{1000 \ J}{1 \ kJ}\right)\right] +$$

$$[(25.0 \ g)(2.0 \ J \cdot g^{-1} \cdot °C^{-1})(102 \ °C - 100 \ °C)]$$

$$q = 76,100 \ J \times \frac{1 \ kJ}{1000 \ J} = 76.1 \ kJ$$

A total of 76.1 kJ of energy are require to convert 25.0 grams of ice at –15 °C to steam at 102 °C.

PRACTICE:

The heating curve for a pure substance at a given pressure is shown below.

(a) What are the melting and boiling points of the substance?
(b) At which point on the heating curve are chemical bonds broken?
(c) Is the specific heat capacity greater for the substance in its liquid state or its solid state?

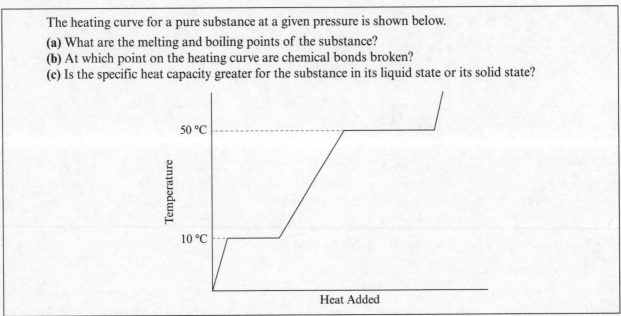

(a) The melting point of the substance is 10 °C. The first plateau in the curve represents the conversion of solid to liquid. This occurs at the melting temperature. The boiling temperature is 50 °C. The second plateau represents the conversion of liquid to gas.

(b) The heating of the substance involves a physical process. The average kinetic energy of the particles is increasing, and during melting and boiling, intermolecular forces are being disrupted, but at no point are chemical bonds broken.

(c) The slope of the heating curve of the solid state is steeper, which means it requires more heat to raise the temperature of the substance in the liquid state by 1 °C than it does to raise the temperature of the substance in the solid state by 1 °C. The specific heat capacity of the liquid form is greater than the specific heat capacity of the solid substance.

PRACTICE:

A block of ice with a mass of 10.0 grams and a temperature of –10.0 °C is added to 100.0 mL of water at 40.0 °C. What is the final temperature of the mixture? (ΔH_{fus} = 6.01 kJ·mol^{-1}, c_{ice} = 2.1 J·g^{-1}·°C^{-1}, and c_{liq} = 4.18 J·g^{-1}·°C^{-1})

This type of problem can be treated exactly like a calorimeter problem. The heat gained by the ice as it warms, melts to a liquid, and continues to warm until thermal equilibrium is reached is equal to the heat lost by the water until both are at the same temperature, T_{final}. The number of grams of water is equal to the volume of the water multiplied by the density of water, 1.00 g·mL^{-1}. The number of moles of ice is the mass divided by the molar mass, 18.02 g·mol^{-1}.

The energy lost by the 40.0 °C water is equal in magnitude to the energy that is gained by the ice.

$$q_{lost} = -q_{gained}$$
$$m_{liq}c_{liq}\Delta T = -(m_{ice}c_{ice}\Delta T + n_{ice}\Delta H + m_{liq}c_{liq}\Delta T)$$

$$\left[\left(100. \text{ mL} \times \frac{1 \text{ g}}{1 \text{ mL}}\right)\left(4.18 \text{ J} \cdot \text{g}^{-1} \cdot {}^{\circ}\text{C}^{-1}\right)\left(T_f - 40.0 \text{ }^{\circ}\text{C}\right)\right] = -\left[\left(10.0 \text{ g}\right)\left(2.1 \text{ J g}^{-1} \cdot {}^{\circ}\text{C}^{-1}\right)\left(0 \text{ }^{\circ}\text{C} - (-10.0 \text{ }^{\circ}\text{C})\right)\right]$$

$$-\left[\left(10.0 \text{ g} \times \frac{1 \text{ mol}}{18.02 \text{ g}}\right)\left(6.01 \text{ kJ} \cdot \text{mol}^{-1}\right)\left(\frac{1000 \text{ J}}{1 \text{ kJ}}\right)\right]$$

$$-\left[\left(10.0 \text{ g}\right)\left(4.18 \text{ J g}^{-1} \cdot {}^{\circ}\text{C}^{-1}\right)\left(T_f - 0 \text{ }^{\circ}\text{C}\right)\right]$$

$$T_f = 28.7 \text{ }^{\circ}\text{C}$$

Endothermic and Exothermic Reactions

Enthalpy changes associated with chemical reactions were introduced in Big Idea 3 (Chapter 3, "Chemical Reactions"). When reactants have higher potential energy than products, a reaction is **exothermic.** When products have higher potential energy than reactants, a reaction is **endothermic.**

The **potential energy** of a molecule is the energy it possesses by virtue of the attractions and repulsions among its constituent atoms and between the molecule and the surrounding particles.

In an exothermic reaction, heat is released and $\Delta H_{rxn} < 0$. In an endothermic reaction, heat energy is gained and $\Delta H_{rxn} > 0$.

Energy is required to break bonds, and energy is released when bonds are formed. In other words, *bond breaking is endothermic and bond formation is exothermic.* The average amount of energy required to break a particular type of bond is the **bond enthalpy** or **bond energy.** The higher the bond energy, the stronger the bond.

Bond energies can be used to estimate the enthalpy change of a reaction in which all reactants and products are in the gas phase. The energies of the bonds in the products are subtracted from the energies of the bonds in the reactants.

$$\Delta H_{rxn} = (\Sigma \text{ Bond energies of reactants}) - (\Sigma \text{ Bond energies of products})$$

For example, suppose a chemist would like to know the enthalpy of reaction for the addition in the gas phase of HBr to ethylene, C_2H_4, to form bromoethane, CH_3CH_2Br. A table of bond energies provides the following data.

Bond	Bond Energy (kJ·mol⁻¹)
C — C	348
C ═ C	612
C — H	412
Br — H	363
C — Br	276

The Lewis structures for reactants and products show the number of each kind of bond present.

Bromoethane Formation

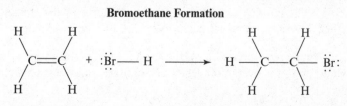

The reactants contain one C=C bond, four C-H bonds, and one H-Br bond. The product contains one C-C single bond, five C-H bonds, and one C-Br bond. The enthalpy change is calculated using the tabulated values.

$$\Delta H_{rxn} = [(1 \times 612 \text{ kJ} \cdot \text{mol}^{-1}) + (4 \times 412 \text{ kJ} \cdot \text{mol}^{-1}) + (1 \times 363 \text{ kJ} \cdot \text{mol}^{-1})] - [(1 \times 348 \text{ kJ} \cdot \text{mol}^{-1})$$

$$+ (5 \times 412 \text{ kJ} \cdot \text{mol}^{-1}) + (1 \times 276 \text{ kJ} \cdot \text{mol}^{-1})]$$

$$\Delta H_{rxn} = -61 \text{ kJ} \cdot \text{mol}^{-1}$$

Notice that this technique works equally well when only the bonds that are broken and formed are considered. The broken bonds are the C=C bond and the H-Br bond. The bonds formed are the C-C, C-Br, and C-H bonds.

$$\Delta H_{rxn} = (\Sigma \text{ Energy of bonds broken}) - (\Sigma \text{ Energy of bonds formed})$$

$$\Delta H_{rxn} = [(1 \times 612 \text{ kJ} \cdot \text{mol}^{-1}) + (1 \times 363 \text{ kJ} \cdot \text{mol}^{-1})] - [(1 \times 348 \text{ kJ} \cdot \text{mol}^{-1}) + (1 \times 412 \text{ kJ} \cdot \text{mol}^{-1}) + (1 \times 276 \text{ kJ} \cdot \text{mol}^{-1})]$$

$$\Delta H_{rxn} = -61 \text{ kJ} \cdot \text{mol}^{-1}$$

PRACTICE:

Use the tabulated bond energies below to find the enthalpy of reaction for the nitrogen gas with fluorine gas to produce nitrogen trifluoride gas.

Bond	Bond Energy (kJ·mol⁻¹)
N $\equiv$ N	944
F — F	158
N— F	270

The Lewis structures of reactants and products should be determined first.

$$N_2 + 3 F_2 \rightarrow 2 NF_3$$

There is one N-N triple bond and there are three F-F single bonds in the reactants. The product contains six N-F single bonds. The enthalpy of reaction is determined as follows.

$$\Delta H_{rxn} = [(1 \times 944 \text{ kJ} \cdot \text{mol}^{-1}) + (3 \times 158 \text{ kJ} \cdot \text{mol}^{-1})] - (6 \times 270 \text{ kJ} \cdot \text{mol}^{-1})$$

$$\Delta H_{rxn} = -202 \text{ kJ} \cdot \text{mol}^{-1}$$

A second method for calculating the enthalpy of a reaction involves the use of **Hess's law.** Hess's law states that enthalpy change for a process is equal to the sum of the enthalpy changes for reaction steps that add up to the process, regardless of whether those steps were actually involved in the chemical reaction mechanism.

When using Hess's law to determine reaction enthalpy, the steps for which the enthalpy changes are known must be rearranged so that they add up to the overall process. For example, consider the reaction of graphite with oxygen.

$$C(gr) + \frac{1}{2}O_2(g) \rightarrow CO(g) \qquad\qquad \Delta H = ?$$

The following two known reaction enthalpies can be used to elucidate the enthalpy of reaction for the oxidation of graphite to carbon dioxide.

$$C(gr) + O_2(g) \rightarrow CO_2(g) \qquad\qquad \Delta H = -393.5 \text{ kJ} \cdot \text{mol}^{-1}$$
$$CO(g) + \frac{1}{2}O_2(g) \rightarrow CO_2(g) \qquad\qquad \Delta H = -283.0 \text{ kJ} \cdot \text{mol}^{-1}$$

These two equations must be manipulated so that they add up to the overall transformation of interest. Graphite, $C(gr)$, is a reactant in the overall equation, so the first step should be used as written. The second equation, however, needs to be reversed so that $CO(g)$ is a product. When the equation is reversed, the sign of the enthalpy change for the second equation is also reversed. The sum of the two steps results in the equation that represents the overall reaction between graphite and oxygen to form carbon monoxide. So, the sum of the enthalpy changes gives the enthalpy of this reaction.

$$C(gr) + \frac{\cancel{2}^{1}}{2}O_2(g) \rightarrow \cancel{CO_2(g)} \qquad\qquad \Delta H = -393.5 \text{ kJ} \cdot \text{mol}^{-1}$$

$$\cancel{CO_2(g)} \rightarrow CO(g) + \frac{1}{2}\cancel{O_2}(g) \qquad\qquad \Delta H = -(-283.0 \text{ kJ} \cdot \text{mol}^{-1})$$

$$\overline{C(gr) + \frac{1}{2}O_2(g) \rightarrow CO(g) \qquad\qquad \Delta H = -110.5 \text{ kJ} \cdot \text{mol}^{-1}}$$

It is sometimes necessary to multiply an equation by some factor in order to produce the equation that represents the overall reaction. When this is the case, the enthalpy of the corresponding reaction must be multiplied by that factor. For instance, suppose the enthalpy of reaction for the decomposition of sulfur trioxide, SO_3, is needed.

$$2\,SO_3(g) \rightarrow 2\,SO_2(g) + O_2(g) \qquad\qquad \Delta H = ?$$

The following information is given.

$$S(s) + \frac{3}{2}O_2(g) \rightarrow SO_3(g) \qquad\qquad \Delta H = -395.7 \text{ kJ} \cdot \text{mol}^{-1}$$
$$S(s) + O_2(g) \rightarrow SO_2(g) \qquad\qquad \Delta H = -296.8 \text{ kJ} \cdot \text{mol}^{-1}$$

In this case, the first equation must be reversed. Both equations must be multiplied by 2.

$$2\,SO_3(g) \rightarrow 2\,\cancel{S(s)} + \frac{\cancel{6}^{2}}{2}O_2(g) \qquad\qquad \Delta H = -(-395.7 \text{ kJ} \cdot \text{mol}^{-1})2$$

$$2\,\cancel{S(s)} + \frac{4}{2}\cancel{O_2}(g) \rightarrow 2\,SO_2(g) \qquad\qquad \Delta H = (-296.8 \text{ kJ} \cdot \text{mol}^{-1})2$$

$$\overline{2\,SO_3(g) \rightarrow 2\,SO_2(g) + O_2(g) \qquad\qquad \Delta H = 197.8 \text{ kJ} \cdot \text{mol}^{-1}}$$

PRACTICE:

The chemical equations and enthalpy changes of the following reactions are given.

$$4\,HCl(g)+O_2(g) \rightarrow 2\,H_2O(l)+2\,Cl_2(g) \qquad \Delta H = -202.4\ \text{kJ}\cdot\text{mol}^{-1}$$

$$H_2O(l) \rightarrow H_2(g)+\tfrac{1}{2}O_2(g) \qquad \Delta H = 285.8\ \text{kJ}\cdot\text{mol}^{-1}$$

$$HF(l) \rightarrow \tfrac{1}{2}H_2(g)+\tfrac{1}{2}F_2(g) \qquad \Delta H = 299.8\ \text{kJ}\cdot\text{mol}^{-1}$$

Determine the enthalpy of reaction for the reaction of HCl with F_2.

$$2\,HCl(g)+F_2(g) \rightarrow 2\,HF(l) + Cl_2(g) \qquad \Delta H = ?$$

The first equation is the only one in which HCl appears. It is divided by 2. The third equation is the only one in which HF appears. Reversal and multiplication of the third equation by 2 results in the correct number of HF moles in the products. Since H_2O, H_2, and O_2 do not appear in the overall equation, the second equation is left as it is written in the problem.

$$2\,HCl(g)+\tfrac{1}{2}O_2(g) \rightarrow H_2O(l) + Cl_2(g) \qquad \Delta H = (-202.4\ \text{kJ}\cdot\text{mol}^{-1})\tfrac{1}{2}$$

$$H_2O(l) \rightarrow H_2(g) + \tfrac{1}{2}O_2(g) \qquad \Delta H = 285.8\ \text{kJ}\cdot\text{mol}^{-1}$$

$$\underline{H_2(g) + F_2(g) \rightarrow 2\,HF(l) \qquad \Delta H = (-299.8\ \text{kJ}\cdot\text{mol}^{-1})2}$$

$$2\,HCl(g) + F_2(g) \rightarrow 2\,HF(l) + Cl_2(g) \qquad \Delta H = -415.0\ \text{kJ}\cdot\text{mol}^{-1}$$

The third method for determining the enthalpy change for a reaction involves the use of standard molar heats of formation of the reactants. The **standard molar heat of formation,** $\Delta H°_f$, of a substance is the enthalpy change that occurs when mole of a substance is formed from its constituent elements in their standard states. The **standard state** of an element is its form under thermodynamic standard conditions. *The standard molar heat of formation of an element in its standard state is zero.*

In thermodynamics, standard conditions are defined as 1 atmosphere pressure or 1 atm of partial pressures in a gas mixture or 1 M solution. (Often the standard temperature reported in thermodynamic tables is 25 °C, unlike standard temperature for gas law calculations, which is 0 °C).

In order to calculate the enthalpy of a reaction, the sum of the standard molar enthalpies of formation of the reactants is subtracted from the sum of the standard molar enthalpies of formation of the products.

$$\Delta H°_{rxn} = \sum n\Delta H°_{f(products)} - \sum n\Delta H°_{f(reactants)}$$

The enthalpy of reaction for the combustion of propyne, C_3H_4, for example, can be calculated using the tabulated heats of formation.

$$C_3H_4(g) + 4\,O_2(g) \rightarrow 3\,CO_2(g) + 2\,H_2O(l)$$

Substance	$\Delta H°_f$ (kJ·mol^{-1})
$C_3H_4(g)$	184.9
$CO_2(g)$	−393.5
$H_2O(l)$	−285.8

The enthalpies of formation are multiplied by the number of moles, n.

$$\Delta H^\circ_{rxn} = \left[(3(-393.5 \text{ kJ} \cdot \text{mol}^{-1})) + (2(-285.8 \text{ kJ} \cdot \text{mol}^{-1}))\right] - \left[(1(184.9 \text{ kJ} \cdot \text{mol}^{-1})) + (4(0 \text{ kJ} \cdot \text{mol}^{-1}))\right]$$
$$\Delta H^\circ_{rxn} = -1937 \text{ kJ} \cdot \text{mol}^{-1}$$

PRACTICE:

Determine the amount of energy absorbed or released when 30. moles of solid iron are produced from iron(III) oxide by the following reaction.

$$Fe_2O_3(s) + 3 CO(g) \rightarrow 3 CO_2(g) + 2 Fe(s)$$

Substance	ΔH°_f (kJ·mol^{-1})
$Fe_2O_3(s)$	−824.2
$CO_2(g)$	−393.5
$CO(g)$	−110.5

The overall enthalpy change for the reaction can be determined using the standard molar enthalpies of formation.

$$\Delta H^\circ_{rxn} = \sum n\Delta H^\circ_{f(products)} - \sum n\Delta H^\circ_{f(reactants)}$$
$$\Delta H^\circ_{rxn} = \left[(3(-393.5 \text{ kJ} \cdot \text{mol}^{-1})) + (2(0 \text{ kJ} \cdot \text{mol}^{-1}))\right] - \left[(1(-824.2 \text{ kJ} \cdot \text{mol}^{-1})) + (3(-110.5 \text{ kJ} \cdot \text{mol}^{-1}))\right]$$
$$\Delta H^\circ_{rxn} = -25 \text{ kJ} \cdot \text{mol}^{-1}$$

The enthalpy change "per mole of reaction" is the enthalpy change when two moles of iron are formed (using the stoichiometric coefficient). The amount of heat released when 30. moles of iron are formed is determined using the stoichiometry of the reaction.

$$30. \text{ mol Fe} \times \frac{1 \text{ mol reaction}}{2 \text{ mol Fe}} \times \frac{-25 \text{ kJ}}{1 \text{ mol reaction}} = -370 \text{ kJ}$$

The amount of heat released for every 30. moles of iron formed is 372 kJ. Reported to two significant figures, this is 370 kJ.

Notice that the standard molar enthalpy change is not rounded until the end of the calculation. When the calculated value is used, the amount of heat released is 370 kJ rather than 380 kJ (rounded up from 375).

The Second Law of Thermodynamics

A reaction that is thermodynamically favorable will spontaneously proceed in the forward direction. Although "spontaneous" is a description that is no longer used on the AP Chemistry exam, a very large number of chemistry (and physics) resources use the word to describe a thermodynamically favored process. Once a thermodynamically favored process begins, no intervention is necessary for it to continue, although spontaneity should not be confused with speed. Some spontaneous processes, like the rusting of a solid sheet of iron in the presence of oxygen and moisture, are very slow.

Consider a balloon filled with air. If the balloon is punctured and bursts, it releases its gaseous contents to the surroundings. The release of gas is thermodynamically favored (or spontaneous). The reverse of this process is non-spontaneous, or thermodynamically disfavored. The gas molecules will not re-assemble into a balloon-shaped volume.

Enthalpy changes alone do not predict whether a process will be thermodynamically favored or disfavored. In the balloon-bursting example, little if any heat is exchanged between the system and the surroundings, yet the process is thermodynamically favored. Examples of both exothermic processes, like the combustion of hydrocarbons, and endothermic processes, like the melting of ice on a warm countertop, are thermodynamically favored. If thermodynamic favorability is to be predicted, both enthalpy and entropy have to be taken into account.

Entropy, S, is the range of positional states experienced by the particles in a system or the dispersal of energy in a system. It is generally reported with units of $J \cdot mol^{-1} \cdot K^{-1}$. (Be aware that this differs from the units of ΔH, which are usually $kJ \cdot mol^{-1}$.) Any change that increases the range of motion of a collection of molecules increases their entropy, $\Delta S_{sys} > 0$. Such changes include phase transitions that allow molecules to move more freely—like melting and boiling, increases in temperature or volume, and mixing. Also, the system entropy increases for reactions in which gaseous products outnumber gaseous reactants.

It is important to remember that while the entropy of the system increases when solids or liquids are dissolved in liquids, when gases are dissolved in liquids, entropy of the system decreases.

PRACTICE:

Which of the following processes likely involve an increase in entropy of the system and which involve a decrease?

(a) The freezing of ethanol, C_2H_6O

(b) Dissolving a crystal of sodium chloride in water

(c) Solid calcium carbonate decomposes to form solid calcium oxide and gaseous carbon dioxide

(d) A sample of helium at constant temperature expands from a volume of 2 liters to a volume of 3 liters

(e) A sample of helium in a rigid 3-liter container is heated from 25 °C to 35 °C

(a) The freezing of ethanol involves a decrease in system entropy, $\Delta S_{sys} < 0$. When ethanol freezes, the molecules' positions become fixed at their crystal lattice points, and this decreases their dispersal.

$$C_2H_6O(l) \rightarrow C_2H_6O(s)$$

(b) System entropy increases, $\Delta S_{sys} > 0$, upon the dissolution of a crystal of sodium chloride in water. The sodium and chlorine ions are more dispersed and free to move in the aqueous solution than they are in fixed crystal lattice points.

$$NaCl(s) \rightarrow Na^+(aq) + Cl^-(aq)$$

(c) When a solid molecule of calcium carbonate decomposes, system entropy increases, $\Delta S_{sys} > 0$. Reactions in which the number of moles of gaseous products is greater than the number of moles of gaseous reactants generally involve an increase in system entropy.

$$CaCO_3(s) \rightarrow CaO(s) + CO_2(g)$$

(d) When a container containing a fixed number of helium atoms expands at constant temperature, the positional possibilities available to each atom increases. This causes the entropy of the system to increase, $\Delta S_{sys} > 0$.

(e) At constant volume, an increase in the temperature of a sample causes the kinetic energy of the molecules to increase. An increase in the motion of the particles increases the entropy of the system, $\Delta S_{sys} > 0$.

The entropy of the universe is always increasing. This is a statement of the **second law of thermodynamics,** which is very different from the first law. The quantity of matter and energy is fixed (first law), but the entropy is not (second law). Stated mathematically, the change in entropy of the system plus the change in entropy of the surroundings is always a positive quantity in spontaneous processes.

$$\Delta S_{univ} = \Delta S_{sys} + \Delta S_{surr}$$
$$\Delta S_{univ} > 0$$

By looking at the effect of a process on the entropy of the universe, the thermodynamic favorability of the process can be predicted.

At constant temperature and pressure, the entropy change of the surroundings is related to the enthalpy change of a process.

$$\Delta S_{surr} = \frac{\Delta H_{surr}}{T}$$

The enthalpy change of the surroundings is determined from the enthalpy change of the system. The amount of heat transferred between system and surroundings is equal in magnitude and opposite in sign, so the change in entropy of the surroundings is opposite in sign to the heat transferred by the system.

$$\Delta H_{surr} = -\Delta H_{sys}$$
$$\Delta S_{surr} = \frac{-\Delta H_{sys}}{T}$$

The entropy change of a system can be calculated from tabulated values of the standard entropies of the products and reactants. An equation similar to the one that was used to determine the enthalpy change for a system can be used to determine the changes in entropy for a system.

$$\Delta S_{sys}^{\circ} = \sum S_{products}^{\circ} - \sum S_{reactants}^{\circ}$$

Consider the highly exothermic reaction of solid sodium metal with chlorine gas.

$$Na(s) + \frac{1}{2}Cl_2(g) \rightarrow NaCl(s)$$

Substance	ΔH°_{f} (kJ·mol^{-1})	S° (J·mol^{-1}·K^{-1})
NaCl(s)	−411.2	72.1
Na(s)	0	51.3
Cl$_2$(g)	0	165

In terms of the entropy of the system, this reaction is disfavored since the entropy decreases. This can be predicted qualitatively since the number of moles of gaseous reactants is greater than the number of moles of gaseous products. This prediction can also be quantified.

$$\Delta S_{sys}^{\circ} = \sum S_{products}^{\circ} - \sum S_{reactants}^{\circ}$$
$$\Delta S_{sys}^{\circ} = 72.1 \text{ J} \cdot \text{mol}^{-1} \cdot \text{K}^{-1} - \left[(1(51.3 \text{ J} \cdot \text{mol}^{-1} \cdot \text{K}^{-1}) + \left(\frac{1}{2}(165 \text{ J} \cdot \text{mol}^{-1} \cdot \text{K}^{-1})\right) \right]$$
$$\Delta S_{sys}^{\circ} = -62 \text{ J} \cdot \text{mol}^{-1} \cdot \text{K}^{-1}$$

Even though the ΔS_{sys} is negative, this reaction occurs spontaneously under appropriate conditions. It generates a large amount of heat, and the heat that is released is transferred to the surroundings, which ultimately leads to an increase in the entropy of the universe. The enthalpy change for the reaction can be used to determine the entropy change for the surroundings at 298 K.

$$\Delta H^\circ_{rxn} = \sum n \Delta H^\circ_{f(products)} - \sum n \Delta H^\circ_{f(reactants)}$$

$$\Delta H^\circ_{sys} = (1(-411.2 \text{ kJ} \cdot \text{mol}^{-1})) - \left[(1(0 \text{ kJ} \cdot \text{mol}^{-1}) + \left(\frac{1}{2}(0 \text{ kJ} \cdot \text{mol}^{-1}) \right) \right]$$

$$\Delta H^\circ_{sys} = -411.2 \text{ kJ} \cdot \text{mol}^{-1}$$

$$\Delta H_{surr} = -\Delta H_{sys} = 411.2 \text{ kJ} \cdot \text{mol}^{-1}$$

$$\Delta S_{surr} = \frac{\Delta H_{surr}}{T} = \frac{411.2 \text{ kJ} \cdot \text{mol}^{-1}}{298 \text{ K}} = 1.38 \text{ kJ} \cdot \text{mol}^{-1} \cdot \text{K}^{-1}$$

The larger resulting entropy increase of the surroundings compensates for the entropy decrease of the system, and the change in entropy of the universe increases. Notice that enthalpy is usually reported in kJ·mol^{-1}, while entropy is reported in J·mol^{-1}·K^{-1}.

$$\Delta S_{univ} = \Delta S_{sys} + \Delta S_{surr}$$

$$\Delta S_{univ} = \left[-62 \text{ J} \cdot \text{mol}^{-1} \cdot \text{K}^{-1} \times \frac{1 \text{ kJ}}{1000 \text{ J}} \right] + 1.38 \text{ kJ} \cdot \text{mol}^{-1} \cdot \text{K}^{-1} = 1.32 \text{ kJ} \cdot \text{mol}^{-1} \cdot \text{K}^{-1}$$

PRACTICE:

The following reaction is thermodynamically favored.

$$NH_3(g) + HCl(g) \rightarrow NH_4Cl(s)$$

Given the information tabulated below,

(a) Calculate the standard enthalpy of the reaction.
(b) Calculate the entropy change of the system.
(c) Explain qualitatively why this reaction occurs as written.

Substance	ΔH°_f (kJ·mol^{-1})	S° (J·mol^{-1}·K^{-1})
NH$_4$Cl(s)	–314.4	94.6
NH$_3$(g)	–45.9	192.8
HCl(g)	–92.3	186.9

(a) The standard enthalpy of the reaction is determined from the standard enthalpies of formation.

$$\Delta H^\circ_{rxn} = \sum n \Delta H^\circ_{f(products)} - \sum n \Delta H^\circ_{f(reactants)}$$

$$\Delta H^\circ_{sys} = (1(-314.4 \text{ kJ} \cdot \text{mol}^{-1})) - \left[(1(-45.9 \text{ kJ} \cdot \text{mol}^{-1}) + (1(-92.3 \text{ kJ} \cdot \text{mol}^{-1})) \right]$$

$$\Delta H^\circ_{sys} = -176.2 \text{ kJ} \cdot \text{mol}^{-1}$$

(b) The entropy change associated with the reaction is determined from the enthalpies of the product and reactants.

$$\Delta S^\circ_{sys} = \sum S^\circ_{(products)} - \sum S^\circ_{(reactants)}$$

$$\Delta S^\circ_{sys} = 94.6 \text{ J} \cdot \text{mol}^{-1} \cdot \text{K}^{-1} - \left[(1(192.8 \text{ J} \cdot \text{mol}^{-1} \cdot \text{K}^{-1}) + (1(186.9 \text{ J} \cdot \text{mol}^{-1} \cdot \text{K}^{-1})) \right]$$

$$\Delta S^\circ_{sys} = -285.1 \text{ J} \cdot \text{mol}^{-1} \cdot \text{K}^{-1}$$

(c) Despite the entropy decrease of the system, the reaction is thermodynamically favored. The reaction must be sufficiently exothermic to increase the entropy of the surroundings enough to offset the entropy decrease of the system, since the change in entropy of the universe is always positive.

The Third Law of Thermodynamics

The **third law of thermodynamics** states that at 0 K, when a substance is a perfect, motionless crystal, the entropy of the substance is zero. As the temperature is raised, the vibrational motion increases the dispersion of the particles making up the crystal. Since this variation of entropy with temperature is understood, the **absolute entropies** of substances can be reported. The values of standard absolute entropies, $S°$, are reported in tables of thermodynamic values.

Unlike the enthalpies of formation of pure elements in their thermodynamic standard states, the absolute entropies of elements and molecules are nonzero. This is because these elements are not perfectly ordered at temperatures above 0 K, and the values reported in the tables are usually for a standard thermodynamic temperature of 298 K.

Absolute entropy increases from solid to liquid to gas. Also, it increases with increasing molecular complexity; the larger the number of electrons in a molecule, the higher the absolute entropy of the molecule, but this effect is not as pronounced as that due to the phase of the molecule.

PRACTICE:

Rank the compounds in order of increasing absolute entropy at 298 K: $H_2(g)$, $Cl_2(g)$, $H_2O(l)$, $HCl(g)$.

Gaseous compounds tend to have higher absolute entropies than liquids, so the entropy of $H_2O(l)$ is predicted to be the lowest. The three gases must be ranked in terms of molecular complexity. Hydrogen gas, H_2, is the least complex. It has only two electrons, so it has a lower entropy than Cl_2 or HCl. Chlorine gas, Cl_2, has the greatest complexity and the largest number of electrons, so it has the highest absolute entropy. The correct ranking of the molecules in terms of increasing absolute entropy is $H_2O(l) < H_2(g) < HCl(g) < Cl_2(g)$.

The actual absolute entropy values are shown for comparison.

Substance	$S°$ ($J \cdot mol^{-1} \cdot K^{-1}$)
$H_2O(l)$	70
$H_2(g)$	131
$HCl(g)$	187
$Cl_2(g)$	223

Gibbs Free Energy

The change in **Gibbs free energy,** ΔG, associated with a process is a predictor of the thermodynamic favorability of the process at constant temperature and pressure. Gibbs free energy provides a value for the maximum amount of useful work that can be obtained from a system. The Gibbs free energy of a system, at constant temperature and pressure, is given by

$$\Delta G = \Delta H - T\Delta S$$

The products of a thermodynamically favored, or spontaneous, reaction have final Gibbs energies that are lower than that of the reactants. In other words, ΔG is negative for a thermodynamically favored process. For a process that is thermodynamically disfavored, ΔG is positive, and for a process in which reactants and products are at equilibrium, $\Delta G = 0$. Processes for which ΔG is negative are sometimes referred to as **exergonic,** and processes for which ΔG is positive are sometimes referred to as **endergonic.**

Standard molar Gibbs free energy values, $\Delta G°$, for thermodynamic standard conditions (1 atm, 1 M solutions, and usually 298 K) are experimentally determined and are tabulated in the scientific literature along with $\Delta H°$ and $S°$ values. Like $\Delta H°$ values, $\Delta G°$ values are zero for elements in their standard states.

The standard molar Gibbs free energy change for a reaction can be determined in the same ways that the enthalpy and entropy changes can be calculated.

$$\Delta G°_{rxn} = \sum n\Delta G°_{f(products)} - \sum n\Delta G°_{f(reactants)}$$

For example, a prediction can be made regarding whether the decomposition of pure hydrogen peroxide is a spontaneous process at 1 atmosphere and 298 K using tabulated values of $\Delta G°_f$.

$$2\ H_2O_2(l) \rightarrow 2\ H_2O(l) + O_2(g)$$

Substance	$\Delta G°_f$ (kJ·mol^{-1})
$H_2O_2(l)$	–120.4
$H_2O(l)$	–237.1
$O_2(g)$	0

The reaction is carried out under standard conditions, so these free energies of formation may be used to determine the overall free energy change for this reaction.

$$\Delta G°_{rxn} = \sum n\Delta G°_{f(products)} - \sum n\Delta G°_{f(reactants)}$$

$$\Delta G°_{rxn} = \left[(2(-237.1\ kJ \cdot mol^{-1})) + (1(0\ kJ \cdot mol^{-1}))\right] - (2(-120.4\ kJ \cdot mol^{-1}))$$

$$\Delta G°_{rxn} = -233.4\ kJ \cdot mol^{-1}$$

The negative value of the change in free energy for the reaction indicates that this is a thermodynamically favored process under standard conditions.

PRACTICE:

Use the standard molar free energies of formation below to determine whether the reaction between solid B_2O_3 and hydrogen gas to form gaseous B_2H_6 and oxygen is spontaneous under standard thermodynamic conditions.

Substance	$\Delta G°_f$ (kJ·mol^{-1})
$B_2O_3(s)$ the negative value of	–1194.3
$B_2H_6(g)$	87.6

The first step is to write and balance the chemical equation.

$$2\ B_2O_3(s) + 6\ H_2(g) \rightarrow 2\ B_2H_6(g) + 3\ O_2(g)$$

The standard free energies of formation can be used to determine the overall change in Gibbs free energy for the process under standard thermodynamic conditions.

$$\Delta G°_{rxn} = \sum n\Delta G°_{f(products)} - \sum n\Delta G$$

$$\Delta G°_{rxn} = \left[(2(87.6\ kJ \cdot mol^{-1})) + (3(0\ kJ \cdot mol^{-1}))\right] - \left[(2(-1194.3\ kJ \cdot mol^{-1})) + (6(0\ kJ \cdot mol^{-1}))\right]$$

$$\Delta G°_{rxn} = 2564\ kJ \cdot mol^{-1}$$

A second method for determining the Gibbs free energy change for a reaction is to use a procedure similar to the one used to find $\Delta H°$ using Hess's law. The steps for which the free energy changes are known must be manipulated so that they add up to the overall process.

When graphite is added to solid copper(II) oxide, the reduction of $CuO(s)$ to solid copper becomes thermodynamically favored under standard conditions.

$$2\,CuO(s) + C(s) \rightarrow 2\,Cu(s) + CO_2(g)$$

The reactions that make up this transformation are:

$$CuO(s) \rightarrow Cu(s) + \frac{1}{2}O_2(g) \qquad \Delta G°_{298\,K} = 129.7\ kJ \cdot mol^{-1}$$

$$C(s) + O_2(g) \rightarrow CO_2(g) \qquad \Delta G°_{298\,K} = -394.4\ kJ \cdot mol^{-1}$$

When the first equation is multiplied by 2, it can be added to the second equation to result in the overall transformation. The $\Delta G°$ for the first reaction is also multiplied by 2. The Gibbs free energy changes can be added to give the overall $\Delta G°$ for the reaction. (This is valid only at 298 K.)

$$2\,CuO(s) \rightarrow 2\,Cu(s) + O_2(g) \qquad \Delta G°_{298\,K} = (129.7\ kJ \cdot mol^{-1})2$$

$$\underline{C(s) + O_2(g) \rightarrow CO_2(g) \qquad \Delta G°_{298\,K} = -394.4\ kJ \cdot mol^{-1}}$$

$$2\,CuO(s) + C(s) \rightarrow 2\,Cu(s) + CO_2(g) \qquad \Delta G°_{298\,K} = -135.0\ kJ \cdot mol^{-1}$$

This example serves to illustrate another important point. The decomposition of copper(II) oxide to solid copper and oxygen gas under standard conditions is thermodynamically disfavored ($\Delta G°_{298\,K} = 129.7\ kJ \cdot mol^{-1}$). The **coupling** of this reaction to one in which the oxygen produced forms bonds with carbon results in a sufficient decrease in Gibbs free energy to make the transformation of copper(II) oxide to solid copper possible.

PRACTICE:

Calculate $\Delta G°$ for the formation of gaseous NO_2.

$$NO(g) + O(g) \rightarrow NO_2(g)$$

Use the following information.

$$2\,O_3(g) \rightarrow 3\,O_2(g) \qquad \Delta G°_{298\,K} = -326.4\ kJ \cdot mol^{-1}$$

$$O_2(g) \rightarrow 2\,O(g) \qquad \Delta G°_{298\,K} = 463.4\ kJ \cdot mol^{-1}$$

$$NO(g) + O_3(g) \rightarrow NO_2(g) + O_2(g) \qquad \Delta G°_{298\,K} = -199.5\ kJ \cdot mol^{-1}$$

The first and second equations, along with their associated $\Delta G°$ values, are algebraically manipulated in the same manner as for ΔH. The first and second equations, along with their associated $\Delta G°$ values, are multiplied by $-\frac{1}{2}$.

Addition of the three equations and their $\Delta G°$ values gives the overall change in Gibbs free energy for the transformation at 298 K.

$$\frac{3}{2}O_2(g) \rightarrow O_3(g) \qquad \Delta G°_{298\,K} = (-326.4\ kJ \cdot mol^{-1})\left(-\frac{1}{2}\right)$$

$$O(g) \rightarrow \frac{1}{2}O_2(g) \qquad \Delta G°_{298\,K} = (463.4\ kJ \cdot mol^{-1})\left(-\frac{1}{2}\right)$$

$$\underline{NO(g) + O_3(g) \rightarrow NO_2(g) + O_2(g) \qquad \Delta G°_{298\,K} = -199.5\ kJ \cdot mol^{-1}}$$

$$NO(g) + O(g) \rightarrow NO_2(g) \qquad \Delta G°_{298\,K} = -268.0\ kJ \cdot mol^{-1}$$

The third method for the determination of the Gibbs free energy change for a reaction is to use the relationship between $\Delta S°$ and $\Delta H°$.

$$\Delta G° = \Delta H° - T\Delta S°$$

The reaction between hydrogen and oxygen gases to form water vapor is thermodynamically favorable at room temperature. (The activation energy for the reaction is high, so a spark must be applied to initiate the reaction. Once the reaction has begun, however, it proceeds.)

$$H_2(g) + \frac{1}{2}O_2(g) \rightarrow H_2O(g)$$

The change in Gibbs free energy for this process can be found by determining the enthalpy and entropy changes at this temperature.

Substance	$\Delta H°_f$ (kJ·mol^{-1})	$S°$ (J·mol^{-1}·K^{-1})
$H_2O(g)$	−237.1	188.8
$H_2(g)$	0	130.7
$O_2(g)$	0	205.2

The enthalpy change for the process is the standard enthalpy of formation of one mole of H_2O.

$$\Delta H° = -237.1 \text{ kJ·mol}^{-1}$$

The entropy change for this reaction is the difference between the standard entropies of products and reactants.

$$\Delta S°_{rxn} = \sum S°_{(products)} - \sum S°_{(reactants)}$$

$$\Delta S°_{rxn} = 188.8 \text{ J·mol}^{-1}\cdot K^{-1} - \left[(1(130.7 \text{ J·mol}^{-1}\cdot K^{-1}) + \left(\frac{1}{2}(205.2 \text{ J·mol}^{-1}\cdot K^{-1}) \right) \right]$$

$$\Delta S°_{rxn} = -44.5 \text{ J·mol}^{-1}\cdot K^{-1}$$

The standard Gibbs free energy change is determined using these values at 298 K.

$$\Delta G° = \Delta H° - T\Delta S° = -237.1 \text{ kJ·mol}^{-1} - \left[(298 \text{ K})(-44.5 \text{ J·mol}^{-1}\cdot K^{-1})\left(\frac{1 \text{ kJ}}{1000 \text{ J}} \right) \right]$$

$$\Delta G° = -223.8 \text{ kJ·mol}^{-1}$$

This equation is useful for determining the spontaneity of a process at temperatures other than the thermodynamic standard temperature, 298 K. The thermodynamic favorability of a process at one temperature can differ greatly from the favorability of the process at a different temperature. Consider the boiling of liquid water. This process is thermodynamically favored ($\Delta G° < 0$) above 100 °C at atmospheric pressure, but it is thermodynamically disfavored ($\Delta G° > 0$) at temperatures below 100 °C.

Since standard enthalpies of formation are relatively constant across a wide range of temperatures, the tabulated enthalpies of formation and standard entropies can be used to predict whether or not a process is favorable at a given temperature.

The standard molar Gibbs free energy for boiling water at 80 °C (353 K) and at 120 °C (393 K) can be calculated as examples. The pressure in both situations is 1 atm.

$$H_2O(l) \rightarrow H_2O(g)$$

Substance	ΔH°_f (kJ·mol^{-1})	S° (J·mol^{-1}·K^{-1})
$H_2O(l)$	−285.8	70.0
$H_2O(g)$	−241.8	188.8

The values of ΔS° and ΔH°_f are determined for the process.

$$\Delta H^\circ_{rxn} = \sum n\Delta H^\circ_{f(products)} - \sum n\Delta H^\circ_{f(reactants)}$$
$$\Delta H^\circ_{rxn} = (1(-241.8 \text{ kJ} \cdot \text{mol}^{-1})) - (1(-285.8 \text{ kJ} \cdot \text{mol}^{-1}))$$
$$\Delta H^\circ_{rxn} = 44.0 \text{ kJ} \cdot \text{mol}^{-1}$$

$$\Delta S^\circ_{rxn} = \sum S^\circ_{(products)} - \sum S^\circ_{(reactants)}$$
$$\Delta S^\circ_{rxn} = 188.8 \text{ J} \cdot \text{mol}^{-1} \cdot \text{K}^{-1} - 70.0 \text{ J} \cdot \text{mol}^{-1} \cdot \text{K}^{-1}$$
$$\Delta S^\circ_{rxn} = 118.8 \text{ J} \cdot \text{mol}^{-1} \cdot \text{K}^{-1}$$

These values are used to determine the Gibbs free energy change at the two different temperatures.

At 80 °C (353 K):

$$\Delta G^\circ = \Delta H^\circ - T\Delta S^\circ = 44.0 \text{ kJ} \cdot \text{mol}^{-1} - \left[(353 \text{ K})(118.8 \text{ J} \cdot \text{mol}^{-1} \cdot \text{K}^{-1})\left(\frac{1 \text{ kJ}}{1000 \text{ J}} \right) \right]$$

$$\Delta G^\circ = 2.1 \text{ kJ} \cdot \text{mol}^{-1}$$

The positive change in Gibbs free energy indicates that boiling water is thermodynamically disfavored at 80 °C.

At 120 °C (393 K):

$$\Delta G^\circ = \Delta H^\circ - T\Delta S^\circ = 44.0 \text{ kJ} \cdot \text{mol}^{-1} - \left[(393 \text{ K})(118.8 \text{ J} \cdot \text{mol}^{-1} \cdot \text{K}^{-1})\left(\frac{1 \text{ kJ}}{1000 \text{ J}} \right) \right]$$

$$\Delta G^\circ = -2.7 \text{ kJ} \cdot \text{mol}^{-1}$$

The negative value for the change in Gibbs free energy indicates that water boiling is a thermodynamically favored process at 120 °C.

At equilibrium, the change in Gibbs free energy for a process is zero. This fact can be used to determine the temperature at which phase changes occur.

At the boiling point of water at 1 atmosphere (the **normal boiling point**), liquid water is in equilibrium with water vapor. The values of ΔH° and S° have already been determined (44.0 kJ·mol^{-1} and 118.8 J·mol·K^{-1}, respectively). The boiling point of water, T, can be determined by setting the change in Gibbs free energy to zero.

$$\Delta G^\circ = 0 = \Delta H^\circ - T\Delta S^\circ = 44.0 \text{ kJ} \cdot \text{mol}^{-1} - \left[T(118.8 \text{ J} \cdot \text{mol}^{-1} \cdot \text{K}^{-1})\left(\frac{1 \text{ kJ}}{1000 \text{ J}} \right) \right]$$

$$T = 370 \text{ K}$$

This is very close to the true normal boiling point of water, 373 K. The difference between the two values can be accounted for by the slight differences in ΔH° and S° at temperatures other than 298 K.

The signs of ΔH° and S° can be indicators of whether the change in Gibbs free energy of a process will be greater than or less than zero, as summarized below. The $T\Delta S$ term in the Gibbs free energy equation relates the temperature to the spontaneity of a process.

$$\Delta H - T\Delta S = \Delta G$$

ΔH	ΔS	ΔG
Negative (–)	Positive (+)	Negative at all temperatures. *Always* thermodynamically favorable.
Negative (–)	Negative (–)	Negative at low temperatures. Positive at high temperatures. Only thermodynamically favorable at *low temperatures*.
Positive (+)	Positive (+)	Negative at high temperatures. Positive at low temperatures. Only thermodynamically favorable at *high temperatures*.
Positive (+)	Negative (–)	Positive at all temperatures. *Never* thermodynamically favorable.

PRACTICE:

> The following reaction is endothermic. Is it thermodynamically favorable at all temperatures, at high temperatures only, at low temperatures only, or at no temperature?
>
> $$2\ CuCl_2(s) \rightarrow 2\ CuCl(s) + Cl_2(g)$$

The enthalpy change for an endothermic process is positive.

This reaction also involves an increase in entropy, since a gas is formed from a solid. This means that ΔS is positive and that $T\Delta S > 0$. The higher the temperature, the larger the positive value that is subtracted from the enthalpy term, and the more negative the overall Gibbs free energy change becomes. The reaction will be thermodynamically favorable only at high temperatures.

PRACTICE:

> Use the data provided to calculate the minimum temperature at which the decomposition of copper(II) chloride occurs according to the reaction in the previous practice problem.
>
> $$2\ CuCl_2(s) \rightarrow 2\ CuCl(s) + Cl_2(g)$$
>
> Assume that the values of $\Delta H°$ and $S°$ are independent of temperature.
>
> | Substance | $\Delta H°_f$ (kJ·mol^{-1}) | $S°$ (J·mol^{-1}·K^{-1}) |
> |---|---|---|
> | $CuCl_2(s)$ | –220.1 | 108.1 |
> | $CuCl(s)$ | –137.2 | 86.2 |
> | $Cl_2(g)$ | 0 | 223.1 |

The enthalpy and entropy changes for the reaction are calculated first.

$$\Delta H^\circ_{rxn} = \sum n\Delta H^\circ_{f(products)} - \sum n\Delta H^\circ_{f(reactants)}$$

$$\Delta H^\circ_{rxn} = (2(-137.2 \text{ kJ} \cdot \text{mol}^{-1})) + (1(0 \text{ kJ} \cdot \text{mol}^{-1})) - (2(-220.1 \text{ kJ} \cdot \text{mol}^{-1}))$$

$$\Delta H^\circ_{rxn} = 165.8 \text{ kJ} \cdot \text{mol}^{-1}$$

$$\Delta S^\circ_{rxn} = \sum S^\circ_{(products)} - \sum S^\circ_{(reactants)}$$

$$\Delta S^\circ_{rxn} = (2(86.2 \text{ J} \cdot \text{mol}^{-1} \cdot \text{K}^{-1})) + (1(223.1 \text{ J} \cdot \text{mol}^{-1} \cdot \text{K}^{-1})) - (2(108.1 \text{ J} \cdot \text{mol}^{-1} \cdot \text{K}^{-1}))$$

$$\Delta S^\circ_{rxn} = 179.3 \text{ J} \cdot \text{mol}^{-1} \cdot \text{K}^{-1}$$

Since both ΔH°_{rxn} and ΔS°_{rxn} are positive, this process is spontaneous at high temperatures. The temperature at which this reaction changes from nonspontaneous to spontaneous is determined by setting ΔG° to zero.

$$\Delta G^\circ = 0 = \Delta H^\circ - T\Delta S^\circ = 165.8 \text{ kJ} \cdot \text{mol}^{-1} - \left[T(179.3 \text{ J} \cdot \text{mol}^{-1} \cdot \text{K}^{-1}) \left(\frac{1 \text{ kJ}}{1000 \text{ J}} \right) \right]$$

$$T = 924.7 \text{ K}$$

Electrochemistry and Gibbs Free Energy

The thermodynamic favorability of an oxidation reduction reaction was shown in Big Idea 3 (Chapter 3, "Chemical Reactions") to be a function of the value of the standard cell potential, E°. The relationship between the change in Gibbs free energy, ΔG°, and the standard cell potential is given on the *AP Chemistry Equations and Constants* sheet (pages 365–366).

$$\Delta G^\circ = -nFE^\circ$$

In this relationship, n is the number of moles of electrons transferred and F is Faraday's constant, also given on the *AP Chemistry Equations and Constants* sheet (pages 365–366).

A positive standard cell potential results in a negative change in Gibbs free energy. This corresponds to a thermodynamically favored process. A negative standard cell potential leads to a positive change in Gibbs free energy, indicating a thermodynamically unfavorable process.

For example, the standard cell potential can be used to calculate the change in Gibbs free energy for the reaction of cobalt with iron(II) ions.

$$Co(s) + Fe^{2+}(aq) \rightarrow Co^{2+}(aq) + Fe(s)$$

Half Reaction	Standard Reduction Potential, E° (V)
$Co^{2+} + 2\,e^- \rightarrow Co$	−0.28
$Fe^{2+} + 2\,e^- \rightarrow Fe$	−0.44

$$E^\circ_{cell} = E^\circ_{reduction} - E^\circ_{oxidation} = -0.44 \text{ V} - (-0.28 \text{ V}) = -0.16 \text{ V}$$

The standard cell potential is then used to determine the Gibbs free energy change for this two-electron transfer. Notice that the conversion factor between volts and joules per coulomb is also given on the *AP Chemistry Equations and Constants* sheet (pages 365–366).

$$\Delta G^\circ = -nFE^\circ = -(2)\left(\frac{96,485 \text{ C}}{1 \text{ mol } e^-} \right)(-0.16 \text{ V})\left(\frac{1 \text{ J} \cdot \text{C}}{1 \text{ V}} \right) = 31,000 \text{ J} \cdot \text{mol}^{-1}$$

The negative cell potential indicates the reduction of $Fe^{2+}(aq)$ by $Co(s)$ is a thermodynamically unfavorable process.

PRACTICE:

Calculate the change in Gibbs free energy for the following unbalanced reaction in acidic solution.

$$Ce^{4+} + I^- \rightarrow I_2 + Ce^{3+}$$

Half Reaction	Standard Reduction Potential, $E°$ (V)
$Ce^{4+} + e^- \rightarrow Ce^{3+}$	1.61
$I_2 + 2\,e^- \rightarrow 2\,I^-$	0.53

Reduction of Ce^{4+} is occurring at the cathode, and oxidation of I_2 is occurring at the anode. In order to balance the overall equation, the reduction of Ce^{4+} is multiplied by 2. Overall, this reaction involves a two-electron transfer, so $n = 2$. For a review of balancing redox equations, see Big Idea 3 (Chapter 3, "Chemical Reactions").

$$2\,Ce^{4+} + 2\,I^- \rightarrow 2\,Ce^{3+} + I_2$$

The standard cell potential is calculated from the half reaction reduction potentials.

$$E°_{cell} = E°_{reduction} - E°_{oxidation} = 1.61 \text{ V} - (0.53 \text{ V}) = 1.08 \text{ V}$$

This value is used to calculate the change in Gibbs free energy.

$$\Delta G = -nFE° = -(2)\left(\frac{96,485 \cancel{C}}{1 \text{ mol } e^-}\right)(1.08 \cancel{V})\left(\frac{1 \text{ J} \cdot \cancel{C}}{1 \cancel{V}}\right) = -210,000 \text{ J} \cdot \text{mol}^{-1}$$

The negative $\Delta G°$ indicates a thermodynamically favorable reaction.

Thermodynamically Unfavorable Processes

Thermodynamically unfavorable processes occur in biological systems and technology. In order for a thermodynamically unfavorable process to proceed, energy must be supplied. Consider again the thermodynamically disfavored reaction in which copper is produced from copper(II) oxide.

$$CuO(s) \rightarrow Cu(s) + \frac{1}{2}O_2(g) \qquad \Delta G° = 129.7 \text{ kJ} \cdot \text{mol}^{-1}$$

When this thermodynamically unfavorable process is coupled with a spontaneous process, the thermodynamically disfavored process becomes favorable.

$$CuO(s) \rightarrow Cu(s) + \frac{1}{2}O_2(g) \qquad \Delta G° = 129.7 \text{ kJ} \cdot \text{mol}^{-1}$$

$$C(s) + O_2(g) \rightarrow CO_2(g) \qquad \Delta G° = -394.4 \text{ kJ} \cdot \text{mol}^{-1}$$

The overall change in Gibbs free energy for the reaction of copper(II) oxide with carbon is -135.0 kJ·mol^{-1}, in contrast to 129.7 kJ·mol^{-1} for the uncoupled process. This was discussed previously on page 247.

PRACTICE:

> The conversion of iron ore to pure iron is thermodynamically unfavorable at temperatures below about 1250 °C. The change in Gibbs free energy at 1225 °C is + 824.1 kJ·mol^{-1}.
>
> $$2\ Fe_2O_3(s) \rightarrow 4\ Fe(s) + 3\ O_2(g) \qquad \Delta G = 824.1\ \text{kJ·mol}^{-1}$$
>
> The oxygen that is produced reacts with coke, a carbon-containing substance similar to charcoal.
>
> $$O_2(g) + C(s) \rightarrow CO_2(g) \qquad \Delta G = -397.8\ \text{kJ·mol}^{-1}$$
>
> What is the overall reaction and change in Gibbs free energy for the conversion of iron ore to pure iron in the presence of coke? Is the overall process thermodynamically favorable?

The second equation and its associated ΔG value must be multiplied by a factor of 3 in order for carbon to react with all the O_2 produced in the first equation. When carbon is added to the iron(II) oxide, the decomposition to solid iron is thermodynamically favorable at 1225 °C.

$$2\ Fe_2O_3(s) \rightarrow 4\ Fe(s) + 3\ \cancel{O_2(g)} \qquad \Delta G = 824.1\ \text{kJ·mol}^{-1}$$
$$3\ C(s) + 3\ \cancel{O_2(g)} \rightarrow 3\ CO_2(g) \qquad \Delta G = 3(-397.8\ \text{kJ·mol}^{-1})$$
$$\overline{2\ Fe_2O_3(s) + 3\ C(s) \rightarrow 4\ Fe(s) + 3\ CO_2(g) \qquad \Delta G = -369.3\ \text{kJ·mol}^{-1}}$$

Other technological methods are applied to nonspontaneous systems to make them thermodynamically favorable. Electrolysis reactions have negative standard cell potentials and positive Gibbs free energy changes. They do not proceed in the absence of an energy source because they are thermodynamically unfavorable. A battery is a device that provides the driving force for such a disfavored process. As was discussed in the electrochemistry section of Big Idea 3 (Chapter 3, "Chemical Reactions"), a battery, which is a galvanic cell or series of galvanic cells, can provide the driving force for the process of electrolysis.

An example is the refinement of copper metal by electrolysis. An impure copper anode and a pure copper cathode are immersed in an aqueous solution of copper(II) sulfate. Oxidation of copper at the anode is produces copper ions in solution. The copper ions are reduced to pure copper at the cathode by coupling the reaction with an external power source provided by a spontaneous reaction.

Coupled reactions are very important for the spontaneity of biological reactions. Many reactions in biology are thermodynamically disfavored and rely on the sharing of intermediates with thermodynamically favored processes. **Adenosine triphosphate,** ATP, is a common molecule used by living systems to provide energy for thermodynamically disfavored processes. ATP is hydrolyzed to ADP, adenosine diphosphate, and inorganic phosphate, P_i. This is a thermodynamically favorable process with a $\Delta G°$ of -30.5 kJ·mol^{-1}.

The Hydrolysis of ATP

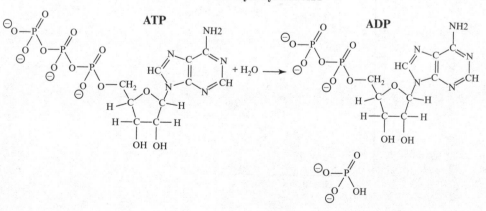

One example of reaction coupling occurs in the first step of glycolysis in the cell. The uncoupled reaction is thermodynamically unfavorable.

$$\text{Glucose} + \text{P}_i \rightarrow \text{glucose-6-phosphate} + \text{H}_2\text{O} \qquad \Delta G° = 13.8 \text{ kJ·mol}^{-1}$$

By coupling this reaction with the hydrolysis of ATP, the cell drives the synthesis of glucose-6-phosphate.

$$\text{glucose} + \cancel{\text{P}_i} \rightarrow \text{glucose-6-phosphate} + \cancel{\text{H}_2\text{O}} \qquad \Delta G° = 13.8 \text{ kJ} \cdot \text{mol}^{-1}$$
$$\underline{\text{ATP} + \cancel{\text{H}_2\text{O}} \rightarrow \text{ADP} + \cancel{\text{P}_i} \qquad\qquad \Delta G° = -30.5 \text{ kJ} \cdot \text{mol}^{-1}}$$
$$\text{glucose} + \text{ATP} \rightarrow \text{glucose-6-phosphate} + \text{ADP} \qquad \Delta G° = -16.7 \text{ kJ} \cdot \text{mol}^{-1}$$

Photosynthesis, the thermodynamically unfavorable synthesis of glucose, $C_6H_{12}O_6$, from carbon dioxide and water, occurs in green plants.

$$6 \text{ CO}_2(g) + 6 \text{ H}_2\text{O}(l) \xrightarrow{\text{light}} C_2H_{12}O_6(s) + 6 \text{ O}_2(g)$$

This reaction has a positive change in Gibbs free energy, $\Delta G° = +2872 \text{ kJ·mol}^{-1}$. The plant cells absorb visible photons of light, which excite the electrons of pigment molecules to higher-energy states. The energy is transferred through a complex system of receptor molecules to ultimately drive the synthesis of ATP. The cell can then use the ATP to provide the energy for the formation of glucose in photosynthesis.

Kinetic Control

As reviewed in Big Idea 4 (Chapter 4, "Kinetics"), the activation energy of a reaction determines its rate at a particular temperature. Some thermodynamically favorable reactions do not occur at a measurable rate due to an insurmountable activation energy for a particular temperature. Factors such as activation energy and presence or absence of a catalyst have no effect on the Gibbs free energy change of a process.

The conversion of diamond to graphite is thermodynamically favored. The Gibbs free energy of graphite is slightly lower than that of diamonds, but diamonds do not generally convert to graphite under familiar conditions. The reason for this is the very high activation energy for the reaction. This is an example of **kinetic control.**

Kinetic Control

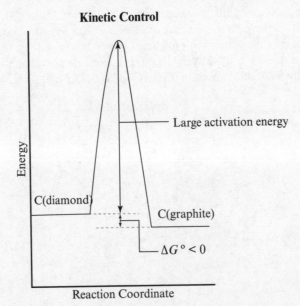

Review Questions

Multiple Choice

Use the following reactions to answer questions 1–2.

Reaction A	$H_2O(g) \rightarrow H_2O(l)$
Reaction B	$2\,H_2(g) + O_2(g) \rightarrow 2\,H_2O(g)$
Reaction C	$CaCO_3(s) \rightarrow CaO(s) + CO_2(g)$
Reaction D	$Ag^+(aq) + Cl^-(aq) \rightarrow AgCl(s)$

1. For which of the reactions is the work done by the system less than zero ($w < 0$) at constant pressure?

   A. Reaction A
   B. Reaction B
   C. Reaction C
   D. Reaction D

2. For which of the reactions is $\Delta S > 0$?

   A. Reaction A
   B. Reaction B
   C. Reaction C
   D. Reaction D

3. The temperature of a 12.0-gram cube of metal increases from 15.0 °C to 35.0 °C when 216 J of energy are added. Based on the following heat capacities, determine the identity of the metal.

Element	Heat Capacity ($J \cdot g^{-1} \cdot {}^\circ C^{-1}$)
Aluminum	0.90
Nickel	0.44
Tin	0.21
Lead	0.16

   A. Aluminum
   B. Nickel
   C. Tin
   D. Lead

4. A block of iron at 95 °C is placed in thermal contact with a sample of gas that is initially at 28 °C. Which change best reflects the effect on the distribution of molecular speeds for the gas?

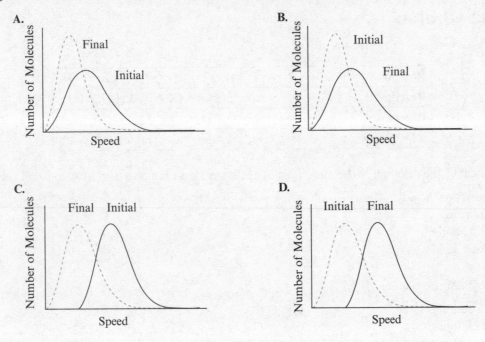

5. A 25.0-mL sample of a 0.500 M solution of aqueous sodium hydroxide is added to a 25.0-mL sample of a 0.500 M solution of aqueous hydrochloric acid in a coffee cup calorimeter. Both solutions are initially at 22.5 °C. After mixing, the temperature of the combined solution reaches a maximum of 26.0 °C. Which statement is true?

   A. The negative value of ΔH_{rxn} that can be calculated from this information is more negative than the true value.

   B. The positive value of ΔH_{rxn} that can be calculated from this information is more positive than the true value.

   C. The negative value of ΔH_{rxn} that can be calculated from this information is less negative than the true value.

   D. The positive value of ΔH_{rxn} that can be calculated from this information is less positive than the true value.

6. A 0.39-kg block of ice at 0 °C is added to 1.0 kg of water at 45.0 °C. Which statement best describes the process that occurs?

   A. The ice cools the water by transferring thermal energy to the surroundings.

   B. The water transfers heat to the ice to first melt it with no change in temperature and then to warm the resulting water.

   C. The water transfers heat to the ice to raise its temperature and then to warm the resulting water.

   D. The ice increases in entropy as it melts and the surroundings experience an increase in entropy as heat is transferred to the system.

7. Which of the following mathematical statements are all true when solid water melts?

   A. $\Delta H < 0, \Delta V > 0$

   B. $\Delta H > 0, \Delta V > 0$

   C. $\Delta H < 0, \Delta V < 0$

   D. $\Delta H > 0, \Delta V < 0$

Use the following equations to answer questions 8–10.

The combustion of methane occurs by the following reaction.

$$CH_4(g) + 2\,O_2(g) \rightarrow CO_2(g) + 2\,H_2O(g) \qquad \Delta H° = -804 \text{ kJ/mol}$$

Reaction	$\Delta H°$ (kJ·mol^{-1})
$2O(g) \rightarrow O_2(g)$	v
$2H(g) + O(g) \rightarrow H_2O(g)$	w
$C(graphite) + 2O(g) \rightarrow CO_2(g)$	x
$C(graphite) + 2H_2(g) \rightarrow CH_4(g)$	y
$2H(g) \rightarrow H_2(g)$	z

8. Which expression represents the heat of combustion of methane?

   A. $v + w + x + y + z$
   B. $-v + w + x - y + z$
   C. $2v + w + x - y + 2z$
   D. $-2v + 2w + x - y - 2z$

9. Which of the values shown are greater than zero?

   A. w, x, and y only
   B. v and z only
   C. v, w, x, y, and z
   D.   None of the values are greater than zero.

10. How much heat is transferred when 0.010 mol of O_2 undergoes combustion with 0.010 mol of methane?

   A.   8.04 kJ are released by the system
   B.   8.04 kJ are absorbed by the system
   C.   4.02 kJ are released by the system
   D.   4.02 kJ are absorbed by the system

11. Which of the following processes involves a decrease in entropy?

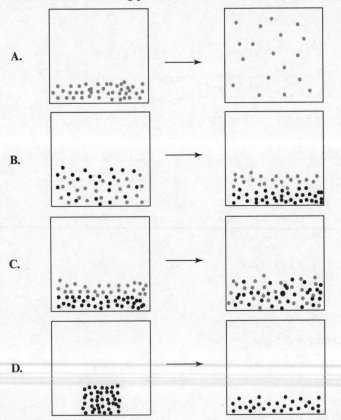

12. The sodium-potassium pump is a trans-membrane protein that transports potassium into a cell and sodium out of a cell. This process is thermodynamically unfavorable. Hydrolysis of ATP to form ADP by the protein is necessary for potassium transport to occur. Based on this information, what is the most likely explanation for the ability of the protein to function?

    A. The hydrolysis of ATP to form ADP is thermodynamically unfavorable, and the overall Gibbs free energy change for the process is positive.

    B. The change in Gibbs free energy for the conversion of ADP to ATP is zero.

    C. The hydrolysis of ATP to ADP by the trans-membrane protein has a negative change in Gibbs free energy, making the overall process thermodynamically favorable.

    D. The higher sodium concentration outside the cell is favored by the resulting increase in the entropy of the system and decrease in the enthalpy of the surroundings.

13. An electrochemical cell was constructed with a tin electrode and tin(II) nitrate at the cathode and a silver electrode and silver nitrate at the anode. Which statement regarding this system is true?

Half Reaction	$E°$ (V)
$Sn^{2+} + 2\,e^- \rightarrow Sn$	−0.83
$Ag^+ + e^- \rightarrow Ag$	1.07

    A. The cell is galvanic and $\Delta G° > 0$.

    B. The cell is galvanic and $\Delta G° < 0$.

    C. The cell is electrolytic and $\Delta G° > 0$.

    D. The cell is electrolytic and $\Delta G° < 0$.

14. The sketch below is a representation of the steps involved in the dissolution of a solid solute in a liquid solvent. For which (if any) of the steps is $\Delta H < 0$?

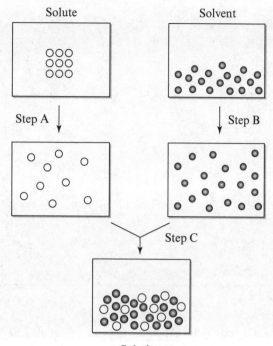

A. Step A
B. Step B
C. Step C
D. $\Delta H < 0$ for all three steps

Questions 15–16 refer to the heating curve shown below.

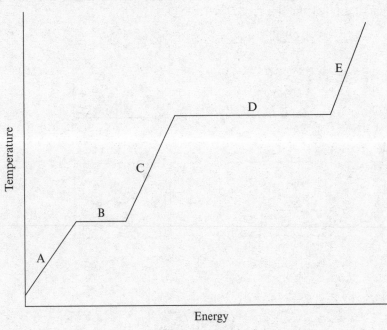

15. For which region on the heating curve does the heat transfer equal $mc_{liq}\Delta T$?

   A.   Region A
   B.   Region B
   C.   Region C
   D.   Region E

16. The heat of vaporization for a substance is the amount of energy that must be supplied to convert a substance from the liquid to the vapor phase. The length of which region of the curve is given by $n\Delta H°_{vap}$?

   A.   Region A
   B.   Region B
   C.   Region C
   D.   Region D

17. At 298 K, which reaction below represents the standard formation reaction of $MgCrO_4(s)$?

   A. $Mg^{2+}(aq) + CrO_4^{2-}(aq) \rightarrow MgCrO_4(s)$
   B. $Mg(s) + Cr(s) + 4\,O(g) \rightarrow MgCrO_4(s)$
   C. $MgO(s) + CrO_3(s) \rightarrow MgCrO_4(s)$
   D. $Mg(s) + Cr(s) + 2\,O_2(g) \rightarrow MgCrO_4(s)$

18. When ammonium chloride is dissolved in water at room temperature, the final temperature of the solution is significantly lower than the initial temperature. Which of the following is true?

   A.   The dissolution is thermodynamically favorable under all conditions.
   B.   The dissolution is thermodynamically favorable only at low temperatures.
   C.   The dissolution is thermodynamically favorable only at high temperatures.
   D.   The dissolution is thermodynamically unfavorable under all conditions.

19. The following is a representation of a system undergoing a change at constant temperature. Select the answer that best describes the heat and work involved in this process.

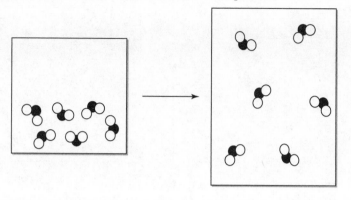

    A. $q > 0, w > 0$
    B. $q > 0, w < 0$
    C. $q < 0, w < 0$
    D. $q < 0, w > 0$

20. Consider the reaction between isooctane, a component of gasoline, and oxygen gas.

$$2\ C_8H_{18}(l) + 25\ O_2(g) \rightarrow 16\ CO_2(g) + 18\ H_2O(g)$$

When gasoline is exposed to oxygen at room temperature, no reaction occurs. Which of the following is the best explanation for this observation?

    A.   The activation energy for the reaction is too high for the reaction to occur at this temperature.
    B.   A catalyst is necessary in order for this reaction to occur.
    C.   The change in enthalpy for the oxidation of isooctane is negative.
    D.   The change in entropy for the oxidation of isooctane is positive.

Long Free Response

1. Ethylene gas, C_2H_4, can undergo hydrogenation, an addition reaction in which hydrogen gas is added in the presence of a heterogeneous platinum catalyst. This reaction produces ethane, C_2H_6.

Use the thermodynamic data provided to answer the following questions.

Substance	ΔG°_f (kJ/mol)
$C_2H_4(g)$	68.4
$H_2(g)$	0
$C_2H_6(g)$	−32.0

Bond Type	Bond Energy (kJ·mol^{-1})
C — C	348
C $=$ C	612
C — H	412
H — H	436

a. **i.** Draw Lewis structures for C_2H_4 and C_2H_6 in the boxes below.

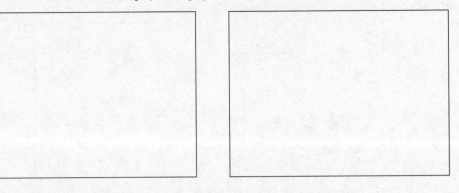

ii. Write and balance the equation for the hydrogenation of C_2H_4.

b. Calculate the change in enthalpy associated with the hydrogenation of ethylene gas under standard thermodynamic conditions.

c. **i.** Calculate the standard change in Gibbs free energy for the reaction.

ii. Calculate the change in entropy associated with the hydrogenation of ethylene gas at 298 K.

d. Calculate the change in Gibbs free energy for the transformation at 100 °C, assuming $\Delta H°$ and $\Delta S°$ are temperature-independent.

e. **i.** What is the purpose of the catalyst in this reaction? Include in your answer a brief description of how the catalyst achieves this purpose.

ii. Explain the effect, if any, of the catalyst on the Gibbs free energy change for the reaction.

Short Free Response

2. When white phosphorus under an atmosphere of oxygen at 25 °C is touched with a hot wire, the following reaction occurs with evolution of heat and bright white light.

$$P_4(s) + 5\,O_2(g) \rightarrow 2\,P_2O_5(s)$$

a. Predict the sign of $\Delta S°$ for the system and discuss how you arrived at your prediction.

b. What is the sign of $\Delta G°$ and how would ΔG change as the temperature of this reaction is increased from 25 °C? Justify your response.

c. Is the potential energy of the reactants higher or lower than that of the products? Explain your answer.

d. When the reactants are placed together at room temperature, no observable reaction takes place until the hot wire touches the phosphorus. Explain why this is true.

3. A student constructed a coffee cup calorimeter in order to determine the enthalpy change for the reaction of ammonia, $NH_3(aq)$, and hydrochloric acid, $HCl(aq)$.

When 50.0 mL of 2.00 M aqueous NH_3 were added to 50.0 mL of 2.00 M aqueous HCl in the calorimeter, the temperature reached 33.1 °C. Both solutions were initially at 23.0 °C.

Assume that the density of all solutions is 1.00 $g \cdot mL^{-1}$ and the heat capacity of all solutions is the same as that of water, $c = 4.18\ J \cdot g^{-1} \cdot °C^{-1}$.

a. Write the net ionic equation for the reaction.

b. What is the enthalpy change in kilojoules per mole of reaction? Assume that the heat transferred between the system and the surroundings is negligible.

c. Would the calculated value for the enthalpy change be higher or lower than the actual value if a significant amount of heat transfer occurred between the solution and the calorimeter? Discuss your response.

d. The student uses chemical literature resources to find the standard molar enthalpy of reaction for an aqueous acid-base reaction.

$$H^+(aq) + OH^-(aq) \rightarrow H_2O(l) \qquad \Delta H° = -54 \text{ kJ·mol}^{-1}$$

Using this information and the information in parts **a** and **b,** determine the enthalpy change for the reaction below.

$$NH_3(aq) + H_2O(l) \rightarrow NH_4^+(aq) + OH^-(aq)$$

Answers and Explanations

Multiple Choice

1. **C.** (EK 5.B.1) A negative value for work indicates that the system is doing work on the surroundings. Since $w = -P\Delta V$, the final volume of the system must be greater than the initial volume. Reaction C is the only choice in which there is a greater number of gaseous products than gaseous reactants, so it is the only one in which the system experiences an increase in volume and, therefore, does work on the surroundings.

2. **C.** (EK 5.E.1) The change in entropy of the system for Reaction C is greater than zero because there is a greater number of gaseous products than gaseous reactants. In all the other choices there are either fewer moles of gaseous products than gaseous reactants (Reactions A and B) or, in the case of Reaction D, the dispersion of the particles of the system decreases as they are converted from dissolved solutes to a solid.

3. **A.** (EK 5.A.2) The heat capacity of the block of metal can be found by rearranging the equation for heat transfer, $q = mc\Delta T$.

$$c = \frac{q}{m\Delta T} = \frac{216 \text{ J}}{(12.0 \text{ g})(20 \text{ °C})} = 0.90 \text{ J·g}^{-1}\text{·°C}^{-1}$$

This is the heat capacity of aluminum (choice A). Without a calculator, one suggestion for estimating this value is to start by expanding the numerator and the denominator.

$$\frac{\cancel{2}(108)}{(12)(\cancel{2})(10)} = \frac{\cancel{10}(10.8)}{(12)(\cancel{10})} \approx \frac{11}{12}$$

The numerical heat capacity value of 0.90 is the closest choice to $\frac{11}{12}$.

4. **B.** (EK 5.A.1, 5.A.2) When the hot object is placed in thermal contact with the gas, heat will be transferred from the object to the gas. This will cause the average kinetic energy to increase, and this will be reflected in the Boltzmann distribution as higher velocities for the gas molecules in addition to a more dispersed distribution of molecular speeds.

5. **C.** (5.B.2, 5.B.3, 5.B.4) The increase in temperature shows that the reaction is exothermic. An exothermic reaction has a negative enthalpy change, $\Delta H < 0$. Because some of the heat given off by the reaction is lost to the calorimeter and the surroundings, the temperature change that is measured is artificially low. This results in a less negative enthalpy change than the actual ΔH for the reaction, as calculated using

$$\Delta H_{rxn} = \frac{q_{rxn}}{n} = -\frac{q_{soln}}{n} = \frac{-mc\Delta T}{n}$$

6. **B.** (5.B.2, 5.B.3) The energy that is transferred to the ice from the warm water only melts it. It does not cause the temperature of the 0 °C water to increase until all of the solid water has been converted to liquid water.

7. **D.** (EK 5.C.2, 5.D.2, 5.E.1) When ice melts, it undergoes an increase in enthalpy, so $\Delta H > 0$. Since solid water is less dense and contains more open space than liquid water, $\Delta V < 0$.

8. D. (EK 5.C.1, 5.C.2) The reactions must be arranged so that their sum results in the overall chemical equation. If the reaction is reversed, its enthalpy sign is reversed. If the coefficients are multiplied by a factor, its enthalpy is also multiplied by that factor. It is simplest to begin with the reaction that contains CH_4.

$$
\begin{array}{ll}
CH_4(g) \rightarrow C(\text{graphite}) + 2H_2(g) & -y \\
C(\text{graphite}) + 2O(g) \rightarrow CO_2(g) & x \\
2[O_2(g) \rightarrow 2O(g)] & -2v \\
2[H_2(g) \rightarrow 2H(g)] & -2z \\
2[2H(g) + O(g) \rightarrow H_2O(g)] & 2w \\
\hline
CH_4(g) + 2O_2(g) \rightarrow CO_2(g) + 2H_2O(g) & \Delta H = -2v + 2w + x - y - 2z
\end{array}
$$

9. D. (EK 5.D) As the reactions are written, all have enthalpy changes that are less than zero. Energy is released when bonds are formed, corresponding to negative values of ΔH.

10. C. (EK 5.B.3, 5.C.2, 3.A.2) The limiting reagent can be determined by determining which reactant leads to the smaller quantity of released energy. Since the energy is released, the value of ΔH is negative.

$$0.010 \; \text{mol } O_2 \times \frac{-804 \text{ kJ}}{2 \text{ mole } O_2} = -4.02 \text{ kJ}$$

$$0.010 \; \text{mol } CH_4 \times \frac{-804 \text{ kJ}}{1 \text{ mol } CH_4} = -8.04 \text{ kJ}$$

Oxygen is the limiting reagent, and 4.02 kJ of energy are released.

11. B. (EK 5.E.1) The diagram in choice B shows a system that is increasing its organization. This is a greater dispersal of matter in the initial diagram than there is in the final diagram, so the entropy change is negative.

12. C. (EK 5.E.4) Reactions that are thermodynamically unfavorable, like the transport of potassium into the cell against its concentration gradient, can be driven by coupling to another source of energy. Since the reaction is coupled to the hydrolysis of ATP, the hydrolysis reaction must have sufficiently negative Gibbs free energy to overcome the positive free energy of the transport.

13. C. (EK 5.E.4) Because the tin electrode is the cathode and the silver electrode is the anode, the cell potential can be calculated using the standard reduction potentials.

$$E°_{\text{cell}} = E°_{\text{cathode}} - E°_{\text{anode}} = -0.83 \text{ V} - (1.07 \text{ V}) = -1.9 \text{ V}$$

The standard cell potential is negative, so the reaction is thermodynamically unfavorable. This is an electrolytic cell with $\Delta G > 0$.

14. C. (EK 5.D.1) Step C is the only step in which intermolecular attractions are causing particles to move closer to one another. As particles approach one another as the result of intermolecular attractions, potential energy decreases and the process is exothermic ($\Delta H < 0$).

15. C. (EK 5.B.3) Region C shows the rise in temperature that occurs as energy is added to the liquid phase of the substance. The heat transferred to or from the substance in the liquid phase is given by

$$q = mc_{\text{liquid}}\Delta T$$

16. D. (EK 5.B.3) Region D shows the plateau in temperature that occurs as added energy causes the liquid phase of the substance to be converted to gas. The amount of heat required to vaporize a given number of moles of the liquid is given by

$$q = n\Delta H_{\text{vap}}$$

17. **D.** (EK 5.C.2) The formation reaction for a compound is the reaction that forms the compound in its thermodynamic standard state (at 1 atmosphere of pressure and 298 K) from its constituent elements in their thermodynamic standard states.

18. **C.** (EK 5.E.3) It is apparent from the decrease in the temperature of the solvent as ammonium chloride dissolves that the dissolution is endothermic and $\Delta H > 0$. Dissolution increases the dispersion and disorganization of the materials, so $\Delta S > 0$. The dissolution is thermodynamically favorable under conditions in which $\Delta G < 0$. The Gibbs free energy change is negative according to $\Delta G = \Delta H - T\Delta S$ when the temperature is high.

19. **B.** (EK 5.B.1, 5.D.1) It is apparent that work is being done on the surroundings by the system and that $w < 0$ because the volume of the sample is increasing at constant temperature. Energy is required to disrupt the intermolecular forces between the molecules as the substance is converted from liquid to gas, so heat is absorbed by the system, $q > 0$.

20. **A.** (EK 5.E.5) The combustion of isooctane is thermodynamically favorable. It does not occur at room temperature, however, because the reactant molecules do not have sufficient energy to overcome the activation barrier for the reaction.

Long Free Response

1. **a. i.** (EK 2.C.4) The Lewis structures of C_2H_4 and C_2H_6 are shown.

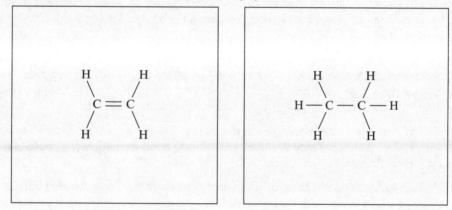

ii. (EK 3.A.1) The balanced chemical equation for this reaction is

$$C_2H_4(g) + H_2(g) \xrightarrow{\text{Pt}(s)} C_2H_6(g)$$

b. (EK 5.C.2) The enthalpy change for the process can be determined from the difference between the sums of the bond energies of reactants and products.

$$\Delta H_{rxn} = (\Sigma \text{ bond energies of reactants}) - (\Sigma \text{ bond energies of products})$$

$\Delta H_{rxn} = [(1 \times 612 \text{ kJ·mol}^{-1}) + (4 \times 412 \text{ kJ·mol}^{-1}) + (1 \times 436 \text{ kJ·mol}^{-1})] - [(1 \times 348 \text{ kJ·mol}^{-1}) + (6 \times 412 \text{ kJ·mol}^{-1})]$

$$\Delta H_{rxn} = -124 \text{ kJ·mol}^{-1}$$

c. i. (EK 5.E.3) The standard change in Gibbs free energy can be found using the equation

$$\Delta G^{\circ}_{rxn} = \Sigma n\Delta G^{\circ}_{f(products)} - \Sigma n\Delta G^{\circ}_{f(reactants)}$$

$$\Delta G^{\circ}_{rxn} = \left[(1(-32.0 \text{ kJ} \cdot \text{mol}^{-1})\right] - \left[(1(68.4 \text{ kJ} \cdot \text{mol}^{-1})) + (1(0.0 \text{ kJ} \cdot \text{mol}^{-1}))\right]$$

$$\Delta G^{\circ}_{rxn} = -100.4 \text{ kJ} \cdot \text{mol}^{-1}$$

ii. (EK 5.E.1, 5.E.3) The value of $\Delta S°$ can be determined by rearrangement of the equation for the change in Gibbs free energy.

$$\Delta G° = \Delta H° - T\Delta S°$$

$$\Delta S° = \frac{\Delta G° - \Delta H°}{-T} = \frac{-100.4 \text{ kJ} \cdot \text{mol}^{-1} - (-124 \text{ kJ} \cdot \text{mol}^{-1})}{-298 \text{ K}} = -0.0792 \text{ kJ} \cdot \text{mol}^{-1} \cdot \text{K}^{-1}$$

d. (EK 5.E.3) A temperature of 100 °C equals 373 K.

$$\Delta G = \Delta H - T\Delta S = (-124 \text{ kJ} \cdot \text{mol}^{-1}) - \left[(373 \text{ K})(-0.0792 \text{ kJ} \cdot \text{mol}^{-1} \cdot \text{K}^{-1})\right] = -94 \text{ kJ} \cdot \text{mol}^{-1}$$

e. i. (EK 4.D.1) The purpose of the catalyst is to increase the rate of the reaction by providing an alternative mechanism with a lower activation energy than the uncatalyzed reaction.

ii. (EK 4.D.1, 5.E.3) The catalyst has no effect on the change in Gibbs free energy because it has no effect on $\Delta H°$ or $\Delta S°$. It affects only the energy of the transition state for the reaction, which alters the rate, not the thermodynamic favorability.

Short Free Response

2. a. (EK 5.E.1) The standard entropy change is likely to be negative because the number of moles of gaseous reactants is greater than the number of moles of gaseous products. This corresponds to a decrease in dispersion of matter.

b. (EK 5.E.3) The reaction is thermodynamically favorable since it proceeds in the direction that is written. For a spontaneous process, the standard change in Gibbs free energy, $\Delta G°$, is negative. The reaction is also exothermic since it gives off heat. Since $\Delta H < 0$, $\Delta S < 0$, and $\Delta G = \Delta H - T\Delta S$, the reaction becomes less spontaneous (ΔG becomes more positive) as the temperature increases.

c. (EK 5.C.2) The reaction is exothermic, which means that less energy is consumed when bonds in the reactants are broken than is released in the process of new bond formation. The potential energy of reactants is greater than that of products.

d. (EK 5.E.5) The reactants do not have sufficient energy to overcome the activation barrier until their energy is increased by contact with the hot wire. Once the reaction is initiated, it proceeds spontaneously.

3. a. (EK 3.A.1) Ammonia is a weak base. It reacts with a strong acid to form an ammonium salt. The overall equation is

$$NH_3(aq) + HCl(aq) \rightarrow NH_4Cl(aq)$$

The total ionic equation is

$$NH_3(aq) + H^+(aq) + \cancel{Cl^-(aq)} \rightarrow NH_4^+(aq) + \cancel{Cl^-(aq)}$$

The net ionic equation is

$$NH_3(aq) + H^+(aq) \rightarrow NH_4^+(aq)$$

b. (EK 5.B.4) The total mass of the solution is given by

$$50.0 \text{ mL} + 50.0 \text{ mL} = 100.0 \text{ mL of the final solution}$$

$$100.0 \text{ mL} \times \frac{1.00 \text{ g}}{1 \text{ mL}} = 100.0 \text{ g}$$

The number of moles of either reactant is

$$50.0 \ \cancel{mL} \times \frac{1 \ \cancel{L}}{1000 \ \cancel{mL}} \times \frac{2.00 \ mol}{1 \ \cancel{L}} = 0.100 \ mol$$

The heat, q, given off by this reaction divided by the number of moles, n, of either reactant or the number of moles of product formed is equal to the enthalpy change for the process.

$$\Delta H_{rxn} = \frac{q_{rxn}}{n} = \frac{-mc\Delta T}{n} = \frac{-(100.0 \ \cancel{g})(4.18 \ \cancel{J} \cdot \cancel{g^{-1}} \cdot \cancel{^\circ C^{-1}})(33.1 \ \cancel{^\circ C} - 23.0 \ \cancel{^\circ C})}{0.100 \ mol} \times \frac{1 \ kJ}{1000 \ \cancel{J}} = -42 \ kJ \cdot mol^{-1}$$

c. (EK 5.B.4) The calculated value of the enthalpy change is less negative (higher) than the actual value because some of the heat released in the reaction is absorbed by the calorimeter and does not result in a temperature change for the solution.

d. (EK 5.C.2) The equation illustrating the reaction of $NH_3(aq)$ with $H^+(aq)$ can be added to the reverse of the equation illustrating the reaction of $OH^-(aq)$ with $H^+(aq)$ to result in an equation representing the overall reaction in question. The sum of the enthalpies results in the enthalpy change for the overall reaction.

$$NH_3(aq) + \cancel{H^+(aq)} \rightarrow NH_4^+(aq) \qquad \qquad \Delta H = -42 \ kJ \cdot mol^{-1}$$

$$\underline{H_2O(l) \rightarrow \cancel{H^+(aq)} + OH^-(aq) \qquad \qquad \Delta H = (-1)(-54 \ kJ \cdot mol^{-1})}$$

$$NH_3(aq) + H_2O(l) \rightarrow NH_4^+(aq) + OH^-(aq) \qquad \qquad \Delta H = 12 \ kJ \cdot mol^{-1}$$

Chapter 6

Chemical Equilibrium (Big Idea 6)

Big Idea 6: Chemical reactions are reversible and proceed to equilibrium, the condition in which the rate of the forward reaction and the rate of the reverse reaction are equal

Although some chemical reactions proceed almost to completion, most do not completely convert reactants to products. In addition, the forward and the reverse reactions occur simultaneously. When this is the case, a reaction is said to be **reversible.**

An example of a reversible process is the freezing and melting of water. A sample of water will freeze when the temperature drops below 0 °C at one atmosphere, and it will melt when the temperature rises above 0 °C. An equilibrium arrow denotes reversibility.

$$H_2O(l) \rightleftharpoons H_2O(s)$$

Another example of a reversible reaction is one in which a messenger molecule binds reversibly to a receptor in a cell. The binding of the messenger causes a change in the receptor that causes a biochemical signal in another portion of the organism. When the messenger molecule is released, the signal stops.

Neurons, or nerve cells, for example, release acetylcholine, a small molecule that binds reversibly to protein receptors on the cell membrane of other neurons. The binding of acetylcholine causes an ion channel to open in the protein, transmitting a signal to the neuron. The signal is terminated when the acetylcholine is released and the ion channel closes.

Chemical Equilibrium

Chemical equilibrium is the stable state in which a reversible reaction is occurring with equal rates in the forward and reverse directions. The reaction has not stopped; the molecules are continually reacting, but the concentrations of reactants and products are no longer changing.

Consider the following reversible reaction.

$$A + B \rightleftharpoons C$$

Suppose reactants A and B are combined in a reaction vessel. The reaction begins to proceed with a faster rate in the forward direction than in the reverse direction.

$$A + B \rightarrow C$$

As C forms, it converts back to A and B in the reverse direction, but until equilibrium is established, the rate of this reverse reaction is slower than the rate of the forward reaction.

$$C \rightarrow A + B$$

As equilibrium is approached, the rate of the forward reaction slows and the rate of the reverse reaction increases until equilibrium is reached. At equilibrium, the rates of the forward reaction and reverse reaction are equal and the concentrations have stopped changing.

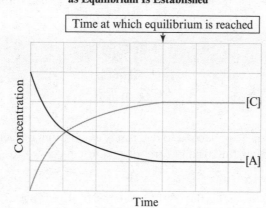

The Disappearance of A and Appearance of C as Equilibrium Is Established

The Equilibrium Constant

Consider the following equilibrium reaction.

$$aA + bB \rightleftharpoons cC + dD$$

The **equilibrium constant**, K_c, for this reaction is related to the equilibrium concentrations (denoted by the subscript, c) of the reactants and products at a particular temperature by the mass action expression. (Note that in the K_c expression, each concentration is raised to the power of its coefficient in the balanced chemical equation.)

$$K_c = \frac{[C]^c[D]^d}{[A]^a[B]^b}$$

The equilibrium constant is determined experimentally for a reaction. For a given reaction, only a change in temperature can change the equilibrium constant. The equilibrium constant is independent of the initial concentrations of reactants and products.

Only dissolved aqueous substances and gases appear in the mass action expression. For the purposes of AP Chemistry, no solids or liquids contribute to the expression, and the equilibrium constant is unitless.

PRACTICE:

Write the mass action expression, K_c, for the reaction between nitrogen gas and hydrogen gas to form gaseous ammonia.

The balanced chemical equation is

$$N_2(g) + 3\,H_2(g) \rightleftharpoons 2\,NH_3(g)$$

The mass action expression is

$$K_c = \frac{[NH_3]^2}{[N_2][H_2]^3}$$

For a reaction in which $K > 1$, products are favored over reactants at equilibrium. For a reaction in which $K < 1$, reactants are favored over products at equilibrium.

Often the equilibrium constant is used to determine equilibrium concentrations of the species in the reaction. For example, suppose 3.00 moles of A_2 are added to 3.00 moles of B_2 in a 1.00-L container. The reactants A_2 and B_2 form the product AB. The equilibrium constant at this temperature, K_c, is 25.0.

$$A_2 + B_2 \leftrightharpoons 2\,AB$$

$$K_c = \frac{[AB]^2}{[A_2][B_2]}$$

A **R.I.C.E. table,** which is a tool that can be used to determine equilibrium concentrations, is an appropriate method. R.I.C.E. stands for reaction, initial concentration, change in concentration, and equilibrium concentration.

At the beginning of the reaction, the molarities of the reactants, $[A_2]$ and $[B_2]$, are known to be 3.00 M. There is no product, so initially [AB] is zero. Let x equal the magnitude of the decrease in the molarities of A_2 and B_2. According to the stoichiometry of the reaction, the concentration of AB increases by $+2x$. In other words, the concentration of AB increases twice as much as the concentration of A_2 or B_2 decreases.

Reaction	A_2	B_2	2 AB
Initial Concentrations (M)	3.00	3.00	0
Change	$-x$	$-x$	$+2x$
Equilibrium Concentrations (M)	$3.00 - x$	$3.00 - x$	$2x$

The equilibrium concentrations are substituted into the mass action expression.

$$K_c = \frac{[AB]^2}{[A_2][B_2]}$$

$$25.0 = \frac{(2x)^2}{(3.00 - x)^2}$$

In this example, x is determined by taking the square root of both sides of the equation.

$$\sqrt{25.0} = \sqrt{\frac{(2x)^2}{(3.00 - x)^2}}$$

$$5.00 = \frac{2x}{3.00 - x}$$

$$15.0 - 5.00x = 2x$$

$$15.0 = 7.00x$$

$$x = 2.14 \qquad (2.142857143)$$

The unrounded value of x is used to calculate $[A_2]$, $[B_2]$, and [AB].

$$[A_2] = [B_2] = 3.00\ M - x = (3.00 - 2.142857143)\ M = 0.86\ M$$
$$[AB] = 2x = 2(2.142857143\ M) = 4.29\ M$$

The equilibrium expression is not always as easily solved as in the example above. In some problems, it is necessary to use the quadratic formula or perform even more labor-intensive operations in order to solve for x. This is extremely unlikely to ever be the case on the AP Chemistry exam. It is much more likely that problems resembling the following practice question will appear.

PRACTICE:

A 5.00-mole sample of $SO_3(g)$ is placed in a rigid, evacuated 10.0-L container at 1000. K. When the reaction reaches equilibrium, the amount of $SO_3(g)$ has decreased to 3.18 moles. What is K_c for the reaction at this temperature?

$$2\ SO_3(g) \rightleftharpoons O_2(g) + 2\ SO_2(g)$$

Because the volume of the container is 10.0 liters, the initial concentration of $SO_3(g)$ is

$$[SO_3]_{initial} = \frac{5.00\ mol}{10.0\ L} = 0.500\ M$$

The final concentration of $SO_3(g)$ is

$$[SO_3]_{final} = \frac{3.18\ mol}{10.0\ L} = 0.318\ M$$

The R.I.C.E. table can be constructed to determine the equilibrium concentrations of the products.

Reaction	2 SO$_3$	O$_2$	2 SO$_2$
Initial Concentrations (*M*)	0.500	0	0
Change	$-2x$	$+x$	$+2x$
Equilibrium Concentrations (*M*)	0.318	x	$2x$

There is enough information about the change in $[SO_3]$ to solve for x.

$$0.500 - 2x = 0.318$$
$$0.182 = 2x$$
$$x = 0.0910$$

The equilibrium concentrations are as follows.

$[SO_3] = 0.500 - 2x = 0.318\ M$

$[O_2] = x = 0.0910\ M$

$[SO_2] = 2x = 2(0.0910) = 0.182\ M$

The equilibrium constant, K_c, is determined using the equilibrium concentrations.

$$K_c = \frac{[O_2][SO_2]^2}{[SO_3]^2} = \frac{(0.0910)(0.182)^2}{(0.318)^2} = 0.0298$$

Other forms of the equilibrium constant are also useful. For reactions in the gas phase, it is sometimes appropriate to determine an equilibrium constant, K_p, as a function of the partial pressures of the reactants and products. A R.I.C.E. table involving K_p should contain the partial pressure values for the reactants and products.

$$a\ A(g) + b\ B(g) \rightleftharpoons c\ C(g) + d\ D(g)$$

$$K_p = \frac{P_C{}^c P_D{}^d}{P_A{}^a P_B{}^b}$$

271

PRACTICE:

> At 2117 K, the reaction of carbon dioxide with graphite proceeds with an equilibrium constant, K_p, of 8.60×10^4. Under equilibrium conditions in which the partial pressure of $CO(g)$ is 4.15 atm, what is the partial pressure of $CO_2(g)$?
>
> $$C(s) + CO_2(g) \rightleftharpoons 2\ CO(g)$$

Graphite is a solid, so it is ignored, and the mass action expression for this reaction is

$$K_p = \frac{P_{CO}^2}{P_{CO_2}}$$

$$P_{CO_2} = \frac{P_{CO}^2}{K_p} = \frac{(4.15)^2}{8.60 \times 10^4} = 2.00 \times 10^{-4}\ \text{atm}$$

Variations of the Equilibrium Constant

When equations representing chemical reactions are reversed, multiplied, and added, their equilibrium constants must be manipulated to reflect the new equations. When the equation of a reaction is reversed, for example, the new equilibrium constant is the reciprocal of the equilibrium constant for the original direction.

$$A + B \rightleftharpoons AB \qquad \text{where } K_{forward} = \frac{[AB]}{[A][B]}$$

$$AB \rightleftharpoons A + B \qquad K_{reverse} = \frac{[A][B]}{[AB]} = K_{forward}^{-1}$$

When an equation for a reaction is multiplied by a factor, its equilibrium constant is raised to the power of that factor.

$$A + B \rightleftharpoons AB \qquad \text{where } K_1 = \frac{[AB]}{[A][B]}$$

$$2A + 2B \rightleftharpoons 2AB \qquad K_2 = \frac{[AB]^2}{[A]^2[B]^2} = K_1^2$$

When two equations representing two chemical reactions are added, the equilibrium constant for the resulting equation is the product of the equilibrium constants of the constituent reactions.

$$A + B \rightleftharpoons AB \qquad \text{where } K_1 = \frac{[AB]}{[A][B]}$$

$$AB \rightleftharpoons C + D \qquad \text{where } K_2 = \frac{[C][D]}{[AB]}$$

$$\overline{A + B \rightleftharpoons C + D} \qquad K = \frac{[C][D]}{[A][B]} = K_1 \times K_2$$

PRACTICE:

> Calculate the equilibrium constant for reaction 1, illustrated by the following equation:
>
> reaction 1 equation: $A_3 \rightleftharpoons A + A_2$
>
> using the information given for reactions 2 and 3, illustrated by the following equations:
>
> reaction 2 equation: $AB + A \rightleftharpoons A_2B$ $K_2 = 4.5$
> reaction 3 equation: $A_3 + AB \rightleftharpoons A_2B + A_2$ $K_3 = 3.1$

The reverse of equation 2 added to equation 3 results in equation 1. The reciprocal of the equilibrium constant for reaction 2 is multiplied by the equilibrium constant for reaction 3.

$$A_2\cancel{B} \rightleftharpoons \cancel{AB} + A \qquad K_2^{-1} = 4.5^{-1}$$
$$A_3 + \cancel{AB} \rightleftharpoons \cancel{A_2B} + A_2 \qquad K_3 = 3.1$$
$$\overline{A_3 \rightleftharpoons A + A_2 \qquad\qquad K_1 = K_2^{-1} \times K_3}$$
$$= 0.69$$

Measuring the Equilibrium Constant

Equilibrium constants are determined experimentally by measuring the relative amounts of reactants and products at equilibrium. A common laboratory exercise is the measurement of the equilibrium constant for the reaction between iron(III) ions, Fe^{3+}, and thiocyanate ions, SCN^-. The product that is formed, $FeSCN^{2+}$, is red, and its concentration can be determined by spectrophotometry.

$$Fe^{3+}(aq) + SCN^-(aq) \rightleftharpoons FeSCN^{2+}(aq)$$

$$K_c = \frac{[FeSCN^{2+}]}{[Fe^{3+}][SCN^-]}$$

PRACTICE:

> A student generated a standard calibration curve for the concentration of $FeSCN^{2+}$ using a spectrophotometer. The student then mixed 5.0 mL of 2.00×10^{-3} M $Fe(NO_3)_3$ with 5.0 mL of 2.00×10^{-3} M KSCN.
>
> When the color stopped changing, the student determined that the concentration of $FeSCN^{2+}$ was 1.3×10^{-4} M. What is the equilibrium constant, K_c, for this reaction?

The initial concentrations of Fe^{3+} and SCN^-, immediately after mixing the two solutions and before any reaction has occurred, can be determined using the dilution formula.

The initial concentration of Fe^{3+}, before mixing the two solutions, was 2.00×10^{-3} M, and the initial volume was 5.0 mL. The final volume of the solution is 10.0 mL.

$$M_{initial} \times V_{initial} = M_{final} \times V_{final}$$

$$(2.00 \times 10^{-3} \, M)(5.0 \, \text{mL}) = M_{final}(10.0 \, \text{mL})$$

$$M_{final} = 1.0 \times 10^{-3} \, M$$

The initial concentrations of Fe^{3+} and SCN^- are equal. A R.I.C.E. table is used for the determination of the equilibrium concentrations.

Reaction	Fe^{3+}	SCN^-	$FeSCN^{2+}$
Initial Concentrations (M)	1.0×10^{-3}	1.0×10^{-3}	0
Change	-1.3×10^{-4}	-1.3×10^{-4}	$+1.3 \times 10^{-4}$
Equilibrium Concentrations (M)	8.7×10^{-4}	8.7×10^{-4}	1.3×10^{-4}

The equilibrium concentrations are used to determine the equilibrium constant.

$$K_c = \frac{[FeSCN^{2+}]}{[Fe^{3+}][SCN^-]} = \frac{(1.3 \times 10^{-4})}{(8.7 \times 10^{-4})(8.7 \times 10^{-4})} = 1.7 \times 10^2$$

The Reaction Quotient

The **reaction quotient**, Q, is a measure of how different the mass action ratio of reactants and products are from the equilibrium value at a given temperature. Comparison of Q with K indicates the direction in which the reaction must proceed in order to reach equilibrium. The reaction quotient is calculated in the same manner as K, except that actual concentrations are used (not necessarily equilibrium values).

The reaction quotient can be compared with K to determine whether a reaction will shift toward products or reactants to reach equilibrium:

- When $Q > K$, the reaction shifts toward reactants. The rate of the reverse reaction is greater than the rate of the forward reaction until equilibrium is established.
- When $Q < K$, the reaction shifts toward products. The rate of the forward reaction is greater than the rate of the reverse reaction until equilibrium is established.
- When $Q = K$, the reaction is at equilibrium. At equilibrium, the rates of the forward and reverse reactions are equal.

The Relationship Between Q and K

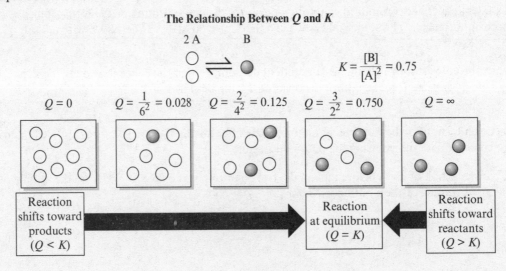

PRACTICE:

The equilibrium constant, K_p, for the reaction of $CO(g)$ with $Cl_2(g)$ at 1000. K is 2.9×10^{-2}.

$$CO(g) + Cl_2(g) \rightleftharpoons COCl_2(g)$$

The partial pressures of the gases are as follows:

$$P_{CO} = 0.40 \text{ atm}$$
$$P_{Cl_2} = 0.60 \text{ atm}$$
$$P_{COCl_2} = 0.020 \text{ atm}$$

Will the reaction shift to produce reactants or products?

The equilibrium quotient, Q, must be calculated and compared with K_p.

$$Q = \frac{P_{COCl_2}}{P_{CO}P_{Cl_2}} = \frac{(0.020)}{(0.40)(0.60)} = 8.3 \times 10^{-2}$$

Because $Q > K$, the reaction shifts toward reactants until equilibrium is established.

Le Chatelier's Principle

When a change is made to a system at equilibrium, the system will respond in a way that re-establishes the equilibrium. This is **Le Chatelier's principle,** and it is used to make qualitative predictions about how a system will react to stress. Alterations in conditions that shift a system from equilibrium include addition or removal of a reactant or product or a change in pressure if gases are produced or consumed. A change in temperature causes the equilibrium constant itself to change, but Le Chatelier's principle can still be used to qualitatively predict the effect of a change in temperature on a system.

Concentration Changes

When a reactant or product is added to a system at equilibrium, that reactant or product will be consumed until a new equilibrium state is reached. It is sometimes said that the reaction "shifts away" from the added species. For example, if compound A is added to the following reaction at equilibrium, C will be produced and A and B will be consumed until equilibrium is reached.

$$A + B \rightleftharpoons C$$

Likewise, if a reactant or product is removed from a system at equilibrium, the system will produce more of that reactant or product until equilibrium is re-established. The system "shifts toward" the removed species.

PRACTICE:

> Hypochlorite, ClO^-, decomposes to form chloride, Cl^-, and chlorate, ClO_3^-, in aqueous solution.
>
> $$3\ ClO^-(aq) \rightleftharpoons 2\ Cl^-(aq) + ClO_3^-(aq)$$
>
> A 1.0-L solution of hypochlorite is allowed to reach equilibrium at 25 °C. The concentrations of the three species in a reaction vessel are determined to be $[ClO^-] = 1.0 \times 10^{-9}\ M$, $[Cl^-] = 2.0\ M$, and $[ClO_3^-] = 2.5\ M$.
>
> **(a)** Without doing any calculations, predict whether the system will shift toward reactants or products when 0.5 mole of NaCl is added to the solution.
>
> **(b)** Calculate K_c and Q for the reaction and state whether these calculated values support the prediction made in part (a).

(a) Upon its addition to the solution, the NaCl dissociates into Na^+ and Cl^-. While the Na^+ ions do not have any effect on the equilibrium, the Cl^- ions do. According to Le Chatelier's principle, addition of one of the products (Cl^-) to the reaction vessel will cause the reaction to shift toward reactants in order to re-establish equilibrium.

(b) The value of K_c is

$$K_c = \frac{[Cl^-]^2[ClO_3^-]}{[ClO^-]^3} = \frac{(2.0)^2(2.5)}{(1.0 \times 10^{-9})^3} = 1.0 \times 10^{28}$$

The added 0.5 mole of Cl^- results in a new Cl^- concentration of 2.5 M. The value of Q is

$$Q = \frac{[Cl^-]^2[ClO_3^-]}{[ClO^-]^3} = \frac{(2.5)^2(2.5)}{(1.0 \times 10^{-9})^3} = 1.6 \times 10^{28}$$

Because $Q > K_c$, the reaction will shift toward reactants as predicted.

Pressure Changes

If a container containing a reaction that produces or consumes a gas is compressed, the system will respond by shifting in the direction that reduces the number of moles of gas present. For example, assume that A, B, and C are all gaseous species. An increase in the pressure in the reaction vessel will cause the reaction to shift toward products, and the total number of moles of gas present will decrease. Notice that the increase in pressure in this case is due to a decrease in the volume of the container.

$$A + B \rightleftharpoons C$$

The Effect of Increased Pressure on a Gaseous Equilibrium

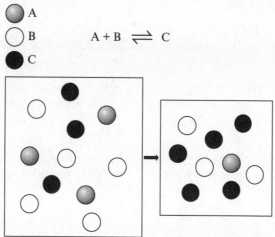

PRACTICE:

For the reactions below, predict the direction that the reaction will shift as a result of an increase in pressure.

(a) $2 Cl_2(g) + O_2(g) \rightleftharpoons 2 Cl_2O(g)$

(b) $H_2(g) + I_2(g) \rightleftharpoons 2 HI(g)$

(c) $CH_4(g) + H_2O(g) \rightleftharpoons CO(g) + 3 H_2(g)$

An increase in pressure causes a reaction to shift toward the side with fewer gas molecules. Due to an increase in pressure, reaction (a) will shift toward products, reaction (b) will undergo no change, and reaction (c) will shift toward reactants.

Tip: It should be noted that addition of an *inert* ideal gas to a system at constant volume will not shift the equilibrium since it has no effect on the concentrations or partial pressures of the other gases present.

Temperature Changes

An equilibrium constant for a reaction is specific for a particular temperature. A change in the temperature of a system (unlike a change in concentration or pressure) changes the value of the equilibrium constant.

An endothermic reaction consumes heat. Therefore, heat is treated like a reactant. So, adding heat to raise the temperature is like adding a reactant: It shifts the reaction toward products. This causes an increase in the value of the equilibrium constant. On the other hand, an exothermic reaction produces heat. Therefore, heat is treated like a product. Adding heat to raise the temperature is like adding a product: It shifts the reaction toward reactants. This causes a decrease in the value of the equilibrium constant.

Note: It is very important to remember that ONLY temperature changes affect the value of K.

The Effect of Temperature on Equilibrium

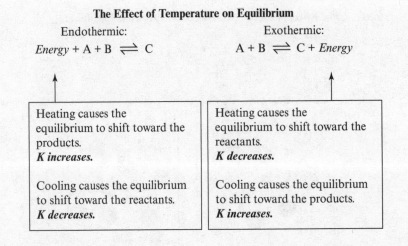

Endothermic:

$$Energy + A + B \rightleftharpoons C$$

Exothermic:

$$A + B \rightleftharpoons C + Energy$$

Heating causes the equilibrium to shift toward the products.
K increases.

Cooling causes the equilibrium to shift toward the reactants.
K decreases.

Heating causes the equilibrium to shift toward the reactants.
K decreases.

Cooling causes the equilibrium to shift toward the products.
K increases.

PRACTICE:

Use the bond energy data to determine whether K will increase or decrease for the reaction of F_2 with O_2 as temperature increases.

$$F_2(g) + \frac{1}{2}O_2(g) \rightleftharpoons OF_2(g)$$

Bond	Bond Energy (kJ·mol^{-1})
F——F	159
O══O	498
O——F	190

First, draw the Lewis structures of each of the reactants and products.

$$:\ddot{F}—\ddot{F}: \quad :\ddot{O}═O: \quad :\ddot{F}—\ddot{O}:$$
$$\underset{\ddot{F}}{\diagdown}$$

Next, we use the bond energies to determine whether the reaction is endothermic or exothermic.

$$\Delta H_{rxn} = (\Sigma \text{ bond energies of reactants}) - (\Sigma \text{ bond energies of products})$$

$$\Delta H_{rxn} = \left[1(159 \text{ kJ} \cdot \text{mol}^{-1})\right] + \left[\frac{1}{2}(498 \text{ kJ} \cdot \text{mol}^{-1})\right] - \left[2(190 \text{ kJ} \cdot \text{mol}^{-1})\right] = 28 \text{ kJ} \cdot \text{mol}^{-1}$$

The reaction is endothermic, so as temperature increases, the reaction will shift toward the products. The equilibrium constant, K, increases.

Acid-Base Chemistry

As discussed in Big Idea 3 (Chapter 3, "Chemical Reactions"), Brønsted-Lowry acids and bases are proton donors and acceptors, respectively. Acid-base dissociation reactions in water are equilibrium reactions.

Strong acids and bases have large equilibrium constants for dissociation in water. The ionization reactions of weak acids and bases have relatively small equilibrium constants.

The Autoionization of Water

Water is **amphoteric;** it can behave as either an acid or a base. Pure water undergoes **autoionization** according to the reaction illustrated below. *Note*: Both H_3O^+ and H^+ are found on the AP Chemistry curriculum. Be prepared to use both.

$$2\,H_2O(l) \rightleftharpoons H_3O^+(aq) + OH^-(aq) \quad \text{or} \quad H_2O(l) \rightleftharpoons H^+(aq) + OH^-(aq)$$

$$K_w = [H_3O^+][OH^-] = [H^+][OH^-] = 1.0 \times 10^{-14}$$

The equilibrium constant for this reaction, K_w, is 1.0×10^{-14} at 25 °C. This extremely small value means that neutral water is ionized only to a very small degree.

The hydronium and hydroxide ion concentrations for pure neutral water are equal.

$$[H_3O^+] = [OH^-]$$

The concentrations of hydronium and hydroxide ions at 25 °C are 1.0×10^{-7} M.

$$K_w = \left[H_3O^+\right]\left[OH^-\right] = \left[H_3O^+\right]^2 = 1.0 \times 10^{-14}$$

$$\sqrt{\left[H_3O^+\right]^2} = \sqrt{1.0 \times 10^{-14}}$$

$$\left[H_3O^+\right] = \left[OH^-\right] = 1.0 \times 10^{-7}\ M$$

PRACTICE:

Use the K_w values of water at various temperatures to determine whether the autoionization of water is endothermic or exothermic.

Temperature (°C)	K_w
25	1.0×10^{-14}
30	1.5×10^{-14}
50	5.5×10^{-14}

Because the equilibrium constant increases as temperature increases, addition of heat to the reaction causes the equilibrium to shift toward the products. The autoionization of water is endothermic.

The pH and pOH Scales

The **pH scale** is a commonly used measure of the acidity of a solution. The **pH** is defined as

$$pH = -\log[H^+]$$

The pH scale ranges from below 0 for strongly acidic solutions to over 14 for strongly basic solutions. At 25 °C, a solution with a pH that is less than 7 is acidic, and a solution with a pH that is greater than 7 is basic.

As discussed previously, for pure, neutral water at 25 °C,

$$[H_3O^+] = 1.0 \times 10^{-7}\ M$$

The pH of pure, neutral water at 25 °C is

$$pH = -\log(1.0 \times 10^{-7}) = 7.00$$

Because pH is based on a logarithm scale, a solution with a pH of 6 is ten times more acidic than pure water at room temperature, which has a pH of 7. A solution with a pH of 5 has 100 times the hydronium ion concentration of pure water, and a solution with a pH of 4 has 1000 times the hydronium ion concentration of pure water.

PRACTICE:

> What is the pH of a solution that has a hydronium ion concentration of 0.0200 M at 25 °C?

The pH of a solution is the negative logarithm of the hydronium ion concentration.

$$\text{pH} = -\log[H_3O^+] = -\log 0.0200 = 1.699$$

The **pOH** of a solution is defined as

$$\text{pOH} = -\log[OH^-]$$

Because pure water at room temperature has a hydroxide ion concentration of 1.0×10^{-7} M, the pOH of water at 25 °C is

$$\text{pOH} = -\log[1.0 \times 10^{-7}] = 7.00$$

Remember that for water at 25 °C,

$$[H_3O^+][OH^-] = 1.0 \times 10^{-14}$$

Therefore,

$$\text{pH} + \text{pOH} = 14.00$$

PRACTICE:

> The pH of a solution is 3.20 at 25 °C. What is the hydroxide ion concentration at this temperature?

The pH is first converted to pOH.

$$\text{pOH} = 14.00 - 3.20 = 10.80$$

The pOH is then used to determine the [OH⁻].

$$10.80 = -\log[OH^-]$$

$$[OH^-] = 10^{-10.80} = 1.6 \times 10^{-11} \ M$$

Strong Acids and Bases: A Review

As discussed in Big Idea 3 (Chapter 3, "Chemical Reactions"), there are six strong acids that should be memorized: HCl, HBr, HI, $HClO_4$, H_2SO_4, and HNO_3. These acids have very large equilibrium constants for the dissociation of a proton. **Dissociation** means that the proton is released completely from the acid to form a charged species (hydronium) in aqueous solution. The pH of any solution of a strong acid is calculated by using the concentration of the acid as the concentration of hydronium. Hydronium should be viewed as a strong acid.

For a sample of nitric acid in water, for instance,

$$[HNO_3] = [H_3O^+]$$

PRACTICE:

What is the pH of a 0.00010 M aqueous solution of HBr at 25 °C? (Notice that you should be able to do this without a calculator.)

Hydrobromic acid is one of the strong acids. It has a very large equilibrium constant for dissociation, so it essentially dissociates completely in aqueous solution.

$$HBr(aq) + H_2O(l) \rightarrow Br^-(aq) + H_3O^+(aq)$$

The concentration of H_3O^+ after the dissociation occurs is approximately equal to the initial concentration of HBr, 1.0×10^{-4} M.

$$pH = -\log(1.0 \times 10^{-4}) = 4.00$$

The strong bases that should be memorized are the hydroxides of the alkali metals: LiOH, NaOH, KOH, RbOH, and CsOH. These species have very large equilibrium constants for their dissociation reactions. In this case, **dissociation** refers to the release of the hydroxide ion from the metal cation in solution. The pOH of any strongly basic solution is calculated using the hydroxide ion concentration. In addition to the group IA hydroxides, hydroxides of the alkaline earth metals, $Sr(OH)_2$ and $Ba(OH)_2$, are considered to be strong.

PRACTICE:

What is the pH of a 1.00×10^{-4} M aqueous solution of $Ba(OH)_2$ at 25 °C?

At low concentrations, $Ba(OH)_2$, a strong base, dissociates completely into Ba^{2+} and OH^-.

$$Ba(OH)_2(aq) \rightarrow Ba^{2+}(aq) + 2\,OH^-(aq)$$

It is apparent from the reaction stoichiometry that 2 hydroxide ions are released for every $Ba(OH)_2$ molecule dissolved, so the concentration of OH^- is 2.0×10^{-4} M.

The pOH can be determined from the OH^- concentration.

$$pOH = -\log(2.0 \times 10^{-4}) = 3.70$$

$$pOH + pH = 14.00$$
$$pH = 14.00 - pOH$$
$$pH = 14.00 - 3.70 = 10.30$$

Weak Acids and K_a

Weak acids are acids that do not dissociate completely in aqueous solution. Acetic acid is an organic acid that is frequently used as an example. Vinegar is usually a solution of about 5% acetic acid in water.

A Weak Acid and Its Conjugate Base

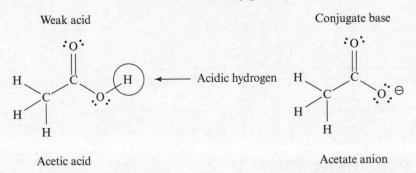

Weak acid

Acidic hydrogen

Conjugate base

Acetic acid

Acetate anion

Although acetic acid dissolves very well in water, it only dissociates to a small extent. The equilibrium constant for the dissociation of a weak acid such as acetic acid is known as the **acid dissociation constant, K_a**. The reaction of the weak acid, HA, with water to form the conjugate base, A^-, and hydronium is illustrated by the equation below. Recall that pure liquids (H_2O in this case) are excluded from the equilibrium expression.

$$HA(aq) + H_2O(l) \rightleftharpoons H_3O^+(aq) + A^-(aq)$$

$$K_a = \frac{[H_3O^+][A^-]}{[HA]}$$

Remember that although hydronium, H_3O^+, is primarily used in this review, it is also acceptable in AP Chemistry to write H^+ in the equation for the dissociation of an acid.

$$HA(aq) \rightleftharpoons H^+(aq) + A^-(aq)$$

$$K_a = \frac{[H^+][A^-]}{[HA]}$$

The K_a for acetic acid is 1.8×10^{-5}, which is quite small. This means that of the acetic acid dissolved in water, only a very small fraction of the molecules are dissociated into ions.

It is often useful to calculate percent ionization and pH for solutions of weak acids given the initial concentration of acid. The **percent ionization** is the percentage of a species in solution that is dissociated.

For example, suppose a question asks for the percent ionization of a 0.100 M solution of acetic acid, CH_3CO_2H, in addition to the pH of the solution. The first step is to write the equation for the dissociation of acetic acid in water.

$$CH_3CO_2H(aq) + H_2O(l) \rightleftharpoons H_3O^+(aq) + CH_3CO_2^-(aq)$$

The next step is to set up a R.I.C.E. table to determine the equilibrium concentrations of the species in solution.

Reaction	CH_3CO_2H	H_3O^+	$CH_3CO_2^-$
Initial Concentrations (M)	0.100	0	0
Change	$-x$	$+x$	$+x$
Equilibrium Concentrations (M)	$0.100 - x$	x	x

The equilibrium constant, 1.8×10^{-5}, is equal to the mass action expression for the dissociation of acetic acid.

$$K_a = \frac{[H_3O^+][CH_3CO_2^-]}{[CH_3CO_2H]}$$

$$1.8 \times 10^{-5} = \frac{x^2}{0.100 - x}$$

In order to solve the expression for x, the quadratic formula is necessary. It is highly unlikely that an AP Chemistry–level exam question will require this kind of solution. Instead, consider the magnitude of the equilibrium constant. An equilibrium constant of 1.8×10^{-5} indicates that very little of the acid is dissociated. So little is dissociated, in fact, that x may be neglected in the denominator since subtraction of x from 0.100 does not significantly change the value of the denominator. Students are expected to be able to provide this justification for simplifying the calculation.

$$1.8 \times 10^{-5} = \frac{x^2}{0.100 - \cancel{x}}$$

$$(1.8 \times 10^{-5})(0.100) = x^2$$

$$\sqrt{(1.8 \times 10^{-5})(0.100)} = \sqrt{x^2}$$

$$x = 1.3 \times 10^{-3} \ M = [H_3O^+] = [CH_3CO_2^-]$$

The pH of the solution is determined using the H_3O^+ concentration. Even though only two significant figures can be reported for the concentration of H_3O^+, the entire calculator result for x is used to calculate the pH. Note that different significant digits rules apply for pH values. The number of significant figures that are valid for the concentration (1.3×10^{-3}) are equal to the number of digits to the right of the decimal that are significant for the pH. Since there are two significant figures in the concentration, 1.3×10^{-7}, the reported pH value will have two digits after the decimal.

$$pH = -\log[H_3O^+] = -\log(1.34164 \times 10^{-3}) = 2.87$$

The percent ionization is the percentage of ionized acetate ion in the total acetic acid/acetate concentration. Again, the unrounded value of the concentration should be used.

$$\% \text{ ionization} = \frac{[CH_3CO_2^-]}{[CH_3CO_2^-] + [CH_3CO_2H]} \times 100\% = \frac{1.3 \times 10^{-3} \ \cancel{M}}{0.100 \ \cancel{M}} \times 100\% = 1.3\% \text{ ionized}$$

PRACTICE:

A sample of 0.0100 M hypochlorous acid, HClO, is 0.17 % ionized at 25 °C. What is the acid dissociation constant for HClO?

The dissociation of HClO is shown by the following equation.

$$HClO(aq) + H_2O(l) \rightleftharpoons ClO^-(aq) + H_3O^+(aq)$$

The concentration of ClO^- is 0.17% of the initial concentration of HClO. This is equal to the hydronium ion concentration.

$$[ClO^-] = (0.0017)(0.0100 \ M) = 1.7 \times 10^{-5} \ M = [H_3O^+]$$

The HClO concentration at equilibrium is the initial concentration minus the portion that ionized.

$$[HClO] = 0.0100 \ M - 1.7 \times 10^{-5} \ M \approx 0.0100 \ M$$

$$K_a = \frac{[H_3O^+][ClO^-]}{[HClO]} = \frac{(1.7 \times 10^{-5})^2}{0.0100} = 2.9 \times 10^{-8}$$

Weak Bases and K_b

Weak bases are those that only weakly ionize in aqueous solution. They ionize according to the reaction illustrated by the equation shown.

$$B(aq) + H_2O(l) \rightleftharpoons BH^+(aq) + OH^-(aq)$$

The equilibrium constant for base dissociation according to this equation is known as K_b.

$$K_b = \frac{[BH^+][OH^-]}{[B]}$$

Weak bases include **amines,** compounds that contain a nitrogen atom bound to carbon or hydrogen. Ammonia, for instance, is a weak base. It is the simplest amine. Other examples of weakly basic amines include methylamine, $(CH_3)NH_2$, and pyridine, C_5H_5N.

Weak Bases

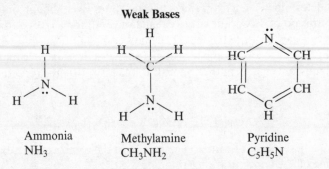

| Ammonia | Methylamine | Pyridine |
| NH_3 | CH_3NH_2 | C_5H_5N |

The pH and percent ionization of a weak base solution are determined in a manner similar to those of a weak acid solution.

PRACTICE:

The K_b of aniline, $C_6H_5NH_2$, is 3.8×10^{-10}. What is the pH of a 0.150 M solution of aniline?

Aniline is a weak base. The dissociation reaction for aniline in aqueous solution is represented by:

$$C_6H_5NH_2(aq) + H_2O(l) \rightleftharpoons C_6H_5NH_3^+(aq) + OH^-(aq)$$

The mass action expression for the K_b is

$$K_b = \frac{[C_6H_5NH_3^+][OH^-]}{[C_6H_5NH_2]}$$

A R.I.C.E. table is used to determine the concentrations.

Reaction	$C_6H_5NH_2$	$C_6H_5NH_3^+$	OH^-
Initial Concentrations (M)	0.150	0	0
Change	$-x$	$+x$	$+x$
Equilibrium Concentrations (M)	$0.150 - x$	x	x

Substitution of the equilibrium concentrations into the expression for K_b and the assumption that x is much smaller than the initial concentration of aniline allow for the calculation of the hydroxide ion concentration.

$$3.8 \times 10^{-10} = \frac{x^2}{0.150 - \cancel{x}}$$

$$x = \sqrt{(3.8 \times 10^{-10})(0.150)} = 7.55 \times 10^{-6} \ M = [OH^-]$$

$$pOH = -\log 7.55 \times 10^{-6} = 5.12$$

$$pH = 14.00 - 5.12 = 8.88$$

pK_a and pK_b

A convenient expression for the acidity or basicity of a substance is given by its **pK_a** or its **pK_b**.

$$pK_a = -\log K_a$$

$$pK_b = -\log K_b$$

The higher the K_a, the lower the pK_a, and the stronger the acid.

The higher the K_b, the lower the pK_b, and the stronger the base.

PRACTICE:

Based on the provided data, is benzoic acid or formic acid a stronger acid? Determine the K_a of each acid.

Acid	pK_a at 25 °C
Benzoic acid	4.20
Formic acid	3.75

The lower pK_a of formic acid indicates that it is a stronger acid. The K_a of formic acid is

$$K_a = 10^{-pK_a} = 10^{-3.75} = 1.8 \times 10^{-4}$$

The K_a of benzoic acid is

$$K_a = 10^{-pK_a} = 10^{-4.20} = 6.3 \times 10^{-5}$$

The larger K_a and lower pK_a of formic acid confirms that it ionizes to a greater extent (and produces more hydronium) than benzoic acid.

Finally, it is important to recognize and remember the relationship between K_a and K_b for a conjugate acid-base pair at a given temperature.

$$K_w = K_a \cdot K_b$$

Since $K_w = 10^{-14}$ at 25 °C, the sum of the pK_a and the pK_b for a conjugate acid-base pair is 14.00 at 25 °C.

$$pK_w = pK_a + pK_b = 14.00$$

PRACTICE:

> The K_a of hydrofluoric acid, HF, is 7.2×10^{-4} at 25 °C. What is the pK_b of the fluoride ion?

The K_b for F⁻, the conjugate base of HF, is determined using the K_a and K_w at 25 °C.

$$K_b = \frac{K_w}{K_a} = \frac{1.00 \times 10^{-14}}{7.2 \times 10^{-4}} = 1.4 \times 10^{-11}$$

$$pK_b = -\log K_b = -\log 1.4 \times 10^{-11} = 10.86$$

Acidic and Basic Salts

Many salts, when added to neutral water, have no effect on the pH of the water. If sodium chloride is added to a sample of pure water at 25 °C, the pH of the water does not change. When a sample of sodium acetate is added to pure water, however, the pH increases. If ammonium chloride is added to water, the pH decreases. Sodium acetate, therefore, is referred to as a basic salt and ammonium chloride is an acidic salt.

A salt that is composed of the cation of a strong base and the anion of a strong acid is a *neutral salt* **and, therefore,** has no effect on the pH of the solution. Sodium chloride, for example, is composed of sodium cations and chloride anions. A sodium ion is the cation of a strong base, NaOH, and a chloride anion is the anion of a strong acid, HCl. When added to pure water, sodium chloride does not cause a change in the pH. For this reason, sodium chloride is referred to as a **neutral salt.** Other examples of neutral salts include KNO_3, LiBr, and $BaCl_2$.

A salt that is composed of the cation of a strong base and the anion of a weak acid, such as sodium acetate, $NaCH_3CO_2$**, is a** *basic salt.* Sodium acetate dissociates completely in water, and the acetate anions that are released increase the pH of an aqueous solution by extracting protons from the water molecules. This results in an increase in the hydroxide ion concentration.

$$CH_3CO_2^-(aq) + H_2O(l) \rightleftharpoons CH_3CO_2H(aq) + OH^-(aq)$$

Other examples of basic salts include KCN, LiF, and Cs_2CO_3.

A salt that is composed of the cation of a weak base and the anion of a strong acid, such as ammonium chloride, NH_4Cl**, is an** *acidic salt.* Ammonium chloride is soluble in water, and it dissociates completely. The ammonium ion releases a proton into the solution and decreases the pH.

$$NH_4^+(aq) + H_2O(l) \rightleftharpoons NH_3(aq) + H_3O^+(aq)$$

PRACTICE:

> Predict whether solutions of the following salts will be acidic, basic, or neutral when added to pure water. Support your predictions with balanced equations for hydrolysis to produce the ions that contribute to an acidic or basic pH.
>
> **(a)** $LiNO_2$
>
> **(b)** NH_4Br
>
> **(c)** $NaClO_4$

(a) Li^+ is the cation of a strong base. NO_2^- is the conjugate base of a weak acid. $LiNO_2$ is a basic salt.

$$NO_2^-(aq) + H_2O(l) \rightleftharpoons HNO_2(aq) + OH^-(aq)$$

(b) NH_4^+ is the conjugate acid of a weak base. Br^- is the anion of a strong acid. NH_4Br is an acidic salt.

$$NH_4^+(aq) + H_2O(l) \rightleftharpoons NH_3(aq) + H_3O^+(aq)$$

(c) Na^+ is the cation of a strong base. ClO_4^- is the anion of a strong acid. $NaClO_4$ is a neutral salt.

PRACTICE:

The K_b for ammonia is 1.8×10^{-5}. Find the pH of a 0.0500 M solution of ammonium chloride.

The dissociation reaction for ammonium is

$$NH_4^+(aq) + H_2O(l) \rightleftharpoons NH_3(aq) + H_3O^+(aq)$$

The ammonium ion is the conjugate acid of ammonia, so it is necessary to work with the K_a.

$$K_a = \frac{K_w}{K_b} = \frac{1.0 \times 10^{-14}}{1.8 \times 10^{-5}} = 5.6 \times 10^{-10}$$

A R.I.C.E. table can be used to find the concentration of H_3O^+.

Reaction	NH_4^+	NH_3	H_3O^+
Initial Concentrations (M)	0.0500	0	0
Change	$-x$	$+x$	$+x$
Equilibrium Concentrations (M)	$0.0500 - x$	x	x

Because the acid dissociation constant is small, the K_a expression can be simplified and x can be neglected from the $(0.0500 - x)$ term.

$$5.6 \times 10^{-10} = \frac{x^2}{0.0500 - \cancel{x}}$$

$$\sqrt{(5.6 \times 10^{-10})(0.0500)} = \sqrt{x^2}$$

$$x = 5.3 \times 10^{-6}\ M = [H_3O^+]$$

$$pH = -\log[H_3O^+] = -\log 5.3 \times 10^{-6} = 5.28$$

PRACTICE:

The K_a for formic acid, H_2CO_2, is 1.77×10^{-4}. What concentration of sodium formate, $NaHCO_2$, would have a pH of 8.00 at 25 °C?

The species of interest is the formate ion, the conjugate base of formic acid. Therefore, K_a must be converted to K_b.

$$K_b = \frac{K_w}{K_a} = \frac{1.00 \times 10^{-14}}{1.77 \times 10^{-4}} = 5.65 \times 10^{-11}$$

The hydrolysis reaction of the formate ion is

$$HCO_2^-(aq) + H_2O(l) \rightleftharpoons H_2CO_2(aq) + OH^-(aq)$$

This time the pH is given, so the final concentration of the hydroxide ion can be calculated.

$$pOH = 14.00 - 8.00 = 6.00$$

$$[OH^-] = 10^{-6.00} = 1.0 \times 10^{-6} \, M$$

Let the initial concentration of the formate ion be x.

Reaction	HCO_2^-	H_2CO_2	OH^-
Initial Concentrations (M)	x	0	0
Change	-1.0×10^{-6}	$+1.0 \times 10^{-6}$	$+1.0 \times 10^{-6}$
Equilibrium Concentrations (M)	$x - 1.0 \times 10^{-6}$	1.0×10^{-6}	1.0×10^{-6}

$$K_b = 5.65 \times 10^{-11} = \frac{[OH^-][H_2CO_2]}{[HCO_2^-]} = \frac{(1.0 \times 10^{-6})^2}{x - 1.0 \times 10^{-6}}$$

$$x = 1.8 \times 10^{-2} \, M$$

The initial concentration of $NaHCO_2$ is $1.8 \times 10^{-2} \, M$.

Sometimes a salt is composed of the conjugate base of a weak acid and the conjugate acid of a weak base. An example of this kind of salt is ammonium acetate, $NH_4CH_3CO_2$. The pH of a solution of this type of salt is determined by the ionization constants of the parent acid and base.

The parent base for ammonium, NH_4^+, is ammonia, NH_3. The acid dissociation constant for the hydrolysis of ammonium ion is determined from the K_b for ammonia.

$$NH_4^+(aq) + H_2O(l) \rightleftharpoons NH_3(aq) + H_3O^+(aq) \qquad K_b \text{ (ammonia)} = 1.8 \times 10^{-5}$$

$$K_a = \frac{K_w}{K_b} = \frac{1.0 \times 10^{-14}}{1.8 \times 10^{-5}} = 5.6 \times 10^{-10}$$

The parent acid for the acetate ion is acetic acid. The base dissociation constant for the hydrolysis of acetate ion is the reciprocal of the K_a for acetic acid.

$$CH_3CO_2^-(aq) + H_2O(l) \rightleftharpoons CH_3CO_2H(aq) + OH(aq) \qquad K_a \text{ (acetic acid)} = 1.8 \times 10^{-5}$$

$$K_b = \frac{K_w}{K_a} = \frac{1.0 \times 10^{-14}}{1.8 \times 10^{-5}} = 5.6 \times 10^{-10}$$

Because the hydrolysis of ammonium produces the same concentration of hydronium as the concentration of hydroxide produced by the hydrolysis of acetate, as shown by the fact that the dissociation constants are equal, an ammonium acetate salt solution is neutral.

If, however, the K_a for the conjugate acid of the weak base is greater than the K_b for the conjugate base of the weak acid, H_3O^+ will be produced to a greater extent than OH^-, and the solution will be acidic. To see why this is the case, consider pyridinium formate, $C_5H_5NHCHO_2$. Pyridinium formate, is composed of a pyridinium cation, $C_5H_5NH^+$, and a formate anion, CHO_2^-. The weak base and weak acid are C_5H_5N ($K_b = 1.8 \times 10^{-9}$) and CHO_2H ($K_a = 1.8 \times 10^{-4}$), respectively. The hydrolysis reactions for the two ions are shown below.

$$C_5H_5NH^+(aq) + H_2O(l) \rightleftharpoons C_5H_5N(aq) + H_3O^+(aq) \quad K_b \text{ (pyridine)} = 1.8 \times 10^{-9}$$

$$K_a = \frac{K_w}{K_b} = \frac{1.0 \times 10^{-14}}{1.8 \times 10^{-9}} = 5.6 \times 10^{-6}$$

$$CHO_2^-(aq) + H_2O(l) \rightleftharpoons CHO_2H(aq) + OH^-(aq) \quad K_a \text{ (formic acid)} = 1.8 \times 10^{-4}$$

$$K_b = \frac{K_w}{K_a} = \frac{1.0 \times 10^{-14}}{1.8 \times 10^{-4}} = 5.6 \times 10^{-11}$$

Because the hydrolysis of pyridinium to form hydronium occurs to a much greater extent (10^{-6} is much greater than 10^{-11}), a solution of the pyridinium formate is acidic.

PRACTICE:

The K_b for ammonia, NH_3, is 1.8×10^{-5}. Given the following acid dissociation constants, predict whether the following salts will form acidic or basic solutions when added to pure water.

(a) NH_4IO_3

(b) NH_4CN

Acid	K_a
HIO_3	1.6×10^{-1}
HCN	6.2×10^{-10}

Since the conjugate acid of ammonia is the cation for each of these species, the K_a for ammonium is needed for comparison.

$$NH_4^+(aq) + H_2O(l) \rightleftharpoons NH_3(aq) + H_3O^+(aq)$$

$$K_a = \frac{K_w}{K_b} = \frac{1.0 \times 10^{-14}}{1.8 \times 10^{-5}} = 5.6 \times 10^{-10}$$

(a) The K_b for IO_3^- is needed.

$$IO_3^-(aq) + H_2O(l) \rightleftharpoons HIO_3(aq) + OH^-(aq)$$

$$K_b = \frac{K_w}{K_a} = \frac{1.0 \times 10^{-14}}{1.6 \times 10^{-1}} = 6.25 \times 10^{-14}$$

Because the base dissociation constant for IO_3^- is less than the acid dissociation constant for NH_4^+, in an NH_4IO_3 solution, the amount of hydronium produced by the hydrolysis of ammonium is greater than the amount of hydroxide produced by the hydrolysis of iodate. Therefore, ammonium iodate is an acidic salt.

(b) The K_b for CN^- is needed.

$$CN^-(aq) + H_2O(l) \rightleftharpoons HCN(aq) + OH^-(aq)$$

$$K_b = \frac{K_w}{K_a} = \frac{1.0 \times 10^{-14}}{6.2 \times 10^{-10}} = 1.6 \times 10^{-5}$$

The K_b for CN^- is greater than the K_a for NH_4^+, so NH_4CN is a basic salt.

Buffer Solutions

A **buffer** is an aqueous solution that resists a change in pH upon addition of small quantities of acids or bases. A buffer is either composed of a **weak acid and its conjugate base** in similar concentrations or a **weak base and its conjugate acid** in similar concentrations.

Consider the buffer solution composed of formic acid, H_2CO_2, and sodium formate, $NaHCO_2$. Formic acid is a weak acid with a K_a of 1.77×10^{-4}. Sodium formate dissociates completely in aqueous solution. The illustration below represents an equimolar mixture of formic acid and formate ion. *Sodium ions and water molecules are omitted from the diagrams for clarity.*

In the first situation, acid is added to the solution in the form of H^+ ions (two H^+ ions are added in this representation). Instead of lowering the pH by increasing the hydronium concentration, the protons react with free formate ions to produce formic acid molecules. This results in a very small pH change.

In the second situation, base is added to the solution in the form of OH^- ions (two in this representation). Protons are removed from two of the formic acid molecules to form water, and again, the pH changes very little.

Resistance of a Buffer to a Change in pH

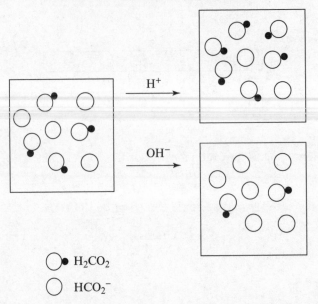

$\bigcirc\!\bullet$ H_2CO_2

$\bigcirc$ HCO_2^-

PRACTICE:

Which of the following pairs of reagents could produce a buffer? Explain your reasoning.

(a) $NaNO_3$ and HNO_3

(b) $NaNO_2$ and HNO_3

(c) $NaNO_2$ and HNO_2

(d) $NaNO_3$ and HNO_2

(a) $NaNO_3$ is the salt of a strong acid and a strong base. HNO_3 is a strong acid. These reagents could not be combined to produce a buffer.

(b) $NaNO_2$ is the salt of a weak acid and HNO_3 is a strong acid. If HNO_3 is added to the NO_2^- from the salt, some HNO_2 will be formed. The amount of HNO_3 added could be adjusted so that a 1:1 molar ratio of $[HNO_2]:[NO_2^-]$ would result. This resulting weak acid/conjugate base pair is a buffer.

(c) $NaNO_2$ is the salt of a weak acid, and HNO_2 is its conjugate acid. This pair forms a buffer when combined in approximately equimolar quantities.

(d) $NaNO_3$ is a neutral salt. It will have no effect on a solution of HNO_2, which is a weak acid. No buffer formation is possible.

The Henderson-Hasselbalch Equation

The Henderson-Hasselbalch equation is a derivation of the acid dissociation equilibrium expression. It relates the pH of a buffer solution composed of a weak acid, HA, and the anion of the weak acid, A^-, to the pK_a of the weak acid. This equation is included on the *AP Chemistry Equations and Constants* sheet (pages 365–366). Students will not be asked to derive the Henderson-Hasselbalch equation, but they are expected to know how to use it.

$$pH = pK_a + \log \frac{[A^-]}{[HA]}$$

A weak acid/conjugate base system produces the most effective buffer when $[HA] = [A^-]$. Under these conditions, the pH of the solution is equal to the pK_a of the weak acid.

When the pH of the buffer solution is less than the pK_a of the weak acid form of the buffer, the concentration of protonated weak acid is greater than the concentration of the anion. When the pH of the buffer solution is greater than the pK_a, the concentration of the anion is greater than the concentration of the weak acid.

$$pH = pK_a: \quad [HA] = [A^-]$$

$$pH < pK_a: \quad [HA] > [A^-]$$

$$pH > pK_a: \quad [HA] < [A^-]$$

The Henderson-Hasselbalch equation can also be modified to describe a buffer composed of a weak base, B, and its conjugate acid, BH^+. Notice the similarities and differences between the acid and base forms of the equation. Because the pOH version of the Henderson-Hasselbalch equation is *not* included on the *AP Chemistry Equations and Constants* sheet, this convenient equation must be memorized in order to be used.

$$pOH = pK_b + \log \frac{[BH^+]}{[B]}$$

A weak base/conjugate acid system produces the most effective buffer when $[B] = [BH^+]$. At this point the pOH of the solution is equal to the pK_b of the weak base. Again, the pOH is dependent on the relative concentrations of base and conjugate acid.

$$pOH = pK_b: \quad [B] = [BH^+]$$

$$pOH < pK_b: \quad [B] > [BH^+]$$

$$pOH > pK_b: \quad [B] < [BH^+]$$

PRACTICE:

> Use the K_a values of the following substances to determine which can be added to one-half of an equivalent of strong base to produce a buffer with a pH of 7.
>
> | Acid | K_a at 25 °C |
> |------|----------------|
> | HF | 7.2×10^{-4} |
> | HN_3 | 1.9×10^{-5} |
> | H_2S | 1.0×10^{-7} |

These acids can be partially reacted with a strong base such as NaOH to produce buffers with pH ranges near the pK_a values of the acids. The pK_a values of HF, HN_3, and H_2S are 3.14, 4.72, and 7.00, respectively. The pK_a of H_2S is equal to the pH that is needed, so H_2S is the correct choice.

By adding one-half of an equivalent of a strong base to H_2S such that $[H_2S] = [HS^-]$, the pH of the solution will be equal to the pK_a.

$$H_2S(aq) + OH^-(aq) \rightarrow HS^-(aq) + H_2O(l)$$

$$pH = 7.00 + \log \frac{[HS^-]}{[H_2S]} = 7.00 + \log 1 = 7.00$$

PRACTICE:

> The pK_a of benzoic acid, $C_6H_5CO_2H$, is 4.19 at 25 °C. When 0.030 mole of NaOH is added to 100.0 mL of a 0.500 M solution of benzoic acid, what is the pH before and after the addition of NaOH? Assume the volume of the solution does not change when the NaOH is added.

Before the addition of the NaOH, the pH is determined by the weakly-dissociating $C_6H_5CO_2H$.

$$C_6H_5CO_2H(aq) + H_2O(l) \rightleftharpoons C_6H_5CO_2^-(aq) + H_3O^+(aq)$$

The K_a of benzoic acid can be calculated.

$$K_a = 10^{-pKa} = 10^{-4.19} = 6.5 \times 10^{-5}$$

Reaction	$C_6H_5CO_2H$	$C_6H_5CO_2^-$	H_3O^+
Initial Concentrations (M)	0.500	0	0
Change	$-x$	$+x$	$+x$
Equilibrium Concentrations (M)	$0.500 - x$	x	x

Because K_a is small, x can be neglected in the denominator.

$$6.5 \times 10^{-5} = \frac{x^2}{0.500 - \cancel{x}}$$

$$\sqrt{(6.5 \times 10^{-5})(0.500)} = \sqrt{x^2}$$

$$x = 5.7 \times 10^{-3} \ M = [H_3O^+]$$

$$pH = -\log [H_3O^+] = -\log 5.7 \times 10^{-3} = 2.24$$

When NaOH is added, some of the benzoic acid is converted to benzoate ion.

$$C_6H_5CO_2H(aq) + OH^-(aq) \rightarrow C_6H_5CO_2^-(aq) + H_2O(l)$$

The initial number of moles of benzoic acid is

$$0.1000 \ \cancel{L} \times \frac{0.500 \ \text{mol} \ C_6H_5CO_2H}{1 \ \cancel{L}} = 0.0500 \ \text{mol} \ C_6H_5CO_2H$$

After the reaction, 0.030 mole of benzoic acid has been converted to benzoate. The number of moles of benzoic acid remaining is

$$0.0500 \ \text{mol} - 0.030 \ \text{mol} = 0.020 \ \text{mol} \ C_6H_5CO_2H$$

The pH can be determined using the Henderson-Hasselbalch equation.

$$pH = pK_a + \log \frac{[C_6H_5CO_2^-]}{[C_6H_5CO_2H]} = 4.19 + \log \frac{\left(\dfrac{0.030 \ \text{mol}}{0.100 \ \text{L}} \right)}{\left(\dfrac{0.020 \ \text{mol}}{0.100 \ \text{L}} \right)} = 4.37$$

The pH of the solution after 0.030 mole of NaOH has been added is 4.37.

Buffer Capacity

Buffer capacity refers to the amount of strong acid or strong base that can be added to a buffer system before the pH of the buffer system begins to change dramatically. The absolute concentrations of acid and conjugate base or base and conjugate acid determine the buffer capacity of the solution. The higher the absolute concentration of the buffer, the more acid or base can be added before the pH begins to change.

Dilution of a buffer system *does not affect the pH of the solution*. To see why this is the case, let's look at the pH values of two buffer systems. Buffer A contains 0.40 mole of HA and 0.60 mole of A⁻ in 1.00 L of solution, and buffer B contains 0.40 mole of HA and 0.60 mole of A⁻ in 0.100 L of solution. The pH values of the two solutions are calculated as follows:

Buffer A:

$$pH = pK_a + \log \frac{[A^-]}{[HA]} = pK_a + \log \frac{\left(\dfrac{0.60 \ \text{mol}}{\cancel{1.00 \ L}} \right)}{\left(\dfrac{0.40 \ \text{mol}}{\cancel{1.00 \ L}} \right)} = pK_a + \log \frac{0.60}{0.40}$$

Buffer B:

$$pH = pK_a + \log \frac{[A^-]}{[HA]} = pK_a + \log \left(\frac{\frac{0.60 \text{ mol}}{0.100 \text{ L}}}{\frac{0.40 \text{ mol}}{0.100 \text{ L}}} \right) = pK_a + \log \frac{0.60}{0.40}$$

Despite the fact that the pH values of the two buffers are identical, buffer B is ten times as concentrated as buffer A, so it has a much larger buffer capacity. It is capable of reacting with a larger quantity of added acid or base before the pH begins to change appreciably.

PRACTICE:

Which of the following weak acid/conjugate base (HA/A$^-$) representations has the highest buffer capacity for addition of strong acids or strong bases?

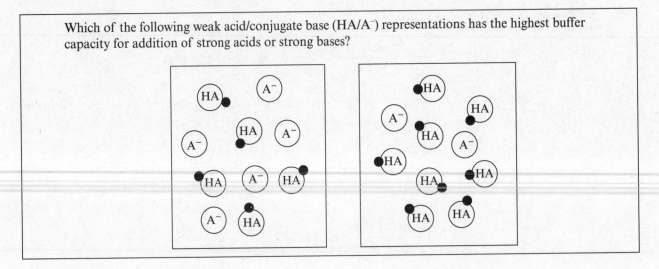

Both diagrams show ten particles. The diagram on the left has an equal ratio of HA and A$^-$, so it has a greater ability to neutralize both H$_3$O$^+$ and OH$^-$. The diagram on the right has a smaller capability to neutralize added H$_3$O$^+$ since it has a larger number of HA molecules and relatively few A$^-$.

Acid-Base Titration Curves

Titration, an analytical technique by which a solution with a known concentration is used to determine the concentration of an unknown, was introduced in Big Idea 2 (Chapter 2, "Bonding and Intermolecular Forces"). Here, **titration curves,** which are plots of pH versus the amount of titrant added to an acid or base solution, will be examined in more detail.

Strong Acid/Strong Base

When a strong base is added to a strong acid, the resulting products are water and a neutral salt. If a strong acid solution of unknown concentration is titrated with a known concentration of a strong base, the volume of base required to reach the equivalence point of the titration is easily determined by the volume of base required to raise the pH of the solution to 7. The net ionic equation for the reaction is

$$H_3O^+(aq) + OH^-(aq) \rightarrow 2 H_2O(l)$$

The equilibrium constant for this process is very large, $K_{eq} \approx 1 \times 10^3$, so the equilibrium greatly favors the products.

Consider the titration curve below, in which 50.0 mL of an unknown concentration of HCl is titrated with a 0.100 M solution of NaOH. When 20.0 mL of the NaOH have been added, the pH rises sharply and passes through an inflection point at a pH of 7. At this point, the number of moles of OH⁻ added are equal to the number of moles of H_3O^+ present initially. This is the **equivalence point** for the titration. The amount of OH⁻ added to reach the equivalence point is sometimes referred to as an **equivalent.**

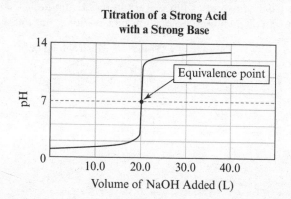

Notice that as base is added, the pH gradually increases until just before the equivalence point. Within 10% of the volume of base required to reach the equivalence point, the pH begins its sharp rise before leveling off when the hydroxide concentration becomes larger than the hydronium concentration.

PRACTICE:

A student titrates a 25.0-mL aqueous sample of HNO_3 with 0.200 M standardized KOH. The titration requires 30.1 mL of base to reach the equivalence point.

(a) What is the initial concentration of HNO_3?

(b) What is the pH of the solution after 15.0 mL of KOH have been added?

(a) The number of moles of base added at the equivalence point is equal to the number of moles of HNO_3 that was initially present. The initial $[HNO_3]$ can be calculated.

$$HNO_3(aq) + KOH(aq) \rightarrow KNO_3(aq) + H_2O(l)$$

$$0.0301 \ \cancel{L \ KOH} \times \frac{0.200 \ \cancel{mol \ KOH}}{1 \ \cancel{L \ KOH}} \times \frac{1 \ mol \ HNO_3}{1 \ \cancel{mol \ KOH}} = 0.00602 \ mol \ HNO_3$$

$$[HNO_3]_{initial} = \frac{0.00602 \ mol \ HNO_3}{0.0250 \ L} = 0.241 \ M$$

(b) The number of moles of HNO_3 remaining after the addition of the base determines the pH. The number of moles of base added is calculated next.

$$0.0150 \ \cancel{L \ KOH} \times \frac{0.200 \ mol \ KOH}{1 \ \cancel{L \ KOH}} = 0.00300 \ mol \ KOH$$

The number of moles of KOH added is equal to the number of moles of HNO_3 that have reacted. Since 0.00602 mole of HNO_3 was initially present, the number of moles that remain can be calculated. The concentration of hydronium is equal to the concentration of HNO_3 remaining since HNO_3 is a strong base and dissociates completely in water.

$$0.00602 \ mol - 0.00300 \ mol = 0.00302 \ mol \ H_3O^+$$

$$[H_3O^+] = \frac{0.00302 \ mol}{0.0250 \ L + 0.0150 \ L} = 0.0755 \ M$$

$$pH = -\log[H_3O^+] = -\log 0.755 = 1.122$$

Weak Acid/Strong Base

The titration of a weak acid with a strong base is more complex than the strong acid/strong base titration since there is a large **buffering region** in which both the weak acid and the anion of the weak acid are present.

The titration curve for the titration of a weak acid, HA, with a strong base, MOH, looks like the one shown below. Several key facts can be gleaned from this plot without any calculations, so it is important to be able to recognize this type of curve and predict which species dominate at each point along the titration curve.

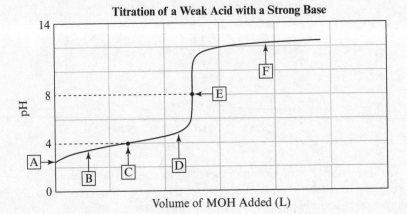

- At point **A**, the pH depends only on the concentration of the weak acid and the acid dissociation constant, K_a.

$$HA + H_2O \rightleftharpoons A^- + H_3O^+$$

- Within regions **B** and **D**, the solution is buffered and the pH is calculated using the Henderson-Hasselbalch equation. The base that has been added has converted some of the HA to A^-.

$$OH^- + HA \rightarrow H_2O + A^-$$

The relative concentrations of HA and A^-, along with the pK_a, determine the pH of the solution.

$$pH = pK_a + \log \frac{[A^-]}{[HA]}$$

- At point **C**, the half-equivalence point, exactly enough base has been added to produce a buffer solution with 1:1 ratio of $[HA]:[A^-]$. At this point in the titration, the pH of the solution is equal to the pK_a of the acid.
- At point **E**, the equivalence point, the number of moles of OH^- that have been added is equal to the number of moles of HA that were initially present. The pH at the equivalence point is determined by the basic salt, A^-, which is the dominant species.

$$A^- + H_2O \rightleftharpoons HA + OH^-$$

- Within region **F**, the OH^- in excess of the HA initially present determines the pOH and thus the pH of the solution.

Titration Curve Region	Major Species in Solution	Minor Species in Solution
A	HA	H_3O^+, A^-
B	HA	A^-, M^+
C	HA, A^-, M^+ (equimolar concentrations)	
D	A^-, M^+	HA
E	A^-, M^+	OH^-, HA
F	OH^-, M^+	A^-

Consider, for example, 100.0 mL of a 0.250 M solution of nitrous acid, HNO_2, at 25 °C. Nitrous acid has a K_a of 4.0×10^{-4}. Before the titration begins, the dominant species in the solution is HNO_2. A very small proportion of the weak acid is dissociated, so the minor components of the system are H_3O^+ and NO_2^-. The H_3O^+ concentration determines the pH of the solution.

$$HNO_2(aq) + H_2O(l) \rightleftharpoons H_3O^+(aq) + NO_2^-(aq) \qquad K_a = 4.0 \times 10^{-4}$$

Reaction	HNO_2	H_3O^+	NO_2^-
Initial Concentrations (M)	0.250	0	0
Change	$-x$	$+x$	$+x$
Equilibrium Concentrations (M)	$0.250 - x$	x	x

$$K_a = \frac{[H_3O^+][NO_2^-]}{[HNO_2]}$$

$$4.0 \times 10^{-4} = \frac{x^2}{0.250 - x}$$

The amount of acid that dissociates is small compared to the initial amount, so x in the denominator may be neglected.

$$4.0 \times 10^{-4} = \frac{x^2}{0.250 - \cancel{x}}$$

$$\sqrt{(4.0 \times 10^{-4})(0.250)} = \sqrt{x^2}$$

$$x = 0.010 \ M$$

$$[H_3O^+] = 0.010 \ M$$

The pH of the solution at point **A** is

$$-\log(0.010) = 2.00$$

Now suppose the solution is titrated with 0.250 M NaOH. How can the pH be determined at the equivalence point? It is first necessary to know how much NaOH must be added. This can be determined stoichiometrically.

$$HNO_2(aq) + OH^-(aq) \rightarrow NO_2^-(aq) + H_2O(l)$$

$$\text{volume NaOH added} = 0.1000 \ \text{L} \ \cancel{HNO_2} \times \frac{0.250 \ \text{mol} \ \cancel{HNO_2}}{1 \ \text{L} \ \cancel{HNO_2}} \times \frac{1 \ \text{mol} \ \cancel{NaOH}}{1 \ \text{mol} \ \cancel{HNO_2}} \times \frac{1 \ \text{L NaOH}}{0.250 \ \cancel{\text{mol NaOH}}}$$

$$= 0.1000 \ \text{L NaOH}$$

Since all of the OH^- and HNO_2 have reacted at the equivalence point, the major species in the solution is NO_2^-. The number of moles of NO_2^- is equal to the number of moles of HNO_2 that were present initially.

$$\text{moles of } NO_2^- = 0.1000 \ \text{L} \ OH^- \times \frac{0.250 \ \text{mol} \ OH^-}{1 \ \text{L} \ OH^-} \times \frac{1 \ \text{mol} \ NO_2^-}{1 \ \text{mol} \ OH^-} = 0.0250 \ \text{mol} \ NO_2^-$$

$$[NO_2^-] = \frac{0.0250 \ \text{mol} \ NO_2^-}{0.1000 \ \text{L} + 0.1000 \ \text{L}} = 0.125 \ M \ NO_2^-$$

The next step in finding the pH is to evaluate NO_2^- as a basic species. The K_b for NO_2^- is K_w at 25 °C divided by the K_a of HNO_2.

$$NO_2^-(aq) + H_2O(l) \rightleftharpoons HNO_2(aq) + OH^-(aq)$$

$$K_w = K_a \cdot K_b = 1.0 \times 10^{-14}$$

$$K_b = \frac{1.0 \times 10^{-14}}{4.0 \times 10^{-4}} = 2.5 \times 10^{-11}$$

Reaction	NO_2^-	HNO_2	OH^-
Initial Concentrations (M)	0.125	0	0
Change	$-x$	$+x$	$+x$
Equilibrium Concentrations (M)	$0.125 - x$	x	x

$$K_b = \frac{[HNO_2][OH^-]}{[NO_2^-]}$$

$$2.5 \times 10^{-11} = \frac{x^2}{0.125 - \cancel{x}}$$

The amount of hydroxide is small compared to the amount of NO_2^-, so x in the denominator may be neglected.

$$\sqrt{(2.5 \times 10^{-11})(0.125)} = \sqrt{x^2}$$

$$x = 1.8 \times 10^{-6} \ M = [OH^-]$$

The pOH of the solution at the equivalence point is determined using the unrounded value.

$$pOH = -\log(1.76776695 \times 10^{-6}) = 5.75$$

$$14.00 = pH + pOH$$

$$pH = 14.00 - 5.75 = 8.25$$

It is very important to note that at the equivalence point of a titration of a weak acid with a strong base, the pH is not 7. The solution has a pH higher than 7 because a basic salt is the major species in solution.

To determine the pH at any point within the buffering region (any point in region **B** or **D** of the titration curve), the Henderson-Hasselbalch equation may be used. The concentrations of HNO_2 and NO_2 are determined stoichiometrically.

$$HNO_2(aq) + OH^-(aq) \rightarrow NO_2^-(aq) + H_2O(l)$$

A buffer is formed after 40.00 mL of the 0.250 M OH^- solution have been added to 100.0 mL of 0.250 M HNO_2 solution. Suppose the pH of this buffer is needed. Because the equivalence point has not yet been reached, OH^- is the limiting reagent. The *numbers of moles* of reactants and products can be tabulated (although this should not be confused with a R.I.C.E. table, which is used to determine equilibrium *concentrations*).

The number of moles of HNO_2 decreases by the amount that reacted with OH^- to form NO_2^-. The OH^- is the limiting reagent, so it reacts completely. The number of moles of NO_2^- increases by the same amount of OH^- that was added.

	HNO_2	OH^-	NO_2^-
Initial Moles	$0.100 \;\cancel{L} \times \dfrac{0.250 \text{ mol}}{1 \;\cancel{L}}$ $= 0.0250$ mol	$0.0400 \;\cancel{L} \times \dfrac{0.250 \text{ mol}}{1 \;\cancel{L}}$ $= 0.0100$ mol	≈ 0
Change in Moles	-0.0100	-0.0100	$+0.0100$
Final Number of Moles	0.0150	0	0.0100
Final Concentration (M)	$\dfrac{0.0150 \text{ mol}}{0.140 \text{ L}} = 0.107 \; M$	0	$\dfrac{0.0100 \text{ mol}}{0.140 \text{ L}} = 0.0714 \; M$

The pH of the solution can now be determined using the Henderson-Hasselbalch equation.

$$pH = pK_a + \log \frac{[NO_2^-]}{[HNO_2]} = (-\log \; 4.0 \times 10^{-4}) + \log \frac{0.0714}{0.107} = 3.22$$

PRACTICE:

A 100.-mL solution of formic acid, H_2CO_2, is titrated with a 1.00 M normalized solution of NaOH. A volume of 38.0 mL of the NaOH solution is required to reach the equivalence point. The K_a of formic acid is 1.77×10^{-4}.

(a) What is the pH at the equivalence point?

(b) What is the pH of the solution after 12.0 mL of NaOH have been added?

(a) The number of moles of NaOH added is equal to the number of moles of formate ion that are present at the end of the titration.

$$H_2CO_2(aq) + OH^-(aq) \rightarrow HCO_2^-(aq) + H_2O(l)$$

$$0.0380 \;\cancel{\text{L NaOH}} \times \frac{1.00 \;\cancel{\text{mol NaOH}}}{1 \;\cancel{\text{L NaOH}}} \times \frac{1 \text{ mol } HCO_2^-}{1 \;\cancel{\text{mol NaOH}}} = 0.0380 \text{ mol } HCO_2^-$$

$$[HCO_2^-] = \frac{0.0380 \text{ mol } HCO_2^-}{0.100 \text{ L} + 0.0380 \text{ L}} = 0.275 \; M$$

The pH at the equivalence point depends on the behavior of HCO_2^- as a weak base.

$$HCO_2^-(aq) + H_2O(l) \rightleftharpoons H_2CO_2(aq) + OH^-(aq)$$

The K_a of formic acid must be converted to the K_b of formate.

$$K_w = K_a \cdot K_b = 1.0 \times 10^{-14}$$

$$K_b = \frac{1.00 \times 10^{-14}}{1.77 \times 10^{-4}} = 5.65 \times 10^{-11}$$

Reaction	HCO_2^-	H_2CO_2	OH^-
Initial Concentrations (M)	0.275	0	0
Change	$-x$	$+x$	$+x$
Equilibrium Concentrations (M)	$0.275 - x$	x	x

The very small K_b allows for the assumption that x is negligible compared with the concentration of HCO_2^-.

$$K_b = \frac{[H_2CO_2][OH^-]}{[HCO_2^-]}$$

$$5.65 \times 10^{-11} = \frac{x^2}{0.275 - x}$$

$$x = \sqrt{(5.65 \times 10^{-11})(0.275)} = 3.94 \times 10^{-6} = [OH^-]$$

$$pOH = -\log 3.94 \times 10^{-6} = 5.404$$

$$pH = 14.000 - 5.404 = 8.596$$

(b) The number of moles of OH^- added is equal to the number of moles of formic acid converted to formate.

$$0.0120 \text{ L NaOH} \times \frac{1.00 \text{ mol NaOH}}{1 \text{ L NaOH}} \times \frac{1 \text{ mol } HCO_2^-}{1 \text{ mol NaOH}} = 0.0120 \text{ mol } HCO_2^-$$

The number of moles of formic acid remaining is the difference between the initial number and the number of moles converted to formate.

$$0.0380 \text{ mol} - 0.0120 \text{ mol} = 0.0260 \text{ mol } HCO_2H$$

Because the total volume of the solution (100. mL + 12.0 mL) cancels out of the equation, the numbers of moles of formic acid and formate can be used directly in the Henderson-Hasselbalch equation.

$$pH = pK_a + \log \frac{[HCO_2^-]}{[HCO_2H]} = (-\log 1.77 \times 10^{-4}) + \log \frac{0.0120}{0.0260} = 3.416$$

Strong Acid/Weak Base

When a weak base, B, is titrated with a strong acid, H_3O^+, the reaction produces BH^+ and H_2O.

The shape of the pH curve for the titration of a weak base with a strong acid has some similarities to the curve for the titration of a weak acid.

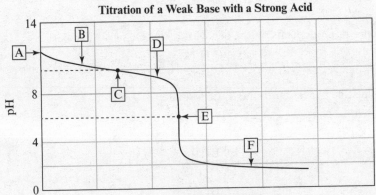

Titration of a Weak Base with a Strong Acid

The curve starts at a high pH value. As acid, HX, is added and converts the base, B, to its conjugate acid form, BH^+, the pH hovers at a value above 7 in the buffering region. At the half-equivalence point, the pH is equal to the pK_b, and at the equivalence point, the pH depends on the concentration of the acidic species, BH^+.

- At point **A,** the pOH depends only on the concentration of the weak base and the base dissociation constant, K_b.

$$B + H_2O \rightleftharpoons BH^+ + OH^-$$

- Within regions **B** and **D**, the solution is buffered and the pOH is calculated using the appropriate form of the Henderson-Hasselbalch equation. The acid that has been added has converted some of the B to BH$^+$. The relative concentrations of B and BH$^+$, along with the pK_b, determine the pOH of the solution.

$$pOH = pK_b + \log \frac{[BH^+]}{[B]}$$

- At point **C,** the half-equivalence point, exactly enough acid has been added to produce a 1:1 ratio of [B]: [BH$^+$]. At this point in the titration, the pOH of the solution is equal to the pK_b of the weak base.

- At point **E,** the equivalence point, the number of moles of H$^+$ that have been added is equal to the number of moles of B that were initially present. The pH at the equivalence point is determined by the acidic species, BH$^+$, which is the dominant species.

$$BH^+ + H_2O \rightleftharpoons B + H_3O^+$$

- Within region **F,** the excess H$_3$O$^+$ determines the pH of the solution.

Titration Curve Region	Major Species in Solution	Minor Species in Solution
A	B	OH$^-$, BH$^+$
B	B	BH$^+$, X$^-$
C	B, BH$^+$, X$^-$ (equimolar quantities)	
D	BH$^+$, X$^-$	B
E	BH$^+$, X$^-$	B, H$_3$O$^+$
F	H$_3$O$^+$, X$^-$	BH$^+$

PRACTICE:

A 0.100-L solution of 0.100 M pyridine, C$_5$H$_5$N, $K_b = 1.7 \times 10^{-9}$, is titrated with 0.100 M HCl. Sketch the titration curve, labeling the axes. Clearly label the pH before any acid has been added, at the equivalence point and the half-equivalence point. Also label the volume of HCl added at the equivalence point and at the half-equivalence point.

Before the titration begins, the pH of the pyridine solution depends on the concentration and K_b for pyridine.

$$C_5H_5N(aq) + H_2O(l) \rightleftharpoons C_5H_5NH^+(aq) + OH^-(aq)$$

Reaction	C$_5$H$_5$N	C$_5$H$_5$NH$^+$	OH$^-$
Initial Concentrations (M)	0.100	0	0
Change	$-x$	$+x$	$+x$
Equilibrium Concentrations (M)	$0.100 - x$	x	x

The value of x is negligible compared to the concentration of pyridine.

$$K_b = \frac{[C_5H_5NH^+][OH^-]}{[C_5H_5N]}$$

$$1.7 \times 10^{-9} = \frac{x^2}{0.100 - \cancel{x}}$$

$$x = \sqrt{(1.7 \times 10^{-9})(0.100)} = 1.3 \times 10^{-5} = [OH^-]$$

$$pOH = -\log 1.303840 \times 10^{-5} = 4.88$$

$$pH = 14.00 - 4.88 = 9.12$$

At the half-equivalence point, the pOH = pK_b for C_5H_5N since $[C_5H_5NH] = [C_5H_5NH^+]$.

$$pOH = pK_b + \log \frac{[C_5H_5NH^+]}{[C_5H_5N]}$$

$$pOH = -\log 1.7 \times 10^{-9} + \log 1 = 8.77 + 0$$

$$pH = 14.00 - 8.77 = 5.23$$

The pH at the equivalence point is determined by the extent of dissociation of the pyridinium ion, $C_5H_5NH^+$, the conjugate acid of pyridine.

$$C_5H_5NH^+(aq) + H_2O(l) \rightleftharpoons C_5H_5N(aq) + H_3O^+(aq)$$

The K_a of $C_5H_5NH^+$ is needed for the determination.

$$K_w = K_a \cdot K_b = 1.0 \times 10^{-14}$$

$$K_a = \frac{1.0 \times 10^{-14}}{1.7 \times 10^{-9}} = 5.9 \times 10^{-6}$$

The concentration of $C_5H_5NH^+$ at the equivalence point is required for the pH determination. When HCl is added to pyridine, the reaction to form pyridinium ion goes essentially to completion.

$$C_5H_5N(aq) + HCl(aq) \rightarrow C_5H_5NH^+(aq) + Cl^-(aq)$$

The concentration of pyridinium is found and used in a R.I.C.E. table to determine the equilibrium concentration of H_3O^+.

$$0.100 \text{ L } C_5H_5N \times \frac{0.100 \text{ mol } C_5H_5N}{1 \text{ L } C_5H_5N} \times \frac{1 \text{ mol } C_5H_5NH^+}{1 \text{ mol } C_5H_5N} = 1.00 \times 10^{-2} \text{ mol } C_5H_5NH^+$$

$$[C_5H_5NH^+] = \frac{1.00 \times 10^{-2} \text{ mol}}{0.100 \text{ L} + 0.100 \text{ L}} = 5.00 \times 10^{-2} \ M$$

Reaction	$C_5H_5NH^+$	C_5H_5N	H_3O^+
Initial Concentrations (M)	5.00×10^{-2}	0	0
Change	$-x$	$+x$	$+x$
Equilibrium Concentrations (M)	$5.00 \times 10^{-2} - x$	x	x

Again, x is negligible compared to the concentration of pyridinium.

$$K_a = \frac{[C_5H_5N][H_3O^+]}{[C_5H_5NH^+]}$$

$$5.9 \times 10^{-6} = \frac{x^2}{5.00 \times 10^{-2} - x}$$

$$x = \sqrt{(5.9 \times 10^{-6})(5.00 \times 10^{-2})} = 5.4 \times 10^{-4} = [H_3O^+]$$

$$pH = -\log 5.4 \times 10^{-4} = 3.27$$

Your sketch should resemble the following. Notice the three labeled pH values, the general shape of the buffering region, and the volumes of HCl added at the half-equivalence point and at the equivalence point.

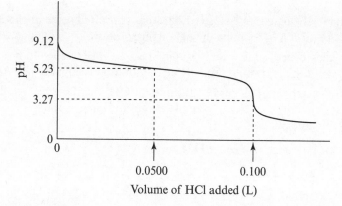

Polyprotic Acid/Strong Base

A polyprotic acid is one that has more than one proton to donate in aqueous solution. Examples include phosphoric acid, H_3PO_4, carbonic acid, H_2CO_3, and sulfuric acid, H_2SO_4.

The acid dissociation constant for the loss of the first proton is called K_{a_1}. The second proton dissociates with a dissociation constant of K_{a_2}, and so on. The dissociation reactions for phosphoric acid are shown below.

$$H_3PO_4 + H_2O \rightleftharpoons H_2PO_4^- + H_3O^+ \qquad K_{a_1} = 7.5 \times 10^{-3}$$

$$H_2PO_4^- + H_2O \rightleftharpoons HPO_4^{2-} + H_3O^+ \qquad K_{a_2} = 6.2 \times 10^{-8}$$

$$HPO_4^{2-} + H_2O \rightleftharpoons PO_4^{3-} + H_3O^+ \qquad K_{a_3} = 4.8 \times 10^{-13}$$

As one equivalent of base is added to a polyprotic acid, one proton from each molecule of acid is removed. Once all the molecules of acid have lost a single proton, a second equivalent of base will remove a second proton from the acid molecules, and so on. The inflection points on the titration curve for the reaction of a strong base with a weak polyprotic acid represent the equivalence points, just as they do in the titration curves for the reaction of strong base with a monoprotic weak acid. The number of acidic protons in a molecule is equal to the number of inflections in the titration curve. The curve shown below is for a diprotic acid.

Titration of a Polyprotic Acid with a Strong Base

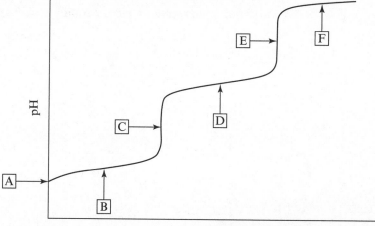

Volume of OH⁻ Added

- At point **A,** the pH depends only on the concentration of the weak acid and the first acid dissociation constant, K_{a_1}.

The pH is determined by the ionization of the weak acid.

$$H_2A + H_2O \rightleftharpoons HA^- + H_3O^+$$

- Between points **A** and **C,** the base that has been added has converted some of the H_2A to HA^-. The relative concentrations of H_2A and HA^- determine the pH of the solution.

- At point **B,** the half-equivalence point, exactly enough base has been added to produce a 1:1 ratio of $[H_2A]:[HA^-]$. At this point in the titration, the pH of the solution is equal to the pK_{a_1} of the weak acid.

- At point **C,** the equivalence point, the number of moles of OH^- that have been added is equal to the number of moles of H_2A that were initially present. The pH at the equivalence point is determined by the species, HA^-, which is the dominant species.

$$HA^- + H_2O \rightleftharpoons A^{2-} + H_3O^+$$

- At point **D,** the second half-equivalence point, exactly enough base has been added to produce a 1:1 ratio of $[HA^-]:[A^{2-}]$. At this point in the titration, the pH of the solution is equal to the pK_{a_2} of the weak acid.

- Between points **C** and **E,** the base that has been added has converted some of the HA^- to A^{2-}. The relative concentrations of HA^- and A^{2-} determine the pH of the solution.

- At point **E,** the second equivalence point, the number of moles of OH^- that have been added is equal to twice the number of moles of H_2A that were initially present. The pH at the equivalence point is determined by the species, A^{2-}, which is the dominant species.

$$A^{2-} + H_2O \rightleftharpoons OH^- + HA^-$$

- Within region **F,** the excess OH^- determines the pOH of the solution.

Titration Curve Region	Major Species in Solution
A	H_2A
B	H_2A, HA^-, M^+
C	HA^-, M^+
D	HA^-, A^{2-}, M^+
E	A^{2-}, M^+
F	OH^-, M^+

PRACTICE:

The curve below is observed when oxalic acid, $C_2O_4H_2$, is titrated with sodium hydroxide.

(a) Write the equations for the acid dissociation reactions and the equilibrium expressions for K_{a_1} and K_{a_2} .

(b) Use the curve to determine the approximate numerical values of K_{a_1} and K_{a_2}. Show how you arrived at your answers.

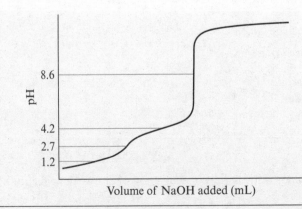

(a) The equations and equilibrium expressions for the hydrolysis of oxalic acid are

$$C_2O_4H_2(aq) + H_2O(l) \rightleftharpoons C_2O_4H^-(aq) + H_3O^+(aq) \qquad K_{a_1} = \frac{[C_2O_4H^-][H_3O^+]}{[C_2O_4H_2]}$$

$$C_2O_4H^-(aq) + H_2O(l) \rightleftharpoons C_2O_4^{2-}(aq) + H_3O^+(aq) \qquad K_{a_2} = \frac{[C_2O_4^{2-}][H_3O^+]}{[C_2O_4H^-]}$$

(b) The acid dissociation constants are most easily determined by the pH at the half-equivalence points of the titration, where pH = pK_a.

At pH = 1.2, $[C_2O_4H_2] = [C_2O_4H^-]$, so $pK_{a_1} = 1.2$.

$$pK_{a_1} = -\log K_{a_1}$$
$$K_{a_1} = 10^{-pK_{a_1}} = 10^{-1.2} = 6 \times 10^{-2}$$

At pH = 4.2, $[C_2O_4H^-] = [C_2O_4^{2-}]$, so $pK_{a_2} = 4.2$.

$$pK_{a_2} = -\log K_{a_2}$$
$$K_{a_2} = 10^{-pK_{a_2}} = 10^{-4.2} = 6 \times 10^{-5}$$

Acid-Base Indicators

Indicators are usually weak acids that exhibit a color change when they are converted from protonated (HIn) to deprotonated form (In⁻). An example of an indicator is bromocresol green, shown below. In the protonated form, HIn, bromocresol green is yellow. In the deprotonated form, In⁻, it is blue. The K_a for the deprotonation of bromocresol green at 25 °C is 1.3×10^{-5}, so the pK_a is 4.89.

$$HIn + H_2O \rightleftharpoons In^- + H_3O^+ \qquad K_a = \frac{[In^-][H_3O^+]}{[HIn]}$$

Bromocresol Green, an Acid-Base Indicator

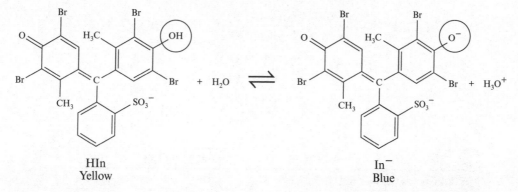

HIn
Yellow

In⁻
Blue

When hydroxide is added to an acidic solution of HIn, the H_3O^+ is neutralized and the equilibrium shifts to the right. When approximately 10% of the indicator molecules have been converted to In⁻, the change from a yellow solution to a green solution is detectable. As additional base is added, more HIn is converted to the In⁻ form.

If, on the other hand, hydronium is added to a basic solution of In⁻, the equilibrium shifts to the left and the indicator is protonated. When approximately 10% of the In⁻ molecules have been converted to HIn, the change from a blue solution to a green solution is detectable.

The useful range for an indicator is within one pH unit of the pK_a of the indicator. For bromocresol green, the equivalence point of a reaction that occurs at a pH of 4.89 ± 1 can be detected effectively.

A wide range of indicators are available. The most appropriate indicator for a particular reaction is one with a pK_a that is closest to the pH at the equivalence point of the reaction under investigation.

PRACTICE:

A researcher has access to the indicators tabulated below.

Indicator (In)	pK_a Range	Color of HIn	Color of In$^-$
Methyl orange	3.2 – 4.4	Red	Yellow
Methyl red	4.8 – 6.0	Red	Yellow
Cresol red	7.0 – 8.8	Yellow	Orange
Thymolphthalein	9.4 – 10.0	Colorless	Violet

(a) What is an appropriate indicator of the equivalence point for the titration of 1.00 L of 0.500 M chloroacetic acid, $ClCH_2CO_2H$, with 0.500 M hydroxide? The K_a of chloroacetic acid is 1.4×10^{-3}.

(b) What is the color of the solution containing the chosen indicator when the pH is equal to the pK_a of chloroacetic acid?

(a) At the equivalence point of the titration, the concentration of chloracetate ion, $ClCH_2CO_2^-$, determines the pH of the solution. The anion behaves as a weak base, so the K_b is needed.

$$ClCH_2CO_2^-(aq) + H_2O(l) \rightleftharpoons ClCH_2CO_2H(aq) + OH^-(aq)$$

$$K_w = K_a \cdot K_b = 1.0 \times 10^{-14}$$

$$K_b = \frac{1.0 \times 10^{-14}}{1.4 \times 10^{-3}} = 7.1 \times 10^{-12}$$

In order to reach the equivalence point, 1.00 L of 0.500 M OH$^-$ solution must be added. At the equivalence point, the number of moles of $ClCH_2CO_2^-$ is equal to the initial number of moles of $ClCH_2CO_2H$. The molarity is determined using this information.

$$1.00 \text{ L } ClCH_2CO_2H \times \frac{0.500 \text{ mol } ClCH_2CO_2H}{1.00 \text{ L } ClCH_2CO_2H} = 0.500 \text{ mol } ClCH_2CO_2H$$

$$0.500 \text{ mol } ClCH_2CO_2H \times \frac{1 \text{ mol } ClCH_2CO_2^-}{1 \text{ mol } ClCH_2CO_2H} = 0.500 \text{ mol } ClCH_2CO_2^-$$

$$\frac{0.500 \text{ mol } ClCH_2CO_2^-}{1.00 \text{ L} + 1.00 \text{ L}} = 0.250 \text{ } M \text{ } ClCH_2CO_2^-$$

Reaction	$ClCH_2CO_2^-$	$ClCH_2CO_2H$	OH$^-$
Initial Concentrations (M)	0.250	0	0
Change	$-x$	$+x$	$+x$
Equilibrium Concentrations (M)	$0.250 - x$	x	x

The value of K_b is small, so x is assumed to be negligible compared to the chloroacetate ion concentration.

$$K_b = \frac{[ClCH_2CO_2H][OH^-]}{[ClCH_2CO_2^-]}$$

$$7.142857 \times 10^{-12} = \frac{x^2}{0.250 - \cancel{x}}$$

$$x = \sqrt{(7.142857 \times 10^{-12})(0.250)} = 1.3363 \times 10^{-6} = [OH^-]$$

$$pOH = -\log 1.3363 \times 10^{-6} = 5.88$$

$$pH = 14.00 - 5.72 = 8.12$$

The pH at the equivalence point of the titration lies within the color-change range of cresol red, so cresol red is the best choice.

(b) The pK_a of chloroacetic acid is

$$pK_a = -\log 1.4 \times 10^{-3} = 2.85$$

At a pH of 2.85, cresol red will be in its protonated form, HIn, which will result in a yellow solution.

The Solubility Product

The **solubility** of a compound is the amount of the compound that dissociates in a given volume of solvent. Ionic compounds exhibit a range of solubilities. Some compounds, like NaCl, are very soluble. The solubility of NaCl in water at 25 °C is 359 grams (6.14 moles) per liter. Other compounds, such as AgCl, are described as "insoluble." In actuality, AgCl has a slight solubility of 1.9 mg (1.3×10^{-5} moles) per liter of water at 25 °C.

The solubility product, K_{sp}, is the equilibrium constant that describes the dissociation of an ionic compound, such as $Mg(OH)_2$, to form a saturated solution. Magnesium hydroxide, $Mg(OH)_2$, has a K_{sp} value of 8.9×10^{-12} at 25 °C. The equation for the dissolution of $Mg(OH)_2$ is shown.

$$Mg(OH)_2(s) \rightleftharpoons Mg^{2+}(aq) + 2\ OH^-(aq) \qquad K_{sp} = [Mg^{2+}][OH^-]^2$$

Notice that $Mg(OH)_2$ does not appear in the solubility product expression since it is a solid.

The number of moles of a substance that will dissolve in one liter of water is the **molar solubility.** The molar solubility of $Mg(OH)_2$ in moles per liter of water at 25 °C can be determined using a R.I.C.E. table. In the R.I.C.E. table below, the $Mg(OH)_2$ column is crossed out because it does not contribute to the mass action expression.

Reaction	$Mg(OH)_2$	Mg^{2+}	$2\ OH^-$
Initial Concentrations (*M*)		0	0
Change		+ x	+ 2x
Equilibrium Concentrations (*M*)		x	2x

The solubility product constant can be used to determine x, the number of moles of Mg^{2+}, that are dissolved per liter. Since one Mg^{2+} is dissociated for each $Mg(OH)_2$ that dissolves, x will be equal to the maximum number of moles of $Mg(OH)_2$ that dissolve per liter of water.

$$K_{sp} = x(2x)^2$$

$$4x^3 = 8.9 \times 10^{-12}$$

$$x = \sqrt[3]{\frac{8.9 \times 10^{-12}}{4}} = 1.3 \times 10^{-4}\ M$$

The molar solubility of $Mg(OH)_2$ at 25 °C is $1.3 \times 10^{-4}\ M$.

PRACTICE:

> Calculate the K_{sp} for $Co(OH)_3$, which has a molar solubility of 5.52×10^{-5} M at 25 °C.

The dissolution of $Co(OH)_3$ occurs according to the following equation.

$$Co(OH)_3(s) \rightleftharpoons Co^{3+}(aq) + 3\,OH^-(aq) \qquad K_{sp} = [Co^{3+}][OH^-]^3$$

The solubility is equal to the maximum number of moles of $Co(OH)_3$ that will dissolve in pure water at this temperature, so it is also equal to the equilibrium $[Co^{3+}]$ for a saturated solution.

Reaction	$Co(OH)_3$	Co^{3+}	$3\,OH^-$
Initial Concentrations (M)		0	0
Change		$+\,5.52 \times 10^{-5}$	$+\,3 \times 5.52 \times 10^{-5}$
Equilibrium Concentrations (M)		5.52×10^{-5}	1.65×10^{-4}

$$K_{sp} = [Co^{3+}][OH^-]^3 = (5.52 \times 10^{-5})(1.65 \times 10^{-4})^3 = 2.51 \times 10^{-16}$$

The Common Ion Effect

The **common ion effect** refers to the decreased dissociation of an ionic compound in solution due to the presence of one of the ions produced.

For example, consider the dissociation of solid CaF_2 in a solution of 1.00 M $Ca(NO_3)_2$. Since nitrate salts are soluble (they have a very large K_{sp}), the solution is already 1.00 M in Ca^{2+}. Calcium fluoride, on the other hand, has a very small K_{sp} of 4.0×10^{-11} at 25 °C.

$$CaF_2(s) \rightleftharpoons Ca^{2+}(aq) + 2\,F^-(aq) \qquad K_{sp} = 4.0 \times 10^{-11}$$

Because Ca^{2+} is already present, the equilibrium shifts to the left, and less CaF_2 dissolves in the solution than would dissolve in pure water.

The number of moles of CaF_2 that could be dissolved in 1.00 L of 1.00 M $Ca(NO_3)_2$ solution can be determined using a R.I.C.E. table.

Reaction	CaF_2	Ca^{2+}	$2\,F^-$
Initial Concentrations (M)		1.00	0
Change		$+\,x$	$+\,2x$
Equilibrium Concentrations (M)		$1.00 + x$	$2x$

Again, the solubility product expression is used, but it becomes apparent that the algebra required to solve for x is complicated beyond the scope of the AP Chemistry exam.

$$K_{sp} = [Ca^{2+}][F^-]^2$$

$$K_{sp} = (1.00 + x)(2x)^2 = 4.0 \times 10^{-11}$$

Rather than solving the resulting polynomial expression for x, the simplifying assumption can be made that x, the number of moles of CaF_2 that dissolve in a 1.00 M solution of Ca^{2+} solution, is negligibly small. In that case, it can be omitted from the $(1.00 + x)$ term.

$$4.0 \times 10^{-11} = (1.00 + \cancel{x})(2x)^2 = 4x^2$$

$$\sqrt{\frac{4.0 \times 10^{-11}}{4}} = x = 3.2 \times 10^{-6} \ M$$

The solubility of CaF_2 in aqueous solution of $1.00 \ M \ Ca(NO_3)_2$ at 25 °C is $3.2 \ 10^{-6} \ M$.

PRACTICE:

Zinc hydroxide, $Zn(OH)_2$, has a K_{sp} of 4.5×10^{-17} at 25 °C. Compare the solubility of $Zn(OH)_2$ in pure water with the solubility of $Zn(OH)_2$ in a 0.250 M solution of $Zn(NO_3)_2$ **(a)** qualitatively and **(b)** quantitatively, by calculating the solubility of $Zn(OH)_2$ in pure water and in 0.250 M $Zn(NO_3)_2$ solution.

(a) The dissolution of $Zn(OH)_2$ occurs according to the reaction shown.

$$Zn(OH)_2(s) \rightleftharpoons Zn^{2+}(aq) + 2 \ OH^-(aq)$$

Zinc hydroxide will be less soluble in a solution containing $Zn(NO_3)_2$ because, according to Le Chatelier's principle, the Zn^{2+} ion present will shift the dissolution equilibrium to the left, in the direction of the reactant.

(b) The solubility of $Zn(OH)_2$ in pure water is calculated as before.

Reaction	Zn(OH)₂	Zn²⁺	2 OH⁻
Initial Concentrations (M)		0	0
Change		+x	+2x
Equilibrium Concentrations (M)		x	2x

$$K_{sp} = [Zn^{2+}][OH^-]^2$$

$$K_{sp} = (x)(2x)^2 = 4.5 \times 10^{-17}$$

$$4.5 \times 10^{-17} = (x)(2x)^2 = 4x^3$$

$$\sqrt[3]{\frac{4.5 \times 10^{-17}}{4}} = x = 2.2 \times 10^{-6} \ M$$

The calculation of the solubility of $Zn(OH)_2$ in a 0.250 M Zn^{2+} solution takes the common ion effect into account.

Reaction	Zn(OH)₂	Zn²⁺	2 OH⁻
Initial Concentrations (M)		0.250	0
Change		+x	+2x
Equilibrium Concentrations (M)		0.250 + x	2x

The value of x is negligible compared with the initial Zn^{2+} concentration.

$$K_{sp} = [Zn^{2+}][OH^-]^2$$

$$K_{sp} = 4.5 \times 10^{-17} = (0.250 + \cancel{x})(2x)^2$$

$$\sqrt{\frac{4.5 \times 10^{-17}}{(0.250)(4)}} = x = 6.7 \times 10^{-9} \ M$$

The solubility of $Zn(OH)_2$ in pure water (2.2×10^{-6} M) is greater than the solubility in a 0.250 M Zn^{2+} solution (6.7×10^{-9} M).

Precipitation Reactions

The K_{sp} for an ionic compound can be used to determine whether or not a precipitation reaction will occur when aqueous solutions of the ions are combined.

The K_{sp} of $BaSO_4$, for example, is very small at 25 °C. Barium sulfate is minimally soluble in water.

$$BaSO_4(s) \rightleftharpoons Ba^{2+}(aq) + SO_4^{2-}(aq) \qquad K_{sp} = 1.1 \times 10^{-10}$$

This solubility product can be compared with a reaction quotient, Q, to determine whether a precipitation reaction will occur under a specified set of conditions.

For example, a student adds 25.0 mL of a 1.0×10^{-4} M solution of $Ba(NO_3)_2$ to a 25.0-mL solution of a 1.0×10^{-4} M solution of Na_2SO_4. Is a precipitation reaction expected to occur?

First, find the number of moles of Ba^{2+} and SO_4^{2-}.

$$\left(0.0250 \text{ L}\right)\left(\frac{1.0 \times 10^{-4} \text{ mol}}{1 \text{ L}}\right) = 2.5 \times 10^{-6} \text{ mol } SO_4^{2-} = 2.5 \times 10^{-6} \text{ mol } Ba^{2+}$$

$$[Ba^{2+}] = [SO_4^{2-}] = \frac{2.5 \times 10^{-6} \text{ mol}}{0.050 \text{ L}} = 5.0 \times 10^{-5} \text{ } M$$
$$Q = [Ba^{2+}][SO_4^{2-}] = (5.0 \times 10^{-5})^2 = 2.5 \times 10^{-9}$$

Because Q is greater than K_{sp}, the dissociation reaction shifts toward the solid reactant. In other words, a precipitation reaction occurs.

PRACTICE:

> Predict whether a precipitation reaction will occur when 125 mL of a 0.0420 M solution of KI are added to 125 mL of 0.0210 M $Pb(NO_3)_2$. The K_{sp} for PbI_2 is 1.4×10^{-8} at 25 °C.

The dissolution reaction for PbI_2 is

$$PbI_2(s) \rightleftharpoons Pb^{2+}(aq) + 2 I^-(aq)$$

The reaction quotient must be determined using the initial concentrations of Pb^{2+} and I^- that results upon the addition of the two solutions.

$$[Pb^{2+}] = \frac{\left(0.125 \text{ L}\right)\left(\frac{0.0210 \text{ mol } Pb^{2+}}{1 \text{ L}}\right)}{0.250 \text{ L}} = 1.05 \times 10^{-2} \text{ } M$$

$$[I^-] = \frac{\left(0.125 \text{ L}\right)\left(\frac{0.0420 \text{ mol } I^-}{1 \text{ L}}\right)}{0.250 \text{ L}} = 2.10 \times 10^{-2} \text{ } M$$

$$Q = [Pb^{2+}][I^-]^2 = (1.05 \times 10^{-2})(2.10 \times 10^{-2})^2 = 4.63 \times 10^{-6}$$

Because Q is greater than K_{sp}, the equilibrium favors the solid reactant, and a precipitation reaction occurs.

The Thermodynamics of Equilibrium

The equilibrium constant is an indication of the thermodynamic favorability of a process at a particular temperature. If a reaction has an equilibrium constant larger than 1, it will occur in the forward direction spontaneously. In other words, $K > 1$ and $\Delta G° < 0$.

On the other hand, if a reaction has an equilibrium constant less than 1, $K < 1$, then $\Delta G° > 0$ for the process.

When a reaction is at equilibrium, $K = 1$ and $\Delta G° = 0$.

The relationship between $\Delta G°$ and K is given on the *AP Chemistry Equations and Constants* sheet (pages 365–366).

$$\Delta G° = -RT \ln K$$

In the K expression, partial pressures must be used for gases, and concentrations must be used for species in solutions. (The reason for this is beyond the scope of the AP Chemistry exam.)

Also, note the R units must be compatible with the $\Delta G°$ units. Therefore, the R used in the above equation is

$$R = 8.314 \text{ J/mol K}$$

PRACTICE:

> Determine the change in Gibbs free energy, $\Delta G°$, for the autoionization of water at 298 K.

The autoionization of water occurs with a K_w of 1.00×10^{-14} at 298 K.

$$\Delta G° = -\left(8.314 \text{ J·mol}^{-1}\cdot\text{K}^{-1}\right)\left(298 \text{ K}\right) \ln 1.00 \times 10^{-14}$$

$$\Delta G° = 7.99 \times 10^4 \text{ J·mol}^{-1}$$

When the reaction quotient, Q, is less than K, $\Delta G < 0$; the conversion of reactants to products is thermodynamically favored. When Q is greater than K, $\Delta G > 0$; the conversion of reactants to products is thermodynamically disfavored.

Below, the free energy of a reaction is plotted against reaction coordinate with pure reactants on the left and pure products on the right. At equilibrium, $Q = K$ and $\Delta G = 0$.

The Relationship Between Free Energy and Equilibrium

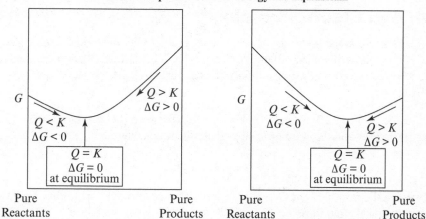

PRACTICE:

> For the formation of gaseous ammonia by the reaction of nitrogen and hydrogen gases, $\Delta H°$ is –92.6 kJ·mol^{-1} and $\Delta S°$ is –199 J^{-1}·K^{-1}. If the partial pressures of NH_3, H_2, and N_2 are 1.5 atm, 0.080 atm, and 0.060 atm, respectively, will the reaction shift toward reactants or products in order to reach equilibrium at 298 K?

The balanced equation is

$$N_2(g) + 3\,H_2(g) \rightleftharpoons 2\,NH_3(g)$$

The value of $\Delta G°$ must first be determined from $\Delta H°$ and $\Delta S°$.

$$\Delta G° = \Delta H° - T\Delta S°$$

$$\Delta G° = \left(-92.6\ \cancel{kJ} \cdot mol^{-1} \times \frac{1000\ J}{1\ \cancel{kJ}}\right) - \left((298\ \cancel{K})(-199\ J \cdot mol^{-1} \cdot \cancel{K^{-1}})\right) = -3.33 \times 10^4\ J \cdot mol^{-1}$$

The value of $\Delta G°$ is used to calculate K.

$$\Delta G° = -RT \ln K$$

$$-3.33 \times 10^4\ J \cdot mol^{-1} \cdot K^{-1} = -\left(8.314\ J \cdot mol^{-1} \cdot \cancel{K^{-1}}\right)(298\ \cancel{K}) \ln K$$

$$\ln K = \frac{-3.33 \times 10^4\ J \cdot mol^{-1} \cdot K^{-1}}{-\left(8.314\ J \cdot mol^{-1} \cdot \cancel{K^{-1}}\right)(298\ \cancel{K})} = 13.4$$

$$K = e^{13.4} = 7 \times 10^5$$

The expression for Q is

$$Q = \frac{P_{NH_3}^2}{P_{N_2} P_{H_2}^3} = \frac{1.5^2}{(0.060)(0.080)^3} = 7.3 \times 10^4$$

Since Q is less then K, the reaction will proceed toward the product.

Equilibrium and Electrochemistry

AP Chemistry exam questions sometimes require students to predict the nonstandard cell potential, E, or the free energy change, ΔG, for an electrochemical cell under nonstandard conditions. (Remember, under standard thermodynamic conditions, the concentrations of solutions are exactly 1 M, pressures are 1 atmosphere, and temperature is 298 K.)

In Big Idea 5 (Chapter 5, "Thermodynamics"), the relationship between the standard Gibbs free energy change for an electrochemical process and the standard cell potential was considered.

$$\Delta G° = -nFE°$$

The relationship between the nonstandard Gibbs free energy change and the nonstandard cell potential is similar to the relationship at standard conditions.

$$\Delta G = -nFE$$

It is important to realize that as a cell reaction proceeds, E and ΔG both approach zero. The concentrations of all reactants and products approach those that satisfy the expression for K. For a battery (or galvanic cell), once the reaction has reached equilibrium, the battery is said to be "dead."

AP Chemistry students are expected to be able to make qualitative predictions regarding cell potentials under non-standard conditions. For example, consider the following redox reaction under standard cell conditions at 25 °C.

$$3 \, Sn^{4+}(aq) + 2 \, Cr(s) \rightarrow 3 \, Sn^{2+}(aq) + 2 \, Cr^{3+}(aq)$$

Half Reaction	Standard Reduction Potential, $E°$ (V)
$Sn^{4+} + 2 \, e^- \rightarrow Sn^{2+}$	0.15
$Cr^{3+} + 3 \, e^- \rightarrow Cr$	–0.74

The standard reduction potential is calculated as usual. For a thermodynamically favorable process, Sn^{4+}, having a greater $E°$ value, gets reduced at the cathode, while Cr gets oxidized at the anode.

$$E°_{cell} = E°_{reduction} - E°_{oxidation} = 0.15 \text{ V} - (-0.74 \text{ V}) = 0.89 \text{ V}$$

This value of $E°$ is valid when $[Sn^{4+}] = [Sn^{2+}] = [Cr^{3+}] = 1.00 \, M$. Consider the case where $[Sn^{2+}]$ is greater than 1.00 M. In terms of the nonstandard reduction potential, E is now *less positive* than $E°$.

A more serviceable method for determining the nonstandard cell potential is to use the Nernst equation. Despite the removal of the Nernst equation from the AP Chemistry curriculum by the College Board, students who are familiar with the Nernst equation and are equipped to use it correctly in support of their responses have the advantage of an enhanced understanding. Although the Nernst equation no longer appears on the *AP Chemistry Equations and Constants* sheet, it is simple to remember and to understand.

$$E = E° - \frac{0.06}{n} \log Q \qquad \text{(only valid at 298 K)}$$

Here, E and $E°$ are the nonstandard and standard cell potentials, respectively; n is the number of electrons transferred in the balanced redox equation; and Q is the reaction quotient. The equation is derived from the relationship between the change in Gibbs free energy and Q.

For example, suppose a galvanic cell is composed of the following two half reactions.

Half Reaction	Standard Reduction Potential, $E°$ (V)
$Pb^{2+}(aq) + 2 \, e^- \rightarrow Pb(s)$	–0.13
$Cr^{3+}(aq) + e^- \rightarrow Cr^{2+}(aq)$	–0.41

The cell potential when $[Pb^{2+}] = 1.00 \times 10^{-2} \, M$, $[Cr^{3+}] = 3.00 \times 10^{-4} \, M$, and $[Cr^{2+}] = 3.00 \times 10^{-4} \, M$ at 25 °C can be calculated using the Nernst equation.

The first step is to determine the standard cell potential. For a thermodynamically favorable process, Pb^{2+} must be reduced, and Cr^{3+} must be oxidized.

$$E°_{cell} = E°_{reduction} - E°_{oxidation} = -0.13 \text{ V} - (-0.41 \text{ V}) = 0.28 \text{ V}$$

The balanced redox equation is

$$Pb^{2+}(aq) + 2 \, Cr^{2+}(aq) \rightarrow Pb(s) + 2 \, Cr^{3+}(aq)$$

There are a total of 2 electrons transferred in the balanced process ($n = 2$).

$$E = E° - \frac{0.06}{n} \log \frac{[Cr^{3+}]^2}{[Pb^{2+}][Cr^{2+}]^2} = 0.28\ V - \frac{0.06}{2} \log \frac{[3.00 \times 10^{-4}]^2}{[1.00 \times 10^{-2}][3.00 \times 10^{-4}]^2} = 0.22\ V$$

The nonstandard cell potential is 0.22 V.

Review Questions

Multiple Choice

1. Given the data in the table below, determine the equilibrium constant for the reaction of $Br_2(g)$ with $NO(g)$ to form $NOBr(g)$.

$$Br_2(g) + 2\ NO(g) \rightleftharpoons 2\ NOBr(g)$$

Reaction	K
$N_2(g) + Br_2(g) + O_2(g) \rightleftharpoons 2\ NOBr(g)$	2.0×10^{-27}
$\frac{1}{2}N_2(g) + \frac{1}{2}O_2(g) \rightleftharpoons NO(g)$	1.0×10^{-15}

A. 2.0×10^{-57}

B. 2.0×10^{-42}

C. 2.0×10^{-12}

D. 2.0×10^{3}

2. What is the correct expression for K_p for the reaction of iron(III) oxide with hydrogen gas?

$$Fe_2O_3(s) + 3\ H_2(g) \rightleftharpoons 2\ Fe(s) + 3\ H_2O(g)$$

A. $\dfrac{[Fe_2O_3]P_{H_2}^3}{[Fe]^2 P_{H_2O}^3}$

B. $\dfrac{[Fe]^2 P_{H_2O}^3}{[Fe_2O_3]P_{H_2}^3}$

C. $\dfrac{P_{H_2O}^3}{P_{H_2}^3}$

D. $\dfrac{P_{H_2O}}{P_{H_2}}$

Questions 3–4 refer to the reaction of CO(g) with H₂O(g).

A 1.0-mole sample of $CO(g)$ and a 2.0-mole sample of $H_2O(g)$ are combined in a rigid, evacuated 1-L vessel. They react to form $CO_2(g)$ and $H_2(g)$. At equilibrium 0.67 mole of $CO_2(g)$ is present in the container.

3. What is the equilibrium constant, K_c, for the reaction?

   A. 0.5
   B. 1.0
   C. 2.0
   D. 4.0

4. The reaction is set up such that the concentrations of the species are as follows.

[CO]	2.0 M
[H₂O]	1.5 M
[CO₂]	3.0 M
[H₂]	2.0 M

Which of the following best describes the results of the reaction?

   A. The reaction will shift toward products to reach equilibrium because $Q > K$.
   B. The reaction will shift toward reactants to reach equilibrium because $Q > K$.
   C. The reaction will shift toward products to reach equilibrium because $Q < K$.
   D. The reaction will shift toward reactants to reach equilibrium because $Q < K$.

Questions 5–7 refer to the decomposition of BrCl(g).

$$2\,BrCl(g) \rightleftharpoons Br_2(g) + Cl_2(g) \qquad K_c = 36 \text{ at a certain temperature}$$

5. A closed, rigid 1.0-L container is charged with 2.00 moles of $BrCl(g)$. What is the equilibrium concentration of $BrCl(g)$ in the container?

   A. 0.15 M
   B. 0.92 M
   C. 1.1 M
   D. 1.8 M

6. Which of the following is true of the reaction as it progresses from pure reactants toward equilibrium?

   A. The rate of the forward reaction decreases until it is equal to the rate of the reverse reaction.
   B. The rate of the forward reaction increases until it is equal to the rate of the reverse reaction.
   C. The rate of the forward reaction and the rate of the reverse reaction are identical throughout the experiment.
   D. The rate of the forward reaction decreases until equilibrium is reached and the reaction stops.

7. If additional $Cl_2(g)$ is added after equilibrium has been established, which graph best shows the effect on the concentration of $Cl_2(g)$?

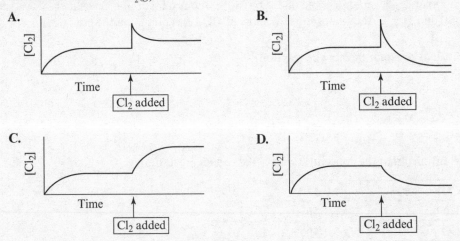

A.

[Cl₂] vs Time — Cl₂ added

B.

[Cl₂] vs Time — Cl₂ added

C.

[Cl₂] vs Time — Cl₂ added

D.

[Cl₂] vs Time — Cl₂ added

8. Hemoglobin, Hb, is an iron-containing metalloprotein that transports oxygen and other gases in the blood of mammals. Carbon monoxide poisoning occurs when CO coordinates with the iron in hemoglobin.

$$Hb(O_2)_4(aq) + 4\,CO(g) \rightleftharpoons Hb(CO)_4(aq) + 4\,O_2(g)$$

Which strategy would be effective for reversing the effects of carbon monoxide poisoning?

A. Exposing the system to a low partial pressure of $O_2(g)$
B. Exposing the system to a high partial pressure of $O_2(g)$
C. Lowering the total pressure of the system
D. Raising the total pressure of the system

9. The reaction of Cl_2 with H_2O forms HCl and O_2. The value of K_c is 1.9×10^{-15} at 298 K.

$$2\,Cl_2(g) + 2\,H_2O(g) \rightleftharpoons 4\,HCl(g) + O_2(g) \qquad \Delta H° = 115\ kJ\cdot mol^{-1}$$

What effect will an increase in temperature have on the equilibrium constant?

A. K_c will decrease because there are more product molecules than reactant molecules.
B. K_c will increase because the reaction is endothermic.
C. K_c will be unaffected because it is constant.
D. The change in K_c depends on the change in enthalpy at the new temperature.

10. What is the pH of a $5.00 \times 10^{-2}\ M$ aqueous solution of $Ba(OH)_2$?

A. 9
B. 12
C. 13
D. 14

11. An acid, HA, has a pK_a of 4.00. What is the approximate percent ionization of a 0.010 M aqueous HA solution?

A. 0.10%
B. 1.0%
C. 10%
D. 100%

12. Which of the following salts is expected to have the highest pH in a 1.00 M aqueous solution?

    A. $NaClO_4$

    B. KBr

    C. MgI_2

    D. $Ca(CN)_2$

13. Given the following acid dissociation constants, select the correct statement.

Acid	K_{a_1}	K_{a_2}	K_{a_3}
H_3PO_4	7.5×10^{-3}	6.2×10^{-8}	4.8×10^{-13}
$H_3C_6H_5O_7$	8.4×10^{-4}	1.8×10^{-5}	4.0×10^{-6}

    A. H_3PO_4 is a weaker acid than $H_3C_6H_5O_7$

    B. HPO_4^{2-} is a weaker base than $C_6H_5O_7^{3-}$

    C. $H_2PO_4^-$ is a stronger acid than $H_2C_6H_5O_7^-$

    D. PO_4^{3-} is a stronger base than $C_6H_5O_7^{3-}$

Questions 14–16 refer to the amino acid glycine.

Glycine, $H_2NCH_2CO_2H$, is the simplest of the twenty amino acids that are commonly found in proteins. It contains a weakly basic amine group, $-NH_2$, and a weakly acidic carboxylic acid group, $-CO_2H$. In very low pH solutions, the amine group is in conjugate acid form and the carboxylic acid group is neutral. In very high pH solutions, the carboxylic acid group is in conjugate base form and the amine group is neutral. The neutral carboxylic acid group is more strongly acidic than the conjugate acid form of the amine group. A 20.0-mL aqueous solution of 0.100 M glycine is titrated with 0.100 M NaOH at 25 °C. The following titration curve results.

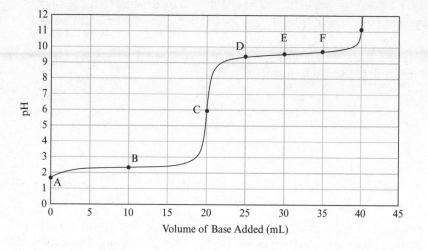

14. Which of the structures below correctly shows the form of glycine at point A in the titration?

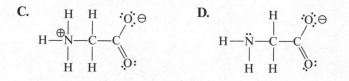

15. A zwitterion is a compound that contains atoms with both positive and negative formal charges. Based on the information above, at what point in the titration curve is the concentration of zwitterionic glycine the highest?

A. Point A
B. Point C
C. Point D
D. Point E

16. Estimate the pK_a for the following reaction of glycine.

$$^+H_3NCH_2CO_2^-(aq) + H_2O(l) \rightleftharpoons H_2NCH_2CO_2^-(aq) + H_3O^+(aq)$$

A. 2.3
B. 6.0
C. 9.6
D. 11.0

17. Use the data in the table to determine which scenario would lead to a buffer with a pH of 6.

Acid	K_a
HF	1×10^{-3}
HOCl	1×10^{-8}

A. 1.0 mole of NaOCl is added to 0.01 mole of HOCl in enough water to make 1.0 L of solution.
B. 0.01 mole of NaF is added to 1.0 mole of HF in enough water to make 1.0 L of solution.
C. 1.0 mole of NaF is added to 0.01 mole of HF in enough water to make 1.0 L of solution.
D. 0.01 mole of NaOCl is added to 1.0 mole of HOCl in enough water to make 1.0 L of solution.

18. At a certain temperature, the K_{sp} of magnesium hydroxide is 4.0×10^{-12}. What is the pH of a saturated solution of magnesium hydroxide at this temperature?

A. 8.6
B. 10.3
C. 11.0
D. 12.0

19. Two reactions have enthalpy changes that are almost identical, yet one of the reactions has an equilibrium constant that is much larger than the other. Which of the following must be true?

A. The reaction with the larger equilibrium constant has the more positive entropy change.
B. The reaction with the larger equilibrium constant has the less positive entropy change.
C. The reaction with the larger equilibrium constant has the larger activation energy.
D. The reaction with the larger equilibrium constant has the smaller activation energy.

20. A galvanic cell is constructed in which a silver electrode is immersed in 50.0 mL of an aqueous 1.0 M $AgNO_3$ solution and a zinc electrode is immersed in 50.0 mL of an aqueous 1.0 M $Zn(NO_3)_2$ solution. The two half-cells are connected by a salt bridge. A 0.010-mg sample of solid NaCl is added to only one of the half-cells. Which choice correctly describes the effect on the cell potential?

Compound	K_{sp}
AgCl	1.3×10^{-10}
ZnCl	1.3×10^2

Half Reaction	Standard Reduction Potential, $E°$ (V)
$Zn^{2+}(aq) + 2\,e^- \rightarrow Zn(s)$	–0.76
$Ag^+(aq) + e^- \rightarrow Ag(s)$	0.80

A. The cell potential is decreased because the reaction quotient, Q, is increased by addition of NaCl to the zinc half-cell.
B. The cell potential is increased because the reaction quotient is decreased by addition of NaCl to the zinc half-cell.
C. The cell potential is decreased because the reaction quotient, Q, is increased by addition of NaCl to the silver half-cell.
D. The cell potential is increased because the reaction quotient is decreased by addition of NaCl to the silver half-cell.

Long Free Response

1. A 1.00-gram sample of solid CO_2 is placed in a rigid, evacuated 1.00-L vessel that contains a negligible volume of a solid metal catalyst. The reaction is heated to 3000. K, and the reaction shown below occurs.

$$2\,CO_2(g) \rightleftharpoons 2\,CO(g) + O_2(g)$$

a. What is the pressure inside the container at 3000. K before any reaction has occurred?
b. When the system is at equilibrium, the total pressure in the container is 6.15 atm. Calculate the partial pressures of $CO_2(g)$, $CO(g)$, and $O_2(g)$ in the container at 3000. K.
c. Write the equilibrium constant expression, K_p, for the reaction.
d. Calculate the value of the equilibrium constant for the reaction at 3000. K.
e. Is the reaction exothermic or endothermic? Support your response with a discussion of the change in Gibbs free energy.
f. If the temperature of the reaction is decreased to 2000 K, will the value of K_p increase, decrease, or remain constant? Explain your response.
g. In a separate experiment, the original partial pressures at 3000. K are shown in the table below. Will the amount of CO_2 in the container increase, decrease, or remain constant? Justify your response with a calculation.

Species	Partial Pressure (atm)
CO_2	5.0
CO	0.20
O_2	0.20

2. The graph below shows the results of the titration of 50.0 mL of a 0.500 M solution of a weak acid, HA, with 0.500 M NaOH.

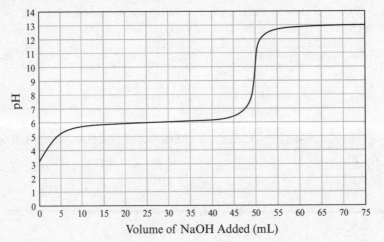

Volume of NaOH Added (mL)

a. Describe three features of the graph that identify HA as a weak acid.

b.

   i. Describe three different ways that the acid dissociation constant, K_a, for HA may be determined.

   ii. Choose one of the methods that you described and use it to calculate the K_a for HA.

c. On the graph above, sketch the curve that would result if 50.0 mL of 0.500 M HNO$_3$ were titrated instead of HA.

d. How will the pH at the equivalence point differ if 1.00 M NaOH is used instead of 0.500 M?

e. What is the pH of the solution after 10.0 mL of 0.500 M NaOH have been added to the HA solution?

f. Would the pH at the endpoint of the titration be higher or lower than the pH at the equivalence point if an indicator with a K_a of 1×10^{-6} had been used instead of a pH meter? Justify your response with a calculation.

Short Free Response

3. At 25 °C, the pH of 25.0-mL of a 0.00300 M aqueous solution of aniline, $C_6H_5NH_2$, is 8.174.

a. Write the balanced net ionic equation for the base dissociation reaction of aniline with water.

b. Determine the pK_b of aniline.

c. What is the pH of a 25.0-mL solution of 0.00300 M aniline to which 25.0 mL of 0.00100 M HCl have been added?

d. When a few drops of additional HCl are added to the solution in part c, the pH does not change detectably. Write a net ionic equation that shows why this is true.

4. A saturated solution of CaF_2 has an F$^-$ concentration of 4.31×10^{-4} M at 25 °C.

a. Write the expression for the solubility product, K_{sp}, for CaF_2.

b. Determine the K_{sp} for CaF_2 at 25 °C.

c. How many moles of CaF_2 will dissolve in a 1.00-L solution that is 0.250 M in NaF?

d. At 25 °C, the pH of a saturated aqueous solution of CaF_2 is 7.10 and the pH of a saturated aqueous solution of MgF_2 is 7.85. A solution of 1.0 M NaF is slowly added to an aqueous solution that is 0.100 M $Mg(NO_3)_2$ and 0.100 M $Ca(NO_3)_2$. Write the net ionic equation for the precipitation reaction that occurs first and explain your answer.

Answers and Explanations

Multiple Choice

1. **D.** (EK 6.A.2) Notice that when the second equation is reversed and multiplied by 2, the sum of the two equations gives the overall transformation. The equilibrium constant for the reaction of N_2 with O_2 must reflect the change to that equation. First, the equation is reversed.

$$(1.0 \times 10^{-15})^{-1} = 1.0 \times 10^{15}$$

Second, the equation is multiplied by 2, so the equilibrium constant must be squared.

$$(1.0 \times 10^{15})^2 = 1.0 \times 10^{30}$$

Third, the two equations are added together, so their equilibrium constants are multiplied.

$$(1.0 \times 10^{30})(2.0 \times 10^{-27}) = 2.0 \times 10^3$$

2. **C.** (EK 6.A.3) The solids do not contribute to the equilibrium expressions. The partial pressures are raised to the powers of the coefficients in the balanced equation.

3. **B.** (EK 6.A.3) The balanced chemical equation is simply

$$CO(g) + H_2O(g) \rightleftharpoons CO_2(g) + H_2(g)$$

The equilibrium concentrations can be determined using a R.I.C.E. table.

Reaction	CO	H$_2$O	CO$_2$	H$_2$
Initial Concentrations (M)	1.0	2.0	0	0
Change	−0.67	−0.67	+0.67	+0.67
Equilibrium Concentrations (M)	0.33	1.33	0.67	0.67

The math is simplified by recognizing that 0.33 is approximately $\frac{1}{3}$.

$$K_c = \frac{[CO_2][H_2]}{[CO][H_2O]} = \frac{\left(\frac{2}{3}\right)^2}{\left(\frac{1}{3}\right)\left(\frac{4}{3}\right)} = 1.0$$

4. **B.** (EK 6.A.2) A comparison of K with Q gives the direction in which the reaction will proceed to establish equilibrium.

$$Q = \frac{[CO_2][H_2]}{[CO][H_2O]} = \frac{(3.0)(2.0)}{(2.0)(1.5)} = 2.0$$

Since Q is greater than K, the reaction shifts to the left. Reactants are formed faster than products are consumed until equilibrium is reached.

5. **A.** (EK 6.A.2, 6.A.3) The equilibrium concentrations are determined using a R.I.C.E. table.

Reaction	2 BrCl	Br$_2$	Cl$_2$
Initial Concentrations (M)	2.00	0	0
Change	$-2x$	$+x$	$+x$
Equilibrium Concentrations (M)	$2.00 - 2x$	x	x

$$K_c = \frac{[Br_2][Cl_2]}{[BrCl]^2}$$

$$\sqrt{\frac{x^2}{(2-2x)^2}} = \sqrt{36}$$

$$\frac{x}{2-2x} = 6$$

$$x = \frac{12}{13}$$

The equilibrium concentration of BrCl is

$$2.00 - 2\left(\frac{12}{13}\right) = 0.15 M$$

6. **A.** (EK 6.A.3) When the reaction begins, the rate of the reverse reaction is negligible compared with the rate of the forward reaction since there is little product to react. As the reaction proceeds, the rate of the forward reaction decreases and the rate of the reverse reaction increases until both rates are equal and there is no net change in the forward or reverse direction (although reaction in both the forward and reverse directions is still continuously occurring).

7. **A.** (EK 6.A.3) When chlorine gas is added, the reaction consumes some of the added chlorine as it shifts back to the reactants. The final chlorine concentration, however, is still greater than it was after the initial equilibrium is established.

8. **B.** (EK 6.A.1, 6.B.1) Increasing the partial pressure of O$_2$ will have the effect of shifting the equilibrium toward $Hb(O_2)_4$, releasing CO.

9. **B.** (EK 6.B.1) The reaction is endothermic, so an increase in temperature will shift the reaction toward products, increasing the equilibrium constant.

10. **C.** (EK 6.C.1) Barium hydroxide is a strong, soluble base. For every mole of $Ba(OH)_2$ dissolved, two moles of OH$^-$ are released in the solution. The concentration of OH$^-$ is

$$\frac{5.00 \times 10^{-2} \text{ mol Ba(OH)}_2}{1 \text{ L}} \times \frac{2 \text{ mol OH}^-}{1 \text{ mol Ba(OH)}_2} = 0.100 \ M \text{ OH}^- = 1.00 \times 10^{-1} \ M \text{ OH}^-$$

$$pOH = -\log[OH^-] = -\log 1.00 \times 10^{-1} = 1$$
$$pH = 14 - pOH = 14 - 1 = 13$$

11. C. (EK 6.C.1) The K_a for the weak acid is 10^{-4}.

$$HA(aq) + H_2O(l) \rightleftharpoons A^-(aq) + H_3O^+(aq)$$

The concentration of ionized HA is determined using a R.I.C.E. table.

Reaction	HA	H_3O^+	A^-
Initial Concentrations (M)	0.0100	0	0
Change	$-x$	$+x$	$+x$
Equilibrium Concentrations (M)	$0.0100 - x$	x	x

$$K_a = \frac{[H_3O^+][A^-]}{[HA]}$$

$$1 \times 10^{-4} = \frac{x^2}{0.0100 - \cancel{x}}$$

$$\sqrt{(1 \times 10^{-4})(1 \times 10^{-2})} = \sqrt{x^2}$$

$$x = 1 \times 10^{-3} \; M = [A^-]$$

$$\% \text{ ionization} = \frac{1 \times 10^{-3}}{1 \times 10^{-2}} \times 100\% = 10\%$$

12. D. (EK 6.C.1) The solution with the highest pH is the one in which the anion is the conjugate base of the weakest acid. The weakest conjugate acid is HCN, so the CN^- released by the $Ca(CN)_2$ produces the most basic solution of the choices given.

13. D. (EK 6.C.1) Given a list of K_a values, the conjugate acid strength of the bases must be compared. The conjugate acid of PO_4^{3-} is HPO_4^{2-}, with a K_a of 4.8×10^{-13}. The conjugate acid of $C_6H_5O_7^{3-}$ is $HC_6H_5O_7^{2-}$, with a K_a of 4.0×10^{-6}. Since HPO_4^{2-} is a weaker acid than $HC_6H_5O_7^{2-}$, PO_4^{3-} is a stronger base than $C_6H_5O_7^{3-}$.

14. B. (EK 6.C.1) At the lowest pH in the titration, the carboxylic acid group has the form $-CO_2H$, and the amine group has the form $-NH_3^+$, where the nitrogen atom has a formal charge of $+1$.

15. B. (EK 6.C.1) The carboxylic acid group is the most acidic, so it reacts with OH^- first to form $-CO_2^-$, where one of the oxygen atoms has three lone pairs and a formal charge of -1. Since the amine group still has the form zwitterionic $-NH_3^+$ at the first equivalence point, the predominant form of glycine at the first equivalence point is zwitterionic. The first equivalence point is at Point C on the titration curve.

16. C. (EK 6.C.1) The form of glycine that is present at the second equivalence point of the titration is the one in which both the carboxylic acid and the amine are deprotonated, $H_2NCH_2CO_2^-$. This form is the conjugate base of the zwitterionic species, $^+H_3NCH_2CO_2^-$, for which the pK_a, ~9.6, can be determined halfway between the first and second equivalence points.

17. D. (EK 6.C.2) The Henderson-Hasselbalch equation can be used to determine which ratio of conjugate acid and conjugate base is appropriate. For the $[OCl^-]:[HOCl]$ ratio of $0.01:1.0$, the pH is equal to 6.

$$pH = pK_a + \log\frac{[A^-]}{[HA]} = 8 + \log\left(\frac{1.0 \times 10^{-2}}{1.0}\right) = 8 - 2 = 6$$

18. B. (EK 6.C.1, 6.C.3) The dissociation equation for $Mg(OH)_2$ is

$$Mg(OH)_2(s) \rightleftharpoons Mg^{2+}(aq) + 2\,OH^-(aq)$$

$$K_{sp} = [Mg^{2+}][OH^-]^2 = x(2x)^2 = 4x^3$$

$$4x^3 = 4.0 \times 10^{-12}$$

$$x = 1.0 \times 10^{-4}$$

$$[OH^-] = 2.0 \times 10^{-4}$$

$$pOH \approx 3 - 4$$

$$pH \approx 10 - 11$$

19. **A.** (EK 6.D.1) The reaction with the larger equilibrium constant has a more negative change in Gibbs free energy, $\Delta G°$. Since both reactions have similar values of $\Delta H°$, the reaction with the more positive entropy change will have a smaller $\Delta G°$ according to $\Delta G° = \Delta H° - T\Delta S°$.

20. **C.** (EK 6.D.1) The standard cell potential is positive for a galvanic cell, so Ag^+ is reduced at the cathode and Zn is oxidized at the anode.

$$E°_{cell} = E°_{reduction} - E°_{oxidation} = 0.80\ V - (-0.76\ V) > 0$$

The overall balanced equation is

$$2\ Ag^+ + Zn \rightarrow 2\ Ag + Zn^{2+}$$

Addition of NaCl to the Ag^+ half-cell will cause AgCl to precipitate, decreasing the concentration of Ag^+ and increasing the reaction quotient, Q.

The Nernst equation can be used to perform a quick logic check.

$$E = E° - \frac{0.06}{n}\ \log\ \frac{[Zn^{2+}]}{[Ag^+]^2}$$

A decrease in $[Ag^+]$ will increase the $\log Q$ term and decrease E.

Long Free Response

1. **a.** (EK 2.A.2) The pressure inside the container is determined using the ideal gas law.

$$1.00\ g\ CO_2 \times \frac{1\ mol\ CO_2}{44.01\ g\ CO_2} = 0.0227\ mol\ CO_2$$

$$P = \frac{nRT}{V} = \frac{(0.0227\ mol)(0.08206\ L \cdot atm \cdot mol^{-1} \cdot K^{-1})(3000\ K)}{1\ L} = 5.59\ atm$$

b. (EK 2.A.2, 6.A.2, 6.A.3) The equilibrium partial pressures are related to one another by the stoichiometric coefficients in the balanced chemical equation.

Reaction	2 CO$_2$	2 CO	O$_2$
Initial Partial Pressure (atm)	5.59	0	0
Change	$-2x$	$+2x$	$+x$
Equilibrium Partial Pressure (atm)	$5.59 - 2x$	$2x$	x

The total pressure in the container is the sum of the partial pressures.

$$P_{total} = (5.59 - 2x) + 2x + x = 6.15\ atm$$

$$x = 0.56\ atm$$

$$P_{CO_2} = 4.47\ atm$$
$$P_{CO} = 1.12\ atm$$
$$P_{O_2} = 0.56\ atm$$

c. (EK 6.A.3, 6.A.4) The equilibrium constant expression is

$$K_p = \frac{P_{CO}^2 P_{O_2}}{P_{CO_2}^2}$$

d. (EK 6.A.3, 6.A.4) The value of the equilibrium constant is determined from the partial pressures of the species present at equilibrium.

$$K_p = \frac{(1.12)^2(0.56)}{(4.47)^2} = 0.035$$

e. (EK 5.E.1, 5.E.3, 6.D.1) The equation $\Delta G^\circ = - RT \ln K_p$ shows the relationship between the change in Gibbs free energy and the equilibrium contstant. For $K_p < 1$, $\Delta G^\circ > 0$. Because the entropy of the system is increasing when two moles of gas react to form three moles of gas, $\Delta S^\circ > 0$. In order for ΔG° to be positive according to the equation $\Delta G^\circ = \Delta H^\circ - T\Delta S^\circ$, ΔH° must be positive. The reaction is endothermic.

f. (EK 6.B.1) A decrease in temperature for an endothermic reaction decreases the equilibrium constant.

g. (EK 6.A.2) In order to determine whether the reaction shifts toward reactants or products, it is necessary to evaluate Q.

$$Q = \frac{(0.20)^2(0.20)}{(5.0)^2} = 3.2 \times 10^{-4}$$

Because $Q < K$, the reaction will shift to the right. This means that the amount of CO_2 in the container will decrease.

2. a. (EK 6.C.1) The three features of the graph that indicate that HA is a weak acid rather than a strong acid are 1) the initial pH is greater than 0.30, which is the expected pH for a 0.5 M solution of a strong acid; 2) there is an initial rise in the pH when base is first added, and then the pH levels off in the buffering region before it undergoes another sharp rise just prior to the equivalence point; and 3) the pH at the equivalence point is greater than 7.

b. **i.** (EK 6.C.1) The acid dissociation constant may be determined by 1) the pH and [HA] of the solution before any base has been added (the K_a is equal to $\dfrac{(10^{-pH})^2}{[HA]}$). 2) At the half-equivalence point of the titration, the K_a is equal to 10^{-pH}. 3) The K_b at the equivalence point can be determined. (It is equal to $\dfrac{\left(10^{-(14-pH)}\right)^2}{[A^-]}$.) The K_a can then be determined by $\dfrac{K_w}{K_b}$.

ii. (EK 6.C.1) The simplest method is the second one, in which pH = pK_a at the half-equivalence point. It can be seen from the plot that the pH at the half-equivalence point, when 25.0 mL of base have been added, is 6.

$$K_a = 10^{-6}$$

c. (EK 6.C.1) If a HNO_3, a strong acid, were titrated, the initial pH would be around 0.3, the curve would not rise initially and then enter a buffer region, and the pH at the equivalence point would be 7.

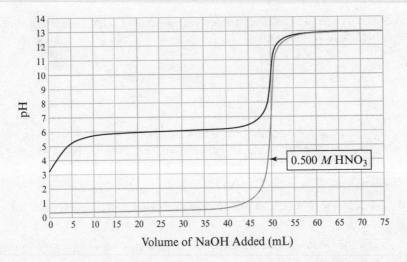

Volume of NaOH Added (mL)

d. (EK 6.C.1) If 1.00 M NaOH were used instead of 0.500 M, a smaller volume of NaOH would be required to reach the equivalence point. The concentration of A^- would be greater since the total volume would be less, resulting in a slightly higher $[OH^-]$, a lower pOH, and a higher pH.

e. (EK 6.C.1) The number of moles of HA present before the titration begins is

$$0.0500 \; \cancel{L\,HA} \times \frac{0.500 \text{ mol HA}}{1 \; \cancel{L\,HA}} = 0.0250 \text{ mol HA}$$

After 10.0 mL of 0.500 M NaOH have been added to the solution, the number of moles of HA that have been converted to A^- is

$$0.0100 \; \cancel{L\,NaOH} \times \frac{0.500 \; \cancel{\text{mol NaOH}}}{1 \; \cancel{L\,NaOH}} \times \frac{1 \text{ mol } A^-}{1 \; \cancel{\text{mol NaOH}}} = 0.00500 \text{ mol } A^-$$

The number of moles of HA remaining are

$$0.0250 \text{ mol} - 0.00500 \text{ mol} = 0.0200 \text{ mol HA}$$

The Henderson-Hasselbalch equation, given on the *AP Chemistry Equations and Constants* sheet, is used to determine the pH of the solution at this point. Notice that the total volume, 60.0 mL, cancels, so number of moles can be used directly instead of concentrations in this calculation.

$$\text{pH} = \text{p}K_a + \log \frac{[A^-]}{[HA]} = 6.0 + \log\left(\frac{0.00500}{0.0200}\right) = 5.4$$

f. (EK 6.C.1) The pH at the endpoint of the titration is determined by the concentration and K_b of A^-. The concentration is

$$\frac{0.0250 \text{ mol } A^-}{0.100 \text{ L}} = 0.250 \; M \; A^-$$

Note that the volume used is the total volume after the addition of 50.0 mL of NaOH to the original 50.0 mL of HA.

The K_b is determined using the K_a of HA and K_w.

$$K_b = \frac{K_w}{K_a} = \frac{1 \times 10^{-14}}{1 \times 10^{-6}} = 1 \times 10^{-8}$$

The base dissociation reaction of A^- is as follows.

$$A^-(aq) + H_2O(l) \rightleftharpoons HA(aq) + OH^-(aq)$$

$$K_b = \frac{[HA][OH^-]}{[A^-]}$$

A R.I.C.E. table is used to determine the equilibrium concentrations.

Reaction	A⁻	HA	OH⁻
Initial Concentrations (M)	0.250	0	0
Change	$-x$	$+x$	$+x$
Equilibrium Concentrations (M)	$0.250 - x$	x	x

Substitution of the equilibrium concentrations into the expression for K_b and the assumption that x is much smaller than the initial concentration of A^- allow for the calculation of the hydroxide ion concentration.

$$1.0\times10^{-8} = \frac{x^2}{0.250 - \cancel{x}}$$
$$x = \sqrt{(1.0\times10^{-8})(0.250)} = 5.0\times10^{-5} \ M = [OH^-]$$
$$pOH = 5.0\times10^{-5} = 4.30$$
$$pH = 14.00 - 4.30 = 9.70$$

If an indicator with a pK_a of 6 had been used, the pH at the endpoint of the titration would be about 5–7, which is lower than the pH at the equivalence point.

Short Free Response

3. a. (EK 3.A.1, 6.C.1) The net ionic equation for the dissociation reaction of aniline with water is shown below.

$$C_6H_5NH_2 + H_2O \rightleftharpoons C_6H_5NH_3^+ + OH^-$$

State symbols are not required for credit, but if they are included, the reaction becomes

$$C_6H_5NH_2(aq) + H_2O(l) \rightleftharpoons C_6H_5NH_3^+(aq) + OH^-(aq)$$

b. (EK 6.C.1) The pK_b can be determined from the K_b. The expression for the K_b is

$$K_b = \frac{[C_6H_5NH_3^+][OH^-]}{[C_6H_5NH_2]}$$

The value of the pH can be used to determine the pOH of the solution.

$$pOH = 14.000 - pH = 5.826$$

The $[OH^-]$ concentration is $10^{-5.826} \ M$, or $1.49 \times 10^{-6} \ M$. This is equal to $[C_6H_5NH_3^+]$. The aniline concentration is the difference between the initial concentration and the concentration of $[C_6H_5NH_3^+]$.

$$[C_6H_5NH_2] = 0.00300 \ M - 1.49 \times 10^{-6} \ M \approx 0.00300 \ M$$

$$K_b = \frac{(1.49\times10^{-6})^2}{0.00300} = 7.43\times10^{-10}$$
$$pK_b = -\log(7.43\times10^{-10}) = 9.13$$

c. (EK 6.C.2) The result of the addition is a buffer solution. The number of moles of $C_6H_5NH_2$ and $C_6H_5NH_3^+$ can be substituted into the base version of the Henderson-Hasselbalch equation.

$$C_6H_5NH_2(aq) + H^+(aq) \rightarrow C_6H_5NH_3^+(aq)$$

$$0.0250 \; \cancel{L\,HCl} \times \frac{0.00100 \; \cancel{mol\,HCl}}{1 \; \cancel{L\,HCl}} \times \frac{1 \; mol \; C_6H_5NH_3^+}{1 \; \cancel{mol\,HCl}} = 2.50 \times 10^{-5} \; mol \; C_6H_5NH_3^+$$

$$0.0250 \; L \; C_6H_5NH_2 \times \frac{0.00300 \; mol \; C_6H_5NH_2}{1 \; L \; C_6H_5NH_2} = 7.50 \times 10^{-5} \; mol \; C_6H_5NH_2 \; \text{initially present}$$

$$7.50 \times 10^{-5} \; mol \; C_6H_5NH_2 - 2.50 \times 10^{-5} \; mol \; C_6H_5NH_3^+ = 5.00 \times 10^{-5} \; mol \; C_6H_5NH_2 \; \text{present at equilibrium}$$

$$pOH = pK_b + \log \frac{\left[C_6H_5NH_3^+ \right]}{\left[C_6H_5NH_2 \right]} = 9.13 + \log \left(\frac{2.50 \times 10^{-5}}{5.00 \times 10^{-5}} \right) = 8.83$$

$$pH = 14.00 - 8.83 = 5.17$$

d. (EK 3.A.1, 6.C.2) The solution is a buffer since it has a base, $C_6H_5NH_2$, and its conjugate acid, $C_6H_5NH_3^+$. The reaction between HCl and aniline allows the solution to resist a change in pH as HCl is added.

$$C_6H_5NH_2 + H^+ \rightleftharpoons C_6H_5NH_3^+$$

State symbols are not required for credit, but if they are included, the reaction becomes

$$C_6H_5NH_2(aq) + H^+(aq) \rightleftharpoons C_6H_5NH_3^+(aq)$$

4. a. (EK 6.C.3) The expression for K_{sp} is based on the dissociation reaction of CaF_2 in aqueous solution.

$$CaF_2(s) \rightleftharpoons Ca^{2+}(aq) + 2 \; F^-(aq)$$

$$K_{sp} = [Ca^{2+}][F^-]^2$$

b. (EK 6.C.3) The concentration of F^- is twice the concentration of Ca^{2+}.

$$[F^-] = 4.31 \times 10^{-4} \; M$$

$$[Ca^{2+}] = \frac{4.31 \times 10^{-4} \; M}{2} = 2.16 \times 10^{-4} \; M$$

$$K_{sp} = (2.16 \times 10^{-4})(4.31 \times 10^{-4})^2 = 4.00 \times 10^{-11}$$

c. (EK 6.C.3) The number of moles of CaF_2 that could be dissolved in 1.00 L of 0.250 M NaF solution can be determined using a R.I.C.E. table.

Reaction	CaF$_2$	Ca^{2+}	2 F$^-$
Initial Concentrations (M)		0	0.250
Change		$+x$	$+2x$
Equilibrium Concentrations (M)		x	$0.250 + 2x$

$$K_{sp} = [Ca^{2+}][F^-]^2$$

$$K_{sp} = (x)(0.250 + 2x)^2$$

Rather than solving the resulting polynomial expression for x, the simplifying assumption can be made that x, the number of moles of CaF_2 that dissolve in 1.0 L of a 0.250 M solution of F^-, is negligibly small.

$$4.0 \times 10^{-11} = (x)(0.250 + \cancel{2x})^2 = 0.0625x$$
$$x = 6.40 \times 10^{-10} \ M$$

A total of 6.40×10^{-10} moles of CaF_2 will dissolve in 1.0 L of a 0.250 M solution of NaF at 25 °C.

d. (EK 6.C.1, 6.C.3) The fluoride ion, F^-, is the conjugate base of a weak acid, HF, so a solution of F^- will have a pH that is greater than 7 due to the reaction

$$F^-(aq) + H_2O(l) \rightleftharpoons HF(aq) + OH^-(aq)$$

Because the saturated MgF_2 solution has a higher pH than the saturated CaF_2 solution, more F^- must be present in the MgF_2 solution. The solubility of MgF_2 is greater than the solubility of CaF_2, so CaF_2 precipitates first.

The net ionic equation for the precipitation reaction that occurs is just the reverse of the dissociation reaction.

$$Ca^{2+} + 2 F^- \rightarrow CaF_2$$

State symbols are not required for credit, but if they are included, the reaction becomes

$$Ca^{2+}(aq) + 2 F^-(aq) \rightarrow CaF_2(s)$$

Chapter 7

Laboratory Review

The College Board requires that 25% of an AP Chemistry course is devoted to laboratory work, and a number of questions on the exam are intended to assess student understanding of experimental chemistry.

Safety

Safety is always the top priority in any school, university, or professional chemistry laboratory. Questions about safety have been asked on past AP Chemistry exams.

In lab work, the adage "measure twice, cut once" should be a guiding principle. Before beginning any lab experiment, make sure you have read and understood the objectives and procedure. Before you begin, ask your teacher to clarify anything that you do not understand. Think ahead and anticipate possible problems. Know the location of the eyewash, shower, or other nearby source of clean, running water. Research the hazards associated with the chemicals that you should be using. Here are some other good practices you should follow in the lab:

- Wear your personal protective equipment. Eye protection is not optional. (Your prescription eyeglasses will not protect your eyes from flying shards of glass.) Lab aprons and gloves are recommended when working with hazardous or irritating substances that may splash. Closed-toe shoes should be worn, and long hair should be tied back.
- Familiarize yourself with the Material Safety Data Sheets, or MSDSs, for the chemicals that you will be using. What are the first-aid procedures for skin contact, inhalation, ingestion, or injection (resulting from cuts with chemical-contaminated glass)? Is the chemical flammable?
  - If a strong acid is spilled on skin, wash the area with plenty of running water, followed by dilute sodium bicarbonate solution, if available.
  - If a strong base is spilled, flush the area with plenty of running water, followed by dilute acetic acid solution, if available.
  - Never rinse your eyes with anything other than running water.
- Does the chemical's disposal require special procedures? Always follow your teacher's disposal instructions.
- Know that one of the serious safety hazards encountered in a lab class is incorrect dilution of strong acids. Always add concentrated acid to water; never add water to concentrated acid.
- Never touch your eyes, nose, or mouth during lab. Nothing should ever go in your mouth during a chemistry lab activity. Gum, food, drinks, pipettes, and your pencil, among other things, can all be contaminated with chemicals and solvents. Always wash your hands at the end of the laboratory session to prevent spreading chemical residues outside of the lab.
- Know the location of fire extinguishers and fire blankets. Never pick up a vessel that contains a substance that has ignited. In case of a fire, alert your teacher and those around you immediately. If the fire is small enough to be extinguished with a watch glass, for example, do so. If the fire is large, follow your teacher's instructions and evacuate quickly.

Glassware and Equipment

The names and uses for the following laboratory glassware should be familiar.

	Beaker	Used to contain solids or liquids. A 100-mL beaker has a precision of ±5 mL.
	Erlenmeyer flask	Used to contain liquids and solutions. A 100-mL flask has a precision of ±5 mL.
	Graduated cylinder	Used to measure volumes of liquids that will be poured into other containers. A 100-mL graduated cylinder has a precision of ±0.5 mL.

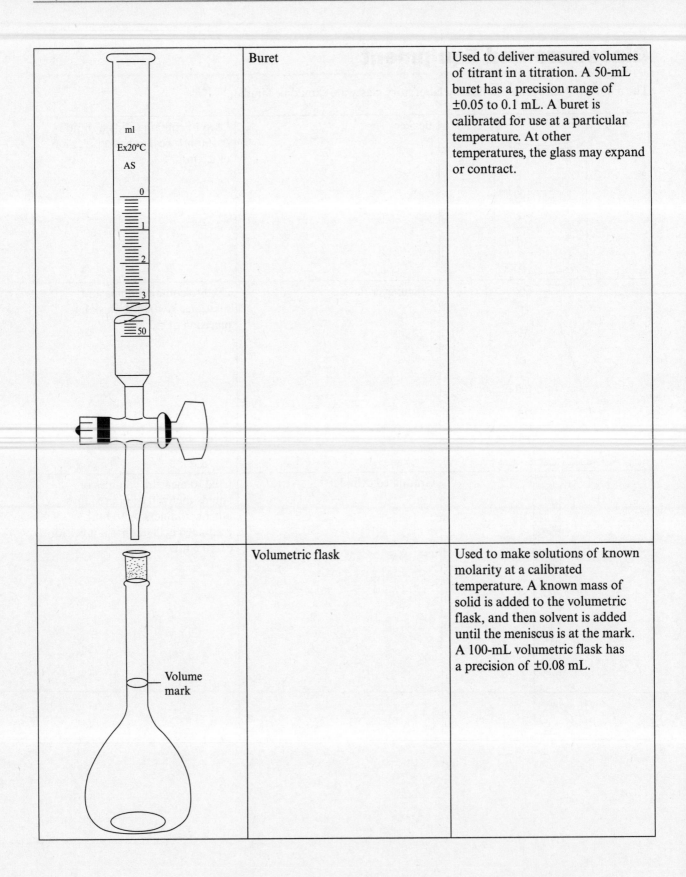

| | Buret | Used to deliver measured volumes of titrant in a titration. A 50-mL buret has a precision range of ±0.05 to 0.1 mL. A buret is calibrated for use at a particular temperature. At other temperatures, the glass may expand or contract. |
| | Volumetric flask | Used to make solutions of known molarity at a calibrated temperature. A known mass of solid is added to the volumetric flask, and then solvent is added until the meniscus is at the mark. A 100-mL volumetric flask has a precision of ±0.08 mL. |

	Volumetric pipet	Used to transfer measured volumes of liquid. When marked "TD," which means "to deliver," the liquid that remains in the tip should not be blown out after the liquid transfer. A 10-mL volumetric pipet has a precision of ±0.02 mL.
Volume mark	Separatory funnel	Used to separate two immiscible liquids. The less dense liquid forms the top layer in the separatory funnel, and the more dense liquid forms the bottom layer. The bottom layer can be drained out of the bottom of the funnel, separating it from the top layer.
Top should be open when draining / Layer A / Layer B	Crucible with lid	Used to contain solids during heating to high temperatures.

Measurement

Any measurement has an inherent uncertainty. For example, when reading the volume of a liquid in a graduated cylinder, the bottom of the meniscus can be read to the nearest marking, and then one more digit is estimated to the researcher's best approximation. No more than one digit should be estimated.

Estimation of a Volume

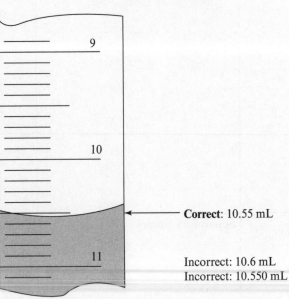

Correct: 10.55 mL

Incorrect: 10.6 mL
Incorrect: 10.550 mL

The number of significant figures for a reported measurement communicates the level of precision with which the chemist made a measurement. In the picture above, the measurement 10.55 mL has four significant figures. The higher the number of significant figures, the more precise the measurement. It is important to be familiar with the conventions for working with significant figures, as discussed on page 5 of the Introduction.

AP Chemistry Experiments

The 16 experiments in the AP Chemistry laboratory manual are briefly summarized below.

The review of laboratory experiments in this book are not meant to replace detailed laboratory procedures, disposal, and safety concerns. Under NO circumstances are the scenarios for the labs to be used as directions for actually performing the laboratory work.

Experiment 1: Measuring Concentration with Spectrophotometry

The purpose of this experiment is to use a spectrophotometer or a colorimeter to determine the concentration of a dye in a commercial beverage by measuring transmittance, T, of a particular visible wavelength. **Transmittance** is the fraction of light of a certain wavelength that passes through a sample. It is related to the absorbance of a substance by

$$A = -\log T$$

PRACTICE:

> What is the absorbance of a sample that transmits 52% of the light at a given wavelength?

The percent transmittance, % T, must be converted to transmittance, T.

$$T = 0.52$$

Absorbance is determined by taking the negative of the logarithm of the transmittance according to the equation below.

$$A = -\log T$$

$$A = -\log (0.52) = 0.284$$

Absorbance measurements of greater than 1.5 mean that the transmittance is less than $10^{-1.5}$. This value is too small to be used with confidence, so dilution of the sample and re-measurement of the transmittance is required.

Several known dilutions of the dye of interest are made in order to create a calibration curve. The transmittance values of the known solutions at a given wavelength are measured and recorded. The transmittance values are converted to absorbance values and plotted versus dye concentration. The absorbance of the blue beverage can be compared with the calibration curve as described in "Measuring Concentration Using Spectrophotometry" on page 118.

Experiment 2: Determining the Composition of an Alloy

In this investigation, spectrophotometry is again used to measure the concentration of a colored solution. The solution is produced when the copper in a sample of brass of unknown composition is converted to Cu^{2+} ions in a precise volume of water.

The mass of a brass sample is determined using a balance, and then the brass is treated with a minimum volume of concentrated nitric acid. This produces blue Cu^{2+} ions in solution.

$$Cu(s) + 4\ HNO_3(aq) \rightarrow Cu(NO_3)_2(aq) + 2\ NO_2(g) + 2\ H_2O(l)$$

The resulting solution is diluted to a precise volume. The absorbance of the sample is measured and compared to a standard curve. (The standard curve is generated using various solutions of known Cu^{2+} concentration.)

PRACTICE:

> A 2.28-g sample of brass is dissolved in 20 mL of concentrated HNO_3. The resulting blue solution is diluted to 100.0 mL in a volumetric flask. A 1.00-mL volumetric pipet is used to transfer a sample of the Cu^{2+} solution to another volumetric flask, and the sample is again diluted to 100.0 mL. Comparison of the absorbance of the resulting solution with a standard curve indicates a Cu^{2+} concentration of 0.00269 M. What is the mass percentage of copper in the original sample of brass?

The final measured concentration of Cu^{2+} was the result of dilution of 1.00 mL of the original solution. The concentration of the original solution can be determined using the dilution equation.

$$M_1V_1 = M_2V_2$$

$$M_1 = \frac{M_2 V_2}{V_1} = \frac{(0.00269 \ M)(100.0 \ \text{mL})}{1.00 \ \text{mL}} = 0.269 \ M$$

The number of moles of Cu^{2+} can be calculated from the volume and the concentration of the original solution. The number of moles is then converted to grams using the atomic weight of copper.

$$100.0 \ \text{mL} \times \frac{1 \ L}{1000 \ \text{mL}} \times \frac{0.269 \ \text{mol}}{1 \ L} = 0.0269 \ \text{mol} \ Cu^{2+}$$

$$0.0269 \ \text{mol} \ Cu^{2+} \times \frac{63.55 \ \text{g Cu}}{1 \ \text{mol} \ Cu^{2+}} = 1.71 \ \text{g Cu}$$

$$\frac{1.71 \ \text{g Cu}}{2.28 \ \text{g brass}} \times 100\% = 75.0\%$$

Experiment 3: Gravimetric Analysis

Gravimetric analysis is an analytical technique in which an insoluble solid is filtered from solution and dried. The mass of the solid is measured and the original concentration of the solution is deduced.

The gravimetric experiment is one in which the concentration of calcium ions present in a sample of water is determined by precipitation, filtration, and drying. An excess of sodium carbonate is added to the unknown Ca^{2+} solution. The product is solid calcium carbonate, which has a K_{sp} of 8.7×10^{-9}. The net ionic equation is

$$Ca^{2+}(aq) + CO_3^{2-}(aq) \rightarrow CaCO_3(s)$$

The solid is filtered through a vacuum filtration apparatus, as shown on page 10. A piece of pre-weighed filter paper is used to collect the solid.

Once the solvent has been removed, the solid is washed with a small amount of deionized water. The filter paper with the wet solid is placed on a watch glass in a drying oven and allowed to dry completely. When the solid is dry, the mass of the filter paper with the solid is determined and the mass of the empty filter paper is subtracted to give the mass of the solid.

It is important to note that if the sample is not rinsed with deionized water before drying, the mass will be too high due to the presence of other ions. If the sample is rinsed with too much deionized water, however, the mass will be too low due to some dissolving of the slightly soluble calcium carbonate.

In addition, it is important to break up the pieces of solid calcium carbonate with a metal spatula between periods of drying in order to release water that is trapped in the interior of the solid.

PRACTICE:

A 1.00-L sample of mineral water is boiled down until about 20 mL remain. Approximately 40 mL of 0.5 M Na_2CO_3 are added to the solution and a precipitate forms. The solid is filtered and dried, and the following data is collected. What is the concentration of Ca^{2+} in the original sample? Report your answer in mol·L^{-1}.

Mass of filter paper	0.238 g
Mass of filter paper + solid after first drying	2.196 g
Mass of filter paper + solid after second drying	2.048 g
Mass of filter paper + solid after third drying	2.042 g
Mass of filter paper + solid after fourth drying	2.041 g

The mass does not change very much between the third and fourth drying periods, so the final mass of the solid plus the filter paper is 2.041 g. The mass of the sodium carbonate solid is

$$2.041 \text{ g} - 0.238 \text{ g} = 1.803 \text{ g}$$

This mass can be divided by the molar mass of $CaCO_3$ to find the number of moles of Ca^{2+} in the 20-mL sample.

$$1.803 \ \cancel{\text{g } CaCO_3} \times \frac{1 \ \cancel{\text{mol } CaCO_3}}{100.09 \ \cancel{\text{g } CaCO_3}} \times \frac{1 \text{ mol } Ca^{2+}}{1 \ \cancel{\text{mol } CaCO_3}} = 0.0180 \text{ mol } Ca^{2+}$$

The molarity of Ca^{2+} in the 1.00-L sample can be determined by recognizing that the total number of moles of Ca^{2+} were present in the 1.00-L sample.

$$\frac{0.0180 \text{ mol } Ca^{2+}}{1.00 \text{ L}} = 0.0180 \ M \ Ca^{2+}$$

Experiment 4: Acid-Base Titration

The concentration of acid in fruit juices and sodas is determined in this experiment by titration of dilute solutions of these beverages with standardized sodium hydroxide. For an overview of titration, refer to "Measuring Concentration Using Titration" on page 121.

Fruit juice contains citric acid, $H_3C_6H_5O_7$, a weak triprotic acid that can be titrated with standardized NaOH.

$$H_3C_6H_5O_7 + 3 \ OH^- \rightarrow C_6H_5O_7^{3-} + 3 \ H_2O$$

The Structure and K_a Values of Citric Acid

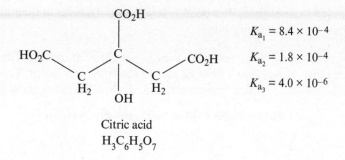

Citric acid
$H_3C_6H_5O_7$

Solid sodium hydroxide is very **hygroscopic.** This means that it quickly absorbs moisture from the atmosphere. This prevents solid sodium hydroxide from being accurately weighed. In order to determine the accurate concentration of a solution of sodium hydroxide, it must be standardized. Usually, the unknown sodium hydroxide solution is used to titrate a solution that contains an accurately known mass of potassium hydrogen phthalate, $KC_8H_5O_4$, or KHP, a monoprotic acid that is not hygroscopic and can be weighed easily.

PRACTICE:

> A 2.0-g sample of sodium hydroxide that has been exposed to the atmosphere is added to a 1-L Erlenmeyer flask. Approximately 500 mL of water are added and the solution is thoroughly mixed. A 1.038-g sample of KHP (MW = 204.22 g·mol⁻¹) is added to a second Erlenmeyer flask and diluted with about 50 mL of water. Three drops of phenolphthalein indicator are added to the KHP solution, and it is then titrated with the sodium hydroxide solution. The indicator turns pink and remains pink after 56.97 mL of NaOH solution have been added. What is the molarity of the NaOH?

Sodium hydroxide and KHP react in a 1:1 mole ratio, so the number of moles of KHP equal the number of moles of NaOH at the endpoint.

$$1.038 \ \text{g KHP} \times \frac{1 \ \text{mol KHP}}{204.22 \ \text{g KHP}} \times \frac{1 \ \text{mol NaOH}}{1 \ \text{mol KHP}} = 0.005083 \ \text{mol NaOH} \quad (0.0050827539)$$

$$\frac{0.0050827539 \ \text{mol NaOH}}{0.05697 \ \text{L}} = 0.08922 \ M \ \text{NaOH}$$

For the titration of fruit juice, an indicator must be chosen that exhibits a color change at the pH of the endpoint. Although the pH at the endpoint is somewhat greater than 7, phenolphthalein can still be used as an indicator. At the endpoint of the titration, the concentration of citric acid can be determined.

PRACTICE:

A 10.00-mL sample of apple juice was transferred to an Erlenmeyer flask and diluted with approximately 20 mL of water. Three drops of phenolphthalein were added, and the acid was titrated to the endpoint with 18.12 mL of 0.03193 M standardized NaOH. What was the concentration of citric acid in the original apple juice sample?

The number of moles of citric acid present is calculated from the volume and concentration of the NaOH required to titrate the sample. Since citric acid is a triprotic acid, 3 moles of NaOH are needed per mole of acid.

$$0.01812 \ \text{L NaOH} \times \frac{0.03193 \ \text{mol NaOH}}{1 \ \text{L NaOH}} \times \frac{1 \ \text{mol citric acid}}{3 \ \text{mol NaOH}} = 1.929 \times 10^{-4} \ \text{mol citric acid}$$

$$\frac{1.929 \times 10^{-4} \ \text{mol citric acid}}{0.01000 \ \text{L}} = 0.01929 \ M \ \text{citric acid}$$

Experiment 5: Paper Chromatography

Chromatography is a technique that separates compounds based on differences in their intermolecular interactions between a mobile phase and a stationary phase.

In this experiment, a mixture of food dyes is separated using paper chromatography. The dyes have varying degrees of polarizability, polarity, and charge, as can be seen in the structures below. Their interactions with the mobile phase (water) and the stationary phase (paper) are sufficiently different to allow good separation.

The Structures of Blue, Yellow, and Red Food Dye

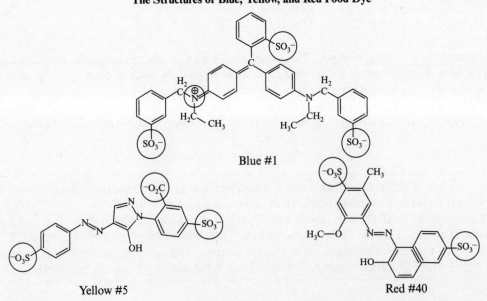

Blue #1

Yellow #5

Red #40

For a review of chromatography and the calculation of retention factor, R_f, see "Separation by Chromatography" on page 122.

Several different solvent systems are used, but the ones that give the best separation of the dyes are water and isopropyl alcohol.

Separation of Food Dyes by Paper Chromatography

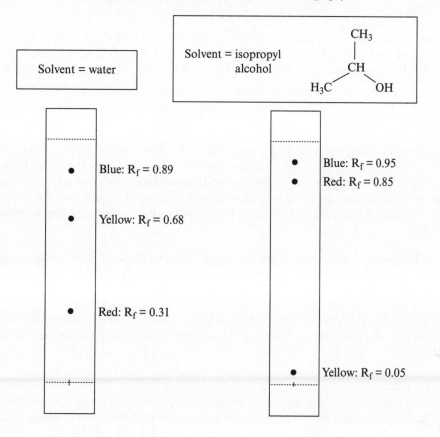

PRACTICE:

> Yellow food dye and red food dye have different retention factors in water and isopropyl alcohol. Which dye (red or yellow) experiences greater intermolecular attractions with water, and which experiences greater attractions with isopropyl alcohol?

Yellow food dye travels farther up the paper when water is used as the mobile phase than it does when isopropyl alcohol is the mobile phase. Red dye travels farther up the paper when isopropyl alcohol is the mobile phase than it does when water is the mobile phase. Yellow food dye experiences greater attractions to water than to isopropyl alcohol, and red food dye experiences greater attractions to isopropyl alcohol than to water.

Experiment 6: Ionic, Covalent, and Metallic Bonds

In this experiment, various unknown solids are classified by bonding type: ionic, polar covalent, nonpolar covalent, or metallic. Unknown substances may include the following:

Ionic	Covalent (polar)	Covalent (nonpolar)	Metallic
NH_4Cl	$C_6H_5CO_2H$ (benzoic acid)	Wax	Aluminum
MgO	$C_{12}H_{22}O_{11}$ (sucrose)	Iodine (I_2)	Magnesium

Methods for determination include assessment of water solubility, pH, melting point, and electrical conductivity.

Solubility in water: All ammonium salts are soluble, so NH_4Cl will dissolve. Also soluble are MgO, $C_6H_5CO_2H$, and $C_{12}H_{22}O_{11}$. Wax, iodine, aluminum, and magnesium are insoluble.

Remember: A compound is not necessarily soluble in water merely because it is ionic. Some ionic compounds have low K_{sp} values.

- The pH of the resulting aqueous solution may be higher or lower than 7. The pH values of solutions of NH_4^+ and benzoic acid are slightly lower than 7. The pH value of MgO is higher than 7 due to the formation of a hydroxide in aqueous solution: $MgO + H_2O \rightarrow Mg(OH)_2$. The sucrose solution is neutral.
- The conductivity of the aqueous solution indicates the presence of ions. NH_4Cl and MgO ($Mg(OH)_2$) are highly conductive strong electrolytes in aqueous solution. Benzoic acid, a weak acid, is weakly conductive, and sucrose is a nonelectrolyte.

Melting point determination can distinguish between molecular solids and ionic solids. The coulombic attraction between oppositely charged ions is much stronger than the intermolecular forces that hold the molecules of a molecular solid together. The melting point of benzoic acid, a molecular solid, is much lower than an ionic compound. A simple test for a low melting point is to place a small amount of the solid on the clean lid of an aluminum can. The lid is placed on a hot plate and heated. If the solid melts, the melting point is reasonably low, and the solid is not ionic.

Metallic solids can be distinguished from nonpolar covalent solids by their electrical conductivity. If a sample is conductive in the solid state, the electron sea model of bonding applies. A solid that is not conductive and not soluble in water is likely to be a nonpolar covalent compound.

A final test for a nonpolar covalent compound is dissolution of the compound in a nonpolar solvent such as hexane. Iodine and wax are soluble in hexane, while metals such as aluminum and magnesium are not.

PRACTICE:

> A solid green crystalline sample appears to be insoluble in deionized water. The solution exhibits slight electrical conductivity, and the pH of the water is greater than 7. When a few drops of aqueous HCl are added to the solution, more of the solid dissolves. The sample is insoluble in hexane, chloroform, and ethanol. When the solid is heated to the maximum temperature that can be achieved with a hot plate, it does not melt. Is the solid ionic, polar covalent, nonpolar covalent, or metallic?

The insolubility of the compound in water does not rule out any of the four possible bonding types.

The high pH of the solution rules out weak acids but not weak bases. The sample is unlikely to be metallic since it is a green crystal. The slight electrical conductivity of the solution confirms that the sample is either an ionic compound with a low K_{sp} or a weakly basic polar covalent compound.

The high melting point and insolubility in solvents such as hexane, chloroform, and ethanol suggest that this solid is an insoluble ionic compound.

Experiment 7: Decomposition Stoichiometry

In this experiment, the composition of a mixture of $NaHCO_3$ and Na_2CO_3 is determined. One of the compounds, $NaHCO_3$, undergoes decomposition upon heating, but the sample is not heated to a temperature high enough to decompose Na_2CO_3.

$$2\,NaHCO_3(s) \xrightarrow{\Delta} Na_2CO_3(s) + H_2O(g) + CO_2(g)$$

By comparing the mass of the mixture with the mass of the decomposed sample, the number of moles of $CO_2(g)$ lost can be determined. This information may be used to find the mass of the $NaHCO_3(s)$ in the original sample.

The technique for heating the mixture involves placing it in a pre-weighed crucible, covering it with the lid askew so that gases do not build up and blow off the lid, and heating the crucible in a ceramic triangle over a Bunsen burner. After the sample is removed from the heat, it is allowed to cool completely before the mass is determined.

Heating a Laboratory Crucible over a Bunsen Burner

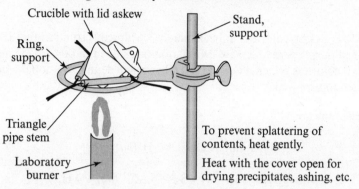

Crucible with lid askew

Ring, support

Triangle pipe stem

Laboratory burner

Stand, support

To prevent splattering of contents, heat gently.

Heat with the cover open for drying precipitates, ashing, etc.

PRACTICE:

A mixture of solid Na_2CO_3 and $NaHCO_3$ has a mass of 1.073 g. The mixture is placed in a crucible with a mass of 23.940 g. After heating to constant mass and cooling, the mass of the crucible plus the sample is 24.728 g.

(a) What is the percentage of $NaHCO_3$ in the original mixture?

(b) Would the calculated percentage be too high or too low if an additional impurity with a very high melting point was present in the mixture?

(a) The mass of the crucible plus the original sample is

$$23.940 \text{ g} + 1.073 \text{ g} = 25.013 \text{ g}$$

The mass of the sample that was lost is

$$25.013 \text{ g} - 24.728 \text{ g} = 0.285 \text{ g}$$

The mass of the sample that was lost is due to a 1:1 ratio of CO_2 (MW = 44.01 g·mol^{-1}) and H_2O (MW = 18.02 g·mol^{-1}). Let x be equal to the number of moles of CO_2 lost and the number of moles of H_2O lost.

$$\text{mass lost} = x(44.01 \text{ g} \cdot \text{mol}^{-1}) + x(18.02 \text{ g} \cdot \text{mol}^{-1}) = 0.285 \text{ g}$$
$$x(44.01 + 18.02) = 0.285$$
$$x = 0.00459 \text{ mol } H_2O = 0.00459 \text{ mol } CO_2$$

The balanced chemical equation shows that the stoichiometric ratio of $NaHCO_3$ to CO_2 is 2:1. Therefore,

$$0.00459 \text{ mol } CO_2 \times \frac{2 \text{ mol } NaHCO_3}{1 \text{ mol } CO_2} \times \frac{84.01 \text{ g } NaHCO_3}{1 \text{ mol } NaHCO_3} = 0.771 \text{ g } NaHCO_3$$

The mass percentage of $NaHCO_3$ in the original sample is

$$\frac{0.771 \text{ g } NaHCO_3}{1.073 \text{ g sample}} \times 100\% = 71.9\% \text{ } NaHCO_3$$

(b) A second impurity would cause the calculated mass of $NaHCO_3$ to be artificially high. The calculated mass percentage, therefore, would also be artificially high.

Experiment 8: Redox Titration

Titrations are not limited to acid-base reactions. Concentrations can be determined by titrations that exploit redox reactivity as well. In this experiment, the concentration of H_2O_2 in a commercial bottle of peroxide is determined by redox titration.

Hydrogen peroxide, H_2O_2, is a clear, colorless, approximately 3% aqueous solution that is used as an antiseptic and bleaching agent. When purple permanganate, MnO_4^-, ions are added to peroxide in acidic solution, they are oxidized to Mn^{2+}, which is colorless. When all of the H_2O_2 has reacted, any additional MnO_4^- added to the solution will cause the solution to turn pink.

The two relevant half reactions are

$$H_2O_2(aq) \rightarrow O_2(g) + 2\ H^+(aq) + 2\ e^-$$

$$MnO_4^-(aq) + 8\ H^+(aq) + 5\ e- \rightarrow Mn^{2+}(aq) + 4\ H_2O(l)$$

The overall balanced equation is

$$5\ H_2O_2(aq) + 2\ MnO_4^-(aq) + 6\ H^+(aq) \rightarrow 5\ O_2(g) + 2\ Mn^{2+}(aq) + 8\ H_2O(l)$$

PRACTICE:

> A 10.00-mL solution of H_2O_2 of unknown concentration is titrated with 61.42 mL of a standardized 0.04020 M MnO_4^- solution. What is the percent by mass of H_2O_2 in the original sample? Assume the density of the H_2O_2 solution is 1.000 $g \cdot mL^{-1}$.

The number of grams of H_2O_2 in the sample is determined by determining the number of moles of MnO_4^-, and then converting to moles of H_2O_2 stoichiometrically. The number of moles of H_2O_2 can be converted to grams by multiplication by the molar mass.

$$0.06142\ \text{L MnO}_4^- \times \frac{0.04020\ \text{mol MnO}_4^-}{1\ \text{L MnO}_4^-} \times \frac{5\ \text{mol H}_2\text{O}_2}{2\ \text{mol MnO}_4^-} \times \frac{34.02\ \text{g H}_2\text{O}_2}{1\ \text{mol H}_2\text{O}_2} = 0.2100\ \text{g H}_2\text{O}_2$$

From the density, we know that the 10.00-mL sample of H_2O_2 solution had a mass of 10.00 g. The percent H_2O_2 by mass in the sample is

$$\frac{0.2100\ \text{g H}_2\text{O}_2}{10.00\ \text{g solution}} \times 100\% = 2.100\%$$

Experiment 9: Liquid-Liquid Extraction

Liquid-liquid extraction is the technique of partitioning a solute between two immiscible liquid phases due to selective solubility in only one of the phases. In this experiment, students separate aspirin from acetaminophen in a separatory funnel.

The analgesics are first dissolved in ethyl acetate, an organic solvent.

The Structures of Aspirin, Acetaminophen, and Ethyl Acetate

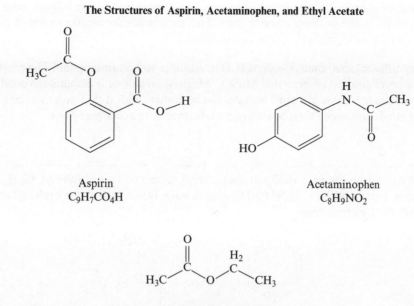

Aspirin
$C_9H_7CO_4H$

Acetaminophen
$C_8H_9NO_2$

Ethyl acetate solvent

The solution is added to a separatory funnel, and then an aqueous solution of $NaHCO_3$ is added. Because water does not mix with ethyl acetate and because water is more dense than ethyl acetate, water forms the bottom layer in the separatory funnel. Neither aspirin nor acetaminophen is soluble in water.

The separatory funnel is next shaken gently (with frequent venting to prevent pressure buildup), exposing the solutes in the ethyl acetate layer to the aqueous $NaHCO_3$. Because aspirin is a weak acid, it is deprotonated by HCO_3^-, forming the sodium salt. The acetaminophen does not react and remains dissolved in the ethyl acetate layer.

The sodium salt of aspirin is no longer soluble in ethyl acetate. As a result of further shaking and venting, the aspirin anion, which is water-soluble, is partitioned into the water layer, or aqueous phase. The resulting H_2CO_3 decomposes into water and carbon dioxide.

$$C_9H_7CO_4H + HCO_3^- \rightarrow C_9H_7CO_4^- + H_2CO_3 \rightarrow C_9H_7CO_4^- + H_2O + CO_2$$

Use of a Separatory Funnel to Separate Aspirin from Acetaminophen

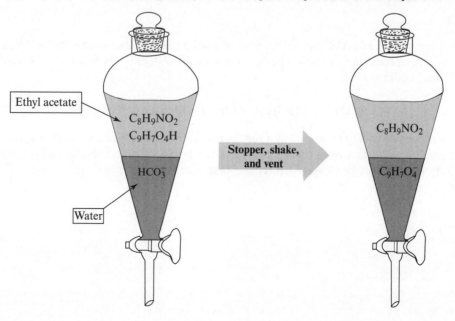

The aspirin sodium salt solution is drained out of the separatory funnel, separating it from the ethyl acetate layer. Aqueous HCl is then added to the drained aqueous layer. This protonates the aspirin so that it is, once again, insoluble in water. It forms a solid precipitate that can be filtered.

The ethyl acetate layer still contains some dissolved H_2O in addition to acetaminophen. The ethyl acetate can be dried by addition of a small amount of insoluble $MgSO_4$. Magnesium sulfate is insoluble in ethyl acetate, but it attracts the water molecules present in the ethyl acetate. The hydrated solid $MgSO_4$ can then be filtered off, taking the water with it. The ethyl acetate can then be evaporated, leaving pure acetaminophen.

PRACTICE:

A solution of dichloromethane, CH_2Cl_2, in a separatory funnel contains biphenyl, $C_{12}H_{10}$, a neutral compound, and 3-nitroaniline, $C_6H_4NO_2NH_2$, a weak base. Describe how the biphenyl might be separated from the 3-nitroaniline.

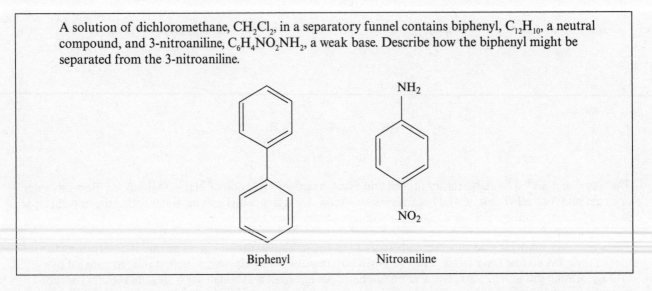

Biphenyl   Nitroaniline

An aqueous solution of HCl can be added to the separatory funnel. The contents of the funnel are shaken and vented to expose the solutes in the CH_2Cl_2 layer to the HCl in the aqueous layer. The 3-nitroaniline will be protonated $-NH_2$ nitrogen, resulting in a water-soluble cation, $-NH_3^+$, while biphenyl will remain in the CH_2Cl_2 layer. The two layers are then separated, and the CH_2Cl_2 layer is dried. The aqueous layer can be neutralized with aqueous $NaHCO_3$, resulting in a neutral 3-nitroaniline precipitate, which can be removed from the water by filtration.

Experiment 10: Measurement of the Rate of a Chemical Reaction

This experiment examines the effect of the surface area of a solid reactant and concentration of an aqueous reactant on the rate of a gas-producing reaction. The reaction under investigation is between solid marble chips, composed of $CaCO_3$, and aqueous HCl.

$$CaCO_3(s) + 2\ HCl(aq) \rightarrow CaCl_2(aq) + H_2O(l) + CO_2(g)$$

The volume of gas collected can be measured as a function of time using either a syringe in a rubber stopper or a eudiometer (see page 345). Alternatively, the reaction flask can be placed on a balance, and the mass, which decreases as CO_2 is released, can be measured at regular time intervals.

Two Pieces of Apparatus for Measuring the Rate of Gas Formation

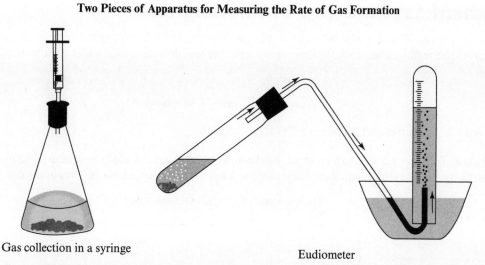

Gas collection in a syringe

Eudiometer

The volume of gas collected is measured at regular, timed intervals, and the data is graphed as shown below.

The Rate of Calcium Carbonate Decomposition

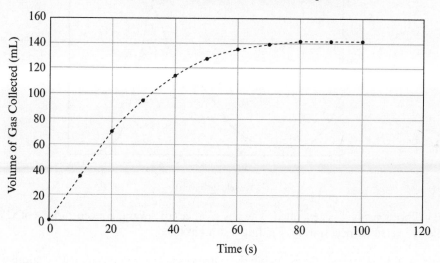

PRACTICE:

> A student places 1-cm³ marble chips in an Erlenmeyer flask, adds excess 1.0 M HCl, stoppers the flask with a gas collection syringe, and records the volume of gas collected at regular intervals. What are two ways in which the student might cause the rate of the reaction to increase?

Two simple ways to increase the rate of the reaction are to increase the surface area of the marble chips by breaking or grinding or to increase the concentration of the HCl used. Both of these actions increase the frequency of sufficiently energetic collisions that have the necessary orientations of reactants for the reaction to occur.

Experiment 11: Rate Law Determination

The rate law for the reaction of a colored reactant can be determined by following the decrease in concentration of the reactant spectrophotometrically. In this experiment, the reaction of crystal violet with hydroxide is investigated.

$$CV^+(aq) + OH^-(aq) \rightarrow CVOH(aq)$$

The unreacted CV^+ is purple, and the reacted CVOH is colorless.

A standard sample of CV^+ is added to a cuvette, and the absorption of crystal violet is measured across the spectrum of visible wavelengths. The wavelength with the greatest absorption is chosen, about 600 nm in the case of CV^+.

The Absorbance Spectrum of Crystal Violet

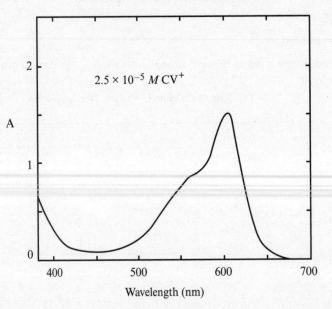

Wavelength (nm)

Next, a standard calibration curve is generated. The absorbances of several concentrations of CV^+ are measured. Absorbance is plotted versus concentration, yielding a straight line.

The concentrations of CV^+ at various times during the data collection are determined by comparing the absorbance of the reaction mixture with the standard calibration curve as described in "Measuring Concentration Using Spectrophotometry" on page 118.

The overall rate law for the reaction is

$$\text{rate} = k[CV^+]^x[OH^-]^y$$

Hydroxide is used in such a large excess that its concentration changes only slightly compared with the change in concentration of CV^+. In other words, the concentration of OH^- is approximately constant. The rate law can be simplified to

$$\text{rate} = k'[CV^+]^x$$

where

$$k' = k[OH^-]^y$$

The concentration of CV^+ as a function of time is used to generate three plots: $[CV^+]$ versus time (zero order), ln $[CV^+]$ versus time (first order), and $[CV^+]^{-1}$ versus time (second order).

PRACTICE:

The following data was collected in a crystal violet fading experiment. What is the order with respect to $[CV^+]$?

Time (s)	$[CV^+]$ (M)
40	1.825×10^{-5}
80	1.742×10^{-5}
120	1.664×10^{-5}
160	1.585×10^{-5}
200	1.509×10^{-5}
240	1.434×10^{-5}
280	1.370×10^{-5}
320	1.300×10^{-5}
360	1.233×10^{-5}
400	1.168×10^{-5}
440	1.110×10^{-5}
480	1.051×10^{-5}

Three plots of the data are shown below. In the classroom, these graphs would be generated using a graphing calculator or a program such as Microsoft Excel. It is highly unlikely that students will be asked to generate plots like these on the AP Chemistry exam, but they will need to do so in class, and they must understand how the plots are generated.

Because all three plots appear linear, notice the correlation of determination, R^2, value underneath the equation for each line. The closer this value is to 1, the better the data fits the calculated linear equation.

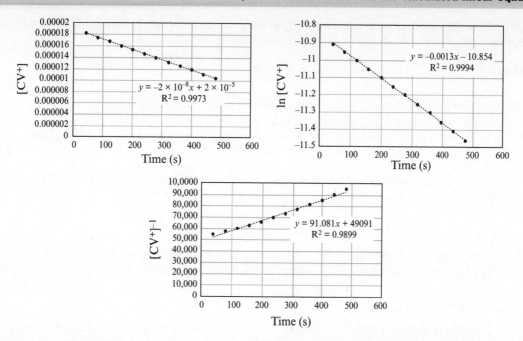

The linear plot of $\ln [CV^+]$ versus time indicates that the reaction is first order with respect to $[CV^+]$.

Experiment 12: Constant Pressure Calorimetry

The purpose of this calorimetry experiment is to determine the amount of heat absorbed or gained when various ionic solids are dissolved in water. For a review of the theory behind coffee cup calorimetry, refer to "Calorimetry" on page 231.

The first requirement is measurement of the calorimeter constant. This is the amount of heat transferred to or from the calorimeter per degree of temperature change. This is measured by adding a volume of warm water to a water sample in the calorimeter and measuring the temperature change of the mixture.

PRACTICE:

> A 25.0-g sample of water at 60. °C is added to a 25.0-g sample of water at 22 °C in a coffee cup calorimeter. After 15 seconds, the combined water in the calorimeter has a maximum temperature of 40. °C. The specific heat capacity of water is $4.18 \ J \cdot g^{-1} \cdot °C^{-1}$. What is the calorimeter constant, c_{cal}? Report your answer in units of $J \cdot °C^{-1}$.

The heat lost by the warm water as it is added to the calorimeter is equal to the heat that is gained by the cool water and the calorimeter.

$$q_{lost} = -q_{gained}$$

$$q_{hot} = -\left(q_{cold} + q_{cal}\right)$$

$$m_{hot} c_{H_2O} \Delta T_{hot} = -\left(m_{cold} c_{H_2O} \Delta T_{cold} + c_{cal} \Delta T_{cold}\right)$$

$$(25.0 \ \cancel{g})(4.18 \ J \cdot \cancel{g^{-1}} \cdot \cancel{°C^{-1}})(40. \ \cancel{°C} - 60. \ \cancel{°C}) = -[(25.0 \ \cancel{g})(4.18 \ J \cdot \cancel{g^{-1}} \cdot \cancel{°C^{-1}})(40. \ \cancel{°C} - 22 \ \cancel{°C}) + c_{cal}(40. °C - 22 °C)]$$

$$c_{cal} = 12 \ J \cdot °C^{-1}$$

The amount of energy absorbed or released by a known quantity of a salt can be used to determine the enthalpy of dissolution.

PRACTICE:

> The calorimeter from the preceding practice problem contains 25.0 g of water at 22.0 °C. A 1.00-g sample of $CaCl_2$ is added, and the solution is stirred. The final temperature of the solution is 27.8 °C. What is the enthalpy of dissolution, ΔH_{soln}, of $CaCl_2$? Report your answer in units of $kJ \cdot mol^{-1}$.

The total amount of heat released by the dissolution, q_{rxn}, is equal in magnitude to the sum of the heat that raises the temperature of the solution, q_{soln}, and the heat that is lost to the calorimeter, q_{cal}.

$$q_{rxn} = -(q_{soln} + q_{cal})$$

The mass, m, of the water is 25.0 g. Notice that only two significant figures can be reported for q_{rxn}, but the entire calculated value should be carried through to the next step to avoid a rounding error.

$$q_{rxn} = -[(mc\Delta T) + (c_{cal}\Delta T)]$$

$$q_{rxn} = -[(25.0 \ \cancel{g})(4.18 \ J \cdot \cancel{g^{-1}} \cdot \cancel{°C^{-1}})(27.8 \ \cancel{°C} - 22.0 \ \cancel{°C}) + (12 \ J \cdot \cancel{°C^{-1}})(27.8 \ \cancel{°C} - 22.0 \ \cancel{°C})]$$

$$q_{rxn} = -680 \ J \quad (-675.7)$$

In order to report the enthalpy change per mole of $CaCl_2$ dissolved, the number of grams of $CaCl_2$ is converted to moles.

$$1.00 \ \text{g CaCl}_2 \times \frac{1 \ \text{mol CaCl}_2}{110.98 \ \text{g CaCl}_2} = 0.00901 \ \text{mol CaCl}_2$$

The total heat divided by the number of moles is the heat of dissolution.

$$\Delta H_{\text{rxn}} = \frac{-675.7 \ \text{J}}{0.00901 \ \text{mol CaCl}_2} \times \frac{1 \ \text{kJ}}{1000 \ \text{J}} = -75 \ \text{kJ} \cdot \text{mol}^{-1}$$

Experiment 13: Le Chatelier's Principle

In this lab, students apply Le Chatelier's principle to equilibrium systems in order to generate solutions of different colors. In order to shift the equilibria and change the color of the solutions, students will apply different "stresses" to the equilibrium systems.

- Bromothymol blue is an acid-base indicator. An aqueous solution of bromothymol blue is green in its neutral form, yellow in the presence of acid, and blue in the presence of base. The equilibrium can be shifted by addition of acid or base.

$$\text{BTB-H} + H_2O \ \rightleftharpoons \ \text{BTB}^- + H_3O^+$$
Yellow   Blue

Addition of acid, H_3O^+, shifts the equilibrium to the left, so the solution appears yellow. Addition of OH^- removes H_3O^+ from solution, shifting the equilibrium back to the right, so the solution appears blue.

- When aqueous solutions of Fe^{3+} and SCN^- are mixed, an equilibrium is established with $FeSCN^{2+}$.

$$Fe^{3+} + SCN^- \ \rightleftharpoons \ FeSCN^{2+}$$
Yellow   Dark red

Addition of Fe^{3+} in the form of $FeCl_3$ shifts the equilibrium to the right, so more of the dark red complex is formed. Addition of SCN^- in the form of KSCN also shifts the equilibrium to the right. Addition of PO_4^{3-} in the form of Na_3PO_4, however, forms an insoluble precipitate, $FePO_4$. This compound removes the Fe^{3+} from the solution, which shifts the equilibrium to the left.

- An aqueous solution of Cu^{2+} ions forms a pale blue precipitate with OH^- when a small amount of NH_3, a weak base, is added.

$$Cu^{2+}(aq) + 2 \ OH^-(aq) \ \rightleftharpoons \ Cu(OH)_2(s)$$
Blue   Pale blue
                         precipitate

When additional NH_3 is added, Cu^{2+} from the $Cu(OH)_2$ precipitate forms a complex ion with NH_3.

$$Cu(OH)_2(s) + 4 \ NH_3(aq) + 2 \ H_2O(l) \ \rightleftharpoons \ [Cu(NH_3)_4(H_2O)_2]^{2+}(aq) + 2 \ OH^-(aq)$$
Pale blue   Dark blue
precipitate

- Addition of Cl^- in the form of HCl to a solution of hexaaquacopper(II) shifts the equilibrium toward the green tetrachlorocopper(II) form. Addition of excess H_2O shifts the equilibrium back toward reactants.

$$[Cu(H_2O)_6]^{2+} + 4\ Cl^- \rightleftharpoons [CuCl_4]^{2-} + 6\ H_2O$$
$$\text{Blue} \qquad\qquad\qquad\qquad \text{Green}$$

- The reaction of a solution of hexaaquacobalt(II) with chloride in ethanol is endothermic. Addition of Cl^- or heating the reaction will cause the equilibrium to shift toward products. Addition of Ag^+ ions will drive the equilibrium toward reactants since AgCl is an insoluble precipitate, removing Cl^- from solution.

$$[Co(H_2O)_6]^{2+} + 4\ Cl^- \rightleftharpoons [CoCl_4]^{2-} + 6\ H_2O$$
$$\text{Pink} \qquad\qquad\qquad\qquad \text{Blue}$$

- A solution of carbonated water, which has been produced by adding CO_2 to water, undergoes several equilibrium processes. Carbonation in water causes added methyl red to appear red.

$$CO_2(g) \rightleftharpoons CO_2(aq) + H_2O(l) \rightleftharpoons H_2CO_3(aq) \rightleftharpoons HCO_3^-(aq) + H_3O^+(aq)$$

The disappearance of H_3O^+ causes methyl red to appear yellow.

The presence of H_3O^+ causes methyl red to appear red.

A syringe is filled with carbonated water to which a few drops of methyl red have been added. The air is expelled from the syringe, and the syringe tip is then closed with a Luer Lock valve.

Syringe with Luer Lock

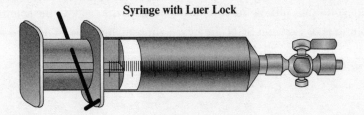

The plunger of the syringe is pulled back to increase the volume and decrease the pressure (it creates a "suction"). This shifts the equilibrium toward reactants, which include $CO_2(g)$, so the methyl red indicator turns yellow.

Experiment 14: Acid-Base Titration Curves

In this lab exercise, students will titrate various strong and weak acids and bases. This titration requires the same practical skills as the previous titrations in experiments 4 and 8. In this experiment, however, students will need to be able to tell whether the acid or base is strong or weak by the shape of the titration curve. Instead of an indicator, a pH meter is used.

For a detailed review of acid-base titration curves, refer to page 294.

When a strong acid is titrated with a strong base, the S-shaped titration curve begins at a low pH, rises steadily until just before the equivalence point, passes through the equivalence point at a pH of 7, and then levels off. When a strong base is titrated with a strong acid, the S-shaped titration curve begins at a high pH, decreases steadily until just before the equivalence point, passes through the equivalence point at a pH of 7, and then levels off. Students are expected to identify the analyte as a strong acid or a strong base by the shape of the titration curve.

Titration Curves for Strong Acids and Strong Bases

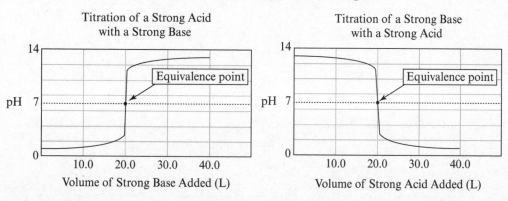

When a weak acid is titrated, the initial pH of the analyte is not as low as that of a strong acid. The pH rises gradually with added strong base in the buffering region until just before the equivalence point. When half of an equivalent of base has been added, the pH of the solution is equal to the pK_a of the weak acid. At the equivalence point, the pH is greater than 7 because the major species in solution, the conjugate base of a weak acid, is a weak base.

Titration of a Weak Acid with a Strong Base

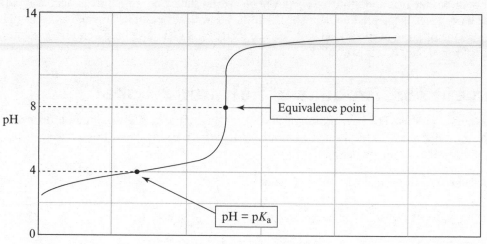

Volume of MOH Added (L)

The pH of a solution of a weak base is less than that of a strong base. The curve features a buffering region in which the pH changes gradually. When exactly half of an equivalent of the strong acid has been added, the pOH of the solution is equal to the pK_b of the weak base. Finally, the pH at the equivalence point of the titration is less than 7, because the conjugate acid of a weak base is a weak acid.

When the salt of a weak acid is titrated with a strong acid, the titration curve is that of a weak base with a strong acid. When the salt of a weak base is titrated with a strong base, the titration curve is that of a weak acid with a strong base.

Titration of a Weak Base with a Strong Acid

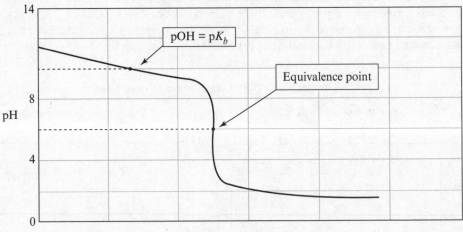

PRACTICE:

> Does it take more, less, or the same amount of 0.100 M NaOH to titrate 25 mL of 0.100 M nitrous acid and 25 mL of 0.100 M nitric acid to the equivalence points? How do the pH values at the equivalence points compare?

The volume of 0.100 M NaOH required to titrate 25 mL of 0.100 M nitrous acid to the equivalence point will be the same as the volume required to titrate 25 mL of 0.100 M nitric acid to the equivalence point. The pH at the equivalence point for the titration of nitrous acid will be greater than 7 because nitrous acid is a weak acid, and its conjugate base, which is the predominant species at the equivalence point, is a weak base. The pH at the equivalence point for the titration of nitric acid is 7, because the H^+ and OH^- have been completely neutralized, and the salt that is formed, $NaNO_3$, is neutral.

Experiment 15: Titrations of Polyprotic Acids

The titration curves produced by the titration of phosphoric and citric acid with sodium hydroxide are more complex than those produced by the titration of monoprotic acids with strong bases. For a review of polyprotic titration curves, refer to the section on page 303.

Phosphoric acid is a triprotic acid with three K_a values.

$H_3PO_4(aq) + H_2O(l) \rightleftharpoons H_2PO_4^-(aq) + H_3O^+(aq)$	$K_{a_1} = 7.5 \times 10^{-3}$	$pK_{a_1} = 2.12$
$H_2PO_4^-(aq) + H_2O(l) \rightleftharpoons HPO_4^{2-}(aq) + H_3O^+(aq)$	$K_{a_2} = 6.2 \times 10^{-8}$	$pK_{a_2} = 7.21$
$HPO_4^{2-}(aq) + H_2O(l) \rightleftharpoons PO_4^{3-}(aq) + H_3O^+(aq)$	$K_{a_3} = 4.8 \times 10^{-13}$	$pK_{a_3} = 12.3$

There are two distinct equivalence points in the titration curve, but the third equivalence point is obscure. This is because PO_4^{3-} is almost as strongly basic as OH^-; no sharp increase in pH is observed.

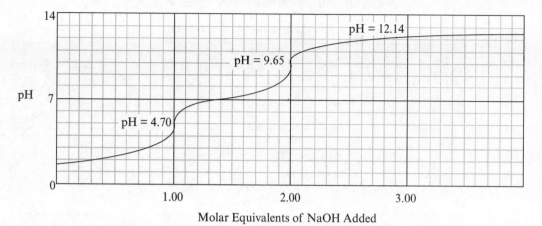

Titration of Phosphoric Acid with NaOH

PRACTICE:

> List the major species present, other than water, in a 30 mL of 0.100 M solution of phosphoric acid in the following scenarios:
>
> **(a)** Before NaOH has been added
>
> **(b)** After 15 mL of 0.100 M NaOH have been added
>
> **(c)** After 30 mL of 0.100 M NaOH have been added
>
> **(d)** After 60 mL of 0.100 M NaOH have been added
>
> **(e)** After 100 mL of 0.100 M NaOH have been added

(a) Before NaOH has been added, the major species in solution is H_3PO_4. (The minor species are H_3O^+ and $H_2PO_4^-$).

(b) After 15 mL of 0.100 M NaOH have been added, halfway to the first equivalence point, H_3PO_4, $H_2PO_4^-$, and Na^+ are the major species in solution.

(c) After 30 mL of 0.100 M NaOH, or one equivalent of OH^-, have been added, $H_2PO_4^-$ and Na^+ are the major species in solution.

(d) After 60 mL of 0.100 M NaOH, or two equivalents of OH^-, have been added, HPO_4^{2-} and Na^+ are the major species in solution.

(e) After 100 mL of 0.100 M NaOH, or three equivalents of OH^-, have been added, PO_4^{3-}, OH^-, and Na^+ are the major species in the solution.

Citric acid, $H_3C_6H_5O_7$, is also a triprotic acid.

$H_3C_6H_5O_7(aq) + H_2O(l) \rightleftharpoons H_2C_6H_5O_7^-(aq) + H_3O^+(aq)$	$K_{a_1} = 8.4 \times 10^{-4}$	$pK_{a_1} = 3.07$
$H_2C_6H_5O_7^-(aq) + H_2O(l) \rightleftharpoons HC_6H_5O_7^{2-}(aq) + H_3O^+(aq)$	$K_{a_2} = 1.8 \times 10^{-5}$	$pK_{a_2} = 4.74$
$HC_6H_5O_7^{2-}(aq) + H_2O(l) \rightleftharpoons C_6H_5O_7^{3-}(aq) + H_3O^+(aq)$	$K_{a_3} = 4.0 \times 10^{-6}$	$pK_{a_3} = 5.40$

The titration curve for citric acid is shown below. Notice that there are not three distinct equivalence points in the titration. Instead, the pH increases steadily until just before the third equivalence point.

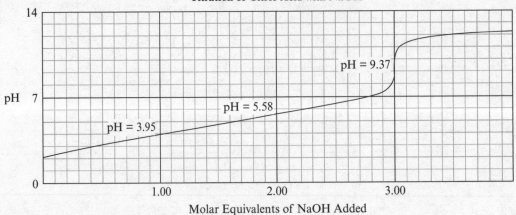

Titration of Citric Acid with NaOH

Because the pH values of the solution at the first two equivalence points are so similar, sharp rises in the pH are not observed. Instead, the buffering regions blend together, resulting in a steadily rising pH.

Experiment 16: Buffer Preparation

The final experiment in the AP Chemistry laboratory program is to generate a buffer of a particular pH and buffer capacity. For a review of buffer solutions, see page 290.

Students are given a list of available materials and a target pH for their buffer. For example, suppose the goal is to produce a 50-mL sample of a buffer that can maintain a pH of 4.74 when HCl or NaOH is added. The materials provided are a 0.1 M solution of CH_3CO_2H and solid CH_3CO_2Na.

The K_a of acetic acid is 1.8×10^{-5}. The pK_a is 4.74. Therefore, a 1:1 mole ratio of $CH_3CO_2H:CH_3CO_2Na$ will result in a solution with a pH of 4.74. The Henderson-Hasselbalch equation can be used to verify this.

$$pH = pK_a + \log \frac{[CH_3CO_2^-]}{[CH_3CO_2H]} = -\log 1.8 \times 10^{-5} + \log 1 = 4.74 + 0$$

In order to generate such a solution, the mass of CH_3CO_2Na that must be added to 50 mL of a 0.1 M solution of CH_3CO_2H must be determined.

$$0.050 \text{ L } CH_3CO_2H \times \frac{0.10 \text{ mol } CH_3CO_2H}{1 \text{ L } CH_3CO_2H} \times \frac{1 \text{ mol } CH_3CO_2Na}{1 \text{ mol } CH_3CO_2H} \times \frac{89.04 \text{ g } CH_3CO_2Na}{1 \text{ mol } CH_3CO_2Na} = 0.45 \text{ g } CH_3CO_2Na$$

PRACTICE:

(a) Calculate the resulting pH after 10 mL of 0.01 M NaOH have been added to 50 mL of a buffer that is orginally 0.1 M in CH_3CO_2H and 0.1 M in CH_3CO_2Na.

(b) Calculate the resulting pH after 10 mL of 0.01 M NaOH have been added to 50 mL of a buffer that is orginally 1.0 M in CH_3CO_2H and 1.0 M in CH_3CO_2Na. Account for the discrepancy in the pH values in parts (a) and (b).

(a) The first task is to determine how many moles of acid and conjugate base are present initially.

$$0.05 \; \text{L CH}_3\text{CO}_2\text{H} \times \frac{0.1 \text{ mol CH}_3\text{CO}_2\text{H}}{1 \text{ L CH}_3\text{CO}_2\text{H}} = 0.005 \text{ mol CH}_3\text{CO}_2\text{H} = 0.005 \text{ mol CH}_3\text{CO}_2\text{Na}$$

Next, the number of moles of OH^- added are needed.

$$0.01 \; \text{L NaOH} \times \frac{0.1 \text{ mol NaOH}}{1 \text{ L NaOH}} = 0.001 \text{ mol OH}^-$$

The OH^- reacts with the CH_3CO_2H to form $CH_3CO_2^-$.

$$CH_3CO_2H + OH^- \rightarrow CH_3CO_2^- + H_2O$$

The OH^- is the limiting reagent, so it reacts completely to yield 0.006 mol $CH_3CO_2^-$ and 0.004 mol CH_3CO_2H.

Because the volume is the same in the concentration ratio, the Henderson-Hasselbalch equation can be solved with the numbers of moles.

$$pH = 4.7 + \log\left(\frac{0.006}{0.004}\right) = 4.9$$

(b) The same procedure is used to determine the pH of the more concentrated buffer after NaOH has been added. The first step is to determine the numbers of moles of acid and conjugate base that are present initially.

$$0.05 \; \text{L CH}_3\text{CO}_2\text{H} \times \frac{1.0 \text{ mol CH}_3\text{CO}_2\text{H}}{1 \text{ L CH}_3\text{CO}_2\text{H}} = 0.05 \text{ mol CH}_3\text{CO}_2\text{H} = 0.05 \text{ mol CH}_3\text{CO}_2\text{Na}$$

The 0.001 mole of OH^- added reacts with the CH_3CO_2H to form $CH_3CO_2^-$.

$$CH_3CO_2H + OH^- \rightarrow CH_3CO_2^- + H_2O$$

The OH^- is the limiting reagent, so it reacts completely to yield 0.051 mol $CH_3CO_2^-$ and 0.049 mol CH_3CO_2H.

Because the volume is the same in the concentration ratio, the Henderson-Hasselbalch equation can be solved with the numbers of moles.

$$pH = 4.7 + \log\left(\frac{0.051}{0.049}\right) = 4.7$$

The pH change is less for the more concentrated buffer because it has a higher buffer capacity. It is able to neutralize more base before a significant pH change is observed.

Review Questions

Multiple Choice

1. Which chemical is NOT a good choice for neutralizing an acid spill?

    A. Na_2CO_3

    B. $NaHCO_3$

    C. $CaCO_3$

    D. KOH

2. A sample transmits 10.0% of incident light at a given wavelength. What is the absorbance of the sample?

    A. 0.100
    B. 0.900
    C. 1.000
    D. 9.000

3. What volume should be reported for the buret reading shown below?

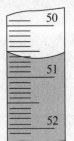

    A. 50.65 mL
    B. 50.6 mL
    C. 50.650 mL
    D. 51.3 mL

4. A student is performing a gravimetric analysis on a solution of Ca^{2+}. The student causes the calcium to precipitate by adding Na_2CO_3. The student filters the solid using a Buchner funnel and a piece of filter paper. Which of the following is LEAST likely to lead to an error in the mass of $CaCO_3$ determined?

    A. Neglecting to wash the sample with a small amount of deionized, neutral H_2O.
    B. Failing to add an excess of Na_2CO_3.
    C. Breaking up the wet solid with a spatula before allowing it to dry for an additional length of time.
    D. Washing the sample with large amounts of deionized, neutral H_2O.

5. Compound A and compound B are separated by paper chromatography in which hexane, C_6H_{12}, is used as the mobile phase. Compound A has an R_f of 0.75, and compound B has an R_f of 0.25. Which of the following is true?

    A. Compound B is less polar than compound A and experiences greater intermolecular attractions with hexane than with paper.
    B. Compound A is less polar than compound B and experiences greater intermolecular attractions with hexane than with paper.
    C. Compound B is polar and experiences greater dipole-dipole attractions with hexane than with paper.
    D. Compound A is nonpolar and experiences greater London dispersion forces with hexane than with paper.

6. A lustrous, brittle gray solid is insoluble in water but soluble in CCl_4. It does not conduct electricity in its solid form. The solid has a melting point of 114 °C. What kind of bonding is likely to be present in the substance?

    A. Metallic
    B. Ionic
    C. Polar covalent
    D. Nonpolar covalent

7. Dichromate ions, $Cr_2O_7^{2-}$, are orange in aqueous solution, while chromate ions, CrO_4^{2-}, are yellow. In aqueous solution, the following equilibrium is established.

$$Cr_2O_7^{2-}(aq) + 3\ H_2O(l) \rightleftharpoons 2\ CrO_4^{2-}(aq) + 2\ H_3O^+(aq)$$

Which method would cause an aqueous solution of $Cr_2O_7^{2-}$ to appear yellow?

A. Addition of NaOH
B. Addition of HCl
C. Addition of $Na_2Cr_2O_7$ or NaOH
D. Addition of Na_2CrO_4 or HCl

8. A student would like to measure the enthalpy change for the reaction of dilute solutions of aqueous NaOH with H_2SO_4. Which of the following would NOT cause an incorrect result?

A. Assuming the heat capacities of the solutions are higher than the heat capacity of water
B. Failing to measure the calorimeter constant in order to account for heat lost to the surroundings
C. Assuming that the densities of the solutions are equal to the densities of pure water
D. Using initial solutions that are initially at different temperatures

9. Which of the following titration curves does NOT show the pH change when a triprotic acid is titrated with a strong base?

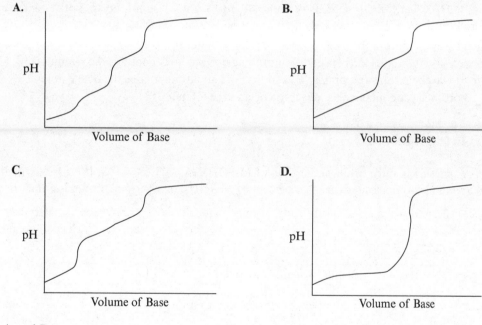

A. A and B
B. B and D
C. B, C, and D
D. D only

10. Beta carotene and vitamin B$_5$ are both compounds that are found in sweet potatoes. The structures of the two compounds are shown below.

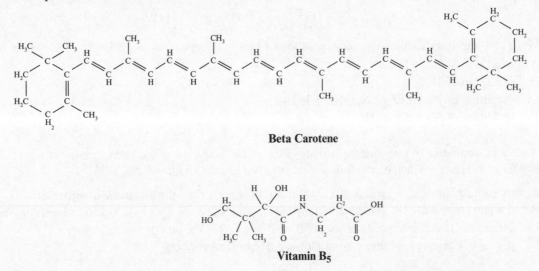

Beta Carotene

Vitamin B$_5$

A food scientist mixes a 1-g portion of finely ground sweet potato in a dish with 10-mL portion of ethanol. The solids are filtered, and the ethanol filtrate is added to a separatory funnel. A 100-mL portion of isooctane, $(CH_3)_3CCH_2CH(CH_3)_2$ (density = 0.692 g·mL^{-1}), and a 100-mL portion of water are added. The separatory funnel is stoppered and shaken with venting. When the layers settle,

A. the top layer contains the beta carotene and the vitamin B$_5$.

B. the top layer contains the beta carotene and the bottom layer contains the vitamin B$_5$.

C. the top layer contains the vitamin B$_5$ and the bottom layer contains the beta carotene.

D. the bottom layer contains the beta carotene and the vitamin B$_5$.

Long Free Response

1. Milk of magnesia is a milky white suspension of $Mg(OH)_2$ ($K_{sp} = 1.8 \times 10^{-11}$). It is used as an antacid. A student would like to determine the mass percent of $Mg(OH)_2$ in a particular brand of milk of magnesia.

A dropper is used to add approximately 1 mL of milk of magnesia to a pre-weighed vial and the mass is recorded.

Mass of vial (g)	17.873 g
Mass of vial with milk of magnesia (g)	20.369 g

The contents of the vial are rinsed into a 500-mL Erlenmeyer flask with plenty of distilled water, then the sample is diluted to a volume of about 100 mL. At this point the student observes a cloudy white color.

A buret is filled with 0.500 M standardized HCl, and 13.00 mL are added to the analyte. The solution turns clear, and when it is touched to a piece of litmus paper, the paper turns pink.

a. **i.** Write a net ionic equation for the reaction between $Mg(OH)_2$ and HCl.

ii. Explain why the litmus paper has turned pink.

b. A few drops of phenolphthalein are added to the analyte. Describe the expected appearance of the resulting solution.

c. The student standardizes a 0.1 M solution of NaOH. A 0.740-g sample of the monoprotic acid potassium hydrogen phthalate, KHP (MW = 204.23 g·mol^{-1}), is weighed into a second 500-mL Erlenmeyer flask. About 100 mL of distilled water are added. Phenolphthalein indicator is added to the solution, and then the solution is titrated with the NaOH solution. A total of 32.35 mL of NaOH are required to reach the endpoint.

What is the molarity of the NaOH solution?

d. The standardized NaOH is used to titrate the acidified milk of magnesia. A color change is observed after 8.17 mL of NaOH have been added.

How many moles of $Mg(OH)_2$ were present in the original sample?

e. What is the mass percent of $Mg(OH)_2$ in the original drugstore sample of milk of magnesia?

f. Phenolphthalein has a pK_a of 9.3. Compare this to the pH at the equivalence point of the titration of the acidified milk of magnesia sample and explain why phenolphthalein is or is not a suitable indicator for this titration.

2. A chemistry teacher is asked to prepare 500 mL of a buffer with a pH in the range of 10–11 for a special project in the biology classes.

The materials available are:

1000-mL Erlenmeyer flask   beakers of various sizes deionized water

500-mL graduated cylinder   pH meter

balance   thermometer

The teacher tests the pH of the available acid solutions in the biology storeroom:

Acid Solution	Concentration	pH at 25 °C
H-MES*	0.25 M	3.38
H-MOPS**	0.25 M	3.90
H-CAPS***	0.25 M	5.58

* H-MES: 4-Morpholineethanesulfonic acid
** H-MOPS: 4-Morpholinepropanesulfonic acid
*** H-CAPS: [3-(cyclohexylamino)-1-propane sulfonic acid

The available sodium salts are:

Sodium Salt	Molar Mass (g·mol⁻¹)
NaMES	217.22
NaMOPS	231.25
NaCAPS	243.31

a. What are the K_a values of the acids H-MES, H-MOPS, and H-CAPS? Show your calculations and fill in the table provided below.

Acid	K_a
H-MES	
H-MOPS	
H-CAPS	

b. Which acid, H-MES, H-MOPS, or H-CAPS, should be used to prepare the buffer? Show how you arrived at your answer.

c.   **i.** Write a brief procedure for the preparation of 500-mL buffer with the target pH.

     ii. What is the expected pH of the buffer the teacher prepared using this method?

d. The teacher tests the ability of the solution to behave as a buffer by adding 25 mL of 0.2 M NaOH. What is the new expected pH of the solution?

e. How might your procedure be altered if the teacher needed to prepare a solution with a higher buffer capacity? (You are *not* limited to the chemicals already listed.)

Answers and Explanations

Multiple Choice

1. **D.** Acid spills are most safely neutralized by solutions of weak bases. Addition of a strong base may cause a strongly exothermic reaction. All of the compounds shown are weak bases except for KOH, which is a strong base. Therefore, KOH is not a good choice for neutralizing an acid spill.

2. **C.** Absorbance is related to transmittance by

$$A = -\log T$$

A transmittance value of 10.0%, or 0.100, has an absorbance of 1.000.

3. **A.** The buret reading is between 50.6 mL and 50.7 mL. The reading should include one estimated digit, and 50.65 is a good estimate.

4. **C.** Breaking up the wet solid to allow the interior to be exposed to the atmosphere will decrease the likelihood that trapped water will cause the measured mass to be artificially high. Therefore, choice C is the least likely to introduce an error in the mass calculation. Failing to wash the sample (choice A), failing to add an excess of Na_2CO_3 (choice B), or washing the sample with too much H_2O (choice D) are all likely to lead to substantial errors in the mass calculation.

5. **B.** Compound A has a higher R_f value than B, which means that its intermolecular attractions to hexane are greater than those of B, but it does not necessarily mean that compound A is completely nonpolar.

6. **D.** Despite the compound's luster, its inability to conduct electricity in the solid state rules out the possibility of a metal. The low melting point rules out the possibility of ionic bonding. The solubility of the compound in CCl_4, a nonpolar solvent, provides evidence that the bond is nonpolar covalent.

7. **A.** In order to turn the solution yellow, the equilibrium must be shifted toward the products. Removal of a product, H_3O^+, by reaction with NaOH will drive the reaction toward CrO_4^{2-}.

8. **D.** Using initial solutions that are at identical temperatures is unnecessary as long as both temperatures are measured accurately before addition of the reactants to the calorimeter. The temperature changes can still be calculated for both solutions.

9. **D.** Only D, the strong acid titration curve with the single inflection point, is not a triprotic titration curve. Curve A has three obvious inflections, so it is unquestionably triprotic. Although there are not three clear equivalence points in curves B and C, overlapping buffering regions for the acidic protons can explain the shapes of the curves.

10. **B.** Because isooctane is less dense than water, it forms the top layer. Isooctane is a hydrocarbon, so beta carotene is likely to be soluble in isooctane, while vitamin B_5, which has polar and hydrogen-bonding functional groups, is not.

Long Free Response

1. **a. i.** The net ionic equation for the reaction between the solid $Mg(OH)_2$ suspended in the antacid and an aqueous solution of HCl is

$$Mg(OH)_2(s) + 2\,H^+(aq) \rightarrow Mg^{2+}(aq) + 2H_2O(l)$$

The state symbols are not required in order for the answer to receive credit

$$Mg(OH)_2 + 2\,H^+ \rightarrow Mg^{2+} + 2\,H_2O$$

ii. In order for the litmus paper to turn pink, which indicates an acidic solution, excess H^+ must have been added.

b. Phenolphthalein is colorless in acidic solution and pink in basic solution. The analyte solution is acidic, so its appearance is clear and colorless.

c. The number of moles of the NaOH is determined by first finding the number of moles of KHP that were titrated. KHP is a monoprotic acid, so it reacts with NaOH in a 1:1 molar ratio.

$$0.740 \text{ g KHP} \times \frac{1 \text{ mol KHP}}{204.23 \text{ g KHP}} \times \frac{1 \text{ mol NaOH}}{1 \text{ mol KHP}} = 0.00362 \text{ mol NaOH}$$

Next, the molarity of NaOH is determined by dividing the number of moles by the volume.

$$\frac{0.00362 \text{ mol NaOH}}{0.03235 \text{ L NaOH}} = 0.112 \; M \text{ NaOH}$$

d. The titration reaction is between the excess acid and the NaOH.

The number of moles of excess acid is

$$0.00817 \text{ L NaOH} \times \frac{0.112 \text{ mol NaOH}}{1 \text{ L NaOH}} \times \frac{1 \text{ mol HCl}}{1 \text{ mol NaOH}} = 0.000915 \text{ mol HCl} \quad (0.00091504)$$

The initial amount of acid added to the solution is

$$0.01300 \text{ L HCl} \times \frac{0.500 \text{ mol HCl}}{1 \text{ L HCl}} = 0.00650 \text{ mol HCl}$$

The difference between the number of moles of initial HCl and the number of moles of excess HCl is the number of moles that reacted with $Mg(OH)_2$.

$$0.00650 \text{ mol HCl} - 0.00091504 \text{ mol HCl} = 0.00558 \text{ mol HCl} \quad (0.00558496)$$

The number of moles $Mg(OH)_2$ reacted is

$$0.00558496 \text{ mol HCl} \times \frac{1 \text{ mol } Mg(OH)_2}{2 \text{ mol HCl}} = 0.00279 \text{ mol } Mg(OH)_2 \quad (0.00279248)$$

e. The mass of $Mg(OH)_2$ is determined using the molar mass.

$$0.00279248 \text{ mol } Mg(OH)_2 \times \frac{58.32 \text{ g } Mg(OH)_2}{1 \text{ mol } Mg(OH)_2} = 0.163 \text{ g } Mg(OH)_2 \quad (0.1628574)$$

The mass of the original sample is

$$20.369 \text{ g} - 17.873 \text{ g} = 2.496 \text{ g}$$

The mass percent of $Mg(OH)_2$ in the original sample is

$$\frac{0.1628574 \text{ g } Mg(OH)_2}{2.496 \text{ g}} \times 100\% = 6.52\%$$

f. Although the pK_a of phenolphthalein, 9.3, is more than one pH unit different from the pH of 7 at the equivalence point, the volume required to change the pH drastically at the equivalence point consists of only a drop or two of titrant. Because this does not result in a large change in volume, the volume measured is not significantly different from the volume required to titrate the analyte.

2. a. The K_a values are found using the concentration and the pH. For the first solution, H-MES, the $[H^+]$ is

$$[H^+] = 10^{-pH} = 10^{-3.38} = 4.17 \times 10^{-4}$$

The K_a value can be determined from the concentration of all species in solution.

$$H\text{-MES} + H_2O \rightleftharpoons MES^- + H_3O^+$$

Reaction	H-MES	MES⁻	H₃O⁺
Initial Concentrations (*M*)	0.25	0	0
Change	-4.17×10^{-4}	$+4.17 \times 10^{-4}$	$+4.17 \times 10^{-4}$
Equilibrium Concentrations (*M*)	0.25	4.17×10^{-4}	4.17×10^{-4}

$$K_a = \frac{[MES^-][H_3O^+]}{[H\text{-MES}]}$$

$$K_a = \frac{(4.17 \times 10^{-4})^2}{0.25} = 6.95 \times 10^{-7}$$

The values of H-CAPS and H-MOPS are found similarly, and the tabulated values are as follows.

Acid	K_a
H-MES	6.95×10^{-7}
H-MOPS	6.34×10^{-8}
H-CAPS	2.77×10^{-11}

b. In order to determine the best acid to use for the buffer, the pK_a values must be calculated. A buffer works best when the pK_a of the acid is closest to the desired pH range for the buffer.

For H-MES,

$$pK_a = -\log K_a = -\log (6.95 \times 10^{-7}) = 6.158$$

For H-MOPS,

$$pK_a = -\log K_a = -\log (6.34 \times 10^{-8}) = 7.198$$

For H-CAPS,

$$pK_a = -\log K_a = -\log (2.77 \times 10^{-11}) = 10.558$$

The third acid, H-CAPS, has a pK_a in the desired range, so it is the best choice for the buffer.

c. i. A possible procedure for producing the buffer is:

- Place a small beaker on the balance and zero the balance.
- Weigh 30 g of NaCAPS into the beaker. (The number of grams is found by calculating the number of moles of H-CAPS that are in 500 mL of a 0.25 *M* solution. The number of moles is multiplied by the molar mass of NaCAPS. See below for the calculation).
- Add the NaCAPS to the 1000-mL Erlenmeyer flask.
- Fill the graduated cylinder with 500 mL of the 0.25 *M* H-CAPS.
- Add the H-CAPS solution to the NaCAPS in the 1000-mL Erlenmeyer flask.
- Swirl the solution until the NaCAPS has dissolved completely.
- The calculation of the mass of NaCAPS is as follows.

$$0.5 \text{ L H-CAPS} \times \frac{0.25 \text{ mol H-CAPS}}{1 \text{ L H-CAPS}} \times \frac{1 \text{ mol NaCAPS}}{1 \text{ mol H-CAPS}} \times \frac{243.31 \text{ g NaCAPS}}{1 \text{ mol NaCAPS}} = 30 \text{ g NaCAPS}$$

ii. Using the method shown, the number of moles of NaCAPS is equal to the number of moles of H-CAPS. This means the concentrations are equal and

$$\frac{[CAPS^-]}{[H\text{-}CAPS]} = 1$$

The pH should equal the pK_a of H-CAPS.

$$pH = pK_a + \log\frac{[CAPS^-]}{[H\text{-}CAPS]} = 10.558$$

d. The added OH^- reacts with H-CAPS in the buffer.

$$H\text{-}CAPS + OH^- \rightarrow CAPS^- + H_2O$$

The number of moles of H-CAPS and $CAPS^-$ present initially is

$$0.5 \;\cancel{L\,H\text{-}CAPS} \times \frac{0.25\text{ mol H-CAPS}}{1 \;\cancel{L\,H\text{-}CAPS}} = 0.125\text{ mol H-CAPS (all digits from the calculator are shown)}$$

The number of moles of OH^- added is

$$0.025 \;\cancel{L\,OH^-} \times \frac{0.2\text{ mol }OH^-}{1 \;\cancel{L\,OH^-}} = 0.005\text{ mol }OH^-$$

The new amounts of H-CAPS and $CAPS^-$ are

$$0.125 - 0.005 = 0.12\text{ mol H-CAPS}$$

$$0.125 + 0.005 = 0.13\text{ mol CAPS}^-$$

The expected pH of the solution can be determined from the Henderson-Hasselbalch equation.

$$pH = 10.558 + \log\left(\frac{0.13}{0.12}\right) = 10.593$$

e. To produce a buffer with a higher buffer capacity, a more concentrated solution of H-CAPS and a larger mass of NaCAPS could be used.

PERIODIC TABLE OF THE ELEMENTS

1 H 1.008																		2 He 4.00
3 Li 6.94	4 Be 9.01											5 B 10.81	6 C 12.01	7 N 14.01	8 O 16.00	9 F 19.00	10 Ne 20.18	
11 Na 22.99	12 Mg 24.30											13 Al 26.98	14 Si 28.09	15 P 30.97	16 S 32.06	17 Cl 35.45	18 Ar 39.95	
19 K 39.10	20 Ca 40.08	21 Sc 44.96	22 Ti 47.90	23 V 50.94	24 Cr 52.00	25 Mn 54.94	26 Fe 55.85	27 Co 58.93	28 Ni 58.69	29 Cu 63.55	30 Zn 65.39	31 Ga 69.72	32 Ge 72.59	33 As 74.92	34 Se 78.96	35 Br 79.90	36 Kr 83.80	
37 Rb 85.47	38 Sr 87.62	39 Y 88.91	40 Zr 91.22	41 Nb 92.91	42 Mo 95.94	43 Tc (98)	44 Ru 101.1	45 Rh 102.91	46 Pd 106.42	47 Ag 107.87	48 Cd 112.41	49 In 114.82	50 Sn 118.71	51 Sb 121.75	52 Te 127.60	53 I 126.91	54 Xe 131.29	
55 Cs 132.91	56 Ba 137.33	57 *La 138.91	72 Hf 178.49	73 Ta 180.95	74 W 183.85	75 Re 186.21	76 Os 190.2	77 Ir 192.2	78 Pt 195.08	79 Au 196.97	80 Hg 200.59	81 Tl 204.38	82 Pb 207.2	83 Bi 208.98	84 Po (209)	85 At (210)	86 Rn (222)	
87 Fr (223)	88 Ra 226.02	89 †Ac 227.03	104 Rf (261)	105 Db (262)	106 Sg (266)	107 Bh (264)	108 Hs (277)	109 Mt (268)	110 Ds (271)	111 Rg (272)								

*Lanthanide Series

58 Ce 140.12	59 Pr 140.91	60 Nd 144.24	61 Pm (145)	62 Sm 150.4	63 Eu 151.97	64 Gd 157.25	65 Tb 158.93	66 Dy 162.50	67 Ho 164.93	68 Er 167.26	69 Tm 168.93	70 Yb 173.04	71 Lu 174.97

†Actinide Series

90 Tn 232.04	91 Pa 231.04	92 U 238.03	93 Np (237)	94 Pu (244)	95 Am (243)	96 Cm (247)	97 Bk (247)	98 Cf (251)	99 Es (252)	100 Fm (257)	101 Md (258)	102 No (259)	103 Lr (262)

AP Chemistry Equations and Constants

On the exam, the following symbols are defined as noted here unless specified otherwise:

L, mL	=	liter(s), milliliter(s)	mm Hg	=	millimeters of mercury
g	=	gram(s)	J, kJ	=	joule(s), kilojoule(s)
nm	=	nanometer(s)	V	=	volt(s)
atm	=	atmosphere(s)	mol	=	mole(s)

Atomic Structure

$E = hv$

$c = \lambda v$

E = energy

v = frequency

λ = wavelength

Planck's constant, $h = 6.626 \times 10^{-34}$ J s

Speed of light, $c = 2.998 \times 10^{8}$ m s^{-1}

Avogadro's number $= 6.022 \times 10^{23}$ mol^{-1}

Electron charge, $e = -1.602 \times 10^{-19}$ coulomb

Equilibrium

$$K_c = \frac{[C]^c[D]^d}{[A]^a[B]^b}, \text{ where } a\,A + b\,B \rightleftharpoons c\,C + d\,D$$

$$K_p = \frac{(P_C)^c (P_D)^d}{(P_A)^a (P_B)^b}$$

$$K_a = \frac{[H^+][A^-]}{HA}$$

$$K_b = \frac{[OH^-][HB^+]}{[B]}$$

$K_w = [H^+][OH^-] = 1.0 \times 10^{-14}$ at 25 °C

$\quad = K_a \times K_b$

$pH = -\log[H^+]$, $pOH = -\log[OH^-]$

$14 = pH + pOH$

$$pH = pK_a + \log\frac{[A^-]}{[HA]}$$

$pK_a = -\log K_a$, $pK_b = -\log K_b$

Equilibrium Constants:

K_c molar concentrations

K_p gas pressures

K_a weak acid

K_b weak base

K_w water

Kinetics

$\ln[A]_t - \ln[A]_0 = -kt$

$$\frac{1}{[A]_t} - \frac{1}{[A]_0} = kt$$

$$t_{1/2} = \frac{0.693}{k}$$

k = rate constant

t = time

$t_{1/2}$ = half-life

Gases, Liquids, and Solutions	
$$PV = nRT$$ $$P_A = P_{total} \times X_A, \text{ where } X_A = \frac{\text{moles A}}{\text{total moles}}$$ $$P_{total} = P_A + P_B + P_C + \ldots$$ $$n = \frac{m}{M}$$ $$K = {}^\circ C + 273$$ $$D = \frac{m}{v}$$ $$KE \text{ per molecule} = \frac{1}{2}mv^2$$ Molarity, M = moles of solute per liter of solution $$A = abc$$	$P =$ pressure $V =$ volume $T =$ temperature $n =$ number of moles $m =$ mass $M =$ molar mass $D =$ density $KE =$ kinetic energy $v =$ velocity $A =$ absorbance $a =$ molar absorbtivity $b =$ path length $c =$ concentration Gas constant, $R = 8.134$ J mol^{-1} K^{-1} $= 0.08206$ L atm mol^{-1} K^{-1} $= 62.36$ L torr mol^{-1} K^{-1} 1 atm = 760 mm Hg = 760 torr STP = 273.15 K and 1.0 atm Ideal gas at STP = 22.4 mol^{-1}
Thermodynamics/Electrochemistry	
$$q = mc\Delta T$$ $$\Delta S^\circ = \Sigma S^\circ \text{ products} - \Sigma S^\circ \text{ reactants}$$ $$\Delta H^\circ = \Sigma H^\circ_f \text{ products} - \Sigma H^\circ_f \text{ reactants}$$ $$\Delta G^\circ = \Sigma G^\circ_f \text{ products} - \Sigma G^\circ_f \text{ reactants}$$ $$\Delta G^\circ = \Delta H^\circ - T\Delta S^\circ$$ $$= RT \ln K$$ $$= -nFE^\circ$$ $$I = \frac{q}{t}$$	$q =$ heat $m =$ mass $c =$ specific heat capacity $T =$ temperature $S^\circ =$ standard entropy $H^\circ =$ standard enthalpy $G^\circ =$ standard Gibbs free energy $n =$ number of moles $E^\circ =$ standard reduction potential $I =$ current (amperes) $q =$ charge (coulombs) $t =$ time (seconds) Faraday's constant, $F = 96{,}485$ coulombs per mole of electrons $$1 \text{ volt} = \frac{1 \text{ joule}}{1 \text{ coulomb}}$$

Practice Exam 1 Answer Sheet
Section I: Multiple Choice

1 Ⓐ Ⓑ Ⓒ Ⓓ	21 Ⓐ Ⓑ Ⓒ Ⓓ	41 Ⓐ Ⓑ Ⓒ Ⓓ
2 Ⓐ Ⓑ Ⓒ Ⓓ	22 Ⓐ Ⓑ Ⓒ Ⓓ	42 Ⓐ Ⓑ Ⓒ Ⓓ
3 Ⓐ Ⓑ Ⓒ Ⓓ	23 Ⓐ Ⓑ Ⓒ Ⓓ	43 Ⓐ Ⓑ Ⓒ Ⓓ
4 Ⓐ Ⓑ Ⓒ Ⓓ	24 Ⓐ Ⓑ Ⓒ Ⓓ	44 Ⓐ Ⓑ Ⓒ Ⓓ
5 Ⓐ Ⓑ Ⓒ Ⓓ	25 Ⓐ Ⓑ Ⓒ Ⓓ	45 Ⓐ Ⓑ Ⓒ Ⓓ
6 Ⓐ Ⓑ Ⓒ Ⓓ	26 Ⓐ Ⓑ Ⓒ Ⓓ	46 Ⓐ Ⓑ Ⓒ Ⓓ
7 Ⓐ Ⓑ Ⓒ Ⓓ	27 Ⓐ Ⓑ Ⓒ Ⓓ	47 Ⓐ Ⓑ Ⓒ Ⓓ
8 Ⓐ Ⓑ Ⓒ Ⓓ	28 Ⓐ Ⓑ Ⓒ Ⓓ	48 Ⓐ Ⓑ Ⓒ Ⓓ
9 Ⓐ Ⓑ Ⓒ Ⓓ	29 Ⓐ Ⓑ Ⓒ Ⓓ	49 Ⓐ Ⓑ Ⓒ Ⓓ
10 Ⓐ Ⓑ Ⓒ Ⓓ	30 Ⓐ Ⓑ Ⓒ Ⓓ	50 Ⓐ Ⓑ Ⓒ Ⓓ
11 Ⓐ Ⓑ Ⓒ Ⓓ	31 Ⓐ Ⓑ Ⓒ Ⓓ	51 Ⓐ Ⓑ Ⓒ Ⓓ
12 Ⓐ Ⓑ Ⓒ Ⓓ	32 Ⓐ Ⓑ Ⓒ Ⓓ	52 Ⓐ Ⓑ Ⓒ Ⓓ
13 Ⓐ Ⓑ Ⓒ Ⓓ	33 Ⓐ Ⓑ Ⓒ Ⓓ	53 Ⓐ Ⓑ Ⓒ Ⓓ
14 Ⓐ Ⓑ Ⓒ Ⓓ	34 Ⓐ Ⓑ Ⓒ Ⓓ	54 Ⓐ Ⓑ Ⓒ Ⓓ
15 Ⓐ Ⓑ Ⓒ Ⓓ	35 Ⓐ Ⓑ Ⓒ Ⓓ	55 Ⓐ Ⓑ Ⓒ Ⓓ
16 Ⓐ Ⓑ Ⓒ Ⓓ	36 Ⓐ Ⓑ Ⓒ Ⓓ	56 Ⓐ Ⓑ Ⓒ Ⓓ
17 Ⓐ Ⓑ Ⓒ Ⓓ	37 Ⓐ Ⓑ Ⓒ Ⓓ	57 Ⓐ Ⓑ Ⓒ Ⓓ
18 Ⓐ Ⓑ Ⓒ Ⓓ	38 Ⓐ Ⓑ Ⓒ Ⓓ	58 Ⓐ Ⓑ Ⓒ Ⓓ
19 Ⓐ Ⓑ Ⓒ Ⓓ	39 Ⓐ Ⓑ Ⓒ Ⓓ	59 Ⓐ Ⓑ Ⓒ Ⓓ
20 Ⓐ Ⓑ Ⓒ Ⓓ	40 Ⓐ Ⓑ Ⓒ Ⓓ	60 Ⓐ Ⓑ Ⓒ Ⓓ

Practice Exam 2 Answer Sheet
Section I: Multiple Choice

1 Ⓐ Ⓑ Ⓒ Ⓓ	21 Ⓐ Ⓑ Ⓒ Ⓓ	41 Ⓐ Ⓑ Ⓒ Ⓓ
2 Ⓐ Ⓑ Ⓒ Ⓓ	22 Ⓐ Ⓑ Ⓒ Ⓓ	42 Ⓐ Ⓑ Ⓒ Ⓓ
3 Ⓐ Ⓑ Ⓒ Ⓓ	23 Ⓐ Ⓑ Ⓒ Ⓓ	43 Ⓐ Ⓑ Ⓒ Ⓓ
4 Ⓐ Ⓑ Ⓒ Ⓓ	24 Ⓐ Ⓑ Ⓒ Ⓓ	44 Ⓐ Ⓑ Ⓒ Ⓓ
5 Ⓐ Ⓑ Ⓒ Ⓓ	25 Ⓐ Ⓑ Ⓒ Ⓓ	45 Ⓐ Ⓑ Ⓒ Ⓓ
6 Ⓐ Ⓑ Ⓒ Ⓓ	26 Ⓐ Ⓑ Ⓒ Ⓓ	46 Ⓐ Ⓑ Ⓒ Ⓓ
7 Ⓐ Ⓑ Ⓒ Ⓓ	27 Ⓐ Ⓑ Ⓒ Ⓓ	47 Ⓐ Ⓑ Ⓒ Ⓓ
8 Ⓐ Ⓑ Ⓒ Ⓓ	28 Ⓐ Ⓑ Ⓒ Ⓓ	48 Ⓐ Ⓑ Ⓒ Ⓓ
9 Ⓐ Ⓑ Ⓒ Ⓓ	29 Ⓐ Ⓑ Ⓒ Ⓓ	49 Ⓐ Ⓑ Ⓒ Ⓓ
10 Ⓐ Ⓑ Ⓒ Ⓓ	30 Ⓐ Ⓑ Ⓒ Ⓓ	50 Ⓐ Ⓑ Ⓒ Ⓓ
11 Ⓐ Ⓑ Ⓒ Ⓓ	31 Ⓐ Ⓑ Ⓒ Ⓓ	51 Ⓐ Ⓑ Ⓒ Ⓓ
12 Ⓐ Ⓑ Ⓒ Ⓓ	32 Ⓐ Ⓑ Ⓒ Ⓓ	52 Ⓐ Ⓑ Ⓒ Ⓓ
13 Ⓐ Ⓑ Ⓒ Ⓓ	33 Ⓐ Ⓑ Ⓒ Ⓓ	53 Ⓐ Ⓑ Ⓒ Ⓓ
14 Ⓐ Ⓑ Ⓒ Ⓓ	34 Ⓐ Ⓑ Ⓒ Ⓓ	54 Ⓐ Ⓑ Ⓒ Ⓓ
15 Ⓐ Ⓑ Ⓒ Ⓓ	35 Ⓐ Ⓑ Ⓒ Ⓓ	55 Ⓐ Ⓑ Ⓒ Ⓓ
16 Ⓐ Ⓑ Ⓒ Ⓓ	36 Ⓐ Ⓑ Ⓒ Ⓓ	56 Ⓐ Ⓑ Ⓒ Ⓓ
17 Ⓐ Ⓑ Ⓒ Ⓓ	37 Ⓐ Ⓑ Ⓒ Ⓓ	57 Ⓐ Ⓑ Ⓒ Ⓓ
18 Ⓐ Ⓑ Ⓒ Ⓓ	38 Ⓐ Ⓑ Ⓒ Ⓓ	58 Ⓐ Ⓑ Ⓒ Ⓓ
19 Ⓐ Ⓑ Ⓒ Ⓓ	39 Ⓐ Ⓑ Ⓒ Ⓓ	59 Ⓐ Ⓑ Ⓒ Ⓓ
20 Ⓐ Ⓑ Ⓒ Ⓓ	40 Ⓐ Ⓑ Ⓒ Ⓓ	60 Ⓐ Ⓑ Ⓒ Ⓓ

Chapter 8

Practice Exam 1

Section I: Multiple Choice

60 questions
90 minutes

Calculators are not allowed for Section I.

Note: For all questions, assume the temperature is 298 K, the pressure is 1.0 atm, and solutions are aqueous unless otherwise specified.

Directions: Each of the questions or incomplete statements below is followed by four suggested answers or completions. Select the one that is best in each case and then fill in the corresponding circle on the answer sheet.

1. Which choice best describes the reaction represented by the particulate diagram?

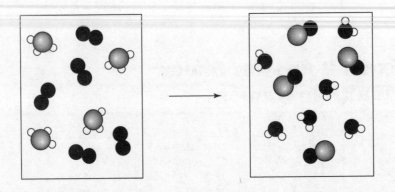

   A. Phosphorus trichloride and oxygen react to form phosphite and chlorine monoxide.
   B. Ammonia is oxidized to form nitrogen monoxide and water.
   C. Methane, the simplest hydrocarbon, undergoes combustion to form carbon monoxide and water.
   D. Chlorine reacts with hydronium to form chlorine dioxide and hydroxide.

2. Which properties are expected to be exhibited by solid potassium chloride?

   A. It melts at a temperature that is lower than the melting point of pure potassium.
   B. It is an electrical conductor.
   C. It dissociates into molecules in aqueous solution.
   D. It has a higher melting point than solid potassium bromide.

GO ON TO THE NEXT PAGE

Questions 3–5 refer to the experiment described below.

A student researcher performs an oxidation of borneol, $C_{10}H_{17}OH$, by treating it with CrO_3 and H_2SO_4 to produce camphor, $C_{10}H_{16}O$.

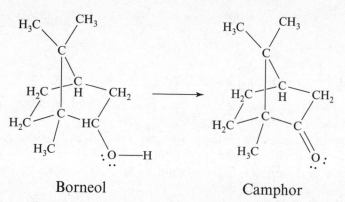

Borneol   Camphor

3. The paper chromatograph below shows pure borneol in lane 1 and the reaction mixture in lane 2. Chloroform, $CHCl_3$, was used as the mobile phase. What can be concluded from this analysis?

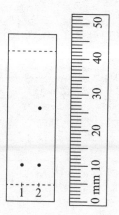

    A. Borneol experiences stronger intermolecular attractions with the mobile phase than camphor.
    B. Borneol experiences weaker intermolecular attractions with the mobile phase than camphor.
    C. Borneol bonds covalently with the stationary phase and does not move with the mobile phase.
    D. Camphor bonds covalently with the stationary phase and does not move with the mobile phase.

4. Which choice correctly matches each compound with its R_f in the chromatograph?

	Borneol	Camphor
A.	0.24	0.62
B.	0.62	0.24
C.	0.14	0.57
D.	0.57	0.14

5. Which statement about this experiment is correct?

    A. The camphor was produced in a 50% yield.
    B. The camphor was produced in a 100% yield.
    C. The yield of the camphor was less than 100%.
    D. The reaction has 100% atom economy.

GO ON TO THE NEXT PAGE

6. Which of the following correctly ranks the gaseous compounds in order of decreasing standard molar entropy?

   A. $HCl > SiCl_4 > CF_4$

   B. $CF_4 > SiCl_4 > HCl$

   C. $HCl > CF_4 > SiCl_4$

   D. $SiCl_4 > CF_4 > HCl$

7. Which of the statements concerning interstitial alloys is correct?

   A. The atomic radii of the elements in the mixture are similar, and the electron sea model of bonding serves to explain the conductivity and malleability of the alloy.

   B. The atomic radii of the elements in the mixture are different, and the electron sea model of bonding serves to explain the conductivity and malleability of the alloy.

   C. The atomic radii of the elements in the mixture are similar, and n-doping serves to explain the conductivity and malleability of the alloy.

   D. The atomic radii of the elements in the mixture are similar, and p-doping serves to explain the conductivity and malleability of the alloy.

8. Use the data below to determine the enthalpy of reaction for the reaction of aluminum metal with chlorine gas.

   $$2\ Al(s) + 3\ Cl_2(g) \rightarrow 2\ AlCl_3(s) \qquad \Delta H° = ?$$

Reaction	$\Delta H°$
$2\ Al(s) + 6\ HCl(aq) \rightarrow 2\ AlCl_3(aq) + 3\ H_2(g)$	w
$HCl(g) \rightarrow HCl(aq)$	x
$H_2(g) + Cl_2(g) \rightarrow 2\ HCl(g)$	y
$AlCl_3(s) \rightarrow AlCl_3(aq)$	z

   A. $w + 6x + 3y - 2z$

   B. $-w - 6x - 3y + 2z$

   C. $w + 3x + 2y - 3z$

   D. $-w - 3x - 2y + 3z$

9. Addition of solid zinc oxide-chromium(III) oxide to the gases shown in the reaction below causes the system to reach equilibrium more quickly than it would in the absence of zinc oxide-chromium(III) oxide. This is because

   $$CO(g) + 2\ H_2(g) \rightleftharpoons CH_3OH(g)$$

   A. the equilibrium constant is shifted such that the reaction does not have to proceed as far to reach equilibrium.

   B. the number of collisions and energy of collisions between reactant molecules is increased.

   C. the reaction is provided with an alternate mechanistic pathway that has a lower activation energy.

   D. the average kinetic energy of the reactants is increased.

10. The molecular geometry and polarity of SiF_4 and SeF_4 are

    A. the same because the molecular formulas are similar.

    B. the same because Si and Se are in the same period.

    C. different because Si and Se are in different groups.

    D. different because Si and Se have different electronegativity values.

GO ON TO THE NEXT PAGE

11. What is the best method for determination of the concentration of an aqueous solution of HNO_3?

    A. Gravimetric analysis by precipitation with an aqueous solution of Pb^{2+} ions

    B. Spectrophotometric or colorimetric determination utilizing Beer's law analysis

    C. Titration with a standardized solution of $NaOH$

    D. Distillation to remove the water from the solution

12. A 0.100 M solution of which substance would have the lowest pH?

    A. $HClO_3$

    B. HNO_2

    C. HCO_2H

    D. NH_3

Questions 13–15 refer to the following reaction.

$$H_2S(aq) + H_2O(l) \rightleftharpoons HS^-(aq) + H_3O^+(aq) \qquad K_a = 9 \times 10^{-8}$$

13. What is the approximate pH of a 1.00 M solution of H_2S?

    A. 1.5

    B. 3.5

    C. 5.5

    D. 7.5

14. Which species are acting as Brønsted-Lowry acids in the reaction?

    A. H_2S and H_2O

    B. H_2O and HS^-

    C. H_2O and H_3O^+

    D. H_2S and H_3O^+

15. Which species in the reaction has the largest K_b?

    A. H_2S

    B. H_2O

    C. HS^-

    D. H_3O^+

16. Carbon dioxide from the atmosphere dissolves at the surface of a body of water and forms carbonic acid.

$$CO_2(g) + H_2O(l) \rightarrow H_2CO_3(aq)$$

The carbonic acid is a weak, diprotic acid that dissociates in water according to the following equilibrium equations.

$$H_2CO_3(aq) + H_2O(l) \rightleftharpoons HCO_3^-(aq) + H_3O^+(aq)$$

$$HCO_3^-(aq) + H_2O(l) \rightleftharpoons CO_3^{2-}(aq) + H_3O^+(aq)$$

Which of the following processes are expected to decrease the pH of the body of water?

    A. A decrease in the partial pressure of CO_2 in the atmosphere

    B. A decrease in the partial pressure of N_2 in the atmosphere

    C. A decrease in the temperature of the water

    D. An increase in the dissolved carbonate concentration

GO ON TO THE NEXT PAGE

17. A 1.00-g sample of an unknown metal at 100.0 °C is added to 20.0 g of water at 25 °C. The final temperature after thermal equilibrium is reached is 25.3 °C. What is the identity of the metal if the water/metal system is perfectly insulated? The specific heat of water is 4.184 $J \cdot g^{-1} \cdot K^{-1}$.

Metal	Heat Capacity ($J \cdot g^{-1} \cdot K^{-1}$)
A	0.107
B	0.192
C	0.274
D	0.336

  A. Metal A
  B. Metal B
  C. Metal C
  D. Metal D

Questions 18–19 refer to the following reaction.

$$CH_3CH_2NH_2(g) \xrightarrow{\Delta} C_2H_4(g) + NH_3(g) \qquad \Delta H^{\circ}_{rxn} = 55 \text{ kJ} \cdot \text{mol}^{-1}$$

18. Which of the following plots best represents the relationship between ΔG° and temperature for this reaction?

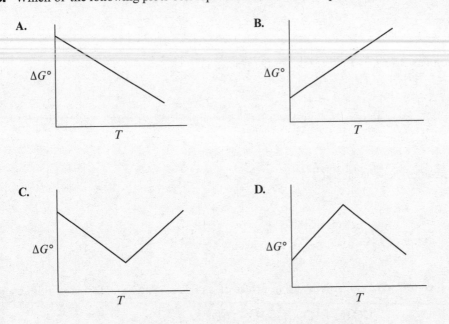

19. What is the approximate energy of a mole of C-N single bonds?

Bond	Bond Energy ($kJ \cdot mol^{-1}$)
C——H	412
C——C	347
C═══C	611
N——H	389

  A. 296 kJ
  B. 379 kJ
  C. 708 kJ
  D. 1120 kJ

GO ON TO THE NEXT PAGE

20. Which of the following is true of a phase change of a pure substance from a liquid state to a gaseous state?

    A. The process is exothermic because the temperature of the gas is higher than the temperature of the liquid.
    B. The temperature of the system does not change during the phase change because all of the energy transferred is needed to overcome intermolecular attractions.
    C. The temperature of the system increases during the phase change because heat is being added to the system.
    D. The temperature of the system does not change because the intermolecular forces remain unaltered during the phase change.

21. For which of the processes listed is $\Delta H° > 0$?

    A. $Na(l) \rightarrow Na(s)$
    B. $F(g) + e^- \rightarrow F^-(g)$
    C. $Na(g) \rightarrow Na^+(g) + e^-$
    D. $Na^+(g) + F^-(g) \rightarrow NaF(s)$

22. A sample of gas has a density of 2.00 g·L^{-1} at 268 K and 1 atm. What is the identity of the gas?

    A. NH_3
    B. N_2
    C. CO_2
    D. NO_2

23. Which choice correctly shows the compounds in order of decreasing C–O bond length?

    A. $H_3COH > (CH_3)_2CO > CH_3CO_2^-$
    B. $(CH_3)_2CO > CH_3CO_2^- > H_3COH$
    C. $H_3COH > CH_3CO_2^- > (CH_3)_2CO$
    D. $CH_3CO_2^- > (CH_3)_2CO > H_3COH$

24. A cast iron skillet can be heated over an open flame without undergoing vigorous oxidation, but when powdered iron is exposed to a flame, it rapidly ignites to form Fe_2O_3. Which is the best explanation for this observation?

    A. The activation energy for the reaction of the powdered iron is greater than that of the skillet.
    B. The impurities in the iron powder act as a catalyst for the combustion.
    C. The greater surface area of the powdered iron compared to the skillet leads to an increased rate of oxidation.
    D. The enthalpy change of the reaction of powdered iron is more negative than that of the skillet.

25. Which arrangement shows the following atoms in order of increasing energy of the $2p$ electrons in the PES spectrum?

    A. $F < N < O < C$
    B. $F < O < N < C$
    C. $C < O < N < F$
    D. $C < N < O < F$

26. Which of the following ions will experience the greatest degree of deflection in a mass spectrometer?

    A. $^2H_2^{16}O^+$
    B. $^1H_2^{16}O^+$
    C. $^1H^2H^{16}O^+$
    D. $^1H_2^{17}O^+$

GO ON TO THE NEXT PAGE

27. The decomposition of dinitrogen pentoxide forms nitrogen dioxide and oxygen according to the equation:

$$2 \, N_2O_5(g) \rightarrow 4 \, NO_2(g) + O_2(g)$$

The concentration of N_2O_5 was determined at various times in the experiment, and the data were used to generate the following linear plot.

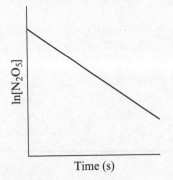

Which statement must be true of this decomposition reaction?

A. The rate of the reaction is independent of the concentration of N_2O_5.
B. The reaction is second order.
C. The rate has been accelerated by the addition of an appropriate catalyst.
D. The half-life of N_2O_5 is independent of its initial concentration.

28. The plot below shows the first ionization energies for the elements with atomic numbers 5 to 9. Which explanation best accounts for the deviation of the first ionization energy of the element with atomic number 8 from the overall ionization energy trend?

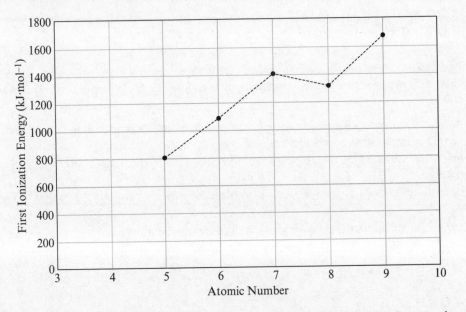

A. The valence electrons of oxygen experience greater shielding of the nucleus by core electrons than the valence electrons of nitrogen.
B. A repulsive interaction exists between the electrons in the doubly occupied oxygen $2p$ orbital.
C. The effective nuclear charge of oxygen is greater than that of nitrogen.
D. The atomic radius of oxygen is greater than that of fluorine, so the coulombic attraction between the valence electrons and the nucleus of oxygen is less.

GO ON TO THE NEXT PAGE

29. The marble in many monuments is composed of calcite, a form of calcium carbonate. When unpolluted rain, which has a pH of about 5.6, falls on calcite, the following is one of the reactions that occurs.

$$CaCO_3(s) + H_3O^+(aq) \rightleftharpoons Ca^{2+}(aq) + HCO_3^-(aq) + H_2O(l)$$

When the pH of rainwater drops below 5.6, which of the following is true?

A. $Q < K$, so more of the marble dissolves.
B. $Q > K$, so more of the marble dissolves.
C. $Q < K$, so less of the marble dissolves.
D. $Q > K$, so less of the marble dissolves.

30. Each solid sphere below represents a molecule of A, and each hollow sphere represents a molecule of B. The volume of the container is 1.0 L. Which drawing best illustrates an equilibrium mixture of A and B if A decomposes to form B according to the reaction below?

$$A \rightleftharpoons 2\,B \qquad K_c = 6$$

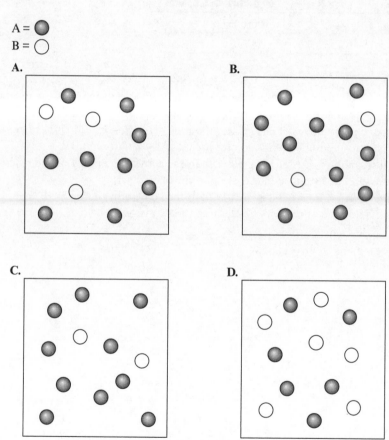

Questions 31–32 refer to the reaction below.

$$SbCl_5(g) \rightleftharpoons SbCl_3(g) + Cl_2(g) \qquad K_c = 43 \text{ at } 373 \text{ K}$$

31. At a given point in an experiment, a 100-L rigid reaction vessel contains 20 moles of $SbCl_5$, 50 moles of $SbCl_3$, and 60 moles of Cl_2 at 373 K. Which of the following describes how the pressure in the vessel will change and why it will change as the reaction approaches equilibrium at constant temperature?

    A. The pressure will increase because $K_c > Q_c$.
    B. The pressure will increase because $K_c < Q_c$.
    C. The pressure will decrease because $K_c > Q_c$.
    D. The pressure will decrease because $K_c < Q_c$.

32. Consider two evacuated 100-L rigid reaction vessels, vessel 1 and vessel 2. Equal amounts of liquid $SbCl_5$ are added to the two vessels at room temperature. A small amount of solid $FeCl_3$ is added to vessel 2. Both vessels are sealed and heated to 373 K. The rates of the reactions are measured and tabulated below.

Vessel	Time to Reach Equilibrium (seconds)
1	1000
2	200

Which of the following describes the two systems?

    A. The activation energy of the reaction in vessel 1 is greater than the activation energy of the reaction in vessel 2, and the total pressure at equilibrium is greater for vessel 1 than for vessel 2.
    B. The activation energy of the reaction in vessel 2 is greater than the activation energy of the reaction in vessel 1, and the total pressure at equilibrium is greater for vessel 1 than for vessel 2.
    C. The activation energy of the reaction in vessel 1 is greater than the activation energy of the reaction in vessel 2, and the total pressures at equilibrium are equal in the two vessels.
    D. The activation energy of the reaction in vessel 2 is greater than the activation energy of the reaction in vessel 1, and the total pressures at equilibrium are equal in the two vessels.

33. Which structure contains an atom that is sp^2 hybridized?

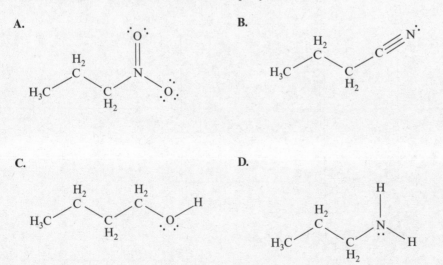

A.

B.

C.

D.

GO ON TO THE NEXT PAGE

34. The Mohs hardness scale ranks solids according to their ability to scratch other solids. The higher the Mohs hardness, the harder the substance. The hardness values of several substances are shown below.

Compound	Hardness
KCl	2
?	2.5
CaF_2	4
Diamond	10

Which of the following compounds is expected to have a hardness of 2.5?

A. NaCl
B. KI
C. SiO_2 (quartz)
D. Steel

35. Cyclohexane, C_6H_{12}, does not absorb electromagnetic radiation in the ultraviolet region of the spectrum, but benzene, C_6H_6, does. Which choice best describes the reason for this observation?

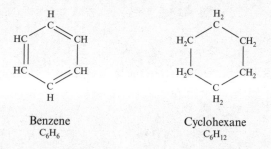

Benzene
C_6H_6

Cyclohexane
C_6H_{12}

A. The π electrons in benzene are capable of transitioning to higher-energy states by absorption of UV photons.
B. The carbon-hydrogen σ-bonds in benzene are capable of vibrating at frequencies corresponding to ultraviolet energies.
C. The nuclei of benzene are capable of transitioning to higher-energy states when ultraviolet photons are absorbed.
D. The π C-C bonds in benzene vibrate with a frequency that corresponds to an ultraviolet energy.

Questions 36–37 refer to the following data.

Four 1-liter containers at 273 K contain equal numbers of moles of pure gases.

Container	Gas	Pressure (atm)
1	H_2	1.0
2	CH_4	1.0
3	CF_4	?
4	CCl_4	0.68

36. The average speed of the gas particles is

A. greatest in container 1.
B. greatest in container 2.
C. greatest in container 4.
D. equal in the four containers.

GO ON TO THE NEXT PAGE

37. The pressure in container 3 is expected to be

    A. less than the pressure in container 4 because the C-F bond is more polar than the C-Cl bond.

    B. less than the pressure in container 2 because the C-F bond is more polar than the C-H bond.

    C. less than the pressure in container 4 because CF_4 experiences weaker London dispersion forces than CCl_4.

    D. less than the pressure in container 2 because CF_4 experiences stronger London dispersion forces than CH_4.

38. Which of the following reactions does not involve an oxidation-reduction?

    A. $NaBr + AgNO_3 \rightarrow AgBr + NaNO_3$

    B. $2\, MoS_2 + 5\, O_2 \rightarrow 2\, MoO_3 + 4\, SO_2$

    C. $2\, C_6H_6 + 15\, O_2 \rightarrow 12\, CO_2 + 6\, H_2O$

    D. $2\, NH_4Cl + 2\, MnO_2 + Zn \rightarrow 2\, NH_3 + Mn_2O_3 + ZnCl_2 + H_2O$

39. Which of the following species is most easily reduced?

    A. H_2

    B. Cl_2

    C. Cu^+

    D. Na^+

40. When ammonium chloride is dissolved in water, the temperature of the solution decreases. Which enthalpy change below is the largest?

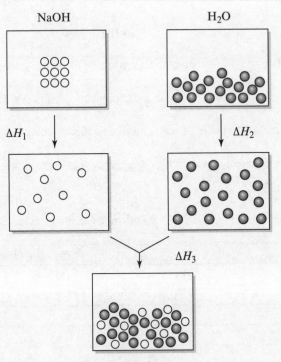

Solution

    A. ΔH_3

    B. $\Delta H_1 + \Delta H_3$

    C. $\Delta H_1 + \Delta H_2$

    D. $\Delta H_2 + \Delta H_3$

GO ON TO THE NEXT PAGE

41. The table below shows the K_a values for two weak acids. Which of the following pairs of solutions results in a buffer with a pH closest to 7.4?

Acid	K_a
$HClO_2$	1.2×10^{-2}
$HOCl$	3.5×10^{-8}

- **A.** 50 mL of 1.00 M $HClO_2$; 50 mL 0.50 M NaOH
- **B.** 50 mL 1.00 M NaOCl; 50 mL 0.50 M HCl
- **C.** 50 mL of 1.00 M $HClO_2$; 50 mL 1.00 M $NaClO_2$
- **D.** 50 mL 1.00 M HOCl; 50 mL 1.00 M NaOH

42. A student sets up the same chemical reaction in two different test tubes and labels them A and B. Test tube A is allowed to react at room temperature, 27 °C, and test tube B is placed in a 60 °C water bath. The student measures a larger rate constant for the reaction in test tube B than for test tube A. Which of the following is the best explanation for this observation?

- **A.** More of the colliding particles in test tube B have the proper orientation for the reaction to occur.
- **B.** A greater fraction of the molecules in test tube B collide more frequently with sufficient average kinetic energy to overcome the activation barrier for the reaction.
- **C.** The activation barrier for the reaction in test tube B is lower because of the relatively greater potential energy of the reactants.
- **D.** The reactant molecules in test tube B have a greater average velocity so they collide more frequently and have a statistically greater chance of reacting.

43. The titration curve shown below best represents the titration of

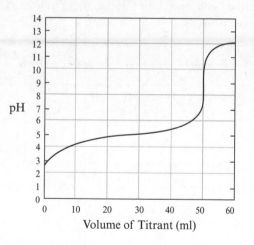

- **A.** phosphoric acid with sodium hydroxide.
- **B.** hydrofluoric acid with sodium hydroxide.
- **C.** sulfuric acid with sodium hydroxide.
- **D.** hydrochloric acid with ammonia.

GO ON TO THE NEXT PAGE

44. The following graph shows the trend in boiling points for PH_3, AsH_3, and SbH_3. Does point X or point Y reflect the boiling point of NH_3, and why is this the correct point?

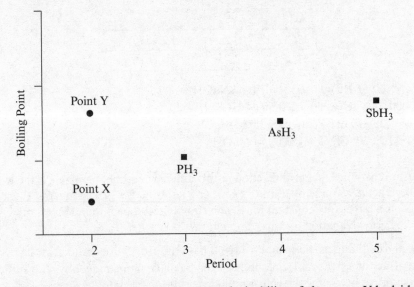

A. NH_3 boils at point X because it has the lowest polarizability of the group V hydrides.
B. NH_3 boils at point Y because it has the lowest polarizability of the group V hydrides.
C. NH_3 boils at point X because it is capable of hydrogen bonding.
D. NH_3 boils at point Y because it is capable of hydrogen bonding.

Questions 45–47 refer to the following information.

Isomers are compounds that have the same molecular formula, but different atomic connectivity. The compounds *n*-hexane and 2,3-dimethylbutane are isomers.

Name	*n*-hexane	2,3-dimethylbutane
Molecular Formula	C_6H_{14}	C_6H_{14}
Structural Formula	H_3C — $\overset{H_2}{C}$ — $\overset{H_2}{C}$ — $\overset{H_2}{C}$ — $\overset{H_2}{C}$ — CH_3	H_3C — $\overset{CH_3}{\underset{H}{C}}$ — $\overset{CH_3}{\underset{H}{C}}$ — CH_3

45. Which of the following compounds can exist as more than one isomer?

A. CH_4
B. C_2H_2
C. C_2H_4
D. C_3H_6

GO ON TO THE NEXT PAGE

46. Geometric isomers are compounds that may exhibit isomerism due to restricted rotation around π-bonds. Which of the compounds below may exhibit geometric isomerism?

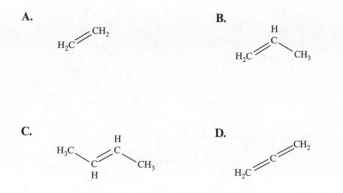

A.

B.

C.

D.

47. Which statement concerning isomers is true?

    A.   Only geometric isomers usually have identical physical and chemical properties.

    B.   Isomers usually have different chemical and physical properties.

    C.   Only changes in the number and type of atoms in a compound change the properties of the compound.

    D.   Neither of the isomers of hexane shown experience London dispersion forces.

48. Addition of which of the following elements to germanium would lead to a p-doped semiconductor?

    A.   B

    B.   Si

    C.   Se

    D.   Sn

Questions 49–50 refer to the following reaction and initial rate data.

Iodide is oxidized to hypoiodite in a basic solution of hypochlorite.

$$I^-(aq) + ClO^-(aq) \xrightarrow{\;OH^-\;} IO^-(aq) + Cl^-(aq)$$

The initial rates of the reaction were measured using various initial concentrations of the reactants.

Trial	Initial [I⁻] (*M*)	Initial [ClO⁻] (*M*)	Initial [OH⁻] (*M*)	Initial Rate (*M·s⁻¹*)
1	5.00×10^{-3}	1.00×10^{-2}	5.00×10^{-3}	6.0×10^{-2}
2	1.00×10^{-2}	5.00×10^{-3}	5.00×10^{-3}	6.0×10^{-2}
3	5.00×10^{-3}	5.00×10^{-3}	5.00×10^{-3}	3.0×10^{-2}
4	5.00×10^{-3}	5.00×10^{-3}	1.00×10^{-2}	1.5×10^{-2}

49. What is the rate law for the reaction?

    A.   rate = k[ClO⁻][OH⁻]

    B.   rate = k[I⁻][ClO⁻]

    C.   rate = k[ClO⁻][I⁻][OH⁻]⁻¹

    D.   rate = k[ClO⁻][I⁻][OH⁻]

GO ON TO THE NEXT PAGE

50. What are the units of the rate constant?

A. $M^{-1} \cdot s^{-1}$
B. $M \cdot s^{-1}$
C. $M^{-2} \cdot s^{-1}$
D. s^{-1}

51. Solid potassium and oxygen gas react to produce solid potassium peroxide, K_2O_2. Assume the reaction between 39.1 grams of potassium and 32.0 grams of oxygen proceeds to completion. Which choice best reflects the final contents of the reaction vessel?

	Mass of Potassium (grams)	Mass of Oxygen (grams)	Mass of K_2O_2 (grams)
A.	0	16.0	55.1
B.	0	0	71.1
C.	0	16.0	110.2
D.	19.6	0	51.5

52. The reaction of nitric oxide with chlorine is second order in NO and first order in Cl_2.

$$2 \, NO(g) + Cl_2(g) \rightarrow 2 \, NOCl(g)$$

$$\text{rate} = k[NO]^2[Cl_2]$$

Which statement about this reaction is most likely to be true?

A. The reaction mechanism is likely to involve more than one step.
B. Tripling [NO] will increase the rate of the reaction by a factor of 6.
C. Doubling $[Cl_2]$ will increase the rate of reaction as much as doubling the concentration of [NO].
D. At some point in the reaction mechanism, N_2O_2 must be formed.

53. Determine whether the electrochemical reaction between lead sulfate and iodide is thermodynamically favored as written under standard conditions.

$$Sn^{4+} + 2 \, Fe^{2+} \rightarrow Sn^{2+} + 2 \, Fe^{3+}$$

Reaction	$E°$ (V)
$Sn^{4+} + 2 \, e^- \rightarrow Sn^{2+}$	0.15
$Fe^{3+} + e^- \rightarrow Fe^{2+}$	0.77

A. $E°_{cell} = -1.39$ V; the reaction is thermodynamically disfavored as written.
B. $E°_{cell} = -0.62$ V; the reaction is thermodynamically disfavored as written.
C. $E°_{cell} = -1.39$ V; the reaction is thermodynamically favored as written.
D. $E°_{cell} = -0.62$ V; the reaction is thermodynamically favored as written.

54. A current of 25.0 A is continuously applied through an aqueous solution of potassium chloride. The reaction that occurs at the cathode is

A. $2 \, H_2O + 2 \, e^- \rightarrow H_2 + 2 \, OH^-$
B. $2 \, Cl^- \rightarrow Cl_2 + 2 \, e^-$
C. $2 \, H_2O \rightarrow O_2 + 4 \, H^+ + 4 \, e^-$
D. $K^+ + e^- \rightarrow K$

GO ON TO THE NEXT PAGE

55. Which pair of molecules is expected to exhibit the greatest dipole-induced dipole interactions?

    A. Br_2 and Cl_2

    B.   HCl and HBr

    C.   HBr and Br_2

    D.   HCl and Br_2

56. The rate constant of a reaction was measured at several temperatures. Which of the plots below is expected to result in a slope of $-\dfrac{E_a}{R}$, where E_a is the activation energy of the reaction?

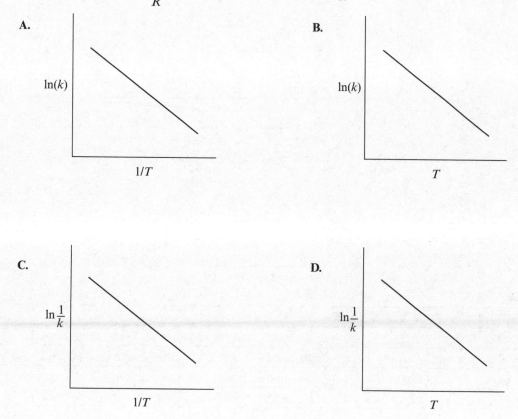

Questions 57–58 refer to the following reaction of barium carbonate.

Barium carbonate, $BaCO_3$, decomposes according to the reaction represented below.

$$BaCO_3(s) \rightleftharpoons BaO(s) + CO_2(g)$$

At 1500 K, the equilibrium constant, K_p, is 6.4×10^{-2}.

57. Some solid $BaCO_3$ is placed in a previously evacuated container and heated to 1500 K. When equilibrium is reached, some of the solid $BaCO_3$ remains. What is the pressure in the container at equilibrium at 1500 K?

    A. 2.5×10^{-1} atm

    B. 1.3×10^{-1} atm

    C. 6.4×10^{-2} atm

    D. 4.1×10^{-3} atm

GO ON TO THE NEXT PAGE

58. The value of $\Delta G°$ for the decomposition of $BaCO_3$ at 1500 K is

    A. positive.

    B. negative.

    C. zero.

    D. unpredictable from the information given.

59. A plot of potential energy as a function of internuclear distance between two molecules, X and Y, is shown below. Which of the following choices shows the correct curve correspondence, along with the correct reasoning?

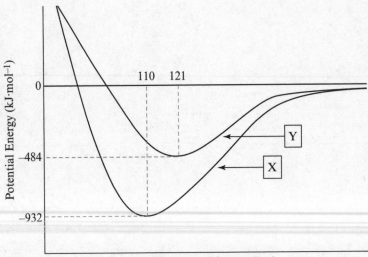

Internuclear Distance (pm)

	X	Y	Reason
A.	N_2	O_2	A triple bond is shorter and stronger than a double bond.
B.	N_2	O_2	A triple bond is longer and weaker than a double bond.
C.	O_2	N_2	A triple bond is shorter and stronger than a double bond.
D.	O_2	N_2	A triple bond is longer and weaker than a double bond.

GO ON TO THE NEXT PAGE

60. Which particulate diagram best illustrates the bonding responsible for the conductivity and malleability of metals?

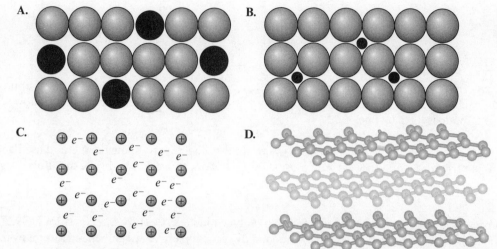

Section II: Free Response

7 questions

105 minutes

You may use your calculator for Section II.

Directions: Long free-response questions (questions 1–3) are worth 10 points each; allow yourself approximately 23 minutes for each one. Short free-response questions (questions 4–7) are worth 4 points each; allow yourself approximately 9 minutes for each one.

Include examples and equations in your responses where appropriate. Clearly show the method used and the steps involved in arriving at your answers. You must show your work to receive credit. Be mindful of significant figures.

1. **a.** A researcher is studying the effect of bleach on blue food dye, $C_{37}H_{34}N_2O_9S_3Na_2$ (MW = 792.86 g·mol^{-1}). The researcher weighs 0.200 gram of the solid dye onto a piece of weigh paper. How many moles of dye molecules are present?

    b. The researcher would like to make a stock solution of the dye by adding distilled water. Should the researcher use a volumetric flask or a graduated cylinder to prepare an accurately known concentration? Briefly explain your answer.

    c. Water is added to the 0.200 gram of dye so that the final volume is 500. mL. What is the molarity of the dye solution? Be sure to show your calculation.

    d. A 0.50-mL aliquot of the solution is diluted with distilled water to prepare 100.0 mL of stock solution. What is the concentration of the stock solution?

    e. The stock solution is placed in a spectrophotometer and its absorbance is measured. The following plot of absorbance versus wavelength is generated. What wavelength should be selected in order to analyze the concentration of the food dye? Justify your response by referring to the data.

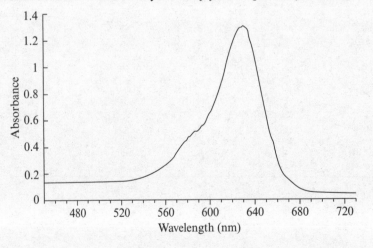

GO ON TO THE NEXT PAGE

f. A known excess of bleach is added to a 5.0×10^{-6} *M* sample of the dye solution. The solution is mixed well and placed in a dry cuvette. The absorbance of the solution is measured as a function of time, and the following data are obtained.

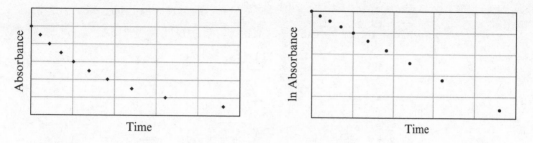

i. What is the order of the reaction with respect to the dye?

ii. When the concentration of dye is held constant and the concentration of bleach is doubled, the rate doubles. What is the rate expression for the reaction of bleach with dye?

2. Morphine, $C_{17}H_{19}O_3N$, is a weak base that is used to treat severe pain. The hydroxide ion concentration in a 0.0621 *M* aqueous solution of morphine is 3.17×10^{-4} *M* at 25 °C. For the following questions, assume that the temperature remains constant and that the volumes are additive.

a. Write the equation for the reaction of $C_{17}H_{19}O_3N(aq)$ with water.

b. Write the base dissociation constant expression for the reaction of $C_{17}H_{19}O_3N(aq)$ with water.

c. Determine the pH of the 0.0621 *M* morphine solution.

d. Determine the base dissociation constant, K_b, for morphine.

e. Determine the percent ionization of morphine in a 0.0621 *M* solution.

f. A chemist titrates a 25.0-mL sample of the 0.0621 *M* morphine solution with 0.0500 *M* HCl(*aq*).

    i. Determine the volume of 0.0500 *M* HCl(*aq*) required to reach the equivalence point.

    ii. Determine the pH of the solution at the equivalence point.

    iii. Determine the pH of the solution after 14.0 mL of 0.0500 *M* HCl have been added.

g. On the axes below, sketch the titration curve for the titration of morphine with HCl(*aq*). Label the pH values at the beginning of the titration, halfway to the equivalence point, and at the equivalence point. Label the volume of HCl added at the half-equivalence point and at the equivalence point.

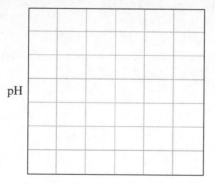

GO ON TO THE NEXT PAGE

3. An electrochemical cell is constructed with two cadmium electrodes. The cathode contains a 1.00 M solution of $Cd(NO_3)_2$, and the anode contains 1.00 M Na_2S.

$$Cd^{2+}(aq) + 2\,e^- \rightarrow Cd(s) \qquad\qquad E° = ?\ V$$

$$CdS(s) + 2\,e^- \rightarrow Cd(s) + S^{2-}(aq) \qquad\qquad E° = -1.210\ V$$

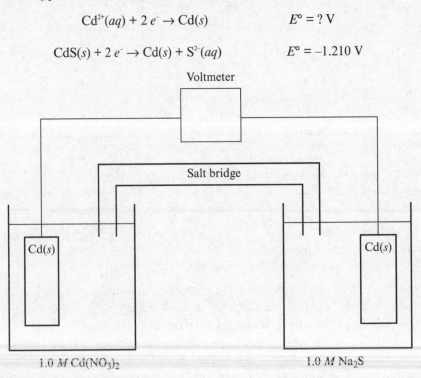

a. When the half-cells are connected, an overall potential of 0.807 V is measured. What is the standard reduction potential, $E°$, for the reduction of Cd^{2+}?

b. Clearly describe the function of the salt bridge in this cell.

c. Write the overall net ionic equation for the electrochemical cell.

d. If the cell is assembled with 0.500 M $Cd(NO_3)_2$ instead of 1.00 M $Cd(NO_3)_2$, what effect would this have on the cell potential? Provide a qualitative explanation of your response.

e. What is the standard free energy change, $\Delta G°$, at 25 °C for the overall reaction? Report your answer in units of $kJ \cdot mol^{-1}$.

f. Calculate the solubility product, K_{sp}, at 25 °C for $CdS(s)$.

g. Solid CdS is added to a 0.100 M solution of Na_2S at 25 °C. Calculate the solubility of CdS in 0.100 M Na_2S. Report your answer in units of $mol \cdot L^{-1}$.

GO ON TO THE NEXT PAGE

4. The reaction between solid sodium hydride, NaH, and water produces hydrogen gas and sodium hydroxide. A sample of NaH was added to excess water and the reaction was allowed to proceed until gas production stopped. The gas collected in the cylinder is in thermal equilibrium with the water.

The depth of the cylinder is adjusted so that the water levels inside and outside of the cylinder are the same.

The barometric pressure is 757 torr and room temperature is 24 °C. The vapor pressure of water at 24 °C is 22.5 torr.

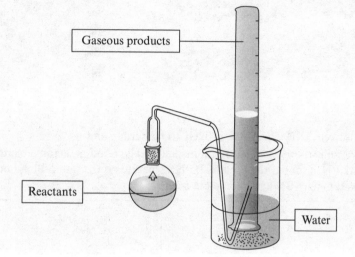

    a. Write the balanced equation for the gas-forming reaction.

    b. The collected gas occupies 19.2 mL. How many moles of gas have been collected?

    c. The collected gas is dried over a dessicant, or drying agent. What volume is occupied by the dry gas at 757 torr? Express your answer in units of mL.

    d. An equal number of moles of dry HCl gas is collected in a separate experiment. Is the volume occupied by the HCl equal to, less than, or greater than the volume occupied by the hydrogen? Explain your answer.

GO ON TO THE NEXT PAGE

5. Boron nitride, BN, exists in several allotropic forms. One allotrope, a-BN, consists of sheets of six-membered rings similar to graphite, and the other allotrope, β-BN, is arranged in a manner similar to diamond.

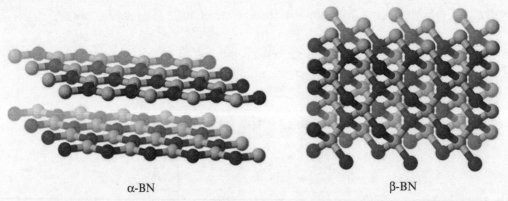

α-BN   β-BN

a. Which allotrope, α-BN or β-BN, is likely to be harder, and why?

b. Unlike graphite, α-BN is an electrical insulator. The bonding arrangement of the boron and nitrogen atoms in α-BN is similar to graphite. In the structure on the right, fill in bonds and formal charges so that each atom in α-BN has a complete octet.

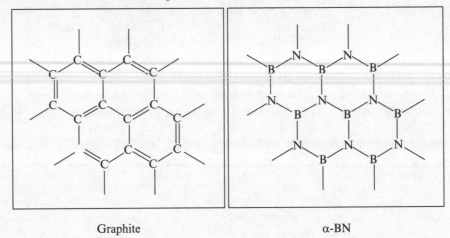

Graphite   α-BN

c. What is the hybridization and geometry of the boron atoms in α-BN?

d. A second binary nitride is composed of nitrogen and element X in a 1:1 mole ratio. The compound is 34.18% nitrogen by mass. What is the identity of element X? Show your calculation.

GO ON TO THE NEXT PAGE

6. The balanced equation for the complete combustion of acetylene, C_2H_2, in oxygen is shown below.

$$C_2H_2(g) + \frac{5}{2} O_2(g) \rightarrow 2\,CO_2(g) + H_2O(l)$$

a. Use the data in the table below to determine $\Delta H°$ for the reaction. Report your answer in units of $kJ \cdot mol^{-1}$.

Substance	$\Delta H°_f$ ($kJ \cdot mol^{-1}$)
$C_2H_2(g)$	227.4
$CO_2(g)$	−393.5
$H_2O(g)$	−241.8

b. Calculate the quantity of heat released when 500.0 g of acetylene reacts completely with oxygen. Report your answer in units of kJ.

c. The standard free energy change, $\Delta G°$, for the reaction is −1227 $kJ \cdot mol^{-1}$. Estimate the standard entropy change, $\Delta S°$, for the reaction at 298 K. Report your answer in units of $J \cdot mol^{-1} \cdot K^{-1}$.

d. Use the data in the table below to estimate the bond energy of the C-C triple bond in acetylene. Report your answer in units of $kJ \cdot mol^{-1}$.

Bond	Bond Energy ($kJ \cdot mol^{-1}$)
C—H	412
O=O	495
C=O	799
O—H	467

7. Solid ammonium carbamate, $NH_4CO_2NH_2$, decomposes at 25 °C to form gaseous ammonia and carbon dioxide.

a. Write the balanced chemical equation for the decomposition reaction described above.

b. A 100.0-g sample of $NH_4CO_2NH_2$ was introduced into an evacuated, rigid container. When the reaction reached equilibrium, the total pressure inside the container was 0.270 atm.

   i. Determine the partial pressures of NH_3 and CO_2 at equilibrium.

   ii. What is the equilibrium constant, K_p, for the decomposition of ammonium carbamate at 25 °C?

c. An additional quantity of CO_2 gas was added to the equilibrium mixture so that the total pressure was 0.370 atm. A student claims that when equilibrium is reestablished, the new total pressure will be less than 0.270 atm due to Le Chatelier's principle. Explain why you agree or disagree with this statement.

IF YOU FINISH BEFORE TIME IS CALLED, CHECK YOUR WORK ON THIS SECTION ONLY. DO NOT WORK ON ANY OTHER SECTION IN THE TEST.

Answer Key

Section I: Multiple Choice

1. B	**13.** B	**25.** D	**37.** D	**49.** C
2. D	**14.** D	**26.** B	**38.** A	**50.** D
3. B	**15.** C	**27.** D	**39.** B	**51.** A
4. C	**16.** C	**28.** B	**40.** C	**52.** A
5. C	**17.** D	**29.** A	**41.** B	**53.** B
6. D	**18.** A	**30.** D	**42.** B	**54.** A
7. B	**19.** A	**31.** A	**43.** B	**55.** D
8. A	**20.** B	**32.** C	**44.** D	**56.** A
9. C	**21.** C	**33.** A	**45.** D	**57.** C
10. C	**22.** C	**34.** A	**46.** C	**58.** A
11. C	**23.** C	**35.** A	**47.** B	**59.** A
12. A	**24.** C	**36.** A	**48.** A	**60.** C

Answers and Explanations

Section I: Multiple Choice

1. B. (EK 3.A.1) Ammonia is represented by the gray and white spheres. Oxygen is represented by the black spheres. The overall equation is

$$4 NH_3 + 5 O_2 \rightarrow 4 NO + 6 H_2O$$

2. D. (EK 2.D.1) A bromide ion has a larger ionic radius than a chloride ion, so the distance between ions in potassium bromide is greater than the distance in potassium chloride. This leads to a lower coulombic attractive force between potassium and bromide compared to that between potassium and chloride. The lower attractive force results in a lower melting point for potassium bromide.

3. B. (EK 2.A.3, 2.B.3, 5.D.2) In paper chromatography, substances that have stronger intermolecular forces with the mobile phase will move up the paper more quickly than substances that experience weaker intermolecular forces with the stationary phase. Since borneol (shown in lane 1) does not move as far up the paper as camphor (shown as the higher spot in lane 2), it experiences weaker intermolecular attractions with the mobile phase than camphor does.

4. C. (EK 2.A.3) The R_f value for a compound in a particular solvent is calculated by taking the ratio of the distance travelled by the compound to the distance travelled by the solvent.

Borneol:

$$\frac{10-5}{42-5} = \frac{5}{37} \approx \text{around } \frac{1}{7} \text{ or } 0.14$$

Camphor:

$$\frac{26-5}{42-5} = \frac{21}{37} \approx \frac{3}{5} \text{ or } 0.6$$

The actual value of the R_f of camphor is 0.57, so this is a good approximation.

$$\frac{21}{37} = 0.57$$

5. C. (EK 3.A.2) Since borneol was still present in the reaction mixture in lane 2, the reaction was not complete, and the yield was less than 100%.

6. D. (EK 5.E.1) Generally, the larger the number of electrons in a gaseous compound, the more complex the molecule is, and the higher its standard molar entropy. The $SiCl_4$ has the most electrons and the highest standard molar entropy, followed by CF_4. HCl is the smallest molecule, with the lowest standard molar entropy.

7. B. (EK 2.D.2) Interstitial alloys are composed of mixtures of primarily metal atoms, such as iron, with smaller atoms such as carbon in the interstices of the crystal lattice. The conductivity and malleability of the alloy can still be understood in terms of the electron sea model of metallic bonding.

8. A. (EK 5.C.2) The equations can be rearranged to add up to the overall transformation. The $\Delta H°$ values must be changed to reflect the changes made to the equations. The sum of the $\Delta H°$ values is the overall $\Delta H°$ for the reaction.

Reaction	$\Delta H°$
$2\ Al(s) + 6\ HCl(aq) \rightarrow 2\ AlCl_3(aq) + 3\ H_2(g)$	w
$[HCl(g) \rightarrow HCl(aq)] \times 6$	$6x$
$[H_2(g) + Cl_2(g) \rightarrow 2\ HCl(g)] \times 3$	$3y$
$[AlCl_3(s) \rightarrow AlCl_3(aq)] \times (-2)$	$-2z$

9. **C.** (EK 4.D.1) The increase in the rate of the reaction suggests that zinc oxide-chromium(III) oxide is a heterogeneous catalyst. Catalysts increase the rate of a reaction by providing an alternative mechanism with a lower activation energy than that of the uncatalyzed process.

10. **C.** (EK 2.C.4) Atoms in the same main group on the periodic table have the same number of valence electrons and tend to exhibit similar bonding patterns. Since Si and Se are in different groups on the periodic table, the resulting structures have different geometry and polarity. SiF_4 is a tetrahedral, nonpolar molecule, and SeF_4 is a "see-saw" shaped (or diphenoidal), polar molecule.

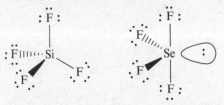

11. **C.** (EK 1.E.2, 3.A.2) HNO_3 is a strong acid. Its concentration is best determined by titration of a standardized solution of a base such as NaOH.

12. **A.** (EK 3.B.2, 6.C.1) The stronger an acid, the lower the pH of the solution. $HClO_3$ is the only strong acid among the choices, so a solution of $HClO_3$ will have the lowest pH.

13. **B.** (EK 6.C.1) It is clear from the small K_a that H_2S is a very weak acid. The pH of a weak acid solution is formally determined using a R.I.C.E. table, although students with sufficient practice can perform this calculation without writing out the table.

Reaction	H_2S	H_3O^+	HS^-
Initial Concentrations (M)	1.00	0	0
Change	$-x$	$+x$	$+x$
Equilibrium Concentrations (M)	$1.00 - x$	x	x

The value of x may be neglected in the denominator. Because the equilibrium constant is so small, subtraction of x from 1.00 does not significantly change the value of the denominator.

$$K_a = \frac{[H_3O^+][HS^-]}{[H_2S]}$$

$$9 \times 10^{-8} = \frac{x^2}{1.00 - \cancel{x}}$$

The pH of the solution is estimated to be between 3 and 4.

$$\sqrt{(9 \times 10^{-8})} = \sqrt{x^2}$$

$$x = 3 \times 10^{-4} \ M = [H_3O^+]$$

$$pH = -\log (3 \times 10^{-4}) \approx 3 - 4$$

14. **D.** (EK 3.B.2) Brønsted-Lowry acids are proton donors in solution. The species that behave as Brønsted-Lowry acids are H_2S in the reactants and H_3O^+ in the products.

15. **C.** (EK 3.B.2) Brønsted-Lowry bases are proton acceptors in solution. The species that behave as bases in the reaction are HS^- in the products and H_2O in the reactants. Because the acid dissociation constant is small, the equilibrium lies to the left. Because the equilibrium favors the side of the reaction with the weaker acid and base, H_2O is a weaker base than HS^-. The K_b of HS^- is larger than the K_b of H_2O.

16. **C.** (EK 6.A.1) Since gases dissolve in water in an exothermic process, a decrease in the temperature of the water increases the solubility of gaseous CO_2. This results in an increase in the concentration of H_2CO_3, which drives the acid dissociation reaction toward products. The resulting increase in the H_3O^+ concentration leads to a decrease in pH.

17. **D.** (EK 5.B.2, 5.B.3, 5.B.4) The metal can be identified by its heat capacity. The heat gained by the water is equal to the heat lost by the metal.

$$q_{lost} = -q_{gained}$$

$$\text{where } q = mc\Delta T$$

$$(1.00 \text{ g})(c)(25.3 - 100.0 \text{ °C}) = -(20.0 \text{ g})(4.184 \text{ J} \cdot \text{g}^{-1} \cdot \text{°C}^{-1})(25.3 - 25.0 \text{ °C})$$

$$c = \frac{(20.0 \text{ g})(4.184 \text{ J} \cdot \text{g}^{-1} \cdot \text{°C}^{-1})(0.3 \text{ °C})}{(1.00 \text{ g})(74.7 \text{ °C})} \approx \frac{6 \times 4.18}{75} \approx \frac{25}{75} \approx \frac{1}{3} \approx 0.33$$

18. **A.** (EK 5.E.3) In this reaction, one mole of gas becomes two moles of gas, so entropy increases. Because $\Delta H°$ and $\Delta S°$ are both positive, as temperature increases, the larger the $T\Delta S°$ term becomes in the equation $\Delta G° = \Delta H° - T\Delta S°$. In other words, as T increases, $\Delta G°$ decreases.

19. **A.** (EK 5.C.2) The difference between the sums of the bond energies of the reactants and the bond energies of the products gives an estimate of $\Delta H°_{rxn}$.

$$\Delta H°_{rxn} = \left(\Sigma \text{ bonds broken}\right) - \left(\Sigma \text{ bonds formed}\right)$$

$$= [\cancel{3}^{1}(BE_{\text{C-H single}}) + 1(BE_{\text{C-C single}}) + \cancel{2(BE_{\text{N-H}})} + 1(BE_{\text{C-N single}})] - [1(BE_{\text{C-C double}}) + \cancel{4(BE_{\text{C-H single}})} + \cancel{3}^{1}(BE_{\text{N-H}})]$$

$$55 \text{ kJ} \cdot \text{mol}^{-1} = 412 \text{ kJ} \cdot \text{mol}^{-1} + 347 \text{ kJ} \cdot \text{mol}^{-1} + BE_{\text{C-N single}} - [611 \text{ kJ} \cdot \text{mol}^{-1} + 389 \text{ kJ} \cdot \text{mol}^{-1}]$$

$$BE_{\text{C-N single}} = 296 \text{ kJ} \cdot \text{mol}^{-1}$$

20. **B.** (EK 2.A.1, 5.B.3) The energy that is transferred to a liquid as it undergoes a phase transition to the gaseous state does not raise the temperature of the liquid; during the phase transition, intermolecular forces are overcome and the individual particles of the substance separate from one another as energy is added.

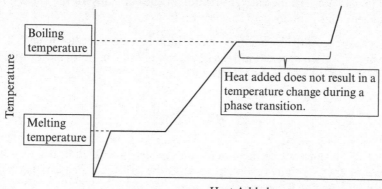

21. **C.** (EK 5.C.2) The positive $\Delta H°$ indicates an endothermic process. Energy is required to overcome the attraction between a sodium ion and an electron.

22. **C.** (EK 2.A.2) The density, temperature, and pressure of a gas can be used to determine the molar mass of the gas. Three equations, all available on the *AP Chemistry Equations and Constants* sheet, can be combined to solve for the molar mass.

$$D = \frac{m}{V}$$

$$n = \frac{m}{M}$$

$$PV = nRT$$

Where D is density, m is mass, V is volume, n is number of moles, M is molar mass, P is pressure, R is the gas constant, and T is temperature.

Substitution and rearrangement to solve for the molar mass gives

$$M = \frac{dRT}{P} = \frac{(2.00\ g \cdot L^{-1})(0.08206\ L \cdot atm \cdot mol^{-1} \cdot K^{-1})(268\ K)}{1\ atm} = 44\ g \cdot mol^{-1}$$

This is the molar mass of CO_2.

23. **C.** (EK 2.C.5) Double bonds are shorter than single bonds, so the C-O bond length in $(CH_3)_2CO$ is less than that in H_3COH. The bond in $CH_3CO_2^-$, a resonance hybrid, is of intermediate length. It is longer than a double bond, but shorter than a single bond.

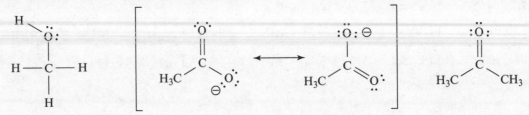

24. **C.** (EK 4.A.1) Increased surface area of a reactant increases its exposure to the other reactant(s), allowing the reaction to proceed at a faster rate.

25. **D.** (EK 1.B.1) Across a period, effective nuclear charge increases, causing the attraction of the electrons in a given sublevel to increase. The increased attraction of the electrons for the nucleus results in a larger energetic requirement for the removal of an electron from the sublevel.

26. **B.** (EK 1.D.2) Ions are separated by mass-to-charge ratio in a mass spectrometer. The lower the ratio, the higher the deflection. All four species have the same charge (+1), but the species with the lowest mass, and therefore the lowest mass-to-charge ratio, is $^1H_2^{16}O^+$.

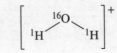

27. **D.** (EK 4.A.1, 4.A.2) The linearity of the plot of time versus $\ln[N_2O_5]$ indicates that the reaction is first order with respect to N_2O_5. For any first order process, the half-life depends only on the rate constant, not on the initial concentration of the reactant.

28. **B.** (EK 1.B.1) The first ionization energy is slightly lower for oxygen than it is for nitrogen due to repulsion between the two electrons in the first doubly occupied *p*-orbital of oxygen.

29. A. (EK 6.B.1, 6.B.2) At a lower pH, rainwater has a higher concentration of H_3O^+. An increase in the concentration of H_3O^+ decreases Q and causes the reaction to shift to the right, meaning more of the marble dissolves.

$$Q = \frac{[Ca^{2+}][HCO_3^-]}{[H_3O^+]}$$

30. D. (EK 6.A.4) The equilibrium expression for the hypothetical reaction is

$$K = \frac{[B]^2}{[A]}$$

The figure that depicts equilibrium is the one in which $[A] = 6\ M$ and $[B] = 6\ M$ (choice D).

$$6 = \frac{6^2}{6}$$

31. A. (EK 6.A.3) The concentrations of the three species in the 100-L container are

$$[SbCl_5] = \frac{20\ mol}{100\ L} = 0.2\ M$$

$$[SbCl_3] = \frac{50\ mol}{100\ L} = 0.5\ M$$

$$[Cl_2] = \frac{60\ mol}{100\ L} = 0.6\ M$$

The equilibrium quotient can be compared with the equilibrium constant.

$$Q_c = \frac{[SbCl_3][Cl_2]}{[SbCl_5]} = \frac{(0.5)(0.6)}{0.2} = 1.5$$

Since $Q_c < K_c$, the reaction will shift toward products. Because one mole of gaseous reactant becomes two moles of gaseous products, the pressure will increase.

32. C. (EK 4.D.1) The solid catalyst increases the rate of the reaction in vessel 2 by decreasing the activation energy of the reaction but the equilibrium constant is unchanged, so the total equilibrium pressures are equal in both vessels.

33. A. (EK 2.C.4) The nitrogen structure in choice A has three regions of electron density (two single bonds and one double bond). It is sp^2 hybridized.

34. A. (EK 2.A.1) Both quartz (a network covalent solid) and steel (an interstitial alloy) are harder substances than NaCl, KI, KCl, and CaF_2, which are ionic compounds. Sodium chloride (NaCl) is harder than potassium chloride (KCl) because the sodium ion has a smaller radius than the potassium ion, resulting in a stronger coulombic attraction with the chloride anion. Sodium chloride is softer than calcium fluoride (CaF_2) because the 2+ charge of calcium (in addition to the smaller radius of the fluoride ion) leads to a stronger coulombic attraction between Ca^{2+} and F^- than that between Na^+ and Cl^-. Therefore, NaCl (choice A) is expected to have a hardness of 2.5.

35. A. (EK 1.D.3) Absorption of ultraviolet photons leads to electronic transitions in atoms and molecules.

36. A. (EK 2.A.2, 5.A.1) Because the four gases have equal temperatures, they have equal kinetic energies. For gases of similar kinetic energy, smaller molecular weight gases have greater average speeds. Because H_2 has the smallest molecular weight of the choices listed, the average speed of the gas particles is greatest in container 1.

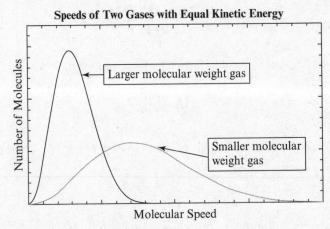

Speeds of Two Gases with Equal Kinetic Energy

37. D. (EK 2.A.2) Fluorine atoms have more electrons and are more polarizable than hydrogen atoms, so the London dispersion forces experienced by CF_4 are greater than those experienced by CH_4. Greater intermolecular attractions decrease the pressure inside the container.

38. A. (EK 3.B.3) None of the elements in the reaction of NaBr with $AgNO_3$ undergoes a change in oxidation number. This is a double replacement reaction.

39. B. (EK 3.B.3) The halogens are some of the most easily reduced elements on the periodic table. Addition of an electron to a neutral chlorine atom achieves a noble gas electron configuration.

40. C. (EK 2.A.3, 5.E.3) The decrease in temperature indicates that the dissolution is endothermic. In order for $\Delta H = \Delta H_1 + \Delta H_2 + \Delta H_3$ to be positive overall, the magnitude of the sum of the two endothermic steps, $\Delta H_1 + \Delta H_2$, must be greater than the magnitude of the exothermic step, ΔH_3.

41. B. (EK 6.C.2) A buffer is formed from approximately equal numbers of moles of a weak acid and its conjugate base. When one-half of an equivalent of HCl, a strong acid, is added to OCl^-, equal numbers of moles of HOCl and OCl^- result. The pH of the buffer solution is equal to the pK_a of the acid. For HOCl

$$pK_a = -\log K_a = -\log(3.5 \times 10^{-8}) \approx 7.4$$

42. B. (EK 4.B.1, 4.B.2) Temperature is a measure of average kinetic energy. The higher the average kinetic energy or temperature of a system, the more frequently the molecules collide with sufficient energy to overcome the activation barrier.

43. B. (EK 6.C.1) The pH at the equivalence point of the titration, when about 50 mL of titrant have been added, is about 9. The high pH at the equivalence point, in addition to the shape of the curve, show that the titration is of a weak monoprotic acid with a strong base.

44. D. (EK 2.B.1, 2.B.2, 2.B.3) The boiling point trend of the group IV hydrides is generally increasing because as the size and polarizability of the electron clouds increase, the stronger the London dispersion forces are among the molecules. However, ammonia deviates from this general trend and has a much higher boiling point than expected because it is capable of hydrogen bonding.

45. D. (EK 2.C.4) Of the choices given, only the compound with three carbons can exist as more than one isomer (it can either contain a double bond or exist as a ring).

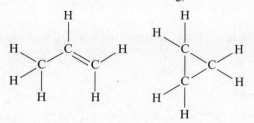

46. C. (EK 2.C.4) Only 2-butene (choice C) can exist as two geometric isomers due to restricted rotation about the π-bond. Rotation about the π-bond would lead to different isomer.

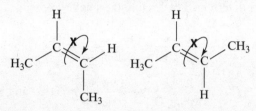

47. B. (EK 2.C.4) Many physical and chemical properties of isomers are very different. For instance, *n*-hexane and 2,3-dimethylbutane have different boiling points because they have different surface areas, which leads to different degrees of intermolecular attractions.

48. A. (EK 2.D.3) Boron has fewer valence electrons than germanium, so addition of boron will result in positive holes in the semiconductor.

49. C. (EK 4.A.2) The rate law can be determined by comparing the trials.

The order with respect to I^- can be determined from trials 2 and 3.

$$\frac{\text{rate}_2}{\text{rate}_3} = \frac{k[I^-]_2^x[ClO^-]_2^y[OH^-]_2^z}{k[I^-]_3^x[ClO^-]_3^y[OH^-]_3^z}$$

$$\frac{6.0 \times 10^{-2}}{3.0 \times 10^{-2}} = \frac{\cancel{k}(1.00 \times 10^{-2})^x(\cancel{5.00 \times 10^{-3}})^y(\cancel{5.00 \times 10^{-3}})^z}{\cancel{k}(5.00 \times 10^{-3})^x(\cancel{5.00 \times 10^{-3}})^y(\cancel{5.00 \times 10^{-3}})^z}$$

$$2 = 2^x$$

$$x = 1$$

The order with respect to ClO^- can be determined from trials 1 and 3.

$$\frac{\text{rate}_1}{\text{rate}_3} = \frac{6.0 \times 10^{-2}}{3.0 \times 10^{-2}} = \frac{\cancel{k}(\cancel{5.00 \times 10^{-3}})^x(1.00 \times 10^{-2})^y(\cancel{5.00 \times 10^{-3}})^z}{\cancel{k}(\cancel{5.00 \times 10^{-3}})^x(5.00 \times 10^{-3})^y(\cancel{5.00 \times 10^{-3}})^z}$$

$$2 = 2^y$$

$$y = 1$$

The order with respect to OH^- can be determined from trials 3 and 4.

$$\frac{\text{rate}_3}{\text{rate}_4} = \frac{3.0 \times 10^{-2}}{1.5 \times 10^{-2}} = \frac{\cancel{k}(\cancel{5.00 \times 10^{-3}})^x(\cancel{5.00 \times 10^{-3}})^y(5.00 \times 10^{-3})^z}{\cancel{k}(\cancel{5.00 \times 10^{-3}})^x(\cancel{5.00 \times 10^{-3}})^y(1.00 \times 10^{-2})^z}$$

$$2 = \left(\frac{1}{2}\right)^z$$

$$z = -1$$

The rate law is written as

$$\text{rate} = k[ClO^-]^x[I^-]^y[OH^-]^z = k[ClO^-][I^-][OH^-]^{-1}$$

50. D. (EK 4.A.3) The overall order of the reaction is the sum of the orders with respect to the reactants.

$$x + y + z = 1 + 1 - 1 = 1$$

The first order rate constant has units of $time^{-1}$.

51. A. (EK 3.A.2) It is first necessary to write and balance the chemical equation for the reaction.

$$2\,K(g) + O_2(g) \rightarrow K_2O_2(s)$$

The theoretical yield can be determined by finding the smallest possible number of moles of K_2O_2 formed.

$$39.1\ gK \times \frac{1\ mol\ K}{39.10\ gK} \times \frac{1\ mol\ K_2O_2}{2\ mol\ K} = 0.500\ mol\ K_2O_2$$

$$32.0\ gO_2 \times \frac{1\ mol\ O_2}{32.00\ gO_2} \times \frac{1\ mol\ K_2O_2}{1\ mol\ O_2} = 1.00\ mol\ K_2O_2$$

This shows that K is the limiting reagent and half (16 grams) of the O_2 is left over. The molar mass of K_2O_2 is 110.2 g·mol^{-1}.

$$0.500\ mol\ K_2O_2 \times \frac{110.2\ g\ K_2O_2}{1\ mol\ K_2O_2} = 55.1\ g\ K_2O_2$$

52. A. (EK 4.C.1) Because of the unlikelihood of three molecules of gas colliding simultaneously with the correct orientation and energy for a reaction to occur, a trimolecular elementary step, which would occur if the reaction proceeded in the single step that is shown, is very rare.

53. B. (EK 3.C.3) The oxidation number of Sn changes from +4 to +2. It becomes less positive, so Sn is being reduced. The oxidation number of Fe changes from +2 to +3. It becomes more positive, so Fe is being oxidized.

$$E^\circ_{cell} = E^\circ_{reduction} - E^\circ_{oxidation} = 0.15\ V - 0.77\ V = -0.62\ V$$

The negative cell potential is indicative of a thermodynamically disfavored process.

54. A. (EK 3.C.3) The electrolysis of KCl will result in one of two reductions at the cathode.

$$K^+ + e^- \rightarrow K$$

or

$$2\,H_2O + 2\,e^- \rightarrow H_2 + 2\,OH^-$$

Because the alkali metal cations are very difficult to reduce (a neutral alkali metal atom achieves noble gas configuration easily by *losing* an electron), the reduction of water takes place at the cathode, as shown in choice A.

55. D. (EK 2.B.2, 5.D.1) Dipole-induced dipole attractions occur between a polar molecule and a nonpolar molecule. Proximity to the polar molecule causes the electrons of the nonpolar molecule to temporarily polarize, resulting in an intermolecular attraction. HCl is the most polar molecule included in the choices, and Br_2 is a nonpolar molecule, so the most important intermolecular force between the two molecules will be dipole-induced dipole attractions.

56. A. (EK 4.B.3) The plot of $\ln(k)$ versus T^{-1}, as shown in the plot in choice A, gives a straight line with a negative slope equal to $-\dfrac{E_a}{R}$.

57. C. (EK 6.A.3) Carbon dioxide is the only gaseous product of the reaction, so the total pressure inside the container is equal to the partial pressure of CO_2, as shown in choice C.

$$K_p = P_{CO_2}$$

58. A. (EK 6.D.1) The change in Gibbs free energy is related to the equilibrium constant.

$$\Delta G° = -RT \ln K$$

Because K is less than 1, $\ln K$ is negative and $-RT \ln K$ is positive.

59. A. (EK 2.C.1, 5.C.1) Triple bonds, in general, are stronger and shorter than double bonds. An N-N bond in N_2 is a triple bond and an O-O double bond in O_2 is a double bond, so X corresponds to N_2 and Y corresponds to O_2. (This is a simple explanation that does not take the diradical nature of O_2 into account; it is sufficient for AP-level justification.)

60. C. (EK 2.C.3) The "electron sea" model of metallic bonding (choice C), in which conductive electrons are shared among fixed metallic nuclei, is responsible for the conductivity and malleability of metals.

Section II: Free Response

1. a. (EK 1.A.1, 1.A.3)

$$0.200 \text{ g dye} \times \frac{1 \text{ mol dye}}{792.86 \text{ g dye}} = 2.52 \times 10^{-4} \text{ mol dye}$$

b. (EK 2.A.3) A volumetric flask is a precisely calibrated piece of glassware that is designed to contain an accurately-known volume of solvent at a particular temperature. A volumetric flask is more accurate than a graduated cylinder, so it should be chosen.

c. (EK 2.A.3)

$$[\text{dye}] = \frac{2.52 \times 10^{-4} \text{ mol}}{0.500 \text{ L}} = 5.05 \times 10^{-4} \ M$$

d. (EK 2.A.3)

$$M_1 \times V_1 = M_2 \times V_2$$

$$M_2 = \frac{M_1 \times V_1}{V_2}$$

$$M_2 = \frac{(5.05 \times 10^{-4} \ M) \times (0.50 \text{ mL})}{100.0 \text{ mL}} = 2.53 \times 10^{-6} \ M$$

e. (EK 1.D.3) The dye shows a maximum absorbance at about 630 nm, so this wavelength is a good choice for the absorbance measurements.

f. i. (EK 4.A.1, 4.A.2) The reaction is first order with respect to the dye, since the plot of ln absorbance versus time is linear.

ii. (EK 4.A.1, 4.A.2) Because the reaction rate doubles when the concentration of bleach doubles, the reaction is first order in bleach. The rate expression is

$$\text{rate} = k[\text{dye}][\text{bleach}]$$

2. a. (EK 6.C.1) State symbols —(*aq*), (*l*), etc.—are not required for full credit unless otherwise stated on the exam.

$$C_{17}H_{19}O_3N(aq) + H_2O(l) \rightleftharpoons C_{17}H_{19}O_3NH^+(aq) + OH^-(aq)$$

b. (EK 6.C.1)

$$K_b = \frac{[C_{17}H_{19}O_3NH^+][OH^-]}{[C_{17}H_{19}O_3N]}$$

c. (EK 6.C.1)

$$pOH = -\log[OH^-] = -\log(3.17 \times 10^{-4}) = 3.499$$

$$pH = 14.000 - 3.499 = 10.501$$

d. (EK 6.C.1)

Reaction	$C_{17}H_{19}O_3N$	H_2O	$C_{17}H_{19}O_3NH^+$	OH^-
Initial Concentrations (*M*)	0.0621		0	0
Change	-3.17×10^{-4}		$+3.17 \times 10^{-4}$	$+3.17 \times 10^{-4}$
Equilibrium Concentrations (*M*)	0.061783		3.17×10^{-4}	3.17×10^{-4}

$$K_b = \frac{[C_{17}H_{19}O_3NH^+][OH^-]}{[C_{17}H_{19}O_3N]} = \frac{(3.17 \times 10^{-4})(3.17 \times 10^{-4})}{0.061783} = 1.63 \times 10^{-6}$$

Notice that the calculated value is 1.6264830×10^{-6}. This unrounded value should be used in question 2.f.ii. below.

e. (EK 6.C.1)

$$\%\text{ ionization} = \frac{3.17 \times 10^{-4}}{0.0621} \times 100\% = 0.510\%$$

f. i. (EK 6.C.1)

$$HCl(aq) + C_{17}H_{19}O_3N(aq) \rightleftharpoons C_{17}H_{19}O_3NH^+Cl(aq)$$

$$25.0 \; \cancel{\text{mL morphine}} \times \frac{1 \; \cancel{\text{L morphine}}}{1000 \; \cancel{\text{mL morphine}}} \times \frac{0.0621 \; \text{mol } \cancel{\text{morphine}}}{1 \; \cancel{\text{L morphine}}}$$

$$\times \frac{1 \; \cancel{\text{mol HCl}}}{1 \; \text{mol } \cancel{\text{morphine}}} \times \frac{1 \; \text{L HCl}}{0.0500 \; \cancel{\text{mol HCl}}} = 0.0311 \; \text{L}$$

ii. (EK 6.C.1)

$$C_{17}H_{19}O_3NH^+(aq) + H_2O(l) \rightleftharpoons C_{17}H_{19}O_3N(aq) + H_3O^+(aq)$$

$$M_1 \times V_1 = M_2 \times V_2$$

$$M_2 = \frac{M_1 \times V_1}{V_2}$$

$$M_2 = \frac{(0.0621\ M) \times (25.0\ \cancel{mL})}{(25.0 + 31.1)\ \cancel{mL}} = 0.0277\ M$$

$$K_a = \frac{K_w}{K_b} = \frac{1.00 \times 10^{-14}}{1.6264830 \times 10^{-6}} = 6.15 \times 10^{-9}$$

Reaction	$C_{17}H_{19}O_3NH^+$	H_2O	$C_{17}H_{19}O_3N$	H_3O^+
Initial Concentrations (M)	0.0277		0	0
Change	$-x$		$+x$	$+x$
Equilibrium Concentrations (M)	$0.0277 - x$		x	x

$$K_a = \frac{[C_{17}H_{19}O_3N][H_3O^+]}{[C_{17}H_{19}O_3NH^+]} = \frac{x^2}{0.0277 - \cancel{x}} = 6.14 \times 10^{-9}$$

Because K_a is very small, x can be neglected in the denominator. (Rounding takes place only after the final calculation.)

$$x = \sqrt{(0.0277)(6.14 \times 10^{-9})} = 1.30 \times 10^{-5} = [H_3O^+]$$
$$pH = -\log(1.30 \times 10^{-5}) = 4.884$$

iii. (EK 6.C.1)

$$14.0\ \cancel{mL\ HCl} \times \frac{1\ \cancel{L\ HCl}}{1000\ \cancel{mL\ HCl}} \times \frac{0.0500\ \cancel{mol\ HCl}}{1\ \cancel{L\ HCl}} \times \frac{1\ mol\ C_{17}H_{19}O_3NH^+}{1\ \cancel{mol\ HCl}} = 7.00 \times 10^{-4}\ mol\ C_{17}H_{19}O_3NH^+$$

$$25.0\ \cancel{mL\ morphine} \times \frac{1\ \cancel{L\ morphine}}{1000\ \cancel{mL\ morphine}} \times \frac{0.0621\ mol\ morphine}{1\ \cancel{L\ morphine}} = 0.00155\ mol\ morphine$$
$$\text{initially present}$$

$0.00155\ mol - 7.00 \times 10^{-4}\ mol = 8.53 \times 10^{-4}\ mol$ morphine remaining after HCl was added

(notice that the value generated by the calculator is 8.525×10^{-4}).

$$pOH = pK_b + \log\frac{[BH^+]}{[B]} = -\log(1.63 \times 10^{-6}) + \log\left(\frac{7.00 \times 10^{-4}}{8.525 \times 10^{-4}}\right) = 5.702$$
$$pH = 14.000 - pOH = 8.298$$

Notice that the numbers of moles can be used directly in the Henderson-Hasselbalch equation since both numbers of moles are divided by the same volume.

$$\frac{\left(\dfrac{7.00 \times 10^{-4}}{39\ \cancel{mL}}\right)}{\left(\dfrac{8.525 \times 10^{-4}}{39\ \cancel{mL}}\right)} = \frac{7.00 \times 10^{-4}}{8.525 \times 10^{-4}}$$

g. (EK 6.C.1) The titration curve of morphine begins at a pH of 10.501. The equivalence point occurs at 4.884. Halfway to the equivalence point, when about 15.5 mL of HCl have been added, the pOH of the solution is equal to the pK_b.

$$pK_b = -\log(1.63 \times 10^{-6}) = 5.788 = pOH$$

$$pH = 14.000 - 5.788 = 8.212$$

The sketch should resemble the following.

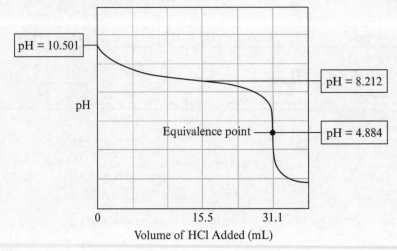

3. a. (EK 3.C.3)

$$E°_{cell} = E°_{cathode} - E°_{anode}$$

$$0.807\ V = E°_{cathode} - (-1.210\ V)$$

$$E°_{cathode} = -0.403\ V$$

b. (EK 3.C.3) The salt bridge maintains electrical neutrality in the half-cells. It allows for the passage of cations into the cathode to replace the ones that are removed from solution during reduction, and it allows anions to migrate into the anode where cations are being released into the solution. The salt bridge also connects the two half-cells while preventing their contents from mixing.

c. (EK 3.C.3)

$$Cd^{2+} + S^{2-} \rightarrow CdS$$

State symbols are not required for credit on the **AP Chemistry exam**, but if they are included, the equation becomes

$$Cd^{2+}(aq) + S^{2-}(aq) \rightarrow CdS(s)$$

d. (EK 3.C.3, 6.B.1, 6.B.2) A decrease in the concentration of Cd^{2+} would have the effect of decreasing the overall cell potential. The equilibrium quotient would be greater than the equilibrium constant, favoring the reactants.

Although the Nernst equation is not required for this answer, it is a helpful method for logic-checking.

$$E = E° - \frac{0.06}{n} \log Q$$

$$Q = \frac{1}{[Cd^{2+}][S^{2-}]}$$

Because $[Cd^{2+}]$ is decreased, Q is increased, and a larger value of $\log Q$ is subtracted from $E°$.

e. (EK 3.C.3)

$$\Delta G° = -nFE° = -(2)(96{,}485 \text{ C} \cdot \text{mol}^{-1})\left(\frac{1 \text{ J}}{1 \text{ V} \cdot \text{C}}\right)(0.807 \text{ V})\left(\frac{1 \text{ kJ}}{1000 \text{ J}}\right) = -156 \text{ kJ} \cdot \text{mol}^{-1}$$

f. (EK 3.C.3, 6.C.3, 6.D.1) First, the reaction is reversed to show the dissociation of CdS, and the sign of $E°$ changes.

$$CdS(s) \rightarrow Cd^{2+}(aq) + S^{2-}(aq)$$

$$E° = -0.807 \text{ V}$$

$$\Delta G° = -RT \ln K = -nF E°$$

$$-(8.314 \text{ J} \cdot \text{mol}^{-1} \cdot \text{K}^{-1})(298 \text{ K})(\ln K_{sp}) = -(2)(96{,}485 \text{ J} \cdot \text{V}^{-1} \cdot \text{mol}^{-1})(-0.807 \text{ V})$$

$$K_{sp} = e^{-62.9} = 5.042 \times 10^{-28}$$

g. (EK 6.C.3)

Reaction	CdS(s)	$Cd^{2+}(aq)$	$S^{2-}(aq)$
Initial Concentrations (M)		0	0.100
Change		$+x$	$+x$
Equilibrium Concentrations (M)		x	$0.100 + x$

$$K_{sp} = [Cd^{2+}][S^{2-}]$$

$$K_{sp} = (x)(0.100 + x) = 5.042 \times 10^{-28}$$

Because the K_{sp} is very small, the simplifying assumption can be made that x, the number of moles of CdS that dissolve in a 0.100 M solution of S^{2-}, is negligibly small. In that case, it can be omitted from the (0.100 + x) term.

$$5.042 \times 10^{-28} = x(0.100 + x) = 0.100x$$
$$x = 5.042 \times 10^{-27} \text{ mol}^{-1} \cdot \text{L}^{-1}$$

4. a. (EK 3.A.1)

$$NaH(s) + H_2O(l) \rightarrow NaOH(aq) + H_2(g)$$

b. (EK 2.A.2)

$$T = 24 \text{ °C} + 273 = 297 \text{ K}$$

$$P = 757 \text{ torr} \times \frac{1 \text{ atm}}{760 \text{ torr}} = 0.996 \text{ atm}$$

$$n = \frac{PV}{RT}$$

$$n = \frac{(0.996 \text{ atm})(0.0192 \text{ L})}{(0.08206 \text{ L} \cdot \text{atm} \cdot \text{mol}^{-1} \cdot \text{K}^{-1})(297 \text{ K})} = 7.85 \times 10^{-4} \text{ mol}$$

c. (EK 2.A.2)

$$P_{H_2} = P_{total} \times X_{H_2}$$

$$P_{H_2} = P_{total} - P_{H_2O}$$

$$757 \text{ torr} - 22.5 \text{ torr} = (757 \text{ torr}) \times X_{H_2}$$

$$X_{H_2} = 0.970$$

$$n_{H_2} = (0.970)(7.85 \times 10^{-4} \text{ mol}) = 7.61 \times 10^{-4} \text{ mol}$$

$$V = \frac{nRT}{P} = \frac{(7.61 \times 10^{-4} \text{ mol})(0.08206 \text{ L} \cdot \text{atm} \cdot \text{mol}^{-1} \cdot \text{K}^{-1})(297 \text{ K})}{0.996 \text{ atm}} = 0.0186 \text{ L} = 18.6 \text{ mL}$$

d. (EK 2.A.2) The volume of HCl is less than the volume occupied by the H_2. HCl is a polar molecule in contrast to H_2, which is nonpolar. While H_2 experiences only London dispersion forces, HCl also experiences dipole-dipole attractions. This causes the volume of HCl to be less than the volume predicted by the ideal gas law.

5. a. (EK 2.D.3) The β-BN allotrope is expected to be harder than the α-BN allotrope because all the boron atoms are covalently bound to all the surrounding nitrogen atoms in the β-BN form. The α-BN form resembles graphite in that the layers experience noncovalent intermolecular attractions. These are easily overcome, causing α-BN to be softer.

b. (EK 2.C.4)

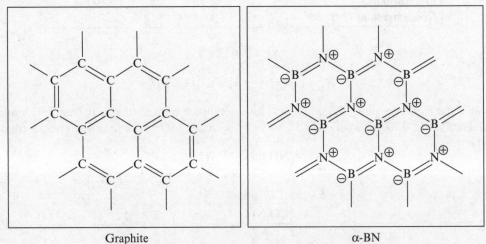

Graphite   α-BN

c. (EK 2.C.4) The boron atoms are sp^2 hybridized with trigonal planar geometry.

d. (EK 1.A.1) Assume there are 100 g of the unknown compound. If nitrogen comprises 34.18 g, element X must make up the other 65.82 g. The number of moles of nitrogen present can be determined.

$$34.18 \ \cancel{g \, N} \times \frac{1 \ \text{mol N}}{14.01 \ \cancel{g \, N}} = 2.440 \ \text{mol N}$$

Since the elements are present in a 1:1 mole ratio, there must also be 2.440 moles of element X.

$$M = \frac{65.82 \ \text{g}}{2.440 \ \text{mol}} = 26.98 \ \text{g} \cdot \text{mol}^{-1}$$

The element is aluminum.

6. **a.** (EK 5.C.2)

$$\Delta H^\circ_{\text{rxn}} = \sum n \Delta H^\circ_{\text{f(products)}} - \sum n \Delta H^\circ_{\text{f(reactants)}}$$

$$\Delta H^\circ_{\text{rxn}} = \left[(2(-393.5 \ \text{kJ} \cdot \text{mol}^{-1})) + (-241.8 \ \text{kJ} \cdot \text{mol}^{-1}) \right] - [227.4 \ \text{kJ} \cdot \text{mol}^{-1}]$$

$$\Delta H^\circ_{\text{rxn}} = -1256.2 \ \text{kJ} \cdot \text{mol}^{-1}$$

b. (EK 5.B.3) The molar mass of acetylene is 26.04 g·mol⁻¹.

$$q = n \Delta H^\circ_{\text{rxn}} = (500.0 \ \cancel{g}) \left(\frac{1 \ \cancel{\text{mol}}}{26.04 \ \cancel{g}} \right) \left(\frac{-1256.2 \ \text{kJ}}{1 \ \cancel{\text{mol}}} \right) = -24{,}120 \ \text{kJ}$$

c. (EK 5.E.1, 5.E.2)

$$\Delta G^\circ = \Delta H^\circ - T\Delta S^\circ$$

$$\Delta S^\circ = \frac{\Delta H^\circ - \Delta G^\circ}{T} = \frac{\left[-1256.2 \ \text{kJ} \cdot \text{mol}^{-1} - (-1227 \ \text{kJ} \cdot \text{mol}^{-1}) \right]}{298 \ \text{K}} = -0.0980 \ \text{kJ} \cdot \text{mol}^{-1} \cdot \text{K}^{-1} = -98.0 \ \text{J} \cdot \text{mol}^{-1} \cdot \text{K}^{-1}$$

d. (EK 5.C.2)

$$\Delta H^\circ_{\text{rxn}} = (\sum \text{bonds broken}) - (\sum \text{bonds formed})$$

$$-1256.2 \ \text{kJ} \cdot \text{mol}^{-1} = \left[(2 \times 412 \ \text{kJ} \cdot \text{mol}^{-1}) + \text{BE}_{\text{C-C triple}} + \left(\frac{5}{2} \times 495 \ \text{kJ} \cdot \text{mol}^{-1} \right) \right]$$
$$- \left[(4 \times 799 \ \text{kJ} \cdot \text{mol}^{-1}) + (2 \times 467 \ \text{kJ} \cdot \text{mol}^{-1}) \right]$$

$$\text{BE}_{\text{C-C triple}} = 812 \ \text{kJ} \cdot \text{mol}^{-1}$$

7. **a.** (EK 3.A.1)

$$NH_4CO_2NH_2(s) \rightleftharpoons 2 \ NH_3(g) + CO_2(g)$$

b. i. (EK 2.A.2)

Reaction	$NH_4CO_2NH_2(s)$	$2 \ NH_3(g)$	$CO_2(g)$
Initial Concentrations (M)		0	0
Change		+2x	+x
Equilibrium Concentrations (M)		2x	x

$$2x + x = 0.270 \text{ atm}$$

$$x = 0.0900 \text{ atm} = P_{CO_2}$$

$$P_{NH_3} = 2x = 2(0.0900 \text{ atm}) = 0.180 \text{ atm}$$

ii. (EK 6.A.3)

$$K_p = P_{NH_3}^2 P_{CO_2} = (0.180)^2(0.0900) = 0.00292$$

c. (EK 6.A.3) Disagree with this statement. When equilibrium is re-established, the product of the partial pressure of CO_2 and the partial pressure of NH_3 squared will still equal K_p. This means that the total pressure after equilibrium is re-established will still be 0.270 atm.

Chapter 9

Practice Exam 2

Section I: Multiple Choice

60 Questions
90 Minutes

Calculators are not allowed for Section I.

Note: For all questions, assume the temperature is 298 K, the pressure is 1.0 atm, and solutions are aqueous unless otherwise specified.

Directions: Each of the questions or incomplete statements below is followed by four suggested answers or completions. Select the one that is best in each case and then fill in the corresponding circle on the answer sheet.

1. Combustion of which of the following in excess oxygen results in a 2:1 mole ratio of CO_2 to H_2O?

    A. CH_4
    B. C_2H_2
    C. C_2H_4
    D. C_3H_6

GO ON TO THE NEXT PAGE

2. A conductivity experiment is conducted as shown in the figure below.

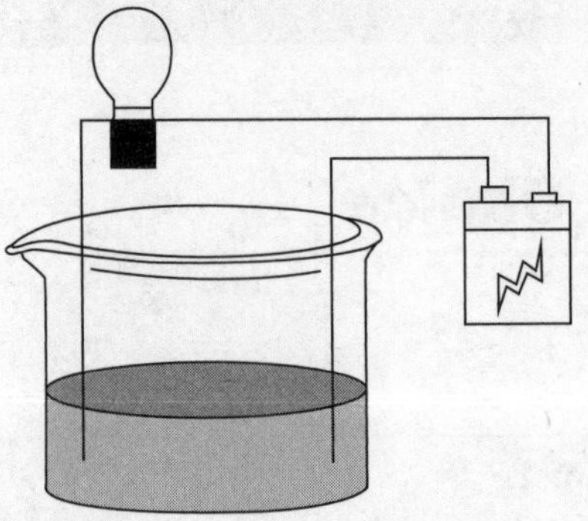

When a 1.00 *M* solution of ammonia, NH_3, and a 1.00 *M* solution of acetic acid, CH_3COOH, are mixed, the bulb glows brightly.

Which particulate diagram best explains this result? Water is not shown.

- Carbon
- Nitrogen
- Oxygen
- Hydrogen

A.

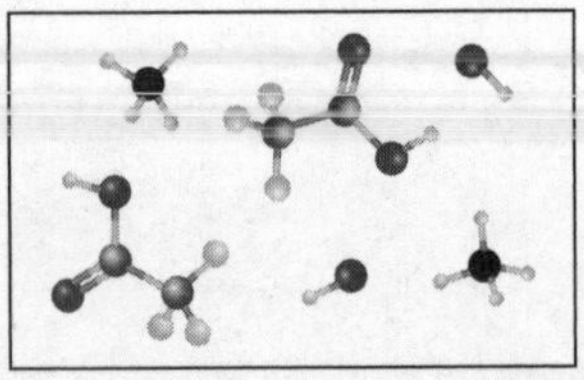

B.

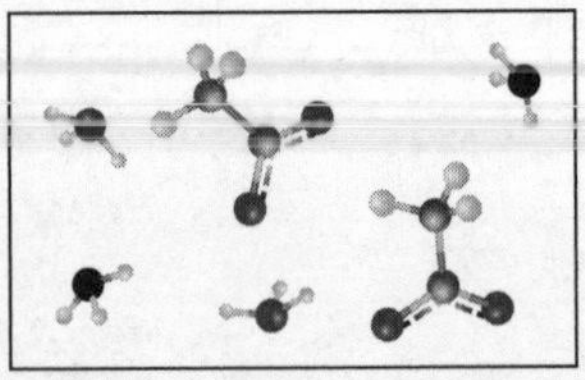

C.

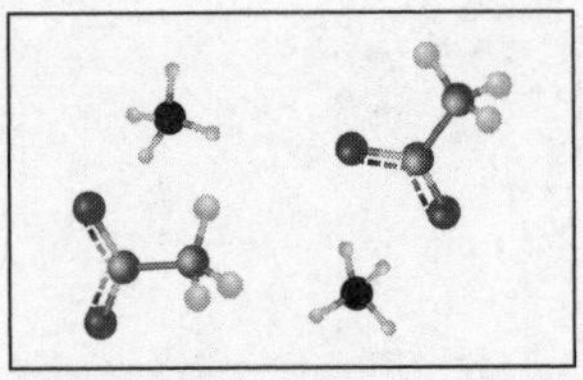

D.

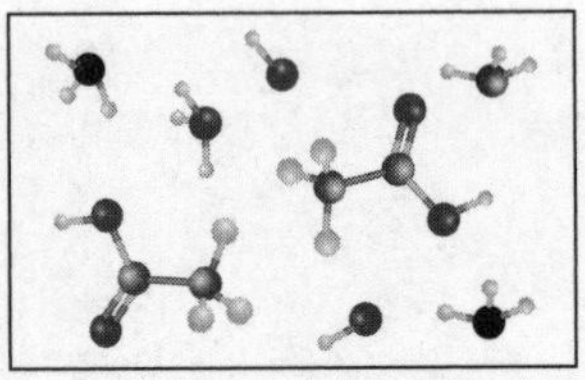

3. Stainless steel is an alloy of iron and carbon. Which of the following provides the best explanation for the unreactive nature of the surface of the alloy?

A. Ionic bonds between iron and carbon prevent atmospheric oxygen from reacting with the metal.
B. A thin film of chromium oxide at the surface of the metal prevents reaction with oxygen.
C. Both iron and carbon are unreactive toward gaseous components of the atmosphere.
D. The iron in stainless steel is enriched such that the unreactive iron isotope makes up the majority of the iron atoms.

GO ON TO THE NEXT PAGE

Use the photoelectron spectra for pure elements X, Y, and Z to answer questions 4–7.

Element X

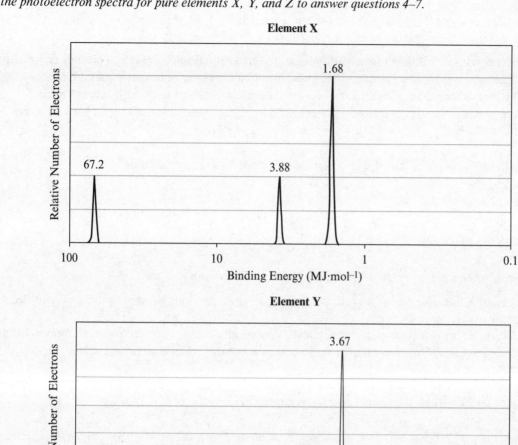

Element Y

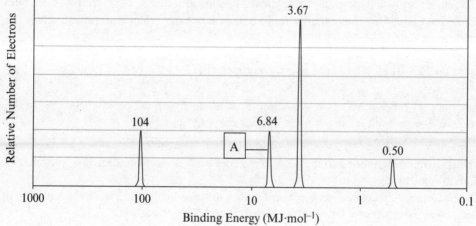

Element Z

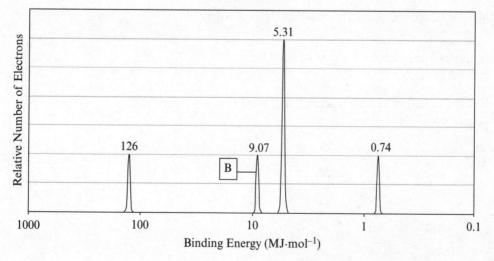

GO ON TO THE NEXT PAGE

4. Niels Bohr is credited with the "shell" model of the atom, which explains the atomic emission spectrum of hydrogen. How would these three photoelectron spectra differ if the shell model was a correct representation of the arrangement of the electrons in a polyelectronic atom?

   A. All the peaks would have lower binding energies due to equal shielding of the orbitals in a shell.
   B. All but the highest-energy peaks would have lower binding energies due to equal orbital shielding.
   C. The spectra would have fewer peaks because the shells would not be divided into subshells.
   D. The spectra would have more peaks because each orbital in each subshell would have a slightly different energy.

5. Which element(s), X, Y, and/or Z, is/are expected to ionize by gaining electrons?

   A. X only
   B. Y only
   C. Z only
   D. Both Y and Z

6. Which neutral element is expected to have the largest atomic radius?

   A. Element X, because it has the smallest nuclear charge of the three elements and its valence electrons experience the least shielding
   B. Element Z, because it experiences the most shielding and the greatest electron-electron repulsions
   C. Elements X and Y will have similar radii; both will be larger than element Z because they have smaller nuclear charges
   D. Element Y, because it has a smaller nuclear charge than element Z and its valence electrons experience more shielding than the valence electrons of element X

7. Compare the peak labeled "A" in the spectrum for element Y with the peak labeled "B" in the spectrum for element Z. Why does peak A have a lower binding energy than peak B?

   A. Element Y has a lower effective nuclear charge than element Z.
   B. The electrons contributing to the peak experience greater electron-electron repulsions in element Z than in element Y.
   C. The coulombic attraction between the electrons and the nucleus is less in element Y than in element Z due to a smaller distance between the electrons and the nucleus.
   D. Peak A arises from electrons in a $2s$ sublevel, while peak B arises from electrons in a $2p$ sublevel.

8. A yellow crystalline solid exhibits the following properties:

   ■ It is insoluble in water.
   ■ It does not conduct electricity in its solid form.
   ■ It melts at 115 °C.

   Which of the following substances could be the solid?

   A. KOH
   B. Au
   C. S_8
   D. HBr

GO ON TO THE NEXT PAGE

9. Which of the following solutions has the highest pH at 25 °C?

   A. 1.00 M NaF
   B. 1.00 M NaBr
   C. 1.00 M CH_3OH
   D. 1.00 M CH_3CO_2H

10. Which compound exhibits the highest degree of ionic character?

    A. CH_3Br
    B. $PbBr_2$
    C. NBr_3
    D. $CHBr_3$

11. Which of the statements regarding elemental silicon is false?

    A. Elemental silicon forms a network covalent solid similar to diamond since it is capable of forming four covalent bonds.
    B. The conductivity of silicon increases with increasing temperature since the number of electrons in the conduction band decreases.
    C. Silicon, like water, is less dense in its solid state than it is in its liquid state.
    D. Elemental silicon has a melting point that is higher than that of mercury or aluminum, but lower than that of elemental carbon.

12. Which structure below is expected to make the greatest contribution to the resonance hybrid structure of $HClO_4$?

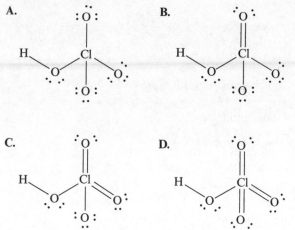

13. Which of the following correctly describes the shape of the $TeCl_5^-$ ion?

    A. The ion has an electronic geometry similar to SF_6 and a molecular geometry similar to BrF_5.
    B. The ion has an electronic geometry similar to PF_5 and a molecular geometry similar to PF_5.
    C. The ion has an electronic geometry similar to SF_6 and a molecular geometry similar to $SbCl_5$.
    D. The ion has an electronic geometry similar to PF_5 and a molecular geometry similar to SbF_4^-.

GO ON TO THE NEXT PAGE

14. Which of the following correctly ranks the bonds according to increasing bond strength?

    A. C-C double bond < C-C single bond < Si-Si single bond

    B. C-C single bond < C-C double bond < Si-Si single bond

    C. Si-Si single bond < C-C double bond < C-C single bond

    D. Si-Si single bond < C-C single bond < C-C double bond

15. Which of the following processes is expected to be endothermic?

    A. Ionization of a neutral atom due to absorption of a photon

    B. Emission of a photon from a neutral atom due to relaxation of an electron from an excited state to the ground state

    C. Condensation of gaseous helium atoms at 4 K and 1 atm

    D. Dissolution of sodium hydroxide in distilled water

Questions 16–17 refer to the hypothetical reaction below.

At a given temperature, the equilibrium constant, K_p, for the following reaction is 1.0×10^{10}.

$$2\, AB_3(g) \rightleftharpoons A_2(g) + 3B_2(g)$$

16. What is the value of K_p for the reaction below at this temperature?

$$\frac{1}{2}\, A_2(g) + \frac{3}{2}\, B_2(g) \rightleftharpoons AB_3(g)$$

    A. 1.0×10^5

    B. 1.0×10^{-5}

    C. 1.0×10^{-10}

    D. 1.0×10^{-20}

17. Consider the decomposition of gaseous AB to form gaseous A and B atoms.

$$AB(g) \rightarrow A(g) + B(g)$$

Which choice is likely to be true of the system in the reverse direction?

    A. $\Delta S > 0;\ \Delta H > 0$

    B. $\Delta S < 0;\ \Delta H < 0$

    C. $\Delta S > 0;\ \Delta H < 0$

    D. $\Delta S < 0;\ \Delta H > 0$

18. A saturated solution of CaF_2 has a Ca^{2+} concentration of x mol·L^{-1}. What is the K_{sp} of CaF_2?

    A. x^2

    B. x^3

    C. $2x^3$

    D. $4x^3$

GO ON TO THE NEXT PAGE

19. The oxidation of glucose during the fermentation process is exothermic, and the equilibrium constant, K_p, is 9×10^{39} at 298 K.

$$C_6H_{12}O_6(s) \rightleftharpoons 2\,C_2H_6O(l) + 2\,CO_2(g)$$

Which statement is true of the fermentation reaction?

A. The change in entropy for the reaction is negative.
B. The reaction is thermodynamically disfavored at high temperatures.
C. The equilibrium can be shifted toward products by increasing the temperature of the reaction.
D. The equilibrium constant can be increased by decreasing the temperature of the reaction.

20. Which of the following statements regarding enzyme catalysis is false?

A. The enzyme has a binding pocket in which the substrate may be positioned in a reactive orientation.
B. The enzyme raises the energy of the transition state of the reaction compared with the transition state of the uncatalyzed reaction.
C. The enzyme may provide an alternative reaction pathway with a transition state that is different from the uncatalyzed reaction.
D. The enzyme's three-dimensional structure is a result of intermolecular interactions between its amino acid residues and the aqueous surroundings.

21. The equation for the decomposition of nitryl chloride and the rate law for the reaction are shown below.

$$2\,NO_2Cl \rightarrow 2\,NO_2 + Cl_2$$

$$\text{rate} = k[NO_2Cl]$$

A researcher proposes two different mechanisms for the reaction.

Mechanism 1		Mechanism 2	
$NO_2Cl \rightarrow NO_2 + Cl$	(slow)	$2\,NO_2Cl \rightleftharpoons N_2O_4 + Cl_2$	(fast)
$Cl + NO_2Cl \rightarrow NO_2 + Cl_2$	(fast)	$N_2O_4 \rightarrow 2\,NO_2$	(slow)

Based on this information, which of the following is true?

A. Only mechanism 1 is consistent with the rate law.
B. Only mechanism 2 is consistent with the rate law.
C. Both mechanism 1 and mechanism 2 are consistent with the rate law.
D. Neither mechanism 1 nor mechanism 2 is consistent with the rate law.

22. Which statement is incorrect regarding crystalline solids, such as quartz, and amorphous solids, such as obsidian?

A. Crystalline solids have a sharp melting point, while amorphous solids melt over a temperature range.
B. Crystalline solids shatter into regularly shaped fragments, while amorphous solids do not.
C. A crystalline solid is composed of regularly spaced atoms, while the atoms of an amorphous solid are distributed randomly.
D. A crystalline solid, which has a regular long-range structure, is referred to as a glass.

GO ON TO THE NEXT PAGE

23. A reactant, A, undergoes decomposition according to the reaction below. Use the data to determine the order of the reaction with respect to reactant A.

A → products

Time (min)	[A]	ln [A]	[A]$^{-1}$
0.00	1.00	0	1.00
10.0	0.800	−0.223	1.25
20.0	0.667	−0.405	1.50
40.0	0.500	−0.693	2.00

    A.   Zero order
    B.   First order
    C.   Second order
    D.   Cannot be determined from the information given

24. Which procedure could be used to change the equilibrium constant for a reaction?

    A.   Increase the temperature of the reaction.
    B.   Decrease the volume of the reaction vessel.
    C.   Add solvent to the reaction vessel.
    D.   Add additional reactant to the reaction vessel.

25. Use the $E°$ values in the table to determine which reaction would have the largest equilibrium constant as written.

Reaction	$E°$ (V)
$Al^{3+} + 3\,e^- \rightarrow Al$	−1.66
$Fe^{2+} + 2\,e^- \rightarrow Fe$	−0.44
$Pb^{2+} + 2\,e^- \rightarrow Pb$	−0.13

    A. $3\,Pb^{2+} + 2\,Al \rightarrow 3\,Pb + 2\,Al^{3+}$
    B. $3\,Fe^{2+} + 2\,Al \rightarrow 3\,Fe + 2\,Al^{3+}$
    C. $3\,Pb + 2\,Al^{3+} \rightarrow 3\,Pb^{2+} + 2\,Al$
    D. $3\,Fe + 2\,Al^{3+} \rightarrow 3\,Fe^{2+} + 2\,Al$

GO ON TO THE NEXT PAGE

26. Which of the following diagrams best represents the change in electrical conductivity of a solution of HF(*aq*) as a solution of NaOH(*aq*) is added?

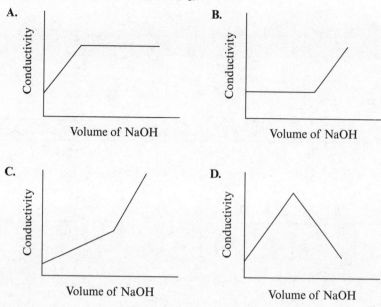

27. Which of the following statements is false?

    A.   Strong acids and strong bases are approximately 100% ionized in dilute aqueous solutions.
    B.   A conjugate acid is formed when a proton is added to a base.
    C.   Water is considered to be amphiprotic, but not amphoteric.
    D.   All strong bases appear to have the same strength in aqueous solution.

28. When a 50.0-mL solution of 0.100 M KI is titrated with 0.0500 M $K_2Cr_2O_7$ in acidic solution, the products of the reaction are I_2 and Cr^{3+}. What volume of $K_2Cr_2O_7$ is required to react completely?

    A.   6.67 mL
    B.   16.7 mL
    C.   30.0 mL
    D.   60.0 mL

29. How many grams of aluminum would be produced if a sample of Al_2O_3 was electrolyzed for 96,500 seconds using a 3.00-amp current?

    A.   9 g
    B.   18 g
    C.   27 g
    D.   54 g

Questions 30–31 refer to the unbalanced redox reaction below.

$$MnO_4^- + SO_3^{2-} \rightarrow MnO_4^{2-} + SO_4^{2-}$$

30. Which ion in the equation above contains the element that is undergoing reduction?

    A. MnO_4^-
    B. SO_3^{2-}
    C. MnO_4^{2-}
    D. SO_4^{2-}

GO ON TO THE NEXT PAGE

31. What is the smallest whole-number coefficient of OH⁻ in the balanced equation when the reaction occurs in alkaline solution?

    A. 1
    B. 2
    C. 3
    D. 4

Use the following data to answer questions 32–33.

	Structure	Boiling Point (°C)	Molar Mass (g·mol⁻¹)	Density (g·mL⁻¹)
Propanol	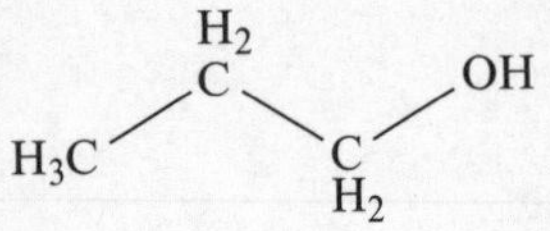	98	60.11	0.802
Propionaldehyde	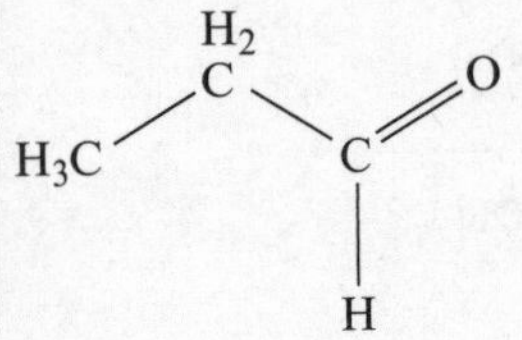	50	58.09	0.807

32. A chemist has 100.0 mL of a clear, colorless liquid composed of 5.0 mL of propanol dissolved in 95.0 mL of propionaldehyde. Which method should the chemist use in order to separate the mixture?

    A. Paper chromatography
    B. Filtration
    C. Centrifugation
    D. Distillation

33. What is the approximate molarity of propanol in the solution?

    A. 0.67
    B. 0.83
    C. 13
    D. 16

34. Which choice provides the best explanation for the thermodynamic favorability of the freezing of benzene at 6 °C and 1 atm of pressure?

    A. The decrease in the entropy of the system is offset by a sufficient increase in the entropy of the surroundings.
    B. The increase in the entropy of the system is offset by a sufficient increase in the entropy of the universe.
    C. The change in Gibbs free energy is negative because the process is highly endothermic.
    D. The entropy of the system increases because of attractive London dispersion forces between the benzene molecules.

GO ON TO THE NEXT PAGE

35. When a reactant's concentration is tripled, the rate of the reaction increases by a factor of 27. What is the order of the reaction with respect to the reactant?

    A. 2

    B. 3

    C. 9

    D. 27

36. A student uses a balance to weigh 169.88 g of $AgNO_3$. Another student uses a more precise balance to weigh 0.120 g of $AgNO_3$. The solids are combined and transferred to a beaker. The graduated cylinder shown below is used to add 100 mL of water with as much precision as possible. How many significant figures should be reported for the calculated molarity?

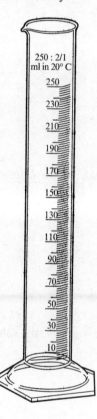

    A. 3

    B. 4

    C. 5

    D. 6

37. Which of the following statements regarding real gas behavior is false?

    A. A real gas behaves more ideally at high temperature and low pressure than it does at low temperature and high pressure.

    B. Molecules of a real gas occupy significant volume.

    C. Intermolecular attractions between gas molecules are most significant when the molecules are in the process of colliding.

    D. Neon gas is expected to deviate very little from ideal behavior since neon atoms occupy volume but do not experience intermolecular attractions.

GO ON TO THE NEXT PAGE

38. The rate law for the dimerization of hexafluoropropene, C_3F_6, was determined to be second order overall. A linear plot was obtained as shown below. What labels should be used for the x and y axes, respectively?

$$2\,C_3F_6 \rightarrow C_6F_{12}$$

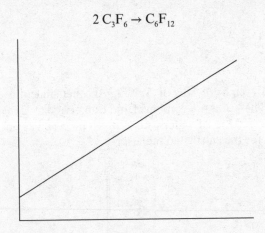

    A.   Time; $[C_3F_6]$

    B.   Time; $[C_3F_6]^{-1}$

    C.   Time; $\ln\,[C_3F_6]$

    D. $[C_3F_6]$; Time

Refer to the structures of toluene, ethylbenzene, chlorobenzene, and aniline to answer questions 39–40.

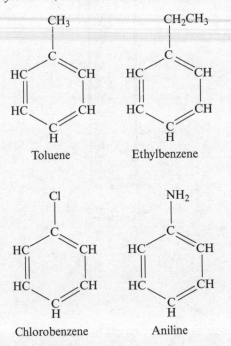

39. Which of the liquids has the greatest surface tension and why?

    A.   The surface tension of aniline is the greatest because it is capable of hydrogen bonding.

    B.   The surface tension of ethylbenzene is greatest because it experiences the strongest London dispersion forces.

    C.   The surface tension of chlorobenzene is greatest because it has the highest molar mass and is thus most polarizable.

    D.   The surface tension of toluene is greatest because its small size results in the greatest coulombic attraction between molecules.

GO ON TO THE NEXT PAGE

40. How is the surface tension of toluene expected to change with increasing temperature?

   A. The surface tension will increase because the intermolecular forces increase at higher temperatures.
   B. The surface tension will decrease because the intermolecular forces increase at higher temperatures.
   C. The surface tension will increase because the kinetic energy of the molecules is greater at higher temperatures.
   D. The surface tension will decrease because the kinetic energy of the molecules is greater at higher temperatures.

41. At constant external pressure, for which process is $w < 0$?

   A. $I_2(g) \rightarrow I_2(s)$
   B. $Br_2(l) \rightarrow Br_2(g)$
   C. $N_2O_5(g) + H_2O(l) \rightarrow 2\,HNO_3(l)$
   D. $H_2O(l) \rightarrow H_2O(s)$

42. For which equation is the equilibrium constant equal to the base dissociation constant, K_b, for the HSO_3^- ion?

   A. $HSO_3^-(aq) + H_2O(l) \rightleftharpoons H_2SO_3(aq) + OH^-(aq)$
   B. $HSO_3^-(aq) + OH^-(aq) \rightleftharpoons SO_3^{2-}(aq) + H_2O(l)$
   C. $H_2SO_3(aq) + OH^-(aq) \rightleftharpoons HSO_3^-(aq) + H_2O(l)$
   D. $SO_3^{2-}(aq) + H_2O(aq) \rightleftharpoons HSO_3^-(aq) + OH^-(aq)$

43. A sample of liquid ethanol and a sample of solid ethanol are at equilibrium at $-114\ °C$ and 1.0 atm. Which of the following statements is false?

   A. The average kinetic energies of the liquid and the solid are equal.
   B. The entropy of the solid is less than the entropy of the liquid.
   C. The rate of melting is equal to the rate of freezing.
   D. The enthalpy change for the melting process is zero.

GO ON TO THE NEXT PAGE

44. Which axes labels correctly describe the following plot of an ideal gas relationship?

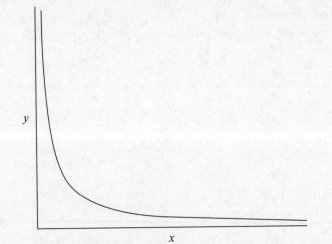

	x	y
A.	[Pressure]⁻¹	Volume
B.	Volume	Temperature
C.	Volume	Pressure
D.	Pressure	Temperature

GO ON TO THE NEXT PAGE

45. Mercury(II) ions form red complexes with the reagent $C_{12}H_7S_2N_3O_3$.

A 200.0-mL sample of dental wastewater was evaporated to dryness. It was re-dissolved in 1.0 mL of H_2O and mixed with 1.0 mL of an acidic solution of excess $C_{12}H_7S_2N_3O_3$. The absorbance of the complex was compared with the Beer's plot below.

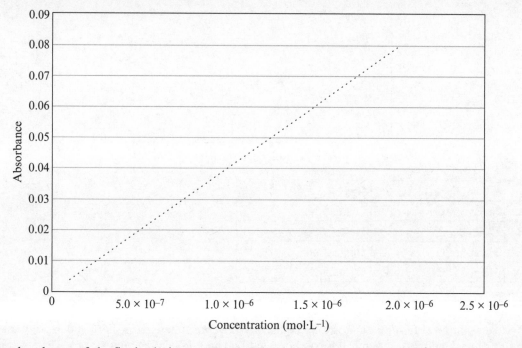

The absorbance of the final solution was 0.040. What is the concentration of Hg^{2+} in the wastewater?

A. $5.0 \times 10^{-8}\ M$

B. $1.0 \times 10^{-8}\ M$

C. $5.0 \times 10^{-6}\ M$

D. $1.0 \times 10^{-6}\ M$

46. Which experimental result provides evidence for the assertion that not all boron atoms are identical?

A. There are three peaks in the photoelectron spectrum of a sample of pure boron.

B. There are two peaks in the mass spectrum of a sample of pure boron.

C. The fourth ionization energy of boron is almost seven times as large as the third ionization energy.

D. Boron can combine with oxygen to form boron trioxide, B_2O_3, or boron suboxide, B_6O.

GO ON TO THE NEXT PAGE

47. Which of the following choices best describes the identities and temperatures of both Gas A and Gas B as represented in the Maxwell-Boltzmann distribution below?

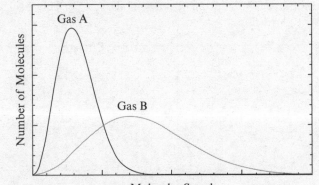

	Gas A	Gas B
A.	He at 35 °C	O$_2$ at 35 °C
B.	O$_2$ at 35 °C	He at 35 °C
C.	He at 35 °C	He at 25 °C
D.	He at 35 °C	O$_2$ at 25 °C

Questions 48–49 refer to the following scenario.

When KI(*aq*) and Pb(NO$_3$)$_2$(*aq*) solutions are combined, a yellow precipitate results. A 0.400 *M* solution of KI(*aq*) is added to a 20.0-mL solution of Pb(NO$_3$)$_2$(*aq*) until no additional precipitate forms. The resulting solid is filtered and thoroughly dried. The mass of the solid is determined to be 2.31 g.

48. How many moles of Pb(NO$_3$)$_2$ were initially present?

  A. 2.00×10^2
  B. 2.00×10^{-2}
  C. 5.01×10^{-2}
  D. 5.01×10^{-3}

GO ON TO THE NEXT PAGE

49. Which of the following diagrams best represents the filtrate solution?

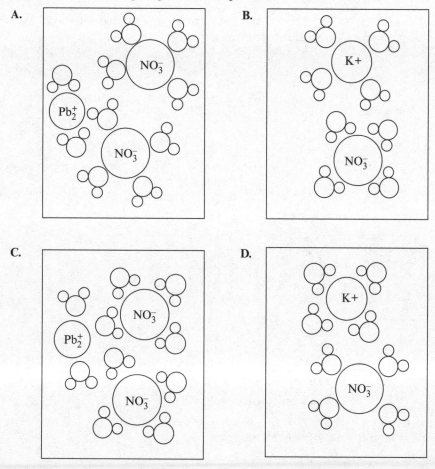

50. Which choice correctly identifies the conjugate acid and conjugate base of HSO_4^-?

	Conjugate Acid	Conjugate Base
A.	H_3O^+	SO_4^{2-}
B.	H_2SO_4	OH^-
C.	H_2SO_4	SO_4^{2-}
D.	SO_4^{2-}	H_2SO_4

51. The hydrolysis of maltose at pH 7 and 298 K is exergonic.

$$\text{maltose} + H_2O \rightleftharpoons 2 \text{ glucose} \qquad \Delta G° = -15.5 \text{ kJ·mol}^{-1}$$

Which of the following is true?

A. $K < 1$ and the reaction is exothermic.
B. $K > 1$ and the reaction is endothermic.
C. $K < 1$ and no information about the change in enthalpy can be determined.
D. $K > 1$ and no information about the change in enthalpy can be determined.

GO ON TO THE NEXT PAGE

Questions 52–55 refer to the experiment described below.

A 25.0-mL solution of phosphoric acid, H_3PO_4, with an unknown concentration is titrated with 0.100 M NaOH, and the following plot of pH versus volume of base added is obtained.

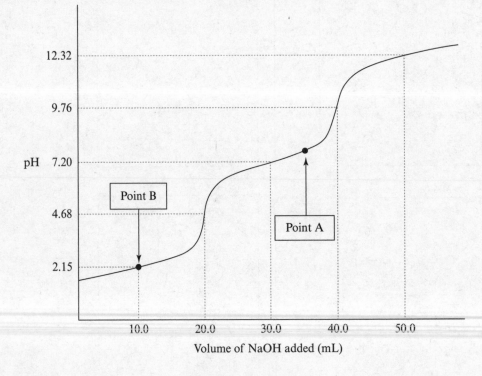

Volume of NaOH added (mL)

52. Using the plot to estimate, what is the K_{a_2} of phosphoric acid?

    A. 5.0×10^{-12}
    B. 1.7×10^{-10}
    C. 6.3×10^{-8}
    D. 2.0×10^{-5}

53. Which laboratory scenario would cause the concentration of the acid at the first equivalence point to appear to be lower than the true value?

    A. The chemist used a buret that was wet with distilled water before the sodium hydroxide solution was added.
    B. The chemist neglected to drain sodium hydroxide solution into the tip of the buret before beginning the titration.
    C. The chemist diluted the acid in the Erlenmeyer flask with an unknown quantity of water.
    D. The chemist used an indicator that had a pK_a of less than 3.5.

GO ON TO THE NEXT PAGE

54. At point A in the titration, which particle diagram best represents the composition of the solution? Water is not pictured.

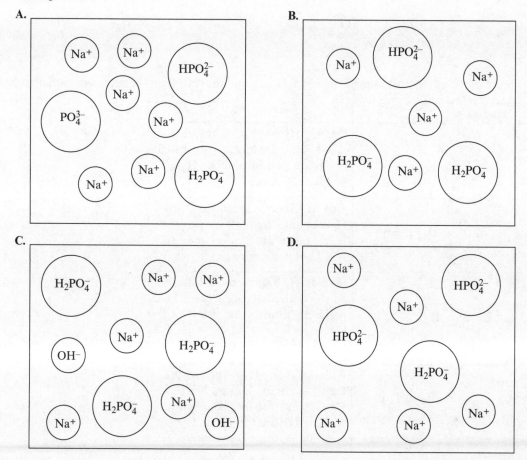

55. At point B in the titration, 10.0 mL of base have been added. At this point, when several drops of base are added, the pH does not change substantially. Which reaction best accounts for this observation?

A. $H_3PO_4 + OH^- \rightarrow H_2PO_4^- + H_2O$

B. $H_2PO_4^- + OH^- \rightarrow HPO_4^{2-} + H_2O$

C. $HPO_4^{2-} + OH^- \rightarrow PO_4^{2-} + H_2O$

D. $H_3O^+ + OH^- \rightarrow 2\ H_2O$

GO ON TO THE NEXT PAGE

56. The reaction between $Hg_2Cl_4(g)$ and $Al_2Cl_6(g)$ to form $HgAlCl_5(g)$ has a heat of reaction that is close to zero.

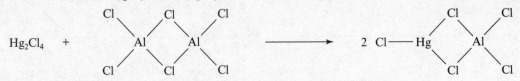

Which choice provides the most likely structure of Hg_2Cl_4 and the reason for the near-zero enthalpy change?

	Structure	Reason
A.	Cl, Cl, Hg—Hg, Cl, Cl	One Hg-Hg bond is broken, two Al-Cl bonds are broken, two Al-Cl bonds are formed, and two Hg-Cl bonds are formed.
B.	Cl, Cl—Hg, Hg—Cl, Cl	Two Al-Cl bonds are broken, two Hg-Cl bonds are broken, two Hg-Cl bonds are formed, and two Al-Cl bonds are formed.
C.	Cl, Cl, Hg—Hg, Cl, Cl	One Hg-Hg bond is broken, four Al-Cl bonds are broken, two Al-Cl bonds are formed, and two Hg-Cl bonds are formed.
D.	Cl, Cl—Hg, Hg—Cl, Cl	Four Al-Cl bonds are broken, two Hg-Cl bonds are broken, four Hg-Cl bonds are formed, and four Al-Cl bonds are formed.

57. A reaction with which energy profile would proceed the fastest at a given temperature? All reactions proceed from reactants on the left to products on the right.

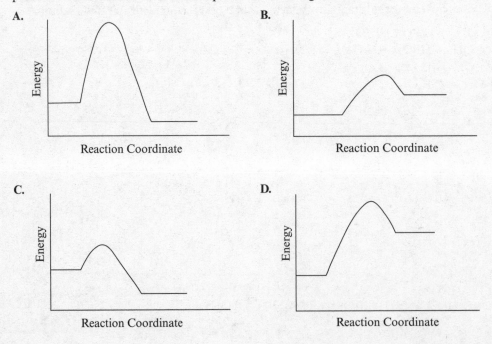

A.

Energy

Reaction Coordinate

B.

Energy

Reaction Coordinate

C.

Energy

Reaction Coordinate

D.

Energy

Reaction Coordinate

GO ON TO THE NEXT PAGE

58. A reaction under kinetic control will form

    A. the product with the lowest activation energy.

    B. the product that can be formed in the smallest number of steps.

    C. the product with the lowest potential energy.

    D. the product with the highest potential energy.

59. Which choice shows the correct arrangement of compounds in order of increasing lattice energy?

    A. MgF_2, $CaCl_2$, GaF_3, $InBr_3$

    B. GaF_3, $InBr_3$, MgF_2, $CaCl_2$

    C. $CaCl_2$, MgF_2, $InBr_3$, GaF_3

    D. $CaCl_2$, $InBr_3$, MgF_2, GaF_3

60. The solubility of elemental iodine in water at 20 °C is about 1.00 g per 3.5 L. Which intermolecular force is responsible for this solubility?

    A. Ion-dipole

    B. Dipole-induced dipole

    C. Hydrogen bonding

    D. Dipole-dipole

IF YOU FINISH BEFORE TIME IS CALLED, CHECK YOUR WORK ON THIS SECTION ONLY. DO NOT WORK ON ANY OTHER SECTION IN THE TEST.

Section II: Free Response

7 Questions

105 Minutes

Directions: Long free-response questions (questions 1–3) are worth 10 points each; allow yourself approximately 23 minutes for each one. Short free-response questions (questions 4–7) are worth 4 points each; allow yourself approximately 9 minutes for each one.

Include examples and equations in your responses where appropriate. Clearly show the method used and the steps involved in arriving at your answers. You must show your work to receive credit. Be mindful of significant figures.

1. Iron(II) sulfate is a white solid. It forms a green hydrate when exposed to water. A 5.000-g impure sample of the hydrated form of iron(II) sulfate is heated until the mass stops changing and only a white solid remains. The mass of the anhydrous sample is 2.755 g.

   a. How many moles of water were released from the hydrate?

   b. The impure anhydrous iron(II) sulfate was diluted with approximately 100 mL of water in an Erlenmeyer flask and acidified with sulfuric acid. It was then titrated with a 0.0521 M standardized potassium permanganate solution. Note that the impurity does not react with any other components of the titration.

      i. Write the balanced net ionic equation for the reaction between Fe^{2+} and MnO_4^- to form Fe^{3+} and Mn^{2+} in acidic solution.

      ii. A volume of 68.33 mL of MnO_4^- is required to titrate the Fe^{2+} solution to the equivalence point. How many moles of Fe^{2+} are present?

   c.
      i. How many water molecules are associated with each formula unit of iron(II) sulfate in the original crystal? Write the molecular formula of the hydrate.

      ii. Why is it unnecessary to measure the exact volume of water used to dilute the iron(II) sulfate sample?

      iii. How would the experimentally determined formula be affected if the mass of the sample had not stopped changing before the mass of water released was determined?

   d. How many grams of the hydrated form of iron(II) sulfate were present in the original 5.000-g sample?

   e. What was the percent purity of the original hydrated sample of iron(II) sulfate?

2. a. Hypochlorous acid has a pK_a of 7.50 at 25 °C.

      i. Write the K_a expression for hypochlorous acid in water.

      ii. Calculate K_a for HClO at 25 °C.

   b. Calculate the pH of a 0.225 M aqueous solution of HClO.

   c. Write the net ionic equation between HClO and NaOH in aqueous solution.

   d. A 25.0-mL sample of 0.225 M aqueous HClO is titrated with 0.125 M NaOH. Calculate the number of moles of NaOH required to reach the equivalence point.

   e.
      i. Calculate the K_b for ClO$^-$.

      ii. Calculate the pH of the solution in the flask after the NaOH addition.

   f. What molar ratio of ClO$^-$:HClO must be achieved in order for the pH of the solution to equal 8.00?

GO ON TO THE NEXT PAGE

3. Azulene, $C_{10}H_8$, is a deep blue molecule that is present in botanicals such as wormwood.

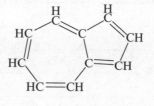

Azulene
$C_{10}H_8$
MW = 128.17 g·mol⁻¹

A 10.0-mg sample of azulene is dissolved in a mixture of 5 mL of ethanol and 25 mL of water to form a bright blue solution. This mixture is added to a separatory funnel, shown below. A 30-mL portion of cyclohexane, C_6H_{12}, is added to the funnel. The solutions in the funnel are mixed well and allowed to separate into two layers.

Compound	Boiling Temperature (°C)	Melting Temperature (°C)	Density (g·mL⁻¹)	Color
Azulene	242	99	1.04	Blue
Water	100	0	1.00	Colorless
Ethanol	78	–114	0.79	Colorless
Cyclohexane	81	6	0.78	Colorless

a. When the layers have separated, which solvent, water or cyclohexane, makes up the top layer and which makes up the bottom layer?

b. When the layers have separated, one layer is blue and the other layer is colorless. Which solvent layer is blue? Explain your response in terms of intermolecular forces.

c. How many π bonds are present in a molecule of azulene?

d. What is the hybridization and approximate bond angles of the carbon atoms in azulene?

e. How might azulene be isolated from the solution in the separatory funnel? Briefly describe a procedure for recovering the 10.0 mg of pure azulene.

f. Write the balanced equation for the combustion of azulene in excess oxygen using the lowest possible whole-number coefficients.

g. Use the following bond energy data to estimate the enthalpy of combustion of azulene in the gas phase. Express your answer in units of kJ·mol⁻¹.

GO ON TO THE NEXT PAGE

Bond Type	Bond Energy (kJ·mol⁻¹)
C−C	348
C=C	612
C−H	412
O=O	498
C=O	728
O−H	463

4. Brass is an alloy consisting of copper and zinc in various proportions. A 1.50-g sample of brass and a 1.50-g sample of pure copper are connected to a voltage source and placed in a solution that is 0.200 M in $CuSO_4$. The orientation of the electrodes is such that the copper electrode serves as the cathode and the brass electrode serves as the anode.

    a.   Is brass a substitutional or an interstitial alloy? Use a particulate sketch to illustrate a brief explanation of your response.

    b.   Write the equation for the half reaction for the process that occurs at the cathode.

    c.   Does the cathode or the anode increase in mass as the reaction proceeds? Provide reasoning for your answer.

    d.   Determine the mass of copper that is deposited after a current of 0.20 amperes is applied for 2.0 hours.

5. When equimolar quantities of $SbCl_3$ and $GaCl_3$ are mixed under appropriate conditions, they react according to the equation below.

$$SbCl_3 + GaCl_3 \rightarrow SbGaCl_6$$

A research group would like to determine whether the structure of $SbGaCl_6$ has the form $[SbCl_2]^+[GaCl_4]^-$ or $[GaCl_2]^+[SbCl_4]^-$. They use a spectroscopic technique to determine that the cation has a bent molecular geometry.

    a.   Which of the two forms is the correct structure and why? Draw Lewis structures of both possible cations to support your response.

    b.   The spectroscopic technique gave the researchers information about the geometry of the molecule. Was the spectroscopic technique one that utilized infrared radiation or one that utilized ultraviolet/visible radiation? Explain your answer.

    c.   What is the molecular geometry of the anion? Draw a Lewis structure to support your conclusion.

GO ON TO THE NEXT PAGE

6. Sodium-24 is a radioactive isotope of sodium.

    a.   In terms of atomic structure, how do sodium-24 and the stable isotope of sodium, sodium-23, differ?

    b.   The rate of decay of ^{24}Na was determined experimentally and the results are plotted below.

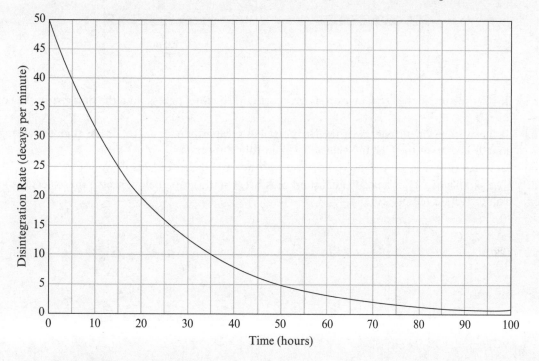

        i.   Determine the half-life of ^{24}Na.

        ii.   Determine the rate constant for the decay of ^{24}Na. Remember to include appropriate units.

    c.   The data can be used to show that the decay is first order, as indicated on the graph below. Label the vertical axis of the graph.

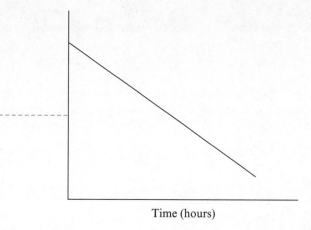

Time (hours)

GO ON TO THE NEXT PAGE

433

7. Consider two containers, each with a volume of 10.0 L at 298 K, as shown below. One container holds 1.0 mol He(*g*) and the other holds 1.0 mol CH_4(*g*). Assume that the He and CH_4 gases exhibit ideal behavior.

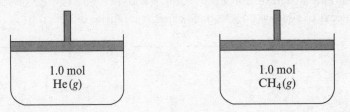

1.0 mol He (*g*)

1.0 mol CH_4(*g*)

    a. Is the pressure in the container of He greater than, equal to, or less than the pressure in the container of CH_4?

    b. Is the average kinetic energy of the He molecules greater than, equal to, or less than the average kinetic energy of the CH_4 molecules? Explain your answer.

    c. In which container do the molecules have a greater average speed? Justify your answer.

    d. The sample of CH_4 is heated at constant pressure. On the graph below, sketch the expected plot of volume versus temperature.

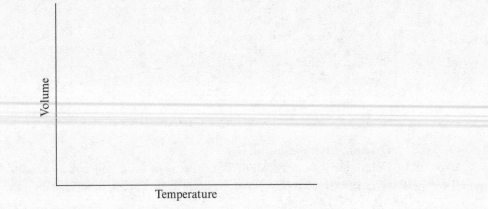

Temperature

IF YOU FINISH BEFORE TIME IS CALLED, CHECK YOUR WORK ON THIS SECTION ONLY. DO NOT WORK ON ANY OTHER SECTION IN THE TEST.

Answer Key

Section I: Multiple Choice

1. B	13. A	25. A	37. D	49. B
2. C	14. D	26. C	38. B	50. C
3. B	15. A	27. C	39. A	51. D
4. C	16. B	28. B	40. D	52. C
5. A	17. B	29. C	41. B	53. D
6. D	18. D	30. A	42. A	54. D
7. A	19. D	31. B	43. D	55. A
8. C	20. B	32. D	44. C	56. B
9. A	21. A	33. A	45. B	57. C
10. B	22. D	34. A	46. B	58. A
11. B	23. C	35. B	47. B	59. C
12. D	24. A	36. B	48. D	60. B

Answers and Explanations

Section I: Multiple Choice

1. **B.** (EK 3.A.2) The ratio of CO_2:H_2O in the overall balanced equation is 4:2 or 2:1.

$$2\,C_2H_2 + 5\,O_2 \rightarrow 4\,CO_2 + 2\,H_2O$$

2. **C.** (EK 2.A.3, 6.C.1) When ammonia, a weak base, is added to acetic acid, a weak acid, ammonium acetate, a strong electrolyte, is formed. The diagram in choice C shows NH_4^+ and $CH_3CO_2^-$ and is the correct choice.

$$NH_3(aq) + CH_3CO_2H(aq) \rightarrow NH_4^+(aq) + CH_3CO_2^-(aq)$$

3. **B.** (EK 2.D.2) Chromium oxide is used to coat the surface of stainless steel to prevent oxidation of the surface of the alloy.

4. **C.** (EK 1.B.1, 1.B.2, 1.D.1) If the Bohr model of the atom were correct, the shells would not be divided into subshells, and there would be fewer peaks in the spectra. There would also be different relative numbers of electrons per peak.

5. **A.** (EK 1.B.1, 1.C.1) Element X has the electron configuration, $1s^2 2s^2 2p^5$, which corresponds to an atom of fluorine. Elements Y and Z are sodium and magnesium, respectively. Of these three elements, only fluorine ionizes by gaining electrons.

6. **D.** (EK 1.C.1) Increasing nuclear charge causes the atomic radii to decrease from left to right across the periodic table.

7. **A.** (EK 1.B.1) The lower effective nuclear charge of sodium results in a lower binding energy for its 2s electrons than that of the 2s electrons in magnesium.

8. C. (EK 2.D.4) The electrical insulating properties, relatively low melting point, and the insolubility of the compound in water suggest that it is a molecular solid. By contrast, KOH is an ionic solid that is expected to be soluble in water. Au is a metal, so it is not expected to be an electrical insulator. Since HBr is a strong acid and is soluble in water, the solid must be sulfur, S_8.

9. A. (EK 6.C.1) The F^- ion is the conjugate base of a weak acid, which means it behaves as a base in aqueous solution. The more basic a solution, the higher its pH.

10. B. (EK 2.C.1, 2.C.2) Compounds with the largest electronegativity differences between the atoms participating in bonding have the highest degree of ionic character. The bond between lead, a metal, and bromine, a nonmetal, is the most ionic bond among the choices.

11. B. (EK 2.D.3) The conductivity of a semiconductor increases with increasing temperature because the number of electrons in the conduction band increases with increasing temperature. Therefore, the statement in choice B is the false statement.

12. D. (EK 2.C.4) When formal charges are assigned to the atoms in the choices, only the structure in choice D has zero formal charges. All of the other structures have separation of charge, so they are predicted to be less important contributors to the structure.

13. A. (EK 2.C.4) $TeCl_5^-$, SF_6, and BrF_5 all have octahedral electronic geometry. $TeCl_5^-$ and BrF_5 have square pyramidal molecular geometry.

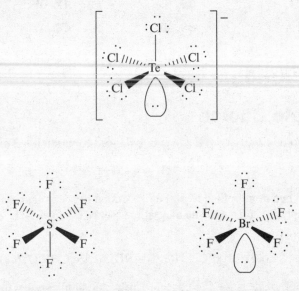

14. D. (EK 2.C.4, 5.C.1) Silicon atoms are larger than carbon atoms; the bond between two silicon atoms is longer and therefore weaker than the bond between two carbon atoms. A double bond, in general, which is composed of one σ and one π bond, is shorter and stronger than a single bond. Therefore, choice D correctly ranks the bonds according to increasing bond strength: Si-Si single bond < C-C single bond < C-C double bond.

15. A. (EK 5.E.4) Ionization is endothermic. Absorption of a photon causes the potential energy of the products to be greater than the potential energy of the reactants.

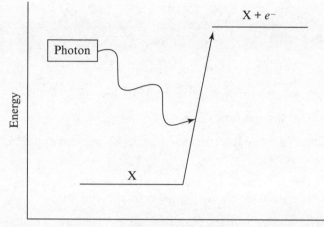

Reaction Coordinate

16. B. (EK 6.A.1, 6.A.2) The reaction has been reversed, so the new equilibrium constant is the reciprocal of the equilibrium constant in the forward direction. The coefficients have been divided by 2, so the new equilibrium constant must be raised to the power of $\frac{1}{2}$.

$$K = (Kp^{-1})^{\frac{1}{2}} = K^{-\frac{1}{2}} = (1.0 \times 10^{10})^{-\frac{1}{2}} = 1.0 \times 10^{-5}$$

Multiplication of the exponent by $-\frac{1}{2}$ gives the new equilibrium constant.

17. B. (EK 5.C.2, 5.E.1) In the reverse reaction, two gaseous atoms come together to form one gaseous atom. This involves a decrease in entropy ($\Delta S < 0$). Bond formation releases energy, so the reverse process is exothermic ($\Delta H < 0$).

18. D. (EK 6.C.3) Calcium fluoride dissociates according to the equation

$$CaF_2(s) \rightleftharpoons Ca^{2+}(aq) + 2\ F^-(aq)$$

The solubility product expression is

$$K_{sp} = [Ca^{2+}][F^-]^2$$

Since $[Ca^{2+}] = x$, then $[F^-] = 2x$

$$K_{sp} = x(2x)^2 = 4x^3$$

19. D. (EK 3.C.2, 5.B.3, 6.B.1) In an exothermic process, heat can be thought of as a "product" of the reaction. As temperature is decreased, the equilibrium constant increases and more products must be formed to achieve equilibrium.

20. B. (EK 4.D.2) Enzymes lower the energy of the transition state compared with the transition state of the uncatalyzed reaction. Thus, choice B is the false statement.

21. A. (EK 4.C.1, 4.C.2, 4.C.3) The rate law for mechanism 1, based on the slow step, is

$$\text{rate} = k\ [NO_2Cl]$$

The rate law for mechanism 2 is based on the slow step.

$$\text{rate} = k\ [N_2O_4]$$

Because an intermediate is not included in the rate law, the equal rates of the forward and reverse reactions in the fast step are taken into account.

$$k_1[NO_2Cl]^2 = k_{-1}[N_2O_4][Cl_2]$$

The overall rate for mechanism 2 is

$$\text{rate} = k[NO_2Cl]^2[Cl_2]^{-1}$$

Only mechanism 1 is consistent with the experimental rate law.

22. D. (EK 2.A.1) A glass is an amorphous solid, not a crystalline solid.

23. C. (EK 4.A.2) Notice that for every 10.0-minute interval, $[A]^{-1}$ increases by 0.25. This linear relationship indicates a second order process.

24. A. (6.A.2, 6.A.3) For a given reaction, only a change in temperature can change the equilibrium constant. All the other changes mentioned merely change the equilibrium quotient.

25. A. (EK 3.C.3, 6.D.1) The reaction with the most positive standard cell potential has the largest equilibrium constant. The value of $E°$ is determined by

$$E°_{cell} = E°_{reduction} - E°_{oxidation}$$

The combination of reactions that leads to the most positive overall cell potential is that of the reduction of Pb^{2+} and the oxidation of Al, as shown in choice A.

26. C. (EK 2.A.3, 3.B.2, 6.C.1) As NaOH, a strong base, is added to HF, a weak acid, the conductivity of the solution increases as an HF/NaF buffer solution is formed.

$$HF + OH^- \rightarrow H_2O + F^-$$

Once the HF has reacted completely, additional NaOH will increase the conductivity at a different rate as Na^+ and OH^- are added; the diagram in choice C best represents this change.

27. C. (EK 3.B.2, 6.C.1) Water is both amphoteric, which means it can behave as both an acid and a base, and amphiprotic, which means it can behave as both a proton donor and a proton acceptor. Therefore, the statement in choice C is false.

28. B. (EK 3.B.3) This redox titration calculation requires a balanced net ionic equation.

$$6\,I^- + 14\,H^+ + Cr_2O_7^{2-} \rightarrow 3\,I_2 + 2\,Cr^{3+} + 7\,H_2O$$

$$0.050\ \cancel{L\,I^-} \times \frac{0.100\ \cancel{mol\,I^-}}{1\ \cancel{L\,I^-}} \times \frac{1\ \cancel{mol\,Cr_2O_7^{2-}}}{6\ \cancel{mol\,I^-}} \times \frac{1\ L\ Cr_2O_7^{2-}}{0.05\ \cancel{mol\,Cr_2O_7^{2-}}} = 0.0167\ L\ Cr_2O_7^{2-} = 16.7\ mL$$

29. C. (EK 3.B.3) The electrolysis of Al^{3+} is a 3-electron transfer.

$$Al^{3+} + 3\,e^- \rightarrow Al$$

$$96{,}500\ \cancel{s} \times \frac{3\ \cancel{C}}{1\ \cancel{s}} \times \frac{1\ \cancel{mol\,e^-}}{96{,}500\ \cancel{C}} \times \frac{1\ \cancel{mol\,Al}}{3\ \cancel{mol\,e^-}} \times \frac{27\ g\ Al}{1\ \cancel{mol\,Al}} = 27\ g\ Al$$

30. A. (EK 3.B.3) The oxidation number of Mn is going from +7 to +6 as the reaction proceeds to the right; therefore, choice A is correct.

31. B. (EK 3.B.3) The coefficient for OH^- in the overall balanced equation in alkaline solution is 2.

$$2\,MnO_4^- + SO_3^{2-} + 2\,OH^- \rightarrow 2\,MnO_4^{2-} + SO_4^{2-} + H_2O$$

32. **D.** (EK 2.A.3) Propionaldehyde and propanol are miscible liquids with similar densities. They have sufficiently different boiling points to be separated by distillation.

33. **A.** (EK 2.A.3) The molarity is the number of moles of solute per liter of solution.

$$5 \text{ mL} \times \frac{0.802 \text{ g}}{1 \text{ mL}} \times \frac{1 \text{ mol}}{60 \text{ g}} \approx \frac{4}{60} = \frac{1}{15} \text{ mol}$$

$$\frac{\left(\frac{1}{15} \text{ mol}\right)}{\left(\frac{1}{10} \text{ L}\right)} = \frac{2}{3} = 0.67 \ M$$

34. **A.** (EK 5.E.1) Freezing decreases the entropy of a liquid as it is converted to a solid, but this is offset by the increase in entropy of the surroundings.

35. **B.** (EK 4.A.1) Let [X] be the concentration of the reactant. The ratio of rate 2:rate 1 is 27.

$$\frac{\text{rate 2}}{\text{rate 1}} = \left(\frac{3[\text{X}]}{[\text{X}]}\right)^x$$

$$27 = 3^x$$

$$x = 3$$

36. **B.** (EK 2.A.3) The addition of the two masses yields five significant figures.

$$169.88 \text{ g} + 0.120 \text{ g} = 170.00 \text{ g}$$

When this mass is divided by the molar mass, the number of moles can be reported to five significant figures.

The graduated cylinder can be read to the nearest 0.1 mL. (If the meniscus is exactly on the 100-mL mark, the student should report this as 100.0 mL.) There are four significant figures in the volume reading.

The number of moles divided by the volume provides the molarity, so a maximum of four significant figures should be reported.

37. **D.** (EK 2.A.2, 2.B.1) London dispersion forces are present between all molecules. The intermolecular forces in neon are weak, but they exist.

38. **B.** (EK 4.A.2) For this second order reaction, a plot of $[C_3F_6]^{-1}$ (y axis) versus Time (x axis) is linear.

39. **A.** (EK 2.B.3) Hydrogen bonding is the strongest intermolecular force and has the greatest influence on surface tension. The $-NH_2$ group in aniline is capable of hydrogen bonding.

40. **D.** (EK 5.A.1) As temperature, or average kinetic energy, of the molecules increases, they become increasingly capable of overcoming intermolecular forces. This increase in average kinetic energy results in a decrease in surface tension.

41. **B.** (EK 5.B.1) Negative work is work done by the system. In order to do work on the surroundings, the system expands against the constant external pressure. This is true for the situation is which bromine liquid is converted to bromine gas.

42. **A.** (EK 6.C.1) The base dissociation constant is the equilibrium constant for the reaction of a base (HSO_3^-) with water, where the base accepts a proton from water to form the conjugate acid (H_2SO_3) and hydroxide.

43. **D.** (EK 5.A.2, 6.A.1) The process of melting is endothermic; energy is being absorbed by the system, so the enthalpy change is not zero. Choice D is the false statement.

44. **C.** (EK 2.A.2) At constant temperature, the pressure of an ideal gas is inversely proportional to volume, so the axes labels should be Volume (x-axis) and Pressure (y-axis), as is choice C.

45. **B.** (EK 1.D.3) The absorbance can be used to find the Hg^{2+} concentration in the final solution. An absorbance of 0.04 corresponds to a concentration of 1.0×10^{-6} M. The original concentration of mercury in the dental wastewater can be determined using the dilution equation.

$$M_1 V_1 = M_2 V_2$$

$$(1.0 \times 10^{-6}\ M)(2.0\ \text{mL}) = M_2(200.0\ \text{mL})$$

$$M_2 = 1.0 \times 10^{-8}\ M$$

46. **B.** (EK 1.D.2) The two peaks in the mass spectrum provide the proof that boron exists as two isotopes that differ by the number of neutrons in the nucleus.

47. **B.** (EK 2.A.2) The temperature of both gases in choice B is the same, so the curve corresponding to Gas A represents a larger gas, because the molecules have a lower average velocity. The curve corresponding to Gas B represents a smaller gas because the molecules have a higher average velocity.

48. **D.** (EK 3.A.2) The solid formed is PbI_2. The number of moles of $Pb(NO_3)_2$ can be determined using the stoichiometry of the chemical equation.

$$Pb(NO_3)_2(aq) + 2KI(aq) \rightarrow PbI_2(s) + 2KNO_3(aq)$$

The molar mass of PbI_2 is 461 g·mol^{-1}.

$$2.31\ \text{g PbI}_2 \times \frac{1\ \text{mol PbI}_2}{461\ \text{g PbI}_2} \times \frac{1\ \text{mol Pb(NO}_3)_2}{1\ \text{mol PbI}_2} = 5.01 \times 10^{-3}\ \text{mol Pb(NO}_3)_2$$

49. **B.** (EK 3.A.1) When the precipitation reaction is complete, only the spectator ions remain. Notice that in diagram B, the large oxygen atoms of the water molecules are oriented toward the K^+ cations and the small hydrogen atoms are oriented toward the NO_3^- anions.

50. **C.** (EK 3.B.2) The conjugate acid, H_2SO_4, has an additional hydrogen and a charge that is +1 greater than HSO_4^-. The conjugate base, SO_4^{2-}, has lost a hydrogen and has an additional negative charge.

51. **D.** (EK 6.D.1) An exergonic reaction is one in which $\Delta G < 0$. Since $\Delta G° = -RT \ln K$, the equilibrium constant is greater than 1. No information is given about whether the reaction is endothermic or exothermic.

52. **C.** (EK 6.C.1) The pK_{a_2} is equal to the pH halfway between the first and second equivalence points. The pK_{a_2} is 7.20.

$$K_{a_2} = 10^{-7.20}$$

This is estimated to be close to 6.3×10^{-8}.

53. **D.** (EK 6.C.1) In order to accurately determine the equivalence point of a titration, the indicator selected must have a pK_a within 1 pH unit of the pH of the equivalence point of interest. If the indicator changed color before the equivalence point was reached, the concentration would appear to be lower than the true value.

54. **D.** (EK 6.C.1) At point A in the titration, addition of OH^- deprotonates $H_2PO_4^-$. The point is more than halfway to the second equivalence point, so HPO_4^{2-} anions outnumber $H_2PO_4^-$ anions, as shown in the particle diagram in choice D.

55. **A.** (EK 6.C.1) At point B in the titration, within the first buffering region of the curve, addition of OH^- deprotonates H_3PO_4, as shown in the reaction in choice A.

56. **B.** (EK 5.C.2) The correct structure is the one in which the bonds broken and the bonds formed are approximately equivalent.

57. C. (EK 4.B.3) The reaction with the lowest activation energy will proceed the fastest at a given temperature. The activation energy is the energy difference between the reactants, which are on the left, and the transition state, which is the highest point on the reaction profile. In choice C, this energy difference is the smallest.

58. A. (EK 5.E.5) A reaction under kinetic control will form the product with the lowest activation energy.

59. C. (EK 2.C.2) Coulombic attractions between anions and cations increase with the product of the charges and decrease with increasing ionic radii. Therefore, the correct arrangement of compounds in order of increasing lattice energy is shown in choice C: $CaCl_2$, MgF_2, $InBr_3$, GaF_3.

60. B. (EK 2.B.2, 2.B.3) Iodine is a nonpolar solute and water is a polar solvent. Iodine dissolves in water due to dipole-induced dipole attractions.

Section II: Free Response

1. a. (EK 1.A.3, 3.B.3)

$$(5.000 \text{ g impure sample}) - (2.755 \text{ g impure anhydrous sample}) = 2.245 \text{ g } H_2O$$

$$2.245 \text{ g } H_2O \times \frac{1 \text{ mol } H_2O}{18.02 \text{ g } H_2O} = 0.1246 \text{ mol } H_2O$$

b. i. (EK 3.A.1, 3.B.3)

$$5 Fe^{2+} + 8 H^+ + MnO_4^- \rightarrow 5 Fe^{3+} + Mn^{2+} + 4 H_2O$$

ii. (EK 1.E.2, 3.A.2, 3.B.3)

$$68.33 \text{ mL } MnO_4^- \times \frac{1 \text{ L } MnO_4^-}{1000 \text{ mL } MnO_4^-} \times \frac{0.0521 \text{ mol } MnO_4^-}{1 \text{ L } MnO_4^-} \times \frac{5 \text{ mol } Fe^{2+}}{1 \text{ mol } MnO_4^-} = 0.0178 \text{ mol } Fe^{2+}$$

c. i. (EK 3.A.2)

$$\frac{0.1246 \text{ mol } H_2O}{0.0178 \text{ mol } Fe^{2+}} = 7$$

$$FeSO_4 \cdot 7 H_2O$$

ii. (EK 3.B.3) It is unnecessary to measure the exact volume of water used to dilute the analyte because only the ratio of the number of moles of water that was originally removed by heating to the number of moles of iron is needed to determine the formula of the hydrate. The concentration does not affect the result.

iii. (EK 1.E.2) When the mass stops changing, all of the water has been removed and the mass of the anhydrous sample can be accurately determined. Before the mass stops changing, water is still present, the sample is not anhydrous, and fewer H_2O molecules per $FeSO_4$ formula would be obtained.

d. (EK 1.A.1, 3.A.2) Formula weight of $FeSO_4 \cdot 7 H_2O = 278.05 \text{ g·mol}^{-1}$.

$$0.0178 \text{ mol } FeSO_4 \cdot 7 H_2O \times \frac{278.05 \text{ g } FeSO_4 \cdot 7 H_2O}{1 \text{ mol } FeSO_4 \cdot 7 H_2O} = 4.95 \text{ g } FeSO_4 \cdot 7 H_2O$$

e. (EK 1.A.1, 1.A.2)

$$\frac{4.95 \text{ g pure } FeSO_4 \cdot 7 H_2O}{5.000 \text{ g sample}} \times 100\% = 99.0\%$$

2. a. i. (EK 6.C.1)

$$K_a = \frac{[H_3O^+][ClO^-]}{[HClO]}$$

ii. (EK 6.C.1)

$$K_a = 10^{-pK_a} = 10^{-7.50} = 3.2 \times 10^{-8}$$

b. (EK 6.C.1)

Reaction	HClO	H₂O	ClO⁻	H₃O⁺
Initial Concentrations (*M*)	0.225		0	0
Change	−x		+ x	+ x
Equilibrium Concentrations (*M*)	0.225 − x		x	x

$$K_a = \frac{[H_3O^+][ClO^-]}{[HClO]} = \frac{x^2}{0.225 - \cancel{x}} = 3.2 \times 10^{-8}$$

Because K_a is very small, x can be neglected in the denominator.

$$x = \sqrt{(0.225)(3.2 \times 10^{-8})} = 8.4 \times 10^{-5} \ M = [H_3O^+]$$
$$pH = -\log(8.4 \times 10^{-5}) = 4.07$$

No rounding occurred until after the final calculation.

c. (EK 3.B.1, 3.B.2)

$$HClO + OH^- \rightarrow H_2O + ClO^-$$

If state symbols are included, the equation becomes

$$HClO(aq) + OH^-(aq) \rightarrow H_2O(l) + ClO^-(aq)$$

d. (EK 1.E.2, 3.A.2, 6.C.1)

$$0.0250 \ \cancel{L\ HClO} \times \frac{0.225 \ \cancel{mol\ HClO}}{1 \ \cancel{L\ HClO}} \times \frac{1 \ \cancel{mol\ OH^-}}{1 \ \cancel{mol\ HClO}} \times \frac{1 \ \cancel{L\ OH^-}}{0.125 \ \cancel{mol\ OH^-}} \times \frac{1000 \ mL\ OH^-}{1 \ \cancel{L\ OH^-}} = 45.0 \ mL\ NaOH$$

e. i. (EK 6.C.1) At the equivalence point, all the HClO has been reacted with OH⁻. The base dissociation constant for ClO⁻ is needed to find the pOH.

$$ClO^- + H_2O \rightleftharpoons HClO + OH^-$$

$$K_w = K_a \cdot K_b$$
$$K_b = \frac{K_w}{K_a} = \frac{10^{-14}}{3.2 \times 10^{-8}} = 3.2 \times 10^{-7}$$

ii. (EK 6.C.1)

$$0.0250 \ \cancel{L\ HClO} \times \frac{0.225 \ \cancel{mol\ HClO}}{1 \ \cancel{L\ HClO}} \times \frac{1 \ mol\ ClO^-}{1 \ \cancel{mol\ HClO}} = 0.00563 \ mol\ ClO^-$$

$$\frac{0.00563 \ mol\ ClO^-}{0.0250 \ L \ + \ 0.0450 \ L} = 0.0804 \ M \ ClO^-$$

Reaction	ClO⁻	H₂O	HClO	OH⁻
Initial Concentrations (M)	0.0804		0	0
Change	− x		+ x	+ x
Equilibrium Concentrations (M)	0.0804 − x		x	x

$$K_b = \frac{[HClO][OH^-]}{[ClO^-]} = \frac{x^2}{0.0804 - \cancel{x}} = 3.2 \times 10^{-7}$$

Because K_b is very small, x can be neglected in the denominator.

$$x = \sqrt{(0.0804)(3.2 \times 10^{-7})} = 1.6 \times 10^{-4} = [OH^-]$$
$$pOH = -\log \ (1.6 \times 10^{-4}) = 3.80$$
$$pH = 14.00 - 3.80 = 10.20$$

f. (EK 6.C.2)

$$pH = pK_a + \log \frac{[ClO^-]}{[HClO]}$$

$$8.00 = 7.50 + \log \frac{[ClO^-]}{[HClO]}$$

$$\frac{[ClO^-]}{[HClO]} = 10^{(8.00-7.50)} = 3.2$$

3. a. (EK 2.B.3) Because cyclohexane and water are the major components of the mixture, they are the solvents, and ethanol and azulene are the solutes. Cyclohexane is less dense than water, so cyclohexane makes up the top layer and water makes up the bottom layer.

b. (EK 2.B.3) The cyclohexane layer is blue because azulene is soluble in cyclohexane rather than water. Azulene is a nonpolar molecule. London dispersion forces are responsible for its solubility in cyclohexane, a nonpolar hydrocarbon. Azulene is much less soluble in water, which is polar and capable of hydrogen bonding.

c. (EK 2.C.4) Five π bonds are present in azulene.

d. (EK 2.C.4) The carbon atoms are sp^2 hybridized with approximate 120° bond angles.

e. (EK 2.A.3) The water layer could be drained from the bottom of the separatory funnel, leaving the cyclohexane layer. The cyclohexane layer could be poured into a distillation flask and the cyclohexane could be removed from the solid azulene by distillation. (Alternatively, all the solvents could be evaporated.)

f. (EK 3.A.1)

$$C_{10}H_8 + 12 \ O_2 \rightarrow 10 \ CO_2 + 4 \ H_2O$$

g. (EK 5.C.2)

$$\Delta H^\circ_{rxn} = (\Sigma \text{ bonds broken}) - (\Sigma \text{ bonds formed})$$

$$\Delta H^\circ_{rxn} = \left[\left(5 \times 348 \text{ kJ} \cdot \text{mol}^{-1}\right) + \left(6 \times 612 \text{ kJ} \cdot \text{mol}^{-1}\right) + \left(8 \times 412 \text{ kJ} \cdot \text{mol}^{-1}\right) + \left(12 \times 498 \text{ kJ} \cdot \text{mol}^{-1}\right) \right]$$
$$- \left[\left(20 \times 799 \text{ kJ} \cdot \text{mol}^{-1}\right) + \left(8 \times 463 \text{ kJ} \cdot \text{mol}^{-1}\right) \right]$$

$$\Delta H^\circ_{rxn} = -5.00 \times 10^3 \text{ kJ} \cdot \text{mol}^{-1}$$

4. a. (EK 2.E.2) Brass is a substitutional alloy. Copper and zinc are adjacent to one another on the periodic table and have similar atomic radii. Some of the copper atoms in the metal are substituted with zinc atoms.

Your sketch should resemble the following.

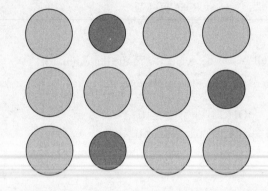

b. (EK 3.C.3)

$$Cu^{2+} + 2e^- \rightarrow Cu$$

c. (EK 3.C.3) The cathode increases in mass because as Cu^{2+} is reduced to neutral copper, it leaves the solution and is plated onto the electrode.

d. (EK 3.C.3)

5. a. (EK 2.C.4) $SbCl_2^+$ has a trigonal planar electronic geometry and bent molecular geometry; $GaCl_2^+$ has linear electronic and molecular geometry. The product must be $[SbCl_2]^+[GaCl_4]^-$.

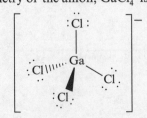

b. (EK 1.D.3) Infrared spectroscopy gives information about the types of bonds that are present in a molecule. The bond angle in the cation was determined by infrared spectroscopy rather than ultraviolet/visible spectroscopy, which gives information about electronic transitions.

c. (EK 2.C.4) The molecular geometry of the anion, $GaCl_4^-$ is tetrahedral.

6. a. (EK 1.D.2) Sodium-24 has one more neutron in its nucleus than sodium-23.

b. i. (EK 4.A.3) According to the graph of disintegration rate versus time, half of the ^{24}Na has decayed at 15 hours.

$$t_{1/2} = 15 \text{ h}$$

ii. (EK 4.A.3) Nuclear decay is always a first order process.

$$t_{1/2} = \frac{0.693}{k}$$

$$k = \frac{0.693}{t_{1/2}} = \frac{0.693}{15 \text{ h}} = 0.46 \text{ h}^{-1}$$

c. (EK 4.A.2) The vertical axis of the graph should be labeled "ln A" or "ln (disintegrations)."

7. a. (EK 2.A.2) Equal numbers of moles of ideal gases occupying equal volumes at the same temperature exert the same pressure.

b. (EK 2.A.2) Both gases have the same average kinetic energy because both are at the same temperature.

c. (EK 2.A.2) The molar mass of He is less than the molar mass of CH_4, so the helium molecules have greater average speed.

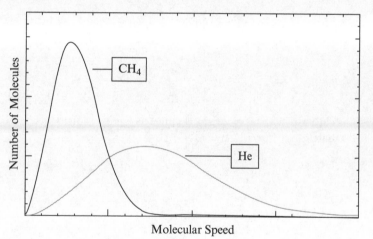

d. (EK 2.A.2) The volume of an ideal gas is directly proportional to temperature. The sketch should show a straight line with a positive slope.

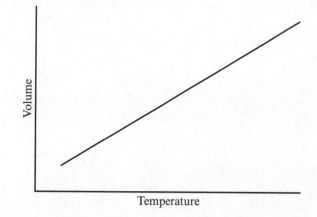

445